THE BURDEN OF TIME

THE FUGITIVES AND AGRARIANS

The Burden of Time

THE FUGITIVES AND AGRARIANS

THE NASHVILLE GROUPS OF THE
1920'S AND 1930'S, AND THE WRITING OF
JOHN CROWE RANSOM, ALLEN TATE, AND
ROBERT PENN WARREN

By JOHN L. STEWART

1965 · PRINCETON UNIVERSITY PRESS

PRINCETON, NEW JERSEY

TO LESLIE AND ANN

"... now, dreaming, you serve me ..."

ACKNOWLEDGMENTS

IN WRITING this book I have incurred many debts but none so great as those to the Fugitives and Agrarians.

All of us who have studied their work owe more than we can say to Donald Davidson. One of his colleagues once remarked to me, "Don has always known more and cared more about the Fugitives and Agrarians than the rest of us. Whatever you want to know, he's the one to ask." And so it was when I talked with him and examined the materials, now in the Joint University Library at Nashville, which he had gathered through the years. His memory of Fugitive and Agrarian affairs is remarkable for its scope and accuracy, and he willingly saves the investigator hours of searching by directing him to the sources he needs. It is, therefore, a particular pleasure to be able to testify to his courtesy and generosity toward all who come seeking his aid. Without him our understanding and appreciation of a significant part of American literary history would be diminished.

The others I consulted were as kind. During the last three years of his life Merrill Moore spent much time reminiscing about the old days in Nashville and describing Fugitive meetings he had attended. He lent me copies of scarce works and helped me find others. The late Sidney Mttron Hirsch twice sat up almost until dawn with me, answering questions, interpreting poems, and astonishing me, as he used to astonish the Fugitives, with the range and variety of his learning. The late Frank Owsley spun yarns about some of the mighty conflicts between the Agrarians and their opponents among Southern historians and social scientists—battles that had brought him furious pleasure and pleasurable fury. Andrew Nelson Lytle sent me a long account of how the roots of Agrarianism reached back into the lives of early settlers and described the attempts of the Agrarians to affiliate with other groups opposed to the direction of modern American life.

One of the treasures of contemporary literature is the collection of letters from his friends and fellow writers which Allen Tate began accumulating soon after *The Fugitive* was founded and which he deposited twenty years later in the Princeton University Library. He generously gave me permission to examine them. It was all I could do to keep my attention on Fugitive and

Acknowledgments

Agrarian matters. Subsequently, John Crowe Ransom allowed me to quote at length from the remarkable sequence of letters in which he argued out the ideas that formed the bases of his theories of poetry, myth, cultural values, and literary criticism. Robert Penn Warren let me reproduce his long explanation to Tate of the dominant themes in *Night Rider*. Without such cooperation and without the care and thoroughness with which these three men, who are the principal figures in this study, replied to my inquiries into all aspects of their work, it would have been impossible to have undertaken a book that tries to do what this one aims at. Part of the aim is to honor them for their achievement. Perhaps I have repaid a little of what I owe them.

I am under special obligations to the staffs of the Joint University Library in Nashville and the Princeton University Library, where the most valuable collections of relevant materials are kept. At other times I have used the New York Public Library and the libraries of Dartmouth College, The Ohio State University, The University of California at Los Angeles, Northwestern University, Harvard University, and Columbia University. Everywhere assistance was promptly and courteously given me.

Time for study and writing and freedom from other responsibilities were made possible by two fellowships which enabled me to take entire years away from the classroom. The first was granted for 1953-1954 by the George A. and Eliza Gardner Howard Foundation. The second, a Faculty Fellowship, was granted for 1962-1963 by Dartmouth College. For it and for assistance in meeting the cost of preparing the typescript I am indebted to the Trustees of the College, Provost John Masland, and Professor Arthur E. Jensen, formerly Dean of the Faculty. The entire book was written during the time that I was a member of the Dartmouth faculty, and much of whatever merit it may have is owing to the setting in which it was conceived and the encouragement which I was given while part of the college.

I am grateful to the persons and firms here listed for permission to quote from works by or pertaining to the Fugitives and Agrarians:

Walter Clyde Curry, for lines from his poem "To a Curious Modest Lady."

Donald Davidson, for excerpts from his poems published in

viii

Acknowledgments

The Fugitive; *An Outland Piper*, copyright 1924 by Donald Davidson, renewed, 1952, by Donald Davidson; *The Tall Men*, copyright 1927, by Donald Davidson, renewed, 1955, by Donald Davidson; and *Lee in the Mountains and Other Poems Including The Tall Men*, copyright 1938 by Donald Davidson.

William Yandell Elliott, for an excerpt from a letter to the Fugitives.

Miss Helen E. Frank, for lines from "The Fugitive Unbound," by James M. Frank.

Harcourt, Brace and World, Inc., for excerpts from *Modern Science and the Nature of Life*, by William S. Beck; *Professor*, by Stanley Johnson; *God without Thunder*, by John Crowe Ransom; and *All the King's Men*, by Robert Penn Warren.

Harper and Row, Publishers, Inc., for excerpts from *Critique of Religion and Philosophy*, by Walter Kaufmann; and from "Statement of Principles," "Reconstructed but Unregenerate," by John Crowe Ransom, "A Mirror for Artists," by Donald Davidson, "Remarks on the Southern Religion," by Allen Tate, and "The Irrepressible Conflict," by Frank Owsley, from *I'll Take My Stand*, by Twelve Southerners, copyright 1930 by Harper & Brothers, renewed 1958 by Donald Davidson.

Dr. Nathaniel D. M. Hirsch, for lines from "The Little Boy Pilgrim," by Sidney Mttron Hirsch.

Holt, Rinehart and Winston, Inc., for excerpts from "Sunset," "The Swimmer," "Noonday Grace," "Prayer," and "Under the Locusts," from *Poems About God*, by John Crowe Ransom. Copyright 1919 by Holt, Rinehart and Winston, Inc. Copyright 1947 by John Crowe Ransom.

Mrs. Ruby Johnson, for the poem beginning, "You owe allegiance to so many gods," and lines from "Sermons" and "Pier," by Stanley Johnson.

Alfred A. Knopf, Inc., for excerpts from *The Mind of the South*, by W. J. Cash, copyright 1941 by Alfred A. Knopf, Inc.; from *The South Old and New*, by Francis B. Simkins, copyright 1947 by Alfred A. Knopf, Inc.; from *Chills and Fever*, by John Crowe Ransom, copyright, 1924 by Alfred A. Knopf, Inc., renewed 1952 by John Crowe Ransom; from *Selected Poems*, by John Crowe Ransom, copyright 1924, 1927 by Alfred A. Knopf, Inc., renewed

Acknowledgments

1952, 1955 by John Crowe Ransom; and from *Poems and Essays* by John Crowe Ransom, copyright 1955 by Alfred A. Knopf, Inc.

Mrs. Ann Leslie Moore, for the poems "Abschied" and "Afternoon Date in a Corner Drugstore," by Merrill Moore.

The New Republic and Mr. Kenneth Burke, for excerpts from his essay, "Property as an Absolute," copyright 1936 by *The New Republic*.

G. P. Putnam's Sons, for excerpts from *The Fire Regained*, by Sidney Mttron Hirsch, copyright 1913 by G. P. Putnam's Sons; *Stonewall Jackson, The Good Soldier*, by Allen Tate, copyright 1928 by G. P. Putnam's Sons; and *The Fathers*, by Allen Tate, copyright 1938 by G. P. Putnam's Sons.

Random House, Inc., for excerpts from *Night Rider*, by Robert Penn Warren, copyright 1939 by Random House, Inc.; *World Enough and Time*, by Robert Penn Warren, copyright 1950 by Random House, Inc.; *Brother to Dragons*, by Robert Penn Warren, copyright 1953 by Random House, Inc.; *Promises*, by Robert Penn Warren, copyright 1957 by Random House, Inc.; and *Selected Essays*, by Robert Penn Warren, copyright 1958 by Random House, Inc.

John Crowe Ransom, for excerpts from *The New Criticism*, by John Crowe Ransom, copyright 1941 by New Directions; and essays by Mr. Ransom originally published in *The Fugitive* and *The Kenyon Review*.

The Reporter Magazine Company and Eric Hoffer for an excerpt from "The Awakening of Asia," by Eric Hoffer, copyright 1954 by the Fortnightly Publishing Company; and the Reporter Magazine Company and George Steiner for an excerpt from "Half Man, Half Beast," by George Steiner, copyright 1963 by the Reporter Magazine Company.

The Saturday Review and John Crowe Ransom, for an excerpt from "Classical and Romantic," by John Crowe Ransom, from *The Saturday Review of Literature*, September 14, 1929.

Charles Scribner's Sons for excerpts from *The World's Body*, by John Crowe Ransom, copyright 1938 by Charles Scribner's Sons; and *Poems*, by Allen Tate, copyright 1960 by Charles Scribner's Sons.

The Sewanee Review and John Crowe Ransom for an excerpt from "Flux and Blur in Contemporary Art," by John Crowe Ran-

Acknowledgments

som; *The Sewanee Review* and Edward Shils for an excerpt from "Daydreams and Nightmares: Reflections on the Criticism of Mass Culture," by Edward Shils; and *The Sewanee Review* and Robert Penn Warren for an excerpt from "Knowledge and the Image of Man," by Robert Penn Warren.

Sheed and Ward, Ltd., for an excerpt from *The American Heresy*, by Christopher Hollis, copyright 1927 by Sheed and Ward, Ltd.

Shenandoah and James Boatwright, editor, for permission to reprint the essay, "The Poetry of John Crowe Ransom," by John L. Stewart.

Alec B. Stevenson, for lines from "Now This is Parting" and for the poems "Imprisonment" and "Fiddler's Green."

Alan Swallow, publisher, for excerpts from *Collected Essays*, by Allen Tate. Copyright 1960 by Allen Tate.

Allen Tate, for excerpts from "The Fugitive: 1922-1925: A Personal Recollection Twenty Years After"; *Jefferson Davis: His Rise and Fall*, by Allen Tate, copyright 1929 by G. P. Putnam's Sons; and *Reactionary Essays*, by Allen Tate, copyright 1936 by Charles Scribner's Sons.

The Virginia Quarterly Review, for an excerpt from "A Liberal Looks at Tradition," by Dudley Wynn, copyright 1936 by *The Virginia Quarterly Review*, The University of Virginia.

Robert Penn Warren, for lines from "The Golden Hills of Hell," "Crusade," "After Teacups," and "The Wrestling Match," and excerpts from "Proud Flesh," *John Brown, The Making of a Martyr*, copyright 1929 by Payson and Clark, Inc., and *Selected Poems 1923-1943*, copyright 1944 by Robert Penn Warren.

The Yale Review, for an excerpt from "Three Critics," by Herbert Muller, copyright 1942 by *The Yale Review*.

CONTENTS

THE BURDEN OF TIME
THE FUGITIVES AND AGRARIANS

CHAPTER ONE

THE FUGITIVES: BEGINNINGS

....

"A seven of friends exceeds much multitude."
—*John Crowe Ransom, "Ego" in* THE FUGITIVE, I, *no. 1*

....

I

*W*ITHOUT Sidney Mttron Hirsch[1] contemporary American letters would not be quite the same. Though he published only one book, a verse-play called *The Fire Regained* which appeared nearly fifty years ago and has since been wholly forgotten, he put his mark on our literature and literary studies. Lacking him, they would be different in essential and significant ways.

Any roll of those writers, critics, editors, and teachers who have done most to define the present character of American letters would certainly include the names of John Crowe Ransom, Allen Tate, and Robert Penn Warren, three of the sixteen men who foregathered long ago in Nashville, Tennessee, to talk about poetry, criticize each others' verses, and publish the nineteen issues of a tiny magazine called *The Fugitive.* Perhaps Pound, Faulkner, or Hemingway could be said to have had more effect as individuals. These matters are hard to determine and the comparisons probably do not mean as much as they seem to. But no contemporary *group* has made such a lasting impression as have the Fugitives, and without Sidney Hirsch this group would never have come into being or continued long enough to matter. Working apart, Ransom, Tate, and Warren might have written much and well, but without the community which began far back under the aegis of Hirsch, their work would not have had its singular and cumulative influence in our culture.

Circumstances of background and environment were extraordi-

[1] Mttron comes from the Kabbala, wherein it is the name of an archangel of immense and mysterious powers associated with the sun. It is pronounced Ma-*ta-tron*, the first syllable being so lightly stressed as to give an effect of Mm-*ta*-tron or simply *Ta*-tron. Mr. Hirsch also signed himself Sidney Mttron-Hirsch. He died on April 7, 1962.

3

narily propitious. Looking back one gets the impression that these men and their friends could scarcely escape coming together to talk about poetry, as, indeed, they did before the Fugitive group took it up, in the classrooms of Vanderbilt University and in the meetings of the Calumet Club, a literary society for undergraduates in which some alumni on the faculty or in the community kept their membership. But such random meetings lacked the depth and concentration that Hirsch made possible by holding the Fugitives together and directing their conversations long enough to establish that community which was to be so important in the work of the three best-known members of the group—a community which, though attenuated, still prevails. This is not to suggest that his ideas were predominant in the group. Most of the members rejected them, and insofar as there was any one man to whom they looked for guidance, that man was Ransom. Yet three decades after the group had broken up, one who had been in it from the beginning and had come back to Nashville to join the others, now full of years and accomplishment, for a Fugitives' reunion recalled that Hirsch was the "true begetter," to which his friends assented. Today Hirsch is unknown even to students and admirers of the Fugitive writers. Indeed, though he lived in Nashville all his life, until the reunion others of the group had not seen him for years. He insisted that he liked his obscurity. But it was not always thus.

There was a time when he and his writing were talked about in the State Department and he was the moment's greatest man in Nashville, where he was born in 1885. (Fond of little mysteries, he himself refused to give the exact date of his birth.) As public attention went, this was the peak of a bizarre career which began with Hirsch's running away from home to join the Navy. His family was a happy one, and his father, an immigrant tradesman, was respected and well-liked in the community. But Hirsch, who was big for his age and exceedingly restless, became bored with school and had to be off. Once in the service he took up boxing and before long had fought his way to the heavyweight championship of the Pacific Fleet. Though he had found schoolwork tedious, he had great curiosity and a love of learning—provided he could come at it in his own darting and roundabout fashion. During a two-year period in which he was stationed in China he began an erratic but persistent study of Buddhism and Taoism. It was the turning point of his life. Fascinated with the ideas he had picked up in his random excursions, Hirsch began a course of self-instruction in mysticism of all forms, from the most subtle and profound to the naive and absurd, and in time he became a rarely learned man. Oriental philosophies, Rosicrucianism, mystical numerology and etymology, astrology, the more remote passages of Hebraic lore—these and countless other matters were jumbled together in the vast warehouse of his mind, waiting to be brought forth to baffle or amuse his listeners.

After his tour of duty in China, Hirsch slowly made his way home through Korea and India, where he stopped off for more studies in mysticism. Eventually he reached Nashville; but though his family hoped he might stay to complete his formal education, soon he was off for Paris. Boxing had left him unmarked, and he had grown into an unusually handsome man. His figure was magnificent and his head, which he held very high, had great distinction. To pick up a little money he worked as a model. Rodin used him for several statues and introduced him to artists and writers, among them A. E. (George Russell) and Gertrude Stein.[2] Impressed, Miss Stein claimed to have discovered some distant connection between them and called him her cousin, but though she may have encouraged Hirsch in his explorations on the frontiers of language, he was much too independent to sit at her feet. The contact with A. E. was more significant, for the Irish poet and mystic urged him to look below the surface of even the most ordinary poem for the true meaning which might be unrecognized by the author himself. To penetrate more deeply, Hirsch began to teach himself languages, and with his predilection for the esoteric, turned to the dead or neglected tongues—the more remote the better. Eventually he gained a wide if sometimes inaccurate knowledge of Greek and Latin; he learned to read ancient Hebrew; and he picked up enough from dictionaries to grope his way through passages of Babylonian, Syrian, Chaldean, Arabic, Sanskrit, and ancient Egyptian. He gathered a bewildering congeries of facts

[2] From a conversation with Hirsch on September 24, 1946. In her richly informed study, *The Fugitive Group: A Literary History* (Baton Rouge, 1959), Louise Cowan writes that Hirsch went abroad with a tutor named Chase, who was a sculptor, and in his company made his way among the studios and ateliers.

about roots and cognates, to which he added some wild and wonderful hypotheses of his own. At their first encounter he told Allen Tate that "*woode* in Middle English meant 'mad,' and that the Trojan horse being the wooden horse must be the mad horse; and that since madness is divine, the Trojan horse is the esoteric and symbolic horse,"[3] and to this writer he once solemnly explained that hermetic meanings, which he was not free to divulge, were present in the term *hamlet* as a consequence of its referring to a play, a prince, an egg dish, and a small village. When anyone tried to explain that there was no historical justification for some of the connections he found, he retorted that it was precisely because of their insistence upon historical validation that others missed the meanings which he discovered by intuition.

From Paris he went to New York, where he became the model and friend of the sculptress Gertrude Vanderbilt Whitney. With her patronage he was able to push on with his studies of the occult and to make his first serious effort to establish himself as a writer. He tried one-act plays and even a libretto for an opera, but he was more successful at cultivating friends among the literati. He was particularly drawn to Edwin Arlington Robinson, who, unlike some of the Fugitives at a later time, was genuinely interested in the meanings Hirsch found in his works. The two corresponded until Robinson's death in 1935 and exchanged many letters on the homonymous associations in "Luke Havergal" and the light-darkness symbolism of Robinson's Arthurian romances.

Mrs. Whitney made several statues of Hirsch which were placed in galleries and parks in the East, but his writing did not get the attention he hoped for. So, still restless and churning with inspiration and conglomerate learning, he went back to Nashville, where a weird and wonderful triumph awaited him. It was all his, and only he could have had just that kind.

Nashville had celebrated its centennial in 1898, and to mark the occasion with a monument appropriate to the character and aspirations of the "Athens of the South," a full-scale replica of the Parthenon had been built of concrete and crushed marble in Centennial Park. The builders had measurements made of the ruins on the Acropolis and casts taken from the Elgin Marbles and

---

[3] Allen Tate, "The Fugitive 1922-1925," *The Princeton University Library Chronicle*, III (April, 1942), 76.

studied copies of all surviving records. The product of their dili-
gence might seem anachronistic to the finicky, but it certainly was
handsome, and over the years, as it settled into the landscape, it
took on dignity. It made a magnificent backdrop for the May
Festival which the Nashville Art Association and the Board of
Trade planned for the spring of 1913. The Association thought of
Oberammergau, while the Board wondered if the Festival would
do as well as the New Orleans Mardi Gras at pulling in out-of-town
shoppers. Music and dancing teachers counted on showing off their
pupils. The pageant chosen to launch what all hoped would become an annual affair was Hirsch's *The Fire Regained*, which he
had published during the previous February.

The civic energy that got the Parthenon up now went into preparations for the festival. A cast of 600 spent three months in re-
hearsal under a teacher from Ward-Belmont College. Professional
drivers were engaged to race in chariots drawn by four white and
four black horses. Huge papier-maché wings were prepared for the
stallion representing Pegasus. Three hundred sheep and 1,000
pigeons were made ready. The railroads reduced their fares for
out-of-town visitors drawn to Nashville by full-page advertise-
ments inviting them to see "The Flight of a Thousand Doves,
the Revel of the Wood Nymphs, the Thrilling Chariot Race, the
Raising of the Shepherd from the Dead, the Orgy of the Flaming
Torches." The revels and orgies were fairly circumspect, for they
were presided over by a former first lady of Tennessee, known for
her "musical readings," who consented to play Athene. Nevertheless, the trolley company had to run special cars to accommodate
the 5,000 people who turned out for the six performances given
between May 5 and 8.

Like the celebrated funeral of the commissioner's step-sister, *The
Fire Regained* was a roaring success, though it lacked some of the
style and logic of Norman Douglas' ceremony. In fact, it not only
lacked logic, it was often totally incomprehensible. The action,
when not stopped dead in its tracks by the poetry, went something
like this: Awakened by the kisses of the (debutante) Muses, a
shepherd is informed by Athene that one of the virgins guarding
the sacred Athenian flame has been falsely accused of unchastity
and that only he can save her. Having, at some length, promised
to do his best, the shepherd promptly dies and is placed in an ad-

7

jacent grave which happens conveniently to be there. Eros then leads in Pegasus, and the shepherd just as promptly returns to life, unburdens himself of an ode invoking divine aid, and leaves for Athens. In the second act one of the virgins goes into hysterics, and the priests take this as a sign that she is the guilty party. She is forced to undergo trials by ordeal that involve the pigeons, a ceremony with rams, and the chariot race. All seem to signify her fall from virtue, and she is led to the flames. Hermes appears and puts off the dread moment by announcing that messengers are on the way. Servants of the chthonian gods, who are behind all the mischief, come staggering in, followed by the shepherd bearing the shield of Athene, which can turn the beholder to stone. He calcifies the enemy, wins the race, and sets free the maiden, who turns out to be Athene herself, helmeted and triumphant.

Probably no one had much time for asking why the shepherd after his resurrection went running around when Pegasus was there or just what Athene thought she was doing all along, because odder things might happen at any moment; on the second day one of the chariots upset in a fine uproar of dust and shouting. But if anyone *had* looked for an explanation, he would have been up against some fairly baffling diction which included words such as *corymbus, helaic, mephitic, eristic, essorant, empherean, sminthian,* and *lumest*. Supposing that these had not stayed him, he would have soon found himself entangled in the fearful syntax and the arcane allusions which had no apparent bearing upon the action. Hirsch was indulging to the utmost his love of the remote and mysterious, and the result was an almost total verbal and dramatic disorder.

Obscure as these might be, they were a relief from the clichés and the stamping-mill rhythms of most of the verse. Wakened by the belles of Nashville, the shepherd apostrophized:

> Ye Sun! Consoling light, O Earth!
> Ye trees and shadowed streams, ye sky-lined hills,
> O bleating lambs, ye rams, ye pebbled rills,
> I've dreamed a dream! a vision rare vouchsafed to me,
> A maid, three heavenly maids,
> Came down and kissed my mouth,
> And breath of theirs was sweeter far than any flower!

8

Sweeter than waters from a native youth-known well
Drunk upon a parchèd midnight palate!
Sweeter than a love child's earliest lisp
Upon the youngest mother's breast,
O sweet it was and balmy past the telling! . . .

The audience, meanwhile, was presumably wondering what was
going on, but as it took the shepherd this long merely to describe
the kisses that woke him, the audience had to wait more than a little
while to find out, if it ever did. Eventually, the pageant neared
its awful climax, and the priests intoned:

The sins that mar our pristine state
Demand propitiation!
The clay that clogs our truest fate
Demands an immolation!
Nor Pity's tear scald fertile earth
Nor heave the windy sigh!
The laws immute that brought us birth
Demand a victim die!
O Justice send thy dire decrees.
Choose thou a maiden of one of these!

To which the nervous maidens answered:

O Hestia! Virgin votaries we,
Attend our tremulation.
Come Astraea from cerulean seas,
To fend our tribulation.
O guard they doves within the cote
That is thine own afflatus,
Defence devise that shall defeat
Storm shades would devastate us!
O Pallas! clearest eyed and brow'd
Save thou thy maid from flaming shroud!

Happily there were all those pigeons.

What emerges from the text is an imagination that has surrendered utterly to the lure of the far and lost, that has only a
rudimentary sense of structure and is willing enough to violate
that for the sake of mystification. But this did not for the present

9

overshadow Hirsch's triumph. Newspapers called the pageant "the most magnificent production ever given in the South or the entire country" and published poems in praise of the author. On the third evening Hirsch was brought out to receive an ovation. And all this seemed only the beginning. A movie made during the production was shown throughout the nation. Plans got underway at once for a festival for the following year, and for this Hirsch wrote a sombre and even more obscure work called "The Mysteries of Thanatos." When it was put on in the spring of 1914 it was received with respectful unenthusiasm, but during the year "The Fire Regained" was staged in Washington with the aid of 600 Marines and caused even more of a sensation than it had in Nashville. It was now that Hirsch came to the attention of the State Department, where there was serious talk of taking the pageant abroad and staging it on the Acropolis as a gesture of good will.

Encouraged, Hirsch had gone back to New York, where one of his pieces, "The Passion Play of Washington Square," was a minor success when staged off Broadway by semi-professionals. But his luck did not hold. The outbreak of war in Europe put an end to the idea of taking "The Fire Regained" abroad and provided the Nashville merchants, who had been uncertain after the less favorable reaction to the festival in 1914, with a readymade reason for dropping plans for yet another in 1915. Profoundly disappointed but full of plans, Hirsch returned once more to Nashville. Again a triumph awaited him, one slow to develop, quiet, but far more significant than all the uproar over "The Fire Regained."

In 1915, Nashville was a small city that had kept the friendly casualness of a town. Nearly 100,000 people, one third of them Negroes, lived there; yet it still seemed as if everyone knew everyone else. Most citizens were natives of the region with family ties long and deeply woven into a way of life that took its tempo and attitudes from the many little farming communities of that genial countryside. Industry had stayed small and diversified, and the fact that the Cumberland River and the coming together in Nashville of several railroads and important highways had made the city a focus of Southern commerce had not spoiled the easy, relaxed atmosphere which had always included a friendly though not very earnest interest in the arts and letters. Between 1900 and 1914, the city had grown and shifted its economy more and more toward industry. Yet the transition had charged the air not with nervous tension so much as with that civic ebullience that had gone into staging the May Festivals.

During the war the government built a great arms plant not far from Andrew Jackson's old farm. Migratory workers poured in. Space was short, rents rose, and the cheerfully sleepy city began to change abruptly. After the war, when the nation returned to a peacetime economy, Nashville managed to escape the fearful slump into which the rest of the South fell. Shutdown of the arms plant brought momentary confusion, but other, recently established heavy industries, which shared in the prosperity of Northern manufacturing, absorbed the labor force and soon needed more manpower. The population of the city grew 30 percent and many more thousands moved into the suburbs and surrounding towns. Yet the growth did not disrupt the smalltown intimacy so long established among the older families. Change seemed exhilarating, not oppressive, and many hoped Nashville would once more be in fact the intellectual leader of the Middle South. There had always been a cultural tradition of sorts. At dinner clubs members read essays on local history. Poets, most of them ladies, published verses in the literary columns of the local papers, and literature was always well spoken of if not diligently read. But there was no symphony orchestra; musical interest was accommodated by sentimental songs around the upright piano or the lightest of light classics. No painter or sculptor of distinction worked in Nashville, and architecture languished under the weight of Methodist Gothic. The "Athens of the South" was not really an oasis in what H. L. Mencken coarsely termed "The Sahara of the Bozart."

Its one sure claim to distinction rested upon its schools and universities. A number of good private academies had been long established in and near the city and had helped to educate several generations of the same families of the region. In addition to unaccredited colleges maintained by Fundamentalist sects, there were Ward-Belmont, one of the better junior colleges for women in the South, the George Peabody College for Teachers, among the best of its kind in the nation, and Fisk University, foremost of the Negro institutions of higher learning. At the top was Vanderbilt University, whose faculty members and their wives were counted among the leaders in the social and cultural life of the city.

In 1915 Vanderbilt's contribution to that life was not so rich and varied as it would become, but for the previous four years it had given the citizens something to argue about. The university had been established in 1875 on what were then the western outskirts of the city with money provided by "Commodore" Cornelius Vanderbilt. His generosity had made possible the dream of the Southern Methodist Church to train young men, especially young Methodist ministers, for the task of rebuilding the South. Though not all members of the faculty were Methodists, no conspicuous deviation from Wesley's *Sermons* and Watson's *Institutes* was encouraged. Forty years after its founding, the university seemed a little retarded and backward-looking when compared with other American schools of comparable size and endowment. But not in Nashville, where much excitement and seemingly endless argument had been furnished by the struggle between Chancellor James M. Kirkland, head of the University, and Bishop E. E. Hoss, of the Southern Methodist Church. Hoss was the passionate, impatient leader of those churchmen who feared contamination of the university by unorthodox teaching and were determined to prevent this by controlling appointments. Kirkland, made chancellor in 1893, had been working to enlarge the university and raise its academic standards and status, but his methods were not approved by the bishop. In the end he won the battle through a decree of the Supreme Court of Tennessee, which established the independence of the university and denied the right of the church to meddle in its affairs. Still, Kirkland found it difficult to hold on to good men, who tended to look North for better jobs and higher pay. Instruction in the classics under Dean Herbert Cushing Tolman, one of the best philologists in the country, was excellent, and Herbert Charles Sanborn, of the Philosophy Department, attracted many young men by his brilliance in the classroom and the quantity of his writing. But instruction in the other departments tended to lag behind that found elsewhere in the country. The English Department, for example, had, until recently, consisted of one professor of literature, an assistant professor of philology, who gave part of his time to the German Department, and one instructor, who taught freshman composition. Edwin Mims had been appointed chairman of the department in 1912 and was slowly reorganizing the staff and extending the instruction, but before his arrival the emphasis had been upon grammar and rhetoric, and young men interested in literature as such tended to gravitate to Tolman and the classics.[4]

Mims came to Vanderbilt with a reputation as a progressive Southerner, an heir of Henry Grady and Joel Chandler Harris, and he brought great energy, interest in contemporary writing, and useful contacts with teachers and scholars throughout the country. He was fond of power, and in the thirty years during which he served as chairman of the English Department he was able to make uncomfortable any younger men who seemed likely to threaten his control or to divert attention from himself. One of his first moves toward strengthening the department was to bring in Walter Clyde Curry, a specialist in medieval literature who joined the faculty in 1915 just after receiving his doctor's degree from Stanford. His appointment followed by one year that of another man who would add even more luster to the department. For in 1914 John Crowe Ransom, who had no graduate training in English literature and who had spent the past year teaching Latin in a New England academy, came back to Vanderbilt.

Born on April 30, 1888, in Pulaski, a small town about seventy-five miles south of Nashville, Ransom had passed most of his life in central Tennessee, where his father was a Methodist minister. But his background was not wholly rural, for his father, who had served as a missionary in Brazil and Cuba, was a skilled linguist and scholar who had translated the Bible into Portuguese, and Ransom had come up to Nashville to attend a preparatory school at eleven. Well coached in the classics, he had entered Vanderbilt when only fifteen, had left to teach school at seventeen, and had returned and graduated *summa cum laude* in 1909. After another year of teaching, Ransom went to Christ's College, Oxford, as a Rhodes Scholar and student in the Literary Humanities (classical literature and philosophy). In his three years at Oxford he became the close friend of

---

[4] Edwin Mims, *History of Vanderbilt University* (Nashville, 1946), p. 441; *Fugitives' Reunion: Conversations at Vanderbilt*, ed. Rob Roy Purdy (Nashville, 1959), pp. 91 *et passim*; conversations with John Crowe Ransom, August 24, 1946, and Merrill Moore, July 7-8, 1956.

Christopher Morley, who founded a literary club called "The Midwives," through which Ransom had his first significant contact with nineteenth-century and contemporary literature in his own language. Reading modern poetry made him vaguely discontented with the classics, and his dissatisfaction increased during his year in New England. Not knowing which way to turn, he applied for a position in the English Department at Vanderbilt. On the strength of his brilliant undergraduate record and his Rhodes scholarship he was accepted. Mims may have thought he was getting a bargain by hiring a man without a degree in English. He was.

In going back to Vanderbilt, Ransom had acted upon a conviction and an impulse, both a bit hazy at the time but no less strong for that; together they comprised his earliest intellectual recollection and were to become a significant force in his thinking throughout his adult life, and a source of many themes, assumptions, and attitudes of his writing. He had come to believe that modern man is crippled by a dissociation of the reason and sensibility which results in an imbalance whereby the reason, armed with abstract principles which have been spectacularly successful in supplying the material needs of the body, tyrannizes over the sensibility and restricts its innocent, profitless delight in the vividness and variety of the world. With this conviction went a "fury against abstractions" and a desire to restore the sensibility to its proper eminence in man and his society and to enable it to enjoy its harmless indulgences.[5]

This was curious equipment for an Oxford-trained classicist and philosopher. It had come to Ransom not from his studies but from his own experiences and observations; though modified through the years by his reading in Kant, Hume, Bergson, Freud, and many others, it owed its origin to no other man. When he compared the classics, in which the idealism of Plato appeared to overbalance the rich particularity of Homer, with English literature, they seemed too abstract and dogmatic for a lifetime of study and teaching. He preferred the greater spontaneity, the rougher surfaces, the seemingly more intense feeling of English poetry. He soon had a chance to find out whether his choice was a good one. Vanderbilt

[5] From a conversation with Ransom, August 26, 1946.

not only took him in, it presented him with a class in Shakespeare. One of his students was Donald Davidson.

That gifted young man had come to Vanderbilt attended, as he later wrote in *The Tall Men*, by

> Dust of battles, creak of wagons, vows
> Rotting like antique lace; the smiles of women
> Broken like glass; the tales of old men blown
> From rheumy beards on the vague wind; silk gowns
> Crumbling in attics; ruffled shirts on bones
> Of gentlemen in forgotten graves; rifles,
> Hunting-shirts, Bibles, looms, and desperate
> Flags uncrowned.

Like Sidney Hirsch, he yearned for things faint, far, and lost.

Born in 1893 at Campbellsville, a tiny village a few miles away from Pulaski, Davidson had spent all his life in south-central Tennessee, where his father was a schoolteacher and where his forebears had held their land against Indians, Britishers, and Yankees. Davidson knew where the Cherokees had whooped, where the blood of tall Tennessee men had darkened the ground. But though he had an unusual loyalty to his region, he took it more or less for granted. His greatest interests at the moment were music and poetry. He had come to Vanderbilt in the fall of 1909 shortly after Ransom had graduated, but after one year he was compelled to withdraw for lack of funds. He spent the next four years teaching in preparatory schools and dallying with the notion of becoming a professional musician. His mother was a gifted performer and teacher; from her he had taken his first lessons on the piano, and he had taught himself elementary harmony from books in her library. In the years after he had withdrawn from the university he had written a musical play for children which had been performed with great applause more than a dozen times. Overlooking his own training, he thought that all artistic creation, be it in music, verse, or whatever, took place when the mind was in a near-trance. Talk about aesthetics bored him.

In those days Vanderbilt boys went about in small groups on Sunday afternoons to call on pretty local girls and their families. One of the most popular was Goldie Hirsch, Sidney's younger half-sister. The Hirsch family had a large house near the campus,

and students were always welcome. In the summer of 1915 Davidson had stayed in Nashville to work and had met Goldie. His friend
Stanley Johnson, a Nashville boy who had entered the university
in 1911, knew the Hirsch family well through Sidney's younger
half-brother Nat. He took Davidson with him to call on Goldie
and introduced him to Sidney, who was restless since his return
from New York and longing for someone to talk to. Johnson
enjoyed arguing with Sidney, but Davidson preferred to listen.
He was impressed by Sidney's reputation (for Nashville still talked
of "The Fire Regained"), and though he was but little interested
in most of Sidney's ideas, he was flattered when the older man took
him off for long walks and talked about his own attempts at poetry.
Hirsch quite agreed with him that creation was a mysterious, largely intuitive act and, pointing out that few people were endowed
with the necessary powers, insisted that to be a poet was the greatest
distinction a man could enjoy and that Davidson should do more
writing. After such an evening Davidson would go back late to his
room with his head in a whirl and his self-esteem greatly enlarged.

It occurred to Davidson and Johnson, who had also studied under Ransom, that their teacher was the right man to stand up to
Hirsch, for Ransom was trained as a philosopher and had had considerable experience with debating while an undergraduate. For all
his dissatisfaction with abstractions, he was fond of speculation and,
under his gentle manner, a hardheaded sceptic. They took him with
them, and soon Ransom was one of those who sat late into the mild
summer nights trying to pin down the protean Sidney. Also part
of the group was William Yandell Elliott, a classmate of Nat from
Murfreesboro, Tennessee. In the fall, Alec Brock Stevenson, the
son of a member of the Vanderbilt faculty, joined the discussions.
Another friend of Nat, Stevenson had entered the university in
1912. He was a strong addition to the now fairly frequent discussions, for he had grown up among the debates of scholars and
was unusually well read. The talk went on through the school year
of 1915-1916, impelled by the extraordinary Sidney, who fascinated the others with his offhand references to distant places and
famous names and the incredible baggage of his learning. His manner was lofty and his observations were sometimes exasperating,
but his interest in them and their ideas was friendly and perfectly

sincere and he drew them farther and farther from the shelter of the conventional. The meetings were informal, but the talk always ran on the highest levels. Sidney kept it there. Without knowing it he had found his real métier. The Fugitive group, unnamed, unorganized, was being established. Then, on a warm afternoon in May of 1916, something happened which would ultimately do much to change the character of the group and make possible its special contribution to American literature. John Crowe Ransom asked Davidson to step out onto the Vanderbilt campus with him: he had something to show his friend. It was "Sunset," Ransom's first poem.[6]

Sometimes it is easy to look back upon the work of a distinguished poet and, assured of his later achievements, discover signs of his idiom and vision in even his earliest verses. But it is difficult to find anything much resembling Ransom's later poems in what he read to Davidson:

> I know you are not cruel,
> And you would not willingly hurt anything in the world.
> There is kindness in your eyes,
> There could not very well be more of it in eyes
> Already brimful of the sky.
> I thought you would someday begin to love me,
> But now I doubt it badly;
> It is no man-rival I am afraid of,
> It is God.

> The meadows are very wide and green,
> And the big field of wheat is solid gold,
> Or a little darker than gold.
> Two people never sat like us by a fence of cedar rails
> On a still evening
> And looked at such fat fields.

[6] Information about the origin of the group was gathered in conversations with Hirsch, September 24, 1946; Davidson, September 26, 1946; Ransom, August 26, 1946; and Merrill Moore, July 7-8, 1956. The order of some of the details was clarified by Mrs. Cowan's excellent study referred to above. Those desiring more information, particularly about the family backgrounds of the Fugitives, should consult her work.

I am stirred,
I say grand and wonderful, and grow adjectival,
But to you
It is God.

The drab and spastic lines lurched on through an explanation of how the speaker thought his sweetheart's preoccupation with the Infinite unnatural and alarming. The poem ended:

I will try to be as patient as Rover,
And we will be comrades and wait,
Unquestioningly,
Till this lady we love
And her strange eyes
Come home from God.

It would be more polite to look the other way and pass on, but certain features of the poem compel attention. One is the humorous self-depreciation of the speaker, which makes lingering over the poem less cruel than it would be if the piece were as pretentious as most first flights in verse. This was to be the tone of many of Ransom's later poems which, like this, took the form of a little anecdote or fable. More important, however, is the fact that in his first effort, Ransom made clear his preference for the immediate natural object (if one may so designate a pretty girl) and his distrust of the noumena which took attention from the substantial world and denied the sensibility its little satisfactions. Concomitants of his fury against abstractions, they opposed the whole direction of the ideas Hirsch poured out upon his hearers.

Davidson did not care much for the poem, but he was too gracious to say so and Ransom felt encouraged to try again. Soon he wrote three more and sent them, with "Sunset," to *The Independent*, which took them all. Then Ransom's Oxford friend, Christopher Morley, accepted still others for his column in *The Philadelphia Public Ledger*. Before the year was out Ransom had placed poems in *The Liberator* and *Contemporary Verse* as well. Looking through these poems, which were collected in Ransom's first volume, *Poems About God*, one is surprised that most of them were ever published, though "The Swimmer," one of the first four, is a fairly witty and well-made piece; but one can only be grateful to the editors who took them, for Ransom, a modest man, was twenty-eight when he began writing, and without such encouragement he might easily have given up.[7]

Yet, though Davidson and Johnson were also writing verse and Stevenson was concerned that more good writing was not being done at Vanderbilt, the discussions at the Hirsch home continued to be mostly about philosophy. Then abruptly the meetings came to an end. The United States entered the First World War and, just a year after he had written his first poem, Ransom left Vanderbilt for the Officers' Training Corps at Fort Oglethorpe. After four months' training he was sent to France. Davidson, too, was at Fort Oglethorpe, and he and Ransom sometimes got away for a talk about literature before they went overseas. Just before he sailed, Ransom sent copies of his poems to Morley, who determined to get them published. Eventually they were accepted by Henry Holt and appeared under the title *Poems About God* in the spring of 1919 with a little preface by the poet, written in France a year earlier, in which he indicated his dissatisfaction with their naïveté. Stevenson, Johnson, and Elliott, too, were in the services, so that Hirsch was left with only his family for an audience. He went to New York for a time, but returned to Nashville much depressed by the failure of all his plans since 1914. He felt that he was neglected by the Vanderbilt intellectuals because he was self-taught. Added to his burdens was the agony of watching the collapse of another brother who had been developing into an illustrator of great promise.

It was in this interval that Hirsch went to live with his sister Rose and her husband, James Marshall Frank, a well-to-do manufacturer of shirts and pajamas. Then in his early fifties, Frank was an educated and sensitive man who so admired his brilliant brother-in-law that he was happy to support him while Sidney studied and wrote. Neither man found anything awkward in their arrangement, for they came from Jewish families in which it had been traditional for those who succeeded in making money to contribute to maintenance of the scholars, who should be free to devote themselves wholly to learning. Assured by the backing of Frank, Hirsch began to withdraw from the world and to find pleasure in obscurity. Gradually he came to believe that any moment

---

[7] For a further discussion of Ransom's early poems, see Chapter Five, pp. 207-215.

there are scattered in widely different parts of the world seven mystic seers to whom are given insights denied other men and that he was one of the seven then living. These men might not publish their knowledge. They were obliged to wait for those who deserved to learn to seek them out. The very fact that those who came to them had known where to look was proof that the seers might divulge to them some of their wisdom. But when none came to them, they must study and follow their visions ever more deeply into their own beings.

At the same time Hirsch developed an indefinite injury near the base of his spine which doctors were unable to diagnose or treat. Sure that they could never help him, he spent his time lying upon a couch—a drastic change from the days when he had been a champion boxer and his great body had been much admired by artists and sculptors. Moreover, his own ordeal convinced him that a man must suffer a mystical injury to his spine in order to realize his inward nature. Later he was to argue that the poet must be maimed, and though none of his friends accepted this idea, his constant invoking of the image of the poet as sufferer and fugitive was to have some effect on the ideas and attitudes of Davidson and other members of the group. Long after the Fugitives had disbanded he recovered, but throughout the years of their meetings he would receive visitors in the Franks' living room, reclining under a full-length painting of his nearly nude torso which had been executed in Paris during the days of his greatest physical vigor. The conjunction had a significance which Hirsch, with all his love of the symbolic, perhaps did not wholly realize.

II

But Fortune had not turned her face from Sidney Hirsch. While so many other gifted young men of their generation stayed on in Paris or settled in New York City after the war, those who had sat with him to talk philosophy came back to Nashville one by one. At first some of them lingered in France to take advantage of the government assistance to veterans who wished to study at foreign universities. Ransom attended Grenoble for a time and, Louise Cowan reports, thought of leaving teaching for journalism, but the offer of an assistant professorship brought him back to Vanderbilt in the fall of 1919.[8] Elliott, who had taken his degree in 1917, studied for a time at the Sorbonne, then decided to return to Vanderbilt in the fall of 1919 to work for a master's degree in English. Stevenson went to Clermont then back to Philadelphia, where he had worked for a short time as a journalist before going into the army. After a few months he, too, came back to Nashville, where he tried journalism again but gave it up to enter banking. Davidson had not remained abroad when mustered out. He had taken his degree in 1916 and had taught for a year. Before going overseas he had married, and as soon as he could he returned to his wife and to teaching in Kentucky. After a year at tiny Kentucky Wesleyan College, where he served as head of the English Department, he was glad to accept Mims's offer that he come back to Vanderbilt as an instructor in English to work for a master's degree. Thus, by the spring of 1920, all of the group except Stanley Johnson were back in town and before long had fallen into the old way of going out to talk with Sid. When Stanley Johnson returned in the fall of 1921 to work for *his* degree in English, things were about as they had been before the war.[9] But not for long.

Ransom for a time shared rooms with Walter Clyde Curry, whose hobby was writing sonnets which he sent to the minuscule *American Poetry Magazine*. At Curry's urging Ransom tried some sonnets of his own, and one of these, an early version of "Winter Remembered," appeared in *The Sewanee Review* for January, 1922. It shows that Ransom had trouble fitting the narrative im-

[8] *The Fugitive Group*, p. 28.
[9] However, Elliott had been granted a Rhodes Scholarship and left for Balliol College in the autumn of 1921. Henceforth he met with the Fugitives only in the summers when he returned to Nashville for the long vacations. Another who sat in on the discussions just after the war was William Frierson, a Tennessee boy who had attended preparatory school in Nashville and had entered Vanderbilt in 1915. After serving in the army he returned to Vanderbilt and graduated in June, 1920. He preceded Elliott as a Rhodes Scholar at Balliol in the autumn of 1921, and like Elliott could attend meetings only during the summers. After 1923 he dropped out of the group altogether. For a time both men were designated members *in absentia*, and their names were carried on the rolls of the group to the end; but though Elliott kept in close touch by letter and attempted some long-distance criticism of the poems and ideas presented in the meetings, neither he nor Frierson contributed much to the group. Elliott's six poems in the magazine and Frierson's two are without interest.
    Mrs. Cowan reports that Johnson spent two years teaching at the University of Manila before coming back to Vanderbilt. *The Fugitive Group*, p. 35.

pulse which from the beginning had been most natural to him to the confines of the form, but the many sonnets written in this period, which have not survived, helped to keep alive his interest in writing poetry.[10] At the same time he was deep in a program of reading which was to have a profound and lasting effect upon his style. Davidson, too, was studying earlier literatures with an intensity that soon showed itself in his poems. After reading Amy Lowell's *Tendencies in Modern American Poetry* while he was in the army, he had tried some free verse which turned out wretchedly. Now he was deep in William Blake, whose style and vision were to have a more lasting and happier effect. But for all this, studying and teaching were often tedious, and Ransom, Davidson, and Johnson liked to get away by going over to see Sid. Often Curry went along, too. Their visits had just a trace of defiance in them. The autocratic Mims was annoyed that in looking for an older companion in the realm of ideas they went outside the university and the department, and the young men, who were restive under his one-man rule, enjoyed doing something he disliked but could not prevent. Hirsch, for all his considerable vanity and his claim to having left the world behind, was genuinely interested in them and their ideas and could be counted on to say something that would start an argument.

Now that he was an invalid, the discussions took place in the living room of the Franks' house in a pleasant suburb west of the university. Jim Frank, too, joined the young men sitting in chairs around the walls (no one ever sat on the floor) and listening to Hirsch discourse with grave formality while they traced the patterns in the Persian rug at their feet or studied the brushstrokes in the great painting of their friend which hung above his couch. Gradually their meetings shifted from Sunday afternoons to Saturday nights and assumed a fairly regular schedule of fortnightly sessions, for they had become intentionally intellectual gatherings and not just social calls. When the talk began to subside around eleven o'clock, Mrs. Frank would put aside the curtains which separated the talkers from the adjoining dining room, and everyone

[10] Later, in "Good Ships" and other sonnets, Ransom showed that he could use the Italian sonnet to achieve a brilliant combination of the fable and the mild but shrewdly penetrating comment by a retiring bystander—the combination which so often appears in his most characteristic and effective poems in other forms.

22

would help himself to cold cuts, sausages, potato salad, cheeses, several kinds of bread, and, if he wished, beer or wine, which were not hard to come by in Nashville despite the new Prohibition Laws.

Then in the autumn of 1921 the whole tenor of the discussions changed. Despite his heavy teaching load and his reading program, Ransom had become more and more committed to poetry, and his work was going through an abrupt metamorphosis. Uncertain of the effectiveness of a style that was new in virtually every way, Ransom brought some of his poetry to one of the meetings to try on his friends. They made a good audience of close critics. Davidson wrote steadily and was actually more interested in poetry than in the abstract speculations which up to now had formed the substance of the discussions. Johnson had written a novel (never published) and hoped eventually to make his way as a writer. Curry put his literary research ahead of his sonnets, but managed time to write many of them and was interested in problems of technique. Stevenson had done imaginative writing as an undergraduate and had only recently given up journalism. And Hirsch, for all the awkwardness and obscurity of his own verse, was immersed in Robinson, A. E., Hardy, and the Greek poets, and delighted in making comparisons which were sometimes outrageous and sometimes richly illuminating and instructive.[11] The evening turned out to be so exciting that the others followed Ransom's example and brought their own verses. In a short time the emphasis had shifted from general philosophical problems to the particular poems brought by the members; ideas still figured in the discussions, but they came in as they bore upon the poems under scrutiny. Hirsch amiably went along with the interests of his friends, and thus, some six years after the casual encounters in the summer of 1915, the Fugitive group assumed its distinctive character.

At the same time that the shift toward poetry was taking place, another definitive element had been added: Davidson asked Allen Tate to come to a meeting, and shortly afterward he was invited to attend regularly. Tate, a native of Kentucky with family ties going back on his mother's side to Virginia, was twenty-two at the time and a senior well known to the faculty for his brilliance

[11] See Donald Davidson, *Southern Writers in the Modern World* (Athens, 1958), p. 12.

and his incorrigibly independent ways. Arrogant, patronizing toward his classmates and teachers, gifted but unsure of himself, he
much resembled the young James Joyce. He had picked up a good
knowledge of the classics before coming to Vanderbilt and thus was
able to appreciate the learning of Herbert Tolman. Curry, too,
had earned his approval. But the most profound effect on his thinking had come from Herbert Sanborn, not because Tate accepted
Sanborn's views but because Sanborn, by the rigor of his arguments and intolerance of anything but the most impeccable reasoning, taught him to relish exact discriminations among ideas and
values.[12] Tate was not easy to get along with and his first poems
were painful to read, but there were those, particularly Ransom,
who appreciated the distinction of his mind.

III

Throughout the winter of 1921-1922 the poems piled up until
on an afternoon in March as they chatted together about the group,
Hirsch suggested to his brother-in-law that they ought to start a
magazine to publish them. Frank liked the idea so well that Hirsch
brought it up at the next meeting, pointing out that they already
had enough material for several issues. Some of the group were
hesitant, but they took fire from Hirsch's own excitement. They
decided to go ahead at once.

Word got out. Many of their friends thought it folly, and Mims
tried angrily to argue them out of it. When one recalls the power
that he had over the careers of Ransom, Davidson, Curry, and Johnson, one can get some measure of their commitment to poetry. (However, it should be noted that when the Fugitives had established
themselves, Mims was proud of their achievement and their connection with the department. He encouraged interest in their writing by reading it at public meetings and dwelling on the high
moral content he said he found in it. And, as Louise Cowan has
pointed out, he had the good sense to value creative writing as highly as literary research. The Fugitives under him were not handi-
capped professionally by writing poems instead of articles about

---

[12] From a letter, Allen Tate to the writer, September 10, 1953. See also
Fugitives' Reunion, pp. 108-112. More information about Tate's background is
given in Chapters Seven and Eight.

poets.[13]) It might seem, therefore, that they chose to name the magazine *The Fugitive* with some reference to their situation and the early opposition to their project, but in fact they were not thinking of themselves at all. Years later it was hard for them to recall who actually proposed the name; some thought the suggestion had come from Hirsch, though Davidson and Stevenson believed that it was the latter who first put it forward. But, whatever the source, the name was selected in consequence of Hirsch's many allusions to the archetypal fugitive in poetry, the outcast wanderer with a mysterious knowledge.[14] The idea of the magazine had been his, and the others were happy to give it a name so close to his dearest interest. Moreover, though they did not feel oppressed in the genial atmosphere of Nashville, some of them were attracted by the glamorous image of the Poet as a sad, superior exile standing in lonely splendor on the far horizon. But insofar as the name had any immediate relevance to their relations with their surroundings, it was of the order described by Ransom in his unsigned editorial for the first issue. *The Fugitive*, he wrote, fled "from nothing faster than from the high-caste Brahmins of the Old South. Without raising the question of whether the blood in the veins of its editors runs red, they at any rate are not advertising it as blue. . . ." In any event, the name had one important use. As Tate has pointed out, it got attention.

At least in Nashville. Five hundred copies of the first issue were run off by a firm of Negro printers and placed on sale in local stores on April 12. Most of these went quickly, and the rest were given to friends or sent to newspapers and magazines in other parts of the country or to famous authors (who never acknowledged receiving them). The whole episode had a carnival air about it. Indeed, while the idea was new and local interest ran high, editing the magazine was more of a game than a chore. As an editorial in the third issue pointed out, "The procedure of publication is simply to gather up the poems that rank highest, by general consent of the group, and take them down to the publisher."[15] As part

[13] From conversations with Hirsch, September 24, 1946, and Moore, July 7-8, 1956. See Allen Tate, "The Fugitive, 1922-1925," p. 75, and Cowan, p. 48.
[14] *Fugitives' Reunion*, pp. 124-127; Tate, p. 79.
[15] "Editorial," *The Fugitive*, I (October, 1922), 66.

25

of the gaiety, the poets took pseudonyms for the first two issues, and these helped bring in buyers. Who was Robin Gallivant and who Henry Feathertop? What self-images had led to the choice of Roger Prim or L. Oafer? But the gaiety did not infect *The New York Times*, which remarked sourly that the poems in the first issue were "extremely mediocre." The local press, if patronizing, was more cordial. *The Nashville Tennessean*, for example, found the verse "marked by considerable breadth and scope of imaginative imagery, and it certainly has the virtue of dealing with themes that are worth considering." The most ambiguous comment came from H. L. Mencken. Writing in *The Baltimore Sun* he called *The Fugitive* "at the moment, the entire literature of Tennessee," which the Athenians of the South probably took as a compliment, as he went on to say that he liked the magazine better than most that came to his desk and was recommending it to his friends.[16]

And well he might, for two of Ransom's poems, the sad, lovely "To a Lady Celebrating Her Birthday" and the sardonic "Night Voices," were among the most original being written by an American at the moment, and only the poems of Tate and Hirsch were downright clumsy and incompetent. However, for all their distinc-

---

[16] The contents of the first issue were:

"Forward," Unsigned, but written by John Crowe Ransom.

"Ego," "Night Voices," "To a Lady Celebrating her Birthday," "The Handmaidens," by Roger Prim [John Crowe Ransom]. "Ego" was revised and reprinted in Ransom's *Chills and Fever* as "Plea in Mitigation." "The Handmaidens" was a revision of "The Power of God," which had been previously published in Ransom's *Poems About God*.

"A Demon Brother," "The Dragon Book," "Following the Tiger," by Robin Gallivant [Donald Davidson]. "A Demon Brother" was revised and retitled "An Outland Piper" in Davidson's first volume of poems, to which it gave its new name.

"To Intellectual Detachment," "Sinbad," by Henry Feathertop [Allen Tate].

"Imprisonment," "The House of Beauty," "To a Wise Man," by Drimlonigher [Alec Brock Stevenson]. For the second number of the magazine, Stevenson took the name "King Badger."

"Sermons," "An Intellectual's Funeral," "The Lifted Veil," by Jonathan David [Stanley Johnson].

"I Have Not Lived," by Marpha [Walter Clyde Curry].

"The Little Boy Pilgrim," by L. Oafer [Sidney Mttron Hirsch].

James Frank was not represented in the first issue. For the second issue, which appeared in June, 1922, and contained his poem "Fugitive Unbound," he chose the name "Philora." The Fugitives used their own names in the third issue, which appeared in October, 1922, and in all subsequent issues.

The poems are discussed in later chapters. Consult the index for comment on particular works.

tion of style and conception, Ransom's poems did not *look* particularly remarkable when put beside the experiments attempted in the other little magazines. In that same spring, for example, tumultuous, brilliant, *Secession* was launched and pointed in the direction (for all the calculated show of indirection) already taken by *S4N* (1919), *Contact* (1920), and *Broom* (1921). The Fugitives fled from the professional custodians of the Old South and all their gift-book phrases about moonlight and roses; yet the idiom and attitudes of their poetry were closer to the manner they repudiated than to that of the aggressively *avant-garde* journals. The magazine came to be well regarded by Louis Untermeyer and by William Stanley Braithewaite, who chose several of its poems for inclusion in his annual anthology of best magazine verse, but not until they began to publish outside the magazine did any of the Fugitives become well known. An attempt at counter sales in New York City failed miserably. Wanamakers and Brentanos sold one copy each, while the Washington Square Bookstore managed to dispose of four. A friend thought the cover was too dull to compete with the "screeching oranges and greens" of the other little magazines, but no change of format was made and the effort was dropped.[17]

New York may not have been impressed, but Nashville was, and several others wanted to join the group. Soon after the first issue was out Merrill Moore stopped Tate on the campus and showed him some quatrains entitled, "To a Fetish." Tate remembers that the talk went thus:

> " 'What do you think of it?' Merrill asked. 'I think it is wonderful,' I said. Then he asked me if I thought it would qualify him for 'membership' in the group. I told him that I was certain that it would. I took the poem to Donald Davidson, and Merrill came to the next meeting. . . ."[18]

More than that, "To a Fetish" was published in the next issue under the pseudonym "Dendric." It was not, as Tate had supposed, Moore's first poem.

Moore was another Nashville boy. Born eighteen years earlier

---

[17] From letters, Mrs. Sadie Frank to Donald Davidson, February 17-21, 1923, and April 20, 1923.
[18] Tate, p. 78.

in Columbia, which is a little north of the towns where Ransom and Davidson were born, he had lived since childhood in a large farmhouse on the edge of Nashville and had known Hirsch and his family for many years. His father, John Trotwood Moore, was a man of great charm and energy and popular throughout the state. Beginning as a gentleman farmer, he had taken to writing casual pieces on horses and racing and had turned novelist in his forties. After writing five sentimental novels, a collection of stories, and much elegiac verse, all saved from oblivion by their wealth of carefully recorded details of life and customs in earlier Tennessee, he had been for three years historian for the state and director of its libraries and archives. He was a kindly man, but his very ebullience bore heavily on his son, who had to resist him to keep any kind of identity. Writing was but one way whereby Merrill asserted himself, and he had been active in the literary clubs and on the campus publications ever since he entered Vanderbilt. As loquacious and tireless as his father, Moore from the start was incredibly prolific. Later in life he came to believe that the earliest and most powerful force behind the torrent of his verse was a feeling that he had to write constantly lest he disappear.

If all had gone according to schedule, Tate would have graduated in June following the establishment of the magazine. Then, if the familiar pattern had prevailed, he would have spent a year or so away from Vanderbilt before returning to do graduate work in English. Actually, he did leave and return. Forced by ill health to withdraw from the university in May just a few weeks before graduation, he spent the next months at home or in the mountains of North Carolina resting, writing poetry, corresponding with Davidson, and planning a career as a man of letters. He returned to Nashville for the second semester of the 1922-1923 year and took his degree at the 1923 commencement. Meanwhile, his place as the bold irritant in the group was partly filled by Ridley Wills, who, with his cousin Jesse, joined the group in the autumn of 1922. Jesse Wills had written some poems of distinction in courses taken with the older Fugitives. After graduating in June of 1922, he had decided to go into business in Nashville, where his family lived. Sensitive and retiring, he liked to listen to the others arguing and reading their poems and attended regularly, though he contributed only eleven poems to the magazine. His cousin, who was five years older than he, was still an undergraduate when he joined and more than made up for Jesse's quietness. A native of Brownsville, in the western part of the state, Ridley had entered Vanderbilt before the war but had left to serve in the army. After an absence of five years during which he had worked as a reporter and written a novel, *Hoax*, which had been published without his name during the previous spring, he had come back to Vanderbilt to get his degree. In a foreword to the novel he explained that the decision to publish it anonymously was due to its partially autobiographical material and his fear that his native community might "be inclined to exaggerate its inferential significance. . . . The truth is," he concluded, "[the author] wants to go home sometime."

The pages that followed described the tribulations of a purportedly brilliant, brooding veteran who wants to be a novelist but is inhibited by a sense of obligation to the girl he left behind. By the end of the novel he has found another girl and published his novel anonymously. The story is told by the protagonist's father, a curious point of view for a first novel involving autobiographical material, for in this genre the father is usually commander-in-chief of The Enemy. From this anomaly come its few small interests. For the most part it is utterly commonplace: the characters are almost as stereotyped as the Bobbsey twins, and the writing is banal and platitudinous, for Wills could not refrain from using the perspective of the older narrator to incorporate gratuitous observations on Life. Yet bad as the novel is, there are scattered through it occasional insights into the self-deceptions of a young man bemused with the notion of being a Writer. But these were not enough to save it from the oblivion into which it disappeared almost at once, even though *The Literary Review* called the style "excellent," and *The New York Times*, which also liked the style, termed it "an unusually interesting book."

The author was an effervescent little man, exceedingly gay, eccentric, and charming though the four poems he contributed to *The Fugitive* were surprisingly dull. After graduating in 1923, he remained in Nashville to work as a reporter. He lived a hand-to-mouth existence for a time and brought to the meetings queer little versicules which were not published. Later he married and left to work at journalism in New York. In 1924 he brought out under his own name a novel called *Harvey Landrum*, a study of a weak man who hides behind bluster and cruelty until he is exposed in the intimacy of marriage. Like *Hoax* it mixed some incisive passages with flabby clichés, and it quickly failed. Today Wills is remembered for his friendship with Tate and Robert Penn Warren, with whom he roomed during his last year at Vanderbilt.

Tate had been away during the first term of that year, but he returned in February of 1923 and met Wills through Warren. He and Wills were at once enchanted with each other and soon became inseparable. Their points of view, particularly as they looked at their professors and the callow undergraduates about them, were so close that they liked to speak jokingly of themselves as an entity. They stimulated each other in crankish whims and sudden outbreaks of wild hilarity. Some of this excitement found outlet in a queer little pamphlet of verse, *The Golden Mean*, which they scribbled in one spring night and published at their own expense. Significantly, Wills encountered Tate just when the latter was cultivating eccentricity in his writing, and the more extravagant the phrases, the more violent and abrupt the shifts, in Tate's poems, the more Wills approved. Together they were a powerful stimulus to young Warren, who turned eighteen that spring. Dazzled by their casual allusions to writers he had never heard of and their scorn of traditional forms and established writers, he read desperately to catch up with them and attempted poems full of esoteric allusions and world-weariness to earn their approval.[19] Wills did not add much to the poetry of the Fugitives, but he charged those meetings he attended with liveliness and humor and was much missed when he dropped out. Without him the writing of Tate and Warren might have been somewhat different.

So it was that by the end of 1922, nearly eight years after the first casual encounters, the Fugitive group was firmly established. The magazine was a going concern, and most of the members were committed to the serious pursuit of poetry. The "seven of friends" to whom Ransom addressed a poem in the first issue had become eleven—thirteen when Elliott and Frierson rejoined the group in the summer. During the next three years, three more members were to be added, one of them Warren, but they made no sig-

[19] The impact of two such energetic older men upon the exceptionally sensitive and gifted boy had a profound and lasting effect that is discussed in Chapter Nine, pp. 431-435.

nificant difference in the intellectual climate. Hirsch's power over it was now at its peak. Extraordinary, ineffable, he had brought the Fugitives together in the first place, had been the pole around which they had reassembled after the war, had started them on the magazine, and had kept them meeting for conversation of rare distinction. In the years that followed, others—Ransom, Davidson, Tate, and Warren—made the Fugitives' reputation. But if any man can be said to have done so, Sid Hirsch made the Fugitives.

CHAPTER TWO

THE FUGITIVE GROUP: 1922-1928

....

"It was a game to make words ring. . . ."

—Jesse Wills, "Proem," in EARLY AND LATE (*1959*)

....

I

*T*HE history of the Fugitive group falls into three distinct intervals. First is the long gestation, just described, which reached fulfillment in 1922. Then came a period measured by the life of the magazine and ending in December of 1925: a period of significant accomplishment for one or two of the Fugitives and of invaluable preparation for others. Finally came a long twilight as the group slowly fell apart and most of the members withdrew into silence while Ransom, Davidson, Tate, and Warren pushed on toward Agrarianism.[1] It is difficult to place the end of this last interval, for those who remained in Nashville met occasionally for old time's sake long after the gatherings had lost their literary character. Perhaps 1928 does best, for in that year appeared an anthology of Fugitive poetry which was the last joint effort of the group. Already Ransom, Davidson, and Tate had begun their defense of values inherited from the Old South, and Warren was working at a biography of John Brown which would help to bring him, along paths of his own, to their side. Their attention was taken up by new ideas with which the other Fugitives had little or no sympathy.

The three intervals were characterized by differing relationships between Sidney Hirsch and the group. During the first he came as near to dominating it as any man could. He had dreamed of an international reputation, and, listening to his stories of Paris and New York and remembering the clamor over *The Fire*

---

[1] Merrill Moore, of course, kept on with poetry, becoming not less but more astonishingly fertile. Jesse Wills, a successful businessman in Nashville, returned to poetry three decades later. His *Early and Late*, made up of work published in *The Fugitive* and some 27 poems written between 1953 and 1959, was published by the Vanderbilt University Press in 1959.

32

Regained, the others had not thought his aspirations altogether preposterous. By the last interval he had slipped into virtually total obscurity, and within the group itself he was hardly more than just another member. During the second period, our present concern, he was moving from the dominance of the first interval to the obscurity of the last, and each new achievement by the group or its members modified and diminished his influence. The Fugitives were acquiring by the means he had given them both the assurance to resist him and the standards which made the measure of his own accomplishments seem less. Such awe as they might once have felt vanished when they confronted the poems he submitted for the magazine. These were judged to be so bad that in all the nineteen issues only five were published: one in each of the four numbers for 1922 and one in the second number of 1923. Yet in many ways he remained throughout the period of the magazine the nearest thing to a leader they had.

Without any rule or calendar, the Fugitives now met almost every fortnight during the school year and as often in the summertime as there were enough of them in town. Usually six or eight members sat around Hirsch's couch in the living room of the Frank home, and sometimes as many as a dozen were in attendance, for the Fugitives were encouraged to bring guests. Among those who met with them were Witter Bynner, Louis Untermeyer, and A. E. (George William Russell), as well as local writers such as Merrill Moore's father. Despite heavy teaching loads, Ransom and Davidson almost never missed a meeting, and even the undergraduates were surprisingly faithful—a fact which Moore later attributed to the abundance of good food at the end of the evening, though even this was sometimes not enough and the younger men went off to eat spaghetti and talk till dawn. Meetings began around eight and broke up between ten-thirty and eleven, but any who wanted to stay and argue with Sid were welcome.

Often there was much still to be said at the end of the evening, for Hirsch took the lead in getting the meetings started and brought up provocative topics whenever the talk fell away. In recognition of this and all he had done for them, the Fugitives elected him their first president in October, 1923, after they had decided that they needed officers. It seemed quite natural for him to preside, not only from long habit, but also from the force of his personality, which remained immense. His courteous dignity and imperious gravity were remarkable for one still in his thirties, and he expected—even managed to get—an appearance of some submission from the others. At first the newer and younger members were bewildered by the strangeness and scope of his learning. But in time they became irritated with his manner and thought many of his opinions simply crazy—even a bit fraudulent. Their impatience made for occasional strain, which the older men tried to ease, for they knew how much Hirsch needed the Fugitives and how much the group depended on him, however pompous and annoying he might seem at times to be.[2]

The commitment to poetry and the magazine brought new seriousness and intensity to the meetings, but the old casual manner still prevailed. The evenings usually began with Hirsch's saying, "Well, gentlemen, we are all here now. Does anyone have a poem he would like to read?" There was rarely any delay. Davidson and Ransom kept at their writing so faithfully that usually one or the other would respond at once, and somewhere in one of their poems would be an image, a recondite word, or a trick of meter that would tease the group and start it talking. Not long after poetry had become the main business of the gatherings, Hirsch suggested that those with new poems to read bring carbon copies so that the others could study the text more closely. Such careful scrutiny from an informed audience accustomed to dealing with problems of diction and organization, backed up by the possibility of seeing their work printed in the magazine, greatly stimulated the Fugitives and helped to fix high standards. Though they were vigorous men long accustomed to disagreeing with each other, the Fugitives desired the group's approval and—except for Merrill Moore and Ridley Wills—worked hard over their lines, a fact which hastened the development of the more talented members. Moreover, the assurance of faithful attention gave them some of the momentum needed to keep them writing when they might have turned to other, less demanding recreations.

But making carbon copies had, in the opinion of some of them, a distinct disadvantage: it opened the way to Hirsch's interpreting

[2] From conversations with the Fugitives.

the Fugitives' own poems to them. Having long believed that all literary works have an outer and an inner meaning and that he was singularly fitted for bringing the hidden to light, he could not be kept from pursuing to the farthest limits any idea suggested by an unusual word or a supposed parallel between the work in hand and some remote writing known only to himself. If the writer objected to his interpretation, Hirsch blandly replied that to disavow it was to disavow one's own visionary powers without which one never could have written in the first place. That the writer might not have intended the meaning Hirsch found was quite beside the point. It was there. How it got there was too mysterious for any of them to explain. With equal imperturbability Hirsch brushed aside the objection that some of his readings were based upon incredible etymologies. This merely showed how remarkably the poet was endowed and how fortunate it was that Hirsch could see beyond the shroud of mundane circumstance. There was no getting around him, and the others had to give up before his massive, friendly assurance. But for all their impatience with his ponderous omniscience, he could rouse them to the liveliest excitement and debate, and he kept the talk at an extraordinarily high level. Looking back after years spent among poets and scholars of great distinction, those who sat with him still marvel at the wit, range, elegance, and substance of those conversations.

Remembering those great arguments, the Fugitives stress that there never was a "Fugitive type," and that generalizations about "Fugitive poetry" tend to be unsound. Though individuals among them might be drawn to some writer or school, the group never studied a particular poet or period or issued pronunciamentoes on the true nature of poetry. After reading their letters[3] and hearing them describe the battles over Tate's poems—always a source of conflict—one can accept Ransom's recollection of them as "a group of very stubborn individuals that couldn't be coerced, if any one

[3] Particularly important are Tate's letters to Davidson, now deposited with the Joint University Library at Vanderbilt, and those of Davidson and Ransom to Tate, now deposited (but available for study only by permission) with the Princeton University Library. Significant portions of many of these letters have been printed in Louise Cowan's fine study, *The Fugitive Group: a Literary History* (Baton Rouge, 1959).

had tried."[4] Such insistence on their difference is needed because some readers, aware of the close communion among Ransom, Tate, and Warren which, in fact, began after the Fugitives had broken up, and knowing how important in that communion were some of Ransom's ideas, have supposed that in the time of the Fugitives, Ransom was their acknowledged leader and even that the others imitated him as much as they could. Moreover, some of these readers assume that the group was much influenced by John Donne because Ransom's own poems have some of the same "metaphysical" wit. Actually, at that time none of them had read Donne with much attention, and Ransom himself has said that Donne was not an influence on them.

But even after such misunderstandings have been disposed of, the extent of Ransom's influence on the others is hard to assess. He constantly attacked certain kinds of poetry, notably English poetry of the late nineteenth century, which some of the others much admired and *did* imitate. He differed with Tate to the point of a near quarrel on the merits of T. S. Eliot's poetry, and frequently defended form and tradition against experiments that would abandon them; yet when the group divided, as it often did, over tradition and experiment, Ransom, far from being the spokesman for the traditionists, was regarded as the true leader of the modernist faction. Moreover, the Fugitives were well aware of the force of his mind and example, and they ungrudgingly conceded that he was the best poet among them, but they were annoyed when outsiders spoke of the group or the magazine as "his," and they tried to resist being like him. They did not succeed all the time. Writing from Oxford, where he was a Rhodes Scholar, William Yandell Elliott warned the Fugitives that they were coming to resemble each other too much, and added:

> "I should say it is a subtle tribute to the attraction of Johnny's bag of tricks. You all draw on it.
> "Perhaps this is no more than to say Johnny was the first modern among us. He it was who castigated sentimentality whenever it showed its simple head and first set up the Baal of complexity for worship."[5]

[4] *Fugitives' Reunion: Conversations at Vanderbilt*, ed. Rob Roy Purdy (Nashville, 1959), pp. 79-80.
[5] To the Fugitives, October 11, 1923.

Tate was the one who campaigned for modernism. Ransom, as he said later, followed the course of "not letting the question of the old and new get into my mind at all," preferring to keep up "a certain heat of composition in the faith that the imagery will be sufficient unto the day and unto the nature of my subject."[6] Yet Elliott was right. For beneath the mock-medieval fustian and the brilliantly varied traditional forms of his poems, Ransom was more truly skeptical and irreverent than Tate, and far more experimental; he did not simply follow impulse or the example of the more extravagant new magazines but tried to get wholly new views of his subjects. Even as he demanded order in poetry, he insisted far more than Tate upon the disorder and ambiguity of the world—but he did not think these especially modern conditions. And, for all his defense of older conventions, he mistrusted all generalizations about poetry and spoke always in terms of the poem immediately before the group and not according to any doctrine or rules. His comments were mild, but unusually specific and apt. At the same time, he wanted to help the others discover themselves. It was he, for example, who first urged Merrill Moore to experiment with the sonnet form and break up its usual patterns. For him the first question to put to a fellow poet was always, "What are *you* trying to do?" He never asked how the poem was supposed to incorporate some principle, preferring to wait and see what principle the poem defined by being itself. How was it that the others wrote in manners enough like his own to warrant Elliott's complaint? Perhaps the fact that he had been a teacher of a good many of them had something to do with it. More likely, however, is the fact that the Fugitives, being more than usually sensitive to poetry, and being, as will be shown, especially interested in unusual dictions and idioms, could not despite their resolution resist the brilliance and originality of his example when they stood so near to it.

Certainly whatever qualities their work had in common did not result from any agreement on the nature of poetry. Like Ransom they preferred to approach a new poem by one of the group in whatever terms the poem itself suggested. During this interval Ransom put down his first, very tentative speculations on the nature of poetry and tried some of them out in letters to

[6] From a letter to Tate, September 13, 1926.

37

Tate, but the group as a whole rarely discussed aesthetics and only occasionally spoke of poetic technique apart from the problems presented by a poem then under their scrutiny.[7] The intense concern with poetics which Ransom shared with Tate and, eventually, Warren, though it looks back to ideas he first began to formulate at this time, really began in 1926 after both Tate and Warren had been out of Nashville for some time and Ransom himself had started to turn away from poetry. The only overt agreement among the Fugitives was on the importance of eschewing sentimentality and functionless "poetic" ornament, particularly the languid nostalgia and the orotund clichés of the newspaper poetesses and other elegists of the Old South. Ransom was especially energetic in attacking these whenever they threatened to appear, but consensus in the group came not so much from his influence as from boredom with the bad poetry of the past.

They knew they were spoken of as Nashville or Tennessee poets, and were proud to be so named, but they did not regard themselves as Southern poets, Old or New. When Harriet Monroe, reviewing DuBose Heyward's and Hervey Allen's *Carolina Chansons* for *Poetry* in May, 1923, suggested that Southern writers should concentrate on the "soft silken reminiscent life . . . of a region so specialized in beauty, so rich in racial tang and prejudice, so jewel-weighted with a heroic past," Davidson fired off a saucy letter, shortly after printed in *The Fugitive*, saying, "Undoubtedly the Old South is literary material to those who may care to write about it. But many may not. . . . They will create from what is nearest and deepest in experience—whether it be old or new, North, South, East, or West—and what business is that of Aunt Harriet's?" Tate, too, opposed her suggestion: "We who are Southerners know the fatality of such an attitude— the old atavism and sentimentality are always imminent. . . ." When Margery Swett, Exchange Editor for *Poetry*, protested the tone of their letters, the Fugitives reiterated in an unsigned editorial, "We fear to have too much stress laid on a tradition that may be called a tradition only when looked at through the haze of a

[7] Conversations with Ransom, August 24, 1946; Warren, October 26, 1953; Moore, July 7-8, 1956; and a letter from Tate to the writer, September 10, 1953.

generous imagination."[8] As for all the hubbub over the New South stirred up by editors, Rotarians, and investment counsellors, in this they took no interest, and they never spoke of politics or public affairs whether regional or national. When Allen Tate reviewed Ransom's *Two Gentlemen in Bonds* and attributed what he called its "Rationalism" and "Noblesse Oblige" to Ransom's Southern heritage, Ransom wrote to say that he thought the terms, as Tate defined them, were good for the occasion but added, "I don't write [poetry] consciously as a Southerner or non-Southerner."[9] For though Ransom had by this time begun to look with new interest at his region and its history, he still followed the Fugitive habit of regarding himself and the rest of the group as men of the world, members of an international community of letters quite as much as poets living in Chicago, New York, or Paris. Nevertheless, they were Southerners; apart from their gift for poetry, the most significant thing about them was the fact that they were all from Nashville or the country round about it.

Few aspects of contemporary American literature have been more discussed of late than the inaccurately named "Southern Renaissance"—that quickening of the imagination which began among Southern writers in the early twenties. The Fugitives are often cited as examples of it, and so they are. But when trying to see just how they are, one must be careful to look back beyond all the things that Ransom, Davidson, Tate, and Warren said about Southern writers after they had become Agrarians. Much of what they claim applies only to writers in whom a commitment to the values of the Southern past is strong enough to provide a conscious frame of reference in the shaping of works of literature, even when these are not directly about the South. They themselves had not in their Fugitive days been brought to this pitch of awareness and commitment.

It was true, of course, that, as they liked to point out afterwards, the Fugitives came from rural Southern backgrounds. It counts

[8] Donald Davidson to Margery Swett, June 22, 1923; [Donald Davidson], "Merely Prose," *The Fugitive*, II (June-July, 1923), 66; [Unsigned], "The Other Half of Prose," *The Fugitive*, II (August-September, 1923), 99; Allen Tate to Margery Swett, June 22, 1923 [copy]. The unsigned editorial was probably written by Tate.

[9] From a letter dated February 20, 1927. Tate's review appeared in *The New Republic* on March 30, 1927. Ransom had seen an advance copy of it. See also Ransom's remarks in *Fugitives' Reunion . . . ,* p. 235.

that Davidson's people had farmed the same land for over a century; that Ransom had grown up in small towns economically dependent on the farms around them; that Moore's father raised horses and his family lived on a farm just outside Nashville. But it counts no less that Ransom's father was a scholar and a much-travelled man and that Ransom had studied for three years at Oxford; that Moore's father had been a writer and that Moore, in an attempt to assert his individuality, had gone abroad; that Hirsch had roamed the world and lived among the salons and ateliers of Paris and New York and that he and Frank were part of a highly cultivated and thoroughly urbanized Jewish community with roots going back to Europe. In looking beyond their region and thinking of themselves as cosmopolites, the Fugitives were behaving much as other residents of Nashville who thought their city a progressive and thoroughly American one, or as the officers and students of Vanderbilt, who took pride in the position of the university among American institutions and in the new intellectual energy manifested in a program of postwar expansion and reorganization. Only Tate and Johnson felt inhibited by their surroundings.

In many respects the Fugitives were like young American writers everywhere in those times. But deep down—deeper even than the consciousness of the region and its past which they were later to claim for the Southern writer—was a rapport with their time and place and with one another so natural that they thought no more of it than of breathing. It made possible that remarkable communication among men strong in nature and various in age, experience, and interests. Much could be taken for granted among them or in their dealings with their neighbors; much left unsaid, or said simply with an inflection or a movement of the hand. Southern, too, was the way they had come back from the experience of the war with that rapport virtually undisturbed and the old lines of communication intact. In this they differed from many other young ex-soldiers in that world of letters to which they thought they belonged. Reading such an account as Malcolm Cowley's *Exile's Return* one finds it a bit strange that Ransom, Davidson, Stevenson, Johnson, Elliott, Frierson, and Ridley Wills could come back to Vanderbilt and Nashville and settle at once into their old ways. True, Elliott and Frierson soon moved on—

but as Rhodes Scholars, not as rebels against the community. Only Tate had any of the younger generation's passion for "new thresholds, new anatomies," as Hart Crane called them, and when he had finally made it to New York, he quickly recognized and affirmed the value of his regional background.

Years afterward, when trying to explain what it was that bound the Fugitives together, what bound even himself despite his restless urge to get away, Tate wrote:

> "The great universities of the East could have boasted in that period groups of writers quite as good as ours, or better, though I doubt it; yet they were not groups in our sense, being associated only through the university and having a cosmopolitan range of interest without, I think, a simple homogenous background which they could take with them to the university where it might suffer little or no break in continuity. I would call the Fugitives an intensive and historical group as opposed to the eclectic and cosmopolitan groups that flourished in the East."[10]

Earlier he had written that "Fugitive poetry turned out to be profoundly sectional in that it was supported by the prejudices, feelings, values into which the poets were born."[11] How, then, did this bone-deep, unselfconscious regionalism manifest itself in the poetry of men who seemed not to know it was there and who, at the moment, thought themselves about as eclectic and cosmopolitan as the gentlemen in the Eastern universities?

In the work of the leading figures of the "Renaissance," one sees beneath the details of Southern landscape, occupations, implements, customs and manners, beneath the florid language pursued, it so often seems, for its own sweet sake, beneath whatever portion of the legend of the Old South and its displacement by the New is retold, an image of man toward which all the regional material tends—an image that lifts the work far above that of local colorists for whom the Southern idiom and mode were ends in themselves. It is an image at once essential and definitive and it constitutes the special contribution of contemporary Southern writ-

[10] "*The Fugitive* 1922-1925: A Personal Recollection Twenty Years After," *The Princeton University Library Chronicle*, III (April, 1942), 83.
[11] "American Poetry Since 1920," *The Bookman*, LXVIII (January, 1929), 504.

ing to American literature. There will be need later in this study to look closely at that image, but for now it is enough to say that it is stoutly anti-progressive, anti-rationalist, and anti-humanist, for it insists on the irreducible mystery in life, the all-pervasiveness of evil in human affairs, and the limitations of man's capacity to understand and control his environment and his own nature. Rejecting modern conceptions of evil as a finite and merely temporary absence of physical and psychic adjustment and ease, the writers of the Southern Renaissance presented it in figures going back at last to the Old Testament, the doctrine of Original Sin, and the Protestant habit of searching the private heart. To them evil was ultimately immanent and indefinable, permeating all experience but beyond man's understanding. Here, of course, they resembled not only the evangelical preachers of their region but earlier writers of New England, from Woolman and Edwards to Hawthorne and Melville, in whom the metaphors of Calvinism loomed strongly. Yet there were differences: born in a land that had undergone defeat in war, they had that special sense of the past possible only in people compelled to search the record of agony, humiliation, and loss asking, "Why? Why did it happen to us? Wherein did we do wrong?" Thus the image was projected not only in religious terms but historic as well. And the view of history was curiously bifocal: because of the mystery, the lack of human control, the ambiguity, life to them was a flux and blur of persistent change within time; yet life was also outside time and changeless because man, for whom progress was not possible, was always the same beneath the shifting temporal surface. In short, their image of man was mythopoeic, and insofar as their writing embodies much or all of that image (in comparison, say, with the writing of Pound, Hemingway, Dos Passos, Sherwood Anderson, Thornton Wilder, Cummings, Stephen Vincent Benet, Carl Sandburg, Hart Crane, or James T. Farrell) one may call these writers—Faulkner, Katherine Anne Porter, Caroline Gordon, Eudora Welty, even Erskine Caldwell and Tennessee Williams—Southern. By the same measure one may so designate Tate and Warren and, somewhat less positively despite his use of regional materials, Davidson. Indeed, both Tate and Warren have insisted on just these qualities as the distinction of modern Southern literature. But they themselves can be so named only for the writing they did *after* the

Fugitive group had entered the third stage and both Tate and Warren had left it. Evil and violence appear in many of their Fugitive poems, to be sure, but mainly because these elements made a fine uproar and shocked the onlookers. It is only here and there—as in Tate's "Procession," "Prayer for an Old Man," and "Homily," and in Warren's "Death Mask for a Young Man" and "Easter Morning: Crosby Junction"—that one begins to see dimly the image that appears in "The Wolves" and *The Fathers* or "Original Sin" and *Brother to Dragons*. Indeed, in the time of the Fugitives, only Ransom might be said to have been a Southern writer in this sense. No one better understood the ambiguity of man and nature or the permanence in the midst of change of the human condition than the author of "Necrological" and "Armageddon." Yet Ransom's perception in the days of *The Fugitive* seems to go back to his fury against abstractions and his inveterate skepticism rather than to any regionalism. And the past to which he looked and from which he took his imagery was not Southern but one found on the pages of English literature. The Southern image of man did not manifest itself in enough Fugitive poetry to justify calling that poetry "sectional."

Or again, the Southerner has long had the reputation of esteeming florid language as a precious object in itself. His supposed affection for the ornate phrase, the resonant polysyllable, and the learned allusion, whether used for humorous extravagance or solemn moralizing, has been remarked innumerable times. He likes, we are told, the extraordinary. Certainly the Fugitives did. Hirsch's fascination with hermetic terms has been noted already. Ransom studded his poems with scholarly words. Davidson and Tate had some of Hirsch's enchantment with the rare and strange— Tate so much that Stanley Johnson wrote a cruel and funny parody of his patched-up lines. Yet, though a Southern love of language may have made the Fugitives less self-conscious about their sometimes gaudy diction, one gathers from the kind of words they chose that temperament and their immersion in literary studies account for it better than their regional background. Ransom's poetry shows a unique mixture of fastidiousness and daintiness— amounting at times to preciousness—with an irony so harsh as to be almost morbid, a mixture quite as independent of any time or place as the similar one to be found in the poetry of Wallace

Stevens.[12] The queer words in the poems of Hirsch, Davidson, and Tate, are, as will be seen, at least partly a form of self-assertion, a way of signifying the superiority of the artist to ordinary men. In this respect some of the Fugitives, at least, might seem to have been nearer the young rebels and experimenters of New York and Paris than their Southern background.

But apart from Tate, they were not. When they wanted to show their difference, when, despite their opposition to ornament and sentimentality, they wanted to be poetic and mysterious and hint of things too ecstatic or fearful to be spoken of in the terms of ordinary discourse, they turned back to Blake, Keats, Tennyson, Poe, the pre-Raphaelites, and Swinburne. Malcolm Cowley writes that the young American poets he knew had wallowed in Swinburne and the English Decadents while in college before going off to war. Afterwards they found these writers too soft and silly for men who had been under fire and had lost all their pretty allusions. Of course they found new illusions: that Laforgue, skyscrapers, and jazz bands were somehow more "real" than Ernest Dowson and swirling veils. But beside the tough new romanticism of Cowley, Hart Crane, and their friends with its iconoclastic bravado, its glorification of the clown as waif, and its curiously sexless eroticism, the Fugitives' dim landscapes and moonlit glades, *belles dames sans merci*, and poets as divinely possessed children seem far behind the times.

Here, by virtue of their apathy toward the new tendencies in American poetry more than by any special attitude regarding language or any unique sensibility, they may truly have been sectional and Southern. For despite the boldness of the retorts to Harriet Monroe, much of their poetry would look to the outsider to be more like the *Carolina Chansons*, and even the attitudes and idioms of the "high-caste Brahmins of the Old South," than like the really significant work being done in the world of letters to which they fancied they belonged. As a group they were cut off from the literary centers and all the ritual of manifestoes, anti-social behavior, expatriotism, and intramural warfare waged among the constantly shifting groups and loyalties. They missed a lot of

[12] There is a touch of this mixture in Robert Frost, too, and something much like it in the cranky, whimsical, and frequently violent music of Charles Ives, another New Englander.

silliness, but they also missed the invigorating and broadening influence of the forces then shaping the new American poetry: the new dimensions of the French Symbolists, the discipline of Flaubert (via Pound), the attempt to assimilate Freudian concepts, the attempt to make poetry of the ideas and metaphors taken over from the new astronomy, physics, and technologies, the theme of the city as Inferno, and the interest in primitives—tramps, Italian immigrants, Navahos, African sculptors, and Harlem musicians. Amateurs writing for the fun of it and addressing their poems to some ideal citizen of Nashville like themselves (Vanderbilt graduate, classicist, gentleman, admirer of nineteenth-century English verse), they had no need to keep up, to catch the eye of Ezra Pound or the editors of *Broom*. Except for Tate they were spared all the rage and uncertainty—and the spur in the side—of those young men and women in Greenwich Village or on the Left Bank who struggled to live by and for their writing.

Not that the Fugitives were ignorant of the new tendencies. While Ransom was stationed in France, some young ladies introduced him to French poetry, and he was attracted and perplexed by the Symbolists and decidedly conscious of them from 1919 on. Tate had read Baudelaire, the Symbolists, and Pound before he joined the group. So had Warren.[13] Most of them admired *The Smart Set* and looked into *The Dial*, and as fast as he discovered a new little magazine, Tate called it to the attention of the others. Warren was impressed and Davidson tried to understand what Tate put before him, but most of the others were just bewildered or bored and too much out of sympathy with *avant-garde* writing to respond. Even Davidson sometimes had too much. When Tate sent him a copy of *Secession* in the summer of 1922, he called it ". . . very smart, very sophisticated, but nevertheless hokum." Its poetry he thought "absolutely pitiful." "Honestly," he went on, "if you can throw some light on them—point out even one little bit of art in them—I will be very much obliged."[14] The rest were not at all humble or ready for instruction (though Warren, not yet a Fugitive, was decidedly both). Thus, when they did try to make contact with other writers, they sent copies of *The Fugitive* to Yeats, Masefield, Bridges, Graves, William Alexander Percy,

[13] *The Fugitives' Reunion*, pp. 99-101.
[14] From a letter, Davidson to Tate, July 15, 1922.

Irving Babbitt—and eventually to Hart Crane and Kenneth Burke, when these men became Tate's friends. They sent copies to *The Bookman, The Yale Review, Poetry, Midland, The New York Times, The Chicago Tribune, The London Times Literary Supplement*, but not to the experimental journals. Rather, it was in such little magazines as *The Lyric* (Norfolk) and *Palms* that they sought their counterpart. Only *The Double Dealer*, of those with which the Fugitives corresponded, might be called somewhat advanced; it published early work by Hemingway and Faulkner (which was wholly conventional in form and content) and some of Hart Crane's less peculiar poetry, but its tone was set more by Louis Untermeyer: the Imagists were about as far as it wanted to go. And when Davidson was looking for outside contributors in 1923, he went to the members of the Poetry Society of South Carolina. Thus of all the non-members published in *The Fugitive* only Crane could be called a modernist.[15]

Crane had read a poem of Tate's in *The Double Dealer* for May, 1922, and written Tate about it, remarking that it seemed to be influenced by Eliot.[16] Though he read some of the poets who formed the background of Eliot's work, Tate had not yet read Eliot. He answered Crane's letter, and Crane immediately replied, this time referring not only to Eliot but to Donne, Webster, Pound, and Stevens, as well. Thus began a friendship of critical importance in Tate's development.[17] He at once read the writers mentioned by Crane and soon afterward claimed Crane and Eliot as his principal mentors. When he returned to Vanderbilt early in 1923, he was convinced that Crane was the greatest living American poet, and he began a campaign to make the Fugitives pay more attention to the modernists, particularly to Eliot. Already the group was divided over the matter—and over the poems Tate had been sending in for Davidson to read at the meetings. Urged on by Tate, Davidson bought Eliot's poems, and by the time "The

[15] From the official records and correspondence of the Fugitives now in the Joint University Libraries at Nashville.
[16] The poem was "Euthanasia." The first stanza does have a little of Eliot's early manner:

> No more the white refulgent streets,
> Never the dry gutters of the mind,
> Shall he in hellish boredom walk
> Again, for death is not unkind.

[17] For an extended discussion of its influence on Tate's poetry, see Chapter Eight.

Waste Land" was published in *The Dial* in November, 1922, he
had come around enough from his earlier opposition to read it with
some bafflement but much excitement. Hirsch, generally one of the
most conservative of the group, delighted in its esoterica. (Later,
after the group had dwindled away, he became a close student of
Eliot's poetry.) But the rest of the Fugitives were not drawn to
Eliot. Ransom thought his poetry too fragmentary—too nearly the
raw stuff of experience and too little formed upon a coherent philosophy.[18]

Looking back on his campaign to modernize the Fugitives, Tate
has remarked with winning candor that he was a bit of a prig.[19]
Probably his manner and his poetry had more than a little to do
with rousing some of the group from indifference to outright opposition to new forms and idioms. Apparently fearful that his considerable gifts might not be fully recognized, he seems to have
wanted to command attention by assertiveness, contradiction, and
the cultivation of the curious. He was particularly attracted by the
figure of Rimbaud, the *enfant terrible* who had startled and irritated the elder poets he was cast among, and Tate liked to encourage by carefully placed hints the impression that he was himself pretty wild and decadent. In many of his poems he was out to
shock by oblique allusions to terrible but indefinite sins and by rare
words, remote references, and fantastically mixed metaphors, but
the Fugitives were more annoyed than impressed. Tate won no real
converts, and when he finally left Nashville there was no real
spokesman for experimentalism.

But why, apart from whatever irritation Tate aroused, was there
so little sympathy among the Fugitives toward the new forces in
American poetry? Was it because they were Southern? Perhaps.
One reason many young men and women from other regions left

[18] From a letter to Tate, December 17, 1922, now deposited in the Princeton
University Library. See below, p. 74. Warren, who was not a Fugitive at this
time, was much excited over "The Waste Land" when Davidson, one of his
instructors and already a good friend, showed it to him. After Tate returned
to Vanderbilt, Warren roomed with him and for a short time there were many
echoes of Eliot and Pound in the poems Warren wrote. Following the summer
vacation they lived together in a cottage on the grounds of one of the faculty
members during the autumn of 1923, for Tate, who had graduated in June,
had no regular work and could not afford to go to New York. However, by this
time Warren had started to develop a personal style in which there were virtually
no traces of Eliot and Pound.
[19] *"The Fugitive . . . ,"* p. 81.

home for the cities where these forces were strongest was that they intended to make a career of writing and they wanted to be at the center of all the new developments for the sake of stimulus and contacts with publishers and editors. But the Fugitives were essentially amateurs, even dabblers. Johnson and Ridley Wills had some indefinite notions of becoming writers (and both wound up as journalists), but only Tate had anything like the dedication to writing as a profession and way of life to be found among the young writers who headed for New York and Paris. In this the Fugitives, for all their sense of being part of the world of letters, may have been influenced by the Southern tradition that honored the gentlemanly trifler but had no real respect for the artist or man of letters —until he was dead. A more likely explanation, however, is the fact that so many of the new tendencies resulted from an effort to represent aspects of experience which had far less significance for the teacher-scholar-poet in Nashville than for the undernourished ex-soldier in Greenwich Village. Technology and urbanization were not nearly so far advanced in the South as in the East and Middle West, whence came so many of the young writers. Thus new words, images, symbols, and themes for the experience of the city were less immediately relevant to the Southern sensibility. In the South, occupations and recreations were not yet so specialized as to force men into smaller and smaller groups—or out of groups altogether.

For all the old Southern and Protestant tradition of examining the conscience which was to be important in the later work of Tate and Warren, the Fugitives as a group, being less outsiders, were less thrown back upon themselves and less inclined to turn inward than many other writers of their generation.[20] Apparently they did not need new techniques to record the inward exaltation and agony, and though Freud was talked of around Vanderbilt, they felt none of the excitement or urgency that sent writers elsewhere looking in his pages for material and made psychoanalysis a popular parlor game. Except, once more, for Tate they shared a sufficiency of beliefs, attitudes, and customs with those around them to prevent their being driven back upon private whims and sanctions. A sig-

[20] Again, as so often in any discussion of any aspect of the Fugitives, one must make an exception of Tate. As already noted, there seem to have been fewer of the communal bonds in his background, and there was almost from the beginning a strong inward direction to much of his poetry. This aspect of his work is treated at length in Chapter Eight.

nificant instance of this is their response to the war. Davidson had some bitter memories of the neglect of the veterans which he put into *The Tall Men*, but for the most part the Fugitives were little affected by the nihilism that shook the "lost generation" as a consequence of measuring their inheritance against their observations and experiences during and just after the war. In rejecting part of the past—as they claimed to do in the first issue of the magazine— the Fugitives were putting aside a rhetoric and an implied conception of poetry, not a way of life. They did not believe they had been betrayed by their society, and they had kept enough of the past not to feel a desperate need of the future. Apart from Tate they did not have to make up a new way of life and a new technique of poetry in order to define themselves as men and writers.

Was their comparative isolation from modernism bad for their poetry? At first it might seem that they were out of touch with their times, and that is reported to be a limitation for poets. But were they? It could be argued that their indifference came about just because they were *not* out of touch with their times *in their place*: to have run after modernism would have been the sign of being out of touch. It is noteworthy that Ransom, Tate, and Warren, the three really important writers among the Fugitives, never steadfastly resisted modernism (despite Ransom's doubts about Eliot) and each, in his own way and at his own good pace, came around to accepting that part which was significant for himself, though Tate, who was the only one to *embrace* it for its own sake, had in the end the most difficult adjustment to make. Noteworthy, too, is the fact that when Davidson eventually turned against modernism in every form, his writing, for all its mellow music, fell away into local-colorism and snobbish nostalgia. In these earlier days, bits of old-fashioned ornamentation got into some of the Fugitive poems along with stereotyped phrases and attitudes that would have been hooted down among the bright young people of the *avant-garde*. But if the Fugitives had been saved from these they might well have gone in for a good deal of exhibitionist nonsense, and it is unlikely that the criticism of the young people in the cities, so programmatic for all the defiance of programs, would have been any more helpful to their poetry than close discussion in a group where the example of Ransom was ever at hand.

It might seem at first that the Fugitives lacked certain important resources developed by the modernists to explore the human condition—the daringly mixed rhythms and figures of speech and the images based upon depth psychology, post-Newtonian physics, machinery, and the new developments in music, the visual arts, and the ballet. But they no more lacked them than did Shakespeare or Wordsworth. For one thing they had kept, along with some outmoded figures of language, many resources of the older poets, particularly those that depended for their effect upon variations of established patterns. Moreover, Ransom could be almost as daring and inventive as Shakespeare and Wordsworth, though perhaps less obviously so than Cummings and Pound, and both Moore and Warren showed that, young as they were, they could reach far down into the human consciousness while staying within more-or-less traditional forms. As for Tate, it was *after* he had stopped running after modernism that he began to write most revealingly about the present state of the human spirit. Taking everything into account, it is hard to believe that the Fugitives missed much. Living in places and among conditions which would have made them more responsive to the new forces and directions in American poetry would also have made such a group as theirs extremely unlikely. This being so, they were probably much better off as they were.

Thus, if we go back to the question proposed earlier and ask once more how the unselfconscious regionalism of the Fugitives manifested itself in their poetry there seems to be only one answer not disqualified by many reservations: it helped to keep them together for that long exchange of encouragement and criticism from which their poetry came. Apart from the work of Ransom that poetry was nothing remarkable, but the meetings helped make his work what it was and provided training and stimulus from which later work of the highest distinction by Tate and Warren—and, in new areas, by Ransom himself—would flower. This may have been all they got at that time from their Southernism, but it was more than enough.

II

The amateurism, the comforting assurance of belonging to the community, and the old-fashionedness of the Fugitives are nowhere more marked than in the poems that some of them wrote about the artist as exquisite exile. Later in this study we shall need to look longer at the tradition of the poet as rebel and seer, for Tate took it seriously indeed, and though he outgrew its more sentimental aspects it influenced his thought and work from the first to the last. But he alone among the Fugitives hoped to be a professional poet; he alone put making poems (as distinct from making a living by his pen, which both Ridley Wills and Stanley Johnson hoped to do) at the head of his occupations. He may have begun with strutting in the role, but as soon as he went to New York and joined Crane's circle it became a matter of desperate seriousness. But for the other Fugitives who wrote about the artist—and whose interest in his alienation had some effect upon Tate's own—the image of the superior outcast was scarcely more than a self-congratulatory fantasy. Hirsch and Davidson came nearest to Tate in meaning business, but they took none of the risks that he did. They may well have felt put upon and unappreciated, but their complaints are passive and singularly bookish. Their poems do not bear the marks of experience which may be seen in Tate's even when he is most self-consciously posing.

The mysterious genius turned up in the first issue of *The Fugitive* among some poems of excruciating silliness and sentimentality such as Hirsch's "The Little Boy Pilgrim":

> I am the little boy pilgrim,
> I wander the wold and the sea,
> And far past the reach of the star-rim
> I mingle my mad minstrelsy.
>
> . . .
>
> I dance in the fragrance of living;
> I shriek till my nose is a-thrill.
> Then I see that the rustics are peeping
> From their boast of the common-sense hill. . . .

The wrenched diction and knock-kneed meters turned up again in his "Quodlibet," published a year later, and with them the superior, childlike soul fleeing the cage of the ordinary. In this poem the escape is effected by dissolving the outlines of consciousness and personality in a vaporous fantasy evoked by such terms as *mad, mystical, rhapsody, melt, ecstatic, secret, necromancy, phantom*, and *dream*. Even the practical James Frank felt the charm of withdrawal from the rub of the ordinary. In his "The Fugitive Unbound" (*The Fugitive*, 1, 2 [June, 1922]) he wrote:

> Into my soul I groped one day,
> As I found it there at rest;
> In a timorous, quivering dream it lay,—
> All that of me was best.
>
> . . .
>
> From its dream it rose with a quaking cry,
> And broke its shackles: free!
> With a bound it mounted to the sky.
> Now, Lord, it rhythms Thee!

Davidson, too, liked the figure of the singer as orphan and exile. In the first two issues of the magazine he published five poems developed upon variants of this image. One of these, "A Demon Brother," which appeared in the first number, he so esteemed that after some small revisions and a new name, he made it the title-poem of his first volume, *An Outland Piper*:

> *Old man, what are you looking for?*
> *Why do you tremble so at the window peering in?*
> *—A Brother of mine! That's what I'm looking for!*
> *Some one I sought and lost of noble kin.*
>
> I heard strange pipes when I was young,
> Piping to songs of an outland tongue.
> I heard, and was agape to see
> How like that piper was to me.
> Playing a tune to the rabble's whim
> He marched away; I followed him.

After the mob had been left behind, the piper turned and ordered the narrator to follow no further, for,

> ". . . Though I be of thy father bred,
> And though I speak from thine own blood,
> Yet I am but of demon brood;
> And follow not my piping sweet
> To find the walking world a cheat;
> And cherish not my outland grace,

Nor pride in likeness of my face—
I am thy demon Brother," he said,
And into the deeper shadow sped.

But the narrator followed and now in old age cried,

—A Brother of mine! That's what I'm looking for!
The sight of a kinsman's face before I am dead.

In the other poems the frail exquisite, all a-tremble with wonder
and contempt for the jostling rabble, went forth, as had Hirsch's
"little boy pilgrim," in search of a lost and magical beauty. In "The
Valley of the Dragon" (1, 2, June, 1922) he took his child-bride
to a refuge

where the Dragon never came,
And one roof sealed against the hostile firmament;
Under the eaves a bench was set in a flowery frame
Where colored flies on honeyed errands came and went. . . .

His beloved sang in the evening and

all the flame
Of many sunsets lifted their drifted gold with her
And moons their silver melted with her voice and dulcimer.

But the Dragon came at last, bringing "serpent-thoughts of men,"
and threatened their "singing magic remote from human ken." So
the wanderer set out once more, this time to find "a Charm,—/ A
Spell, a Sword, a Faith beyond the strange sea's foam" with which
to kill the brute, whom an unsympathetic reader might take to be,
among other things, an unwitting and somewhat overwrought symbol of the realities and responsibilities of adulthood.

When the "outland piper," as we may call the protagonist, so
well does the phrase fit all his manifestations, did at last escape
the gross limits of mere "human ken," the fulfillment of the fantasy was immolation rather than stoic defiance. Amidst a melodious
blur achieved by an incantatory piling up of words such as *sweet,
lost, melt, drift, tremble, faint, strange, alien,* and *unknown,* his
half-dissolved consciousness sank down in blissful surrender to a
mother-mistress. "The Tiger-Woman" (1, 2, June, 1922), a quite
shockingly naive poem, is explicitly though probably unintentionally

masochistic: the piper met a *belle dame sans merci* on a dark and secret jungle way where she has been caressing a tiger and with delicious horror took the kisses from her blood-smeared lips. He and the lady set up a *ménage à trois* where he was general flunky and second-best man to her curious pet. But in "Following the Tiger" (1, 1, April, 1922) the animal led the protagonist, "weary of toiling," to the house of the "long-lost Queen of the Faeries":

> And then was the latch-string lifted.
> And there were the lovely Three—
> God, and his Queen, and the Tiger!
> And God's hand welcomed me.
> The Tiger slept on the Hearthstone;
> The Faery gave me her Ring;
> My Rose began to blossom;
> My Lute began to sing.
> *It sang how the ways of the Tiger*
> *Led me to beauty and God*
> *To the door of the Hut of the Faery*
> *By paths men had never trod.*

It would be cruel without purpose to linger over these lines were it not that the image of the poet which stands forth so clearly had considerable interest for several members of the group and invested the group's name with more, and more explicit, meaning than probably any of them except Hirsch would have intended. The persistence in Davidson's poetry of the symbolic flight from the human condition, the deliquescent diction, the emphasis on such qualities as softness, weakness, and weariness suggest much about the sensibilities and the attitudes toward the artist which formed such poems. One seems to glimpse behind them an imagination much attracted by failure and lost causes and inclined to see in them a delicacy and distinction too fine for the world and the hurly-burly from which comes victory—indeed, such an imagination as would be particularly responsive to the notion that the Old South was too good to survive the challenge of the noisy, dirty, ill-bred North and that those who would keep alive its memory should withdraw from the bustle and confusion and cloddish egalitarianism of the present and defend what is left of Arcadia haughtily, gallantly, but, in the end, hopelessly. The wonder is that Davidson

took so long to reach such an attitude. The whole story of the
Fugitives is, in the main, so genial that one is inclined to look
back upon such poetry with indulgence—until one is brought up
short by Ransom. The most damning measure of the silliness and
sentimentality of the treatment of the wayfaring child is Ransom's
own poem on the same subject, "First Travels of Max," which appeared in the magazine for June, 1923. Little Max

> in a chevroned sailor's blouse
> And tawny curls far from subdued to the cap,
> Had slapped old Katie and betaken himself
> From games for children

to go off to Fool's Forest, where the devil dwelt.

> "Become Saint Michael's sword!" said Max to the stick,
> And to the stone, "Be a brand-new revolver!"
> Then Max was glad that he had armed so wisely,
> As darker grew the wood, and shrill with silence.
> All good fairies were helpless here

in the wood full of reptiles and "people of age and evil/ That
lay on their bellies and whispered." In all that rottenness

> The only innocent thing . . . was Max,
> And even he had cursed his little sisters.

He finds a tarn:

> Bubbles were on it, breath of the black beast
> (Formed like a spider, white bag for entrails)
> Who took that sort of blackness to inhabit
> And dangle after bad men in Fool's Forest.
> "Must they be bad?" said casuistical Max.
> "Mightn't a good boy who stopped saying his prayers
> Be allowed to slip into the spider's fingers?"
> Max raised his sword—but what can swords do
> Against the Prince of the Dark? Max sheathed his point
> And crept around the pool.

Later he comes upon a Red Witch "with a wide bosom yellow as
butter," who "knew him, it appeared, would know him better,"
for all of his family had come to her before him. But he defied her:

"When I am a grown man I will come here
And cut your head off!" That was very well;
Not a true heart beating in Christendom
Could have said more, but that for the present would do.
Max went straight home. . . ,

accompanied on his way by the witch's laugh and his own fright.
But now

Max is more firmly domiciliated.
A great house is Van Vrooman, a green slope
South to the sun do the great ones inhabit
And a few children play on the lawn with the nurse.
Max has returned to his play, and you may find him,
His famous curls unsmoothed, if you will call
Where the Van Vroomans live; the tribe Van Vrooman
Lives there, at least, when any are at home.

Quietly, inexorably the poem makes its point: there is no escape
from the world. Max in his time will leave the sunny lawn and
follow the rest of his family into Fool's Forest for a longer visit.

It would almost seem that Ransom had deliberately set out to
turn the tables on Hirsch, Davidson, and the others, so exactly
does he use each of their favorite elements in just the opposite
way: the startling diction ("casuistical," "domiciliated"), the secret
place, the innocent child, the flight from the fetters of the ordinary,
the *femme fatale* and the mysterious and perverse sexuality—all
are there, but what a different meaning and tone they bear. As in
his other poems about children, "Bells for John Whiteside's
Daughter" and "Janet Waking," Ransom skillfully manipulates
stock figures and attitudes to ridicule the sentimental idealizing
of childhood. Despite its fairy-tale atmosphere, its witty mixture
of formal, even pedantic, rhetoric with colloquial terms and
rhythms, and its offhand manner, the poem is as dark and terrible
an account of a child's first experience with evil and the terror lurk-
ing just beyond the sunny lawn as Warren's later poems and stories
on the same theme, which it much resembles.[21] The difference,

[21] See, for example, Warren's "Letter From a Coward to a Hero" and
"Revelation," or his story "Blackberry Winter." Particularly close to his work
is the description of the dark pool and the spider with the monstrous bag of
entrails. These aspects of Warren's work are discussed in Chapters Nine and Ten.
The nature of Ransom's poetry is taken up in Chapter Five.

finally, between this poem and those his friends were writing, is in the point of view. Instead of writing in the first person and inviting the reader to join the poet in identification with the fairy child, Ransom studies and reports his material from the position of an anonymous, ironic adult. Max is a real boy, not an elf, and the proper object of wry amusement at his pathetic idealism and ignorance and of sympathy for his involvement in the inescapable human condition.

If the Fugitives sometimes looked alike because, as Elliott said, they dipped into "Johnny's bag of tricks,"[22] they borrowed Ransom's mannerisms but not his manner or his view of man from which the manner came. How little Ransom's attacks on sentimentality really counted as well as how little the Fugitives responded to the new forces in American poetry can be seen in their use of diction and conventions which go right back to late nineteenth-century verse. When Ransom took over as editor of *The Fugitive* early in 1925, he wrote sternly of the public's outmoded conception of poetry and singled out for special depreciation the melodies of Swinburne and the "sinister naïveté" of the pre-Raphaelites.[23] He was simply publishing what he had long been saying in the meetings. Others in the generation of the Fugitives ridiculed this conception for a decade or more. But for some of the Fugitives it had lost little of its appeal. Thus Stanley Johnson's "Sermons" in the first issue:

> I paused beside a temple, and I heard one say,
> "Come give your hearts, my children, to God this day;
> Lay flesh and blood and laughter
> And wine and women's hair
> And eyes and lips thereafter
> Upon the altar there."

An unpleasant shambles. The speaker paused by a tavern, resisted the temptation to sleep "Where red poppies grow," and walked off into the "ashes of dead leaves" and silence. Here, and in Johnson's "The Lifted Veil," in the same issue, is the stale old mixture that some of the Fugitives still found delicious: the hints of satiety and longing for God and lost innocence, the dolor, the mysterious guilt,

[22] See above, p. 36.
[23] "Mixed Modes," *The Fugitives*, IV (March, 1925), 28-29.

the hair fetishism, the clichés of lips and wine, the opiates. So, too, in Curry's "To a Curious, Modest Lady," which appeared in the second issue:

> Haste not to violate my shuttered mind
> Lest you should shiver at its chill and blackness;
> Its inwardness is strange, its goings trackless,
> And I myself stand somewhere there behind . . .
>
> . . .
>
> You must not know how I have visioned you,
> Your posturings, the shifting veils you wore . . .
> Beware of desecrations; close the door!

Allen Tate had read much Swinburne earlier, and though he was now looking for more manifestly sophisticated stuff, the old recipe retained some appeal. His "Sinbad," published in the first issue, referred in the good old gorgeous way to lips and poppies and orgies that drove men mad, while his "Parthenia," which came out in *The Double Dealer* during the following July, was even more markedly derivative in its pseudo-hellenism, perfunctory sadism, and allusions to phallic rituals and the deflowering of virgins. Traces of Swinburne and the Decadents lingered on in his poetry for several years but finally disappeared when he went to New York City. But Davidson, having begun with mildly perverse fantasies about the Imperious Woman, was especially susceptible, and in a group of poems beginning with "The Amulet," published in *The Fugitive* for October, 1922, and extending through "Drums and Brass," in the issue for April-May, 1923, he followed Swinburne and the Decadents closely. Having a sensitive ear and being, perhaps, more akin in temperament, he was far more successful with his imitation, as may be seen from these lines from "Drums and Brass":

> We are children spun and blown of an old pleasure,
> And the feet return where the dancing feet began . . .
>
> . . .
>
> We shall move with the living pulse of a dusk that is dead
> Till the untold morning be come and the dancers be fled.

Now Davidson's pursuit of the far and lost had moved on to midnight glade where veils float, white flesh gleams, lithe girls twist in Bacchic dances, and fauns and satyrs leap. But the poems are timid and withal rather circumspect; the real drive is not toward defiance but withdrawal, and the erotic imagery seems esteemed more for remoteness than sexuality. The true direction of the poetry is best seen in the arcane language: *runes, cruse, sudatorium, carcanet, sistrum, channering, mountance,* and so forth. Ransom might have used *sudatorium* mockingly, but the other words were such as had long fascinated Hirsch and were now turning up in some of Tate's poems. Out of them Davidson fashioned mild little verses in which Swinburne's intentionally shocking combination of learned religiosity and salaciousness was reduced to gentle wistfulness.

One Fugitive who had left Swinburne behind was Alec Brock Stevenson, whose work most resembled Ransom's in both style and vision. But his fables of kings, castles, and the pageantry of knighthood tended to lead away from reality whereas in Ransom's work they provided a new perspective on it. Yet until Merrill Moore suddenly developed unexpected skill and maturity, Stevenson was, with Davidson and Johnson, the best of the Fugitives after Ransom, and his sonnet "Imprisonment," which he published in the first issue under the pseudonym "Drimlonigher," might almost be mistaken for one of Ransom's own little essays on mortality and the sad fumblings of a lover trying to cheer his mistress:

> The lightning feet of years appalled her heart,
> Swift days that left a restless love uncrowned.
> She sighed, and smiled at me with piteous art,
> Wishing for ending, death, or sleep as sound.
>
> With bitter Spring and hateful silence stricken,
> Choked with expository word unsaid,
> I stopped her lips with mine, quaked lest I quicken
> The shouting fear that love might yet lie dead.
>
> The moon assisted, and the present stars:
> They went unheeded, we were blind that night,
> Blundered against our own dear prison bars
> And loosed our listless hands and groped for light.
>
> Forgetfulness shall drown me many things,
> But never how the April cricket sings.

A modest poem, but it shows more control of the medium, more deftness in fitting form and sense, than most of the group could manage. The only real interest, however, comes from those touches of Ransom's idiom: the ironic pedantry of *expository word*, which suggests the speaker's homiletic manner, or the flatness of *present stars*, which turns the convention inside out and suggests thereby how little the lovers can be helped by the familiar—and meaningless—trinkets of romance. Effective as these touches are, they cannot raise the poem much beyond the dead level of the second line, and one feels that Stevenson might be more at ease with the conventions he tries to mock than with the critical irony he has awkwardly taken up. More sophisticated—and more like Ransom's poetry—is the sonnet "Now This is Parting," published in the second issue under the pseudonym of "King Badger," a portion of which reads:

> The sour mist like marshy waters moving,
> Comes up at dawn and the young splendid sun,
> Quenched of his flame, thinks this is evil done
> And further race unworthy of the proving.

But the mark of his friend was strongest upon "Fiddlers' Green," published in the magazine in the spring of 1923 and probably Stevenson's best poem:

> This was a splendid city, and its sitting fair to be seen.
> This was a lovely city, and it risen in a day.
> The walls had never seen the new moon's sudden silver hollow
> Before the siegers were upon them, armored kings from far away,
> Brave mailed kings with quick-seeing eyes, and bold to follow....
> It's overthrown they were through much desire for that city's
>   queen.
>
> Oh, it was seemly and strong, and its palace shining forth
>   with a court;
> Banners and mounts like men do never be seeing had this town,
> And the smooth white walls it had, pierced by nine gates
>   of much report;
> The kings, and they battering, never battered them down.

Nor was it a fey place, nothing inhuman, nothing immortal,
For it was a stranger, and him walking, that entered the portal.

There was the town, and it shining up with its mounts
    and towers;
Eh, grand it was, you who do be after beauty early and late,
But I was looking at a grander sight, after a
    mort o' hours,
When I was seeing the young king, and him coming out of
    the narrow gate.

A pleasant poem, though the confusion of idioms—British guide book ("Its sitting fair"), Walter Scott ("it was seemly and strong"), literary folksy ("Eh, grand it was, you who do be . . ."), backwoods ("and him walking"—a syntax much favored by the yokels in Warren's novels), and, of course, Ransom ("nine gates of much report")—makes the reader uneasy. But the poem does not get anywhere. The chivalric details are present to display their own quaint charms, whereas, as we shall see, in Ransom's poems they furnish a critical view of the whole mystique of chivalry and the excesses of romantic idealism.

Stanley Johnson, a better poet than Stevenson, was more successful with the "bag of tricks." During the Fugitive years, Ransom often turned, as we have observed in "First Travels of Max," to the materials and conventions of children's fairytales: hamlets, bustling *hausfrauen*, pretty millers' daughters, bumpkins named Dick, aged eccentrics chasing visions of beauty, and so forth. It may be that far from dipping into Ransom's bag, Johnson was the one who got him interested in this sub-genre, which Ransom used so effectively. Be that as it may (for the matter of priority is of little importance), both men published their first poems of this kind in the issue for October of 1922. Ransom's poem was "Boris of Britain." Johnson's was entitled "Pier":

It is Pier by his candle, thinking one has called;
Grips his pen and stares at the words he has scrawled,
Mutters as he slips lean fingers through his hair,
To shiver in the silence: "There is really no one there!"

While the neighbors whisper, Pier dreams that Eva is calling him.

Cackle witted, pain footed, Pier sold his house—
Plain to be seen his poor wit's on carouse.
Wandered off to the forest; he never came back,
And, for all we'd known of him, it was no great lack.

Oh, he caught her at last, at least in his way,
On a strip of water where new moonlight lay;
And he fathomed her out, this Eva he had known,
Holding in his foolish hand a dripping stone.

Pier walks in the forest—you've heard of Pier?
Owned the small house—it's been many a year.
Starting and peeping behind the trees' black boles,
You'd say, if you saw him, he was stalking souls.

The poem comes to rest somewhere between Hirsch's and Davidson's maundering over the outcast dreamer and the comic ruefulness
of Ransom's "Conrad at Twilight," which was published in the
spring of 1923, or "Captain Carpenter," best of Ransom's poems
on noble crackpots, which came early in 1924. Johnson did not go
on with this kind of work, but he continued to resemble Ransom
in other ways. His sequence, "Sonnets of the Yellow Leaf," published in the magazine from December, 1923, to June, 1924, took
up the mortality of beauty and romance and came much nearer than
had Stevenson's "Imprisonment" to Ransom's equipoise of sadness
on a self-deprecating comedy:

You owed allegiance to so many gods
And I was least of all with whom you strove—
You could not heed the sound of bursting pods
The summer long, nor fill one cubicle with love.

The poplar leaves one day were sternly driven;
Black sorcery of crows came figured on
Our patch of sky, and you said, "Even
Now they have much need of me at home."

You set the cover of the bed aright,
You made the broth for the baby's lips to drink,
And in the narrow room in the waning light
Made me hold the puny hands—and think.

The Fugitive Group: 1922-1928

Outside the storm rode, driving God to cover,
While I kept house, the wet-nurse, the grand lover!

A bit removed from Ransom's "Philomela" or "The Good Ships." Still, where Stevenson had more of the manner, Johnson had the matter.

In his meanderings Davidson, too, veered toward Ransom during what might be termed a third period of his poetic development, one that began with "Iconoclast" in February, 1923, and extended through "Avalon" and "The Old Man of Thorn" to "Prelude in a Garden," published in April, 1924. With "Alla Stoccata" (*The Fugitive*, August-September, 1923) he moved into what was for him really new territory:

> Here's one Phineas
> Out for a walk,
> Tired of skulls
> And bones that talk,
> Aching from words
> That jump and jabber.
> Books have curdled
> His brains to clabber.

Attacked by ogres, Phineas drags them out into the sun; then,

> They sizzled and squeaked.
> They boomed like a drum.
> But they all swelled up
> Worse than Fee-Fo-Fum,
> And they steadily rose
> Past the tops of the trees
> With a strained expression
> Of ill-at-ease.
>
> Higher and higher . . .
> A mess of black dots!
> Phineas gathers
> Forget-me-nots,
> Heave-ho's home
> With a rondelay,

And butters his bread
In the good old way.

Gone were the rarities which had moved Witter Bynner to write
Davidson that "what constantly intruded between your work and
me is the shadow of an academician collecting dead phrases. You
have your own magic, but seem to immerse it in a bath of books."[24]
Perfumy pastel words were supplanted by vigorous colloquialisms
that collided in unexpected rhymes—a trick Ransom liked to manipulate, as in "The Miller's Daughter," to underscore the inadequacy of learning in coping with the world of homely things. Here,
and in "Avalon" and "The Old Man of Thorn," Davidson's attitude toward the *outré* character is wholly different from what it
had been. The eccentric is approved for his sturdiness in confronting
the mob and not for his flight. But where Ransom, in "Old Man
Playing with Children" or "Bells for John Whiteside's Daughter"
(both of this same period), came dangerously near cuteness and
yet by steely control made the poems rebuke such easy self-indulgence, Davidson could not refrain from that feyness which had
marred his work from the beginning.

Where the poet's mastery weakened, the sentimentality latent
in the material ceased to be an object of implicit criticism, as in Ransom's poems, and dominated the tone. Thus Davidson's "Prelude
in a Garden," which resembles Ransom's "Spectral Lovers" of a
year earlier, relaxes in the last line and becomes just one more soft
verse about the confusions of love. He began well, using two of
Ransom's favorite themes: the conflict of desire with conventional
morality, and sexual passion as the beginning of destruction and
death. Davidson even displayed his lovers in the analogue of a
military siege, which Ransom later used in "The Equilibrists":

> Having once idly blushed, she could not startle
> Runaway messages to cover again.
> Trembling was at her lips, and her petulant eyelids
> Drooped, proclaiming him victor in that campaign.
>
> Yet still unyielding to his urgent whispers
> She veiled her silence with reluctant looks,

[24] In a letter dated January 16, 1923.

While he, with creeping tenderness of fingers
Clutched at her hands. Thus lovers plead, in books.

Believing themselves safe in their garden, they suddenly felt a presence, and

Their bodies, that were sealed for dissolution,
Chilled in the fragrant air. The somber breath
Smote on their flesh with hindering strange assailment
Reminding them that love begins with death.

Or death begins with love. They named it not.
After the magic pause were charmed no more.
Too gallant to remember they were mortal,
They kissed, as they had minded to before.

Truly Davidson had come far from "The Valley of the Dragon," but he did not hold his new ground. In the next issue of *The Fugitive* he published "Swan and Exile," wherein he reverted to the theme of the superior outcast and entered still another phase of his poetry—one differing from the first in a significant way. For in these later poems the outcast did not come to cuddling and cosiness; instead he ended in despair:

Slender upon the pond and white,
All motion lost save that I see,
The exile lulls his dead white soul
Without threnody.

. . .

And drifting sees the pale shadow
Of himself, as I have seen
My forgotten self in a cold pool
Dangerously serene.

Swan, where is the flock of eld?
What secrecy keeps us here
Circling within a rim of eyes
Silent in fear?

In "Palingenesis," published in the same issue, the narrator speaks to his own soul, seeking to assuage the hurt of "Thunder or stone or pestilence/ That men contrive for thee," and "words that bit thy beauty." The nadir was not reached until "Lines for a Tomb," published in *The Fugitive* for September, 1925, which began:

> Recite the dangers chiselled on this face:
> How I was clipped by scorn and maimed by lies;
> How conscience hedged my soul; law chilled my eyes;
> Ropes cut my grace. . . .

Sensitive, shy, responsive to the impress of strong personalities and distinctive styles, Davidson had gone quickly from Blake, with perhaps a touch of Hirsch, to Swinburne and the Decadents, and finally to Ransom (and, here and there to Edwin Arlington Robinson). But the sinewy realism of his friend was exactly opposite the set of his temperament. With his fine ear he could parody Ransom's manner more closely than any other Fugitive, but none of them, not even Hirsch, was farther from the disposition behind it. Drawn by the fascination which failure and flight had for him, he returned to the image of the enchanted child fleeing on torn wings. In all his mournful music there is none of that prickly defiance or gay bravado which characterized the poems, novels, and manifestoes of the young expatriates of the time who had really fled. Nor is there any clear statement of what the wanderer was fleeing, only the vague reiterations that the world was cruel, stupid, and all-powerful. Though the tones of melancholy and—it must be said—self-pity are strongest in his work, they are present in many of the poems of Stevenson, Johnson, Curry, Frank, and Jesse Wills, and give substance to Tate's comment, in a letter to Davidson dated November 26, 1925, a year after Tate had settled in New York, that the Fugitive poetry ". . . *was* much alike, in spite of technical inequalities, for it was the expression of defeated men." Tate himself could not at that moment write poetry, he said, because he lacked the idiom for a Vita Nuova. "It will take a long time for me even to understand it. For poetry is the triumph of life, not a commentary on its impossibility."[25] Occasionally Davidson wrote poems such as "Not Long Green" or "Portrait of a Wasp" (both published in *The Fugitive* for June, 1925) filled with winsomeness and gaiety. To judge from his letters and the

---

[25] Cf. Cowan, 218. Tate did not hold to this view for long, as the poems of the next few years make clear.

recollections of his friends, this was the more usual expression of his own spirit. Yet one comes away from reading most of his poems from the Fugitive period with the impression of a sad, gentle spirit escaping into fantasies wherein ultimate defeat and immolation approve and justify all.

The Fugitive who came nearest to sharing Ransom's vision of man was, of all people, Merrill Moore—at least until Warren joined the group early in 1924 and began to write occasional pieces having some of Ransom's perception of the mutations below the bland surface of circumstance. Except for one sonnet Moore never wrote more than three or four lines that sounded even remotely like Ransom's; moreover, of the Fugitives he was the least influenced by Ransom's emphasis upon decorum and control. Yet he, too, had his insights into the complexity of the commonplace, and he, too, confronted it with much of the same cheerful resiliency. In all other respects he was unlike *any* of the Fugitives, and during this period he was, after Ransom, in many ways the most independent and original poet among them. But not at first.

Moore's Fugitive poetry falls quite markedly into two periods. The pieces published through June, 1923, were almost all in forms other than the sonnet and were absolutely without signs of anything but the most ordinary undergraduate talent. Then, after a six months' interval, Moore began publishing again and his new pieces, almost all in the sonnet form, included some of the best poetry to come from the Fugitives. Moore had written many poems before his "To a Fetish" earned him membership in the group, but neither this poem nor those of the year following its appearance had a particle of distinction. Familiar topics were treated in wholly predictable ways: the diction consisted mainly of ready-made phrases such as *soft wind, gleaming tresses, warm shower, sweet song,* and *golden light*; the rhymes were as bland and foreseeable as the ideas, except when they were as outrageous as the combination of *month* and *eleventh* (with the meter compelling the reader to stress the first and third syllables of the latter).

In the summer of 1923, Moore worked his way to Europe. Inflation enabled him to live regally on a dollar a day. Far off the tourist highways he saw such suffering as he had never imagined, though he had not lived under shelter, and he was compelled to use his French and German, at which he proved to be unexpectedly adept. The summer awakened him to language and to the weight of words. In addition to French, which he had begun in child-hood, and German, which he had taken up in Vanderbilt, he knew Latin and Spanish from preparatory school, and he had studied Greek with H. C. Tolman, who had made him more sensitive to the subtle filaments of meaning between language and life and had helped to prepare his imagination for the complex and crucial ex-periences of his summer abroad. Thus aroused, Moore took up Sanskrit and Hebrew and after graduation worked at his languages faithfully, reading some of their literature each day and touching upon each of them not less than once a week. Many years later he learned Maori during the two years he was stationed with the army in New Zealand and mandarin Chinese during the year he was in Nanking. All this helped to develop an unusual verbal memory and power of swift recall, so that his working vocabulary became im-mense and fluid; yet, curiously, he never yielded to a love of strange or rare words for their own sake, and the diction of his verse was notable for its easy colloquialism. More than anything else it was, he later believed, the combination, fused during that summer of rambling, of a habit of looking for the unexpected with an acute awareness of words which made possible the unique qualities and the staggering quantity of his poetry. It enabled him to compose sonnets with a swiftness and fertility never before seen and to move through words toward subjects that had never before been used in poetry. But it also made possible an immeasurable amount of drivel.

For the trip his father gave him letters of introduction to George Moore, an old friend (but no relative), and Thomas Hardy, and Hirsch gave him another to Gertrude Stein. He went down to see Hardy in Wessex, and learned that the old man had heard of the Fugitives even though he had never acknowledged the compli-mentary copies of the magazine they sent him. The visit with George Moore led to a letter of introduction to James Joyce, who said politely that he, too, had heard of the Fugitives, and perhaps he had. In Germany Moore called on Rilke, who later became with Goethe one of the two writers he loved and read most, though one cannot find a trace of Rilke in his sonnets. Such flattering at-tention, such opportunities to observe at first hand men ranging from beggars in Berlin to elderly novelists embowered in the gentle English countryside, and such roving independence abruptly matured Moore, who had been struggling so long to find himself in the shadow of his father. The change was immediately apparent in his writing.

Bad as his earlier work had been, it had lucidity and an easy syntax. The phrases may have been hackneyed, but they were never pretentious or strained: they were such as turn up in conversation or a letter written hurriedly to an old friend. The poetry Moore now began to write was, if anything, even more relaxed and informal, despite the sonnet form, and even more colloquial, for it was no longer clogged with dead metaphors. Abruptly he had found his characteristic style, the one in which he wrote virtually all of his poetry until his death in the summer of 1957. Except that it takes fewer liberties with the sonnet form, "Afternoon Date in a Corner Drugstore," which was published in *The Fugitive* for December, 1923, might have come from *M, A Thousand Autobiographical Sonnets* (1939), or *A Doctor's Book of Hours* (1955):

> Over the counter in this drug-store where
> Pepsol and grape juice so many times have passed
> Slow fans muddle the cool summer air;
> We sip from frosty straws and suck the last
> Cold drops of purple from among the lumps
> Of cracked ice in the bottom, with the noise
> Of great delight to little girls and boys
> While the attendant polishes the syrup-pumps.
>
> This is the summer of a lost content
> We may discuss. But out of doors the rain
> Thumps on the awning, eddies in the drain,
> And no one tells just what this shower has meant
> That drove us into the drug-store where we drink
> Coca-cola and limeade and other things, and think.

It is easy to underestimate this poem: it does not *look* poetic; it does not seem meant to be taken seriously. Yet it is both. The language, by itself, is virtually devoid of interest except for an occasional assonance and the terseness, after stringy sentences and chaffering rhythms, of the last phrase, which sums up the meaning of the poem. The whole thing has the homeliness of a Brownie snapshot, and the kind of sad, startling truth one comes across in an album; for Moore caught exactly the moment of suspense and aimless sorrow that comes at the leaving of childhood and the onset of sexual tension and social insecurity. The details are absolutely authentic. Out of all those available, Moore took just those which carried most authority and arranged them so that, however commonplace when taken one by one, they worked together to evoke a precise image and its attendant feeling. Because it is the image of an ordeal—protracted, obscure, understood, if at all, only long afterward—we all live through, it rises to a quasi-symbol and gives to a universal experience a local habitation and a name.

Yet even Moore came momentarily under Ransom's spell. He greatly admired Ransom's poetry, particularly his sonnets, which had helped to interest him in the form. He had taken Ransom's course in creative writing, and Ransom had encouraged him to write in his own way of his own experiences (as so few of the Fugitives did) and to loosen up the sonnet form. Though he took this advice, he could not resist trying his hand just once at Ransom's own idiom, which he used for "It Is Winter I Know" (*The Fugitive*, April, 1924). With his flair for languages Moore might have imitated those poets he admired and failed to realize his own modest but genuine distinction. How easily he could have done it is suggested in this poem by the phrase "the birds' *indeclinable* twitter," an exact duplication of Ransom's combination of formal, scholarly terms with homely details. Or again one may see Ransom's exaggerated daintiness in "treading but lightly on all the delicate grasses," or his deliberate and mocking ponderousness in "There are too many Nays now confronting/ The obdurate soul that would trick itself. . . ." But though the imitation is superbly clever, the best thing in it is Moore's own: the image of the small birds peppering the sky. Again and again he would write sonnets, many far less engaging than this one, which would have at least one such memorable detail. A good example is "Abschied," which was published in *The Fugitive* for March, 1925. It is entirely his own.

> And—after the dance was over he
> Went up to the ones who were sitting in the car
> And told them all how much he'd like to be

Invited again and whistled them a bar
Of music from the song he'd liked the best,
The one they'd played while he had danced and she
Had remarked what everyone wore—how each was dressed,
And they all agreed and laughed content[ed]ly.

But somehow he felt as far away by then
As if instead of the car he peered into
He was a hunter looking into a pit
Where, in the dark, in fur, were one or two
Fierce bears whose sharp claws tore, whose white teeth bit
The flesh that chanced unarmed to fall within.

Rapid and casual, like so many of his little narratives and sketches, this one is notable for its awesome glimpse of the horror, the dark violence crouching just under the surface of the ordinary. Those bears mean more than all of Davidson's dragons and tigers. The poem compares well with Ransom's "Prelude to an Evening," Tate's "The Wolves," or the eleven terrible poems "on the same theme" which Warren wrote between 1939 and 1942. It comes unexpectedly from a boy of twenty-one who had recently written so much drivel. How exactly it is all *there*: the shy adolescent, his sense of being just on the edge and yet out of things, his awkward attempts to appear at ease, his moment of enthusiasm and self-forgetfulness, followed so abruptly and with such effective contrast, by the shocked awareness of animal savagery and sexuality. Again a snapshot which, blundered on years afterward, makes the heart turn over.

That is the art of Merrill Moore. At its best a stab of insight into the subterranean; at its worst, a catalog of details that lie, inert and lumpy, where they have been flung on the page. Rarely does it achieve intensity because Moore chose to forego many of the resources of the sonnet. With his sensitive ear and his immense vocabulary, constantly kept on the ready by his reading and writing, he swiftly found some sort of words for his anecdotes and portraits, which were almost always sharp and amusing, no matter how casually they had been put down. But he chose to work with the syntax and diction of familiar middle-class conversation and so diminished the range of ideas, feelings, degrees of emphasis avail-

71

able to him. Moreover, as he made less use of the sonnet conventions, he was less able to achieve meanings and modulations of tone through those parallelisms, contrasts, proportions and disproportions which the form makes available to those who will submit to its demands. One has only to put his witty, observant "Mrs. Broderick was a Very Unusual Woman"[26] beside Ransom's "Miriam Tazewell" or "Of Margaret" to discover how much more could be said in as many lines by one who had Moore's own kindly good humor and acceptance of the crankiness of ordinary people.

Moore never surpassed his work of the Fugitive period. Davidson, Tate, and Warren went on to write better things—poems superior to the finest that Moore ever brought off. But between 1922 and 1925, he outdid them with "Abschied," "Chronicles of an Acquaintance," and one or two other poems, and established himself in second place behind—well behind—Ransom. For one so happy-go-lucky in his methods that was quite an achievement.[27]

III

1923, when Moore abruptly emerged as man and poet, was an exceptional year for the whole group. Davidson came out of the mists of melancholy, tied for second place in the South Carolina Poetry Society Contest, broke a lance with the editors of *Poetry*, served as the first official editor-in-chief of *The Fugitive*, and had his first volume, *An Outland Piper*, accepted for publication. Tate returned to graduate and stayed on for the rest of the year, during which he argued in print with Ransom over Eliot and the new

---

[26] *Clinical Sonnets* (New York, 1949), p. 23.

[27] Once he had taken to the sonnet, Moore rarely wrote anything else, though many of his "sonnets" may be called that only out of courtesy. In a lifetime of incredible activity as physician, psychiatrist, professor of medicine, army officer, author of numerous articles on alcoholism and other medical problems, he found time and energy for the writing of so many sonnets that fairly sober estimates put the number at more than 100,000. Most of these remained in manuscript (many were in shorthand) and filled huge boxes in the summer house adjacent to his home at Squantum, Massachusetts, on the shore of Quincy Bay. From time to time he and friends would look over the latest ones and gather up enough for a volume. By this method he published eighteen collections in all. There are some penetrating and often hilarious pieces in *Clinical Sonnets* (1949), but his work fell off after 1940 (even though the bulk of his published poems were written after then), and the best collections are *The Noise that Time Makes* (1929), *Six Sides of a Man* (1935) and *M, A Thousand Autobiographical Sonnets* (1938).

sensibility, published *The Golden Mean* with Ridley Wills, befriended young Red Warren, helped Davidson with editing the magazine, and finally and fully made up his mind to become a man of letters. For a time, too, it seemed that a book of his poems might be published by Lieber and Lewis. For Warren, soon to become a member of the group, it was a year of constant excitement and discovery stimulated by the tumultuous talk of Ridley Wills and Tate.

Ransom, now in the full course of his powers, continued his extraordinary productivity. His "Armageddon," actually begun in 1922, took first place and the "Southern Prize" over Davidson's "Avalon" and a poem by William Alexander Percy in the contest just referred to.[28] In 1923 he also began to think closely on the nature of poetry and wrote his first real essay in criticism and poetics. He had previously written an innocuous little review of Robert Graves's *On English Poetry* for the third issue of *The Fugitive*, which came out in October, 1922. In passing he observed that American poets "abhor the thought of changing the considered phrase that perfectly expresses them in the interest of an irrelevance called meter." But, he continued gently, perhaps the "determinate mathematical regularities of meter" have as much to do with the total effect of a poem as the "determinate geometrical regularities of outline" have to do with the total effect of architecture.

Here, quite without his knowing it, was the crux to which all his later meditations on the nature of poetry, art, science, tradition, myth, and religion would return: how, he wondered, do the abstract patterns admired by the reason consort with the particular details enjoyed by the sensibility? Moved by his fury against abstractions, he had written poems on the division between the Idea and Experience; now he began to wonder how it might affect the very organization of the poems themselves. Later he wrote to Tate, "Poetry is always the exhibit of Opposition and at the same time Reconciliation between the Conceptual or Formal and the Individual or Concrete. An obvious case of the formal is meter; which nevertheless does not seem to impair the life and effectiveness of the Concrete Experience. They coexist." Then in the margin beside this dictum, he added, "This obvious fact was what started

[28] The contest was really a competition among the Fugitives and Percy. Later an officer of the society wrote to Davidson that the Fugitives had sent "about the only real poetry" entered for the prize. ("J. B. W." January 14, 1924.)

me off years ago into this whole way of reasoning."[29] Yet with characteristic skepticism and diffidence, he noted in his review of Graves that it was dangerous to dogmatize in such matters, for Tate's poem "Horatian Epode to the Duchess of Malfi," printed in the same issue, was a good instance of irregular meters and diction so satisfying that one would hesitate to make any change in the interest of regularity.

This demurrer did not satisfy Tate, who was deep in the study of Eliot. He replied with a long essay, "Whose Ox," published in the next issue, in which he defended Eliot's "aberrant" versification on the grounds that it was necessary for the true representation of complex contemporary life. "The Waste Land," he went on, demonstrated "for all time" the necessity of unconventional techniques for certain kinds of subjects. To this Ransom responded in a friendly letter, asserting that "The Waste Land" did not satisfy him and that in "poem after poem" Eliot was trying for form but had not got it. The reason, Ransom believed, was that

> "The art-thing sounds like the first immediate transcript of reality, but it isn't; it's a long way from the event. It isn't the raw stuff of experience. The passion in it has mellowed down— emotion recollected in TRANQUILITY, etc. etc. . . . . There must not be a trace of the expository philosophical method, but nevertheless the substance of the philosophical conclusion must be there for the intelligent reader. . . . I can't help believing more and more (it must be the trace that classical pedagogy has left on me) that the work of art must be perfectly serious, ripe, rational, mature—full of heart, but with enough head there to govern heart."[30]

This was all very well for a letter, but when Ransom expanded his views on Eliot in an essay entitled "Waste Lands," which appeared on July 14, 1923, in *The Literary Review*, a supplementary section of the *New York Evening Post*, Tate felt compelled to retort. Going far beyond the asides of his review of Graves's book, Ransom now claimed that Eliot's new poem was fragmentary and inharmonious because of its random juxtaposing of attitudes, pe-

---

[29] In a letter dated "September 5." Internal evidence and its relation to other dated letters make it clear that the letter was written in 1926.

[30] The letter is dated "Sunday 12/17." References to Tate's poetry in *The Fugitive* for December, 1922, show the year to be 1922.

riods, and styles and warned young men not to abandon established conventions for mere novelty, the cause of the extreme incoherence in Eliot's work. Ransom's own poetry was distinguished by juxtaposition, which was one of the good reasons why William Yandell Elliott could designate him the "first modernist" among the Fugitives, since the forcing together of unlikely elements and edges is a fundamental technique—perhaps supremely *the* fundamental technique—of modern art. But there was nothing random about it, for Ransom managed to bring this off within the older forms, thereby giving his startling conjunctions a reassuring appearance of order and syntax: he left in the connectives which Eliot, on instructions from Pound, had left out. Nothing could have been more likely than Ransom's essay to arouse Tate, who was enchanted with Eliot and, obliged to remain in Nashville for want of anything to do after graduation, impatient to leave the stodgy South for New York and all the new movements. He fired off a letter to *The Literary Review* charging that Ransom restated "superannuated theories of consciousness." He also sent a copy to Ransom, who immediately wrote a letter of his own, and the two were published on August 4 and August 11. Ransom's acknowledged Tate's as a token of "final emancipation" from his own influence as teacher, but charged that it exhibited those very defects of Eliot's verse—and of the young critics under Eliot's spell—over which he had expressed concern: it was "specious" and used "its glittering scraps of comment and citation without any convincing assurance that the subject has been really studied." This hurt, and Tate nearly resigned from the Fugitives. Gradually the coolness between them disappeared, and when Ransom once more took up the nature of poetry in an essay entitled "The Future of Poetry," published in *The Fugitive* for February, 1924, and again defended form and tradition against modernism, Tate replied in the next issue with "One Escape from the Dilemma." This new exchange led to a renewal of correspondence from which would come profound friendship and an exchange of ideas that would affect the whole character of criticism and the study of literature in our time.[31]

Yet 1923, which was to be so filled with excitement, achievement,

[31] This exchange is examined at length in Chapter Six.

and promise of still further achievement, began inauspiciously. The magazine was in trouble. The novelty of getting it out had worn off; editing it was now more of a nuisance than a romp. Mrs. Cowan reports that subscriptions had fallen to eighteen with only twenty-three renewals.[32] Counter sales, which had never amounted to much outside Nashville, were going down even in that city; readers thought the Fugitives too eccentric and obscure (while elsewhere their sales were low because they were thought too conservative). Much correspondence was required to hold onto the subscribers they had, and when the magazine was opened to outsiders in the last issue for 1922, a flood of contributions came in, most of them from people who did not subscribe yet did not hesitate on that account over making work for the unpaid editors. The magazine had become absolutely essential to the morale and further development of the Fugitives—perhaps even to their continued existence—but some organization was needed to keep it going. Yet with all the feeling over the conflict between tradition and experiment it seemed unlikely that the Fugitives could agree on any proposals.

In the spring Curry offered a plan of organization for the magazine that was tabled. By summer the affairs of the magazine were in such a state that Johnson and Tate—good friends despite their disagreement over modern poetry—drew up a plan calling for an editor-in-chief and associate editor to be elected yearly. Both men wanted Davidson for the top position. Then Johnson and Jesse Wills prepared a resolution calling for the adoption of the plan with Davidson at the head and Tate as his assistant and wrote to Davidson, who was out of Nashville for the summer, urging him to accept. He was the only one on whom a majority of the Fugitives could agree, and without him, they said, the magazine would go under.[33] Tate, too, prodded him, but Ransom, strangely, was against the whole scheme. Nevertheless, Davidson did accept, and the next issue came out under his editorship, though Tate, who was still in Nashville, did most of the plain busywork. In October the Fugitives decided to elect officers and chose Hirsch to be president and Stevenson treasurer. An advisory committee for the magazine was established and Johnson, Ransom, and Curry appointed

[32] *The Fugitives*, p. 95.
[33] Johnson to Davidson, July 23 [1923].

members.[34] Meanwhile, Jacques Back, a young advertising man then head of the Associated Retailers of Nashville, got the curious idea that the magazine might be put on a paying basis and offered to assume all expenses and business responsibilities in return for a share of the profits.[35] His proposal was accepted and this, with Davidson's taking over the editorial duties, made the magazine less of a burden to the group and really kept it going.

Casting about for ways to increase circulation, the Fugitives came up with the idea of annual poetry contests. They persuaded the Associated Retailers to offer a prize of one hundred dollars to help toward "the further placing of Nashville on the map as 'The Athens of the South,'" as they told the secretary of the Association; they also persuaded Ward-Belmont, a junior college for women in Nashville, to offer a prize of fifty dollars in a separate contest. When the contests were announced in the issue for April-May, 1923, four hundred poets sent entries from all forty-eight states, Mexico, the Philippines, Belgium, Canada, and Hawaii. Yet, though they made the Fugitives better known in the end, the contests did little to increase circulation.

The Fugitives had decided that poems deserving serious consideration for the prizes would be published in the magazine in advance of picking the winners. Among those entered for the "Nashville Prize" was "Crusade," by Robert Penn Warren, which was included in the issue for June, 1923. Just eighteen and in his second year at Vanderbilt, Warren had been rooming with Ridley Wills and Tate since February. He was a shy but independent boy who had come from Guthrie, a village about fifty miles to the northwest of Nashville and just over the border in Kentucky. Soon after his arrival at the university, he joined Blue Pencil, a writing club for freshmen and sophomores, and later he helped to organize the Verse Guild, an inner group devoted to poetry, which published a little pamphlet called *Driftwood Flames* in the spring of 1923. Encouraged by the acceptance of "Crusade" and the enthu-

[34] From a copy of the by-laws, dated October 6, 1923, and an undated typescript in the Fugitive records.

[35] Mrs. Cowan says that his share was to be twenty-five percent (*The Fugitives*, p. 118), but some of the members recall that he was to get all the profits. Since none of the poets, who had a far better notion of the market value of their commodity than any business man, expected more than a token profit, the point does not matter much. In the end Back lost $450 by the arrangement, which lasted for a year and a half.

siasm of Tate, Warren sent more poems to *The Fugitive*, and "After Teacups," though not entered for either contest, was printed in the issue for August-September, 1923.

Warren was already known to Davidson, Ransom, and Curry, with whom he had taken courses in his sophomore year, but it was Tate who really stirred him. Both poems in *The Fugitive* showed how much Tate's talk about the experimentalists had excited him. (However, it was Davidson, not Tate, who showed him "The Waste Land," and first talked with him about Eliot.) "Crusade" bore conspicuous traces of Pound's later manner, and "After Teacups" of Eliot's *Prufrock and Other Observations*—thereby indicating a flair for suggesting the idiom and rhythms of widely varying styles which would later give such vividness and authority to Warren's characterizations and dialog. Perhaps it was his unusual independence which prevented his imitating either Ransom or Tate, the only Fugitives whose styles had even a momentary influence on his own, until after he had left Vanderbilt. But his work resembled Tate's in one respect: a predilection for violence manifest in both poems for *The Fugitive* and in "Iron Beach," one of the five pieces Warren contributed to *Driftwood Flames*. This predilection may have helped to steer him away from Swinburne, still an influence among undergraduate writers at Vanderbilt and, as we have seen, the Fugitives themselves. Only one poem, "The Golden Hills of Hell," displaying purple lilies and a repentant satyr, was in the Decadent manner. On the other hand, he was attracted for a time by the arcane language that appealed so much to Hirsch, Davidson, and (with certain important differences) to Tate. But this, too, Warren soon gave up, though he was always to be fascinated by language for its own sake and to have a weakness for letting wild and wonderful rhetoric take precedence over dramatic fitness and even at times over sense.[36]

Looking back upon these earliest poems one thoroughly immersed in Warren's later work can discover, here and there, the faintest of signs of the writer to come, but it would be foolish to claim that they showed any remarkable talent. When he wrote them Warren was already recognized as one of the most brilliant men ever to come to Vanderbilt (by the time he graduated two years later,

---

[36] For more discussion of these poems and their relation to Warren's development and style, see Chapter Nine, pp. 431-435.

he had compiled the highest record yet made at the university), and Tate, who was rather possessive in his attitude toward the younger man, energetically sponsored him among the Fugitives. Still, it was not until the middle of the next school year (just before Tate finally left Nashville to take a job as a high school teacher in West Virginia) that Warren was admitted to the group.

As a Fugitive he was aligned on the modernist side. Frank and Hirsch made him impatient with all their talk about the necessity for lofty themes in poetry.[37] Yet for all his interest in the *avant-garde*, he did not follow Tate in identifying himself with it. Not that he was sluggish or indifferent. He listened with interest to his roommates' talk about the newest poetry and read the little magazines Tate passed on to him; but in neither his comments at the Fugitive meetings nor his writing did he show any need to compel attention by aggressive or extravagant expressions aimed at surpassing the eccentricities of the Symbolists or the latest journal from abroad. For one thing, young and shy as he was, he already had received some flattering recognition. For another, he came from a closely knit, happy family that watched his development with affection and approval. Moreover, among the Fugitives Warren was somewhat restrained by the difference in age between himself and the leaders. Ransom, Davidson, and Johnson, for example, seemed more august and professorial to him than they did to Tate or Ridley Wills. Indeed, it was not until his senior year, when they worked together as editors of the magazine, that he knew Ransom well, and their real friendship did not begin until 1932, when they became colleagues in the English Department at Vanderbilt.[38]

Nor did Warren have any interest in the outland piper or the lost Golden Age. The lonely protagonists of such early poems as "Iron Beach" were not fleeing the coarse multitude; Warren had put them down amidst violent surroundings which allowed him to deploy some of his favorite diction and imagery. When he

[37] More than three decades later Hirsch could still get a rise out of Warren by the assertion that great poetry required lofty themes. During the Fugitives' reunion in the spring of 1956, Hirsch referred to the old arguments and Warren was moved to an eloquent, though somewhat diffuse, statement that what counted was not the big subject but the *real* subject. See *The Fugitives' Reunion*, pp. 142ff.

[38] When Warren joined the department in the fall of 1931, Ransom was away on a year's leave of absence.

came later to describing egotists in flight from the familiar condition of ordinary men, he stressed not their superiority nor the moral triumph of their disengagement but their inadequacy and failure. If they fulfilled themselves, it was by returning and accepting the life they had tried to flee. And though he had listened to his grandfather's stories of the Civil War and had long been a reader of history, Warren was not yet aware of the past in any personal way. Of all the Fugitives, he was to have the most profound sense and understanding of the inweaving of the past within the present, but at this point it was something quite separate from his life and times—a fascinating subject for reading, but not at all the repository of values or refuge that it was to Hirsch, Davidson, and some of the others. He was a bit like Jack Burden reading, without comprehending their meaning for himself, the papers of Cass Mastern. When a sense of the past was awakened in Warren, it resembled Ransom's: it was height from which to look upon the present, not a secret valley in which to hide.

In several ways, then, Warren was a little apart from the others; yet being taken into the Fugitives was one of the most fortunate occurrences of his life, as he himself attests. Though only hints and flickers of the themes, ideas, and style of his later work appear in the poetry of this period, simply writing it was supremely important to his development, for now he could gain most from being held to high standards and stimulated by the example of men older and more experienced than he. His apprenticeship in the group far surpassed anything to be had in the finest courses, even when the teachers were as adroit as Ransom and Davidson in attracting and developing talented undergraduates.[39] Warren took more from the group than he gave, but he quite repaid his debt by the honor he brought the Fugitives.

One thing he did not take from the group was the Nashville Prize. Gorham Munson, editor of *Secession*, rated his "Crusade" fourth among the entries, but apart from Hart Crane's "Stark Major," which he put in first place, Munson thought all the entries—including, presumably, Warren's—"hopelessly trademinded." Still,

[39] The men they have helped—Andrew Nelson Lytle, Cleanth Brooks, George Marion O'Donnell, Randall Jarrell, Robert Lowell, Robie Macauley, Peter Taylor, and so many others in addition to Tate, Warren, and Merrill Moore—comprise a fair share of the most distinguished names in contemporary American letters.

if the other judges had thought a little better of his work he might have won, for the ratings turned out to be so bewilderingly diverse that the Fugitives were compelled to strike some sort of average. Both William Alexander Percy and Jessie Rittenhouse put "Stark Major" in twelfth place (the last among those rated at all). Beyond that they could not agree. When the Fugitives got through with their arithmetic, Joseph Auslander's "Berceuse," which Munson had rated second, had tied with Rose Henderson's "A Song of Death," which he had rated tenth. The winning poems were better than Warren's "Crusade," but Crane's entry, though certainly one of his lesser pieces, was about the only work of any literary interest today. The years have vindicated Munson.[40]

Ransom and Tate were greatly taken with the poetry sent in by Laura Riding Gottschalk—so much so that Tate wrote asking her to send more poems for the magazine. This intense, unhappy woman, then just twenty-two years old, had been born in New York City and educated at Cornell and the University of Illinois. Not long before the Fugitives heard of her she had moved to Louisville, where her husband was an assistant professor of history in the university. She had written an unpublished novel and was at work on another, and she had published poems in *Poetry* and several other little magazines; but the notice of the Fugitives was the first real encouragement she had received since beginning to write seriously. At their invitation she sent in sheaves of poems widely varying in quality. Meanwhile, despite the added work entailed by the correspondence with contestants and judges, the Fugitives had decided to go on with the contests, adding a third prize donated by the Presbyterian Bookstore. In 1924 they acted as judges themselves, and at the year's end awarded the Nashville Prize to Mrs. Gottschalk, not for any single poem, but for the whole corpus of her work appearing in the magazine during 1924.

She deserved something from them. By April of 1924 the magazine was in such trouble that a special committee recommended that it be discontinued. Back had lost much by his arrangement with the Fugitives, and, as the committee grimly observed, "Old subscribers approached for renewals take amazing pains to write ex-

[40] From letters, W. A. Percy to Donald Davidson, November 6, 1923; Jessie Rittenhouse to Donald Davidson, undated; Gorham Munson to Donald Davidson, November 6, 1923, and November 16, 1923.

pressing their definite disinclination to subscribe again." The committee put the blame for alienating readers on the Fugitives' uncompromising poetic standards.[41] Mrs. Gottschalk took a brighter view. Hearing of their troubles, she wrote on July 20, 1924, to the "Dear Present Editor of the Fugitive" (it was Davidson) suggesting that they go after donations from wealthy Louisville dowagers. Soon after she began her own collection campaign which was pathetic, funny, and unsuccessful in its attempt to flatter and cajole support from prominent people who had never heard of the group. Taking all this and her winning the Nashville Prize into account, the Fugitives asked her to attend a meeting. Other poets and writers had been their guests, but until her visit, late in 1924, no woman had been allowed to sit in with them, and a number of the wives of members were annoyed by this invitation.

As soon as she appeared, the Fugitives saw that she was not at all their type. Not only was she frighteningly intense, but she wanted Life on terms of immediate, instinctive action, however grotesque or absurd it might seem to others, and she expected a more emotional involvement with her fellow poets than any of them cared for. Impatient with all forms and reflection, she claimed that her consciousness of a situation *was* the poetry of that situation. Yet even though her visit was not successful, Ransom remained so impressed with her work (despite the principle behind it, which was exactly the one he had been opposing in his arguments with Tate) that he proposed that she be made an honorary member, and the Fugitives, mainly to oblige him, elected her one early in 1925. Later she made a second visit to Nashville, during which she overstayed her welcome at the hospitable Frank home. She left at last in a temper and the Fugitives saw her no more, though they listed her as a member right down to the end of the magazine and published much of her work throughout 1925. In 1926 she divorced her husband and went abroad, where she began a long association in writing and publishing with Robert Graves. When the Fugitives were preparing an anthology of the group's poetry, she made clear that she thought she had outgrown the group and did not wish to be closely identified with it. Nevertheless, she sent some of her later poems for it, and these helped to call attention to

[41] "Report of Committee on Disposition of the Fugitive," April 7, 1924 [carbon copy of typescript].

the volume, for by this time her name was becoming known. Despite the disagreeableness attending it, the behavior of the Fugitives had been generous and wholly the result of goodwill toward a gifted fellow poet suffering, as some of them had suffered, from lack of recognition, and they gave her much needed encouragement at a critical time. There was a lot of farce in the business, but the Fugitives look none the worse for that.[42]

IV

Despite Laura Riding's excitement and all that election to membership meant for Warren, 1924 showed a marked slackening after the turmoil and achievements of 1923. In 1924 Ransom published *Chills and Fever* and Davidson *An Outland Piper*, and the group was getting to be known outside Nashville by more than just friends and relations. In this year, too, Ransom and Tate resumed their debate on form in modern poetry. But for all the individual interests and achievements, the group as a whole was beginning to fall apart. The committee which had recommended discontinuing the magazine at the end of the year also noted that attendance at the meetings and participation in discussions were becoming perfunctory, and as Mrs. Cowan has observed, the summer of 1924 was the last time any considerable number of the group were around.[43] Writing, or at least writing worthy of inclusion in the magazine, was also falling off, though Tate struggled to maintain it by mailing in remarkably thorough appraisals and generous encouragement of his friends' work. Davidson and Warren particularly appreciated this and Ransom wrote that among the Fugitives Tate was *"persona gratissimo . . .* a priceless value to a dull and stodgy group" because he inspired them to rededicate themselves in honest criticism.[44] Ransom's own poetry was never better—the first issue of *The Fugitive* for 1924 carried "Bells for John Whiteside's Daughter" and "Captain Carpenter." Davidson was profiting from following his friend, and Warren was leaving behind the pastiches of Eliot and Pound and beginning, very tentatively, to develop his

---

[42] From conversations with the Fugitives and correspondence: Laura Riding Gottschalk to Allen Tate, October 23, 1923, and December 12, 1923; to Donald Davidson, July 25, 1924, November 20, 1924, and December 15, 1924; undated letters to Davidson, written in 1926, regarding the anthology.

[43] *The Fugitives*, p. 170.

[44] In a letter to Tate dated May 6, 1924.

own style. Nevertheless, among the others, the thinness of their talents was beginning to show under the strain of meeting the standards and deadlines of the magazine, and the decline of writing of the group as a whole grew steeper in 1925. Ridley Wills, Frierson, and Hirsch had published nothing since 1923. Stevenson published only one more poem after the first issue of 1924. Elliott published one poem in 1924, two in 1925. Jesse Wills, a steady contributor in 1924, published only one poem in 1925, and Johnson and Curry, both busy on other projects, published nothing in the latter year. Even Tate had only three poems in the magazine during 1925, and these were notably inferior to the poems he had begun to place in *The Nation*. In fact, in the final year most of the space in the magazine was taken up by just five of the Fugitives: Ransom, who never had fewer than two poems in any issue and who published 59 poems in the 19 issues of *The Fugitive*, thereby qualifying as its leading contributor; Davidson, who also never missed an issue and stood second with a total of 49; Moore, who published more poems than anyone else during the last two years and had a total count of 46; Warren, who published 20 in the last two years; and Laura Riding, who had a total of 27 and stood next to Moore in the number of poems placed during the last year. Almost all of the rest of the space was taken up by the syrupy verse of outsiders such as Joseph Auslander. Despite this, however, the final volume, edited by Ransom with the assistance of Warren, was by far the best even though it was the least representative of the group itself. In the first number, published in March, 1925, Ransom spoke out strongly against outdated conceptions of poetry and the influence of Swinburne and the Pre-Raphaelites, and though the magazine continued to publish poems written under that influence (including some by Davidson), these were offset by the originality and modernity of Ransom's own work, some of Moore's finest sonnets (such as "Abschied," "The Noise That Time Makes," and "Shot Who? Jim Lane!"), three strong poems by Hart Crane, and some irregular but promising work from Warren.

Though the final year went so well, it was clear that it would be the last. The excitement of seeing themselves in print had long passed for the Fugitives, and all were weary of the pressure of writing for the meetings and the magazine. At the same time, contributions were coming in at the rate of four to five hundred a month, requiring heavy work that none of them wanted to undertake. In December of 1925 they voted to suspend the magazine temporarily, and Ransom's last editorial spoke of their resuming publication at some unspecified future date. But this was the end. By accident, the cover for the nineteenth and final issue was black.

So, surprisingly, was the latest entry in the Fugitive ledgers. After all the struggles to raise funds—at the end of 1924 the members had been assessed $25 apiece to help pay off debts—the Fugitives had found enough patrons in the last year to make it possible for the magazine to go on indefinitely had any of them really wanted to keep it going. It is pleasing to observe that they never gave up in the face of difficulties and that their reason for bringing the magazine to an end was the best possible one: those who seriously wanted to continue writing were ready for other, larger media and different audiences. It was *The Fugitive* which had prepared them.

Once the magazine was suspended, it became increasingly difficult to bring the group together. What meetings took place were more for sociability than for the exchange of criticism and ideas, though members still brought poems when they had any to show. Many of the productive members were gone. Tate had settled at last in New York City in October, 1924, and soon afterward he submitted his resignation from the Fugitives but was persuaded to withdraw it and accept an "associate membership" instead. Johnson resigned from the English Department at Vanderbilt late in December of 1924 and, made confident by the forthcoming appearance of his novel *Professor*, went to New York City, where he lived for a short time with Tate, in hopes of supporting himself by fiction and journalism.

Johnson's *roman à clef*, based on his observations at Vanderbilt and the Fugitive meetings, was so poorly written that it gave little reason to suppose that he would win the blazing success he had so long hankered for. Nevertheless, it was read with great excitement in Nashville, for in describing his protagonist Johnson paid off a longstanding score by reporting the goatish inclinations of a well-known figure in the university who had often tyrannized over Johnson and his friends. This aspect of the novel, at least, was effective enough to persuade a number of reviewers that they knew the very man—at other universities. Today the only interest of this clumsy package of spitefulness lies in its account of a group of young English instructors and students who start a magazine and publish it under pseudonyms. It is not difficult to recognize elements of Hirsch in Burke, the self-educated president of the poetry group, or of Tate in Tyson Ware, the young modernist who explicates his poetry to his backward associates with elaborate patience.[45] Though it is obvious that here, too, Johnson was getting a bit of his own back, winning, as it were, the arguments he usually lost in the meetings, some notion of how the discussions went and of how the personalities lined up among the Fugitives can be had from his narrative.

Warren, too, was gone, having graduated in June, 1925. He entered the University of California at Berkeley the following fall to work for a master's degree in English literature. Frierson and Elliott had long been out of touch. Ridley Wills had left Nashville a year before. Curry gave almost all of his time after teaching to historical scholarship. His work *Chaucer and the Medieval Sciences*, on which he had labored for many years, was soon to be published and to bring him an international reputation. Ransom and Davidson were being asked to take on more and more committee work, and other duties at the university, and though they continued to write poetry, they, too, were turning to other interests—Ransom to speculations on aesthetics and Davidson to reading American, particularly Southern, history and developing the book page he had begun in the *Nashville Tennessean* early in 1924. Only Hirsch and Moore were as enthusiastic as ever about the meetings—Hirsch because he had so little else in his life to distract him and Moore because, though he had a hundred other things to distract him (he had entered the Vanderbilt Medical School after graduation), he had so much energy that he was now writing more poetry than ever. Alfred Starr, the last man to join the group, did not liven things. Long a friend of the Fugitives, he had been sitting in with his brother, Milton, as their guest from time to time since 1921. But he had never written any poetry, and the invitation to become one of the Fugitives was a compliment to his amiable interest in the work of the others. About the only times that the old fire flared up among the Fugitives still in Nashville came

[45] See also Chapter Eight, pp. 366-367.

when visiting poets such as Robert Frost stayed up late to argue with them.

Several of the meetings in 1926 and 1927 were called to discuss getting out an anthology of Fugitive poetry. The idea of publishing a book of their best work had come up even before the magazine was suspended, and in his final editorial Ransom suggested that henceforth the Fugitives might put out an annual volume. But when Davidson began writing to the absent members and gathering material, it became obvious that the original conception of a book made up of work done since the magazine had come to an end would have to be changed. Some of the Fugitives, particularly Tate, Warren, and Davidson himself, had on hand new work representing a genuine advance beyond points they had reached by the end of 1925, but most of the others had only one or two poems not already published, and the volume would be more of a summing up of past achievements than a supplement to the magazine. Its *Foreword* tried to have it both ways. After giving an abbreviated history of the group, it concluded, "This volume is a survey of the past, . . . [but] it may also be taken as a prospectus." However, nothing was said about subsequent volumes, and no other ever appeared.

When the anthology finally came out in February, 1928, after a number of publishers had refused it, eleven of the sixteen Fugitives were represented. Hirsch, Curry, Ridley Wills, Frierson, and Starr were absent, but the rest made a good appearance, having selected their pieces with surprising acumen. Stevenson, Johnson, and Moore chose their poems from their best work in *The Fugitive*. Of his nine pieces Ransom took six from the magazine, including the early "Necrological" and the late "Equilibrists," which showed him at his peak. Tate took only one poem, "Procession," from *The Fugitive*. The rest included two short poems, "Death of Little Boys" and "Mr. Pope," written since his removal to New York City and marking both the high point and the approaching end of his first period of development, and two long reveries, "Causerie II" and the first version of "Ode to the Confederate Dead," which signified his progress toward a distinctly different kind of poetry and in which could be seen for the first time those passions and as yet shadowy conceptions that were to take him on into Agrarianism.

87

His contributions, at least, fulfilled the original purpose of the book and justified calling it a "prospectus."

So did some of the poems sent in from California by Warren. Inserted among four pieces from the magazine, which represented the best he had done while an undergraduate, were "Letter of a Mother" and "Pro Vita Sua." In these poems he took up for the first time the parent-child relationship which was to become so significant in all his writing from this point forward and within which he would develop so many narratives about the struggle to evade self-knowledge and its burden of responsibility. Two other poems, the first of his Kentucky Mountain Farm series, showed that in his far removal from his region Warren was taking a new interest in its history and its landscape, the setting of so many of the subsequent stories of evasion and acceptance. Davidson, too, was turning to the regional past for the materials of his long poem *The Tall Men*, on which he worked throughout 1926 and 1927 and from which he took "Fire on Belmont Street" for the anthology. His other poems, from *The Fugitive*, were well chosen and included none of the fairychild pieces, though the damp hand of Swinburne lay heavily on "Corymba" and "Drums and Brass." "Avalon," one of his best poems from the Fugitive period, testified to the brief, astringent influence of Ransom, and "Apple and Mole" showed what gay whimsy Davidson could sometimes bring off without a stumble. But "Fire" was manifestly his showpiece and properly so. Like Tate's long poems, it was a mixture of rumination and narrative, and like them it dealt with the decline of the present from the heroic past, which Davidson measured more by the enfeeblement of action and endurance than by the confusion of the moral intelligence which was Tate's principal concern. To stress the vigor and hardiness of the past Davidson went back to Anglo-Saxon literature and particularly to the fragmentary *Fight at Finnsburg* for certain of his images, allusions, and idioms; but while these were markedly different from the soft, deliquescent materials he had favored in the past, they showed that he was still inhibiting his development by a tendency to turn from experience to the library and to depend too little upon observation and too much upon his ability to assume the coloring of any strong verse or strong personality that happened to interest him at the moment. Though the details selected from the past seem clearly intended to serve him as antiquarian materials served Ransom and furnish a perspective on the present, they often failed in this function and appear to have been included mainly for their intrinsic interest. Nevertheless, "Fire on Belmont Street" showed that Davidson, always particularly sensitive to the sounds of poetry, had developed new deftness in varying the rhythms and pace of blank verse and was moving into areas of experience unexplored until now. And in this poem, as in Tate's new poems, could be seen the first signs of those concerns that were to impel the friends toward Agrarianism.

With these auguries, the Fugitives came to the end. When the anthology appeared in the spring of 1928, Ransom had virtually given up writing poetry and was finishing *The Third Moment*, a book of aesthetics which he never published but which served as a testing ground for many of the ideas he subsequently put into *God Without Thunder* and other books and essays over the next two decades. He had just published "The South—Old or New" in the *Sewanee Review* and he and Davidson were corresponding with Tate about the possibility, first raised by Tate in 1927, of a book defending the Old South. Warren, now at Yale, was working on his biography of John Brown. Tate's new biography of Stonewall Jackson was out and in a few months he would be leaving for France on a Guggenheim fellowship to work at a biography of Jefferson Davis. But the other Fugitives did not share this new interest in the Southern past. Moore, about to leave Nashville for further study at Harvard, was inclined to sever rather than affirm his ties with the region and the past, and he had no sympathy with what he regarded as a reactionary and hopeless attempt by his friends to revitalize outmoded values and behavioral patterns. Hirsch, whose family ties were with the Jewish community and its central European background, had never had much interest in the Southern past, and insofar as he paid any attention to them, he regarded the new ideas of his friends as utterly wrongheaded. He would have nothing to do with their discussions and plans, so Ransom and Davidson turned to others—Frank Owsley, who had recently joined the History department, and Herman Nixon, social scientist and another newcomer to the campus, for example—and found the new talk was as invigorating as any in the early days of the Fugitives. Little by little they forgot Sid, who sat alone among his queer books in Jim Frank's house. Ransom, remembering old times and thinking the references to the Kabbala and the defense of myths and symbols would interest him, dedicated *God Without Thunder* to "S. M. H.," but Hirsch dropped so completely out of the lives of those Fugitives still living in Nashville that when the group reunited in 1956 some of them had not seen him for over two decades. Young men from the university hearing stories of the Fugitives would sometimes seek him out and come away dazed and doubtful, but leaving him confirmed in his belief that he was one of the seven seers whose lore must be given only to those who came for instruction. Nevertheless, the great days when he was the leader and, in his oblique way, the teacher, too, of some of America's most gifted literary men were finished.

CHAPTER THREE

TOWARD AGRARIANISM

....

"The form requires the myth."
—Allen Tate, *"Horatian Epode to the Duchess of Malfi"*

....

I

*I*N the spring of 1925, diners at the Commercial Club heard much talk of prosperity and progress in Nashville. Things were going badly in the rest of the South, and there had been a time just after the war when the closing of a government arms plant had caused a serious surplus of labor in the Nashville region, but by now new industries had managed to absorb the surplus and attract even more workers. Many lived in ugly cottages or dilapidated mansions which had been converted into apartment and boarding houses; yet so far Nashville had escaped the squalid slums of the great Southern mill towns. Its industries were still generally small and diversified. Some heavy manufacturing was moving in, but its development was limited by a power shortage. Consequently, a large proportion of the new workers were skilled or semi-skilled and, at least by Southern standards, fairly well paid. By virtue of its location, on the navigable Cumberland River at the intersection of a number of important railroads, Nashville was essentially a center of banking and commerce. Though many of the rents and profits entered on the books downtown were simply passing through on their way north to absentee owners, there was an appearance of energy and bustle in the banks and business houses that pleased the boosters and seemed to give substance to their brave words.

In other parts of the South farmers lived under appalling deprivation, but when Nashville motorists went out for a Sunday drive, they saw small and generally pleasant farms and villages. The rich soil of the surrounding basin provided some of the best pasture land in the country, and the earth had not been leached by unbroken successions of tobacco or cotton crops. Good roads made it easy for the farmers to drive to the small county seats and other towns, and most rural families had at least a model T to go visiting in. A lot of them had battery radios and tuned in the A & P Gypsies just like folks in the city. All in all, life in and around Nashville appeared to be good and likely to get better.

Even in the regions where life was anything but good, there was great faith in progress and a passion for education as the means of bringing it to the blighted lands. Everywhere money was being laid out for schools, and the Southern colleges and universities were conspicuous emblems of pride and hope for all men. Vanderbilt University had been expanding swiftly since the end of the war and had brought in distinguished scholars from all parts of the country to strengthen its faculty. Since Chancellor Kirkland's triumph over conservative Methodism, the university had been regarded as an especially bright symbol of the new enlightenment that would bring all good things, and many of its officers, such as Edwin Mims, who had recently published his *The Advancing South*, talked as often and as confidently about progress and the New South as the luncheon speakers at the Commercial Club. Nashville's air, then, echoed with cheery babble about the condition of the New York Exchange, the money to be made on real estate out near the university, and the winning ways of the Vanderbilt teams. More and more the city looked like Ann Arbor, Columbus, Madison, or any other middlewestern metropolis full of football fans and civic boosters. Their words and ways might annoy the sensitive; they might be a little too ready to follow the Yankees and measure a community by its power plant, paved sidewalks, and inside plumbing; but it was hard to dissent without seeming to be an old crank when they talked excitedly of the future.

Elsewhere it was different. The talk of progress was not so much exuberant as desperate, and the catchwords had other connotations. "Freedom" did not mean what it meant in a Vanderbilt classroom: it did not include freedom to organize mill workers and tenant farmers or freedom to protest the prices at the company store or plantation commissary and to shop somewhere else. For many Southern towns and regions were in a deep depression, and the people took anything they could get and scrabbled for the rest. If they didn't like what they got, there were always plenty of others eager to have it. There had been a time during and immediately following the war when prices had been high, wages were up, and crops were good, but by 1925 that time was long gone. The market in naval stores fell off sharply. The demand for textiles diminished just as English products were reappearing and as industrial expansion and cheap labor were making it possible for the Japanese to undersell the world. In the mill towns wages were cut, the stretchout system was brought in, and shutdowns were frequent. The sleazy tenements put up during the boom years by careless workers using unseasoned lumber were sagging into ruins that no one could afford to repair, and the towns were ringed with slums that stank of misery, disease, and decay. Strikes were useless. With a labor surplus, owners did not need to keep troublemakers and critics could easily be silenced with the threat of using Negro workers.

In much of the South the condition of the farmers was just as bad or worse. Whether they owned their places or worked for others, most of them raised "cash crops" such as cotton and tobacco, which they could not consume themselves. Since these crops had only exchange value, the farmer's well-being depended wholly on the market, now at a very low point. Both cotton and tobacco depleted the soil and compelled the farmer to buy increasing quantities of increasingly expensive fertilizer. The long growing season kept him short of cash and forced him to go into debt to the banks and supply merchant or to trade his labor for goods under the sharecropping system. During the war, the value of cash crops had risen, and many farmers had brought more and more land under cultivation to take advantage of this. But afterward prices fell off and the farmer was in the same position as the industrialist who had over-expanded: there was a surplus of his product. When the boll weevil limited the cotton crop and sent prices up, it sent the cost of raising cotton up, too. Furthermore, it enticed the farmers once more into planting too much in order to make something on a good market, with the result that bumper crops produced new surpluses which promptly drove the prices down farther than ever. Many farmers or their sons and daughters, despairing of any improvement, abandoned their farms and left for the cities, where they swelled the labor surplus and brought wages still lower.

Even in good times, the South held an unfavorable position in the national economy and could not hope to keep up with the prosperity of the North. Essentially, its economy was colonial: the South sent its cotton, tobacco, and other staples North or abroad for fabrication and bought the finished products at high prices kept up by tariffs favorable to the more industrialized regions. The price of the products was further increased by freight rate differentials which meant that it cost Southerners about 40 percent more to move their materials out of their region and the finished products back into it. In some parts of the South the differential meant that Southerners paid 75 percent more than their rivals in the Northeastern regions. Finally, a great deal of Southern industry, all the major railroad systems, and most of the utilities were owned or controlled by the North; the profits from them went North—often by way of Nashville—and did not return.

Poets may shudder at stamping mills and composers stuff their ears to keep out the uproar of trucks and taxis, but publishers, great libraries, bookstores, galleries, symphony orchestras, and string quartets get started and survive only where there is money to pay for them, and for many generations only the big cities had enough industry and commerce to be able to afford the fine arts. The outlook for Southern arts and letters offered little encouragement to the boosters. In some of the cities there were adult education programs, lecture and concert series, women's music clubs, and reading groups. Mass media brought a superficial worldliness enabling a suburbanite to chatter about movie stars with a visitor from Evanston or Shaker Heights. But things stood just about where they were when Mencken wrote his "Sahara of the Bozart": in culture the Southerners were almost wholly consumers, and what they consumed were the standard products sent down, like other products, from the North. They could not afford anything else.

Except, of course, in literature. Here again one must be careful to see the Southern Renaissance for what it really was—especially to Southerners of the time. In 1925, it had barely begun. After fiddling with newspaper sketches and languishing fin-de-siècle verses, Faulkner was about to publish *Soldier's Pay*, his first novel and a failure. Katherine Anne Porter was doing journalism. Thomas Wolfe was still a student dreaming of becoming a playwright. Ransom had begun to have a small—a very small—audience for his elegant ironies, but Davidson was really no more than a melancholy trifler, Tate one of the least noticed of the clamorous young men in New York, Warren a complete unknown, while *The Fugitive* itself, as we have seen, had virtually no readers beyond the Nashville vicinity except for relatives of its editors and a few widely scattered critics and fellow poets. Not one Southerner in a hundred thousand had ever heard of it—or of *The Double Dealer, Lyric, The Wave*, and other tiny journals in New Orleans, Charleston, and Richmond. "Southern writers" meant Ellen Glasgow, who said disagreeable things about Virginia and embarrassed her family, and James Branch Cabell, who was crazy and wrote dirty books.

To Southerners, then, the Renaissance actually meant little, and when recognition came at last, it began outside the South. So, as is sometimes forgotten, did many of the quickening impulses: from Ransom and Hirsch's travels abroad, from Tate's correspondence with Crane and his immersion in Eliot, Pound, and the Symbolists, from Faulkner's contacts with Sherwood Anderson, and from Katherine Anne Porter's wanderings as a free-lance journalist. Not much could be expected from even the most progressive Southerners. As Francis B. Simkins says,

> "Perhaps the most striking characteristic of upper-class Southern society was its almost complete absence of intellectual interests. Leaders of the post-Reconstruction era were Confederate heroes, primitive men whose strength lay in geniality and physical prowess rather than in mental attainments. The next generation of leaders grew up during the cultural famine of war and Reconstruction; some were city-bred with an aristocratic heritage, but the majority sprang from the uncultured yeomanry. Although members of the third generation of leaders were often college-bred, they usually specialized in 'campus courses,' football, and fraternities. They were induced by editors to support museums and orchestras, but displayed little understanding or enjoyment of these institutions. Theirs was the company of the perpetual Philistines to whom it meant social suicide to discuss intellectual or esthetic subjects."[1]

For many writers the Renaissance began with a repudiation of the regional ways and values and particularly of the past in which they were rooted. At first this might seem little different from the repudiation of one's place and heritage that has figured in so much

[1] *The South, Old and New* (New York, 1947), pp. 291-292.

twentieth-century art and writing. But far more was involved. The Fugitives themselves, in flight from the "Brahmins of the Old South," show how the South and its history were more significant for the young Southern writer than the other regions of the United States could ever be for their native sons. If he tried to repudiate them, the violence of his rebellion demonstrated that the South and its history were inexorably a part of his being; his sensibility could no more exist without them than his body could get along without nerves and blood. If he lived the life of the imagination fully, he had, in the end, to come to terms with his place and the past. Indeed, this might become his only subject because, since the South and its patrimony so permeated his being, it took in all the other subjects and furnished the images through which they might be represented and interpreted.

If the Southern writer did not understand this already—and we know that the Fugitives did not—then events of the summer of 1925 made it inescapably clear.

II

Actually, the writers of the Southern Renaissance inherited two kinds of South, two kinds of regional past. For a long time—well into the young manhood of most of them—many people thought there had been only one Old South. But when the historians began to look into it, they found that this Old South was mostly a legend and that there actually had been many Old Souths. Recognition of the two kinds, the legendary and the actual, and of the great diversity of the latter was one of the unavoidable and definitive moments in the artistic maturing of these writers. For some such as Faulkner and Miss Porter this recognition provided the ultimate source of many of their most intensely moving and meaningful fictions: untangling the threads of the actual from the glamorous fabric of the legendary furnished them with story after story, while refurbishing the legend to serve as a means of binding up and giving shape and meaning to the pile of lint which was "what really happened" was the most difficult profound problem confronting them.

"What really happened" was not just lint, of course. There was a fabric underneath. But it looked enough like lint to show how risky it was to generalize about the South before the Civil War. Still, there were many forces that gave the Southern regions and people distinctions which surmounted their differences—forces such as the climate, the economy based upon staple crops requiring great quantities of land and large labor forces, the presence of slaves, and, perhaps most important, the fact that after the 1830's the people of the South were a minority group constantly under attack by others who assumed without bothering to look into the matter that all Southerners were alike and followed the same beliefs. The attack not only struck at the foundations of much of their economic welfare (for many not directly employed in the plantation system were inextricably bound to it because it dominated the economy of their region) but impugned their honor and even their ordinary human decency and charity. Nothing was so likely to make the Southerners of every region conform in all their public appearances and statements as the feeling that they were surrounded by hostile and accusing eyes and that nothing they could do or say would make any difference. From this actual unity and from the defensive rhetoric came much of the substance for the legend impelled by implacable disapproval and the Southerner's own deeply suppressed awareness that slavery was evil and the outsider's disapproval, malevolent and unreasonable as it might be, was partly justified. Nothing so helps in the formulation of such a fantasy as the need to defy and defend when one knows at the heart that the facts and one's own sense of human justice are against one.

So beneath the legend there was, despite the important diversities, a true Old South that was very different. Modern historians have shown that its people were mostly lower and middle bourgeois of humble and surprisingly mixed origins. There were some gentry among the first Southern settlers, but even in the Chesapeake Region, where the most deliberate and sustained effort was made to emulate the ideal of the English country gentlemen, few families had any close connection with English gentlefolk or any background of elegance and privilege. Despite the fact that as early as 1649 Governor Berkeley invited royalists to seek asylum in Virginia, Thomas Lord Fairfax, who settled at Greenway Court in 1747, was the only British peer who made his permanent residence in the colonies. Those gentlemen who followed the standard of Prince Rupert at Naseby or of Bonnie Prince Charlie at Culloden were more likely to flee to France than to the colonies, while those who had made their peace with the authorities in power had a good thing in England's constantly expanding economy.

Eventually, a gentry was established in the Bay area and around Charleston and New Orleans, and the accounts of life at Shirley and Nomini Hall, two great residences belonging to branches of the Carter family, show that some of its members did succeed in matching the lavishness of the great English county families. This gentry was no closed group, and as the career of Washington shows, men could enter it by the possession of land which they had gained through careful trading and speculation in tobacco. Elsewhere, however, there simply was not time to transform the rough, crude, hard-drinking, hard-swearing, hard-fighting frontiersmen, traders, rivermen, and farmers into aristocrats. It was from these that there emerged the strong, pushing, and ambitious men who made up the ruling class in most of the South in the period before the war. As Cash has observed, such men had the very qualities needed to transform a wilderness into the cotton kingdom over a few decades, but more time was needed to gentle them.[2]

Taking in the whole spectrum from the First Families of Virginia to the Sutpens on whose land the stumps still smoldered, there were in 1850 about 100,000 big planters out of a total white population of over eight million. Few of these had inherited their powers and privileges from the eighteenth-century gentry, and most were, as R. S. Cotterill has remarked, self-made business men engaged in large-scale production. But if small in number, the planters set the tone of Southern society, not only because of their place in the Southern economy but also because the small-scale yeomen farmers whose land adjoined theirs dreamed of becoming planters too and took the manners and the politics of the group they hoped to enter. In the argument over slavery, the yeomen, outraged by Abolitionist literature which lumped all Southerners together as lecherous tyrants, supported the planters even though they themselves had no hope of owning slaves and even suffered deprivation as a consequence of their inability to compete in the market with the big owner-producers. Though often dressed in rags, they thought they had more in common with the planters

[2] W. J. Cash, *The Mind of the South* (New York, 1941), p. 14.

who went in broadcloth than with any factory workers in New England no better off than themselves; they aped the planters' pride of place and what Simkins calls their "barely perceptible flourish" and thought themselves superior to any laborer in the North.

Of all the things the planters contributed to the culture of the Old South, none is more important in the history of Southern letters than the cult of chivalry, for in it the real Old South blurs into the legendary one. Climate, seasonal idleness, isolation, traces of the old frontier violence, black men who gave their owners such a flattering sense of power and the most abject white man someone to look down on, suppression of a criticism in the face of attack from the outside over the slavery issue—all these helped to encourage the wonderful daydream that virtually all the planters were gentlemen in the formal sense and to foster the trappings of the cult: the duel, the tournament and horse race, the homemade heraldry and patrician place-names, the hypersensitivity to nuances of tone or bearing which might suggest lack of a proper regard for a gentleman's dignity. From Byron, Bulwer-Lytton, Disraeli, Dumas, and above all Walter Scott they took idealized self-images. Out of the pages of *Ivanhoe* came names for everything from the new big house on the raw hill to the latest coon dog.[3]

It would be foolish to deny the grace and charm which the cult of chivalry gave to Southern life by its emphasis upon courtesy, decorum, hospitality, indifference to money and contempt for those who spoke much about it, and *noblesse oblige*. Nevertheless, it is sometimes hard to choose between smiling at the humorous pretentiousness that went with these agreeable qualities and pitying a people so uncertain and bewildered by the need to give dignity and meaning to their lives that they turned to such insubstantial and delusive materials for their measure of man. When all the struggle to get started was over and the planters had time to stop and look about them, they suddenly found themselves alone in great reaches of time and space without traditions of leisure, art, or true learning to sustain them. They showed imagination and persistence in converting rigamarole of the Waverley romances into a code of conduct, but their taking these novels so seriously

[3] See Rollin G. Osterweis, *Romanticism and Nationalism in the Old South* (New Haven, 1949), pp. 13-17, 27-28, 38-39, 42-56.

suggests the desperation of their need and the meagerness of their resources.

Yet somehow the code worked. It did give some direction to their lives. So much, indeed, that in the bleakness of our times life in the Old South seems particularly rich. But the richness is partly legendary. We know now that few of the homes were so grand, few of the young men so courtly, few of the young ladies so beautiful, few of the older women so goodhumored and wise in the ways of the heart, and few of the older men so learned. Thomas Moore and Byron had taught Southerners to pay lip-service to the classics, and virtually all of the three thousand academies which flourished in the South in 1850 offered a curriculum that included some Latin and Greek "in response to the firm conviction of the Southern people that these two languages were the foundation of all education."[4] But it is easy to overestimate the learning and literary taste of the Old South. We have so often met in fiction the old gentleman who sat under the poplar tree sipping toddies and murmuring lines from Horace and Aeschylus that we quite believe in him. Yet according to Bridenbaugh, "the average planter owned only a few books, and these were confined largely to religious and devotional works, or to subjects related to his immediate concerns, such as books on farming, commerce, surveying, law, and household medicine. In other words, the planter read for practical reasons rather than for entertainment or self-improvement, and such literary culture as he possessed came, as Patrick Henry and George Gilmer readily admitted, from conversation, not from reading."[5] Intelligent but not intellectual, is the way he sums up the gentry of the Tidewater. In Charleston, however, there was a small, truly elegant group which kept in closer touch with London and supported music and a good theatre. It was too given to dining and gossip to have much time for reading, and at best its culture was passive and dependent upon paid performers from outside rather than indigenous and creative. The cultivation of the arts was to a considerable extent a means of displaying wealth and position.[6]

To these groups the new societies farther west looked for

[4] R. S. Cotterill, *The Old South* (Glendale, 1936), pp. 290-291.

[5] C. Bridenbaugh, *Myths and Realities/Societies of the Colonial South* (Baton Rouge, 1952), pp. 33-36, 40.

[6] Bridenbaugh, pp. 76-79, 99.

guidance. If literature and the fine arts had such a comparatively minor place in the life of the leaders, it is not surprising that where the planters had more recently established themselves, such ritual behavior as veneration of the classics was backed by less substantial learning and taste. There had not been as much time to acquire them. Moreover, the new societies were emerging at a time when inflammatory oratory and journalism had become the popular forms of literary expression in the South because they were political weapons as well. The critical spirit essential to any significant achievement in the arts was suppressed lest it weaken the defenses against the Abolitionists. Southern liberalism of the eighteenth century, which gave the nation the Declaration of Independence, was repudiated. The embattled orator was a folk hero to planter and poor white alike, and the contemplative life of letters had little attraction for talented young men. Those few who took literature seriously had almost no audience: rural people were indifferent, and educated men of the towns had the habit of looking beyond the South for what they read. The consequence of such neglect may be seen in the career of William Gilmore Simms, who, Simkins says, "wasted his words in a wilderness."[7]

Then came the Civil War and the end of the Old South. Its place in the Southern imagination was taken by the legend. The "classical form" of that legend has been described by W. J. Cash with great wit—and cruelty, mainly because it is so accurate:

"It was a sort of stage piece out of the eighteenth century, wherein gesturing gentlemen moved soft-spokenly against a background of rose gardens and dueling grounds, through always gallant deeds, and lovely ladies, in farthingales, never for a moment lost their exquisite remoteness which has been the dream of all men and the possession of none. Its social pattern was manorial, its civilization that of the Cavalier, its ruling class an aristocracy coextensive with the planter group—men often entitled to quarter the royal arms of St. George and St. Andrew on their shields, and in every case descended from the old gentlefolk who for many centuries had made up the ruling class of Europe.

"They dwelt in large and stately mansions, preferably white

[7] Simkins, p. 106.

and with columns and Grecian entablature. Their estates were feudal baronies, their slaves quite too numerous ever to be counted, and their social life a thing of Old World splendor and delicacy. What had really happened here, indeed, was that the gentlemanly idea, driven from England by Cromwell, had taken refuge in the South and fashioned for itself a world to its heart's desire: a world singularly polished, and mellow and poised, wholly dominated by ideals of honor and chivalry and *noblesse. . . .*"[8]

It was known, of course, that there were some white men who did not fulfill the gentlemanly ideal. There were two ways of accounting for them. According to one they were "white trash" descended from convicts and indentured servants. But the happier view made them out to be sturdy yeomen too fond of the outdoors to be at ease in drawingrooms. They had, of course, a pride, a natural grace and courtesy, a distinction of bearing whereby they might have taken their place among gentlemen if they had wished, but with lovable eccentricity they preferred forests to furbelows and hounds to harpsichords. Laconic, level-eyed, absolutely dead shots, they were supposed to be regarded pretty much as equals by the aristocrats who often hunted and drank with them, and they were suitably contemptuous of Northerners—townsmen and tradesmen all.

The whole self-congratulatory fantasy seems infinitely silly when not merely irritating in its snobbishness. Yet when amusement and annoyance have subsided, one begins to understand that the legend was an act of compensation by a people who had suffered terribly in war and who, in defeat, had been forced to undergo a humiliation rarely inflicted upon those even so utterly crushed as they—the humiliation of being told and of hearing their conquerors teach their children that they had been defeated not by superior military might but by the invincible force of God's own good. The moral cant of the victors was made more, rather than less, insufferable by the knowledge that the Southern way of life had indeed included great evil.

The legend took hold because it gave comfort amidst fearful uncertainties. Even as the cultural deprivation of Southerners be-

[8] Cash, p. ix.

fore the war could be measured in part by the pretentiousness and absurdity of the cult of chivalry, so the far greater deprivation of the survivors and their heirs could be gauged from the unreality of the legend which evolved from the cult. The legend asserted that life in the Old South had been a thing too rare, refined, and exquisite to endure in a world of boors who understood only the crudest facts of money and manufacturing and who, in their boorish envy, were compelled to destroy what they could never attain and what, by its very existence, incessantly reminded them of their inferiority. Having taken hold, the legend flourished because the war had obliterated much of the evidence which might be used against it, because critical skepticism now seemed a greater disloyalty than ever, and because its idolatry of the Confederate captain and the reputed aristocrats served well the ends of business men who were beginning to grow rich through trading in the mortgages and miseries of the survivors. By recruiting the captains, by making them nominal officers in their banks and other enterprises, the business men protected themselves against criticism. Any attempt to write about the Old South in realistic terms was regarded as Yankee meddlesomeness and met with silence and hostility. Amidst this genteel necrophilia, the Southern literary arts withered.

Yet the forces from which the Southern Renaissance would come were accumulating. The difference between the vision and reality which stifled creativity was to become the central issue of an agonizing drama of the most profound significance. Moreover, underneath all the vanity and self-deception of the cult of chivalry and the legend which evolved from it lay a noble impulse: the consciousness that a man must have something outside himself and larger than himself, some code or system of images, beliefs, and values, which will give his life meaning and an organizing center. However foolish the Southerners may have seemed, they had tried to make their conduct matter, had tried to make themselves responsible to something. The writers of the Renaissance came of an environment in which it was assumed that a man had to commit himself in order to know himself and define his being. The extreme consciousness of the past in that environment meant ultimately that in coming to terms with himself a Southerner would have to come to some sort of terms with the history of his region. These writers were not taken in by the clamor about Progress. They had seen a way of life which aspired to grandeur fall into the grandiose and suffer a terrible defeat. In asking what the past meant to them, they had to ask why this had happened. With that problem before them they brought forth a literature which, taken as a whole, is the best to come out of America in our time.

Beaten, humiliated, and impoverished, the Southerners had been forced to watch from amidst their misery the incredibly swift expansion of Northern industry and commerce after the Civil War. Observing how the economy of the North worked, many Southerners were convinced that cash crops, which in a way resembled the products of factories, would bring in the capital needed to stop the decline of their region and eventually to restore the old way of life. Even subsistence farmers, who consumed what they grew and got along with little ready money, began to give up their independence and went into raising cotton and tobacco, which made them servants of the market. But the cash crops required a large initial investment and a long waiting period before any returns came in, and few men had enough money to get started. Furthermore, the Negroes who had come back to work in the fields could not understand the nature of a contract with long-postponed wages. They just knew they had to get food and clothing and had nothing to give for them. Thus there came about a system of using the crops themselves, or more accurately the *promise* of the crops, as legal tender to pay for seed, equipment, housing, food, and clothing—the system of sharecropping. All those going into the system, whether owners, tenants, or croppers, were compelled to sell part of the promise of their crop to the supply merchants. And since the promise was tenuous, that part had to be large. With the shortage of cash, the long season, the uncertainty of the crop, the surpluses that so frequently drove prices down, the growers and their hands were soon tangled beyond rescue in debts and mortgages and subsided slowly into deeper poverty and despair.

Anyone who managed to get a little cash—an extraordinarily difficult thing to do—could by skillful lending and determined insistence on payment rise swiftly to power and the possession of great estates. The storekeepers and bankers who furnished the farmers with seed, fertilizer, and equipment, or the money to buy them, were in the best position to do this. Simkins claims that:

> "The most important development in Southern society after the Civil War was the shift of control from the agricultural aristocracy to men of industry and commerce. . . . The storekeeper assumed the position of the planter, and Bourbon political leaders, despite their fine manners and old-fashioned oratory, were modern enough to heed the demands of business men, the actual masters of the counties and states they represented. Just as the enterprising citizen of the Old South aspired to become a planter with slaves and broad acres, his counterpart in the New South was eager to become a wealthy business man with holdings in town property and mortgages on farm lands. He knew that the continued pursuit of farming involved low prices and probable economic ruin, while a mercantile career might lead to material success."[9]

But the aristocrats and their descendants still had great social prestige, and the emergent leaders took care to link themselves with the legend of the Old South—to search out real or imagined ancestors among the great planters and to furnish themselves with a crest and *hauteur*.

It was while the many were slipping downward and the few who were more lucky or grasping were moving swiftly upward that the dream of the New South came into being, a dream of raising the level of at least the whites by building schools and factories which would give them the capital to escape the vicious cash-crop system. Notions of this kind had been going around ever since the end of the war, but it took a speech by Henry W. Grady, delivered in 1886 before the New England Society of New York and reprinted many times throughout the country, to give form and passion to the dream—and to give it that talismanic phrase, the New South. Grady was managing editor of the *Atlanta Weekly Constitution* and a man of great charm and energy. Without taking time to consider whether the nation could support more factories of the kind he proposed for the South, without looking into the

[9] Simkins, p. 283.

problems of transportation, the labor surplus, the lack of investors in the region, and so forth, he went about stirring up the people to frenzies of hope. Under the chairmanship of ministers, school-teachers, and other respected local figures, towns issued bonds to build factories far from railroads or navigable rivers.

It was not the pastors and their flocks who made the money, but Northern and foreign investors and those Southerners who managed the outsiders' affairs. They saw the advantages of low taxes, longer hours of labor, lower wage scales, an unorganized labor pool, and the fact that any resistant organization could always be broken up by the threat to bring in Negro workers.[10] Yet the investors encountered little local opposition. The dream, as Grady sketched it, was almost irresistible to a people in such misery. Furthermore, it seemed to offer a way up for the socially ambitious who did not belong to the old aristocracy. Best of all, the New South did not really oppose the Old South: it promised a means of restoring the lost golden age. Nostalgia and lost-cause sentiment could hence be enlisted on the side of the new industrialism and expansion.

Not all the factories were built by well-meaning persons with no business experience who then advertised in the Northern papers for Yankees to come in and pillage the district tax-free. Some industries were established near rail centers and began to do well at once under experienced management. As a consequence, many people moved in from the farms and the urban population increased from 15 percent of the total in 1900 to 30 percent by 1930. Young people, particularly after the First World War, rebelled against the tedium of rural life and hurried to the cities to catch the tail of Progress. Yet except for the period of the war when competition from abroad went down just as the demand for tobacco, cotton, textiles, and naval stores went up, the South as a whole remained poor, and the condition of the factory worker was quite as bad as that of the sharecropper. Efforts to improve conditions at the bottom encountered resistance at all levels. Management, allied with the local political bosses who had come into final power with

[10] See C. V. Woodard, *Origins of the New South* (Baton Rouge, 1937), pp. 115ff.; Broadus Mitchell and George S. Mitchell, *The Industrial Revolution in the South* (Baltimore, 1930), p. 38; R. B. Nixon, *Henry W. Grady* (New York, 1943).

the failure of the Populist revolt in the 1890's and the firm establishment of the single-party system, fought all reform legislation
affecting working hours, conditions, and wages. The workers and
tenant farmers resisted organization as an infringement on their
independence, still as much a matter of "techy" pride as ever,
despite the fact that they were manacled in economic slavery.
Whenever they showed signs of banding together, appeals to sectional pride and conservatism (the reformers and organizers were
depicted as foreigners and radicals) or to their fear of the Negroes
as competitors could be counted on to turn unorganized laborers
against the proposals. By the 1920's some of the townsmen were
doing well, and all over the South Rotarians and Boosters were
babbling about a commercial and industrial expansion that would
soon enable the South to catch up with the Harding-Coolidge
prosperity of the North. Many of them agreed with the Southern
liberals in the universities and the editorial rooms of the big newspapers that it was about time to forget the Old South.

Then in 1925 occurred an event that showed how strong the
Past still was. It embarrassed the liberals and spokesmen of
Progress and at last awakened some young men in Nashville to the
problem of coming to terms with the past—the real past.

From the earliest frontier days revivalists and fundamentalist
sects had been a powerful force among the lower classes, and their
often turbulent meetings had been outlets for the violence and
boredom of the people. Leaders of the New South movement
had found it embarrassing and had tried to minimize its power
and importance; they talked as if the new schools and the spread
of learning would slowly and without commotion or inconvenience
liberalize the Fundamentalists and ameliorate their harsh ways.
Certainly the enthusiasm for learning that spread just after the
turn of the century gave them some reason to expect such a change.
What they could not see was that the very fears and misery that
made the people enthusiastic about new schools and colleges made
them seek surcease in the more bloody books of the Old Testament,
in the Revelation of Saint John, and in the belief in a Second
Coming, when the mighty would be brought down and the poor
cropper and mill hand would go marching up to glory. So great
was the comfort they took from the most literal belief in the "raw
Bible" and from the apocalyptic visions that education could make

no way against them: science and talk of social reforms fell back before the Word. When a choice had to be made, millions of people in the South were in no doubt.

But some of the young folks were after they had gone to the shiny new high schools and agricultural colleges. It was time to take action against newfangled Yankee ideas, as well as against uppity Negroes, aliens, Jews, Catholics, Socialists—all the vaguely terrifying figures associated with change which, for so many of these people, had been a steady change for the worse. In 1915 a second Ku Klux Klan was founded to support White Supremacy and fundamentalist orthodoxy. At first it made little progress. Just at the moment things seemed to be getting better, and one could be a little more tolerant when money jingled in the jeans. But after 1921, when hard times returned and the jobless worker or the cropper who ended the season more deeply in debt than he had begun it needed a release from his fears and frustrations, membership rose swiftly to an estimated peak of 6,000,000 in 1924. Many clergymen from fanatical sects became officers and set out to make the Klan a mighty fortress against skeptics, scientists, and outsiders. Terrifying parades by the white-robed knights of the Invisible Empire, occasional floggings and mutilations, and great political influence gave the Klan a power that was immensely satisfying to its pathetic little members. Moreover it enabled them to put through laws against the teaching of evolution in the schools of Tennessee in 1925 and shortly afterward of Mississippi. For Darwinian doctrines were, as Cash says, "no more than the focal point of an attack for a program, explicit or implicit, that went far beyond evolution laws: a program . . . having as its objective the stamping out of all the new heresies and questioning in the schools and elsewhere—the restoration of that absolute conformity to the ancient pattern under the pains and penalties of the most rigid intolerance: the maintenance of the savage ideal, to the end of vindicating the Old Southern will to cling fast to its historical way."[11]

The Old South of the Fundamentalists (which was not the same as the Old South of the aristocrats though the Klan made good use of the adulation of Confederate captains and had borrowed

[11] Cash, p. 339.

some of the trapping of chivalry) collided head on with the New South at Dayton, Tennessee, in the summer of 1925, when John Scopes, a twenty-four-year-old high school science teacher went on trial for violating the state's new anti-evolution laws. Clarence Darrow led the defense, and though he made a fool of William Jennings Bryan, the spokesman for the Fundamentalists, Scopes was found guilty. Bryan, who had stamped out the new heresy, was a hero to many Southerners. But not to all.

Actually, there were two trials, the one in the Tennessee courtroom and another in the Northern press. Neither allowed a fair hearing either to Fundamentalism or to Southern liberalism. Catching Bryan in misquotations, contradictions, and errors of the simplest fact, Darrow quickly showed that his opponent had only a casual acquaintance with the Word, no understanding whatever of its textual problems, and but a hazy notion of the doctrines he was supposed to be defending. Yet the Fundamentalists idolized the great Commoner and thought his ignorance proof that he was not contaminated with forbidden knowledge and satanic logic. Darrow, playing the role of village freethinker and crackerbarrel philosopher and unabashedly pressing an *ad hominem* attack, was scarcely representative of the beneficence of the new thought. All in all, the antics at Dayton were a cruel parody of debate between orthodoxy and free inquiry. This was bad enough in itself, but the press took it up and made it something much worse. These were the heydays of boob-baiting and the most crudely sensational journalism, and the Dayton trial provided almost unlimited material for both—and for that parochialism which so resents any customs and beliefs different from its own, especially when they have been represented, as those of the South so long had been in the sentimental literature, as belonging to a superior order. Many papers sent sports writers, such as Westbrook Pegler, who wrote ribald accounts treating the trial as a back-country wrestling match. They sought out "characters" when the court was not in session and lovingly put down their quaint idioms without making any effort to understand what the Southerners were trying to tell them. Often the characters they quoted were moonshiners, for a good share of their off hours were spent in a search for corn whiskey. For most of them it was a crazy picnic with all expenses paid, presided over by H. L. Mencken, who sat in a nearby hotel under one of the few electric fans in that part of the country and topped them all in aphorisms upon the congenital idiocy of the state, which in turn was supposed to be representative of the entire South. With cartoons and caricatures they built up an image of the South which soon quite overshadowed the moonlight and magnolias image of the legend.

Nowhere was this picture of the South more resented than in Nashville. The outsiders, supposing that all the people of the state were like the men from the eastern hill country who squatted patiently in the shade of the courthouse during the noon recess and approved of the anti-evolution laws, had redefined "Tennessean" to stand for ignorance, obstinacy, and sloth. The bustling disciples of the New South at the Commercial Club were furious: the trial and the press made them look like fools and might have a bad effect on Northern investors. But the sense of outrage was even greater on the Vanderbilt campus, where the academic body took pride in Chancellor Kirkland's triumphant struggle for freedom of thought and inquiry against the Southern Methodist Church. When the first shock and embarrassment over the spectacle at Dayton had begun to subside, Edwin Mims suggested to his associates that they write letters and essays pointing out to Northerners that Tennessee and the South were not at all as Mencken and Pegler made them out. He particularly sought the support of Ransom, Davidson, and other members of the English Department whose writings had a small audience and some approval in the North.

III

But what did all the hullabaloo at Dayton mean to the Fugitives? And the dream of the New South or the legend of the Old? Little enough early in the summer of 1925.

For at first the trial seemed no more than a bit of midsummer madness that made copy for the evening paper. Warren, for example, was spending the summer at Guthrie, putting in the time between graduation from Vanderbilt and going west to the University of California by halfheartedly getting his poems together to submit to a publisher. It never struck him that the trial might be worth going to Dayton to see. As for the New South, it was old stuff around Nashville—just some more of the Boosterism of Colonel Luke Lea and his friends which alternately amused and annoyed the Fugitives when they noticed it at all. Nashville had been prosperous for a long time, and those Fugitives who had come up from the country around, were from regions that had been spared the ruinous economy of the cash crops. The legend of the Old South was something from which they had always tried to dissociate themselves, being convinced that there was nothing that they could use in the Southern literary tradition as it had come down to their time.

As the trial went on, Ransom, now the senior editor of the magazine, was intermittently following up an interest that had begun as far back as the autumn of 1922, though until recently it had had to wait upon his poetry: he was trying to get a little nearer to understanding the nature of poetry by comparing it with the supposed nature of science. As he pushed on, he tended to make more and more of the difference and division between poetry and science, which he linked to those between the sensibility and the reason—the theme of a number of his poems for *The Fugitive*. With each advance he showed an increasing hostility toward science and technology, though he sometimes made a gesture of granting them their modest due. Science and technology, he believed, were withering contemporary life, the poverty of which he described through poems such as "Morning," "Man Without Sense of Direction," and "Persistent Explorer." Yet when he looked toward the past for a better life against which to measure the present, he paid scant attention to the Old South. It was the interval beginning with the end of the medieval period and lasting through the age of Milton toward which he was drawn—an interval beginning with courtly love and the *Morte d'Arthur* and coming down to Prince Rupert and the Cavaliers. This, of course, was the era from which, by way of Scott and the romancers, the Southerners had taken material for the cult of chivalry and the legend of the Old South, and it may be that his Southern background made Ransom somewhat more receptive to the antiquarian appeal of the period. Yet even here his habitual skepticism made him mistrust his own affections; as "Necrological," "Philomela," and other poems show, he used the very details which charmed him against the sentimental fantasy into which they tended to invite one. He could understand the suffering, beneath the "base pretense" of kinship with a noble house, of a Southern family which had lost its last, feeble little heir and with him the dynastic dream that made life worthwhile. In "The Dead Boy" (*The Sewanee Review*, April, 1924) he expressed an admittedly reluctant admiration for the gestures of courtesy, concomitants of that same vain pretense, which upheld the family in its bad time. In "Antique Harvesters" (*The Southwest Review*, April, 1925), he so antici-pated many of his subsequent convictions that it would seem that the poem must belong to a much later period. Ignoring all the flummery, he went directly to the genuinely human core which had enabled the legend to prevail for so long despite the abuses of advertisers and politicians who traded in it: to that nostalgia for ceremony which can dignify the humblest work and the sense of belonging to a place. But he could not have written these poems, he could not have become the kind of Southerner he was soon to be, had he not been solidly planted in the present, however disagreeable he found it, and had he not resisted all temptation to retreat from it into the past. When events at last compelled him to examine his regional heritage, he was prepared to use even the seemingly insubstantial material of the legend to get a better view of the present, which was, in the last analysis, what he had been writing about all along.

Donald Davidson had always been proud of his Southern back-ground. Yet he had not used the Old South in any of his Fugitive poems of flight from the gross ordinary world, perhaps because the Old South which appealed most to him was not that of "the chivalry" but that of Daniel Boone and the men of the Western waters. For his refuges he went to books, having some of Ransom's attraction toward the quaint, but he chose, as we know, to look in the pages of Blake, Keats, Tennyson, and the pre-Raphaelites. He used his dim paths, secret valleys, and outland pipers quite as many Southerners used the legendary Old South and the aristocrats in a flattering vision of the superior few, doomed to an inevitable martyrdom by their grace and sensitivity. Like those Southerners Davidson had not so much come to terms with the past as wrapped himself in it.

For Tate, the past was at first principally a storehouse of

recondite allusions to baffle and dumbfound the reader. When he escaped the South and settled in New York City he published a bumptious and ill-informed essay, "Last Days of the Charming Lady," in *The Nation* for October 28, 1925, which made clear his attitude toward his own background was much like that of young writers coming up to the city from other regions. "The modern Southerner," he said flatly, "does not inherit, nor is he likely to have, a native culture compounded of the strength and subtlety of his New England contemporary's. But he may be capable, through an empiricism which is his only alternative to intellectual suicide, of a cosmopolitan culture to which his contemporary in the East is emotionally barred." It would not be difficult to name one modern Southerner Tate thought eminently capable of that "cosmopolitan culture." Asserting that the Old South never had a culture of ideas, though there was probably never any society in the United States so distinguished for the graces of living as those which flourished in Charleston and the Tidewater between 1800 and 1850, he claimed that an "essential" Southern literature was impossible because Southerners could not repudiate "outmoded general notions which have lost their roots in an existing reality" and so had "no tradition of ideas, no consciousness of moral and spiritual values" and had "simply lost a prerogative based on property." At this moment, it would seem, Tate had solved the Southern writer's problem of coming to terms with the past by claiming that there never really was one that counted.

Probably the only Fugitive who could match Davidson's sense of the physical texture of the region and his interest in its past was Warren, in whose poems of that period may be found lines that show an exceptional sensitivity to the "feel" of the land and the touch of its shifting weathers. Moreover, though this scarcely appears anywhere in these early pieces, he had a remarkable ear for the cadence and rhythm of folk speech and memory for the anecdotes of rambling yarns of aged veterans and country gaffers. As a boy he had tramped the country around Guthrie and his grandfather's lonely farm in Twigg County, and he knew the landscape so well that he could close his eyes and virtually put his hand on some limestone outcropping or smell the sycamores in a creek bottom after the spring floods had gone and the sun was beginning to bear down. Both his father and grandfather were great readers of history and encouraged him to follow them, and the older man had many memories of the fighting he had seen in the Civil War. But Warren showed no special preference for Southern history. Years after he remembered that two of his favorite books when he was a boy were Buckle's *History of Civilization,* which seemed at the time to have the answer to everything, and Prescott's *The Oregon Trail.*[12] Yet all the time he was soaking up stories of the tobacco wars and the old frontier which he would put to good use many years afterward. One acquainted with Warren's later works and the recurring struggle to understand the past in order to understand the present might suppose that the past, and particularly, the history of his own region, meant more to Warren at this time than it actually did. Like Davidson, he seems to have taken it wholly for granted and to have looked elsewhere for his material, though in "Sonnets of Two Summers" (*The Fugitive,* August, 1924) and "Easter Morning, Crosby Junction" (*The Fugitive,* June, 1925) he made a little use of his sense of the place. And like Tate, Warren was looking beyond the region, beyond the present and such absurdities as the Dayton trial, to the world outside the South—to San Francisco.

But then, abruptly, all this changed. It was the tragi-comedy of the Scopes trial that did it.

The Fugitives began to pay attention to what Mencken and the others were saying about Tennessee, about their own region, about the South as a whole. Mencken had praised the Fugitives on their first appearance, and he had long been an idol of the literary young men at Vanderbilt. Years afterward Jesse Wills remarked that even Tate went around with Mencken under his arm, and Tate owned that he had.[13] One would expect the Fugitives, proud of their sophistication and freedom from provinciality, to side with the journalists and laugh at the yokels. But the descriptions of the Tennessee people, the stories filed by reporters savage with hangovers and heat, and the cartoons in the Northern papers were so offensive that there could be no passing them off with a tolerant smile. When Mims came to Ransom with his suggestion that the intellectuals of Vanderbilt write to the Northern journals disavow-

---

[12] *Writers at Work,* ed. Malcolm Cowley (New York, 1959), pp. 186-187.
[13] Adding, "But not Cabell." See *Fugitives' Reunion,* p. 92.

ing the goings-on at Dayton, he met a furious refusal. Ransom not only turned him down, he argued in defense of the Fundamentalists. At the same time Davidson was dumbfounded to discover the apparent contempt, often joined to an implacable hostility, with which so many Americans regarded the land and the people of whom he was so affectionately proud. All at once he began to see the Southern yeomen, heirs of the tall pioneers, as haughty outcasts from a progressivist society on the Northern plan, as the last remnants of a lost time and cause that became ever more glamorous and precious as they receded. As "The Tall Men" and his subsequent essays would show, the country men of the Middle South quickly replaced the outland piper as the projected self-image of superiority withdrawing from the pullulating welter of ill-begotten ordinary men.

Warren, meanwhile, was still untroubled by the trial and the attacks on the South. During the next few years he was to be cut off from his friends except for occasional visits with the Tates in New York and Paris between 1927 and 1929. It was not Dayton but the experience of leaving home and living in the San Francisco area which awakened him to a sense of his region. Even in Nashville he had been among people so much of his own kind that it was not until he went West that he first knew intense loneliness, first began to realize the special qualities of the men and the places he had left behind. A consequence of this removal was the poem "History Among the Rocks," written during the winter of 1925-1926, which was the first of a series bearing the overall title of "Kentucky Mountain Farm." In this and the poems of the series that followed through the next four years as he roamed from California to New Haven and on to Oxford he showed his extraordinary sensitivity to the texture of the land, the dark, strained violence beneath even the most bland and sunny scenes, and the mysterious, nameless guilts and anxieties they evoked.

It was leaving the region that awakened Tate, too. He had been living in New York since the previous October, and already he was disenchanted with the *avant-garde* and disgusted by the filth and confusion of the city. The postures with which he had sought to impress Nashville meant nothing in the infinite indifference of the city, where so many other young writers from the provinces were trying to startle the citizens. The glamorous image of the defiant modernist, shaping his poems by the twists and dartings of his most private impulses, had long been the actual—if never quite acknowledged—basis for his ideas concerning art and the artist. In his debates with Ransom he had claimed absolute autonomy for the poet and the poetry. But now as he argued over the role of the artist this image began to fail him and he saw how self-defeating and nihilistic it was. Late in the fall of 1925, he and his wife, Caroline Gordon, moved out to Patterson, a village about fifty miles north of the city near the Connecticut border, where with Hart Crane they rented one half of a farmhouse. Nearby was a little community of young writers—friends of the Tates and Crane—established in or around Patterson and Sherman, Connecticut, which was just across the line, and Tate sat up many nights for conversations with Matthew Josephson, Malcolm Cowley, Slater Brown, and Crane which would permanently influence his thought. Again and again they came back to the need of contemporary man for myths to shape his conduct, beliefs, and art— a need especially intense for Tate, with his background of tumult and insecurity, now that the Poet as Cosmos entire and indwelling within himself was proving insufficient. He could not share Crane's hopeful picture of the bridge as the way into the future, and while he admired Crane's struggle to create an American myth around that image, he did not believe it could succeed.

It had been all very well for Tate to ridicule the backwardness of the South as he fumed to get away to New York, but the malice of the Northern press during and just after the Scopes trial was such that even when the journalists were saying things with which Tate might earlier have been inclined to agree, they now evoked only anger, the more acute for the failure of New York literary life to fulfill his hopes. As outraged as Ransom and Davidson, Tate now looked sympathetically toward the South and its past just when he was becoming increasingly convinced of the need for traditional modes of conduct to sustain the man and writer. Even as he was saying in "Last Days of the Charming Lady" that the Old South had never learned "that only through the repudiation of outmoded general notions which have lost their roots in an existing reality, can a society create new forms for the perpetuation of its strength," he had begun to examine the Southern past for those forms and values absent from contemporary culture.[14] So urgently did he himself require those forms and values that of the three important Fugitive writers, Ransom, Warren, and himself, he was to become the one most emotionally committed to the defense of the South, past and present. Only Davidson approached him in the intensity of feeling and violence of statement.

Stung by the attacks, Ransom, Davidson, and Tate wanted to make some reply, but they hardly knew where to begin. After years of ignoring public affairs and social problems and of attempting to eschew their heritage for something larger and, they had hoped, finer, they were unprepared to defend the South. Uppermost in their minds at the moment was a general, but not very definite, disgust with the modes and manners set by the industrial East and Middle West. They wanted a life, as Davidson later said, that had "order, leisure, character, stability, and that would also, in the larger sense, be aesthetically enjoyable," and it seemed that the very backwardness of the South offered hope of this. It did not occur to them to attempt a defense on economic terms, and even if it had, conditions outside their own region did not offer much of an argument against the seemingly endless expansion and prosperity of the North. But literature did not give them much to go on, for that of the Old South was manifestly inferior, while that of their own time was neglected by other Southerners.

As the months passed, Ransom's first anger subsided. His interest in writing poetry gradually diminished while his interest in aesthetics increased. In the fall of 1926 he took his family to Indian Hills in the mountains above Denver, where for several months he worked on a book, to be called "The Third Moment," which would sum up his speculations in aesthetics. By extending the ideas first put forward in the essay "Thoughts on the Poetic Discontent," which was published in *The Fugitive* for June, 1925, he hoped to show how the intellect progresses from Pure Ex-

[14] "Last Days of the Charming Lady," *The Nation*, CXXI (October 28, 1925), 485. These contradictory views of the Southern past were to be found in much of Tate's writing from this time forward and provided the essential problem of his brilliant and far too little appreciated novel, *The Fathers* (1938).

perience, through History (which he defined in terms large enough
to take in science, for by "History" he meant conceptualized knowledge, particularly in the form of abstractions which are utilitarian
and essentially *sub*tractions from the whole), to the Aesthetic, or
Third Moment, during which one becomes aware of the incompleteness and deficiency of the historical record and attempts
through the imagination to recover and dwell in joy upon experience as reconstituted in the arts, dreams, religions, and other
modes of symbolic representation. By February of 1927 he had put
together two hundred pages which he planned to extend and re-
write during the following summer. He had by now virtually
given up poetry, though he was not yet willing to admit this. As
for his interest in Southern affairs, it had been assimilated for the
time being into his concern for living in the Third Moment: he
believed that old-fashioned, easy-going country life such as still
prevailed in most of the South offered the best chance for the
loving recreation and contemplation of nature. As he explained
to Tate: "I subordinate always Art to the aesthetic of life; its function is to initiate us into the aesthetic life, it is not for us the final
end. In the Old South the life aesthetic was actually realized, and
there are the fewer object-lessons in its specific art. The old bird
in the blue-jeans sitting on the stump with the hound-dog at his
feet knew this aesthetic, even."[15] From this time on, with the exception of a few months late in 1930, Ransom's Southernism was
to be somewhat detached and speculative—a matter more of conviction arising from his total view of the good aesthetic life than
of passion. To his friends it always seemed a little cool.

It was in Davidson and Tate that passion prevailed. Except
for Ransom and, in his very private way, Warren, whose growing
interest in the South was not known yet to his friends, the Fugitives
had virtually no sympathy with them. Once the anthology was out,
as we know, the group fell apart, and the other men watched with
only small interest though at times considerable dismay while
their old companions became more and more excited over the South
and its past. When Merrill Moore left Nashville in 1928 to study
more medicine in Boston, where, as it turned out, he was to spend
the rest of his life, he corresponded steadily with the Fugitives,

[15] From a letter to Tate dated "April 3 (and 13)." For a discussion of the
date of the letter see Chapter Six, note 9.

and particularly with Ransom, but his letters dealt mainly with amiable gossip about himself and his family. He regarded the new interest in the Southern past as an extremely sophisticated but essentially dangerous attempt by his friends to escape the pressures of the present, and though he followed their poetry closely, he paid little attention to their essays on the South. The other Fugitives were less assured in trying to account for this new eccentricity, but despite long standing affections, they were no more cordial. Allies and supporters had to be sought elsewhere. They shortly were.

For to Davidson and Tate, the defense of the South became more rather than less important as the Dayton trial receded into the past. Ashamed of his inability to speak for his region in 1925, Davidson had set himself a program of independent reading in Southern history. Soon after he had begun, he was asked by Walter Fleming, who had recently joined the History Department at Vanderbilt, to help build the library's collection of Southern material. Fleming particularly wanted Davidson's aid with Southern literature, and taking the bibliography of Vernon Parrington's *Main Currents of American Thought* for a guide, Davidson surveyed the Vanderbilt holdings to see what should be added. At the same time he determined to read all the books on the South cited in his guide. As he got further into the subject, he began to write a series of seven poems, collected and published in 1927 under the title *The Tall Men*, in which he contrasted the disorder and triviality of life in Nashville during the 1920's with the simplicity, dignity, and determination in the lives of the early settlers in Tennessee. The comparison was made by a veteran of the First World War who had returned and gone into business in Nashville; as he looked with distaste on a world of trolley-cars and typewriters, he recalled stories of the tall men that had come down through his family, men

> Whose words were bullets. They, by the Tennessee waters,
> Talked with their rifles bluntly and sang to the hills
> With whet of axes. Smoke arose where smoke
> Never had been before. The Red Man's lodges
> Darkened suddenly with a sound of mourning.
> Bison, cropping the wild grass, raised their heads
> To a strange wind that troubled them. The deer

Toward Agrarianism

Leaped in the thicket, vainly loathing death
That stung without arrows. . . .

                                 The lips of hunters awoke
With rumor of far lands till Carolina
Firesides were restless, till the tall Virginians hated
The easy warmth of houses, the too-many-peopled
World. In twos and threes the tall men
Strode in the valleys. Their palisades were pitched
In the Cumberland hills. They brought their teeming wives
To rock the hickory cradles and to mould
Bullets for words. . . .

Today, their descendant

                                   sprawls while a little man
Purrs in a patent tone of voice and a sleek
Copyrighted smile. He has a Northern way
Of clipping his words, and with an inevitable curve
Of an arm in a business suit reveals cigars
In the tribal code. Then we are wreathed in smoke
Like friends. He says: "You are so tall, you men,
You Tennesseans. I've never seen so many
Tall fellows riding in elevators.
What makes you then so tall? . . ."

                                 Why, since you ask,
Tallness is not in what you eat or drink
But in the seed of man. I am minded
(Remembering an Indian grave) to speak
As only I can speak of what I am,
What were the loins that begot me, what the breasts
That suckled me in danger, what the blood
Running rebelliously within me still
Of the tall men who walked here when there were
No easy roads for walking or for riding. . . .

The memories go back to the days of Sevier, Jackson, and Crockett,
and come down through tales of the Civil War, which provoke the
veteran to observe,

Toward Agrarianism

The Union is saved. Lee has surrendered forever.
Today, Lorena, it is forbidden to be
A Southerner. One is American now;
Propounds the pig's conception of the state—
The constitution of, by, for the pig—
Meanwhile pushing his trotters well in the trough.
One goes to the movies, motors on Sunday swiftly
On the baked asphalt. . . .

Nevertheless, the veteran has not forgotten the Confederate soldiers. For

This is my body, woven from dead and living,
Given over again to the quick lustration
Of a new moment. This is my body and spirit,
Broken but never tamed, risen from the bloody sod,
Walking suddenly alive in a new morning.

To discover his more immediate past, the "geography of his brain," the veteran recalls his childhood: working in the fields, listening to the stories of his father and Aunt Zif, the colored maid, pondering the relics of the legendary Old South:

Over the Southern fields a moon of ghosts
Enchants me with old tremulous histories
Of slender hands, proud, smiling lips, and halls
Peopled with fragile beauty. Rich is the land,
Rich and impregnable as this magnolia-bloom
Buried among dark lacquered leaves. Breathe not
Into the golden heart, so deep, of this lush flower
Lest it blacken. Take now only its perfume
Drifting so invisibly, seized for a moment
Only, magic only of moonlight lost
And unassailable love that perished here—
Where moonlight builds tall pillars of a house
Lording a shadowy park. Enter the door
So evidently failing. Here is the stair
Where Lady Miranda walked with futile lips
Gallantly firm. And Captain Prosper here
Was laid in agony by this tall window,

Toward Agrarianism

Bleeding from wounds at hands of Caliban,
Mournful as Arthur on the black-draped barge. . . .

The captain is not dismayed at death, for he has seen that

A duller magic rules
Until the blood shall speak again.

It still rules, the veteran thinks. There had been an interval during the World War when some of the Tennessee soldiers recovered the old glory of the pioneers, but afterwards, in the world of Ford and Edison, there seemed to be no place for them. The veteran examines the various means of escape: travel, mysticism, expatriatism, Dada, satyrism, Eliotic intellectualism, but rejects them all. Love for his wife gives a private meaning and shelter. But as a public man, examining his surroundings, he can find no meaning, no heroism, no reason why the city he lives in should not be utterly destroyed, though his ancestors fought to save from the Indians' torches the big forts from which the city grew. The collection ends,

There is a place where beech-trees droop their boughs
Down-slanting, and where the dark cedars grow
With stubborn roots threading the lichened rocks.
There the smooth limestone benches, rubbed
By warm primeval streams, yet hold the crystal
Forms of dead life. There on a summer's evening
The screech-owl quavers and unseen July-flies
Trill their thin songs. And there my father said,
Pointing a low mound out to me: "My son,
Stand on this Indian's grave and plainly ask,
Indian, what did you die for? And he'll say,
Nothing!"

So it was! So it is!
What did you die for? Nothing indeed nothing!
The seed of the white man grows on Indian graves,
Waxing in steel and stone, nursing the fire
That eats and blackens till he has no life
But in the fire that eats him. White man, remember,
Brother, remember Hnaef and his sixty warriors

Greedy for battle-joy. Remember the rifles
Talking men's talk into the Tennessee darkness
And the long-haired hunters watching the Tennessee hills
In the land of big rivers for something.

At first glance, these poems with their images of the old frontier, their fragments of Anglo-Saxon idiom ("when the fair-haired
Goths/ Came a-harrying over the path of the Whale./ Bright was
the hall. . . .") and references to the battle of Burnebrugh, their
details of trench warfare, and their descriptions of the city, seem
utterly different from the little whimsies and delicate maunder-
ings of *An Outland Piper*. The organization, appropriately for a
series of ruminations, is looser, but the movement seems more
energetic until one sees that it is not getting anywhere and that
for all the rough chronology of the series, the poems are variations on the same theme, but variations which do not explore it
with sufficient depth to permit significant differences and real development of an idea or attitude among the poems. Commenting
on "The Tall Men" in "A Note on Three Southern Poets," Warren remarked that "Davidson is not an ironist, although there are
certain ironical effects in the poem. He is concerned with the question of continuity, rather than disparity, in his notion of history in
general and identity of the individual. When the disparities obtrude
themselves, the effect is of shock and desperation, with little of the
acceptance or resolution ordinarily inherent in irony as a mode."
"This implies," Warren reasoned, "the basic difficulty of the poem:
the defect of resolution." Finding the same question restated too
many times in the same tone, Warren claimed that "a more definite,
perhaps dramatic, focus would have clarified the total effect."[16] But,
as Tate had already pointed out in an essay on Edwin Arlington
Robinson, a dramatic treatment requires a comprehensive moral
scheme. To explain the failure of Robinson's *Talifer*, Tate argued
that the modern hero lacks such a scheme and is compelled to fall
back upon a "futile self-assertion in the realm of personal ego."[17]
This is precisely what Davidson's veteran is obliged to do, as the
seventh poem, "The Breaking Mould," makes clear. That he must
do so is, of course, one of the essential points of the series. But be-

[16] *Poetry*, XL (May, 1932), 109.
[17] "Edwin Arlington Robinson," in *Reactionary Essays* (New York, 1936), pp.
194, 199.

cause his personal ego is the lens through which everything is seen, the interpretations and judgments cannot be any greater than that ego, which, the poems repeatedly assert, can find virtually no meaning, no point of reference, outside itself. When we consider the ego more closely, we begin to see how much "The Tall Men" resembles Davidson's earlier poetry and how little he was prepared, despite his immense reading, to undertake a project on so large a scale. For here we find again the same narrow petulance, the same yearning for the far and lost, the same self-congratulatory contempt for the multitude, the same identification with the superior few, and the same yearning to flee to the remote refuge, the Eden-like valley. In place of a comprehensive moral scheme Davidson has only a set of prejudices. The conception, if one can call it that, of what makes a man, of what gives dignity to the human ordeal, is compounded of clichés from boys' books and the legend of the Old South: the grave-eyed hunters, the "teeming" women, the abashed city clerks—these would have appealed to the readers of Zane Grey, just as the magnolias and moon-drenched mansion would have pleased Davidson's old opponent, Harriet Monroe. For though the lines are graceful and melodious, the projected image of the good life is not much more profound. Or real.

From his own experience, his reading, and his talks with other young writers in Patterson and New York City, Tate had developed a firm conviction regarding the "comprehensive moral scheme." In a series of reviews and essays published during 1926 and 1927, he hammered away at the point that "The contemporary poet . . . suffers from a malady of disbelief—which is to say, his attitudes lack the authority and form which only the beliefs can give them." For beliefs of his own he was beginning to look toward medieval Europe. In the meantime he was writing long meditative poems on the drabness and moral relativism of the present, but, like Davidson, he was forced back upon a congeries of attitudes which lacked authority. In its place he tried to evoke a show of force and grandeur by images of a strenuous, semi-militaristic life. Where Davidson went to Anglo-Saxon literature, Tate turned to John Webster's plays and recondite allusions to little-known Greek philosophers. Yet the end result was about the same. The present, it appeared, was condemned mainly for lacking the swagger of the Confederate days or the Italian principalities—as the latter were depicted by Webster, who had never been nearer to Italy than the pages of *The Prince*. Tate was profoundly in earnest, but the poems and essays sometimes looked a little silly.

Meanwhile, his correspondence with Ransom went forward briskly. The two men were in the closest agreement on the inadequacy of the world view of science, but Ransom tried in letter after letter to warn his friend that the absolutes Tate sought could not be had: one would have to settle for a dualist philosophy comparable to Ransom's aesthetic. In the spring of 1927 he wrote, "Perry [Ralph Barton Perry] is right: Value is the supposed responsiveness and manageability of the world under your own heroic dictatorship . . . its capacity to serve your own purpose. Therefore valuation is, pretty obviously, your subjectification of the world, and an escape from the obligation to respect its objectivity. . . . [But the world] ultimately is quite appallingly independent of us, and . . . in realizing this we exhibit our sense of beauty, sense of humor, sense of tragedy, and religiosity." Religion, Ransom claimed, citing Schleiermacher, begins in an awareness of this independence but soon slides downhill into Magic and the attempt first to placate and then control one's surroundings. For the modern man, therefore, art, with its combination of abstract forms and ideas qualified by intractable particularity, offered the best means of viewing experience; but it must be kept free of cosmologies and fixed points of reference or it would quickly become another religion.[18]

But Tate could not accept such a bland and disengaged view of the world. When he sent his poem "Causerie II" to Ransom, the latter gently observed of Tate's verse that its background "might seem to be a truculent or *moral* state rather than a philosophical or *aesthetic* one." There would always be scandals and chorus girls, Ransom continued, but these were insufficient subjects for the poet. He himself had been getting "soft and easy" for some time now, and had come around to believing that the best subjects are individual interests, which are the same in all periods, and that the theme "we are fallen on evil days" was perhaps not so important as it seemed. For one thing, he was not persuaded that it was

[18] From an undated letter now in the Princeton University Library. See Chapter Six, note 9.

such a bad age or that it was even near the nadir of history.[19] Nevertheless, Ransom was still sufficiently disturbed by the attacks on the South to turn back to the idea of a defense based on his recent speculation and his conviction that the Southern provincial life offered the best opportunity for aesthetic satisfaction. During the spring of 1927 he put together an article which he described to Tate as "rather emulsified into pap for popular consumption."[20] And when at just about the same time Tate wrote to suggest that the friends seriously attempt to get up a book about the Old South, Ransom said that he was delighted but, given his habit of defending the good life in aesthetic—which meant virtually literary—terms and values, he had misgivings because there was so little in Southern literature to point the principle. They would have to stress the aesthetic value of the life itself. "Our symposium of authors would be more concerned, seems to me, with making this principle clear than with exhibiting the Southern artists, who were frequently quite inferior to their Southern public in real aesthetic capacity. But there are performances, surely, to which we can point with pride, if you believe the book should be mainly of literary criticism."[21] Ransom had a good point. When he sent the article, now called "The South—Old or New" to *The Nation*, it was rejected because a majority of the staff doubted that the South ever had a significant culture, or that, if it did, that the culture had any chance of survival. It seemed to Ransom that there was some "bad Abolitionist blood" there, but he took hope for what he now termed "the cause" from the fact that so many young Southerners who went North, as Tate had done, found it impossible to "surrender to an alien mode of life."[22]

But while Ransom floundered about in his effort to translate poetics into political theory and to defend the South as he would defend a poem, Tate had gone forward with a biography of Stonewall Jackson, on which he worked throughout 1927. It turned out to be one of the best things he ever did. For here, when he undertook to show in the life of a man of action the greater dig-

[19] Ransom to Tate, September 13, 1926. "Causerie II" was eventually published as "Causerie." It dealt, in part, with a celebrated scandal involving Earl Carroll and Joyce Hawley. "Causerie I" seems to have wholly disappeared.
[20] Ransom to Tate, April 3 and 13, 1927. See Chapter Six, note 9.
[21] *Ibid.*
[22] Ransom to Tate, June 25, 1927.

nity and meaningful order of earlier times, Tate revealed a wholly unexpected feeling for the day-to-day life in the Old South which later gave his novel *The Fathers* such vividness and authority. His description of the Scotch-Irish emigrants scraping a living out of their small farms told far more about the actual touch and texture of life than the stereotypes of Davidson's *The Tall Men*. To get past the difficulty noted by Ransom and account for the supposedly greater satisfaction of life in the Old South, Tate turned to Calhoun's arguments on behalf of a society of fixed classes and to the writings of Spengler, Eliot, and Ramon Fernandez on the ethical insipidness of liberal humanitarianism. Political history was only incidental in this book, but running through it was an assumption which he would develop in many forms over the next decade: moral responsibility depended upon the direct ownership and management of property, and the best property was land given over to diversified, subsistence farming. Where such responsibility prevailed, as, he claimed, it did in most of the Old South, even slavery was not wholly evil. "The institution of slavery," he argued,

> "was a positive good only in the sense that Calhoun had argued that it was: it had become a necessary element in a stable society. He had argued justly that only in a society of fixed classes can men be free. Only men who are socially as well as economically secure can preserve the historical sense of obligation. This historical sense of obligation implied a certain freedom to do right. . . .
>
> "In the North, the historical sense was atrophied, and the feeling of obligation did not exist. . . . The Northern men . . . had come to believe in abstract right. Where abstract right supplants obligation, interest begins to supplant loyalty. Revolution may follow. When such a revolution triumphs, society becomes a chaos of self-interest. Its freedom is the freedom to do wrong. This does not mean that all men will do the wrong thing; only that no external order exists which precludes the public exercise of wrong impulses; too much, in short, is left to the individual. It was such a revolution that the Northern States were now moving towards."[23]

[23] *Stonewall Jackson, The Good Soldier* (New York, 1928), pp. 39-40.

Perhaps in parts of Virginia and around Charleston there had once been such an order in the Old South. But for the most part the record went against Tate. The South had been a place of unusual fluidity wherein the same sort of men who made fortunes in factories in the North could clear the land and because of its incredible fertility make enough money to set up as gentry in a decade or less. Fortunately the dialectic was overshadowed by the portrait of Jackson and the narratives of the great soldier's battles and death. These were the best defense of the Old South, and until *The Fathers*, which was published a decade later, nothing that Tate would write toward that end would serve the cause so well.[24]

IV

1928 was the turning point for those Fugitives who were to go on to Agrarianism. Everything seemed to happen at once. The Fugitive anthology came out in January, followed almost at once by Tate's biography, which was well received. The critical notices helped him toward a Guggenheim fellowship, and in the fall he sailed for France, where he planned to write a biography of Jefferson Davis and prepare for the press a collection of pieces tentatively entitled "Essays on Poetry and Morality" (which never came to pass). Before the year was out, his first volume of poetry, *Mr. Pope and Other Poems*, was published and the initial period of his development as poet came to an end. He had finished with experiment for its own sake and with taking the creative frenzy or even the medium itself as the true subject of poetry. Henceforth, virtually all of his poetry, like most of his prose, was directed at the problem of belief, particularly as it might be studied in the fate of traditional values and their emblems when immersed in the contemporary scene. From this year forward, the course of his thought and development was set.

In this year, too, Ransom finished "The Third Moment" and sent it to Henry Holt and Company. But even before the publishers reached a decision (and they were not enthusiastic), he changed his mind and withdrew it. Until now he had been much excited by the project and could report to Tate long and close

[24] The book is discussed further in Chapter Seven.

work on it; yet once it was out of his hands and he could review the whole of its argument, he was convinced that it lacked an adequate account of the motivation toward art. At once the search for motivation became a central concern—which it would continue to be over the next thirty years. He did not limit his thought to aesthetics. Believing that art was only one of many ways in which the sensibility pursued its innocent satisfactions in the midst of the drive to satisfy biotic needs—a drive which all too easily passed over into a compulsive urge to accumulate material goods—he wanted an explanation of its motivation which would serve to account as well for the impulse behind religion, dream, ritual, and all other forms of behavior offering aesthetic satisfaction, among which he now put the unhurried way of life in the Old South. The more he thought about it, the more it seemed that the progressivist spirit of the North which denigrated the conservative and leisurely South was one more instance of the tyranny of the unchecked reason and its ruthless abstractions. He, too, found an argument well suited to his temperament, an answer such as he had lacked at the time of the Scopes trial and the (to him) outrageous proposal of Mims.

It came in good season. The proposals for a book replying to the Northern attack had foundered for lack of knowledge of the Southern cultural heritage. A study of Southern literature would have been too weak a rejoinder: as Ransom had said, there wasn't enough good writing to point the case. But after his months of reading on the South and his conversations with Ransom, Davidson was ready with a new approach; the friends should prepare a book setting forth a "philosophy of Southern life" addressed to "mature Southerners of the late nineteen-twenties, in the so-called New South—Southerners who, we trusted, were not so far gone in modern education as to require, for the act of comprehension, coloured charts, statistical tables, graphs, and journalistic monosyllables. . . ." Thus, instead of trying to strike back at the North, they would summon Southerners to respect an ancient culture established upon farming and to defend it against the invasion of industrialism which was "the more disturbing because it was proceeding with an entire lack of consideration for its results on Southern life." The book was particularly needed at this moment,

129

for such Southern opinion as was articulate tended to be uncritically admiring of the effects of the industrial invasion.[25]

Ransom believed he had such a philosophy as Davidson called for. His essay, "The South—Old or New," was published in *The Sewanee Review* for April, 1928. It was his first foray and indicated the terrain he would defend and the weapons he would use except for a brief excursion into economics which he made during 1931 and 1932. The essay, though tentative and ingenuous, deserves some attention, for as things turned out Ransom was to be the philosopher of Agrarianism, and the postulates which the Agrarians, if they thought of them at all, took more or less for granted were here first set forth.

He began with the startling proposition that "the South in its history to date has exhibited what nowhere else on a large scale has been exhibited on this continent north of Mexico, a culture based on European principles which has lasted as long as a century," because the South had been settled by people who admired the established order and who "never conceded that the whole duty of man was to increase material production, or that the index to the degree of his culture was the volume of his material production. His business seemed to be, rather, to envelope his work and his play with a leisure which permitted the maximum activity of intelligence." But the North had won the Civil War and its industrialism, which made both work and play tense and brutal, was no longer counterbalanced and was spreading throughout the nation. Thus the critical question: "How can the Southern communities, the chief instance of the stationary European principle of culture in America, be reinforced in their ancient integrity as centers of resistance to an all-but-devouring industrialism? How can the South develop its resources without being persuaded to make development of its resources the end-in-itself?" Perhaps the most persuasive thing about this little piece was its affability. Even when he was obliged to say harsh things about the North, Ransom's prose was so modest and gentle that one could almost believe in those Southern communities with their European principles. They had the winsomeness of those hamlets one seems

[25] Donald Davidson, *"I'll Take My Stand*: A History," *The American Review,* v (Summer, 1935), 304.

to glimpse behind Ransom's poems such as "Miller's Daughter" or "Conrad at Twilight."

Favored by weather, soil, and the luck of having escaped share-cropping, some of the country around Nashville may have permitted the farmer "to envelope his work and his play with a leisure which permitted the maximum activity of intelligence," but the same can scarcely be said of most of the South. Moreover, where had those settlers who so admired the established order of Europe come from? Ireland, Scotland, the vineyards of France, the stony hills of Italy? Certainly not in any significant numbers from the estates and manors of England, whose idealized county gentry so bewitched the Southern imagination. And if these settlers had thus admired the established order, why had they left Europe for the wilderness of the Southern back countries where men often lived too far apart for an established order on a European model to be possible? There is no need to go on. Despite their coming from farming country, Ransom, his two friends, and those who joined them later seem to have had little idea of what life was really like on most Southern farms. In all their subsequent arguments and essays they failed, as Ransom himself finally conceded long afterward, to provide a substantial and believable image of life on a Southern farm that was capable of satisfying to the degree they claimed for it the spirit and aspirations of man, capable of permitting that maximum activity of intelligence that Ransom remarked here.

Ransom's piece had not been long in print before Davidson made essentially the same points in an essay which by comparison with those he would write later seems remarkably mild and conciliatory. Conceding that Southern development was and would remain largely in the hands of business men, Davidson argued that they must work to preserve Southern ideals while advancing education, the arts, social reform, and as much industrialism as was required to strengthen the regional economy. They must infuse Southern industrialism with the ancient spirit of *noblesse oblige*.[26] Davidson manifestly had no understanding of how business men of the New South used the intense individualism Davidson praised to keep the workers disorganized and weak, or of how the paternal-

[26] "First Fruits of Dayton: The Intellectual Evolution in Dixie," *The Forum*, LXXIX (June, 1928), 896-907.

ism of *noblesse oblige* could be corrupted into a system of flattery which effectively smothered protests against the stretch-out system or degrading working conditions.

Having found a position from which to attack the North, Ransom and Davidson looked about for supporters. During the summer following the publication of their essays, Frank L. Owsley, a member of the Department of History at Vanderbilt since 1920, came back to Vanderbilt from studying in Europe. Soon after, Davidson dropped in to talk over their ideas and learn if he were sympathetic. "Why, man," Owsley almost shouted, "Let me show you some of the things I've written."[27] Now thirty-eight, Owsley had grown up on an Alabama farm, and for a short time had directed an agricultural experiment station. He had worked his own soil with his own hands, and he had a love of the land as strong as Warren's and far stronger than Ransom's or Tate's. He had, too, Davidson's bone-deep affection for rural life and customs. He had been as much infuriated as the others by Northern scorn for his region, and his anger had a special edge because he well understood the system of absentee ownership whereby profits earned by Southern labor went North into the pockets of men who abused the South while taking advantage of its weakness. As a trained historian he knew more than his friends about the place of the South in the patterns of American social and economic development, but, though a most generous and affectionate man, he could be choleric and impulsive to the point of fanaticism where conflicts between the North and South were concerned. Looking at the past, he thought he could discern a series of malevolent, carefully planned attacks on the South which were intended to make easier a ruthless exploitation. It was undeniable that Northern investors took advantage of the region. They still do. But most of his fellow historians in the South found his claims regarding the extent and the thoroughness of the planning behind the exploitation fantastic and ludicrous. Thus, where the former Fugitives needed sober instruction he tended to encourage emotionalism and exaggeration.

A much steadier recruit was Lyle Lanier, a native of Tennessee and a good friend of Warren, who had graduated from Vander-

[27] So he remembered and reported his answer to this writer on September 25, 1945.

bilt in 1923 and, after studying and teaching in the North, had come back in the autumn of 1928 as an assistant professor of psychology. Though younger than the others, Lanier was a man of parts (he was elected president of the Southern Society of Philosophy and Psychology at thirty-three and later served as the editor of the *Psychological Bulletin*) and he brought into the group a patient concern for the facts to counterbalance the rashness of Owsley and Davidson. Such concern was much needed. The group had just discovered a recently published attack on American culture which greatly pleased it; this was *The American Heresy*, by Christopher Hollis, a young English journalist. What set his book off from the boob-baiting of Mencken and Sinclair Lewis on the one hand and the usual reports written by Europeans after a quick tour of Harlem, Pittsburgh, and the Chicago stockyards on the other was its thesis, which exactly suited the mood of the Nashville group. The United States, Hollis kept reiterating, was actually two nations—two cultures doomed to conflict. The heretical North, in attempting to live by disembodied rationalism, had swept aside traditional controls upon behavior and had encouraged the individual to live by his own irresponsible will and wishes. Not having to answer for his conduct to any religious authority, the Northern industrialist or merchant could plunder the land and the people without a tremor of guilt. But the South had remained agrarian, homogenous, traditional, and more faithful to the founders' ideal of stable republicanism under which all men were responsible for the common weal. "The United States," Hollis wrote, "were intended to be static. An agricultural people were to live in freedom on the land, suffering as little as possible from the interference of Government and preserving a simple and ancient way of life rather than continually learning, by invention, new customs. For such a people no method of expansion was provided, because it was not intended that they should expand."[28] Defeat in the Civil War had forced the South to keep to the old ways but had freed the North for reckless expansion of which industrialism was the latest and most gross and inhuman form.

The division, he asserted, had evolved under the intellectual leadership of Jefferson from the division between rationalism and orthodoxy in the eighteenth century. Thus:

---

[28] *The American Heresy* (New York, 1927), p. 79.

"A citizen of this divided world, Jefferson, when he gave to the United States a political philosophy, rightly built that philosophy upon the two principles of human liberty and human equality. These principles he should have deduced from dogmatic religion. Instead he adopted them as sentiments and built his philosophy upon a denial of dogmatic religion. This is the American heresy. America is an example of how the principles of liberty and equality, unregulated by religious authority which can adjust their competing claims, may destroy a state. For it was inevitable that, since he had not reason to compell assent, each man would restate these principles as it suited his convenience. The Jeffersonian state, which came to birth in the War of Independence, died in the Civil War."[29]

To substantiate his thesis, Hollis examined the roles in America's development not only of Jefferson, but of Calhoun, Lincoln, and Wilson as well. The center of his book was a comparison between Calhoun, the spokesman for tradition and government by the responsible landed gentry, and Lincoln, whom Hollis called "the representative of a party, whose declared aim was to deprive the Southern citizen of his full rights, and who was, it seemed, the servant of a powerful financial interest, whose intention was to bleed the South white for the subsidy of the North." These two men stood for two ways of life so radical in antipathy that they must inevitably lead to an economic collision which the Northern expansionists would find intolerable. Moreover, the North was irritated by its pinch-lipped envy of the gracious European culture of the South. These, and not slavery, Hollis insisted, were the things over which the sections fought.[30]

Probably only Owsley knew enough American history to trim the hyperboles and qualify the gaudy simplifications of Hollis's book, but its animus was so resonant with his own that he rejoiced in its extravagance. Indeed, he was soon surpassing Hollis in horrendous narratives of Northern plots against the life of the gentle South. The others were as much impressed by the book, for each found in it something which answered directly to his own most immediate interests. Thus Ransom was pleased by the attack on the abstract rationalism of the North and the description

[29] *Ibid.*, p. 9.   [30] *Ibid.*, p. 196.

of Southern life as "European" in geniality and leisureliness, Tate by the argument that the emptiness of contemporary American life was due to the repudiation of religious traditions, and Davidson by the praise for Southern rural life and approval of its apparent backwardness.

The book's influence is most apparent and pervasive in Tate's biography of Jefferson Davis, which was published by Minton, Balch and Company in 1929. In a bibliographical note, Tate explained that he was attempting to unite under a single point of view the accounts given earlier by William E. Dodd and Hamilton James Eckenrode. Insofar as that point of view was not his own, he said flatly, it was indebted to *The American Heresy*, which "'is incomplete and inaccurately documented, but it is the first effort to comprehend the supposedly mixed forces of American history under a single idea."[31] For a man who had recently read Spengler, who must surely have known Henry Adams, and who should not have dared to take up this subject without looking into Beard, that was quite a testimonial!

Tate wasted no time in putting the single idea to work. Early in the book he announced that in the Civil War, "The issue was class rule and religion *versus* democracy and science."[32] Having gotten such a good purchase he laid about him with fervor:

"The South was permanently old-fashioned, backward-looking, slow, contented to live upon a modest conquest of nature, unwilling to conquer the earth's resources for the fun of the conquest; contented, in short, to take only what man needs; unwilling to juggle the needs of man in the illusory pursuit of abstract wealth. . . . The War between the States was the second and decisive struggle of the Western spirit against the European— the spirit of restless aggression against a stable spirit of ordered economy—and the Western won."

"In a sense, all European history since the Reformation was concentrated in the war between the North and the South. For in the South the most conservative of the European orders had, with great power, come back to life, while in the North, opposing the Southern feudalism, had grown to be a powerful industrial state which epitomized in spirit all those middle-class, urban

[31] *Jefferson Davis, His Rise and Fall*, p. 303.   [32] P. 87.

impulses directed against the agrarian aristocracies of Europe after the Reformation. . . ."[33]

Anyone familiar with the inefficient, greedy, and utterly reckless way in which men of the Old South stripped away forests, raised as much cotton as they could, ruined the soil, and moved west (if they could) in search of new land to pillage would read this description with amazement. "Contented . . . to take only what a man needs" hardly describes the new cotton kings, though it might apply to his less ambitious second cousin who lolled in the sun while his wife scraped the meager soil of her "salat" garden. The epithets, the phrasing, the very rhythms of this passage might have come straight out of Ransom's "The South—Old or New" or his soon-to-be-written *God Without Thunder*. Nevertheless, this was Tate's own book, and in it one finds the first rather vague statements of ideas which were to be central to his later poems, fiction, and essays—the idea, for example, of Nature as a chaos of Quality into which man would vanish were it not for Dogma. Or the idea of moral responsibility as founded upon the direct ownership and management of property. It was under this that Tate attempted to bring together and resolve a fundamental contradiction in his book.

Describing the planters, whom he acknowledged to be only a small minority, Tate wrote,

"In the Lower South everybody was 'on the make.' The profits from one year's crop were often enough to set a man up as a planter, and to set him up in style. . . . The Lower South, which has been sentimentalized over more than any other section of the country as the last stronghold of chivalry and the abode of true romance, is thus seen to have been largely a society of *nouveaux riches*. But like *nouveaux riches* everywhere they speedily took on the customs and manners of the local *haute noblesse*."[34]

And how were a people on the make suddenly transformed into defenders of the traditions of European agrarian aristocracies "contented to live upon a modest conquest of nature"? By responsibility:

[33] Pp. 301-302.   [34] P. 33.

"The impulse of [an] agrarian ruling class is to identify its power with inherited responsibility. This identification of power and responsibility is the best basis for a society. . . . Men are everywhere the same, and it is only the social system that imposes a check upon the acquisitive instinct, accidentally and as the condition of a certain prosperity, that in the end makes for stability and creates the close ties among all classes which distinguished a civilization from a mere social machine. Only the agricultural order in the past has achieved this."[35]

One thinks of the Enclosure Acts and wonders how much Tate really knew about life under the *haute noblesse* of a Europe whose virtues he claimed for the South. Anyway, responsibility, he asserted, even mitigated many of the evils of slavery. The Negro did not suffer from the industrial laborer's feeling of not belonging to an institution or class, and his owner felt a responsibility for the slave. Indeed, "For society as a whole the modern system is probably inferior to that of slavery; the classes are not so closely knit; and the employer feels responsible to no law but his own desire. Industrialism comes in the end to absentee landlordism on a grand scale; this was comparatively rare in the Old South."[36] Jefferson Davis often vanished when Tate, seizing any weapon that came to hand, turned aside to take a whack at Industrialism and the North.

Though he held onto his decorum, Ransom was hardly less aggressive than Tate. In February of 1929 he began a book tentatively entitled "Giants for Gods," in which he hoped to draw together more closely the many strands of his thoughts on art, science, and culture, reworking and adding to the ideas of "The Third Moment." Even while it was under way, he wrote to E. P. Dutton offering to do still another book entitled "Dixie: the Future of the South," that would expand the ideas laid down in "The South—Old and New." By July he still had received no reply (and nothing ever came of the proposal), but he had the satisfaction of seeing "The South Defends its Heritage" published in *Harper's Monthly Magazine* for June.[37] This article, which he

[35] Pp. 55-56.   [36] P. 43.
[37] From a letter, Ransom to Tate, dated July 4, 1929, now in the Princeton University Library.

had first called "Reconstructed but Unregenerate," was essentially the same as "The South—Old or New," and even reproduced some of the latter's phrasing, as in the central proposition that "The South is unique on this continent for having founded and defended a culture which was according to the European principles of culture; and the European principles had better look to the South if they are to be perpetuated in this country."[38] Having failed in his first attempt to interest a national journal of opinion, Ransom probably did not mind the change of title required by the editors of *Harper's*. (He was able to restore his original title when he combined his essays to form his contribution to *I'll Take My Stand*.) This time he dropped his analysis of the pioneer spirit into its masculine and feminine components and concluded with a call to Western and Southern agrarians to unite against industrialism.

Far more energy and originality went into his essays, "Flux and Blur in Contemporary Art," which came out in the *Sewanee Review* for July, and "Classical and Romantic," which appeared in *The Saturday Review of Literature* during September. In both he pushed on with his examination of the epistemological differences between the sciences and the arts. The second essay was particularly important to him, for in it he condensed several chapters from "The Third Moment," which he was then reshaping for inclusion in "Giants for Gods." A most significant development was his coming around to Tate's view that religion offered the "only effective defence" against progress, socialism, and the evils of the American economic system, and was the only real guarantee of security and enjoyment.[39] This assumption was the very heart of the new book—and the proposition Ransom needed for his long-deferred retort to the Northerners who had jeered at the Fundamentalists.

But what a religion Ransom meant! In a letter to Tate written sometime late in the spring of 1927 he had termed himself "a desperate Positivist, Nominalist, Philistine, Sensationalist, and Sceptic," suspicious of all supersensibles, and he was nonetheless so now. But he believed that any aesthetic theory must apply to all the arts and all the sources of aesthetic satisfaction, among which he now placed religion—it must be able, as he told Tate, to

[38] See Vol. CLIX, p. 109.

[39] Ransom to Tate, July 4, 1929. The two essays are discussed in Chapter Six.

show a relation between St. Augustine and the history of painting, music, or architecture. To this end, he worked out a system of correlatives which summed up all his ideas about art, science, industry, the agrarian society, myth, religious ritual, and the contemporary fragmentation of the mind. He had prepared himself by wide reading among such writers as Whitehead, Karl Pearson, Bergson, Hume, Coleridge, Milton, and Paul Elmer More, but his conception of myth—which enabled him to accept Tate's argument for the necessity of the religious sanction and to bring together such seemingly disparate modes under the heading of the "aesthetic"—was all his own, going back to his long-standing belief in the division of the mind into the reason and the sensibility and the need for an environment which satisfied both. Myths, he now argued, were fictions whereby man could represent the whole body of his experience and put himself in the right, the unified relation with the world. But the myths were precarious: there was always the danger that the reason would take them over and turn them into systems of absolutes, taint them with the Spirit of Science and secularize them. That, he told Tate, was what the Christians had done. But the secularizing process had not gone nearly so far with the Fundamentalists. They still had a proper respect for the God of the Old Testament, who was not rational and systematic. They had some of the old mythic sense. They believed in a God *with* thunder.[40]

Ransom tried out some of his assumptions in his letters to Tate, then in Paris, and he read portions of his new book to his friends. He even sent a chapter to Warren, who was now a Rhodes Scholar at Oxford. (This was all that Warren read of the work until 1934.) But only Tate had any strong interest in it. Yet this book, which was retitled *God Without Thunder* when it was published in the summer of 1930, came nearest to fulfilling Davidson's hope that they might write a "philosophy of Southern life" (though Davidson probably did not expect anything so "philosophical" as this). In it may be found the clearest—and most unabashed—statement of the assumptions upon which Agrarianism rested, whether all of its spokesmen recognized these assumptions or not. It should be remembered that even as he was writing the book, Ransom had

[40] Ransom's theory of myth and its relation to other aesthetic activities is examined in detail in Chapter Six.

offered to prepare a philosophy of the South for E. P. Dutton, and much that would have gone into the proposed book found its way into this work. The very heart of it, and of Agrarian philosophy, was Ransom's conceptions of the aesthetic life and the function of myth. Farm labor and an agrarian culture established upon small subsistence farms, he maintained, permitted the proper exercise of the sensibility and enabled the whole man to function as an entity whose total experience can best be represented in myths and the arts. But under an unchecked industrialism the sensibility withered, and the reason, now unopposed, dominated all thought and conduct, producing the dehumanized abstractions and the drab life that characterized the Northern technological culture. Insofar as his friends sought philosophical sanction for their beliefs, it was to these assumptions that they came. Only Tate, the one actually most sympathetic with Ransom's ideas, made any significant departure from them. Ransom, holding to his naturalistic position, maintained that myths resorted to the supernatural in order to represent the fullness of the natural. The "absolutes" of religion were really fictions, and in the end one was left with an infinitely mysterious and ultimately unknowable universe upon which the mind projected such absolutes in order to be able to function at all. Tate, while accepting many of Ransom's explanations of the need for myth and tradition, continued to search for true absolutes and came finally to believing in their existence apart from any projecting or acknowledging mind. Nevertheless, once allowance for this significant difference has been made, it is proper to say that in *God Without Thunder* may be found virtually the whole rationale of Agrarianism.[41]

For all that, it was an intensely personal, even a private, book and not what Davidson and the others had in mind. Long before it appeared the friends had agreed that a symposium would give greater range and appeal to their answer to the North. Ruling out "sentimental conservatives of an extreme type" (what they had called "high-caste Brahmins" in their Fugitive days) and hoping to emphasize "trans-Appalachian Southern thought," according to a memorandum drawn up at one of their informal meetings, they considered asking William E. Dodd, Broadus Mitchell, Gerald

[41] See Chapter Six, pp. 259ff.

Johnson, Stringfellow Barr, Chancellor Kirkland of Vanderbilt, Julia Peterkin, and many others, but they approached only Johnson and Barr, who turned them down. (How little they understood opinion in the South is shown by this list. Johnson was to be one of their most persistent and scornful critics; Barr would soon be involved in public debates with Ransom; and Chancellor Kirkland was vehement in repudiating them.)

In the end, they turned to close acquaintances for contributions. One of the first to be asked to take part was Warren. Except for some correspondence regarding his part in the Fugitives' anthology, he had been out of touch with most of the group, but he had been coming by his own paths to something of the same position. After receiving a master's degree in English from the University of California in June, 1927, he had gone on to Yale for a year and then to New College, Oxford, as a Rhodes Scholar. During his stay in New Haven, he had frequently visited the Tates, and a review, "Hawthorne, Anderson and Frost," which he wrote for the *New Republic*, shows that he was impressed by Tate's argument on the contemporary poet's need for tradition and myth.[42] More important was a contract to do a biography of John Brown which Tate helped him obtain from Payson and Clarke.[43] Warren began work early in 1928. During the summer he spent some time at Harpers Ferry, where he talked with the last surviving witness of Brown's raid, and he kept at the biography after settling in Oxford. Though far from his source material and surrounded by new friends and distractions, he pushed on so rapidly that by March 21, 1929, he was able to report to Tate that the end was in sight. Shortly afterward he was in trouble with it and hoped to get Caroline Gordon's advice.[44] Whether this did the trick or not, he managed to get the book done in time for publication in November. It was easily the most readable account and the most penetrating appraisal of the gaunt fanatic yet to appear, and it earned an admiring review from Allan Nevins. But not many

[42] The review appeared in the issue for May 10, 1928.

[43] When he signed the contract, Warren was twenty-two and had published only two poems in *The New Republic* apart from his work for *The Fugitive*. Perhaps because it took such long chances on unknown young men, Payson and Clarke got into difficulty soon afterward. After an attempt at reorganization, it disappeared in 1931.

[44] From letters, Warren to Tate, March 21 and April 9, 1929, now in the Princeton University Library.

readers; only a few hundred copies were sold in that disastrous season.

Someone was needed to discover the real Brown amidst all the legends and folksay, and the distortions or calculated omissions of earlier partisan biographies. Warren had tried hard to find the man, and, despite inexperience with research and writing, despite his dependence on the very accounts he hoped to supersede, he did well. He could not really explain a man who had never, in all his attempts, been able to explain himself; yet without knowing it Warren had encountered in Brown a prototype of the principal figure in many of his later works: that alienated egotist and victim of aimless and intolerable energies turned inward by monomanic self-absorption and self-deception because, as Tate had helped Warren to see, he had nothing outside himself to which he might refer.[45]

Going out to California had made Warren newly aware of his own region and his awareness had been intensified by his research for the book. Thus, when he paid a quick visit to Nashville during the long vacation from Oxford in 1929, he was prepared to sympathize with the new interests of his old friends. Their comments on the aimlessness of contemporary culture carried more force now that he began to see Brown as an abstract idealist capable of any savagery for the sake of his private vision, and he was much impressed with their crusading zeal. Yet, though a young and highly strung man, he kept his head among all their passions. Not for him was any reduction of the Civil War to a conflict between "class rule and religion *versus* democracy and science," or to a conspiracy by miserly industrialists against courtly squires whose generous affability was an insufferable rebuke. Writing of the Southern reaction to the speeches of the Northern demagogues who would have "made the gallows glorious like the cross," he remarked,

> "These people in the South should have understood that most of the people in the North who listened to the 'higher law' sermons went home, promptly forgot that the gallows was glorious like the cross, and were content to mind their own business and vote, in the process of minding that business, for

[45] The biography is considered more extensively in Chapter Nine.

a high tariff. But the people in the South failed to understand, made their own speeches, and retained their touching faith in the laborious justice of the law."[46]

Warren was not then, nor was he ever to become, a "techy" partisan. Nevertheless, when his friends asked him to contribute an essay on the place of the Negro in the Southern agrarian economy he consented. It was a hard assignment, and after returning to Oxford he worked at it slowly for he wanted to avoid stirring up unnecessary opposition. It was one of the last to be finished.

Andrew Nelson Lytle, on the other hand, had no wish whatever to avoid getting up a row. A native of Murfreesboro, Tennessee, and graduate of Vanderbilt in the class of 1925, he had been a close friend of Warren and other Fugitives and had contributed one poem to the magazine. His family had farmed in Rutherford County since shortly after the Revolution and its ties went back to colonial military and political leaders in North Carolina; thus, though it had been established by plain people, it had some reason to regard itself as part of the Southern aristocracy. After graduation, Lytle had studied drama at Yale and worked for a time in the New York theatre. Now he was living at Monteagle, about eighty miles southeast of Nashville, and working on a biography of Nathan Bedford Forrest. Like Tate he had reacted with extreme disgust to New York, and he had come back to the South to rediscover and rededicate himself to the old values and mores he had long taken for granted. When Ransom and Davidson asked him to take part in the symposium, he accepted at once, seeing here a chance to express feelings toward the North which were exceedingly bitter. So bitter, indeed, that Ransom, who admired his courage, worried lest his piece be unacceptable. But his energy was useful. While Warren was at home during the summer of 1929, Lytle went up to Guthrie for a short visit, and his ferocity and vehemence helped to bring his friend into the plan.

Not so contentious but more valuable for the book was Herman C. Nixon, a native of Alabama who had come to Vanderbilt to teach history after receiving a doctorate from the University of Chicago in 1925, but had left in 1928 for a better position at Tulane. Though he eventually returned to Vanderbilt in 1940, Nixon

---

[46] *John Brown, The Making of a Martyr* (New York, 1929), p. 391.

was away during the whole Agrarian interval and was never part of the inner group around Ransom, Davidson, and Tate, who had come back from Paris in January of 1930 and settled on the Cumberland River just outside Clarksville, Tennessee, within fifty miles of Nashville. Indeed, though at first a strong enthusiast, Nixon later felt compelled to repudiate his ties with the group; but for the present he was a good recruit, for he had done much research in the Populist movement and was well informed on the economic background of Southern problems. A more active member was John Donald Wade, a Georgian then in his mid-thirties, who had joined the English Department at Vanderbilt in 1928 after teaching at the University of Georgia and serving as an editor of the *Dictionary of National Biography*. With the remaining contributors, the connection with the group did not go much beyond mailing in their essays. Stark Young sent a nostalgic piece on the Southern past, but by means of his drama criticism, playwrighting, and free lance journalism he had worked out a satisfactory way of life in the very New York the others so detested. Melancholy John Gould Fletcher, a founder of Imagism and after Young the biggest "name" that they had enlisted, had recently turned to social criticism and was glad to have a medium for his ideas about life in America, which were not so welcome in the journals as his poems. Lastly, Henry Blue Kline, who had just received a master's degree in English from Vanderbilt, was flattered to be asked. Ransom had written to Tate early in 1930 that it would be easy to make proselytes and had proposed that the symposium be limited to a few "charter members." Actually, recruiting Kline, whose essay was the feeblest in the collection, shows how little significant support they could muster. Once the book was out he, along with Young and Fletcher, ceased to have any connection with the group.

V

By late summer in 1930, *I'll Take My Stand*, "By Twelve Southerners," was in the press. It had not been easy to get it there. The essays had been slow in coming in, there had been disputes over the title,[47] and some of the leaders had been so discouraged early in

[47] Tate and Warren had wanted to call the book "A Tract Against Communism." When *I'll Take My Stand* was finally chosen, Warren thought it a

the year as to propose abandoning the project for the time being and aim at publication in 1931. Surprisingly, it was the usually diffident Ransom who insisted on keeping at it. He recognized that they might be making fools of themselves; yet he was so on fire with "the Cause," as he and his friends called it, that he even hoped they might be able to buy a weekly county newspaper with the profits from the book and make it not only an organ for their views but a means of publishing tracts and a periodical of some sort. He was weary of academic life and ready to take on journalism if enough money could be made from it.[48] This scheme died quickly, but once the book was safely with the publishers, the others began to be as excited as Ransom. More and more it seemed that the book, far from being the culmination of a single effort, would be the beginning of a great campaign to awaken the region from the hypnotic dream of a New South on progressive Northern lines. Ransom, Tate, and Davidson, who were more fired up than they had been even in the glorious days of launching *The Fugitive* (though Davidson had his moments of melancholy indecision which greatly inconvenienced the others), did not even want to wait for the book to come out. They thought of publishing a manifesto in advance to stir up interest. This, too, was put aside (though Ransom's version of one developed into the "Statement of Principles" that headed the book), but they soon had their chance to make an impression. During the summer *The Virginia Quarterly Review* published a seemingly innocuous essay by Stringfellow Barr (whom the Agrarians had once thought of enlisting) entitled "Shall Slavery Come South?" His argument was simply that by encouraging a controlled industrialism, the South might strengthen its position in the nation while avoiding the evils, the "slavery," of the system. This was about what Davidson himself had said in his essay, "First

---

terrible title—"the god-damnedest thing I ever heard of." (From a letter to Tate dated May 19, 1930, now in the Princeton University Library.)

[48] From letters to Tate dated January 5, 1929, and "Saturday the 15th," now in the Princeton University Library. On the first Tate has added an initialed note pointing out that the year should be 1930, for the letter had been written to welcome Tate home from his stay in France as a Guggenheim Fellow, and he returned early in 1930. The slip would be easy to make just after New Year's Day. Internal references to the progress of negotiations for a contract make clear that the second letter was written early in 1930. Professor Virginia Rock has appended a note to it suggesting that the date is February 15, 1930, because a contract for the book was signed on February 25.

Fruits of Dayton." The only serious fault they could find in Barr's essay was its proposal that the region invest in equipment at a time when the nation as a whole had developed its industrial plant in excess of its real market. Barr's recommendations would only make worse those conditions which had brought about the Great Depression, now well into its first year but still unrecognized for the disaster it was. But this was not what roused the three friends. By now their feelings over industrialism in the South were so high that *any* suggestion for expanding it touched them on the raw. Here was the chance to get their ideas before the public ahead of their book's appearance, and on September 20, 1930, they signed and sent off to *The Virginia Quarterly Review* and a number of influential Southern newspapers, including the *Nashville Tennessean*, an open letter in which they denounced Barr's proposal and asserted that industrialism would be the ruin of the South whereas the only way to preserve the good life indigenous to the region was to encourage an agrarian economy based upon small subsistence farms. Their argument, however, was presented from an aesthetic rather than an economic position and emphasized the superior satisfactions of life on a Southern farm rather than the dangers of industrial expansion at this time. But because the South, always far below the rest of the nation in per capita income, had begun to feel the Depression (even in Nashville people were beginning to talk about hard times), their letter attracted much attention, particularly as its recommendations were exactly contrary to those Southerners had grown used to hearing. Not all the attention was cordial. Chancellor Kirkland, moving quickly to dissociate Vanderbilt University from the proposals of several of its best-known faculty members, issued a statement for the papers in which he called their proposals impractical and "academic." (A small but telling irony that the head of an institution for higher learning used "academic" as a pejorative term.) Others were not so ready to dismiss them. George Fort Milton, usually an advocate of closer rapport with Northern business, suggested in his *Chattanooga News* on October 18 that a debate be held between the Nashville group and any young men from Richmond who agreed with Barr. The *Richmond Times-Dispatch* took up the idea and made arrangements for Ransom to confront Barr in the Richmond civic auditorium on November 14. For days in advance the *Times-Dispatch* published front-page stories on the "national" excitement over the debate, the celebrities who would attend, the number of Boy Scouts needed to handle the crowd. "Intellectually and popularly," it boasted, "the event is expected to prove the most brilliant affair of the kind ever presented in Richmond."

It was hardly that, though the blame did not rest with Ransom. The audience was immense: nearly 3,500 people came, including several governors and other distinguished figures from literary, political, and academic circles. Ellen Glasgow, Henry S. Canby, Norman Thomas, Howard Mumford Jones, and Henry Mencken attended, and Sherwood Anderson took the chair. When it came time to introduce the speakers, Anderson made a speech of his own in which, without any prior warning, he preempted some of Ransom's key points concerning the miseries under industrialism and what they did to prepare the way for Communism. Ransom, who spoke first, had to drop out pages from his prepared speech and improvise transitions on the spot in order to avoid going over the same ground. Nevertheless, he spoke for nearly fifty minutes and developed the argument already put forward in his essays and in *God Without Thunder*: industry robbed work of its satisfaction, destroyed leisure and the enjoyment of the arts, and made impossible the right attitude toward nature on which all humane living depended. When Ransom finished, Barr rose and for twenty minutes fired off witticisms at Ransom's expense. Insofar as he tried to make an argument of it, he maintained that industrialism was already established and that attitudes such as Ransom's simply made more difficult the effort to control it and mitigate its evils. Neither man looked deeply into the economic imbalance industrialism had brought upon the whole nation. No winner was announced when the debate was over, but Davidson, who reported on it for the *Chattanooga News*, thought that Ransom got a little the better of the applause. The crowd had come in a sober mood and Barr's flippancy had offended many.

The affair helped publicize *I'll Take My Stand*, which came out shortly afterward, and it showed that there was widespread interest in any serious discussion of Southern affairs. But the book was misunderstood and most of the reviews were hostile. The essayists had too readily supposed that other Southerners would grant their assumptions, accept their partial definitions, and concur with their attitudes. For example, they referred constantly and almost casually to *the* Southern tradition, by which they meant a way of life to be found in small farming communities in some (but certainly not all) parts of the South and going back, so they supposed, to the forms and customs to be found in small European communities, particularly in outlying English villages. But this is not what the Southern tradition meant to many of their readers. As Dudley Wynn later pointed out, "For most English and American people, tradition, if they are aware of it at all, includes the Reformation, the Enlightenment, the democratic movement, the industrial movement." This certainly was not what Tate would have meant by the term. Then, turning to the meaning of the term for Southerners, Wynn added,

> "There is another element in the 'tradition' of the South which must not be overlooked. If many plantation owners in the Old South were Toryish squires, many others were Whiggish children of the Enlightenment, skeptics, devotees of Reason, and ardent apostles of democracy.... Their doctrines were radically republican and not authoritarian. Appeal to the tradition of the Old South means appeal to many ideas of the French Revolution period, which are, at bottom, progressivist ideas. Take away the Jeffersonian, reasonable gentlemen of the Old South, and then take away the mass of Fundamentalists and bourgeois rugged individualists, and there is little left as a basis for revival of a stable authoritarian polity.... Tradition in the South ... includes the Protestant and progressivist traditions, and any appeal to tradition is likely to uncover some amazing contradictions and surprises."[49]

With no clear conception of the meaning of many of the key terms used, readers were likely to take their definitions from Lytle's reckless piece, "The Hind Tit," by far the most flamboyant and memorable essay in the book, and to suppose that the Agrarians wanted to go back to cottage crafts and a way of life which had vanished from all but the most remote sections. This seems to explain a contemptuous editorial in the *New York Times* which called *I'll Take My Stand* "a sort of boys' Froissart set of tales" and the essayists "Twelve Canutes, ... without any Saxon conquests to

[49] "A Liberal Looks at Tradition," *VQR*, XII (January, 1936), 71-72.

their credit, bidding the waves of the industrial North Sea to fall back."[50] Southern papers were not so harsh. Though opposed to the position taken by Lytle, which they, too, believed to be more representative of the book as a whole than it really was, they welcomed the essays as stimuli to self-appraisal. But descriptions of the book so distorted its true nature that the favorable interest aroused by the debate in Richmond was dissipated and sales were poor. Discouraged by the reviews, Harper and Brothers virtually dropped the book. Except where further debates stirred up a brief local interest, the public soon forgot all about it.

Though the public soon forgot it, the literary scholars did not, and over the years there have been so many allusions to *I'll Take My Stand* that it becomes easy to think of the book as a unified work rather than as the collection of miscellaneous essays that it actually was. The introduction, subtitled "A Statement of Principles," served notice that apart from a little consultation on the topics to be covered there had been no further collaboration and each man was responsible only for the views in his essay. However, all the essays, in the words of the introduction, "tend to support a Southern way of life against what may be called the American or prevailing way; and all as much as agree that the best terms in which to represent the distinction are contained in the phrase, Agrarian *versus* Industrial." But what was the Southern way? At first a reader might be put off by apparent differences among the contributors. As Stark Young described it, it resembled in tempo and manner the supposed life of the great English county families, whereas Ransom seemed to liken it to life in the outlying villages of England. H. C. Nixon called for an ordinary middle-class society no different from that found in farming communities all over the United States, while Lytle seemed to want a return to a rough-and-ready, homespun life only a little distance removed from the frontier. And though Ransom would admit a limited industrialism, Lytle spoke up for the wholly self-sufficient family that wove its own clothes and mended its own shoes.

[50] February 15, 1931.

Nevertheless, by the "Statement of Principles," to which all contributors subscribed (though it was actually written by Ransom alone) and by the total effect of the book there was defined an image of the good agrarian life which, though blurred at the edges, prevailed over the differences among the essays. It was based upon the life of the yeoman farmers of small communities in the Mississippi Valley and in its essentials it bore little resemblance to life in the Old Dominion or Charleston or on the great plantations of the legend of the Old South. Still, the contributors did ornament their account of the yeoman's life with details from the aristocratic tradition. After describing the simple food, clothing, games, and folk-arts of the communities, they went on to claim for them a cultivated humanism that stressed familiarity with the classics, Shakespeare, and the eighteenth-century essayists, an authoritarian religion, social arts, and a paternalistic socio-political structure controlled by affable old gentlemen. In this genial life the fine arts were valued in proportion to their contribution to the charm of social occasions. All in all, people lived happily and at a low intensity; they were unlikely to produce any ideas, works of art, or personalities of much originality or profundity.

Throughout the book the contributors repeatedly and emphatically rejected concepts of economic determinism. When they referred to the Civil War as a struggle between agrarianism and industrialism, they used these terms to describe cultures rather than economies. Nonetheless, when they attempted to describe the Enemy, industrial society, when they wrote—almost always with capitals—about Industry, the North, the North East, Business, and the Banks, they fell back upon abstractions as simplistic as those of the most dogmatic Marxist, and like him they attributed to these bogeys but two animating forces: an insatiable lust for money and an implacable hatred of anything, such as love of nature, which in any way seemed to impede the acquisition of wealth. These abstractions loomed monstrously before the backdrop of the City, a symbol made up of the most hideous features of New York, Chicago, Pittsburgh, and Detroit and representing all of America north of the Mason-Dixon line. Conveniently, the writers ignored the farmers of Indiana, New Jersey, and upstate New York; they forgot the men who raised dairy cattle in Ohio, sheep in New Hamp-

shire, and apples in Maine; they overlooked the small tradesmen
and self-employed craftsmen in countless villages of the North.

Such naive parochialism disfigures even Ransom's "Statement of
Principles," which is actually a series of aphoristic *pensées* summing
up his thinking over the preceding eight years. Its central concern,
which was to be the central concern of all the major work of Ransom, Tate, and Warren from this period on, is that man enjoy the
right relation with "mysterious and contingent" nature, which Ransom, following the line of reasoning that went all the way back to
his decision to return to Vanderbilt after Oxford, said was presently
impossible because of the tyranny of the reason over the sensibility.
As in *God Without Thunder*, Ransom argued in the statement and
his own contribution, "Reconstructed but Unregenerate," by a system
of correlatives. Accordingly, industrialism is a consequence of the
reason's subjection of the sensibility. The very division of the nation into the industrial North and the agrarian South is but another
manifestation of the division of the mind. The North—bleak, abstract, materialistic, greedy, arrogant—is the realm of the reason.
The South—florid, concrete, interested in little charming things of
no utility, gentle and inclined to give way rather than quarrel shrilly
—is the realm of the sensibility. For all the elegance and persuasive-
ness of his prose style, this was bad history, worse geography, and
completely impossible psychology.

The heart of Ransom's argument is reached in three paragraphs
at the center of the "Statement of Principles." If it were possible
to claim an explicit philosophy for the book as a whole, it would be
found here. Tate's essay, "Remarks on the Southern Religion," is
by far the most philosophical in manner, but its scope is confined by
its subject and its assumptions are ones to which few of the others
would have assented; moreover, it is a personal statement whereas
the introduction was subscribed to by all contributors. Too much
weight must not be given to that fact, however, as some subscribed
mainly to please Ransom. Still, there is nothing in the introduction
which any personal statement opposes, and most of the essays give
some support to the thesis contained in the three central paragraphs:

"Religion can hardly expect to flourish in an industrial society.
Religion is our submission to the general intention of a nature
that is fairly inscrutable; it is the sense of our role as creatures

within it. But nature industrialized, transformed into cities and artificial habitations, manufactured into commodities, is no longer nature but a highly simplified picture of nature. We receive the illusion of having power over nature, and lose the sense of nature as something mysterious and contingent. The God of nature under these conditions is merely an amiable expression, a super-fluity, and the philosophical understanding ordinarily carried in the religious experience is not there for us to have.

"Nor do the arts have a proper life under industrialism, with the general decay of sensibility which attends it. Art depends, in general, like religion, on a right attitude to nature; and in particular on a free and disinterested observation of nature that occurs only in leisure. Neither the creation nor the understanding of works of art is possible in an industrial age except by some local and unlikely suspension of the industrial drive.

"The amenities of life also suffer under the curse of a strictly-business or industrial civilization. They consist in such practices as manners, conversation, hospitality, sympathy, family life, romantic love—in the social exchanges which reveal and develop sensibility in human affairs. If religion and the arts are founded on right relations of man-to-nature, these are founded on right relations of man-to-man."

In "Reconstructed but Unregenerate," Ransom repeated—in virtually the same words—the claim he had made in "The South—Old or New" and "The South Defends Its Heritage" that Southern culture was founded upon "European principles." These, he asserted, encouraged the right relation with nature and one's fellow men because they tempered by humility and a respect for leisure: "It is the European intention to live materially along the inherited line of least resistance, in order to put the surplus of energy into the free life of the mind." The best instance still to be found in Europe might be found in the "self-sufficient, backward-looking, intensely provincial" rural communities of England. But in industrial America, which resembled "a Prussianized state which is strictly organized for war and can never consent to peace," there was no such humility, no respect for leisure:

"Ambitious men fight, first of all, against nature; they propose to put nature under their heel; this is the dream of scientists burrowing in their cells, and then of the industrial men who beg of their secret knowledge and go out to trouble the earth. But after a certain point this struggle is vain, and we only use ourselves up if we prolong it. Nature wears out man before man can wear out nature; only a city man, a laboratory man, a man cloistered from normal contacts with the soil, will deny that. It seems wiser to be moderate in our expectations of nature, and respectful; and out of so simple a thing as respect for the physical earth and its teeming life comes a primary joy, which is an inexhaustible source of arts and religions and philosophies."

The industrialists put a good face on their belligerency by talking about Progress, Service, and divine discontent. These are American slogans, and the South, following "European principles" had assumed that a man should take just as much as he needs from nature and devote the rest of his time to enjoying the fruits of his labors through the social arts of dress, conversation, manners, the table, the hunt, politics, oratory, and the pulpit. "These," Ransom explained, "were arts of living and not arts of escape; they were also community arts, in which every class of society could participate after its kind. The South took life easy, which is itself a tolerably comprehensive art." He conceded that if the old mellow existence were to be recovered, some industrialism would be required to restore prosperity to the region. But it should be accepted "with very bad grace" to keep it in bounds. Toward this end he proposed reawakening the old Southern scorn for materialism, noisy salesmanship, and dollar-chasing and joining forces with Western agrarians, perhaps within the structure of the Democratic party, to work for the preservation of rural life.

The ultimate authority for Ransom's criticisms and proposals for reform was metaphysical: a pattern of interlinking conceptions of Nature, perception, *a priori* values, and the character and function of the will in an indeterminate universe. But the immediate authority was his idea of "European principles" and his image of the Old South. Tate, too, had written much of these "European principles." Yet for all the two men said, the principles remained elusive and obscure. At most they seemed but a love of leisure, an innate suspicion of all things having to do with cities, machinery, and newfangled ideas, and a certain ceremoniousness in manners and tendency to cling to old customs. And where was the Europe of these principles? Ransom tried to place it among the English provinces, but his quadrants were vague:

> "There is no doubt that the English tradition expresses itself in many more or less intangible ways, but it expresses itself most importantly in a material establishment; and by this I mean the stable economic system by which Englishmen are content to take their livelihood from the physical environment. . . . They have elected to live their comparatively easy and routine lives in accordance with the tradition which they inherited, and they have consequently enjoyed a leisure, a security, and an intellectual freedom that were never the portion of pioneers."

This was written after the General Strike of 1926 by a man who admired Hardy, knew his Conrad, and had spent three years in England as a Rhodes Scholar. It might have been written by one whose only acquaintance with England and the Continent came through the works of Trollope and Surtees. Ignoring the great industries of the Midlands and the Ruhr, the canals and railroads, the great ports such as Liverpool, Marseilles, and Hamburg, the cartels, and the slums described by Charles Dickens and Karl Marx, Ransom fixed his eye on quaint market towns, thatched hamlets, and lonely little farms in the outlying counties. What he saw was charming—to the visitor. He overlooked the harshness and the deprivations that impoverished the spirit and induced a miserliness of feeling and imagination, a materialism as fierce as might be found in any industrialist, and a flinty hostility toward aspiration and distinction in the realm of ideas and the arts.

Turning to the South in search of the "European principles" Ransom ignored the acquisitiveness of the self-made planter aristocrats. He did not consider the extent to which the leisure he celebrated was simply vacant idleness made possible for the upper classes by slavery and later by a labor surplus and forced upon the lower classes by poverty, malnutrition, and the growth cycles of staple crops. Speaking of the "free life of the mind" which an agrarian culture made possible, he put aside the intolerance of the Klansmen and the fundamentalist sects and the rigid suppression of any kind of social criticism after 1830; speaking of the "respect for the physical earth and its teeming life" that evoked "a primary joy," he, like Tate before him, put aside the image of gutted forests and eroded farm lands. And the arts: how pleasant to call them "arts of living and not arts of escape," as if the high, intense, and impassioned arts—the arts so rarely found in the country and usually seen in their finest, most humanly significant form in the great cities—were intended for evading life. With that genial phrase he slipped around an exceedingly difficult problem for the Agrarians: the fact that for the fine arts and, indeed, virtually all great achievements of human imagination, the agrarian areas depended upon the industrial and mercantile centers. The arts of the Old South—and most of the New South, for that matter— were utterly meager and insipid when they were not imported. Noisy, dirty, brutal, indifferent as the cities might be, it was to them that the gifted usually went to find the free life of the mind. If some of them left in disgust and retired to the country, they still kept their economic ties with the cities, for it was there that they found the appreciation and the market, small and ill-paying as it might be, for their ideas.

Ransom's criticisms of the American scene were sharp, shrewd, and well-merited, but they were undercut by pretentious claims he made for the Old South and rural life. He was writing fables. In his poetry he had skillfully and successfully used a fictive past to interpret the present. Here, however, he had confused fiction with history.

The task of proving Ransom's assertion that arts and artist prospered more under an agrarian dispensation was taken up by Davidson in "A Mirror for Artists," an essay quite unlike anything a reader of his poetry would expect and much better than Ransom's. Temperate, informed, and withal good-natured, it offers an excellent commentary on the alienation of the contemporary artist even though it does not succeed in proving that

> "the making of an industrial society will extinguish the meaning of the arts, as humanity has known them in the past, by changing the conditions of life that have given art a meaning. For they have been produced in societies which were for the most part stable, religious, and agrarian; where the goodness of life was measured by a scale of values having little to do with the ma-

terial values of industrialism; where men were never too far removed from nature to forget that the chief subject of art, in the final sense, is nature."

Davidson began by looking into the claim that industrialism encourages the arts by giving men more time for them and making possible their wider distribution. In the "Statement of Principles" Ransom had written, "We have more time in which to consume, and many more products to be consumed. But the tempo of our labors communicates itself to our satisfactions, and these also become brutal and hurried." Davidson picked up this point and added:

"The furious pace of our working hours is carried over into our leisure hours, which are feverish and energetic. We live by the clock. Our days are a muddle of 'activities,' strenuously pursued. We do not have the free mind and easy temper that should characterize true leisure. Nor does the separation of our lives into two distinct parts, of which one is all labor—too often mechanical and deadening—and the other all play, undertaken as a nervous relief, seem to be conducive to a harmonious life. . . . The leisure thus offered is really no leisure at all; either it is pure sloth, under which the arts take on the character of mere entertainment, purchased in boredom and enjoyed in utter passivity, or it is another kind of labor, taken up out of a sense of duty, pursued as a kind of fashionable enterprise for which one's courage must be continually whipped up by reminders of one's obligation to culture."

This is eminently sound. But it is not the whole story.

Quite as sound are Davidson's claims that mass methods of reproduction and distribution have served to spread bad art, that all too often "The product of a humanistic education in an industrial age is most likely to be an exotic, unrelated creature—a disillusionist or a dilettante," and that there is a tendency to enshrine high art for worship by the dedicated few. The artificial relation between the arts and the culture of our time, Davidson argues, originated in the disruption of society by the industrial revolution, the rise of science and materialism, and the emergence of the middle class which did not respect art and the artist:

"Thus arise the works of the Romantic school, in which the artist sets forth 'the fundamental contradiction of principle' between himself and society. The artist is no longer *with* society, as perhaps even Milton, last of classicists, was. He is *against* or *away from* society, and the disturbed relation becomes his essential theme, always underlying his work, no matter whether he evades or accepts the treatment of the theme itself. His evasion may consist in nostalgia for a remote past, mediaeval, Elizabethan, Grecian, which he revives imaginatively or whose characteristic modes he appropriates. He has thus the spiritual solace of retreating to a refuge secure against the doubtful implications of his position in contemporary society. His retreat is a psychological compensation, but there is also an appeal to something that has survival value. He does not so much rebel against a crystallized tradition . . . as retire more deeply within the body of the tradition to some point where he can utter himself with the greatest consciousness of his dignity as an artist."

Davidson goes on to describe the career of the poet with a diminishing audience who turns more and more inward, developing an eccentric style and putting sensibility above thought, or who tries to emulate the scientists by being a "realist" and becomes instead a recorder of unassimilated data. The portrait he sketches is concise, persuasive, and historically sound. It bears some resemblance to his "outland piper" and there are features of Tate to be seen in it, too. But one does not find much of Ransom or Warren.

What shall the artist do? Harmony between the artist and society can be reestablished in an agrarian culture, Davidson believed, but only by social effort from which the artist must not remain aloof. "He must learn to understand and must try to restore and preserve a social economy that is in danger of being replaced altogether by an industrial economy hostile to his interests." The best place for such an economy is among the Southern communities, where the arts have always flourished in harmony with the lives of the citizens, as the richness of folk-art shows. But Southern or not, the artist "must be a person first of all, even though for the time being he may become less of an artist. He must enter the common arena and become a citizen. Whether he chooses, as citizen-

person, to be a farmer or to run for Congress is a matter of individual choice; but in that general direction his duty lies."

Thus ends this remarkable essay, which had for Davidson, Ransom, and Tate significance beyond its place in the symposium. It
was an *apologia* for their own extraordinary shift from the indifference characteristic of their Fugitive days to the activist roles
they now played, and as such it has particular interest for those
concerned with the evolution of their ideas. At no other point in
all his writing was Davidson in such close agreement with his two
friends, and this essay contributes much to one's understanding of
Ransom's essays in *The World's Body* and *The New Criticism* and
Tate's essays, his novel, *The Fathers*, and even his long poem,
"The Seasons of the Soul."

Though many other essays on the precarious situation of the arts
and the artist in an industrial society have been written since this
one came out, it remains among the best. But when one reads that
"only in an agrarian society does there remain much hope of a
balanced life, where the arts are not luxuries to be purchased but
belong *as a matter of course* [the italics are mine] in the routine
of his living," one begins to waver and pull back, especially when
one is told that this happy balance obtained in the Old South.
Davidson wrote confidently about the "gracious civilization . . . ,
true and indigenous, well diffused and well established" in the
antebellum South. He found "beauty and stability of an ordered
life" in the old country homes. He cited the ballads, country songs
and dances, hymns and spirituals, old tales, and the crafts of weaving, quilting, furniture-making, and continued, "As for the more
sophisticated [again my italics] arts, the South has always prac-
ticed them as a matter of course. I shall not attempt to estimate
the Southern contribution to literature with some special array of
names; the impassioned scholars who are busily resurrecting Chiv-
ers, Kennedy, Byrd, Longstreet, Sut Lovengood, and such minor
persons, in their rediscovery of American literature, will presently
also get around again to Cooke, Page, Cable, Allen, and the like."

Alas, it is not very convincing, especially when one remembers
how the South treated Poe and Simms, the dreadfulness of the
works of Page, Cooke, and Allen, the total absence of any com-
poser or painter worth even a moment's attention, or, coming

down to more recent times, the fact that the writers of the Southern Renaissance found almost the whole of their first audiences and for a long time virtually their sole support outside the South. This evidently embarrassed Davidson. Conceding, by implication, that Southern art had not been very impressive in performance, he cited the interruption of the Civil War: without it, he claimed, indigenous art would have had a good chance of springing up in the South "as the inevitable expression of modes of life rather favorable to the arts." It might not have been great art, but "We should, however, recognize that the appearance or non-appearance of a 'great' art or a 'great' artist can hardly be accepted as a final criterion for judging a society." Certainly not. But if one is claiming that a society offered "modes of life rather favorable to the arts" then the criterion, if not final, cannot be written off quite so easily.

Davidson wrote shrewdly of the neglect, bewilderment, and insecurity of the modern artist, but he did not show that the vague thing "Industry" was to blame for more than part of the trouble; he did not really establish that a truly gifted and serious artist would be better off in an agrarian society (which is not the same thing as living in the country to get away from the noise of the city: one may still be working in and for an urban, mercantile-industrial society); and, most significant of all, he gave no instance of such an artist truly established in, expressing, and communicating with an understanding and appreciative agrarian community. Just a few years before, Ransom, in a letter to Tate, had warned of the difficulties that would result if one tried to base a defense of the South on its literature. Davidson's essay showed that the difficulties were multiplied rather than diminished when one took in the other arts as well.

In some ways Tate's "Remarks on the Southern Religion" is one of the best essays ever to come from his desk. Saucy and high-spirited just where one expects it to be sober and admonishing, it has many flashing aphorisms which delight as they illuminate odd angles of the problems he sets before the reader. But it is also too often simply glib. Tate's argument, if one can call it that, proceeds by bold assertion, analogy, and piquant metaphor, and as long as it holds to the maxim and the vivid image, it does well. But when it leaves *pensées* for history *qua* history, it all falls into oversimplification, the fault which stands so near to the virtues of the aphorism and toward which Tate with his partisan passions much inclined. In this essay, which is itself directed against the reductive fallacy, he follows Ransom and Davidson in attempting to explain the effects of a tumult of social, economic, and political forces as the consequences of a single aesthetic or religious attitude. He writes of a fabulous North and a blundering monster called Protestantism and commits thereby the very errors he attacks in others: he takes what he would call a "Long View" of Southern history and religion.

The argument evolves directly from his earlier meditative poems and essays on the need for centers of belief and sanctions of values. What is new is an emphasis upon their enabling man to see nature as it is; that is, Tate shifts his focus and places cognition before ethics. Though the essay has none of Ransom's courtly tone and arch colloquialisms, it might almost be a part of *God Without Thunder*, so closely does it agree with his argument on behalf of myth and dogma. This was apparent to Tate when Ransom sent him the manuscript of the book in the fall of 1929, and he delayed mailing in his essay until he was persuaded that the others in the group fully understood that he had written it without consulting Ransom.

In essence its argument comes to this. An object can be viewed in three ways: as a concrete entity exhibiting universals localized among its unique particularities (the whole view which Tate paradoxically calls the "Short View"); as an instance of a universal— whatever universal the viewer, by his needs or commitments, chooses to regard out of the many exemplified (the partial view which Tate, like Ransom, attributes to Science and History and calls the "Long View"); and as an aggregate of particulars having nothing universal about them (another partial view and the one Tate attributes to the Symbolist poets). Traditional religion is the great codification of the Short View, for it acknowledges the presence of the contingent and inexplicable in a Nature which is intractable and resists man's successful domination: religion acknowledges the possibility of failure. But the Southern religion was secularized by History, by the Long View, which, acknowledging only the typical, predicts success through the smooth operation of its abstract principles. Following Spengler's criticism of contemporary philosophies of history, Tate wrote of their inadequate vision of man,

> "You need not feel any great interest in the rival merits of the Greek and Roman cultures; they were both ideas comprehensible after some comparison under a single law. There is no accident or uncertainty, for the illusion of contingency that seemed to beset the ages of the past is dissolved by the Long View. . . . Or, put otherwise, since the Christian myth is a vegetation rite, varying only in some details from countless other vegetation myths, there is no reason to prefer Christ to Adonis. . . . The Short [religious] View holds that the whole Christ and the whole Adonis are sufficiently differentiated in their respective qualities (roughly details), and that our tradition compels us to choose more than that half of Christ which is Adonis and to take the whole, separate, and unique Christ."

The Western mind, unlike the Eastern European mind (which Ransom, too, cited as an intelligence capable of a total view and response) cannot apprehend the whole religious tradition at once because of its habit of abstraction. Thus, Tate maintains, in the Middle Ages, Dogma, a special form of the Long View, was brought to the defense of tradition: abstraction was applied against an excess of itself and reason used to protect "the other than reasonable, the other than natural." The very heart of the system, as he had argued in "The Fallacy of Humanism," was the doctrine that Nature is fundamentally evil, "For the Church knew that the only way to restrain the practical impulses of her constituency was to put into the mouth of nature the words, *Noli tangere.*" But during the Renaissance Europeans discovered that the reason could be used against the irrational elements of Religion, against those elements that, as Ransom would have put it, resorted to the supernatural in order to represent the fullness of the natural, and the Short View began to give way to the Long View with its emphasis upon logical structures which served the practical economy, which "worked."

In the Old South there existed a "feudal" society without a feudal religion. Disagreeing with "a distinguished contributor to this symposium" (obviously Ransom), Tate argued that the Southerners had gone back to an older economy, the agrarian, not because they had been less rebellious against "European stability" than the Northerners but because that economy was more in harmony with the conditions of labor determined by soil and climate. But though the South "could blindly return to an older secular polity . . . it could not create its appropriate religion." Founded by men pursuing a "capitalistic enterprise," who were "already convinced adherents of large-scale exploitation of nature," it kept their religion, which was "Protestant, aggressive, and materialistic . . . , in origin a non-agrarian and trading religion; hardly a religion at all, but a result of secular ambition." Thus it lacked the perspective necessary to account for and defend its way of life.

Not that they went over wholly to the utilitarian Long View. For "The Southern mind was simple, not top-heavy with learning it had no need of, unintellectual, and composed; it was personal and dramatic, rather than abstract and metaphysical; and it was sensuous because it lived close to a natural scene of great variety and interest." The Southerners, "saw themselves as human beings living by a humane principle, from which they were unwilling to subtract the human so as to set the principle free to operate on an unlimited program of practicality." Instead, they hovered indecisively:

> "They had a religious life, but it was not enough organized with a right mythology. In fact, their rational life was not powerfully united to the religious experience, as it was in mediaeval society, and they are a fine specimen of the tragic pitfall upon which the Western mind has always hovered. Lacking a rational system for the defense of their religious attitude and its base in a feudal society, they elaborated no rational system whatever, no full-grown philosophy; so that, when the post-bellum temptations of the devil, who is the exploiter of nature, confronted them, they had no defense. Since there is, in the Western mind, a radical division between the religious, the contemplative, the qualitative, on the one hand, and the scientific, the natural, the practical on the other, the scientific mind always plays havoc with the spiritual life when it is not powerfully enlisted in its cause; it cannot be permitted to operate alone."

Today's Southerner finds "his religious conviction is inchoate and unorganized; it never had the opportunity to be anything else."

Consequently, his sole alternative for preserving his way of life is political, and it must be active to the point of violence. But the political way is Jefferson's way. It holds that "The ends of man are sufficiently contained in his political destiny." The proposition—the Southerner's only instrument—is "so unrealistic and pretentious that he cannot believe in it." Nevertheless, he must use it "to re-establish a private, self-contained, and essentially spiritual life."

Tate is brisk, bold, and exceedingly sophisticated. But as a summary or even a fable on the culture and the spiritual life of the South before the Civil War, the essay is hardly less than absurd. In a polemic against the abstractions of history one finds this:

> "While the South in the nineteenth century trafficked with Europe in cotton, she took in exchange very little of manner, literature, or the arts. The Southerners were another community on the complete European plan, and they had no need, being independent, of importing foreign art and noblemen, commodities that New England became frantic about after 1830. For New England was one of those abstract-minded, sharp-witted trading societies that must be parasites in two ways: They must live economically on some agrarian class or country, and they must live spiritually likewise. New England lived economically on the South, culturally on England."

Only a page or two earlier Tate had referred to the South's taking "a lively mediaevalism from the novels of Sir Walter Scott," but the contradiction between this and his description of the "community on the complete European plan" and glorious in its cultural independence is perhaps the kind of anomaly that would trouble the historian but not a genial adherent to the Short View. No need here to take into account the thousands of little New England subsistence farms whose owners could hardly be accused of parasitic dependence on anything beyond their stone fences. No need to take into account the literature of New England or to compare it with what the community on the complete European plan had produced. Still, it might have been better had Tate asked himself if Herr Spengler and young Mr. Hollis, to whom he owed so much, had not taken a fairly Long View themselves.

Robert Penn Warren's "The Briar Patch" was wholly of another kind. Written while he was still at Oxford and far from his friends' eve-of-battle tension, it was notably restrained and patiently logical and specific in surveying the position of the Negro and what might be done for him. Yet it had a poet's concern for vividness and for avoiding the clichés that usually crowd pages that treat such a topic in sociological and economic terms. Furthermore, it did not rest upon oversimplifications about the North and South. Not so exciting as Tate's piece and nowhere nearly so important in the history of Agrarianism, it was a much sounder argument, for Warren kept clear of the easy generalizations his friends had accepted while proclaiming most loudly their distrust of all abstractions.

His thesis was simple: the welfare of Southern white man was inextricably bound up with that of the Negro, and to have any chance of success a program aimed at preserving the good life of the past for the white must aim as well at a secure, stable, and dignified life for the Negro. Moreover, Warren reiterated, any person who would obstruct the Negro's self-fulfillment did not respect himself as a man: to deny the dignity and humanity of the Negro was to confess his sense of his own inferiority. But industrialism would bring no help to the Negro. Under it he would be exploited as cheap labor and, because he competed with the poor whites for jobs and forced them to work for almost as little as he did, he would become the target of their hatred and violence—as he was already wherever an industrial economy, in the form of the crop lien system, had been established in an agrarian area. The Negro, Warren believed, could live best on a subsistence farm. "In the past the Southern negro has always been a creature of the small town and farm. That is where he still chiefly belongs, by temperament and capacity; there he has less the character of a 'problem' and more the status of a human being who is likely to find in agriculture and domestic pursuits the happiness that his good nature and easy ways incline him to as an ordinary function of his being." For this he required vocational training: education of the Negroes should aim not "to create a small band of intellectual aristocrats . . . [but] to make the ordinary negro into a competent workman or artisan and a decent citizen." Once the Negroes had more economic freedom, as a result of vocational training, they could support Negro doctors, lawyers, and other professional men. As for those

Negroes who went into industry, they should be permitted to organize and should receive pay equal to the whites', for otherwise the Negroes dragged all labor down.

As for segregation, "Equal but separate" appears to be as far as Warren was then prepared to go. One must be careful to avoid underestimating just how far Warren *had* gone when he insisted on respect for the rights and dignity of the Negro as an individual, and one must recognize that the essay is everywhere suffused with a quiet humanity and decency. Yet reference to the Negro's "good nature" and "easy ways" and the almost casual assumption that the farm was his natural setting suggest that Warren, for all his generous spirit, saw both the Negro and the satisfactions of life on the subsistence farm in too simple terms. There is, one feels, too little realization of what humiliation of the individual even such kindly proposals as these might involve—proposals eminently realistic when judged solely in terms of the regional economy of the time and the limited sums available for Negro education. One feels this because in *Segregation* (1956) Warren himself told us exactly what the Negro wanted most: simply to be treated like everyone else, even if that means suffering, being deprived, and failing along with the rest. Anything that comes to the Negro under a system that makes a distinction between white and black, even if it appears to be to his immediate advantage, is an affront. Two thoughtful Negroes explained it to Warren this way: " 'It's not so much what the Negro wants as what he doesn't want. The main point is not that he has poor facilities. It is that he must endure a constant assault on his ego. He is denied human dignity.' " And: " 'It's different when your fate is on your face. Just that. It's the unchangeableness. Now a white man, even if he knows he can't be President, even if he knows the chances for his son are one in many millions— long odds—still there's an idea there.' "[51] But this was a quarter of a century later. As Warren wrote, he could not talk to Negroes. He could not read John Dollard's *Caste and Class in a Southern Town*, that clumsy, startling book, published in 1937, which showed how much of the Negroes' "good nature" and "easy ways" were a protective manner, so habitual as to be quite unconscious, but readily dropped when the Negroes were among their own people

[51] Robert Penn Warren, *Segregation* (New York, 1956), pp. 41, 43.

and hurt pride, hostility, and even contempt could be revealed without fear. But, for all the limitation of his perspective, Warren wrote with that eye for naturalistic detail which already distinguished his poetry and gave this brief excursion into sociology and economics authority and concreteness not found in most of the other essays. Moreover, he had his vision, here so rudimentary when compared to what it would become in his long poems and the novels, of a man's compelling need to fulfill himself. Otherwise, the essay had little connection with or significance for his development as a writer. It was not in the least philosophical, and it was the philosophical bases of Agrarianism which counted most with him.

Close discussion of the other essays in *I'll Take My Stand* is beyond the scope of this study. However, because certain of their ideas were held by the writers with whom it is concerned, some mention must be made of Owsley's "The Irrepressible Conflict" and Lytle's "The Hind Tit." The first was meant to show that the supposition that the Civil War had been fought over slavery was a gross oversimplification and that an irrepressible conflict of economies—ultimately of philosophies of life for which the economies were but two of many manifestations—was quite as important and possibly even preeminent. But the essay soon fell into oversimplifications of its own when Owsley wrote: "Complex though the factors were which finally caused the war, they all grew out of two fundamental differences which existed between the two sections: the North was commercial and industrial, and the South was agrarian. The fundamental and passionate ideal for which the South stood and fell was the ideal of an agrarian society. All else, good and bad, revolved around this ideal. . . ." Northern "Industrialism" had decided, however, that the agrarian sections must be made subservient. Slavery made a convenient political and moral issue with which Lincoln and Seward might cover Northern aggression and whip up votes and the martial spirits of the factory hands. And so the South was crushed. But the irrepressible conflict went on as Northern schoolmarms came South and tried to subvert all respect for the Southern past and the Southern way of life. It still goes on, Owsley insisted, for the Southern devotion to states' rights impedes the efforts of

Big Business and Industry to concentrate all power in the national government, which they control.

To judge from such subsequent writing as Tate's "More About Reconstruction" and Lytle's "The Lincoln Myth," Owsley's views, which coincided nicely with those of Hollis, probably had much influence among the more dedicated Agrarians.[52] Perhaps it is not unfair to put on this professional historian, who so often regretted that Americans made less use of the past than did any other civilized people, a share of the blame for the groups' failure to formulate a believable image of the past that would give meaning and force to its social criticism. In their exultation over carrying the fight to the enemy, it must have been easy for the Agrarians to listen when an authority told them that the Northern schoolteachers had dedicated themselves to "destroying" something "intangible, incomprehensible, in the realm of the spirit" which was the foundation of that ineffable superiority of the Southerner so infuriating and baffling to his conqueror; easy to forget to ask "But *how* many?" when the historian described a South "turned over to the three millions of former slaves, some of whom could still remember the taste of human flesh"; easy to forget to wonder if any were likely to revert to eating their fellow men when he added, that "the bulk of them were hardly three generations removed from cannibalism." Here, as in so many of his later Agrarian essays, Owsley began with an excellent point. The economic rivalry between the regions unquestionably encouraged controversy. The combination of self-righteousness and sadism in the Abolitionist literature he cited does indeed reflect an almost manic hatred in some Northerners. But as Warren had said, most Northerners who listened to the Abolitionist preachers went home and promptly "forgot that the gallows was glorious like the cross." When they voted for high tariff, they were just minding their own business, not taking part in an organized and vicious campaign against the South. The Agrarians may have admired Owsley's version of the wicked North, but professional historians looked upon it with laughter and scorn.

But nothing such as that evoked by Lytle's "The Hind Tit," which did the Agrarian cause incalculable damage. Lytle had been

[52] "More About Reconstruction," *The New Republic*, LXIII (August 13, 1930), 376-377; "The Lincoln Myth," *The Virginia Quarterly Review*, VII (October, 1931), 620-626.

living in Monteagle, Tennessee, since leaving New York City, and when he wrote the essay he was in close contact with Tate and much under his influence. (Tate celebrated their friendship and their agreement on the futility of contemporary life in "The Oath," one of his finest poems.) Still a young man (he was twenty-six) and accustomed to expressing his opinions with more energy than control, Lytle brought to his subject, the good life on an old-fashioned Southern farm, not only his revulsion from the cities of the North but a love of the region and its folkways and a long-pent-up sense of outrage at the attacks on the rural Southerner which matched, if they did not even exceed, those of Owsley. Furthermore, it is quite likely that he was urged on by Tate, whose influence, together with the very different one of Ransom, can be seen in Lytle's defense of the farmers' charms, signs, and omens: "They are just as useful and necessary to an agrarian economy as the same attempts which come from the chemist's laboratory in an industrial society, and far wiser, because they understand their inadequacy, while the hypotheses of science do not." In any event, Lytle had a good case, but he overstated it with such bluster and exaggeration that he made the whole book look foolish indeed.

His description of the yeoman's life was intended to bear out the claims which Ransom and Davidson had made for the aesthetic satisfaction of farming, not just for the farmer but for his family as well. As a further aim, it was to show that the rewards of this life were inseparable from a subsistence economy which needed the cooperation of the whole family for its realization and that the introduction of an industrial economy (raising a single crop for money and thereby converting the land into raw material, implements into the equivalent of factory machines, and the members of the family into ill-paid laborers) corrupted the attitudes of the people toward the land, their work, their pastimes, each other, and finally themselves. Lytle, as his subsequent career would show, had great gifts as a writer, and he had a feeling for the joys of the life he described that was not only based on firsthand experience but was steeped in the affections and loyalties that had come down to him through family stories and legends and all the songs and folktales he had heard as a boy. Consequently, his exuberant description of the riches and pleasures of this life is unusually persuasive. Moreover, he showed, not in terms of statistics on declining markets and

168

abandoned farms, but in terms of the misery of real people who are desperate, baffled, and hopelessly trapped in debt, just how ruinous the cash crop system can be. In this respect his essay is more effective for the general reader than the sober, abstract demonstration in Nixon's "Whither Southern Economy?" which comes to the same conclusion about the system. But Lytle overstated his case: few of the yeomen farmers had it so good, and then only in the fat years. He said nothing about the lean years, the periods of enforced idleness that rotted the soul, the widespread filth and disease, and the fearful drudgery—until rural electrification came along and made possible some labor-saving machines—of the farmer's wife. His account of the play parties and other pastimes, while vividly evoking their unselfconscious gaiety, showed how little they contributed to the development of imagination and sensibility and how drab and dispiriting life could be in the intervals between them. There was a satisfyingly defiant swagger and gusto in writing, "Throw out the radio and take down the fiddle from the wall." But one who has relished country fiddling at its gay, irresistible best may still wonder what is to be done, after the radio has been thrown out, by those who want to hear a Mozart violin concerto without driving many miles in a wicked automobile. In the end, it was not the radio but his argument that Lytle threw away. His readers, after all, could hardly be those who lived the life he had described. Most of them would be persons of such tastes and sympathies that they could respond to his vivid and ebullient description of the happier side of rural life but who, just because of these tastes and sympathies, also appreciated concertos, fine performances of Shakespeare, the pleasures of seeing buildings of dignity and elegance—things which Lytle would have to give up along with good roads and the "industrial bric-a-brac" that could bring them nearer to the farm. In the reckless lunging and exaggerations of his essay, one can see with special clarity a major weakness of the Agrarian position: the insufferable limitations it seemed to put upon the human spirit.

The other half-dozen essays in the collection ranged downward from a brilliant attack on the doctrine of progress by Lyle Lanier to a maudlin and snobbish portrait of a Georgian Colonel Carter by John Donald Wade and an even more sentimental defense by

Henry Blue Kline of a feeble dilettante ill at ease in a world of business men, engineers, and movie-goers. Lanier's piece demonstrated what a trained social scientist endowed with a sense of style could do with cultural history, and his meticulous yet supple scholarship showed up the naïveté and inaccuracy of the "history" in the essays of Ransom, Tate, and Owsley. Starting with its origin in both Christian aspiration toward an after life and Enlightenment utilitarianism, Lanier followed the evolution of the doctrine as it was manipulated to establish a definition of progress as the constantly accelerated consumption of new products and to gain acceptance for the notion, quite without any historical or logical support, that the self-interest and welfare of the individual in America were identical with those of the large corporations. In its latest form the doctrine of progress was used again and again to convince the individual that any restraint upon the corporations was a check upon his own liberty. Though he was endangered far more by the unrestrained power of the corporations, the individual watched with approval as the corporations overexpanded and then, when production outran consumption, brought on depressions which could lead easily to revolutions or wars. Lanier recommended restoring agriculture to a position of respect and power, claiming that the yeoman farmer, content to take most of what he needed from his surroundings and freed by his self-sufficiency to pick and choose among the few other things he required, would act as a restraint upon the nation. His direct responsibility as owner-operator (compared with the irresponsibility of absentee owners who held stock in a corporation but paid no attention to how the firm was run as long as their dividends came in), his humble awareness of how little real progress was made in his ancient way of life, and his lack of ready cash with which to buy in excess of his real needs and so acquire the compulsion to "keep up"—all these would help him exercise individual taste and break out of the exploitative and conformist patterns of mass-production. As will be seen, this argument on the freedom and responsibility of the farmer in comparison to the confinement and irresponsibility of the member of the industrial society was to have a profound effect upon the substance and direction of later Agrarian thought and writing, particularly those of Tate. The remaining essays, with the exception of Nixon's laborious but thoroughgoing account of the evils of sharecropping, seem to have had no importance whatever for Agrarianism except to weaken the force of the symposium. Edmund Wilson, in a particularly shrewd and cruel parody, showed how they affected those uncommitted readers whom Ransom, Tate, and Davidson might have been hoping to win over. In one quiet sentence he summed up all the snobbishness, irresponsibility, and just plain silliness of Wade, Fletcher, Kline, and Young: "Cousin Charles' feeling about the depression is that it serves the 'industrialists' right."[53]

If *I'll Take My Stand* had really meant no more than that, Agrarianism might have ended there. But the men who had started it were anything but irresponsible. If they were sometimes foolish, they were not silly. *I'll Take My Stand* was only a beginning. And though Agrarianism became something very different from what they had hoped and intended, and its effects far from what they had aimed at, it was, as we have already indicated, to be of great importance to American letters. However, the three ex-Fugitives were not thinking of American letters when they made their next move.

[53] "Tennessee Agrarians," *The New Republic*, LXVII (July 27, 1931), 279.

CHAPTER FOUR

AGRARIANISM AND AFTER

....

History . . . gives too late
What's not believed in, or if still believed,
In memory only, reconsidered passion.
—*T. S. Eliot, "Gerontian"*

....

I

IN calling Agrarianism "academic" Chancellor Kirkland showed much prescience, which probably would not have surprised him. The commotion attending *I'll Take My Stand* was confined mainly to editorials and book-reviews (whose authors soon found other matters to occupy them) and to the enflamed imaginations of the Agrarians themselves (who did not). Others who paid it any heed did so because Agrarianism provided a momentary focus for a profound but inchoate concern for their region which troubled all thoughtful Southerners. But Agrarian ideas and their image of the ideal Southern life had little appeal, and before long they vanished into the literary quarterlies and seminars, where they enjoyed a queer, shadowy half-life even after the leading Agrarians themselves had abandoned them. The importance of Agrarianism, therefore, comes almost entirely from its relation to the imaginative and critical writings of some members of the group. The proposals for socio-economic action over which the Agrarians were so busy during the next half-dozen years have been forgotten by all but readers and students seeking a better understanding of the works of Ransom, Tate, and Warren. Agrarianism was from the start just what the chancellor called it, though the term has proved to be far from as unflattering as he meant it to be.

Certainly few terms could have seemed so inappropriate to the Agrarians themselves during the tumultuous months that followed the publication of their book—a hectic, joyous interval of conferences, arguments, manifestoes, and motions to censure, all tending to give the impression that the Agrarians were even more closely joined than the Fugitives had been. Actually, despite all this activity, there never was an Agrarian group comparable to the Fugitive group. Some of the Agrarians took part in impromptu discussions, but no formal meetings were ever held, and, according to Davidson, there was only one group enterprise: *I'll Take My Stand.*[1] The appearance of a group was maintained by a dedicated inner circle made up of Ransom, Davidson, Tate, Owsley, Lanier, and Lytle, who kept in touch much of the time by means of letters. In all the Agrarian interval Tate did not live in Nashville, though he was usually near enough to get to the city or have his friends visit him. Lytle, too, was out of Nashville; Ransom spent the school year of 1931-1932 in Wales as a Guggenheim Fellow; and Davidson spent the school year of 1932-1933 in Georgia with John Donald Wade, returning a more intransigent rebel than ever. But as long as their enthusiasm was high, the separation did not deter them and there was a brisk traffic by mail in proposals, counterproposals, essays, criticisms, and encouragements. It was tacitly understood that when one of them published his views on Agrarianism, he spoke for himself. There was, after all, no organization for him to represent. Nevertheless, the Agrarians corresponded so much, read each other's manuscripts so closely, and borrowed so freely when they agreed with one another that they usually presented a united front to their readers, who naturally formed the impression that behind their writing was an organized movement.

Warren, much of whose major writing carries the mark of Agrarian ideas, was never truly part of the inner band. In the fall of 1930 he came back to his native region as an instructor in English at Southwestern College in Memphis. But though he was near at hand during all the excitement immediately following the publication of *I'll Take My Stand,* he was so busy preparing for classes and working on his first novel, the still unpublished *In God's Own Time,* that he could give little attention to Agrarianism. Then when Ransom went abroad in the fall of 1931, Warren

---

[1] Donald Davidson, "The 'Mystery' of the Agrarians," *The Saturday Review of Literature,* XXVI (January 23, 1943), 6-7. Even calling the book a joint enterprise is misleading. Some contributors did no more than mail in their essays. And H. C. Nixon, whose essay was one of the best, went so far as to record in the preface of his *Forty Acres and Steel Mules* (1938) his dissent from all Agrarian writing since *I'll Take My Stand.* He stood by that book, however, and declared in 1952 that it had gained significance. See "A Symposium: The Agrarians Today," *Shenandoah,* III (Summer, 1952), 29-30.

accepted a temporary appointment at Vanderbilt as his replacement. At once he was back on the old terms with Davidson, and he became more intimate with Owsley, whose gusto and great rages delighted him. (Actually, Owsley was a kindly man. His volcanic wraths were lightened by humor and were rarely directed at individuals, for he tended naturally to like all he met, however abhorrent their opinions.) But it was Lyle Lanier, a friend from student days, who first really interested Warren in Agrarianism. Warren was much persuaded by Lanier's arguments against cash crops, having seen for himself the misery of tobacco farmers dependent on large corporations.

When Ransom returned, Warren was asked to stay at Vanderbilt, and now that their age difference meant less, the two became close friends. Ideas about the contingency and disorder of nature, the uses of tradition, and the differences between science and poetry, which Tate had discussed when Warren came from Yale to visit him, were newly explored in conversations with Ransom, who stressed the ambiguity of the experiences of a divided mind confronting a pluralistic universe. In the end it was these ideas, which had little interest for the other Agrarians apart from Tate, rather than Lanier's economics or the fervor of Davidson and Owsley, which made the significant impression on Warren. He was on hand during the interval when the others were most involved in social action, and when he moved to Louisiana State University in the fall of 1934, he kept in touch with them; but though he used some of their assumptions about the effect of abstract financial power on character in *Night Rider* and *At Heaven's Gate*, he was really not much interested in the programmatic side of Agrarianism. Even so, because of the fundamental importance in his writing of concepts from which Ransom and Tate argued their proposals for social reform, Warren, despite the looseness of his connection with the movement, seems the most Agrarian of them all, and through his work much that was most significant in the thinking and the social criticism of the group reached the world at large.

At the outset, though they agreed to answer any challenges to their ideas, Ransom, Davidson, and Tate did not plan any action beyond answering letters to editors or participating in debates. Indeed, Tate did not believe that effective reform in the direction of Agrarain concepts was possible.[2] His proposal in *I'll Take My Stand* that Southerners use violence to recover their lost culture was only an outburst of mocking—especially self-mocking—humor. But between the preparation and the publication of the book, the Great Depression set in. Industrialism, which the Agrarians had assumed to be immovably established, at least in the North, now seemed near collapse, and the South, already depressed, was declining into yet more terrible poverty. Between 1929 and 1932, the income from cotton diminished 70 percent. Forced sales of farms increased abruptly, and in the mill towns wages were cut, men were laid off, and factory after factory closed down. Public concern over Southern economy was so great that readers of *I'll Take My Stand* complained because the book offered no proposals for an agrarian reform, and though the Agrarians were disappointed that their defense of traditional Southern values was not considered in the humanistic terms upon which it was established, they decided that they would have to take account of the economic bases of the life they wished to preserve. Mistrustful of contemporary social science, they went back to Jefferson, John Taylor, Edmund Ruffin, and J. C. Calhoun for their arguments.

Except for Ransom. He, who had been the most concerned with the philosophical aspects, now chose to spend much of his Guggenheim fellowship studying the theories of the English economist, J. A. Hobson, in whose *Rationalism and Unemployment* (1931) and other works Ransom found confirmation for his belief, already set down in *God Without Thunder*, that cash crop farming was—at least economically—analogous with industrialism, for both led to overcapitalization and production in excess of demand. From this Ransom concluded that if the American economy were so reordered that the dominant group consisted of farmers who consumed most of what they raised and sold the remainder to pay for the few things they could not make themselves, the economy and the nation would be more nearly stable. In the present crisis, he believed, the government should establish the unemployed on small subsistence farms, thereby freeing them from the humiliation of the dole and creating a new, if limited, market for shut-down industries.

[2] "A Symposium: The Agrarians Today," pp. 22-23, 28.

During the fall and winter of 1931-1932 Ransom developed his ideas in a book-length manuscript. Tate took charge of circulating it among the publishers, who were not encouraging. Finally Ransom decided that for all his intense study he did not know enough economics to defend his ideas should they be attacked, and he withdrew his manuscript. Weary and disappointed, he made up his mind to stick to poetry and philosophy. He was not through with Agrarianism, but signs of doubt and even disaffection could be seen in his work by late 1933, even though a trip to New Mexico in the summer of that year so renewed his interest for the moment that he talked of writing a book on Agrarianism during the following spring. He did get as far as an essay, "The Aesthetics of Regionalism," which restated his conviction that the agrarian life offered the greatest quantity of aesthetic satisfaction and the best circumstances for understanding and coping with the human condition. The book, however, was not really needed: Ransom had already said everything that was his own and deeply felt in *God Without Thunder*.[3]

By the time the Agrarians were well into their economic studies, the only persons who read their essays with much attention were professional students of Southern affairs, who regarded them as sentimental bunglers and attacked them without mercy at the meetings of such groups as the Southern Historical Association. Their most powerful opponents were the members of the Southern Regional Committee of the Social Science Research Council, who had compiled the staggering quantity of data published in Howard Odum's great book, *Southern Regions of the United States* (1936). These men ignored or ridiculed their arguments and shot the Agrarians down with a barrage of facts.[4] For a while it had seemed as if the Agrarians might fare better in the magazines. Tate was appointed Southern editor of *Hound and Horn* in the spring of

[3] See John Crowe Ransom, "The State and the Land," *The New Republic*, LXX (February 17, 1932), 8-10; "Land! An Answer to the Unemployment Problem," *Harper's Monthly Magazine*, CLXV (July, 1932), 216-224; "Happy Farmers," *The American Review*, I (October, 1933), 513-536; "The Aesthetics of Regionalism," *The American Review*, II (January, 1934), 290-310.

[4] Jonathan Daniels, *A Southerner Discovers the South* (New York, 1938), pp. 81-87; Donald Davidson, "Expedients vs. Principles," *The Southern Review*, II (Spring, 1937), 647-669; W. T. Couch, "The Agrarian Romance," *The South Atlantic Quarterly*, XXXVI (October, 1937), 419-430.

1932, and essays by Davidson, Owsley, and Warren were announced for publication, though they never appeared. The inner circle had better luck with *The American Review,* published by wealthy, eccentric Seward Collins, who had been fluttering on the fringe of the literary world since his graduation a few years before from Princeton, where he had been a disciple of Irving Babbitt. In 1932 he purchased *The Bookman,* which had been proceeding with the utmost dignity into bankruptcy, and after trying without success to liven it up and boost its circulation, he renamed it *The American Review* and set out, as he explained in the first issue (April, 1932), "to give greater currency to the ideas of a number of groups and individuals who are radically critical of conditions prevalent in the modern world, but launch their criticism from a 'traditionalist' basis. . . ." W. S. Knickerbocker, editor of the *Sewanee Review,* told him about the Agrarians, and after conferring with them at Lytle's family's farm in Alabama, Collins promised to publish anything they sent him. He did, but unfortunately for the Agrarians he was just as generous toward writers who admired fascism. Indeed, he himself wrote that "the victory of Hitler signifies the end of the Communist threat, *forever,*" and praised Mussolini as the most constructive statesman of the age. Thus so important and politically innocent an essay as Ransom's "Poetry: A Note on Ontology" appeared among rhapsodies on the manly, disciplined brown-shirts, with the inevitable result: the Agrarians were found guilty of proto-fascism by association. At the very time that they were being humiliated at meetings of the Southern Policy Association, the Agrarians had further to endure a silly exchange of letters in *The New Republic* over the company they kept and an article by V. F. Calverton in *Scribner's Magazine* which was a galaxy of ignorance, illogic, invective, and rancor. Ransom replied to Calverton in the same issue and handled his weapons with such courtly grace that he made Calverton look merely loudmouthed. (As it turned out, this essay, which appeared in May, 1936, was Ransom's last public statement on behalf of Agrarianism.) Perhaps one should be glad that some of the group had the stimulus to write and the opportunity to publish certain of their early and important speculations in aesthetics and criticism, but

177

in general the association with Collins made the Agrarians look not so much sinister as silly.[5]

As the Agrarians shifted from treating the problem of man's relation with his environment in aesthetic and epistemological terms to proposing specific programs in economic and political terms, two themes became more prominent in their writing: the dependence of one's sense of responsibility on the individual owner-ship and management of small property (an idea Lanier had put forward in *I'll Take My Stand* and that Tate had brooded upon since 1927) and the political and cultural importance of regions. As these themes emerged, the intellectual initiative within the inner circle tended to pass from Ransom to Tate, Davidson, and Owsley.

With the pages of *The American Review* open to him, Davidson now entered on a period of imaginative excitement and great productivity. In 1933 he began publishing in that magazine a series of essays defending regional cultures and folk art against "sociologists" and "scions of the newer immigrant stock—the expatriated nationals from a medley of European countries—who had no intimate share in the historic experience of any American place" and were, moreover, Freudians, collectivists, atheists, even cynics.[6] Envious of the innocence, candor, and grace of the regional lives they could not share, they were, according to Davidson, trying to convert the whole of America into a suburb economically and culturally de-pendent upon the Eastern cities where they were dominant. Op-posing them were a few right-minded historians and critics who had rediscovered the rich diversity of the regions and were work-ing to preserve their cultural autonomy. In speaking of Southern society Davidson made no bones about his belief that the region should be allowed to keep racial segregation as an essential part of its social structure. He was particularly wrathful toward Pro-fessor John Dollard, of Yale University, for suggesting in *Caste*

---

[5] See "Editorial Notes," *The American Review*, I (April, 1933), 122-127, and I (May, 1933), 243-256; "Fascism and the Southern Agrarians," *The New Republic*, LXXXVII (May 27, 1936), 76; "The Sunny Side of Fascism," *ibid.* (June 10, 1936), 131-132; V. F. Calverton, "The Bankruptcy of Southern Culture," *Scribner's Magazine*, XCIX (May, 1936), 294-298; John Crowe Ran-som, "The South is a Bulwark," *ibid.*, 299-303.

[6] Donald Davidson, "Lands that Were Golden," *The American Review*, III (October, 1934), 553, 554-555.

and Class in a Southern Town (1937) that segregation was cruel to Negroes. Dollard's views, Davidson claimed, might be "a rationalization of the very convenient and practical process by which, through war and emancipation, Connecticut, say, eliminated the economic competition of South Carolina," or "one of the rationalizations by which Yale excuses the exploitative economy that provides it with a large endowment and keeps the University of South Carolina relatively poor."[7]

Such, alas, was the temper and logic of many passages in these essays, which Davidson published in 1938, with slight revisions and the addition of a few pieces first printed in other periodicals, under the title *The Attack on Leviathan: Regionalism and Nationalism in the United States.* The only book wholly devoted to a discussion of Agrarian ideas by one of the group, it was not likely to win them supporters, though it had many sunny pages which were among the best things Davidson ever wrote.[8] With perceptiveness comparable to Warren's he chose the one or two details that recreated for the reader a country parlor lighted by a coal-oil lamp or the odor of a newly plowed field at sundown and thereby suggested with great vividness and charm what he loved so much about life in his region. It was, indeed, exactly that right relation with nature which so concerned Ransom: a modesty and dignity based on knowledge of man's limitations kept wholesome by work on the land. But where Ransom's arguments were part of a dialectic based on long-pondered conceptions of man, Davidson's, for all their abundance of historical data, appeared to rest upon his old nostalgia for anything lost, threatened, or ignored by ordinary men. In describing rural life he dwelt on aspects which were

[7] Donald Davidson, "Gulliver with Hayfever," *The American Review,* IV (Summer, 1937), 163-164.

[8] Ransom, as we know, abandoned his book of Agrarian economics. His *God Without Thunder* contained the philosophical basis of Agrarianism, but was only partly about Agrarian ideas. Tate projected a collection of essays on Agrarian tenets to be called (among other titles) "Ancestors of Exile," but it was never published and its arguments were transmuted into the narrative of his novel, *The Fathers.* His *Reason and Madness* and *Reactionary Essays* contained Agrarian essays but were devoted to other topics as well. In 1935 Troy J. Cauley, of the Georgia School of Technology, published *Agrarianism, A Program for Farmers* (Chapel Hill), in which he tried to integrate his views on farm economics with the scattered writings of the Agrarians. A dull, dispirited book, it had, nonetheless, the virtue of recognizing that the subsistence farm tended to isolate the family unit and to lead to intellectual and moral narrowness and intolerance.

already quaint anachronisms fast disappearing into oblivion. Nevertheless, his descriptions were so sensitive that the reader was likely to surrender to the soft pleasures of sentimental reminiscence until brought up short by Davidson's nearly hysterical harangues against New York intellectuals, Henry Adams, Marx, Freud, Joyce, Faulkner, and Abraham Lincoln as enemies of the gentle old folk and their ways.

It is not hard to see beneath a fury so intemperate a deep despair which is nearer the surface of *Lee in the Mountains and Other Poems,* a collection of verses written during the previous decade which Davidson published in the same year. The poems written since "The Tall Men" (which was included) had their archetypal symbol in the cavalry officer recalling in the midst of soot, automobiles, and civic boosters the "lost forsaken valor," battleflags unfurled on wild hills, and the rebel yell. Grouped around in a frieze straight out of Thomas Nelson Page were a witty folk-philosopher called "Old Timer," a haughty old lady ignoring the proffered hospitality of upstarts who would endure any humiliation for just one stiff little nod of recognition, and a good nigger with manners enough to go to the back door for a handout and sense enough to long for the good old days before he was free. Since "the living do not fight/ And only the dead can ride," these doomed survivors of better times could do no more than abstain from life. Those who felt as they did might flee to the "Sanctuary," a forgotten valley and renew kinship with Tryon, Tarleton, Sam Houston, De Soto, and the Indians who were the first exiles from that land. There they watched the "last wild eagle soar" and the "last enchanted white deer come to drink." One thinks of Quentin Compson, who found time and change too much for a young romanticist stumbling with a head full of dreams of lost glory amidst the fragments of a legendary Old South. He, too, found a magic in the word "last."

II

Late in 1933, Tate wrote to Herbert Agar proposing that he contribute to *The American Review.* Agar was the London correspondent for the *Louisville Courier* and an admirer of the Distributists, a small, loosely organized group led by G. K. Chesterton and Hilaire Belloc which wanted to break up large corporations and land holdings, distribute the property among small owners who would live mainly by subsistence farming, and extend the authority and ceremonies of churches—particularly of the Roman Catholic church—throughout the life of the community. It is impossible to guess how much of a following the Distributists had despite the patent absurdity of their proposals for a nation with a population so much larger than the arable land could support. They were only one of many "back-to-the-land-and-the-things-that-count" movements of those desperate days. Certainly Agar took them seriously, and he was much interested in the similarity between Distributist and Agrarian proposals for reform. He and Tate exchanged letters briskly, and in the summer of 1934, while Agar was lecturing in this country, he came to Tennessee and met the Agrarians. Soon after, he and Tate proposed getting out a symposium representing the Agrarians, Distributists, and other groups opposing the spread of industrialism and urban culture. Agar also hoped to found a confederation to bring the pressure of organized public opinion to bear on the government. Eventually a conference was held in Nashville during 1936 (that unlucky year!). The Agrarians, who were getting rather touchy in their relations with others, were alarmed by the eccentricity of some of the people Agar invited and the confederation came to nothing. Tate stuck by his friend and helped him plan a new magazine which Tate hoped would be dominated by the Agrarians. When it became apparent that the magazine would be centered in New York, the Agrarians lost interest, though when *Free America* was finally launched in 1939, Tate served on its editorial board. Never robust, it withered soon afterward, and Agar returned to England. He came back to Louisville in 1940, but by then Agrarianism was virtually at an end and he did not renew his contact with the inner circle. Out of all the high hopes he and Tate had put into their lively letters came only one real achievement: their symposium, *Who Owns America?*[9]

Much of the force of this interesting and in many ways excellent book derives from the careful organization and balance which Tate

[9] This account is based on the letters of Agar to Tate, 1933-1940, now in the Princeton University Library.

181

and Agar were able to impose on it despite the opposition of some of the contributors. The book has a unity and coherence such as *I'll Take My Stand* never had, and the center of its design was the concept, shared by the Agrarians and Distributists, that a stable society depended upon responsible ownership and direct personal management of small property, particularly small land holdings, by a majority of the people. As we know, Lanier had described the lack of responsibility among its stockholders for the actions of a large corporation and had cited the farmer as one whose control of his property was obvious. Ransom had written about the emotional stability and self-restraint that came from working with nature, but his emphasis was mainly upon the aesthetic satisfaction. Tate, however, was the one who put emphasis upon *moral* stability, the effect of ownership on character, and the relationship between direct management of small properties and the conservative temper that would preserve traditional modes of conduct. Even before he began writing to Agar he proposed a return to small properties as an Agrarian doctrine in a singularly cruel and inept imitation of Swift's "A Modest Proposal," which may have been influenced by what he had already read of Belloc and Eric Gill.[10] His thinking was best summed up in his essay "A Traditionist Looks at Liberalism," which he wrote in 1936, wherein he asserted that "Society based upon property will pass on its heritage in a concrete form . . . property, which means moral control of the means of life. . . . The traditional society will envisage its heritage in moral terms because its members must be personally responsible for the material basis of life." Here, in brief, was the dominant conception of his novel, *The Fathers*, and its explanation of the breakdown of the traditional society of antebellum Virginia.[11] Agar concurred, and together they arranged the symposium to illustrate the validity of the conception. There were four sections. The first, and best, examined the history and structure of corporations and recommended specific legislation to limit their powers. The second described regionalism in America and particularly in the South, where small, distributed property still prevailed, and proposed ways for protecting local economies and cultures. The third, and

[10] See Tate's "The Problem of the Unemployed," *The American Review*, 1 (May, 1933), 129-149.
[11] The novel is discussed in Chapter Seven.

weakest, described the good life in the regions. The last described Western culture in general and sought to show that finance-capitalism and the great corporations were but part of the results of contemporary materialism and spiritual enervation. Though there was some inevitable overlapping among the essays and the various sections, the plan was orderly and effective, with the stronger essays giving support to pieces which, taken alone, would have seemed querulous, self-righteous, and dull.

Tate's "Notes on Liberty and Property," which was first published in *The American Review* in March, 1936, presents the argument, offered in one form or another by most of the essays in the first section, on the need to control large corporations and encourage small, distributed properties. Following *The Modern Corporation and Private Property*, by Adolf Berle, Jr., and Gardiner Means (1932), he described the irresponsibility of stockholders and the ingenious ways used to persuade the small independent business man that any attempt at regulating the big firms was an infringement on his own liberty as a man. There was nothing new in the essay: what was Tate's own, the conception of the dependence of moral responsibility on direct management of small property, had already been put forward elsewhere. Well written and aggressive in tone, it gave force and direction to the symposium, but its only surviving interest comes from its measure of Tate's concern over property and its clarity and vigor in stating his conceptions.

Davidson's "That This Nation May Endure: The Need for Political Regionalism" was placed in the second section. Intended as an argument for a reorganization of the federal government that would give more power to the regions and thereby preserve their indigenous cultures, the essay soon lapsed into a tantrum in which Davidson charged the Northeast with bringing on the depression and sputtered against new roads, new courthouses, steel filing cabinets, morticians, and life insurance. By contrast, Ransom's "What Does the South Want?" which appeared in the same section, seemed almost friendly in spite of Ransom's references to "Big Business" and "the imperial East." But courtesy and the old argument that sensibility was corroded by industrialism were about the only things that distinguished the essay as his. That he, who had been so alert to cast out the stereotyped phrases in the verses of the Fugitives, should have used such flabby clichés without a flicker of irony, suggests that his heart was elsewhere and his interest in Agrarianism was waning when he wrote the piece.

Warren's "Literature as a Symptom," which appeared in the third section, was easily the best contribution from an Agrarian; yet it, too, was far from original. Indeed, it might almost have been written by either Tate or Warren himself a full decade earlier, so exactly does it follow the thesis of Tate's "The Revolt Against Literature" (published in February, 1927) and Warren's "Hawthorne, Anderson, and Frost," which he wrote while studying at Yale and visiting Tate on weekends in New York. Following T. S. Eliot, they had argued that writers of the past had their themes formed for them by their cultures and could concentrate upon form and style as media for a personal vision. To this thesis Warren now added the argument that contemporary writers, lacking such support and hoping to recover a meaningful relationship with a culture, tended to go in for either regionalism or the proletarian movement. Both offered a revolutionary view of the writer's place in society, but they differed greatly. "The Regional movement may be defined," Warren wrote, ". . . as the attempt of a writer to reason himself into the appropriate relation to the past; the proletarian movement, as the attempt to reason himself into the appropriate relation with the future." The regionalist, therefore, is concerned for tradition and ties with a place, which means that he will stress ownership of land and encourage agrarian cultures, whereas the proletarian writer is hostile toward tradition and seeks to establish ties with a class, which means that he will stress ownership of the means of production and encourage industrial cultures. The danger for the regionalist is lapsing into sentimentality, faddism, and nostalgia; that of the proletarian writer, turning literature into propaganda.

The essay has exceptional interest for admirers of Warren's work, for it suggests how Warren, who was to make resourceful use of regional history in his writing, managed in spite of youth and the pressure of such strong personalities as those of Davidson and Owsley, both of whom had succumbed to the dangers of regionalism, to reason himself into the appropriate relation with the past of his own land. It may be stretching a point too far, but one likes to think that he was unusually fortunate in being exposed to Tate's abstract, hardheaded, and vigorous speculation on the uses of the past for the writer just when Warren was discovering his deep emotional ties with his region and its history and before Tate became so intransigent a partisan that his work frequently veered between brilliance and absurdity. Tate's poem "To the Lacedemonians" and the unhappy progress of Davidson's work since 1930 bore out Warren on the risks confronting the regionalist. So, too, did the essays in the third section by two other Agrarians, Andrew Nelson Lytle and John Donald Wade. Yet for all its shrewdness and independence, Warren's essay had two serious weaknesses, both characteristic of all Agrarian speculation on the relation of the writer to the times. First, its explanation of the alienation of the artist took no account of forces having only indirect or even no connection with the decline of tradition— mass-production publication requiring huge sales, the development of a semi-literate market through public education, and the lingering Puritan mistrust of the arts (which was fully as significant for the writer as the Puritan belief in the individual's responsibility to God, which Warren cited as a theme, backed by a culture, giving scope and meaning to the work of a writer who was a participant in or heir to that culture). Second, though Warren himself was manifestly able to establish an effective connection with the culture of his region, nothing was said here about how the writer should go about it, though he was warned to avoid programmatic literature and the "dogma of the appropriate subject." Warren quoted Wordsworth on the "spontaneous overflow of powerful feelings," and the need to think long and deeply while leaving the rest to God. But this was to say, in effect, that if it has been given one to be able to write, then, of course, one *can* write. The tautology ducks the whole problem at which the essay was supposed to be directed and disappoints a reader who, knowing how well Warren managed to solve the problem for himself, and knowing too, that this was *the* problem for Southern writers of the Fugitive-Agrarian generation such as Faulkner, Katherine Anne Porter, Eudora Welty, and Caroline Gordon, would be grateful for more than simply the shrewd statement of the terms of the dilemma and the account, well-substantiated, as it turned out, of what happened to the work of those who failed to cope with it.

Apart from Tate's work as editor, the merit of *Who Owns America?* was due more to other contributors, particularly the professional social scientists such as David C. Coyle and Richard B. Ransom, than to the Agrarians, who tended to reduce all issues to cartoons in absolute black (industrial society) and white (blithe, beautiful, and kindly agrarian society). But the Agrarians set the tone, and to this most reviewers responded. Though more charitable than the reviewers of *I'll Take My Stand* (and well they might be, for it was a less significant but a far better book), the critics noted the inconsistency of demanding massive government intervention and reorganization of society on behalf of a system which, it was believed, would greatly reduce size and power of institutions, including the government itself. Kenneth Burke spoke for the book's most responsible critics when he wrote:

"When things are going well, their ideal private farmer, proud and free in the untrammeled possession of his acres, dismisses the government with dignity. He does as he pleases, without 'interference': if the market is favorable, he sells; if unfavorable, he retains for his own use. No necessities can dispossess him, since his land is inalienable. . . . Perhaps the land is even untaxed, as the logic of the agrarians' position would require, since the farmer must be wholly independent of the market's financial compulsion, otherwise the deterministic genius of the 'money crop' may get him. On the other hand, if there are adversities, the government must be called in. Such matters as flood control, drought relief, education, road building, and medication are to be handled with governmental assistance. The project suggests a 'spoiled child' theory of politics, where the papa-government is dismissed by the proud bearers of 'freedom' as intolerable interference, until it must be called on for help."[12]

III

Who Owns America? was the last appearance together of the former Fugitives and their companions in the Agrarian inner circle, Owsley, Lytle, Lanier, and John Donald Wade. During the year that followed, the group, such as it was, disintegrated as the hopes

[12] Kenneth Burke, "Property as an Absolute," *The New Republic*, LXXXVII (July 1, 1936), 245.

of some of its most active members diminished and their attention focused more narrowly upon literature. Others wanted to go on fighting for The Cause, as the Agrarians, half-mockingly and half-seriously, had termed their enterprise, and they published a few more essays restating their position. But just as one may think of the Fugitive anthology as marking the end of the Fugitive group, so one may think of the symposium as marking the virtual end of Agrarian activity in public affairs. Looking back one sees those who continued in The Cause as caretakers of an abandoned estate. However, the conceptions of man and his right relation with nature and his fellows which brought them to Agrarianism continued to be central in the work of Ransom, Tate, and Warren, and they went on using the terms and images for defining and illustrating those conceptions which they had evolved during the Agrarian interlude. For them the philosophic side of Agrarianism still had a pre-eminent importance. But though Owsley believed in it until his death in 1956 and Davidson, for all his bemusement as poet with flight to a secret refuge, has never ceased battling, the programmatic side came virtually to an end in 1936.

Ransom had long had his doubts. Even in December of 1933, when in a surge of new enthusiasm he was considering a book arguing the superiority of rural life, he admitted:

> "We must have cities, we shall have them, even if suddenly of late we have become conscious of the squalor, the discomfort, the shoddiness, and the pretentiousness which is in them all as we know them. 'Agrarians' may not like cities temperamentally, and talk against the prospects of any big cities in the future, yet they too go to cities and are influenced by cities, and it is a matter of fact that the city focuses all the features of a culture as nothing else does."[13]

A majority of Americans, he pointed out soon afterward in "The Aesthetics of Regionalism," were permanently committed to a civilization dependent upon technology and nothing could dissuade them. He went even further in "The South Is a Bulwark": "It is not likely that the small Distributist-Agrarian group will cause a vast reversal in American economic practice." The most he

---

[13] John Crowe Ransom, "A Capital for the New Deal," *The American Review,* II (December, 1933), 137.

would hope for now was the appearance of a political movement aimed at reforming "Big Business" and that its leaders would somehow be influenced by Agrarian ideas even if they had never heard of the group. It was a long retreat for a man who had once considered leaving teaching to publish Agrarian pamphlets and who had gone to England to study economics. His friends were deeply hurt and charged him with disaffection. And they were right, for in the spring of 1937 Ransom, in the course of letters to Tate, described an essay on his desk as "a sort of postscript to agrarianism as far as I am in it," and a "last act of patriotism."[14] Shortly thereafter he accepted an appointment as Carnegie Professor of Poetry at Kenyon College and moved to Gambier, Ohio.

This was a critical moment in his career, comparable to his return to Vanderbilt to teach English and his defense of the Fundamentalists at the time of the Scopes trial. He was forty-nine years old. He had published only six poems since the appearance of *Two Gentlemen in Bonds*, and his speculations on art and poetry, having appeared for the most part in *The American Review*, which was little read, were scarcely known. Outside Vanderbilt he was regarded as an amiable ex-poet gone cranky on social theories; within the university he was mistrusted as a spokesman for traditionalism in an institution which took pride in its social progressivism. It was time for a new start.

He was ready for it. Such a tumult of fresh ideas churned within him that he was reluctant to reprint his recent essays, though he had a contract to make a book of them, for they seemed to him full of faults. "The fact is," he wrote to Tate soon after settling into Kenyon, "I see so much future for critical studies that my own are just beginning; it's the biggest field that could possibly be found for systematic study. . . . I want to wade right into it."[15] He soon had his chance when Gordon Keith Chalmers, president of Kenyon, asked him to edit a new review devoted to public affairs and arts and letters. One measure of Ransom's change of heart is the fact

[14] The letters, dated March 11, 1937, and April 6, 1937, are in the Princeton University Library. So far as this writer can determine, the essay was never published and "The South is a Bulwark" was Ransom's last piece on behalf of Agrarianism.

[15] From a letter, Ransom to Tate, dated "Oct. 29." Someone has added in pencil "[1937]" and internal evidence supports the choice of this year. The letter is now in the Princeton University Library.

that he requested that the review be limited to arts and letters. His request was granted and in January, 1939, *The Kenyon Review* began publication with Ransom as the chief editor. Over the next decade it was to be a powerful force in American letters and Ransom was to become one of the most influential critics in the nation.

Moving north made a great change in him. He saw the benefits of science and technology. (The village of Gambier was not technologically more advanced than the city of Nashville; rather, Ransom was compelled to take a new look at things which had been before his eyes for years.) He became acquainted with humane and literate positivists and empiricists and discovered that they were not the simplistic fellows he had supposed. He read Dewey and decided that Dewey was right as far as he went but more was needed to account for the complexities and contradictions in human behavior. Slowly Ransom came around to the view that man was forced to wrest a living from his environment by means of his reason and that a technological culture was, for all its faults, the most efficient way of getting the necessary work done. At the same time man was given to forming sentimental attachments to objects in his environment and he needed the arts to establish the value they had for him beyond their mere usefulness and to remind him that the world is, and is valued for, more than appears to reason, however sophisticated its instruments of observation. In short, Ransom continued to believe in the division of modern man which had been the theme of so many of his earlier poems; but now, instead of hoping to heal the division through some combination of myth, art, tradition, and subsistence farming, he accepted it as an inevitable condition of being. The problem, then, was to define and defend the means whereby the sensibility might have its satisfactions within the mixed order. To this he addressed himself as teacher, editor, critic, and theorist.[16] In so doing he did not openly disavow Agrarianism, but he made a notable omission when early in 1938 he published *The World's Body*: though the philosophy of the book went back in a straight line to the assumptions about the natures of art, science, and man developed in *God Without Thunder* and the "Statement of Principles" in *I'll Take My Stand*,

[16] Based upon conversations with Mr. Ransom on August 26, 1946. See also his essay "Art and Human Economy," *The Kenyon Review*, VII (Autumn, 1945), 683-688.

there was not one essay that referred to Agrarian principles for achieving a good life and a right balance among the three. Ransom had no desire to be a spectacular malcontent. He could fight for a cause, but he felt none of the enchantment of a lost one. If Americans were determined to have a technological culture on the Northern plan, he would work within that plan for a mode of life that satisfied both the reason and the sensibility. He had abandoned Agrarianism as a mode, but he had not abandoned his deepest convictions that life could not be confined within the scope and structures of the reason, and the essays are directly in the line he had followed ever since the "fury against abstraction" entered his life a quarter of a century before.[17]

The withering of Agrarianism after its virtually total failure to affect public affairs in the South must have been harder for Tate. Given, as the canny and reserved Ransom was not, to impetuous commitment and strenuous partisanship, he had engaged his life and imagination more deeply and had given them to plans and forays which sometimes brought only humiliation and at best laid a heavy charge upon him. There were signs of doubt and discouragement in an essay, "The Profession of Letters in the South," which he published in the *Virginia Quarterly Review* for April, 1935. After dismissing most of the literature of the Old South in terms almost as contemptuous as those he used in 1925, when he surveyed the achievements of his region from the towers of New York City, Tate went on to remark that there was little decent literature in the South even now and there would not be more until the Southern man of letters could count on an audience whose opinions were not dictated by Northern reviewers. Moreover, as in antebellum days, "The prevailing economic passion of the age once more tempts, even commands, the Southern writer to go into politics. . . . The emergency, real enough, becomes a pretext for ignoring the arts."[18] Since returning from France in the summer of 1933 he had up to the time of the essay's appearance published only two poems, a short story, some book reviews, and the turgid but seminal speculations gathered under the title "Three Types of Poetry."[19] Did he, perhaps, think that he himself had been ignoring the arts?

[17] *The World's Body* is discussed in Chapter Six.
[18] Allen Tate, "The Profession of Letters in the South," *The Virginia Quarterly Review*, XI (April, 1935), 176.
[19] The essay is discussed in Chapter Seven.

In the months that followed he did a little better. He published seven more poems, none of them of much distinction and some having about them a tone suggesting that they had been willed into being with great effort, and he delivered the 1936 Phi Beta Kappa address, "What is a Traditional Society?" at the University of Virginia. His collection, *Reactionary Essays*, was published early in 1936, followed by a very limited edition of his recent poetry, *The Mediterranean and Other Poems*, which got mixed reviews. The reception of *Who Owns America?* was favorable, even among those critics who disagreed with Agrarian-Distributist objectives, but elsewhere Tate and the Agrarians fared ill in this season. At the spring meeting of the Southern Policy Association other members tried to have the Agrarians, who were among its founders, expelled from the group, and Tate himself was cruelly mocked. Soon after he took part in the demeaning exchange of letters in *The New Republic* over the association of the Agrarians with fascism. Finally, the conference between the Agrarians and other supposedly likeminded groups invited by Agar broke down amidst some ill feeling toward Tate's friend. Tate, who had settled down at Monteagle, Tennessee, to work on the final version of his "Ode to the Confederate Dead" and to prepare his *Selected Poems* for the press, might well feel that though he had managed to keep going at poetry and aesthetics he was not getting very far as a man of letters while spending himself upon social action which yielded more trouble than satisfaction.

As it turned out, the Phi Beta Kappa address was Tate's last public effort on behalf of Agrarianism (if one does not count the letters in *The New Republic*) and it came at just about the same time as Ransom's last effort—the essay "The South is a Bulwark." And after completing the final version of his "Ode," Tate published no more poems on specifically Southern themes. Instead, he put all he had learned from Agrarianism and his speculations on tradition and responsibility into a superb novel, *The Fathers*, whose title he had once planned to use for a collection of essays which never came to pass. Its appearance in 1938 signified the end of his involvement in the programmatic side of Agrarianism. Henceforth, like Ransom, he was to be concerned with the philosophy which underlay it and the application of the tenets of that philosophy to the theory and practice of literary criticism.

Ransom, who had consulted Tate in preparing *The World's Body* and acknowledged his indebtedness in a gracious preface to the book, hoped that they might work together in bringing off a revolution in criticism, for he believed that they had already, in his words, "begun a new chapter in poetics." He tried to find for Tate a position at Kenyon on the staff of the new review. When this failed, Tate, who meanwhile had taken a position at the Women's College of the University of North Carolina, succeeded in obtaining a handsome offer from that school for his friend. But by the time it finally came through, Tate himself had accepted a position as Writer in Residence at Princeton, and President Chalmers had managed to get enough foundation support to launch *The Kenyon Review*; so Ransom turned the offer down. They had to go on working by mail to "found criticism."[20]

The first task was to bring down the old and sturdily built walls around perception and understanding, and Tate ignited a bomb when he read his paper, "Miss Emily and the Bibliographer," before the English Club at Princeton in the spring of 1940. It was subsequently published in *The American Scholar* and Ransom printed a summary of it in *The Kenyon Review* and invited comments. He got them. The noise of the explosion was long to echo in the halls and corridors of the academies.

"The formal qualities of a poem," Tate asserted, "are the focus of the specifically critical judgment because they partake of an objectivity that the subject matter, abstracted from the form, wholly lacks."[21] But scholars concentrated upon a warped and truncated version of the subject matter apart from form, studying it in relation to its historical setting as if a work of art were simply the product of determining forces surrounding it and in identifying those sources one said all that was needed. Conceding that we re-

[20] From letters from Ransom to Tate dated "Oct. 29" (to which has been added "[1937]"), "4/xi/37," "New Year's / 1938," "April 22" (to which has been added "[1938]"), "November 29" (to which has been added "[1938]"), "Washington's Birthday" (to which has been added "[Feb. 22, 1939]"), "Mar. 27" (to which has been added "[1939]"), "Mar. 29/39," "April 13" (to which has been added "[1939]"), "April 24" (to which has been added "[1939]"), and "May 13" (to which has been added "[1939]"). The additions are in pencil and internal evidence makes clear that they are correct. The letters are now in the Princeton University Library.

[21] Allen Tate, "Miss Emily and the Bibliographer," *The American Scholar*, IX (Autumn, 1940), 456.

quire all the knowledge we can get to understand literature, Tate charged the scholars with evading the responsibility to judge and with abandoning literature, as literature, altogether.

Ransom's invitation brought in so many comments that he arranged with Cleanth Brooks and Robert Penn Warren, then editing *The Southern Review*, to publish a symposium in their two magazines. Each would publish five of the best. Among those chosen for *The Southern Review* was Tate's "The Present Function of Criticism," which was one of the clumsiest things he ever put on paper. A tirade that charged the social sciences with helping to bring the slave state to America, it claimed that "The tradition of free ideas is as dead . . . as it is in Germany," and praised literature at the expense of the natural sciences. "The high forms of literature," it went on, "offer us the only complete, and thus the most responsible, versions of our experience. . . . Literature is the complete knowledge of man's experience."[22] This was too much for Sidney Hook, who sent a letter to *The Southern Review*, pointing out that "As his [Tate's] statements stand, they justify the inference that since we do not, and cannot, have complete knowledge of man's experience, literature does not and cannot exist." Moreover, since complete knowledge is not the distinction of literature and scientific statements contain knowledge, literary works cannot be distinguished from scientific works. "The very denigration of science to which Mr. Tate is committed herewith becomes pointless."[23] The same issue of the magazine carried another essay by Tate reaffirming his views on literature as knowledge and the inadequacy of the scientific representation of the world. It in no way diminished the cogency of Hook's criticisms. Actually, Tate was only saying badly what he had said a decade before in his "Remarks on the Southern Religion" in *I'll Take My Stand*. He had always had a gift for aphorisms, but sometimes, especially when he was angry, he produced not aphorisms that startled the reader into a new perception and understanding but pretentious half-truths that annoyed by their oversimplifications and their dismissal of all views that did not agree with his own. Critics and literary scholars who might other-

[22] Allen Tate, "The Present Function of Criticism," *The Southern Review*, VI (Autumn, 1940), 236ff.
[23] Sidney Hook, " 'The Late Mr. Tate,' " *The Southern Review*, VI (Spring, 1941), 840.

wise have been more sympathetic with Tate's effort to shift some attention away from the study of sources and back to the poem as poem were offended by Tate's manner and the manifest absurdity of some of his generalizations; moreover, they tended to think that he spoke for and in the manner of his friends, Ransom, Warren, and Brooks. This is not to say that Tate should be held responsible for all the resistance encountered by the New Criticism, as it came to be called. Many students of literature who were profoundly dissatisfied with the prevailing curricula made flippant and ill-informed remarks about literary history and historians that infuriated their elders, and even the genial Ransom could set teeth on edge with his patronizing comments on science. But since many who had not read Eliot, Richards, Blackmur, Burke, or the earlier essays of Ransom, Tate, Warren, and Brooks, thought that the New Criticism began with Tate's talk and the subsequent symposium, his bomb did harm not to the established institutions so much as to the revolution which he and Ransom hoped to bring about.

Warren, who was far away and absorbed in his own affairs when Agrarianism began, was in much the same situation when it came to an end. After three years at Vanderbilt he left in the fall of 1934 to join the English Department of the Louisiana State University. Shortly afterward he and Cleanth Brooks were asked to become managing editors of a new magazine. They were guaranteed $10,000 and told to ask for more if they needed it. With such backing they could move so swiftly that by the following summer the first number of *The Southern Review* was off the press. Meanwhile Warren finished a second novel (still unpublished and untitled) and worked away at short stories and poetry and in the autumn of 1935 published his second book and first volume of verse, *Thirty-Six Poems,* a collection covering the decade since his graduation. During the next year he was awarded a Houghton Mifflin fellowship and began writing *Night Rider*, his first published novel. Even as he worked at it, he continued to write stories and poems, and before the novel was finished he had begun to think about "Proud Flesh," the play which was to evolve into his novel, *All the King's Men.* Somehow, while teaching, editing, and writing, he managed to find time to work with Brooks in preparing their textbook, *Understanding Poetry*, which was published in 1938 and soon became for the study of literature the most influential textbook of our time. During 1939 and 1940 he held a Guggenheim fellowship, which enabled him to live in Italy, where he studied Italian for as many as five hours a day and worked on both his play and still another novel, *At Heaven's Gate*. It is scarcely odd that the end of Agrarianism meant little to him; yet the very works on which he was engaged showed how much living in the midst of Agrarian ideas had affected his thinking.[24]

Thus, since the summer of 1934 the three principal Fugitive-Agrarians have not been together except for short visits, and since *Who Owns America?* they have not participated in any common project, though Ransom and Tate have served together on the faculty of the Kenyon School of English, which Ransom founded in 1949,[25] and Tate and Warren have been advisory editors for *The Kenyon Review* and the University of Minnesota Press. After settling in at Gambier, Ransom continued teaching and editing his review until his retirement in 1959. In 1961-1962 he returned to Vanderbilt as visiting professor. During his two decades at Kenyon Ransom wrote many critical reviews and essays on the nature of poetry and criticism, but though he often spoke of going back to poetry (after five years of silence he had published one poem in 1939) it was not until the spring of 1962—following his visit to Vanderbilt—that any new verse from his pen appeared.

After three years at Princeton, during which he helped to found a remarkably fine weekly discussion program broadcast by the Columbia Broadcasting System, Tate served as Consultant on Poetry for Library of Congress. Following this he became editor of *The Sewanee Review*; though he worked on the magazine for less than two years he completely remodelled it upon the design established by Ransom for *The Kenyon Review* and made it one of the most vigorous of the literary quarterlies. Though it is now in the care of Tate's old friend, Andrew Nelson Lytle, after passing through the hands of two other excellent editors, it still bears the impress of Tate's personality and point of view. After leaving it Tate served for a time as a publisher's editor and a lecturer in English at New

[24] From conversations with Warren on October 26, 1953, and January 6, 1954, and letters from Warren to Tate, beginning February 4, 1935, and continuing through July 8, 1940. The letters are now in the Princeton University Library. The influence of Agrarianism on these works is considered in Chapter Ten.

[25] In 1952 the school was moved to Bloomington, Indiana, and became the Indiana School of Letters.

York University. Since 1951 he has been a member of the faculty of the University of Minnesota.

When his fellowship was up, Warren spent a year teaching at the University of Iowa, and by the time he returned to Louisiana State University, *The Southern Review* was in deep trouble. When America entered the war, the university's support for the magazine was drastically reduced. Ransom, too, was barely managing to keep his review alive. He wrote to Warren, offering to merge their magazines, but the offer was declined. However, when *The Southern Review* suspended publication in the summer of 1942, Ransom took over its subscription list and Brooks and Warren were appointed advisory editors for *The Kenyon Review*. In the autumn Warren moved to the University of Minnesota, and since 1942 he has made his home in the North. In 1944-1945 he followed Tate as Consultant in Poetry at the Library of Congress, and in 1947-1948 he returned to Italy on his second Guggenheim fellowship. In the meantime Brooks had been appointed to the faculty of Yale University, and when his fellowship came to an end, Warren joined him there as professor of playwriting in the Drama School and fellow of Silliman College in 1950. But in 1956 Warren decided to give up teaching and spend all of his time writing—in Connecticut or on the Italian coast northwest of Rome, where his second wife, Eleanor Clark, had leased a section of a partially ruined Spanish fortress and made it over into an apartment. However, having been so many years a teacher, he missed the classroom and in 1961 he went back to part-time teaching in the English Department at Yale.

Davidson stayed at Vanderbilt until his retirement in 1960. His views regarding the South remained unchanged, but apart from an occasional burst of cantankerousness they did not mar his magnificent two-volume history of the region drained by the Tennessee, published by Rinehart and Company in 1946 and 1948 as part of its Rivers of America series. Southern affairs since the war have been to him a cause for great bitterness. Happier is the career of Andrew Nelson Lytle, who published his first novel, *The Long Night*, in 1936, the year in which Agrarianism all but came to an end. As it declined he gave more and more attention to creative writing, and with the publication of *At the Moon's Inn* (1941), *A Name for Evil* (1947), and *The Velvet Horn* (1959) he has been recognized as one of the South's finest contemporary novelists. Brilliant, reckless, and for many years provokingly immature, he was slow to come out of the shadows of provincialism and the influence of the older Agrarians and look at his region under the light of history. Now, however, he deserves to be named with Faulkner, Warren, Katherine Anne Porter, and Caroline Gordon as an interpreter of the Southern past. In 1961 he was made editor of *The Sewanee Review*, and his appointment ensures continuity with the character and excellence which Tate brought to the magazine together with development in new directions befitting his own vigorous and independent imagination.

IV

The New South has come to pass and it has turned out to be much better than the Agrarians had prophesied. With improvements in transportation and factory design, new industries have moved into the region; Southern cities have grown—some to twice their prewar size; mass production and communications media have made the South increasingly like any other part of the nation. However much one regrets the disappearance of many charms and graces of Southern folk culture (and one should keep in mind that the people within that culture, whose independence the Agrarians had praised, usually gave it up quite willingly), life for ordinary people and particularly for the Negroes is far more abundant, not only in simple necessities and comforts of living but in opportunities for self-fulfillment, than it ever was before, even though the region lags behind the nation as a whole in per capita income, education, public health, and housing. One hears so much about resistance to racial integration that one forgets how much progress is being brought about by decent, patient people who would rather live under the laws of the land than under the rule of ancient passions. The Southerner's conservatism, his pride in personal freedom, racial prejudice, and the bogey of Communism, have been used to impede organization of the labor force, which, in comparison with that of other regions, is still underpaid, but laws passed since Agrarianism began and more enlightened management have greatly improved working conditions. More and more farmers have shifted from the ruinous single cash crop to diversified planting and cattle raising, and deep freezing has opened many new markets, though some farmers still deliberately overproduce in order to take advantage of government subsidies.

Mencken's Sahara of the Bozart now has many oases. Television, the mass-circulation magazines, and improved education have encouraged interest in the fine arts and new leisure and higher incomes have made possible the establishment of good community theatres, orchestras, and galleries. But though a younger generation admires Faulkner and Warren, Southerners are still inclined to mistrust contemporary artists. They tend to support those who exhibit or perform works of the past rather than those who create works of the present. And it cannot be denied that much of the new interest in the arts is—as it is elsewhere in the nation—faddish and superficial, a naive form of dignified conspicuous consumption. But one would have to lack faith in the power of art to suppose that, whatever the motives of the audience, more frequent immediate experience with good works leaves unaffected the taste and perceptiveness of people having normal sensitivity and intelligence. Moreover, there are unmistakable signs that the number of truly informed and appreciative patrons is growing, and where there are more patrons there will in time be more creative artists.

The technological developments which have made this possible have turned most Southern yeomen from the folkways admired by the Agrarians and have so altered their lives that they will never go back to them. At the same time these developments have brought to all parts of the land immeasurable amounts of the vulgar and meretricious, which in the mid-Fifties, when, for example, bookstores were closing down and theatres catered to expense-account audiences demanding brassy musicals, seemed to threaten the existence of all ideas, patterns of behavior, and works of art that required discrimination and intelligence. (Since then bookstores—among which are *not* numbered such new outlets for books as drugstores and supermarkets—have increased by fifty percent and good live drama has reappeared in new community and academic theatres all over the country.) Confronting the most distasteful aspects of mass culture, one can easily overlook how much technology has improved lives once "dulled by labor, illness, and fear," lives in which the recreations were all too often not the play-parties and folk dancing praised by the Agrarians but "bear-baiting, cockfighting, drunkenness, tales of witches, gossip about the sexual malpractices of priests, monks and nuns, [and] stories of murders and mutilations."[26] Against the belief that industrialism has impoverished life, Edward Shils has argued that

"The contrary is true. Hunger and imminence of death, work such as we in the West now regard as too burdensome even for beasts, over very long hours, prevented the development of individuality, of sensitivity or refinement in any except those very few in the lower classes who were either extremely strong personalities or extremely talented or extremely fortunate. . . . It would be far more correct to assert that mass culture is now less damaging to the lower classes than the dismal and harsh existence of earlier centuries had ever been. . . . Only the frustrated attachment to an impossible ideal of human perfection, and a distaste for one's own society and for human beings as they are, can obscure this."[27]

As a group the Agrarians suffered from no "distaste for one's own society and for human beings as they are." One of the principal arguments in their attack on industrialism was that it destroyed the conditions necessary for happy and meaningful human relations. But in comparing life under industrialism with the life of earlier times, Professor Shils offers a partial explanation for the failure of the programmatic side of Agrarianism. The small, old-fashioned subsistence farm by which they hoped to restore the Southern economy and preserve its regional culture did not have the capacity which they attributed to it for satisfying the intellectual, aesthetic, religious, and social aspirations of man. For those who had experienced both, life in the city, or on farms so situated that the farmer could make enough money to drive to the city and buy the products of industrialism to relieve his tedium, was preferable to life under the conditions vaunted by the Agrarians.

It is axiomatic that pastoral literature is written by city men. By the time they wrote *I'll Take My Stand* most, probably all, of the Agrarians had become city men who looked at life in the country through eyes weary of the ugliness and disorder to be found in even so agreeable a place as Nashville. Moreover, their vague

[26] See Edward Shils, "Daydreams and Nightmares: Reflections on the Criticism of Mass Culture," *The Sewanee Review*, LXV (Autumn, 1957), 585-608.

[27] Shils, pp. 604-606.

notion of the good life of the past, of the pre-industrial "Europe" to which they liked to refer, was probably much influenced by literary conventions established over the centuries by city men who, as members or dependents of the privileged classes, did not have to endure the heavy labor and narrow confinement of farming. Owsley, of course, knew what farming was like. He loved the soil and the thrust of bunched muscles on a plow handle, but he made no special claims for their aesthetic significance. For him the physical and emotional release of hard work under a hot sun seemed satisfaction enough, though of course it wasn't: he could not have loved farming half so much had he not loved history, teaching, and arguing more—far more. Warren knew, too: knew the stony uplands, the iron frosts, the July storms, the stench of green-mantled ponds and the ineffable loveliness of a windless autumn morning. The accounts he gives of the meagerness and the moments of tenuous sad beauty of farm life are a good retort to the whimsies of Ransom's *God Without Thunder*, wherein, despite the insistence upon the possibility of natural catastrophes which chasten man's vanity, the description of the aesthetic satisfactions of farm life suggests childlike revelling in a bland and everblooming landscape; in what one might call, borrowing a phrase from Ransom's later theories, the "texture" of the country taken as a metaphysical poem. It was Ransom's quasi-literary image of the farm which, from the "Statement of Principles" onward, represented the Agrarian vision, and the critics repeatedly called attention to its incompleteness. "It dwells," wrote W. S. Knickerbocker, "only on the felicities of the patriarchal farmer, as if the small farmer regularly secured a dependable living from the rude forces of nature: as if nature were beneficent, and cared for his wants; and his children were never ill; and his wife were never overburdened with bearing and rearing children." And looking back upon a decade of Agrarianism, Peter Carmichael said flatly, "The visions they have are book-begotten. . . ."[28]

Essentially primitivistic assumptions about the superiority of life on a subsistence farm led some of the Agrarians to still less tenable

[28] William S. Knickerbocker, "Mr. Ransom and the Old South," *The Sewanee Review*, XXXIX (April, 1931), 228; Peter A. Carmichael, "Jeeter Lester, Agrarian Par Excellence," *The Sewanee Review*, XLVIII (January, 1940), 27. See also Gerald W. Johnson, "The South Faces Itself," *The Virginia Quarterly Review*, VII (January, 1931), 157.

assumptions about the conditions which foster good art. Despite having lived in, written for, and drawn all the support for their own art from a complex urban culture, as had most of the other artists—of whatever times—whom they admired, they tended in their programmatic essays (but not in their theoretical essays on aesthetics) to speak of the arts mainly in terms of the folk songs, folk tales, and handcrafts of the country. Forgetting that the best folk art was governed by conventions as formal as those of any high art of the cities (though not usually so complex or potentially expressive) and that the folk audience had been thoroughly trained to appreciate skill in handling these conventions, they attributed its excellence to the fact that rural artists and their audiences were endowed with a natural good taste uncorrupted by urban institutions—a taste which, when the opportunity presented itself, enabled them to respond directly and simply to whatever deserving art the cities and cultures other than their own produced. The Agrarians overlooked the Southern farmer's suspicion of outsiders, especially when they were men of contemplation rather than men of action; overlooked, too, the point so well made by Sir Joshua Reynolds in his thirteenth discourse on art: "It is the lowest style only of arts, whether of painting, poetry, or music, that may be said, in the vulgar sense, to be naturally pleasing. The higher efforts of those arts, we know by experience, do not affect minds wholly uncultivated. This refined taste is the consequence of education and habit. . . ." Thus they were embarrassed by the fact that with so much natural good taste, the leisure the countryman, unhurried by the tempo of the city, was supposed to have, and the opportunity for "a free and disinterested observation of nature," which Ransom thought particularly necessary for creativity, the agrarian South produced so little art and when given the chance took to the worst products of mass culture with the greatest enthusiasm—to its garish lithographs, crude architecture, and maudlin pseudo-folksongs. The truth is that any considerable amount of the education and habit to which Reynolds referred requires nurture by a culture having diversity of opportunities, specialization of occupations, professional training, wealth, independent, critical spirits, and communion among men of varied interests—the kind of culture which cities throughout history have provided. The gentlemen of the Old South who built fine mansions, whose sons knew enough Horace to season a political address, and whose daughters could play Mozart, lived off the culture of Northern and European mercantile-industrial societies, from whence came their education, books, fine china, musical instruments, furniture, draperies, and fashions. As for the subsistence farmers, by and large they weren't having any.

In 1945 Ransom looked back upon Agrarianism and made what was for him a large and handsome concession:

"Without consenting to a division of labor, and hence modern society, we should have not only no effective science, invention, and scholarship, but nothing to speak of in art, e.g., Reviews and contributions to Reviews, fine poems and their exegesis. . . . The pure though always divided knowledges, and the physical gadgets and commodities, constitute our science, and are the guilty fruits; but the former are triumphs of muscular intellect, and the latter at best are clean and wholly at our service. The arts are the expiations, but they are beautiful. Together they comprise the detail of human history. On these terms the generic human economy can operate, and they are the only terms practicable now. So the Southern agrarians did not go back to the farm, with exceptions which I think were not thoroughgoing. And presently it seemed to them that they could not invite other moderns, their business friends for example, to do what they were not doing themselves. Nor could they even try to bring it about that practicing agrarians, such as there might still be in the Old South, should be insulated from the division of labor and confined securely in their garden of innocence. An educator or a writer cannot abandon the presuppositions behind his whole vocation, nor imagine that they have less than a universal validity for the region, and ought to be kept out of circulation as beyond the common attainment. I find an irony at my expense in remarking that the judgment just delivered by the Declaration of Potsdam against the German people is that they shall return to an agrarian economy. Once I should have thought there could have been no greater happiness for a people, but now I have no difficulty in seeing it for what it is meant to be: a heavy punishment. Technically it might be said to be an inhuman punishment, in the case where the people in the natural course of things have left the garden far behind."[29]

Such candor needs no comment.

V

In later chapters we shall discuss the relation of Agrarian ideas to specific works by Ransom, Tate, and Warren. But it is well to pause here to consider in a general way what Agrarianism has meant for our literature since it has turned out to mean next to nothing in our public affairs.

Elsewhere we have mentioned the appeal which the Agrarian image of an ideal society has had for some literary scholars and the peculiar half-life which Agrarian ideas have continued to lead in quarterlies and seminars. These scholars may overestimate the significance of Agrarianism because Tate and Warren wrote important poems and fiction during the Agrarian interval, because Ransom's theories which have influenced our literary studies are obviously closely related to it, and because when they were Agrarians, Ransom, Tate, and Warren shared so many beliefs and attitudes that it becomes difficult to think of their attaining a comparable eminence in American letters apart from the Agrarian communion. Yet Ransom held most of the important tenets of the philosophy underlying his critical theories *before* he turned to thinking and writing on social problems. Even if one removed from his writing all mention of the Agrarian social image, his thought would still be all of a piece—so much so, indeed, that one can suppose that the parts which have importance for literature would have come into being in just about the same form without Agrarianism. It helps us the better to understand and evaluate those parts, but it does not seem to have been one of their significant ideological determinants. Much the same can be said about Tate's ideas concerning the nature of poetry and the need for tradition: in essence these antedate Agrarianism, and there is good reason to believe that their evolution might have been the same without it. Warren, too, had come to the principal themes of his work—the parent-child relation-

[29] John Crowe Ransom, "Art and the Human Economy," *The Kenyon Review,* VII (Autumn, 1945), 687.

ship, the longing for lost innocence, the struggle for self-knowledge and fulfillment, and the meaning of history—before he returned to Tennessee and made contact with the Agrarians. Moreover, it was the conceptions *behind* the Agrarianism of his friends that most influenced his work, and he had already been exposed to them during his conversations with Tate in New York several years before the Agrarian period. Thus in considering the importance of Agrarianism for the dominant themes, ideas, and attitudes in the writing of the three men whose achievement warrants raising the issue, we should probably think of it not as a cause but, like the writing itself, as an effect of forces anterior to them both.

But one must not leave out of account the powerful stimulus which Agrarianism provided. Certain inward experiences and feelings described in the poems and fiction, certain conceptions proposed and defended with special earnestness in the essays on poetics, had, as we shall see, urgency for these writers because they had hoped to live under their Agrarian correlatives. Moreover, in Agrarianism Ransom, Tate, and Warren had reason for working, arguing, and thinking together, for criticizing manuscripts, for trying out new ideas in letters and discussions, and thereby quickening the imagination and raising the standards of performance for one another. And there was more than simply stimulation. Agrarianism furnished means for declaring and questioning what seemed most meaningful to them: it gave them problems of value and behavior around which to organize their random thoughts and observations into beliefs.

Fully to appreciate this we must recall what Tate and Warren had written about the difficulties confronting the writer who suffered from the "malady of disbelief" and whose imagination could find outlet only through inchoate self-assertion. During the years of Agrarianism other American writers solved these difficulties by swearing fealty to Marxism in return for the assurance of a public identity, a place in the group, and the chance to serve a cause larger than themselves. Southerners of their generation found such difficulties especially complex and burdensome because they could be met only by coming to terms with the regional heritage before coming to terms with themselves and their environment. But there were compensations: Southern writers were not so disengaged from their people and their culture. Out of the experience and legends of their region they could make something which served as an ideal larger than the self. This is just what the Agrarians did. And paradoxically, though it had no perceptible effect on social events where Marxism had an immense one, Agrarianism, with all its misconceptions, served as a better link for the writer with his society because its image of man—not his economy but man himself —was more realistic. One might say that though Agrarianism was not nearly as important for the *text* of the literary work as one might expect, it may have been immensely important for the *act* of writing.

It was almost a myth, in Ransom's sense of the term, and like a myth it was intended to enable man to enter into some kind of right relation with a universe too vast and unpredictable for his understanding and so to possess his soul and perform as a man —which, of course, would include man as writer. Agrarianism had its Adamitic hero, the yeoman farmer; its lost Garden, the bountiful subsistence farm of the past; its Satan, the Northern scientist-industrialist; its Hell, the modern city. Implicit everywhere in it was a narrative of fatal knowledge, a fall from grace, a defiance of the supernatural, and after suffering a quest for salvation. There was even a body of the Elect: the Southerners who yet might re-enter the Kingdom. As a myth it was rudimentary, incomplete, and ultimately inadequate, but for a time it worked. Ransom had warned in *God Without Thunder* against taking a myth for science and history. When one did, he argued, the myth proved to be false on the factual level and was likely to be abandoned, however profound its truth as a representation of the world as man experiences it. Taking Agrarianism as an imperative of belief meant taking it as social science and history, and, as we have seen, it failed. But as long as it functioned as an imperative of reference, it served the Agrarians well. Thus, it served our literature well and meant, but not in the expected ways, a great deal indeed.

CHAPTER FIVE

JOHN CROWE RANSOM'S POETRY

....

"A poem is as strong as its strongest link."
—*Ransom, "Old Age of an Eagle"*

....

I

"ALL my poems end inconclusively," John Crowe Ransom once remarked. "And I used to be taken to task by members of my group for that."[1] He was talking with Cleanth Brooks and Robert Penn Warren about his poem "Bells for John Whiteside's Daughter," and it is unlikely that he thought anything could be added to its delicate perfection. He went on to say that while he was given to tinkering with his poems, he had never wanted to change this one. By "inconclusive" he meant not incomplete but ambiguous. His poems never come down foursquare on one side of an issue or offer any resolutions to the situations they present. From "Sunset," his first, to "Master's in the Garden Again," with which in the spring of 1962 he returned to poetry after an absence of more than two decades, they confront the reader with two views of man, each so meaningful that neither can be abandoned for the other.

Throughout his poetry and prose is an awareness of the radical difference between what men yearn for and what they get. It informs the elements which make up his double vision of man: the "fury against abstractions," the conception of the modern mind as divided and at war with itself; the mistrust of monistic philosophies and sciences; the image of a pluralistic universe and the belief that the arts offer the most comprehensive mode of representing it; the argument in support of an agrarian culture; and the irony of his delivery. Only in death, where the difference seems most immense, does it end. And death, Ransom told his friends, is "the greatest subject of poetry, the most serious subject, . . .

[1] Cleanth Brooks, Robert Penn Warren, et al., *Conversations on the Craft of Poetry* (New York, 1961), p. 21.

there's no recourse from death, except that we learn to face it, and to get on speaking terms with it, and then to have the characters who leave us and bereave us pass as magnificently as possible. And then, life must go on. So in many poems of mine I think I intended for a resolution of that sort to be apparent."[2] A resolution, that is, to accept the ambiguity. Poem after poem confronts the reader with that ambiguity, often in a little narrative about one who rejects the actual in favor of the ideal, or who, dismayed by the difference between them, is incapable of action.

The protagonist of "The Swimmer" rejects the actual. This poem, which opens Ransom's first volume, *Poems About God*,[3] was written soon after Donald Davidson had spoken encouragingly of "Sunset" and is markedly better than that fumbling beginning:

> In dog-days plowmen quit their toil,
> And frog-ponds in the meadow boil,
> And grasses on the upland broil,
> And all the coiling things uncoil,
> And eggs and meats and Christians spoil.

The swimmer, having escaped to a shaded pool, thinks,

> I have no home in the cruel heat
> On alien soil that blisters feet.
> This water is my native seat,
> And more than ever cool and sweet,
> So long by forfeiture escheat.

Concluding that he need no longer endure the pain of living, he lets the water close over him. The poem ends,

> Water-bugs play shimmer-shimmer,
> Naked body's just a glimmer,
> Watch ticks every second grimmer:
> *Come to the top, O wicked swimmer!*

Only two or three among the thirty-two poems in the book are up to this level of competence, and in them about the only interest comes from their faint resemblance to Ransom's later poetry.

Even in "The Swimmer," early as it is, it can be seen. Here, as

---

[2] *Loc. cit.*
[3] For an account of *Poems About God*, see Chapter One, pp. 18-19.

in many of the poems for which he is best known, is a notable disparity between the tone and the subject, deriving most obviously from the diction and such riming combinations as *broil, uncoil,* and *spoil.* The curious *escheat,* a learned and technical term from a higher usage level, is made more conspicuous by being rimed with another somewhat formal and uncolloquial term, *seat,* and together they create an effect of slightly arch whimsy.[4] Having a mere watch order the swimmer to return undercuts the sternness of *grimmer* and *wicked* and makes the suicide seem, as it were, a trifling delinquency like the "brown study" which vexes the mourners for John Whiteside's daughter. The disparity is mildly startling —enough to make us pay a little more attention to what is going on. And it helps to make the poem somewhat inconclusive: has the swimmer done right or wrong? Ransom evokes, but not with such a nice balance of powerful forces as he would later achieve, both sympathy and disapproval for one who rebels against the human condition. Life goes on—with the conflict of attitude unresolved.

Far from fulfilling the small promise of wit and irony suggested by the rimes of "The Swimmer," those of "Noonday Grace," which follows, seem to run away with the poem, which begins,

> My good old father tucked his head,
> (His face the color of gingerbread)
> Over the table my mother had spread,
> And folded his leathery hands and said:
> "We thank thee, Lord, for this thy grace,
> And all thy bounties to the race;
> Turn not away from us thy face
> Till we come to our final resting-place."
>
> These were the words of the old elect,
> Or others to the same effect.

The son adds his own thanks:

> Thank God who made the garden grow,
> Who took it upon himself to know

---

[4] Observing that Tate and Warren also were taken with *escheat,* Randall Jarrell wisecracked that with its "backward brother" *estopped* it constituted " 'the little phrase of Vinteuil's' or national anthem of the Fugitives." ("John Ransom's Poetry," *The Sewanee Review,* LVI [Summer, 1948], 385.)

That we loved vegetables so.
I served his plan with rake and hoe,
And mother, boiling, baking, slow
To her favorite tune of Old Black Joe,
Predestined many an age ago.

The poem ends with the mother and God conspiring over a blackberry pie. Fortunately the volume does not remain on this dismal
level. Toward the end comes a poem so near to Ransom's later
manner that it might almost be an unfinished rough draft of a
poem for *The Fugitive*. "Prayer" describes an aged woman plead-
ing for God's help and ends,

Now God sat beaming on his burnished throne
And swept creation with appraising eye,
Finding, I fear, not all was free from blemish,
Yet keeping his magnificent composure;
But wearing certain necessary airs,
To suit with such incumbency of court,
He still at heart was quite a gentleman;
For when he saw that aged lady drooping
And wearying her bones with genuflections
For her unworthiness, he fell ashamed
To think how hard it went with holy women
To ease their poor predicaments by prayer:
There on his heaven, and heard of all the hosts,
He groaned, he made a mighty face so wry
That several serphin [*sic*] forgot their harping
And scolded thus: "O what a wicked woman,
To shrew his splendid features out of shape!"

The hints of the poetry to come measure the space Ransom had
yet to traverse. Though *Poems About God* was written in Ransom's
twenty-ninth year after he had been teaching at Vanderbilt for
three years, it exhibits a taste so ill-formed that even after we have
allowed for the feebleness of the instruction in English during
his undergraduate days, we wonder how a man schooled in the
classics and having latent within him so much originality and sensitivity could have learned so little about poetry or published such
clumsy lines as appear on page after page. He has said that he first

tried verse after he had been reading Browning, whom he much admired. It seemed to him that Browning managed to bring into every line some unexpected word or rhythm to remind the reader that he had poetry before him. Such became the basis of Ransom's whole poetic principle at this time: "Never a prose line, always a punch."[5] From this one would expect more unconventional verse, but in poetry Ransom was still timid, and only toward the end of the year did he begin to go as far as varying the length and position of the pauses within his lines or letting the lines run over. He would always prefer to start from simple, regular forms, which in later years he learned to vary with great ingenuity. Now, however, when he departed from their strict patterns, it was probably because he knew so little about them.

Along with his simple principle, Ransom had some predilections which subsequently helped to form his distinctive style. Already he showed a preference for narratives, and one third of the collection consists of little anecdotes and fables, and all but one poem involve an account of some action. Though he had been trained in philosophy, only two or three poems are at all ruminative. He had difficulty in sustaining any argument in verse, being easily put off by epithets or allusions which pleased his fancy but did not point toward anything in the poem. He was more at ease with narratives and quasi-narrative forms, and for his characters and situations he often went to village settings to which he would return many times later on. "Under the Locusts" faintly foreshadows the world of "Fall of Leaf," "The Vagrant," "Winter's Tale," "Conrad Sits in Twilight," and other poems published in *Chills and Fever*, his second book, which appeared eight years later in August, 1924:

> What do the old men say,
> Sitting out of the sun?
> Many strange and common things,
> And so would any one.
>
> . . .
>
> Dick's a sturdy little lad
> Yonder throwing stones;
> Agues and rheumatic pains
> Will fiddle on his bones.
>
> . . .

[5] From a conversation with Ransom, August 26, 1946.

Jenny and Will go arm in arm.
He's a lucky fellow;
Jenny's cheeks are pink as rose,
Her mother's cheeks are yellow. . . .

This is not the naturalistic setting of "Sunset" and "Noonday Grace," which Ransom quickly abandoned. Rather, it lies not far from the world of the Grimms' fairy tales, Mother Goose, and the *märchen* tradition toward which Ransom was later much attracted and in which he located many of his fables. His interest in narratives, villagers, and simple stanzaic forms owed nothing, now or later, to the example of Hardy, though a number of critics have thought they did. Ransom used them long before he knew Hardy's poetry well. The practice of describing people indirectly through their actions might owe something to Browning, but it is more likely that Ransom relished Browning's work because it answered to an innate interest in people, particularly rebels and eccentrics struggling in the clogs of convention.

Part of Ransom's early difficulties in controlling the progress of a poem seems to have come from his fascination with rime, which took over such poems as "Noonday Grace," "Grace," "Geometry," and "November." He had, as it turned out, an unusual aural memory and a flair for unexpected combinations comparable to Auden's. Later he learned to use rime brilliantly for emphasis and subtle modification of the tone, and some of his witty combinations saved otherwise mediocre poems from failure. But at the outset he had little or no discrimination, and when, under the manifest influence of Shakespeare, he turned to blank verse ("The skies were jaded, while the famous sun/ Slack of his office to confute the fogs/ Lay sick abed . . ."), his poetry improved in coherence and economy of means. It also got away from the flat diction with which he had begun, and moved in the direction of the elegant and learned language of his mature work. Yet even then he mistrusted the exceptional. He had strong sympathy for idealists who aspired to impossible things; yet aware of the difference between their hopes and their accomplishments, he would not so commit himself, no matter how splendid the hope nor how glorious it might be to fail in a struggle beyond the strength of man. Some of this reserve affected his attitude toward remote and strange words. Unlike Hirsch, Davidson, and Tate, he approached them with caution, and there was always in his use of them an irony directed at the diction itself, as if it were at once delightful and faintly absurd. In an early poem, "The School," he made fun of a conceited young pedant whose head is stuffed with high-falutin' dreams and phrases —who condemns the world but in the end meekly comes to terms with it:

> . . . Equipped with Grecian thoughts how could I live
> Among my father's folk? My father's house
> Was narrow and his fields were nauseous.

God "sent a pair of providential eyes" and the young scholar forgot Helen, the fishes "that were purple," and "proud Athens shining/ Upon her hill."

It would be naive to see an autobiographical impulse here; yet it is curious that Ransom put aside the classics when writing his poetry. Though later he mined the literature of the past, he never made reference to Odysseus, Achilles, Hector, Agamemnon, Oedipus, Creon, Aeneas, or the legends of Thebes and Rome, and the only use of the Trojan material is this reference to Helen, another to asphodel in "Necrological," and one to the fall of Troy in "Blackberry Winter." Not one of these requires more acquaintance with the classics than might be found among schoolboys who had never read a word of them. A number of reasons for this suggest themselves: that allusions to the classics were part of the literary tradition of the Old South, which Ransom rejected from the beginning; that in so abruptly turning aside from the discipline in which he had long been schooled, Ransom felt an uneasiness which inhibited his poetic imagination and directed it away from the classics. None of these really suffices and the omission remains, along with the odd fancy for old-fashioned children's stories, a quirk of an unusually independent and original poetic sensibility.

Meters and rhythms, too, were resources which Ransom learned to use sensitively but handled here without imagination or much sense of the appropriateness of their effects to the meaning and tone of the poem. As may be seen in the quotation from "Prayer," he had a tendency to write in long, stringy sentences; even so, he chopped the phrases to fit his metrical units and imposed on them a metronomic regularity and monotony. Later he did not bother adhering to metrical patterns and relied simply on counting the number of strong accents which seemed to occur naturally in a line.[6] By then he had developed great skill with the movement and pace of his lines, which had a tantalizing variety that sometimes strained to the limit the reader's sense of the meter. In these early poems, however, the uniformity of the phrases tended to space the accents as evenly as the ticks of a clock, and where some variant occurred, the lines seemed to lurch and skip to maintain the regularity of the beat. This, with his strange rimes (*trees—centuries, crazily—infancy*), sometimes distorted the pronunciation of key words. Far from being experiments of a restless innovator, his irregularities were manifestly blunders of taste. This poet who would become so original was at the outset meekly but not very successfully conventional.

One reason is that Ransom had no firm base of ideas from which to venture forth. Such a base is certainly not necessary for experimentalism and many—perhaps even most—of our young poets are most experimental when they have none and can dart about trying now this, now that, novelty. But Ransom needed such a base before his imagination could freely explore his forms and subjects. Years afterward he told Brooks and Warren, "I never tried to write and found I couldn't. I just got involved in some of these theoretical questions—philosophical questions—and they just engage my whole mind." [*sic.*] He would make several drafts of a poem, "And then in another week maybe I'd worked up . . . a tension in me which made my reason, my thinking for the argument, and my imagination for the sensibility, more compatible with each other. They began to try to please each other. And then I found I could knock off a pretty fair poem and while I was still at that height I might do three or four poems."[7] The consistency of his style and his way of treating recurring themes bear out this explanation. We may conclude that even though Ransom had recently studied philosophy at Oxford he had when he wrote *Poems About God* no coherent body of conceptions and attitudes so familiar that he could take them for granted and concentrate on the troubling joy of "knocking off" a poem. For these poems wander about from a sketch of business men exercising to a monolog in which God expresses his outrage at the hardships endured by women. The uses of God's name, which the

---

[6] *Conversations*, pp. 19, 22, 31.
[7] *Conversations*, pp. 30-31.

introduction claims as the common concern of the poems, are too varied to signify any consistent ideas at work behind the themes which engaged Ransom's attention.

Yet for all the wandering, many subjects which one expects as a matter of course to find in the early work of a poet of this century are wholly absent. Only one poem touches fleetingly on life in the city, and there are none of the usual images of vacant lots, mildewed lofts, littered streets, clattering machinery, and picturesque bums. There are no outcries over the poet's agonies of maturation, confusions or loss of belief, tormented relations with others, humiliating maladjustments, defiance of society, defense of his own conduct, and so forth. True, some poems in the first person describe the speaker's conflicts with his surroundings, but the tone is mild, the difficulties do not seem acute, and, more often than not, it is the speaker himself who is in the wrong. Andrew Nelson Lytle has said that Ransom grew up in a society that was humane and had a coherent view of life,[8] and we have seen that their sense of participation in the community helps to explain why most of the Fugitives tended to neglect the conventional figure of the alienated intellectual waging total war on the world. (Davidson's outland piper was something else.) Apparently, then, Ransom may have had enough of an inherited point of view to be uninterested in some topics though lacking enough of a philosophy to free his imagination for exploring in depth more compatible themes and forms. Even so, such a description of his situation, if valid, does not account for the curious fact that Ransom, who had so much to say later on about the poet's love of nature, never published a poem on the natural beauties that have moved so many poets: far hills, pastures, woodlots in spring and autumn, riverbanks, waterfalls, lake shores, seascapes, skies full of stars or clouds, lonely houses, and abandoned roads. Nor does it tell us why apart from a passing reference in "Sunset" to a patient dog as a "southern gentleman," Ransom put into his poems not one detail which was unmistakably identified with his region. (Later he wrote four poems on themes related to the history of Southern society, but even in these he did not put anything—a place-name or a genus of animal or plant—which was distinctively Southern.) One can understand that an energetic young

---

[8] "Note on a Traditional Sensibility," *The Sewanee Review*, LVI (Summer, 1948), 372.

man who had studied abroad and was now teaching in one of the most progressive institutions in the South might turn his back on the *literary* heritage of his region, but that is quite another thing from making no allusion to the rich environment in which he had spent most of his life.

Yet even as he skipped about, certain subjects took his fancy more than others and among them we find traces of a distinctive poetic personality. Already Ransom was concerned over death and the fading of youthful energy and beauty. ("Jenny's cheeks are pink as rose,/ Her mother's cheeks are yellow.") Other themes to which he would return in his mature work are lovers' quarrels, especially between gloomy, domineering men and gentle, easily injured women, the conflict of asceticism and innocuous sensuous pleasure, and rebellion against the mundane and sensible, particularly by old men who will not submit to tea and slippers. The poems about lovers, even when written in the first person, are quite without the intensity and often embarrassingly personal tone that one takes for granted in the work of beginners, while the poems about rebellion, if they touch on the disquietude of the sensitive young man, tend, as we have seen in "The School," to belittle his sense of his own importance. Despite some impatience with tight-lipped godly folk, the poems manifest a friendliness toward all kinds of people and none of the tiresome disdain for those who are not poets.

Perhaps if they were laced with some spite against his fellow men, Ransom's first essays in verse would be more interesting. The few outbursts of anger against the injustice of God are smothered by other passages of conventional piety, and in plain truth the collection is tedious except for what it tells us about Ransom's development. In his later poetry he seemed to do with such ease exactly what he wanted that we may not fully appreciate the ingenuity and originality of his style and his perceptions. A casual comparison of the mature poems with the pieces in *Poems About God*, none of which he has chosen to reprint in subsequent collections,[9] helps to make conspicuous the distinctive qualities of the later achievement and suggests how far Ransom had to come in realizing them.

[9] Robert Graves chose some of them for inclusion in *Grace after Meat*, a collection of Ransom's poems which he persuaded Leonard and Virginia Woolf to publish at their Hogarth Press in 1924.

II

Though he had several years of teaching experience behind him, Ransom felt that he needed more training in English and soon after returning to Vanderbilt from service in the Army he began a program of reading in the literature and history of the late medieval and early Renaissance periods and took courses on *Beowulf* and Chaucer. Yet with all these demands on his time he resumed writing poetry and tried many sonnets that he did not think worth saving. The Fugitives had begun to meet again, and Tate, who joined the group in November of 1921, recalls that

> "John Ransom always appeared at the Fugitive meetings with a poem (some of us didn't), and when his turn came he read it in a dry tone of understatement. I can only describe his manner in those days as irony which was both brisk and bland. Before we began to think of a magazine John had written a poem which foreshadowed the style for which he has become famous; it was 'Necrological,' still one of his best poems; I marvelled at it because it seemed to me that overnight he had left behind him the style of his first book and, without confusion, had mastered a new style."[10]

He was thirty-three years old; he had published one book which had no particular merit. Then, suddenly, this:

> The friar had said his paternosters duly
> And scourged his limbs, and afterwards would have slept;
> But with much riddling his head became unruly,
> He arose, from the quiet monastery he crept.

The friar comes to a battlefield where the bodies of the slain had been stripped and left for the wolves.

> But the brother reasoned that heroes' flesh was thus,
> Flesh fails, and the postured bones lie weatherbeaten.

Among the lords of chivalry

> Was a dead warrior, clutching whose mighty knees
> Was a leman, who with her flame had warmed his tent,
> For him enduring all men's pleasantries.

[10] Allen Tate, "The Fugitive 1922-1925," *The Princeton University Library Chronicle*, III (April, 1942), 77-78.

Close by the sable stream that purged the plain
Lay the white stallion and his rider thrown.
The great beast had spilled there his little brain,
And the little groin of the knight was spilled by a stone.

The youth possessed him then of a crooked blade
Deep in the belly of a lugubrious knight;
He fingered it well, and it was cunningly made;
But strange apparatus was it for a Carmelite.

Then he sat upon a hill and hung his head,
Riddling, riddling, and lost in a vast surmise,
And so still that he likened himself unto those dead
Whom the kites of Heaven solicited with sweet cries.[11]

Ransom wrote "Necrological" soon after reading an account of the siege of Nancy, where the body of Charles the Bold, Duke of Burgundy (1433-1477), had been left on the field and eaten by wolves. Mindful of the Southern concern for the rituals and trappings of chivalry, one might suppose that the antiquarianism of the poem was an unmistakable sign of Ransom's Southern background. The background may have had something to do with encouraging his interest, but the critical spirit which puts the poem firmly in the mock heroic tradition was quite Ransom's own. In all the poems, such as "Spectral Lovers," "Armageddon," "Captain Carpenter," and "The Equilibrists," that use material from the feudal world and the chivalric romances, the archaic elements display their curious and brilliant detail, but the tone of the poems serves to diminish their grandeur and make them seem rather quaint and even slightly absurd. In his rambling but delightful poem "Dog," Ransom got much of his fun from presenting a common bull as if it were a gentle prince from the pages of Malory:

> . . . Up the lane the tender bull
> Proceeds unto his kine; he yearns for them,
> Whose eyes adore him and are beautiful;
> Love speeds him and no treason nor mayhem.

[11] This is the version published in *Chills and Fever*. In preparing the poem for inclusion in his *Selected Poems*, Ransom made some minute changes in the punctuation and substituted *wight* for *knight* in the thirty-fourth line—a small but telling improvement.

> But, on arriving at the gap in the fence,
> Behold! again the ubiquitous hairy dog,—
> Like a numerous army rattling the battlements
> With shout . . .

In a great voice the bull demands, "What do you want of my twenty lady kine?" and

> . . . the air trembles to the sorrowing Moo
> Of twenty blameless ladies of the mead
> Fearing their lord's precarious set-to.

The battle is splendid, but a simple churl, the dog's owner, puts an end to it.

> . . . the leonine smarts with pain and disrepute
> And the bovine weeps in the bosom of his family.

Even "Antique Harvesters," which honors the gallantry and grace of the South in part by allusions to chivalric conventions, lacks not the salt of irony. In the description

> Here come the hunters, keepers of a rite;
> The horn, the hounds, the lank mares coursing by
> Straddled with archetypes of chivalry . . . ,

the satiric realism of *lank* and *straddled* tempers the nostalgia of the poem.

Such lighthearted treatment of a subject one expects to be taken solemnly by a Southerner characterizes, as we shall see, Ransom's use of antiquarian elements and is part of the pervasive dualism of his poetry. The dualism permeates all aspects of "Necrological," which may be read as a fable about a man riven by the conflict between the abstract dogma which appeals to his intellect but cannot account for the complexity of human experience and the sensuous appeal of a life of glittering weapons and gaudy ladies which ends up in meaningless destruction. Neither the absolute of contemplation nor that of action fulfills the needs of man. By poising and counterpoising the words, images, details, feelings, literary and historical associations, and even the rhythms of the poem, Ransom explores without direct comment the complexities of the friar's dilemma and shows the wasteful stupidity beneath the glamorous spectacle of the accipitrine warriors and the fatuity of the friar's little truisms. The closest control over the medium was needed to fuse these complicated and contrary elements and keep the poem turning back upon itself instead of scattering in the many directions toward which the vivid details invite attention. Ransom had matured as a poet to a degree that seems incredible if one takes up "Necrological" just after putting down *Poems About God*. Did the war and his experiences overseas quicken his imagination? (This poem was as near as he ever came to publishing a war poem.) Was it the new energy and excitement in Nashville and Vanderbilt following the wartime expansion and the return of the veterans? Lytle, writing on the occasion of Ransom's sixtieth birthday, said that "It was his associations with younger poets and critics, many of them his students, whose training contained the contradictions of their time, which served as the shock to his imagination and set him in the way of his mature work. The younger men more nearly represented the private sensibility before the spectacle of a breakdown in the common sensibility."[12] Ransom, he said, had been slow to recognize the confusion of values of the times which would henceforth provide many topics for his poems. But while these explanations may partially account for the greater comprehensiveness and the more sophisticated attitudes of the poetry, they leave untouched what at first glance is far more impressive—the amazing advance in technical skill. For with this poem Ransom established himself as one of the finest craftsmen of our literature. The explanations point to an important feature of this poem and those to follow: Ransom may have chosen to make no use of the physical details of his surroundings, but he was responding after his own fashion to the experience of his time and place. His antiquarianism was no retreat from the present; rather, it gave him a vantage from which to look upon the life about him and from its odd angle see much that goes unnoticed. The friar of "Necrological" can properly be said to be Ransom's version of contemporary man, drawn toward irreconcilable opposites, which appeal to conflicting sides of his nature, and incapable of decision and meaningful action.

But the style is more than a display of virtuosity and a perspective. It is a sensitive register of an attitude of amused and slightly weary acceptance of the disparities of life which took the place of the occasional bursts of anger and protest in *Poems About God*. A

[12] "Note on a Traditional Sensibility," p. 373.

few years later Ransom gave an account of the progress of the imagination from romance to irony that does well as a general description of what probably took place in his own development, though it gives no hint of the causes. Man, he wrote, begins life as a practical dualist. The world is one, he is another. "His problem is purely the physical one: the application of force at the point where it will do the most good." But after some failures, he assuages his hurts by supposing some transcendental unity to which he belongs, despite his apparent defeats. Then "the romantic constructions of his mysticism are generally obnoxious to the sober observations of his science, and frequently they fall." Since the flattering monism is untenable, he goes on to a new dualism whose characteristic mode is irony. He learns to live with the dream of the ideal and the dismay of the actual:

> "Irony may be regarded as the ultimate mode of the great minds—it presupposes the others. It implies first of all an honorable and strenuous period of romantic creation; it implies then a rejection of the romantic forms and formulas; but this rejection is so unwilling, and in its statements there lingers so much of the music and color and romantic mystery which is perhaps the absolute poetry, and this statement is attended by such a disarming rueful comic sense of the poet's own betrayal, that the fruit of it is wisdom and not bitterness, poetry not prose, health not suicide. Irony is the rarest of the states of mind, because it is the most inclusive. . . ."[13]

Ransom's own irony, as the discussion of his handling of chivalric materials suggested, is particularly obvious in the disparity between the tone and the subject in his poems, which may confuse the reader at first but helps to present Ransom's dualistic view of his subject and to enlarge the reader's understanding and sympathy for the people in the poems, who are caught between the world as it ought to be and the world as it is. There is no better example of this disparity than the often-anthologized "Bells for John Whiteside's Daughter," first published in *The Fugitive* in February, 1924:

> There was such speed in her little body,
> And such lightness in her footfall,

[13] "Thoughts on the Poetic Discontent," *The Fugitive*, IV (June, 1925), 63-64.

It is no wonder that her brown study
Astonishes us all.

Her wars were bruited in our high window.
We looked among orchard trees and beyond,
Where she took arms against her shadow,
Or harried unto the pond

The lazy geese, like a snow cloud
Dripping their snow on the green grass,
Tricking and stopping, sleepy and proud,
Who cried in goose, Alas,

For the tireless heart within the little
Lady with rod that made them rise
From their noon apple dreams, and scuttle
Goose-fashion under the skies!

But now go the bells, and we are ready;
In one house we are sternly stopped
To say we are vexed at her brown study,
Lying so primly propped.

It is a quiet world in which things are done according to rules
and people are sternly stopped by bells. The imperious grown-ups
look down from their heights on little girls who play not with
sticks but with rods (like the shepherdesses of Versailles), and even
the geese are so refined that instead of honking they *cry* "Alas."
But John Whiteside's daughter is a non-conformist. She engages in
noisy warfare (*bruited* suggests how old-fashioned her world is
and how much uproar she makes) and compels the stately geese to
scuttle. Yet she is a lady for all that and light on her feet as a lady
should be; so the adults view her with both pleasure and dismay.
Now, as Warren has said, she has committed her greatest naughti-
ness: proper little girls do not go off into brown studies. We are
puzzled by the tone. This mixture of amusement and annoyance
seems inconsistent with our feelings about the deaths of children.
The disparity, like the ambiguity of the rhythms of the second line,
makes us pause, and as Ransom observed in speaking of those
rhythms, "complicates our reception of the poem." We are compelled to study the situation closely and to recognize how inade-

quate are our "ideal" stereotypes of little girls and our stock responses. A lively child is charming and vexatious; its death might indeed seem an impropriety to the onlooker, though he would scarcely confess to this feeling. Ransom makes us look beyond the image of the storybook and valentine to a real little girl, who might be living next door. An abiding paradox of Ransom's poetry is that it so skillfully uses artifice to present more vividly the real and often seems to intend one feeling while actually evoking another, which may be quite the opposite. Robert Lowell has praised Ransom for "sticking to concrete human subjects—the hardest." Though Ransom works by indirection, that is just what he does. Lowell also cites his "balance, control, matureness, nimbleness, toughness, and gentleness of temperament. All these qualities were necessary for him to write, as few poets in the world have done, of the death of a child, a child's hen, or a childish coquette, without cynicism, sentimentality, or trifling. These are the hardest of poems. . . ."[14]

Such poems are difficult for the inattentive reader, who may stop short of their ultimate meaning. He could not think them sentimental, but he might think some of them, "Necrological," for example, somewhat frivolous. But it is a thoroughly serious poem and, like those that followed it, is established upon a coherent body of convictions which Ransom chose to represent in a few simple themes, all testifying to the ultimate unknowableness of the universe, the tendency of all monistic systems to give man illusions of power over his surroundings and to mislead him into disaster, the ambiguous value of all human experience, and the difference between the simple, carefree, sunny world of the heart's desire and the world we are actually given. He was anything but didactic; yet he believed that a poem had to be formed upon a philosophical core, though as he told Tate, "There must not be a trace of the expository philosophical method."[15] Even so, he did not intend to write philosophical poems. In reviewing Ransom's third volume, *Two Gentlemen in Bonds*, Tate referred to their mingled rationalism and *noblesse oblige* and cited Ransom's "dualistic philosophy"

[14] "John Ransom's Conversation," *The Sewanee Review*, LVI (Summer, 1948), 376. See also Robert Penn Warren, "Pure and Impure Poetry," *The Kenyon Review*, V (Spring, 1943), 228-254, for a sensitive exegesis of the poem, and Brooks and Warren, *Conversations*, pp. 19-24, for Ransom's own comments on its meters.

[15] See Chapter Two, p. 74 and note 30.

with its "assertive element *versus* an element of withdrawal and respect." The pairings coincided with Ransom's image of the opposition between the reason and sensibility, and Ransom wrote to Tate, expressing approval of Tate's terms, but added, "If you are right I am happy—I've put unconsciously into my creative work the philosophy which independently I have argued out discursively." Then looking back on his performance he said,

> "My object as a poet might be something like the following, though I won't promise to stick by my analysis: (1) I want to find the experience that is in the common actuals; (2) I want this experience to carry (by association of course) the dearest possible values to which we have attached ourselves; (3) I want to face the disintegration or multiplication of those values as calmly and religiously as possible. Art is our refusal to yield to the blandishments of 'constructive' philosophy and permit the poignant and actual Dichotomy to be dissipated in a Trichotomy; our rejection of Third Terms; our denial of Hegel's right to solve a pair of contradictions with a Triad. And here's a slogan: Give us Dualism or we'll give you no Art."[16]

He could appreciate those "dearest possible values" and the inability of idealists to confront their disintegration because there lingered in him a sense of what he had earlier called "music and color and romantic mystery." This led Louis Untermeyer into the mistaken notion that *Chills and Fever* represented a "reaction against realism . . . a return of faith; a hope in a bright-colored, romantic world."[17] But Untermeyer utterly misread his text. Ransom had no hope of such a world and was, by his own later definition, a classicist. "In classical art," he wrote, "we begin with a formula for accomplishing an end and propose to test it in an actual course of nature. . . . Classical art becomes tragic in the hands of the serious artist. He is the artist who submits the formula to such a searching and sustained experimentation that finally he comes to the place where it breaks down."[18] Whatever we may

[16] From an undated letter to Tate, someone has added in pencil "[1926][? Spring]." The letter was written in the spring of 1927. For a discussion of the dating see Chapter Six, note 9. The letter is now in the Princeton University Library, as are all the others from Ransom to Tate referred to in this chapter.

[17] Louis Untermeyer, "Seven Against Realism," *The Yale Review*, XIV (July, 1925), 791.

[18] "Classical and Romantic," *The Saturday Review of Literature*, VI (September 14, 1929), 126.

think of this as a general definition, it is a good account of many poems beginning with "Necrological" in which Ransom follows the fortunes of a character to the point where his formula breaks down. However light the tone, Ransom is almost always a serious artist, and the final implication of his work, for those who accept its dearest possible values, is tragic.

One reason for the breakdown of the formula is the inevitable decay of beauty, love, and bodily grace and vigor. Writing to Tate about the destruction of values as the implication of all art, Ransom observed, "Poe's theory of poetry is a very fine application of this principle—the lovely woman seen dead, etc."[19] Mortality, and particularly that of woman's beauty, is the most frequent theme in Ransom's mature poetry and a little over one third of the poems which he chose for his *Selected Poems* touch on it in some manner. Latent in them is an assumption of the superiority of the past in the life of a man, a society, or a race, and we shall see that the poems look back with nostalgia but no sentimentality to a simpler, happier world. But Ransom was no ordinary primitivist. In "Blackberry Winter" he wrote,

> The breath of a girl is music—fall and swell—
> The trumpets convolve in the warrior's chambered ear,
> But I have listened, there is no one breathing here,
> And all of the wars have dwindled since Troy fell.

Yet he had exposed the real character of those wars in "Necrological," using militaristic imagery, not as Tate was doing to show the moral corrosion and cowardice of the present, but to discover the present through its resemblance to the past. For, as he told Tate, he believed that "The fundamental life-history of individuals is about the same in all periods; or at least it may be."[20] There is here a contradiction with Ransom's later Agrarian views, though it is not as great as it seems. We should remember that one thing for which he praised the agrarian cultures of the past was their preparing man to face the inescapable catastrophes of life.

Sexual love in the poems, far from conferring a kind of im-

[19] From a letter to Tate dated "April 3 (and 13)." See Chapter Six, note 9.
[20] From a letter to Tate dated "September 13." The fact that it was written at Indian Hills, Colorado, makes clear that it belongs to 1926.

mortality on man, is destructive. Ransom's lovers fear an act which, if anything, will hasten the body's decay. In "Spectral Lovers" a man frightened by desire thinks:

> Blessed is he that taketh this richest of cities;
> But it is so stainless, the sack were a thousand pities;
> This is that marble fortress not to be conquered,
> Lest its white peace in the black flame turn to tinder
> And an unutterable cinder.

Similarly, in "The Equilibrists," the woman's body is remembered by her lover as

> . . . a white field ready for love.
> On her body's field, with the gaunt tower above,
> The lilies grew, beseeching him to take,
> If he would pluck and wear them, bruise and break.

But honor keeps them apart until

> . . . these lovers fully were come
> Into their torture of equilibrium:
> Dreadfully had forsworn each other, and yet
> They were bound each to each, and they did not forget.

In death they must choose:

> Would you ascend to Heaven and bodiless dwell?
> Or take your bodies honorless to Hell?

> In Heaven you have heard no marriage is,
> No white flesh tinder to your lecheries,
> Your male and female tissue sweetly shaped
> Sublimed away, and furious blood escaped.

> Great lovers lie in Hell, the stubborn ones
> Infatuate of the flesh upon the bones;
> Stuprate, they rend each other when they kiss;
> The pieces kiss again—no end to this.

But they will have neither and so they lie *"perilous and beautiful"* in an equipoise of passion and principle which resembles the bewildered inaction of the friar of "Necrological." Another analog may be found in the futile warfare of "Armageddon," in which neither the hedonistic (but asexual) Anti-Christ nor the ascetic Christ can achieve a clear-cut victory. However, a most significant difference may also be observed in "Armageddon," for the destructive action is initiated by Christ, who personifies the monistic reason given to abstract formulas for Duty, Honor, and the like (and so is associated with the "gaunt tower" of "The Equilibrists"). Anti-Christ, the personification of the sensibility, wishes only to enjoy a gentle, undemanding pleasure in the ephemeral delights of the natural world. Where desire was absent, Ransom tended to take the side of the sensibility in the conflict between the two halves of man's being (which were similar to the traditional and conflicting body and soul), and the ideal world implied in his poems was one which permitted the sensibility free and unhurried indulgence because the reason, with all its plans for reducing nature to a stern and usable order, is virtually absent. That, however, is the ideal, and the poems never suggest that it is possible. In the real world the sensibility has but little time to follow its fancies, for death waits where vitality and beauty seem most assured. The formula must break down. Man and his works fail, and his illusion that he can escape the common fate makes him glorious and absurd.

Seeking "the experience that is in the common actuals," Ransom chose to depict what he later termed "the domestic situations."[21] His poems had, therefore, a human dynamic that made them dramatic, never abstract and speculative. His most constant interest was in human behavior and what it revealed of men's understanding of themselves and their situation. Not surprisingly, then, half of his poems are narratives or quasi-narratives, and most of these are about innocents who from ignorance or just plain stubbornness do not accept the mortality of their "dearest possible values" and resolutely pursue their objectives, which are usually no more than a thoughtless delight in simple movement and beauty. Children, eccentric old men, and charming spinsters grandly and foolishly go their own way until the common fate overwhelms them and destroys their values. Gently bred young ladies flutter helplessly under the dour realism of their domineering sweethearts in yet another analog of the conflict between the sensibility and the reason.[22] Yet the people of these domestic situations are little more

[21] *Conversations*, p. 19.

[22] In *Two Gentlemen in Bonds* Ransom grouped such poems as "Piazza Piece," "Blue Girls," and "Lady Lost" under the heading "The Innocent Doves." In

than types seen from a distance and wholly from the outside. There is, in many instances, an elaborateness amounting to an almost finicky courtliness and gallantry about their conduct which is appropriate to the ironic formality of the poems and need, of course, be no impediment to the "common actuals" though it restricts our view of them to one or two qualities. We draw somewhat nearer to John Whiteside's daughter, to the little girl in "Janet Waking," and to the husband and wife of "Prelude to an Evening." They succeed as *homi ficti*, for what we can see of them creates an illusion of wholeness. But Captain Carpenter, for example, is only a puppet, and for all the intention which Ransom reported to Tate, much of his poetry is not so immediate, vivid, and concrete as Tate's own "Ode to the Confederate Dead" or sections of Davidson's "The Tall Men," despite the burden of speculation which those poems must carry.

In "Judith of Bethulia" Ransom chose to delineate a complex personality by showing its effect on a variety of onlookers. Here the pluralism of his point of view matched the pluralities of his subject—the ambiguous woman, the confusion of feelings she aroused, and the moral dichotomy of her heroic but sadistic behavior. The result is one of his most penetrating and powerful poems:

> Beautiful as the flying legend of some leopard,
> She had not yet chosen her great captain or prince
> Depositary to her flesh, and our defence;
> And a wandering beauty is a blade out of its scabbard.
> You know how dangerous, gentlemen of threescore?
> May you know it yet ten more.
>
> Nor by process of veiling she grew the less fabulous.
> Grey or blue veils, we were desperate to study
> The invincible emanations of her white body,
> And the winds at her ordered raiment were ominous.
> Might she walk in the market, sit in the council of soldiers?
> Only of the extreme elders.

When Bethulia is invaded, Judith first tests her power on the blear visage of the aged men of the city then, knowing "how bright was

---

the next section, "The Manliness of Men," he placed such poems as "Our Two Worthies," "Two in August," and "The Equilibrists."

the weapon unrusted in her keeping," she goes to the drunken leader of the enemy, unmans him with her beauty, and slays him. In wonder the hearers ask, "Nor brushed her with even so much as a daisy?" To which the narrator laconically answers, with an indirect tribute to a force too great for mere words, "She found his destruction easy." So, after that, was the destruction of his army:

> . . . their white bones clutter the holes of foxes,
> And the chieftain's head, with grinning sockets, and varnished—
> Is it hung on the sky with a hideous epitaphy?
> No, the woman keeps the trophy.

> May God send unto the virtuous lady her prince.
> It is stated she went reluctant to that orgy,
> Yet a madness fevers our young men, and not the clergy
> Nor the elders have turned them unto modesty since.
> Inflamed by the thought of her naked beauty with desire?
> Yes, and chilled with fear and despair.

By skillfully balancing the exotic (Judith is like a rare and deadly animal so far above the ordinary that its legend flies) with the naturalistic (the desperate peeping of the men and their desire for vicarious participation in the violation of their fearful heroine), Ransom makes the woman extraordinary yet convincing. We are brought near enough to see her imperious beauty, feminized by the soft colors of her veils, and her chilly impersonalness which makes her look upon that beauty not as an offering for a beloved but as a weapon or a treasure to be deposited with a reliable custodian. At the same time, the formal design of the carefully parallel stanzas serves to keep her enough in the distance to preclude any risk of making her seem unreal by overinsistence on her strangeness. Though legendary, she is believable because someone—not the reader but the bystander in the city—has been close enough to have become inflamed and chilled, and on that authority we accept her perverse conduct without demanding more explanation, which might diminish rather than augment her presence. Ransom had achieved a fine equation of suggestion and restraint.

Balancing opposing forces within a harmonious and unified order is the fundamental principle of Ransom's style and the communication of his unique vision of man. When reading one of his mature poems we have a sense of radical diversity, of complicated lines of stress, of collisions among the elements. At the same time we feel threading among these strong filaments which bind the poem together, and in the end we are left with a satisfying impression of wholeness. If, as usually happens, we are offered two views of and attitudes toward the subject, we find on finishing the poem that they have preserved their separate identities. The opposition has not been resolved though it has been assimilated into the total statement of the poem, which itself affects us as a single entity. The two images of Judith as a supremely feminine and desirable woman and as an unsexed and forbidding monster are both present in the last lines of the poem and, far from cancelling each other out, make each other more vivid; yet we feel that the poem, as a statement and as an artistic design, is unified and complete. Working with Ransom's pluralistic philosophy and his almost automatic tendency to look for the opposite of anything his imagination discovered in a subject was a love of form and simplicity. As he later told Tate, he had to struggle hard to satisfy that love, but he succeeded and imposed on his poems a power and beauty commensurate with the richness of their details.[23]

His usual way of obtaining contrast within unity was to play off complex, unexpected, and apparently inappropriate particulars against a plain and strong overall design. Thus he would take a simple little anecdote and fill it with complicated details. He would choose some quite ordinary meter and stanzaic form and carry his variations on their patterns almost to the point of a collapse into prose. In the midst of homely diction and colloquial syntax he would put words that send the reader hurrying to the *Oxford English Dictionary*. This technique gave strong architectonic coherence to the work while making the individual details stand forth. In many ways his poetry resembles Bach's *Art of the Fugue*. There is in both the same working and reworking of a few closely related themes, the same simple outward designs enfolding complex but always perfectly controlled and integrated inward patterns, and the same marvelous counterbalancing among the details of individuality with consistency, of opposition with cooperation.

It seems quite natural that Ransom, who carried his variations so far, should think of himself as a traditionalist and should fre-

---

[23] From a letter to Tate written in the spring of 1927. See Chapter Six, note 9.

quently defend meters. He admired Tate's mind and approved of his adventurous spirit, but he could not go along with Tate's experiments in direct representation of the chaotic life of the mind. "I am unable to see the art-thing in the heterogeneity," he wrote in commenting on a poem Tate had sent to the Fugitives early in 1923. "I require for the satisfaction of my peculiar complex something more coherent than is offered in the mere cross-section of a brain at a given instant. You are attempting an art of the sub-rational. To me that seems as unnecessary and as limited as . . . pure Imagism. . . . Isn't it an assumption that the poetic is antithetical to the rational?"[24] As the argument over free forms ran on Ransom added, "I quite agree that the form is organic with the matter. . . . It is the formal preoccupation that destroys art, which must not appear meditated; nor *be* meditated, for that matter."[25] But organicism of the form did not mean that its shape was identical with the shape of the subject in its existential condition, and he would not concede that the disorderly processes of the mind justified a similar disorder in poetry about those processes. His own precise and delicately articulated effects, which often served to delineate confusion in the characters of his anecdotes, were not meditated but came from subsequent tinkering during which he relied on his feeling for the fitness of the details. As he told Brooks and Warren, "When I wrote most of my poems I was unconscious of the principles of poetic composition—unconscious of meters—and didn't know what I was doing in an articulate sense. I imagine that's the rule with poets—that they go right ahead on their own intuition and then later they wonder what they've done and look at it to see."[26] Even so, when he reached the tinkering stage he had an increasing sense of the emergent whole. For all his pleasure in the odd and precious detail he esteemed the "determinate regularities."

Nothing quite so threatened their prevalence or contributed so much to the excitement and beauty of his poetry as the diction. Ransom, whose father, it will be remembered, was a skilled linguist,

[24] From a letter to Tate dated simply "Monday." Someone has added "[Feb. 1923]," which is probably correct. Ransom was commenting on Tate's poem "The Yellow River," which Tate had sent to Davidson with a letter dated January 14, 1923.
[25] From a letter dated "May 6." Internal references to affairs of *The Fugitive* make clear that it was written in 1924.
[26] *Conversations*, p. 19.

had the Fugitives' love for unusual words, but he was more wary, and the ones he chose and the way he used them were utterly different from those of his friends. Where Hirsch and Davidson invoked the dim and tremulous and softened the focus of their poems and Tate—at least in his Fugitive days—tried to assert the superiority of the poet over the reader and shifted the focus from the matter to the manner, Ransom strove to bring the subject more sharply into view and to achieve a detachment which would encourage an unhurried contemplation of its myriad aspects. Occasionally he, too, used lofty language to shift attention to the manner, but then he wanted to make fun of the subject, the very language itself, and even, it seems, of the poet. In "What Ducks Require," a charming poem, he thus describes the nesting period:

> Furled, then, the quadrate wing
> From the lewd eye and fowler's gun
> Till in that wet sequestering,
> Webtoed, the progeny is done. . . .

No easy sentiments about ducklings here. Instead, we are invited to relish the witty and deliberate overwriting.

Some words, such as *springe, thole, frore, halidom, carline, ounce* (leopard), *bruited, wiven,* and *lordings,* though used in the mock-heroic manner, go back to chivalric tales (and such later imitations as *The Faerie Queene* and *Idylls of the King*). Others, such as *unconcessive, perdure, concumbent, casuistical, diurnity, ambulant, theogony,* and *saeculum,* recall the latinate language of Renaissance scholars—that of Milton, whose diction Ransom was studying with fascination at this time, but even more those of Sir Thomas Browne and Jeremy Taylor. Still other terms, while not associated with an earlier literary period, were learned, formal, and remote from both everyday speech and the usual language of poetry: *dissevers, susceptive, palinode, ogive, obsolescent, tumuli, occipital, intervolved, refulgently,* and *reconstitute.* These he would use with some ordinary detail, as when he described the nesting ducks or referred to his having "pernoctated with the Oxford students." He liked to intensify the contrast by the plainness and brevity of the terms among which the odd words appeared, as when he used the combination *transmogrifying bee* in "Janet Waking." In "Parting at Dawn," he told the lovers

231

> . . . most dry should you drain
> Your lips of their wine, your eyes of the frantic rain,
> Till these be as the barren Cenobite.

Having, as it were, exalted them beyond the realm of domestic situations, he abruptly brings them back to the level of the commonplace:

> And then? O dear Sir, stumbling down the street,
> Continue, till you come to wars and wounds;
> Beat the air, Madame, till your house-clock sounds. . . .

Stumbling, beat, and *house-clock* indirectly disparage the lovers' tendency to regard their relation as out of the ordinary.

The antiquarianism operated on more than one level. Beside the castles and courts of love appears the world of cottages, villagers named Dick, Dorothy, Tom, and Doctor O'Dreary, buxom housewives, scullery maids, dim-witted scholars, and stout yeomen occasionally glimpsed in *Poems About God*. Such homely materials were sometimes used to depreciate the chivalric and learned elements. In "Miller's Daughter," for instance, we are given a "bookish hind" whose head is filled with "too much pudding" of "learned characters and scraps of lore" who helplessly and hopelessly desires the village beauty. Here and in a few other places the antiquarianism is not crisp and wry but almost cute, but Ransom rarely exploited it for its quaintness unless it be, in the end, to disparage the very attitudes toward the past that made it seem merely quaint. Such, for example, was his method in "Necrological": he recreated the imagery of psalters and tapestries and then forced us to see beyond them to the real life of the times. Witter Bynner had complained that Davidson's unusual words made his poems "academic." The same might be said for most of the Fugitive poetry, for the Fugitives went to books rather than to their observations of life for much of their material. So did Ransom. His poetry is obviously the work of a literary scholar and requires of us some scholarship for its full understanding. Even so, in all but a few poems he got beyond the library into the real world of his own time. His learning gave him an eminence from which to examine it.

As with the diction, so with the imagery: Ransom constantly surprises the reader's expectations by pairing the archaic with the contemporary, the elevated with the lowly, the serious with the whimsical, the solemn with the jesting. In "The Tall Girl" we are presented with a little tableau right out of a late medieval dream of fair ladies:

> The Queens of Hell had lissome necks to crane
> At the tall girl approaching with long tread
> And, when she was caught up even with them, nodded:
> "If the young miss with gold hair might not disdain,
> We would esteem her company over the plain . . ."

When the Queen of Heaven appears, we expect to see her in the likeness of the Mary of fourteenth-century Florentine paintings; but instead we are shown "a plain motherly woman," who "made a wry face" and referred to herself as "Just an old woman." (The text is that of the *Selected Poems*.) Even more startling is the image with which Ransom concluded his tender "Winter Remembered." As first published in *The Sewanee Review* for January, 1922, this was a sonnet, possibly one of the many Ransom wrote under encouragement from Walter Clyde Curry in the interval between his return to Vanderbilt and the founding of *The Fugitive*. The first three quatrains were the same as those of the later version. Following them came this couplet:

> Which would you choose, and for what boot in gold,
> The absence, or the absence and the cold?

When reprinting the poem in *Chills and Fever* Ransom dropped this feeble ending and added two more quatrains, the second of which has four of the best lines he ever wrote and his most memorable image:

> Dear love, these fingers that had known your touch,
> And tied our separate forces first together,
> Were ten poor idiot fingers not worth much,
> Ten frozen parsnips hanging in the weather.

No number of rereadings can take away the shock of that image which, far from coarsening the poem, gives by indirection the most delicate sense of the woman's warm and gentle presence and what it means to the speaker.

But Ransom's imagery, taken as a whole, is somewhat less rich and evocative than that of Davidson, Tate, and Warren, which is surprising in view of the emphasis he was to place upon imagery in his later speculations on the nature of poetry. Though far more interesting than the imagery in *Poems About God*, it lacks the sensuousness of Davidson's and the visual clarity and brilliance of Tate's and Warren's. Ransom tended to take his images from restricted areas—the feudal world, the scenery of children's stories, and sometimes from a realm that vaguely suggests Edwardian fiction. Despite his pleasure in the countryside around Nashville (he once told Tate that he walked a great deal and "threw fits" over the beauty of his surroundings) he never, as we know, used details from the Tennessee landscape, and in all his work one finds few images of any kind that do not seem derived from other literature. This is not to say that the poems are thereby necessarily weakened. Some of the force and subtlety of his writing comes from the disparity between the genteel literary configurations of the imagery and the blunt realism of the interpretation of human experience which it embodies—a disparity similar in character and effect to that between the tone and the subject, to which it contributes. Often the imagery and diction serve as an indirect representation of personality for which they are, as it were, an extension. This can easily be seen in "Piazza Piece":

> —I am a gentleman in a dustcoat trying
> To make you hear. Your ears are soft and small
> And listen to an old man not at all,
> They want the young men's whispering and sighing.
> But see the roses on your trellis dying
> And hear the spectral singing of the moon;
> For I must have my lovely lady soon.
> I am a gentleman in a dustcoat trying.

> —I am a lady young in beauty waiting
> Until my truelove comes, and then we kiss.
> But what grey man among the vines is this
> Whose words are dry and faint as in a dream?
> Back from my trellis, sir, before I scream!
> I am a lady young in beauty waiting.

The imagery presents us with a garden out of the romantic fiction on which the girl's character is formed. The artistry is so manifest that we cannot dismiss the poem; teased by this odd conjunction of art and banality, we go back to it and discover how wittily Ransom has exposed the sentimental idealism of the stories by which her dearest values are nurtured. It is a *tour de force* comparable to the Nausicaa episode in Joyce's *Ulysses,* all the more pleasing for not being dragged out. More vivid imagery might appeal to us by its intrinsic interest, but it would not serve the purpose of the poem.

After the clumsiness of *Poems About God* Ransom's mastery in handling the phonetic elements of his poetry seems as miraculous as the change in the diction. His graceful counterpointing of the stresses of the metrical patterns against the natural stresses of pronunciation and sense made his poems, as Warren said, very resonant and compelled the reader to slow down and attend to their delicate suggestions and ambiguities. Take, for example, the opening lines of "Good Ships," a sonnet with only one regular line, the fourth. (Even that one feels more trochaic than iambic.) Where do the stresses fall in "Fleet ships encountering on the high seas"? The best reading seems to be *"Fleet ships* encoun*tering on the high seas,"* emphasizing the key words from which the analogy running throughout the sonnet will evolve. The opening stanza of "Eclogue" is particularly contrapuntal:

> JANE SNEED BEGAN IT: My poor John, alas!
> Ten years ago, pretty it was in a ring
> To run as boys and girls do in the grass—
> At that time, leap and hollo and skip and sing
> Came easily to pass.

To read the first line as plain iambic pentameter destroys the sense. Unless we wish to distinguish one person from another having a partially similar name (giving more weight to *John* in "John Black" in order to distinguish John Black from William Black, or giving more weight to *Black* in order to distinguish John Black from John Brown), we put the same stress on a first and a last name. So *Jane* and *Sneed* would get equal weight. *Began,* the verb and an iamb, demands a stress. *John,* as the name of the person addressed, must have one. *Poor* seems more important than the seemingly perfunctory *my. Alas,* set off by itself, can be read only in the usual way. Then does the line have five or six stresses? If we insist upon five, shall we assign a hovering accent to *Jane Sneed* and two stresses to *poor John*? Why not just the reverse? Not until we have pondered the meaning of more than the line or even the stanza can we make up our minds—and even then we are likely to be teased with uncertainties and sent back to look more deeply into the poem. We cannot say, as we might have said when confronted with a puzzling line in *Poems About God,* that the poet did not know what he was up to. Ransom saw to it that his irregularities occurred at points of importance and did not let the metrical pattern put emphasis where it did not belong. So the little punches work. Feeling this to be so, we study the poem to find out how.

In his earlier work Ransom liked to use fairly long sentences which often coincided with the stanzas. But he varied the position of his pauses, matched his runover lines with places where the sense calls for an acceleration of the pace (as one can see in the stanza from "Eclogue"), and built steadily to a climax. Where a sentence runs through several lines, each one carries more import than the one preceding it. Often, too, the last line of the sentence—particularly if it be the last line of the stanza—is truncated and may consist of a single, terse phrase. In "Bells for John Whiteside's Daughter" Ransom goes even further and uses a variation on his variation. The first and last stanzas each consist of one sentence ending in a shortened line that carries the most significant part of the meaning. Their exact parallelism puts a frame around the middle three stanzas, which conform to the metrical pattern of the first and last—but only to surprise us. Where we expect the shortened final lines of the second and third stanzas to bring us a full stop and a long pause, we find that they run on. Moreover, beginning with the second line of the second stanza we have one sentence eleven lines long which describes the busyness of the little girl. The structure accelerates our reading, and this, as Warren has pointed out, beautifully matches the sense of the passage.[27] After that extended flurry, the brevity of the last line, "Lying so primly propped," is especially emphatic.

The rime schemes of the poems after "Necrological" are usually simple, permitting Ransom to surprise us with some unforeseeable rimes or to try some curious half-rimes. Assured by the pattern, we begin to listen for the rime before it arrives. Often it comes

[27] "Pure and Impure Poetry," p. 239.

on a word which would be among the last to occur to us as a possibility. Sometimes we get a half-rime so odd that only the singular appropriateness or wittiness of the word saves it from rejection. "Survey of Literature" exemplifies, perhaps a little too obviously, the first form of surprise; its opening is as unexpected as any part of the poem:

> In all the good Greek of Plato
> I miss my roast beef and potato.

A subtler melody runs through "Of Margaret," the half-rimes of which illustrate the second form of surprise.

> With the fall of the first leaf that winds rend
> She and the boughs trembled, and she would mourn
> The wafer body as an own first born,
> But with louder destruction sang the wind.
>
> Soon must they all descend, there where they hung
> In gelid air, and the blind land be filled
> With dead, and a mere windiness unchild
> Her of the sons of all her mothering.

After describing Margaret's love for her foster-children, the leaves and flowers, the poem ends:

> Virgin, whose image bent to the small grass
> I keep against this tide of wayfaring,
> O hear the maiden pageant ever sing
> Of that far away time of gentleness.

Ransom had long been fond of alliteration and had used it with great force on occasion ("primly propped"), but he was somewhat slower in mastering the assonance and dissonance that give this poem its appropriately soft music and help to bind it together so that the half-rimes and metrical variations can strain against the unity of the poem without breaking it. The later poems use less unusual language than the early ones, but their sounds are more mellifluous or, if need be, harsh. "Painted Head," like "Of Margaret" published in 1934 after several years of silence, is one of the few pieces after *Poems About God* that do not have even half-rimes. Its argument is close and dense, but the concatenation of sounds is so delicate and pleasing that the reader is drawn back to the poem until gradually the meaning, which the sounds gracefully underline, reveals itself. To study that poem is to learn much about the expressive function of sound, which is the subtlest and most difficult aspect of the art of poetry.

Once we are over our surprise at the unexpected words, the devious rhythms, and the odd consort of tones and subjects in Ransom's poetry, we begin to see how well the elements work together in achieving a unified statement which has a meaning both greater than and different from the sum of the meanings of the elements taken one by one. "An act which produces *effective surprise*," Jerome S. Bruner says, is "the hallmark of a creative enterprise."[28] Almost any of Ransom's mature poems are such acts, and tracing all the lines of force among the elements in them to discover how they interact to strengthen and modify one another and draw one another toward their common end leads to further surprises and appreciation of the creative power behind them. The webs of relationships within the poems are simply too close to be taken in at one reading, however attentive, and after several readings the poems continue to reveal unexpected charms and to grow in richness, precision, and effectiveness. For an example we may take the comparatively short and simple "Blue Girls." (The text used here is that of *Selected Poems*. The original version, first published in *The Fugitive* for June, 1924, was longer and less taut. Ransom revised the poem in virtually the form used here for *Two Gentlemen in Bonds*.)

> Twirling your blue skirts, travelling the sward
> Under the towers of your seminary,
> Go listen to your teachers old and contrary
> Without believing a word.
>
> Tie the white fillets then about your hair
> And think no more of what will come to pass
> Than bluebirds that go walking on the grass
> And chattering on the air.
>
> Practise your beauty, blue girls, before it fail;
> And I will cry with my loud lips and publish

[28] Jerome S. Bruner, *On Knowing, Essays for the Left Hand* (Cambridge, Mass., 1962), p. 18.

Beauty which all our power shall never establish,
It is so frail.

For I could tell you a story which is true;
I know a lady with a terrible tongue,
Blear eyes fallen from blue,
All her perfections tarnished—yet it is not long
Since she was lovelier than any of you.

It is one of Ransom's many poems on the frailty of woman's beauty—and, indirectly, of love, for the young girls are lovable, but the lady, who once was lovelier, is not. As in "A Christmas Colloquy" and "Vaunting Oak" there is here a conflict between gentle, childlike feminine figures, just a little bit pert, who wish only to enjoy an innocent and thoughtless sensuousness and the gloomy, authoritative male (either one of their teachers or a close associate) who looks beyond the moment to the ineluctable conditions of life. He is also the poem's spokesman and thus the source of its inconclusiveness. For does he approve or disapprove of the blue girls? Does he see them as silly and vain or as pathetic? Which is the better wisdom for them, their instinctive little skills in practicing their beauty or his drab realism? The poem does not settle the issue, though it teases us down to the last line with the possibility that the judgment will go against the girls. Then, with superb timing, Ransom has the speaker remark that the fearful lady was *lovelier* and suggests how much he appreciates and regrets the failing of the evanescent beauty in which the girls are absorbed. Perhaps theirs is the better knowledge after all.

The poem is neatly made. All the stanzas are single sentences, but they move at different paces. The first two describe the girls by telling them, in effect, to be themselves. The second stanza picks up a little speed; there are no marked pauses, and the pace suggests a quickening of the speaker's imagination by the swift and buoyant movements of the girls. The third stanza begins as if it were to be more of the same genial instructions to enjoy life, but the turning point of the poem occurs in its first line, which is followed by a pause just where, from the example of the first two stanzas, we would expect no delay. The movement of the sounds coincides exactly with that of the thought and the tone. Where the poem had seemed jesting, it now is tinged with a hint of disapproval. The girls are told to "practice" their beauty, an ambiguous instruction conveying both acknowledgment of their cleverness and the suggestion that their beauty is just a little contrived and has about it a hint of professionalism and self-conscious calculation. Following this, in the short phrase just before the pause, are the harsh words that introduce the theme of mortality. Moreover, the girls' beauty will not fade but *fail*, a slightly more pejorative term that proposes not mere decline but giving way before some challenge. Their beauty and all their practicing, it seems, are just a bit trivial. What does the speaker really think of it? By comparison with the chattering of the girls his publishing with his loud lips seems coarse, even harsh (and linked with the sounds of the terrible tongue). Yet he seems to want to establish the frail beauty, impossible as that would be. Certainly his attitude is mixed.

Having abruptly told us what he may do while they are going their lighthearted way, the speaker explains why in the final stanza. The rhythm emphasizes the gravity of his explanation. For the last lines of the first two stanzas were shorter than the other lines, which helped to mark the division of the ideas; but the last line of the third stanza is not just shorter; it is truncated, which gives a special significance to *frail* and makes a wider division—a pause for a gathering of forces, as it were—between the third and the final stanzas. We hear then of the dark "story which is true." After another pause the lines move on with a harshness reenforced by the explosive consonants, whose effect is made even stronger by alliteration and the similarity of sounds in *tongue* and *tarnished*, *blear* and *blue*. The tone seems to verge on the punitive until we come to *lovelier*, which suddenly changes everything. Once more the girls' gaiety and charm are approved, but in the sad and wistful perspective of their inevitable disappearance. The poem which began somewhat flippantly as if it were a little squib on a subject of no importance whatever ends with pathos. The girls embody "dear" values whose certain destruction is foreseen. But the values are not simple. *We* cannot take them for granted.

The significance of the poem comes not from the truism that beauty vanishes but from its being tested in a specific situation which proves its truth and makes us pay new attention both to it and to the feelings it evokes. Toward this all elements work and from it they take the effectiveness of their little incidental surprises. The poem opens strongly with the parallelism, reenforced by consonance, between the phrases built upon *twirling* and *travelling,* and these emphasize the quick motions of the girls. Their light, bright movements are offset by the solidity and shadows of *sward, towers,* and *seminary,* which suggest authority, oppressiveness, and the obsolescence of the teachers who are old, contrary, and not to be believed. The reference to a seminary, which here designates a private school but carries an association with religious instruction and ascetic conduct, leads toward the Biblical idioms of *will come to pass* and *our power shall never establish.* These, in turn, may link the speaker and his crying with his loud lips with Jeremiah, who lamented the vanities of idle, beautiful women. He is not scornful as Jeremiah was. Nevertheless, the knowledge of the teachers is not really out of date: it is the wisdom of the ages and the prophets, beside which the girls and their pretty little skills seem ephemeral.

I could tell you a story is so simple and casual that its appropriateness might be overlooked. One tells stories to children; usually they have happy endings; they are not true. But this story is true, and there is a chance that the childlike girls who do not care for academic lectures might listen to it and learn the truth about their fate. Evidently the speaker decides that he will not tell the story, though he *could.* This complicates the tone and prepares us for the end, where we learn that he looks on the girls a little bit critically but with a friendly sadness and forbearance. And well he might. The rheumy eyes and spiteful tongue of the lady, emphasized, as we have seen, by the phonetic design, are the more dismaying by contrast with the youthful color (the lady's eyes were once blue themselves) and the chattering of the girls, who dart so lightly above mortal concerns that they are like bluebirds moving not *in* but *on* the air. This last choice, apparently so slight and yet so delicately suitable, gives a little more specificity and subtle precision to *fail, frail,* and the dread *fallen* (linked to one another by their sounds). Another small but important interaction occurs between *white* and *tarnished,* which reach across the intervening space to modify one another. *White* makes more fresh and cool the blueness of the girls and *tarnished* as a consequence gains not only force but the additional suggestion of corruption as well as wear. In its turn, *tarnished*, having a strong visual effect, makes the white seem the purer and brighter and the blue more soft and feminine.

We could linger over the metrical and other intricacies of the poem, but here is evidence enough that at their best Ransom's poems achieve a dynamic integration which results in rich expressiveness and a rare aesthetic pleasure. It also shows how much that is the essence of the meaning and beauty of a poem is communicated not by direct statement but by the contextual relations we have described. Truly, as Cleanth Brooks said, "His poems are as little amenable to paraphrase as are any poems one can think of."[29]

III

Because Ransom's poems are so closely organized and have a consistent style and because they treat a rather limited group of themes in terms of a coherent body of related ideas, they present a well-defined vision of man and his universe. As we might expect, the vision has many dualities, though the poems are no less clear and unified for that. Among these dualities, we have seen, is the disparity between the ideal worlds for which the characters in the poems yearn and the actuality with which they must come to terms, though some, like Captain Carpenter, manage to hold out against it to the end. There is another duality, much like this one and overlapping it in many ways, which must be carefully distinguished from it if we are fully to understand and respond to the poems. This is the disparity between the actual world and an ideal world affirmed *not* by the characters in the poems but *by the poems themselves*. To use Ransom's convenient terms, this ideal world is the image of the dearest values of the poems; it is an important means whereby they interpret the meaning and judge the worth of the actual world and our experience in it.

We approach this ideal world by indirection. Since Ransom was not given to making conceptual statements in his poems, the description of that world is not explicit but is rather one of the contextualized meanings arising from such interactions among the

[29] Cleanth Brooks, *Modern Poetry and the Tradition* (Chapel Hill, 1935), p. 95.

elements as we have just seen in "Blue Girls." Its function in interpreting and judging the actual is also such a consequence of a similar interaction between the ideal and actual, which define and test one another. Since we cannot look directly at the ideal world and the interpretations and judgments in which it participates, we must infer it from the effects of the value-bestowing and value-denying elements in the poems. Our inference, like any attempt at paraphrasing the implicit meanings of the poems, may seem gross and clumsy. Nevertheless, it should be undertaken if we wish to draw nearer to the full artistic and expressive substance of the work.

As we do, we must remember that the ideal world of the poems is not necessarily Ransom's ideal world. It cannot even be assumed that he knew it was evolving from the poems as he wrote them. But if he did, it would still be true that as a man any poet, even the most discursive and didactic, has many beliefs and values which he does not put into his poems, partly because some may not be compatible with his poetic imagination and partly because some of them cannot be expressed within the limits laid down by his style, the medium, and the artistic frame of reference. Moreover, it does not follow that those that he does put into his poetry are the ones which as a private citizen he most esteems. And we must remember that though his poems often arose from his brooding upon a philosophic problem, Ransom did not set out deliberately to deal with that problem in verse. He had told Tate that a poem must not be meditated. He was pleased when Tate found a conformity between his poems and his discursive prose, but he had not been aware of it. For his concern when he wrote his poems was with his art. When he wanted to express his ideas for their own sake, he turned to prose. In the poetry they served as guidelines. As Paul Weiss has said, "Artists are primarily concerned with the process of creation. . . . The ideas they have in mind are not matters of major importance to them; their ideas function merely as plans, suggestions, guides, to be modified and even discarded in the course of the process of creation. Nor is the finally produced work of art at the center of the artist's concern. An artist takes his work to be a residuum of the creative process, a momentary rest in an unending quest. . . ."[30] Perhaps Weiss

---

[30] Paul Weiss, *Nine Basic Arts* (Carbondale, Illinois, 1961), pp. 6-7.

overstates his case a little. Certainly we know of writers to whom ideas were indeed matters of major importance. But Ransom's comments on his way of writing suggests that ideas were not of preeminent importance to him as a poet. And taking all this into account, we must be careful to say that the ideal world of the poems is theirs, not Ransom's; or at most it belongs to that portion of the poetic imagination revealed in the poems. Even as the imagination is not the whole man, so that portion which we can see is not the whole of the imagination. Discretion, then, is in order.

As a "physical" entity the ideal world is severely restricted, is cut off from everything else, and is entire unto itself. It does not much resemble the environment of any particular time or place, in either history or literature, though it gets some of its elements from stories about village life in pre-Industrial England or in rural, trans-Appalachian America. It is a realm of cottages, sunny lawns and gardens where birds dart and call, canopied by cloudless summery skies. Among the people who live in it are none invested with authority for there are no social institutions, no communal problems or enterprises; each person is free to behave as a totally independent individual. The men are shy and agreeably awkward; the women must assume the initiative in all relations with them. The young men are workmen and farmers, and the older ones amiable enthusiasts permitted to indulge their whims and hobbies without stint. The young women are pretty flirts happily absorbed in ribbons and giggles, while the older ones are bustling, cheery housewives or delightful old maids who potter about with pets and flowers. Children pursue their games heedless and secure in their simple joys. Lovers are happy, abashed, and domestic; neither sexual passion nor the clash of wills troubles their friendly affections.

It was probably his sense of this ideal world behind the poems which led Untermeyer to speak of the "hope in a bright-colored, romantic world" that he found in *Chills and Fever*.[31] There was yearning, perhaps, but no hope. Cleanth Brooks was nearer the mark when he remarked on "the contrast between the broken and confused life of the mature man and the innocent and total world of childhood which he has grown out of."[32] But insofar as the

[31] See above, page 223.
[32] *Modern Poetry and the Tradition*, p. 89.

ideal world is such, it belongs to an imagined and not to the real world of childhood, whether of men or of Western society. All of us have dreamed of such a world, hence the hold of the image of Eden on our minds. But no man or society has ever really lived in it, and Ransom says as much in poem after poem. Part of our maturity consists in learning to live with the contrast Brooks refers to. Some of the characters in the poems cling stubbornly to the hope of an ideal world much like it. That is one reason Captain Carpenter and Miriam Tazewell, for example, seem immature. Not contemptibly so, however. In fact, they enjoy in their innocence a rather enviable good fortune.

It is not the world to which Davidson's outland piper wants to withdraw. There is nothing diaphanous or mystical about it. The citizens are pragmatic and naturalistic—brisk, sturdy, and pagan, untroubled by remote and awful abstractions of God, Honor, Duty, Service or by the willful desires which in our broken and confused lives set men to struggling against these abstractions. The lovers of "The Equilibrists" would not be found anywhere in it, though the young ladies of "Blue Girls" would be right at home. For though it is a world of busy energy, it has only low intensity. There is no high art, no impassioned personal relations, no complexity of experience, thought, or feeling, no burdensome responsibility, and little variety. The poems insist that such a world can never be realized; yet it is significant that it so much resembles the image of the Agrarian world Ransom described in his letters, *God Without Thunder*, and his essays in *I'll Take My Stand*—the "Europe" he was given to invoking but which never really existed. And because the ideal world leaves out of account so much that we require in our conception of a satisfactory and meaningful adult life, the poems disappoint us for much the same reason that Agrarianism did not appeal to the Southerners. The extraordinarily candid appraisal of the Agrarian ideal which Ransom published in 1945 and to which we referred in the last chapter applies with even greater cogency to this poetic ideal. It satisfies only part of the "generic human economy" that we are obliged to know and live by. Augustine's City of God is another ideal world beyond our powers, but it is a more comprehensive and hence more satisfactory standard for determining the nature and value of the world in which we live.

Like the style which has so much to do with determining its

outline, the ideal world carries the impress of a powerful imagination. We have already considered some of the qualities that have to do most directly with the artistic achievement: the originality, the sensitivity to nuances of feeling and suggestion, the affinity for unusual diction and antiquarian details, the tendency toward simple narratives filled out with contrasts and surprises. The two most important qualities that determine the vision of the ideal world are tenderness and anxiety. Especially in the poems about children, elderly people, and unhappy lovers one finds a gentle kindliness without a trace of flabbiness or condescension, for it comes not so much from pity as from love and respect for the dignity and worth of others. The irony of the poems underscores human folly, but it is never hostile and unforgiving. Among all the voices of exasperation and self-righteousness in modern poetry this quiet amiability is a relief. Yet just beneath the amiability is a muted sadness arising from a profound and pervasive anxiety manifest in the preoccupation with mortality. The proportion of poems on death and decay is high in *Chills and Fever* and *Two Gentlemen in Bonds*. When Ransom was choosing his best pieces for reprinting in *Selected Poems,* he took fewer than half of those first printed in these books (and none from *Poems About God*). Except for one or two omissions he chose unerringly. These *are* his best poems, and among them the proportion of poems on mortality is even higher. Anxiety appears in the treatment of sexual passion as well. The happy people of the poetry and of the ideal world are either sexless or so young that desire is weak and their feelings for one another are more like those between siblings than those between adult lovers. Physical desire is represented as selfish and destructive and it leads to frustration and quarrels. Later, when he was describing the functions of art, Ransom argued that a work of art arises from a wish to honor a beloved object and that one of its virtues was that it could not be used to satisfy bodily needs but could only be contemplated so that through it the object could be better known and loved. To emphasize his point he contrasted celebrating a woman in a work of art with taking sexual possession of her, which is represented as an aggressive act tending to reduce her to the status of a mere thing.

Linked with the anxieties over mortality and sex is a preoccupation with disagreeable bodily processes. Vomiting, sweating, and signs of aging in the body sometimes appear with an abruptness and disgust that seem out of keeping with the context, even when we allow for Ransom's characteristic modes of contrast and surprise. In "To a Lady Celebrating her Birthday" the conventionality of the figure takes much of the force from "voracious worms" that feed on the woman's beauty, but the lines "This day smells mortuary more than most/ To me upon my post" are too coarse for the overall tone of the poem. *Mortuary* is too general to seem excessive until *smells* makes it specific and spoils the lines. And here we have a hint that a repulsion from gross physical details by a refined sensibility may be not the consequence but the prior cause of the anxiety over sex and the deterioration of the body. Support for this notion, which lies in an area too indefinite for any conclusions to be drawn, comes from an even more obvious preoccupation with the small, dainty, and feminine, which can be seen in the diction, where terms such as *sweet, pretty,* and their derivatives are sometimes used in excess, and in the emphasis upon the withering and tarnishing of the girlish, fragile, and coquettish and the hurts inflicted on children and childlike natures by the shocks and disappointments of adulthood. These, rather than the diminution of intellectual power or of grandeur and aspiration, trouble the poetic imagination.

The anti-romanticism of the poetry may be a means of protecting the imagination against the emotional demands of a romantic commitment to absolutes which, by their nature, ask more of man than all his energy and sacrifice can provide. Among these absolutes seem to be knowledge and even poetry itself. The scholar is an object of mockery, and when a poet appears in the poems he persistently depreciates himself and his authority. Their wisdom threatens the dainty and fragile things so perhaps the intention is to lessen its authority by making its possessors appear a bit obtuse ("I will cry with my loud lips and publish"). In view of the unintellectual quality of the ideal world and the chaff aimed at the scholar and poet we seem to have here a mistrust of knowledge. Significantly, the learned brother in the sonnet sequence which concludes and gives its title to the volume *Two Gentlemen in Bonds* finds no beauty in the world, life itself disgusting, and the love of a charming woman tedious; he retires to a grey tower and longs for death. One must not attribute too much to this, but it is manifest that some of the insistence upon learning to accept the dualistic world as it is, some of the interest in rebellious idealists and their difficulties, some of the uneasiness in the presence of absorbing passions, and some of the fury against abstractions and the defense of the timid and innocuous sensibility may well come from a radical insecurity. If this be so, one can only honor an imagination that elects to confront the images of its insecurity in the poetry rather than use the poetry as a means of escaping into an assuaging fantasy.

IV

Speculation on the character and needs of the poetic imagination may help us to a more appreciative response to the poems, but only if we remember that our business is with the poems as poems and do not read them as exercises in psychotherapy. Conceivably, bad poems could serve such needs of the imagination; indeed, the evidence seems to be that they do. In judging Ransom's poems we may use our inferences about the imagination as guides to understanding but not as standards for determining their poetic value. We must not lose sight of the fact they are beautifully made things from the hand of a master craftsman who delighted in the feel and pliancy of his medium and in the exercise of his skill. For this poetry, like that of Alexander Pope, proclaims rather than hides the maker's virtuosity and holds up for our pleasure its flashing details and their intricate mosaic of relationships.

The care with which it was written can be observed in the revisions Ransom made in preparing his *Selected Poems*. In "Bells for John Whiteside's Daughter" he made three changes: he replaced a semicolon with a comma, he removed another comma, and he inserted a hyphen. The first change simply brought the punctuation of the poem up to date. The second and third changes, also more consistent with contemporary usage, subtly modify the pace of the poem and make it more appropriate to the meaning. Both occur in the fifteenth line. In *Chills and Fever* the line went

> From their noon apple dreams, and scuttle

The revision has

> From their noon apple-dreams and scuttle

This gently hastens the reading of the line and adds to our impression of forward-rushing energy. The change in "Janet Waking" extends the meaning and pathos of the poem. Originally line 10 told us that Janet went

> Running on little pink feet upon the grass

It was revised to read

> Running across the world upon the grass

The first version gives us a pleasant detail but adds little to our understanding. If anything it tends to reduce Janet's image to a stereotype. The second version may seem less specific, but in context it is actually far more so. It offers a precise impression of the child's consciousness of her surroundings: her "innocent and total world" was such that she could run across it between the kitchen door and Chucky's house. And in a moment that world is shattered by Chucky's death and she moves into the confused and broken life in which it is man's fate to dwell.

With concentration as close as this, it is not surprising that Ransom usually did best in his shorter works, for such intensity of attention and control over the elements would be difficult to maintain over extended stretches. Nevertheless, "Necrological," "Armageddon," "Captain Carpenter," "Philomela," and "Judith of Bethulia," though longer than most of his poems, are well sustained, and the first and last are as closely woven as anything he wrote. "The Equilibrists," though one of Ransom's strongest poems, does wander and grope a bit, and some of the other long poems such as "In Mr. Minnit's House," "Fresco," and the sonnet sequence, "Two Gentlemen in Bonds," are lumpish and incoherent. Even among the short poems there are clear signs that fatigue began to set in late in 1924, and it is apparent from such perfunctory pieces as "Miller's Daughter," "Jack's Letter," and "Semi-Centennial" that by the following June the drive which enabled Ransom to write his intricate poems at the average of one each fortnight was beginning to run out. There were still some superb ones in him: "Piazza Piece," "Janet Waking," "The Equilibrists," "What Ducks Require," and the three great poems written early in 1933 and published in 1934—"Of Margaret," "Prelude to an Evening," and "Painted Head." But more and more pieces were beginning to read like parodies of earlier and better ones, and *Two Gentlemen in Bonds*, which was published early in 1927, was markedly inferior to *Chills and Fever*. By then the magazine had been suspended for a year, the Fugitives were breaking up, and Ransom, Davidson, and Tate were following the new interest in their region that brought them to Agrarianism. Ransom's career in poetry was all but over. In five years he had published close to seventy poems (or close to ninety if we count separately the sonnets in the sequence "Two Gentlemen in Bonds"), most of which appeared for the first time in *The Fugitive*. More than fifty are excellent; at least a dozen are among the most skillfully written poems in American literature.

All in all it is a strange record. Ransom began late with little knowledge of his medium and in a single year wrote thirty-three poems good enough to be accepted by a major press but undistinguished. During the next five years there were periods when he wrote nothing and no poems from this interval seemed to him worth keeping. Then abruptly he began writing at his best level and with only an occasional stumble he sustained his performance for almost four years. After another year of mixed work, he virtually stopped. While he was at it he attained an artistry which can be matched among American poets of his time only by Wallace Stevens, Marianne Moore, and Robert Frost—and Frost indulged himself as Ransom never would, even when most weary.[33] Like Stravinsky, Ransom used conventions of earlier periods, mastering and assimilating them into a style so bold and original that it creates its own universe and discovers new meaning in ours.

What is the value of that meaning? To put it another way, how far beyond the ordinary perspectives from which we look at our world do we get by entering the universe created by his style? And once we have come to where we have not been before, how much can we see? Finally, what does it matter to us as human beings? Ransom himself pointed to the compelling need to ask such questions about poetry in a letter to Tate written during April of 1927. Disagreeing with the argument in Tate's essay,

[33] In 1952 Frost told a group at Dartmouth College that Ransom was his favorite among living American poets and spoke with admiration of his technical skill.

"Poetry and the Absolute," which had appeared in January and had argued that a poem is an absolute entirely self-contained, Ransom wrote that a poem had an infinite number of relations with the world beyond it—particularly relations with our values. Then taking up the difference between "major" and "minor" poetry, Ransom argued, "Potency in art is a function of the quantitative or dimensional properties in the situation. . . . Its index is the amount of turnover produced in our gray stuff. The size of the values depends on how much we use them, govern our practical lives by them. . . . The major strain in Milton . . . depends on his ability to read the reigning values of our common life into nearly all his situations, even when they look slight, for these values are more major, more important, integral, central for us than the mere intellectual beliefs."[34]

Some of the poems are little whimsies meant to be no more. "Dog" is one of these. By straining we might call it a satire on the pretensions of chivalric romance, but we run the risk of looking back and finding that the delightful poem has disappeared. R. P. Blackmur has some wise words on the worth of such verses. "To maintain gaiety at a definite level of taste," he has said, "is as difficult and requires as much composed unity of approach and as mature an attitude toward the material as is required to maintain fury or disgust. . . . Gaiety, and especially gaiety in finished form, is the last thing to be caught in a formula of facility. . . ."[35] But for all their lightness of touch, most of Ransom's poems are as serious as anyone could desire. They add to our potentialities as men.

But some of the poems do not add as much as the superb artistry and the seriousness and significance of their subjects lead us to expect. "Blue Girls" explores what seems at first a commonplace situation for which we have ready a set of familiar but somewhat inchoate feelings, but after several readings we know that we have been made to see in it things we had missed, to understand what we had failed to comprehend, and to clarify and order our feelings. This apparently slight poem has done for us what only the best art can do. And yet, and yet—

[34] For a discussion of the date of this letter, see Chapter Six, note 9.
[35] Quoted by Oscar Williams in his introduction to *A Little Treasury of Modern Poetry* (New York, 1946), p. 40.

How shall we express our sense that there is much which the poem has left unexamined without taking away the deserved praise? One way would be to point out that we probably would not think this if the poem had not shown us so well what it has. Our discontent is not with the inconclusiveness but with the quantity of realized substance. We have been instructed by the poem not to expect conclusions; yet we would like to get further under the surface of the situation. This desire is not so much the effect of one poem which, like "Blue Girls," may seem entire and perfect in its own way, as an effect of the poetry taken all together. It quickens our perceptions, arouses our expectations, and seems to stop just when we hope it will engage life more searchingly. This is not simply a matter of Ransom's choosing to write on comparatively few subjects and to omit many that we have come to regard as critical for our times.

Ransom, having elected to write about people and to let his representation be its own comment on itself, uses types which, however well we know them after encountering them in a number of poems, seem capable of only a few motions, only a few responses to their situations. Moreover, the style which presents them with such clarity and discovers for us things that we have overlooked tends also to reinforce their typicalness and reduce their range of action and being. We have here a paradox. The integration among the elements manifestly extends the scope of their meaning by creating contextual relations which communicate much which cannot be said directly. At the same time it puts a definite limit on the extended scope. Let us take, for example, the sonnet "Good Ships." It is constructed upon a witty conceit whereby two potential lovers are likened to "fleet ships" and their encounter and destinations are described in nautical terms. We get a vivid sense of *part* of their natures, *part* of their social world, and within those parts are unexpected and apt meanings for us. But the intricate elaboration of the conceit effectively keeps out of the poem all things that cannot be brought into the maritime analogy, and that very analogy is such as to put a severe limitation on our image of them as people. Miss Ivy Compton-Burnett, whose work resembles Ransom's in a surprising number of ways, uses the same types from one novel to the next, and we have difficulty keeping her books separate in our memories. Their conduct is more mannered and seems to be more remote from ordinary human behavior than that of Ransom's people. Yet among her characters are a few capable of powerful and complex responses, and in presenting them she takes care that her style, terse and concentrated as it is, suggests variety and depth below the surface that we see. These characters seem related to us somewhat as are Shakespeare's central characters, who speak in verse and do things strange to our way of life yet have a richness and vitality that enables them to touch our experience at many points and serve as symbols of ourselves. That relationship can be achieved with the characters of short poems. Yeats brings it about in less than a dozen lines. Ransom has done it in "Janet Waking" and a few other poems. But we do not feel it with Captain Carpenter, Emily Hardcastle, the lady who died of chills and fever, the man without sense of direction, or the young lady in "Parting without a Sequel." Moreover, we do not often come in Ransom's poetry upon one of those heart-stopping moments when we seem to look directly at the naked, infinite face of reality and all matters of style and structure that brought us to that vision are forgotten in the shock. Miss Compton-Burnett provides some of them. After all the melodrama, after all the artificial dialogue, after all the manner that insists upon having our attention (as well it might, for much of our pleasure is in it), there will come an instant that shakes us, as when two children overhear a remark not intended for their ears which bewilders and betrays them and recalls for us a long forgotten hurt and the suffering of childhood that we have managed to forget. Such moments come repeatedly in the poems of Robert Penn Warren, even in some of the earliest and weakest. "Original Sin" is a deeply flawed poem, but no one can easily forget its last stanza describing the guilt that follows us forever:

It tries the lock; you hear, but simply drowse:
There is nothing remarkable in that sound at the door.
Later you may hear it wander the dark house
Like a mother who rises at night to seek a childhood picture;
Or it goes to the backyard and stands like an old horse
    cold in the pasture.

Ransom's frozen parsnips and the sounds of needles clicking and the low wind making a warning sibilance among the pines in

"Prelude to an Evening" are as powerful as Warren's last two lines and take us as far into the heart of the matter, but there are not many such images in all of his poetry.

And here we may have part of the reason for the disappointment we sometimes feel, for that sense of "and yet, and yet—." Those poems in which Ransom is most profound are those in which the splendid articulation gives an added power to vivid and concrete imagery having not just a few appropriate qualities such as "Good Ships" exposed in the metaphor of ships and timbers but as many qualities as are suggested by the veiled sword which is Judith of Bethulia's beauty. Too often the focus of the style comes to rest on details of limited substance and emotive force, and being so splendidly appropriate to the content the style thrusts into prominence rather than hides their limitations.

The depth of penetration of the subject and the sheer quantity of realized substance in the poetic representation of it are not in themselves the measure of a poem's significance for us, though obviously they can affect it. What gives the measure are the significance of the subject *per se* and the significance of the poet's treatment of it. It is the second of these that the penetration and quantity of realized substance affect. Taken alone, the significance of the subject cannot bestow importance on a poem, as we may see from myriad bad poems about subjects of the most profound concern. A brilliantly executed poem about a subject of minor importance is of greater worth to us than a poorly executed one about a subject of major importance. And not simply because of its aesthetic interest, for the same organization of its elements that give it merit as a work of formal beauty will make possible contextual meanings which illuminate our understanding. Even so, a subject of importance offers more opportunity for achieving a poem of importance, and many of Ransom's have as much prepoetic importance as anyone could desire. So the issue of their significance turns upon his handling of them. Does he, in his own terms, really get at their "dearest possible values"?

Some of them, certainly. His style is marvelously expressive within its range, but, as we have said, the range is small. The characters he presents are too limited in their responses, understanding, and actions to encompass much that is in their situations.

Our wish that the poems and people had more scope is not simply a desire for variety and abundance. Though Ransom omits many subjects which have importance for our time, those he takes up matter so greatly that we want to know all we can about them and we want the interpretations and judgments of them by what is clearly a sensitive and subtle imagination. It is an irony which Ransom would appreciate if it were not at his expense: the excellence of his artistry helps to make us aware of the values which the poetry omits.

The ultimate reason for the failure of most of the poems to achieve the significance and greatness which their artistic merit suggests is the insufficiency of the ideal world affirmed by the style and by the too limited people. Ransom's poetry is, as he himself remarked, "inconclusive." It proceeds through all its dualities, contrasts, variations, and surprises to insist upon the disparity between the ideal and the actual. How much it matters to us in part depends, therefore, on how poignant and meaningful the disparity is, and within the poems that disparity in its turn depends on how much the implicit ideal world represents the true aspirations of men. A world in which there are no recognizable forms of mature sexual love, no drive for knowledge, no yearning for freedom (for everyone is free—and does not know it; there is nothing to impose a limitation), or no problem of choosing among competing goods is inadequate as an image of our deepest human values and as a measure of the disparity with which we live and of the world in which we actually dwell. As the poems tell us again and again, we have left behind the "innocent and total world of childhood," and we want to know where we are and what we are. The values of the implicit ideal world are not trivial ones. *Genesis,* Freud—and Warren—show how powerfully they haunt us and control our behavior. But there are other values indispensable to our sense of ourselves, and the poems, for all their crystalline clarity and splendor, leave them out of account. Or most of them do, for we must always except "Winter Remembered," "Janet Waking," "Judith of Bethulia," and the two or three others we have cited so often in this discussion. Apart from these, the poems are exquisite miniatures. But their virtues are rare ones and we should not forget how precious is their beauty, how unique their particular contribution to our sensibilities and our perceptions of the actuals about us in the "domestic situations." There are not many poems that give us so much or add to our humanity by instructing us how to ask for more.

CHAPTER SIX

RANSOM'S THEORIES OF POETRY

AND CRITICISM

....

"The critic in his own speculations is going to have many a moment asking himself if he sees what he thinks he sees, and means what he says he means, and if this is really the life for him."

—Ransom, "Why Critics Don't Go Mad"

....

I

*T*HERE is no mistaking prose from John Crowe Ransom's hand. Be it an editor's note, a review, or yet another essay on the nature of poetry, it bears as surely as any of his poems the signature of a stylist whose phrases are, in Malraux's term, *significations*. For behind each is the imagination that made the poems, even though Ransom wrote the prose for which he is known after he had virtually given up poetry and though many of his propositions are not sustained by his own art. The same predilections inscribe the ideas about science, religion, poetry, and criticism—and restrict them in some of the ways that the poems are restricted. Restricted or not, the ideas have made Ransom one of the influential literary theorists of the present and even among those who disagree with him have improved the study of literature as a fine art. Their effect has been the more easily achieved because the style displays so much modesty and grace. The gestures are not as deft as those in the poems and Ransom sometimes fumbles into coyness. (The insouciance in treating topics usually handled with tedious gravity can be delightful, but when it pretends to be naïveté it is sometimes not amusing and ironic but slightly embarrassing.) Yet for the most part Ransom is unaffectedly himself and so pleasant to read that he can persuade us to consider postulates which, if they came from anyone else, might seem outrageous. Like "Bells

257

for John Whiteside's Daughter," they provoke us into taking another look at familiar things. A good teacher—and Ransom has been a great one—he sends us back to poetry charged with a more alert and discriminating perceptivity.

As in the poetry, the informing principle is contrast. It is everywhere: in the style, in the organization of the discourse, in the topics. Contrast between the tone and the topic; between the sophisticated hypothesis and the homely example; between the colloquial diction and syntax and the learned terms and Great Names; between what Ransom regards as monistic, even totalitarian philosophies and pluralistic, rebellious particulars that will not submit to confinement; between logic and feeling; between science and art; between mind and body; between East and West. And among them all we sense, as we sensed in the poetry, a pervasive sympathy for small and delicate things, especially if they seem to be struggling with gaiety and impudence for their right to be themselves. There are, as there were in the poetry, a mistrust of the reason and its structures and institutions, an anxiety over mortality, and an urgency to enjoy the day. For if the principle is contrast, the conclusion once more is disparity between the ideals men pursue and the actuals to which they must accommodate themselves. Consequently, the final concern of the prose is that of the poetry, the dual nature of the universe and man's right relation to it. (This is not to say that it was Ransom's own principal concern when he was writing the poetry. *That*, we may properly suppose, was usually to do the best job he could with the poem in hand.) The poetry represented portions of the universe, suggested its own kind of ideal universe, and dramatized the successes and failures of men in achieving as much of the ideal universe as was possible within the actual one. The prose comes to the final concern with a different intention. It asks how men shall know the actual universe and shape their conduct on their knowledge. Ransom's Agrarian writing, as we have seen, was devoted to problems of conduct. The prose we shall here consider is devoted to problems of knowledge. It treats of epistemology, cognition, and the ontologies of those discourses in which we present our images of the known.

Fundamental to its treatment is an assumption implicit in poems from "One Who Rejected Christ" and "Friendship" (1916-1917) through "An Address to the Scholars of New England" (1939) and explicit in "Painted Head" (1934), that the mind of man is made up of the reason and the sensibility, which contend for mastery over one another and man's affairs. Or, to be more accurate, the reason so contends, while the sensibility wants only to enjoy its rights. However, it was not until after he had all but abandoned writing poetry that Ransom began to refer directly to the two parts of the mind, and not until *God Without Thunder* did he define their functions. Asserting that "industrialism" sees man as a superior animal with a reason which enables him to satisfy his appetites more swiftly and abundantly and so "to live a life more animal than that of animals," Ransom argued that under an aesthetic view of life man

> "distinguishes himself from the animals not only by the effectiveness of his animal purposes but also by the unique manner in which he chooses to proceed with these purposes. *Man not only lives his animal life but enjoys it.* And that is by the exercise of a faculty that animals possess just as little as they possess his reason: by sensibility. By pure reason man would hasten and brutalize his animal processes, but by his free sensibility he elects to observe them, complicate them, and furnish them with background and accessory detail that cannot enter into the exclusive animal consciousness."[1]

Usually Ransom represented the reason as trying to repress the sensibility so that man might gorge himself more greedily upon nature, but sometimes he apparently reversed himself and represented it as devising abstract moral principles which excessively inhibited man's enjoyment of nature and thus impaired his aesthetic life. Often his conception of the mind resembled that in Freud's earlier speculations—the sensibility being a rough equivalent of Freud's id, and the reason, of his ego. In a late essay Ransom attempted an outright identification of the reason with the ego, which he described as "devoted to aggression against the environment" but "too enterprising, too ambitious; it involved the whole psyche in adaptations which brought anxieties and deprivations too great to be borne." (*Involved* and *brought*, the key words, are so vague that they obscure the contradiction between the reason as lustful and the reason as ascetic.) When it came to the id, Ransom was more tentative. Though convinced that play upon the substance

---

[1] *God Without Thunder* (New York, 1930), p. 189.

of things is a pleasure sought by the id, he wanted more explanation of the satisfactions other than the sexual which it obtained and was not prepared to assign to it all of the role he had been giving to the sensibility.[2] That would not have been possible. Ransom had been reading Freud at least since 1924, when he reviewed Freud's *Beyond the Pleasure Principle,* but his reason and sensibility conform only partially with Freud's ego and id. Often he attributed to the reason functions which Freud had attributed to the superego. When he wrote about drives and instincts Ransom followed the ancient tradition which located them in the sub-capital body rather than in the mind, though he made the reason serve them much as Freud's ego served those of the id. As for the sensibility, it apparently was quite conscious (Ransom always tended to personify the reason and sensibility, giving them cognitions and intentions of their own) and unlike the id obtained its satisfactions *without* possession.

This is a matter of some consequence. So much of Ransom's idea of the right relation between men and the universe, and thus of the cognitive functions of poetry, depends upon his conception of the sensibility that we must not be misled by our familiarity with Freud and by Ransom's rather offhand references to him. The differences in their thinking may be inferred from Ransom's description of romantic love, which he believed to be the motive of art and religion. It is, he wrote,

"among the most delightful of our experiences; most of us would probably name it as the most massive and satisfying of all—provided at least that we do not confine the term to the love between the sexes, but extend it to the love of nature, of works of art, and of God. But this romantic love is not what it might first seem to be, and it may be quickly perverted. At the base of romantic love there is probably an impulse fundamental in our biological constitution, *to be in rapport with our environment.* In the psychological terms of Schopenhauer, this is the impulse *to have knowledge without desire.* Love is conditioned on respect for the object, and what it loves is to contemplate the infinite variety of the object: its demonic and invincible individuality."[3]

[2] "Poetry: II. The Final Cause," *The Kenyon Review,* IX (Autumn, 1947), 656, 655.
[3] *God Without Thunder,* p. 315.

It is not to Freud, then, that we should look for parallels with and influences upon Ransom's image of the mind so much as to Hebraic-Christian doctrine and to the philosophic tradition extending from Plato through Plotinus, Kant, Coleridge, Hegel, and Schopenhauer to Bergson and Santayana. Ransom differed from all of these men (least from Kant, Coleridge, and Bergson; most from Plato and Hegel), but they encouraged him to see the mind as divided into a portion that restlessly sought abstract universals in perceived objects and events and a portion that savored the untidy and contingent particularity of the world's body. Nevertheless, his conception was originally and essentially his own and derived, along with his fury against abstractions, from his observations and experience.

In the opposition of the reason and the sensibility, Ransom was all for the latter because it was proscribed under the present regime, not because he wanted it to dominate human behavior. The ideal world implied in his poetry seemed intended for the effortless gratification of the sensibility and offered little if anything for the reason to do. But the poetry insisted that *any* ideal world was impossible of attainment. The prose argues that the ideal world of science and technology, so utterly different from the ideal world of the poetry (and the ideal world of Agrarianism), would wholly satisfy the reason and deprive the sensibility. It, too, is impossible, but in pursuing it men have gotten near enough to it to pervert normal conduct and impair happiness. What is wanted, then, is a pluralistic cosmology: one that recognizes the worth of both the ideal world of the sensibility (all delicious particularity) and the ideal world of the reason (all orderly and efficient universals) but knows, too, the character of the actual world in which fragments of the two ideals are mixed in unpredictable ways that preclude realization of either one. Under such a cosmology the reason would have its proper role and satisfactions; so would the sensibility. Man would confront his environment realistically and humbly, prepared for the contingency of events and for the eventual decay and disappearance of himself and his works and beloved objects. But for such right cosmology there must be right epistemology, cognition, and ontology. It is with these, therefore, that most of the prose—even most of the Agrarian pieces—is profoundly concerned.

261

II

Ransom began writing about the nature of poetry almost as haphazardly as he had begun with poetry itself. Reviewing Robert Graves' *On English Poetry* in the third number of *The Fugitive*, he turned aside to comment on the vogue for free verse and remarked mildly, "It would seem . . . likely that the determinate mathematical regularities of meter which are imposed upon the words have as much to do with the total effect of a poem as, in a sister art, the determinate geometrical regularities of outline which are imposed upon the stones have to do with the total effect of a work of architecture."[4] Ransom was not thinking very hard: the analogy was visually apt but vague; and he did not say what he thought the total effects of the regularities might be. He himself liked working with meters, but he relied on his ear and his feeling for the rightness of his lines. Yet once the problem had caught his attention, he continued to be puzzled by the apparent reconciliation of the pattern of sound and the pattern of meaning, and some years later, when he was getting into his first comprehensive thinking about the nature of poetry, he told Tate that it was brooding on this reconciliation which had started him off.

In the next issue Tate focused on the "total effect" and helped to give Ransom's speculations the character which they were to maintain over the next four decades and from which was to come their importance in contemporary poetics and theories of criticism. Defending T. S. Eliot's "aberrant versification," Tate argued that traditional forms might not permit an accurate representation of inner experience and that the poet might be compelled to rearrange details from the external world according to a subjective order.[5] Ransom was so interested that in a letter written soon afterward he took up some of Tate's points and thus began an exchange of views which was to last for many years. How closely they agreed on many things can be seen in the momentary embarrassment Tate felt when his essay for *I'll Take My Stand* turned out to follow so closely the central argument of Ransom's *God Without Thunder* and in the efforts the two friends made during 1938 and 1939 to find jobs for each other so that they might work together on criticism. In

[4] J. C. R., "Editorial," *The Fugitive*, I (October, 1922), 68.
[5] Allen Tate, "Whose Ox," *The Fugitive*, I (December, 1922), 99-100.

making his acknowledgments for *The World's Body* in 1938, Ransom wrote, "I am most under obligations to Mr. Allen Tate, with whom I have generally been in close communication, and whose views of poetry I share, so far as I know them, with fewest and slightest reservations. Between us, when the talk was at a certain temperature, I have seen observations come to the surface in a manner to illustrate the theory of anonymous or communal authorship."

They did not agree so well at the outset. In his letter Ransom insisted that a poem was neither a transcript of reality on the one hand nor a philosophical exposition on the other. Yet there must be in it "the substance of a philosophical conclusion," and "Above all things else, the core of experience in the record has been taken up into the sum total of things and its relations then discovered are given in the work of art. That is why its marginal meanings, the associations, the interlinear element of a poem are all-important."[6] Though the terms *core* of experience and *sum total* of things are so broad that they convey little, it is easy to see here the beginning of Ransom's protracted theorizing on the presence and function in a poem of what he took to be a logical argument and a rather loose conglomerate of fortuitous details. We should not attach too much importance to these incidental remarks in a letter from an older man to an undergraduate; yet there is something else about them worth noting. The reference to marginal meanings, associations, and the interlinear element is exquisitely vague; even so, taking it with the allusion to the philosophical core, we might suppose that Ransom would be interested in the kinds of ties that would obtain among these aspects of the poem and between them and the core, that he would be concerned for their intratextual functions and the qualifications these functions would place upon their extratextual references. But in the speculations that followed Ransom seemed to take the ties for granted, and certainly he neglected the intratextual functions and qualifications— so much so that he distorted the nature and exaggerated the scope of the extratextual references. In short, it was the irrelevant rather than the relevant aspects of the marginal meanings, associations, and

[6] The letter was written on December 17, 1922. See Chapter Two, note 38, for a discussion of the date. This and all other letters from Ransom to Tate cited in this chapter are now in the Princeton University Library.

interlinear element that engaged his attention. The reason is not far to seek: his attention was directed by his fury against abstractions and his affection for all little independent things from "blue girls," quixotic old men, and yeoman farmers to the images of a poem that maintained their independence against authoritative systems. Again and again he was to describe the details of a poem as if they were perky, mischievous children. This sympathy gave many of his passages their zest and charm and accounts for some of Ransom's most original insights. But it seems also to have placed some serious limitations on the scope and validity of his ideas about poetry and criticism.

The first contrasting of art and science, which was to become a commonplace in Ransom's speculations, occurred in the essay "Waste Lands," published during the summer of 1923. Citing the leanness of science and the abundance of art and poetry, Ransom said that the "free and unpredictable associations [of art] . . . are impertinences to the scientific temper, but delightful to the soul that in the routine of scientific chores is oppressed with the sense of serving a godless and miserly master."[7] He did not develop the comparison, however, until two years later, when he published "Thoughts on the Poetic Discontent" in *The Fugitive* for June, 1925. Science, he now said, represented man's effort to dominate his environment, and the ironic mode in poetry acknowledged the failure of the enterprise. In the next issue Ransom argued in "Prose, a Doctrine of Relativity" that a poem consists of a "fable" surrounded by contingent details which threaten it with chaos but also give it the widest possible reference and representation. He had moved on from wondering how "prose" sense and meter could coexist in a poem to asking how a poem managed to make some kind of coherent statement even though "there may be a dozen terms, in one little poem, as the fable proceeds, which take the mind away into passionate excursion."[8] The shift of attention is significant. He had moved from the technical aspects to the epistemological and cognitive ones.

---

[7] "Waste Lands," *The Literary Review*, III (July 14, 1923), 826. Copies of *The Literary Review*, a supplement of the *New York Evening Post*, are difficult to find. The essay was reprinted in *Modern Essays (Second Series)*, edited by Christopher Morley (New York, 1924). The passage just cited appears on page 350.

[8] *The Fugitive*, IV (September, 1925), 93.

These were the focus of interest in "The Third Moment," a book on aesthetics which Ransom worked on from the summer of 1926 until the fall of 1928 but never published. (Several years later he destroyed the manuscript; what he considered to be valid in it had already been used in *God Without Thunder* and an essay, "Classical and Romantic," published early in the autumn of 1929.) From a prospectus he sent to Tate in the fall of 1926 and the arguments in four long letters written to Tate during the spring of 1927 we can follow Ransom's thinking during this interval.[9]

Three "moments," Ransom argued, distinguish the historical order of experience. The first is that of the original, the actual, experience, "pure of all intellectual content, unreflective, concrete, and singular; there are no distinctions, and the subject is identical with the whole." The second is the moment of cognition, of reflection on the experience from which come abstract ideas whose ends are practical. The experience has become conceptualized knowledge;

[9] The prospectus is part of a letter to Tate dated simply "September 5." Someone has added in pencil "[1926]." The fact that the letter was sent from Indian Hills, Denver, where Ransom was spending a semester on leave from Vanderbilt, confirms this date. Only one of the four letters that follow is dated, and the order in which they are listed here is an informed guess based on the evolution of the ideas and the internal references. The letter which seems to come first is dated "February 20/27." The second is undated. Someone has added in pencil "[1926] [? Spring]," but this is certainly a mistake. The letter alludes to Tate's review of Ransom's *Two Gentlemen in Bonds*. The book was published in January, 1927; the review was published in *The Nation* on March 30, 1927. In the letter of February 20th, Ransom thanked Tate for an advance copy of the review, which he had just received. In the undated letter Ransom refers to the review in a way that suggests that it is much in his mind, but as he makes no thanks for his copy, this letter seems to have been written after—but not long after—the letter of February 20th. In any event, it was not written in the spring of 1926: Tate could not have reviewed the book that far ahead of publication because it contained poems not in existence at that time. What appears to be the third letter of the series is dated "April 3 (and 13)" and again there is a mistaken addition in pencil: "[1926]." A reference to Hart Crane's "book" (his first one, *White Buildings*, was published in December, 1926, with an introduction by Tate) and the arguments of the letter make virtually certain that the year was 1927. The last letter is dated simply "Tuesday." Someone has added in pencil "[1927] [? Fall]." This may be correct. But the contents follow closely upon the argument of the letter dated "April 3 (and 13)" and there is a reference to a challenge Ransom had made to Tate in the letter dated "February 20/27" (that Ransom was really more radical than Tate) which Tate had apparently taken up and Ransom was now defending. Perhaps it is not the fourth but the third or even the second in the series, though the evolution of the argument strongly suggests that it comes at the end. The chances are that it was written in the first half of 1927 and probably in the late spring or early summer.

whatever is left over passes into memory. In the third moment we become aware that most of the quality of the original experience is missing from the abstract ideas and that synthesizing them will not recover it. Therefore we try to recover it through images. These are adulterated with concepts, but adults cannot exclude practical ideas in order to get back to pure quality. Indeed, "our Aesthetic can never deny science wholly, which would be wildly romantic, and not reasonable; if not quite suicidal. Science is a kind of blindness, but necessary and useful; exactly as the typical successful mercenary appears blind to the poet, but still is indispensable." In the margin Ransom added, "This leads us to a distinction between *Romantic or Pure* tendencies & *Gothic or Mixed* which is like the distinction between the *East* and the *West*." And in a scribbled footnote, "An important detail is, To show why, with our formal cognitive habit or apparatus, we cannot have *fresh experience* of first moments; because they disintegrate as fast as they come. And this Corollary: In Nature as compared with Art, our sense of Wholeness is extremely vague and unsatisfying; the artistic contemplation of Nature is better, a very advanced state, in which we are conscious of the scene as we might have conceptualized it, and at the same time of the scene as we actually do persist in intuiting it. But this is quite like Art: a Mixture." Though he believed that men could reconstitute the first moment through dreams, day-dreams, religion, morals, and art, he based most of his claims on the ontology of poetry, which he said "is always the exhibit of Opposition and at the same time Reconciliation between the Conceptual or Formal and the Individual or Concrete. An obvious case of the formal is meter; which nevertheless does not seem to impair the life and effectiveness of the Concrete Experience. They coexist."

The world, then, appears to us in two aspects: the Quantitative, which appeals to the Occidental mind and from which we make our science and technology, and the Qualitative, which appeals to the Oriental mind and is chaotic. Poetry combines the aspects yet manages to leave the Qualitative "free and contingent." The Oriental mind is inclined toward religious humility and a sense of the infinity and unmanageableness of the universe, but the Occidental mind is inclined toward morals, which Ransom said was a system of values based upon the responsiveness of the environment to control. As man progressed to the third moment through his poetry he learned that the world destroys values. Tragedy, toward which all art tends, was his acknowledgment of his failure to make his values prevail. Chastened, man learned to enjoy the aesthetic experience of contemplating nature, and from this came his love of nature, which is the motive of art.

In February of 1929, having abandoned "The Third Moment," Ransom began work on another book which he called "Giants for Gods" but to which he gave the title *God Without Thunder*, when it was published in the summer of 1930. The fundamental arguments were the same but the focus had shifted from poetry to religious myth as the mode of representing the dual nature of the universe and inducing in man the necessary humility and love of nature. At this time Ransom was deeply engaged in Agrarianism, and the book contained many passages saying that a subsistence farming community offered the best environment for the proper attitudes and realistic and aesthetically satisfying conduct. Indeed, as we have said elsewhere, *God Without Thunder* was the philosophical text and defense for Agrarianism, and Owsley, for one, thought that Ransom had reasoned rather than felt himself into the movement.

How closely Ransom's conceptions of religion and poetry resembled each other can be seen at once in his description of religion as

> "the system of myths which gives a working definition to the relation of man to nature. It always has to join together in some fashion two quite different views of this relation. The first is that of nature as usable and intelligible for man: nature as humane order, devoted to man's welfare, created by a benevolent God for the purpose of man's service. The second is that of nature as unintelligible and contingent, and therefore alien and unusable for man: nature as an order that is not the humane or ethical order."[10]

But Ransom did not believe in suprasensibles. "A myth," he wrote,

> "is frankly a fable: it calmly alleges a miracle or impossible occurrence; it is a *tour de force* which intends to take its representation of the object out of the fatal confinement of science and routine. . . . The scientific account of an event (1) never goes

[10] *God Without Thunder*, p. 156.

out of its natural history, and (2) uses only an abstract or part of that history. But its myth, on the other hand, (1) leaves its natural history altogether and yet (2) attempts to imply the whole of that history. . . . *Myth resorts to the supernatural in order to represent the fullness of the natural.*"[11]

In the right relation to nature, good was enjoyment of the particularity of nature supported by enough practical technique to satisfy the needs of the body without interfering with the contemplation from which the enjoyment came—in other words, a harmony and right proportion in the activities of the reason and sensibility. Evil "manifests itself largely in our failure, as living beings, to keep up an unimpeded activity; that is, in disease and death."[12]

Though little known, *God Without Thunder* holds the central position in Ransom's prose writings. The ideas of the letters and miscellaneous essays preceding it are summarized, systematized, illustrated, and defended in detail. The ideas of the prose of the next three decades are simply extensions, with but a few modifications, of the arguments here set forth. In later years Ransom was sometimes obliged by limitations of space to make assertions or use terms in ways that needed explanation for their fullest understanding. On these occasions his jesting or self-depreciatory tone, taken with the rather abrupt presentation, might mislead readers into supposing that Ransom did not know precisely where he stood on the matter or that he was engaging in ironic exaggeration. Familiarity with *God Without Thunder* helps us to see that he meant what he said. It is invaluable for reading those essays for which Ransom is best known as a theorist. It also clarifies and enriches one's understanding and appreciation of his poetry, for many of its conceptions expand upon convictions and attitudes implicit in the poems. One must, of course, be on guard against reducing the meaning of the poems to the subsequent conceptions, the more so as many of them —those on the role of the reason in formulating inhibiting abstractions, for example—were nowhere nearly so thoroughly worked out at the time that Ransom wrote verse. Remembering this we may take what he says in *God Without Thunder* about mortality, the unmanageableness of the universe, delight in the particularity of nature, the disparity between man's hopes and his fate, and the

[11] P. 65.   [12] P. 178.

need to come to terms with the evil in our environment and use it as a guide toward a more perceptive reading of almost any of the poems but perhaps most obviously such ones as "Miriam Tazewell," "Necrological," "Bells for John Whiteside's Daughter," "Vaunting Oak," "Armageddon," "Eclogue," "Persistent Explorer," and "Painted Head," to name those that come first to mind.

Moreover, the book will serve as a guide in reading the works of Tate and Warren. At the time of its writing Ransom and Tate shared so many attitudes and assumptions and argued out in letters so many of their ideas that it is not possible to say which one originated some conceptions that they held in common. Ransom was right in referring to their "communal authorship." Sometimes they pushed forward on their own and arrived independently at the same place at about the same moment, one instance being in their speculations on the representational functions of myth (in *God Without Thunder* and Tate's "Remarks on the Southern Religion") and another being their suggestions (in Ransom's "Poetry: a Note on Ontology" and Tate's "Three Types of Poetry," which were thought out, though not published, at about the same time) for classifying poems according to their place on a scale between abstract and concrete. We may say that in general Ransom emphasized problems in cognition and representation while Tate emphasized inherited beliefs as guides to organizing and judging conduct. Thus what Ransom says in this book about science, technology, and myth helps us with some of Tate's most difficult poems, such as "The Meaning of Life" and "The Meaning of Death." Warren, of course, was never so close to Ransom; yet between 1931 and 1934 when he was trying his first large-scale works he lived in an intellectual atmosphere charged with Ransom's ideas and was, as he himself says, much influenced by them, though he cannot say (who could?) to what extent. Even if this were not so, *God Without Thunder* would still be helpful in reading Warren, for his major works are all concerned with the disparity between the ideal and the actual and the necessity for accepting the world as it is and avoiding being misled by abstractions or demanding more of man and the world than is possible. His view of scientists, historians, and others who work with ideas and risk oversimplifying experience is much like Ransom's. They differ profoundly, as we shall see, in their conceptions of evil. But if we keep this in mind, *God Without Thunder* can help us understand such determinedly philosophical works as *All the King's Men, World Enough and Time,* and *Brother to Dragons.*

III

Earlier it was said that the informing principle of Ransom's prose is contrast. With his inveterate dualism, the application of this principle resulted again and again in the pairing of supposed opposites, science and religion, prose and poetry, Oriental and Occidental, and so forth. He was, as he reported in "An Address to Kenneth Burke" (1942), a firm believer in speculation by seeking philosophical correlatives; as a consequence, his paired opposites tended to fall into two groups. Recognizing this, Ransom said that he was tempted to offer as definitive of the opposing categories two terms borrowed from politics—"*Leftist,* for the logico-mathematical or Platonic or idealistic philosophy, involving the ontology and the religion and the ethics as well as the politics which that term connotes; and *Rightist,* for the substantival or aesthetic ontology, religion, ethics, and politics."[13] The terms, which he thought might be more useful than Jung's *introvert* and *extrovert,* signify yet another tendency in his speculation: personification, endowing with temperament, aspiration, will, and choice all manner of things from ideas to pebbles. Often he made no distinction between the actor and the act, the thinker and the thought, the creator and the creation, the writer and the text. Dualism, contrast, correlation, and personification—these properties of his theorizing reflect his belief in the division of the mind and the conflict between the reason and sensibility. It is extraordinary how many situations and prob-lems seemed to him to be instances of Leftist, the party of the Reason, against Rightist, the party of the Sensibility. And however unconsciously, Ransom almost always took the side of the oppressed Rightists. This gives his prose much vigor and it furnishes him with some of his best insights. But it also has its risks.

Consideration of the ideas of *God Without Thunder* may best begin with examination of Ransom's conception of the nature and function of science and scientific exposition (he used the terms inter-

[13] *The Kenyon Review,* IV (Spring, 1942), 234.

changeably and endowed both modes with human traits); for, as we have seen, Ransom tended almost from the beginning to define the natures of art, poetry, and myth by comparing them with science and its discourse. "Science," he had written in "Waste Lands," where he first made the comparison, "writes it [nature] down . . . by abstracting a feature and trying to forget all the rest. . . . The excellence of science is its poverty, for it tries to carry away only the abstractions into the record."[14] "*This is why,*" he said later,

> "*a science can never give us an adequate knowledge of the concrete thing.* The concrete thing never capitulates to the scientific enterprise. The essence of the concrete thing is its *variety.* It may seem docile enough as it yields to some specific science, and is ticketed and disposed of very neatly. But all of a sudden we observe that the concrete thing is not really embodied in that science. Only one of its aspects is there. One by one it reveals other aspects, and challenges other sciences to take hold of it and embody it; and the other sciences undertake to do so, but it is inevitable that each one in its turn must fail in precisely the same manner."[15]

Why do the sciences rise so foolishly to challenges when they are so sure to fail? Because they "aim of course at reducing natural phenomena to human understanding, and to that extent they may seem disinterested and innocent. But they also aim, perhaps slyly and half-consciously at first, and then greedily and openly as soon as they can, at reducing them to human prediction and control." The scientific procedures "crucify our organic sensibility while they drive furiously toward their abstracts," and in the end science becomes "an order of experience in which we mutilate and prey upon nature; we seek our practical objectives at any cost, and always at the cost of not appreciating the setting from which we have to take them." By contrast religion, the arts, and poetry are humble, gentle, and affectionate toward nature, and almost contemptuous of the scientific enterprises. "It seems certain," Ransom said, "that art, as a usual thing, is late, post-scientific, rebellious against science, and bent on exposing to scorn the little constants of our scientific thinking when it compares them with the infinites of quality with

14 *Modern Essays (Second Series)*, pp. 348-349.
15 *God Without Thunder*, p. 258.

271

which they are invested in reality. . . . Back of art there is the embittered artist, whose vision of the real has been systematically impaired under the intimidations of scientific instruction, and who seeks with indignation as well as with joy to recover it."[16]

"Ultimately," he told Tate, "this world can neither be understood nor possessed." The abstractions of the scientist, the constructive philosopher, the religious doctrinaire, are drowned in the complexity and contingency of things. "The world has its value—or service—side for us, but . . . ultimately is quite appallingly independent of us and . . . in realizing this we exhibit our sense of beauty, sense of humor, sense of tragedy, and religiosity."[17] The difficulty is that we may forget this and turn religion into magic; that is, we may try to use religion as we use science, to possess the world and make it serve our practical needs. One who resists this behavior is Ransom's "good" Fundamentalist. He begins with sound scientific principles and an awareness of their limitations and of the independence of the world. To satisfy his religiosity and to represent to himself the "fullness of the natural," he enriches his science with the qualities that the principles omit; he makes myths. These do not conflict with science; they simply go beyond it and comprehend areas of experience and cognition which science cannot treat. Enveloped in qualities, the myths gradually come to appear to the imagination of the good Fundamentalist as natural objects. He no longer bothers to remember that they are fictions, but conducts himself toward them as if they were existent. Thus he does not say to himself on each religious occasion, " 'Remember, this is myth, not fact; this is *als ob*, my hypothesis; don't be taken in.' " Instead,

"He takes his God for actual, talks to him, obeys him, makes offerings to him. If the naturalist questions him about this, he will not discuss it: for he has made his decision, and elected his belief, and he does not care what its grounds were and what he meant by it. *In effect the Fundamentalist does not any longer distinguish myth and fact.* But why should he, if the myth is worth believing in? He did distinguish when there was need of distinguishing: but he made the distinction then in order that he would not have to make it every day. In the life of belief

[16] *God Without Thunder*, pp. 22-23, 83, 136; "Flux and Blur in Contemporary Art," *The Sewanee Review*, XXXVII (July, 1929), 362-363.
[17] From letters to Tate, February 20, 1927, and Spring, 1927. See note 9.

there must be a certain economy. It is well to believe a good many things without having to conduct a continuous epistemological discussion about them; to believe without being self-conscious about it."[18]

However, he is not stubborn about the details of his myth and is willing to modify them if they conflict painfully with his science, for he does not make the mistake of the believers at Dayton and suppose that his myth *is* science and that all its features are sacrosanct. "So," Ransom summed up, "the myths rise spontaneously out of the Principles [of the sciences and science-like philosophies], and when they have been selected for institutional purposes, systematized, and perpetuated, they produce Gods. I hope I have not indicated that the natural history of a set of Gods is anywhere or at any time an easy one to follow. What I have given is rather a logic than a history."[19]

Science exhibited a "Rotarian Optimism which does not admit defeat, does not recognize tragedy, and fools itself like a kid with its toys when it contemplates its apparent successes."[20] Liberal churchmen admired science and were inclined to indulge in the same optimism, which infected their image of God, making Him a bland, reasonable, and predictable embodiment of social benevolence and physical welfare who encouraged men to profiteer upon the universe for the satisfaction of their appetites and who was amenable to magical practices and manipulation. We need now a God *with* thunder to represent our helplessness and induce a religious humility and a realistic relation with nature. Such a God would be the author of evil as well as of good. "This," Ransom wrote, "is my orthodox version of the God of Israel at the point where it is most challenging and critical."[21] Without Him man became a vain and fatuous monster.

Though there are many references to the arts wherein poetry is cited as their representative, not much is said directly in *God Without Thunder* about its character and function. Nevertheless, the book indirectly sums up Ransom's speculations on poetry to

[18] *God Without Thunder*, pp. 98-100.
[19] P. 92.
[20] Letter to Tate, late Spring, 1927. See note 9.
[21] *God Without Thunder*, p. 39.

that moment and points to the speculations yet to come. For when Ransom wrote about poetry he concentrated on its epistemological and cognitive roles rather than on the qualities and formal relations which endow it with beauty, and these roles were essentially the same as those which he attributed to myth. In Ransom's system of correlatives myth and poetry were so much alike that in many passages one might use either term without violence to the sense or to Ransom's assumptions. Myth, by Ransom's definition, is virtually a literary form, and *poetry* in many places really stands for all imaginative literature. It is only when he says that myth invites belief in itself as a concrete, existent object and when he speaks of meter in poetry that significant differences appear. *God Without Thunder*, then, is among other things an oblique statement of Ransom's poetics at the time of its appearance.

He did not begin to formulate these poetics as part of his preparation for writing poetry, nor did he pause in mid-career to ponder his medium. When he was writing most of his poetry, he distrusted rules and believed, as he said in "Prose, a Doctrine of Relativity," that poetry is spontaneous and the poet's processes are not rational. The Fugitives cared little for aesthetic theories, though they liked to talk closely about specific technical problems in a poem one of them had written. Only Tate had any interest in the small amount of theorizing Ransom undertook in the days of the magazine. Indeed, Tate was prepared to go far beyond Ransom in conscious attention to the resources of the medium. When he resolved early in his own career as poet to find new means of expression to fit new subjects, Ransom doubted that he would succeed and said that for himself he relied on the heat of composition to supply him with the appropriate materials.[22] Ransom's tightly integrated poetry came from a disciplined imagination following assumptions about the medium which seem to have been felt rather than postulated. Even so, a study of the subsequent theorizing helps us to understand the poetry, for the theories derive from the conceptions of man and

---

[22] Letters to Tate dated "April 22" and "September 13." The first refers to another letter from Ransom to Tate dated "April 15," which can be attributed to 1924 on the basis of its lengthy discussion of Ransom's reading of Tate's essay, "One Escape from the Dilemma," published in *The Fugitive* for April, 1924. From this we may safely assume that the letter of April 22 was also written in 1924. The letter of September 13 was written from Indian Hills, a suburb of Denver, where Ransom was living during the autumn of 1926.

the universe which furnished subjects for the poems. Moreover, the theories make us closer readers of *all* poems, so that we get more out of Ransom's, too.

He began, as we have seen, with simple curiosity over how poetry exhibits successful patterns of both sound and sense; but soon he had gone on to wondering about the more complicated conjunction between an argument and seemingly free details. Inclined at first to defend the "imprecision" of the poetic statement on the ground that its superfluity gave pleasure, he came to believe when he was writing "The Third Moment" that the unforeseen additives were what made poetry superior to science as a means of representing the world as it truly is in its natural fullness. Though he said many times in his letters to Tate that poetic images reconciled the logical and determinate with the contingent and indeterminate, he did not say how but sidestepped the problem with figures of speech about the immersion of universals in particulars. In the summer of 1929 he wrote that "art, as a representation of nature, represents it in its dual capacity as composed in part of constants and in part of contingents. If it were lacking in either feature, it would fail in realism, . . . and it would forfeit our confidence." Then came an ambiguous sentence which seemed to imply a close parallel between the organic structure of the world and the formal organization of a work of art: "A system of constants and an infinite aggregate of contingency enveloping and of course imperilling these constants,— that is the real world, and that is necessarily its competent representation by the arts."[23] The similes and metaphors of poetry invited the reader to excursions away from the logical argument and offered him a larger view of a natural object, which the reader valued for its own sake; for poems, like most works of art, "are doubtless compromises whereby we indulge science and sensibility, or pursue thesis and romance, in *alternating moments.*"[24] [Italics added.] In five years he had added a number of correlatives to his two major categories (later *Rightist* and *Leftist*) but he had not gotten far with explaining the actual, in-the-poem relationship of the constants and contingents.

[23] "Flux and Blur in Contemporary Art," p. 363.
[24] "Classical and Romantic," *The Saturday Review of Literature*, VI (September 14, 1929), 127.

After *God Without Thunder* came Agrarianism, and for the next three years Ransom's attention was engaged with social action and economics. In May, 1933, he published his study of *Lycidas* entitled "A Poem Nearly Anonymous," and from then on all of his prose writings with the exception of three essays on Agrarian topics dealt with art, poetry, and criticism. Religion was cited in "Forms and Citizens" as a mode of controlling the appetites and occasionally it was referred to in other essays as a correlative of art and poetry, but otherwise it vanished from Ransom's published speculations.

In 1938 Ransom gathered up fifteen essays from the previous five years and republished them under the title *The World's Body*. Taken together they were "preparations for criticism, for the understanding and definition of the poetic effects. They [were] about poetic theory itself."[25] Having originally appeared separately, they did not march together very well but tended instead to mill around in the area of two main topics—poetry as knowledge, by imagery, of the fullness and particularity of nature, and the function of form in restraining appetite so that contemplation of the imagery could occur. Much that was said had been said before in *God Without Thunder*. Science was a matter of "infantile or animal practice" the same as that of "the maw and mouth of actual red appetite," and scientists were "deficient exemplars of humanity," with "the same obtuseness which animals characteristically display."[26] And so on. What is new is the emphasis Ransom put upon the importance of the ideas and the logical argument of the poem. Feeling, perhaps, that he had stressed too much the freedom of the details, he wrote that "It is easy to overestimate the gaiety, the abandon, of metered expression. Prose is the supremely single and exclusive experience, possible only by an abridgment of personality. But poetry does not jump to the other extreme and seek the chaos of complete diffusion as its goal. . . . The poem must have logic, meaning, sense. . . ." Some poets, among them Wallace Stevens, Hart Crane, and Allen Tate, had aimed at "pure" poetry having only an aesthetic effect and no moral, political, religious, or sociological values, but

[25] *The World's Body* (New York, 1938), p. vii.
[26] Pp. 225, 49-50, 220, 221.

pleasing as this might be, Ransom thought such poetry unnatural. "The union of beauty with goodness and truth has been common enough to be regarded as natural. It is the dissociation which is unnatural and painful." In a passage that probably reflected his disenchantment with Agrarianism, he observed that "the state of the original Adam [which would be equivalent to what Ransom had called the "first moment"] is not the happiness that has been supposed. . . . Adam, in the absence of technical thought-processes, was incapable of a distinguished aesthetic experience. . . . His integral or unitary experience could not have been like the thing exhibited in a work of art, but must have resembled the life of the uninformed child or . . . the insensitive beasts. The brilliant effect we admire in a poem is the result of compounding many prose effects, and technical or specific ones."[27]

Even so, he maintained that poetry which aimed first at the clear exposition of ideas for the sake of their ethical, psychological, or political interest was of an inferior order, and he rebuked critics who attended only to the argument of a poem and valued it to the extent that it conformed to their own philosophies. Cognition rather than instruction or persuasion was the essential element in the poetic experience. We contemplate the objects and events represented in a poem as we study a landscape in watercolor: "We trace its configuration, colors, planes, objects, till we are satisfied; that is, till we have received the sense of how infinite this particularity may be."[28] Following Kant and Schopenhauer he argued that the form gets between man and the represented object and slows down his aggressive reason. He is unable to hurt the object or disrespect it by taking a practical attitude toward it. The poet, too, is compelled to take a different view of an object when he writes about it. Anticipating Mark Schorer's famous concept of "technique as discovery" Ransom noted that the competent poet is not dismayed to find that his first thoughts will not fit his meter. He is "as sure of his second thoughts as of his first ones. In fact, surer, if anything; second thoughts tend to be richer, for in order to get them he has to break up the obvious trains of associations and explore more widely."[29] Meter, fiction, and tropes increase "the volume of percipienda or sensibilia"—the first two by restraint, the last by "inviting perceptual attention, and weakening the tyranny of

[27] Pp. 259, 72, 241.   [28] P. 208.   [29] P. 11.

science over senses." Tropes perform little miracles comparable to the big ones of religious myth. "The miraculism arises when the poet discovers by analogy an identity between objects which is partial, though it should be considerable, and proceeds to an identification which is complete."[30] As an instance he cited Cowley's line "She and I have exchanged our hearts" and commented:

> "What has actually been exchanged is affections, and affections are only in a limited sense the same as hearts. Hearts are unlike affections in being engines that pump blood and form body; and it is a miracle if the poet represents the lady's affections as rendering her inside into man. But he succeeds, with this mixture, in depositing with us the image of a very powerful affection."

But Ransom does not tell us what is added to the prosaic "They were much in love." He simply says that the miraculism "leaves us looking, marvelling, and revelling in the thick *dinglich* substance that has just received its strange representation."[31]

Obviously the original object or event would have as much "thick *dinglich* substance," but our desire to use it would intrude. An artist might well prefer an imitation on canvas to the view from his window.

> "The studied aesthetician will admit to this fact, but will contend perhaps that the painting is better for the purpose than the view from the window, because the painting has suppressed something, or added something, or distorted something; being quite unable to conceive that its superiority may lie in the simple fact that it is the imitation of something rather than the original. An imitation is better than its original in one thing only: not being actual, it cannot be used, it can only be known. Art exists for knowledge, but nature is an object both to knowledge and to use; the latter disposition of nature includes that knowledge of it which is peculiarly scientific, and sometimes it is so imperious as to pre-empt all possibility of the former."[32]

Thus casually Ransom dismissed such matters as the artistic merit and interpretive function of the formal organization and the artist's pleasure in his medium. To the obvious rejoinder that a

[30] Pp. 130, 133, 139.   [31] Pp. 140, 142.   [32] Pp. 196-197.

photograph, being more precise, would be even richer than a painting, Ransom said that to be particular is to be infinite and the subject of a painting is as particular as the subject of a photograph. The difference between them and the superiority of the painting comes from the arduous pains which the artist endured for his beloved subject. "We are excited by these pains proportionately; they give the painting its human value; and carrying this principle a little farther, we never discover in the work a single evidence of technique, discipline, deliberation, without having the value enhanced further. The pains measure the love."[33]

Fortunately when he criticized specific works Ransom himself was not confined by this queer theory of value. Approaching Shakespeare's sonnets as he might his own, he went straight to a consideration of the organization and its unity, consistency, and appropriateness to the argument. Though he had said much about freedom and contingency, he judged harshly just those details which were most free and contingent because they disrupted the order and harmony of a poem's design. Since he did not cite any details which pleased both his feeling for the form and his theory of infinite particularity, he left the reader wondering just what acceptable freedom and contingency really were. And though he rebuked those "moralistic" critics who evaluated poems as interpretations (rather than simply as lovingly thorough representations), he was quite stern with Edna St. Vincent Millay's verse, which he said was rich in sensibility but deficient in adult understanding of the meaning of experience. To be blunt, there seemed to be little connection between Ransom's critical theory and his practice.

One must remember that essays in *The World's Body* were not written to go together in a book. Confined by the occasions for which they were originally prepared, they could not explore and illustrate many of their most interesting propositions. Shortly before they were sent to the publisher Ransom told Tate that he saw in them so many faults that were it not for his contract he would withdraw them. When they appeared he wrote again to say that he had been reading Yvor Winters' *Primitivism and Decadence*, which so excited him that he had drafted, but had not yet mailed,

[33] P. 209.

a letter to Winters' publisher suggesting a book of his own to supplement it. Perhaps he and Tate could collaborate, using Tate's essay "Narcissus as Narcissus" (an explication of Tate's poem, "Ode to the Confederate Dead") as the center of the volume.[34] Nothing came of the proposal, which was part of their scheming to collaborate on criticism, but Ransom was so stimulated that he pushed ahead with a book-length study of four critics who were interested in the ontology of poetry as a representation of nature. But these "new critics" (three of whom had been writing criticism for years) did no go far enough to suit him, and throughout his comments he scattered observations on what he believed to be the true natures of poetry and criticism. When Delmore Schwartz read the manuscript he suggested that Ransom append a chapter giving his theories in greater detail; so Ransom added "Wanted: An Ontological Critic," in which he brought his theorizing up to date. The book appeared in 1941 under the title *The New Criticism*. Its name was picked up and used as a rallying cry by rebellious graduate students and young teachers of literature grown weary of the conventional historical approach to poetry. There was a bit of a scandal in the academies, and the book became famous, though many who referred to it in the most forceful terms had not read it.

The critics chosen for consideration were I. A. Richards, William Empson, T. S. Eliot, and Yvor Winters. Some of the theories of semantics of the philosopher Charles W. Morris were also discussed in the final chapter. Richards was praised as a sensitive reader who attended closely to the particulars of a poem. But though he had shifted from his early argument that poetry made statements having no validity but useful for exercising the feelings to his later conceptions of poetry as a logical statement enveloped in agreeable irrelevance, Richards, according to Ransom, had failed to see how poetry represented the dual character of the world. Empson, the critic with whom Ransom seemed to have the closest sympathy, was judged to be even more sensitive to the particulars and to have seen the relevance of the free details to the poetic representation; but he failed to account for its relation to the logical statement and the organization of the poem. (Ransom was discussing

---

[34] From letters to Tate dated "Oct. 29" and "April 22." Someone has added in pencil to the first "[1937]" and to the second "[1938]." Abundant references to current events confirm these years.

only Empson's *Seven Types of Ambiguity*.) Eliot received good marks for using his immense learning to make shrewd generalizations about poetry that had the status of "half-truths, or gnomic truths," but these were marred by his assumption that poetry was more important as a release for emotion than as a mode of cognition and by his not requiring poetry to be in its own way factual and capable of commanding belief. Winters, on the other hand, expected poetry to command belief, but, said Ransom, of its total meaning only the ethically significant ideas interested him. A "victim of the moralistic illusion," Winters could not account for the particularity, though he was quick to recognize and respond to nuances of feeling and association.

In explaining what he wanted from an ontological critic Ransom went over much old ground, especially the differences between poetry and science. He had, however, changed his attitude toward the scientists and his idea of their motivation. After quoting a passage from Tate which much resembled the kind of thing he himself used to say, Ransom observed that such a policy, as he called it, had become too rich for his blood. He was impressed by the honesty of the scientists and did not think their behavior such a monstrous villainy or even such a monstrous folly.[35] The proper business of the poet and his critic was to see that scientific knowledge was gentled and complemented by poetic knowledge. Scientists were neither greedy nor stupid; they just tended to forget that there were other valid forms of knowledge besides their own. It was up to poets and ontologists to remind them.

This change of attitude toward the scientists may have had bearing on the even greater emphasis which Ransom now gave to the logical argument and the phonetic patterns—the elements he had called the "scientific" aspects of the poem. Once they had seemed on the one hand to represent the predatory reason serving the appetites and on the other to get between the appetites (if not the reason) and the poem so that the sensibility might luxuriate in the particulars and discover the full and true nature of the subject. As Ransom now saw it, the argument fought to displace the meter, and the meter fought to displace the argument; the poet took liberties with each in order to accommodate the irreducible re-

---

[35] *The New Criticism* (Norfolk, Connecticut, 1941), pp. 201-202.

quirements of the other; and as a consequence, much heterogeneous material got in, loosening up the argument, which inclined to be abstract and scientific, and introducing variations on the metrical pattern. In the end, the poem consisted of "determinate meaning, or such of the intended meaning as succeeds in being adhered to; it may be fairly represented by the logical paraphrase of the poem . . . indeterminate meaning, or that part of the final meaning which took shape not according to its own logical necessity but under metrical compulsion; it may be represented by the poem's residue of meaning which does not go into the logical paraphrase . . . determinate sound-structure, or the meter; and . . . whatever phonetic character the sounds have assumed which is in no relation to the meter." Yet not all of the indeterminate meaning got into the poem as a consequence of the metrical compulsion. Some of it was imported "in order to densify the discourse. The world is dense with its cross-relations and its interpenetrations of content, and why should not the poem represent it so?" "The confusion of our language is a testimony to the confusion of the world. The density or connotativeness of poetic language reflects the world's density."[36] So did the sounds.

If Ransom had mellowed a bit toward science, he had lost none of his pleasure at the prospect of defiant little details getting into the poem and mocking the authority of the structure. Finally he came right out and called them, as he had in *The World's Body*, "irrelevant." He was so taken with the density and particularity of what he called the "texture" of the poem that even though it seemed from his new attention to ideas that he might find a more significant role for them, when it came to that he said that the need for the logical structure "briefly is this: in order to support a local texture."[37] Though nowhere did Ransom say so directly, the tone of his comments strongly suggested at many points that the poetic interest and aesthetic value of a poem were proportionate to the amount of local texture the structure managed to support. But the business of the critic was not with evaluation. Following his account of the elements of a poem, Ransom added, almost as an afterthought, "I cannot but think that the distinction of these elements, and especially of D M [determinate meaning]

[36] *The New Criticism*, pp. 299, 73, 79.
[37] P. 269.

and I M [indeterminate meaning], is the vocation *par excellence* of criticism."[38] In some ways this seems to take us even further from the critic's proper concerns than the notion of the pains as the measure of the human value proposed in *The World's Body*.

V

Despite teaching and keeping *The Kenyon Review* going through the Second World War, Ransom managed during the half dozen years following the appearance of *The New Criticism* to write a series of essays on the nature of art, poetry, and criticism, culminating in "Poetry: I. The Formal Analysis" and "Poetry: II. The Final Cause," which came out in the summer and fall of 1947. ("Poetry: III . . ." was promised but did not appear.) There came a lull of five years during which he published little, for his attention was taken up with establishing the Kenyon School of English and then overseeing its successful transplanting to Bloomington, where it became the Indiana School of Letters. In this interval appeared a sensitive appreciation of Wordsworth and essays on Aristotle's theory of tragedy and on the understanding of fiction, both containing some curious observations on style. Another outburst started in 1952 and lasted into early 1955, when Ransom published the second of a pair of essays which shared the title "The Concrete Universal: Observations on the Understanding of Poetry." Late in 1955 these essays of 1952-1955 were published in the collection *Poems and Essays* (but without the first of the pair on the concrete universal, which was really more a conglomerate of scattered observations than an essay). Since then Ransom has prepared a selection of Thomas Hardy's poems, published with an appreciative essay in 1961, and a few miscellaneous pieces, among which the most interesting for those who have followed the development of his thought is "Our Age Among the Ages," which he read as the Phi Beta Kappa Address at William and Mary College in May of 1958. Here he went against one of the main themes of *God Without Thunder*. To show that the great religious myths embodied a God with thunder, he had earlier cited the story of the Fall and had praised *Paradise Lost* for showing what sin and misery man brought upon himself when

[38] P. 301.

he sought "scientific" knowledge and used it against nature to satisfy his lusts. Now he judged Milton's damning man for his science to be odious: in the tremendous and contingent universe man must have science. The Agrarians, he recalled, had never found words to address to the farmer's wife, who was glad to have any technology she could afford to relieve the drudgery of her existence. He admitted to a tendency to side with the Old Order whenever there was economic or cultural change; he felt uneasy at the neglect of great literature and the prospect that it would become part of a minority culture. Even so, he could be hopeful as he looked upon the vitality and sprawling style of the emergent popular culture, and he thought that high culture might well be due for a transfusion of energy from the lower levels. The address testified to rare honesty, courage, and openmindedness, but those who know Ransom's work well would not be surprised to encounter these qualities again.

The most important essays that have followed *The New Criticism* were written after Ransom had studied the criticism of Kenneth Burke, Cleanth Brooks, R. P. Blackmur, and W. K. Wimsatt. For the most part he restated in them the conceptions of *The New Criticism* and showed his agreement or disagreement with other theorists in terms of those conceptions. The one significant development, which had begun in scattered passages in *The World's Body* and had become more apparent in *The New Criticism*, was in his changing attitude toward what he had been in the habit of calling the "prose core" of a poem. After all he had said about the inutility of poetry and after all the emphasis he had placed upon the freedom of the texture, it was startling to read in "The Inorganic Muses" that he would "subscribe to the modern philosophies to the extent of believing that we cannot accept a poetry, if indeed a poet can want and write a poetry, which does not record some contribution to the biotic organism. . . . I would put the emphasis on the Positive [in the sense of positivistic] or prose elements of the poem first, and regardless of another element ['interpolated material which does not relate to the argument'] which proposes to make a poetry out of it."[39] He was pleased that our age had come to recognize an "irresponsible

[39] *The Kenyon Review*, v (Spring, 1943), 286.

exuberance" in the poetic materials but he thought that "the new critics, careless of the theoretical constitution of poetry, have contrived to create a sense of its disorder."[40] Moreover, he wanted them to pay more heed to the perennial human values of the meanings they were finding by their close readings. "The idea has been that the expanded meanings which the text of poetry yields under the willing hands of the new critics are rewarding in themselves; but it depends upon what the meanings are humanly worth."[41] He found the criticism of R. P. Blackmur brilliant but insufficient because "There is no ideological emphasis; the social or religious ideas are looked at shrewdly, but they are appraised for their function within the work; even though they may be ideas from which, at the very moment, out in the world of action, the issues of life and death are hung."[42] Manifestly he had come a long, long way from the position taken in *The World's Body*, from which he had been inclined to scold critics for having too much ideological emphasis in their writing, though, of course, they were different critics who had neglected the texture. Ransom could take it for granted that with Brooks and Blackmur there would be no such neglect.

His conception of the aesthetic interest of nature, art, and poetry did not change much. "Beauty," he wrote in 1945,

"is the impression we take of the occasion when nature assembles her materials in characteristic luxuriance, not to destroy the human design but to exhibit it well achieved, and at the same time to invest it with natural and contingent brilliance. The investing properties are not functional. The business of aesthetics is to point them out and do what it can with them in theory, while the business of scientific theory is to concern itself with the functional properties."

Among the elements exhibiting functional properties and belonging to the "core of science" were plot, argument, design, form, structure, harmony, composition, the sequence of pragmatic human interest, and the logical organization.[43] However, though he con-

[40] "Poetry: I. The Formal Analysis," *The Kenyon Review*, IX (Summer, 1947), 436.
[41] *Op.cit.*, p. 440.
[42] "More Than Gesture," in *Poems and Essays* (New York, 1955), p. 104.
[43] "Art Worries the Naturalists," *The Kenyon Review*, VII (Spring, 1945), 292, 293.

tinued to distinguish between the logical structure and the investing properties that are the concern of aesthetics, he did come around to saying that in the biotic sense the properties were functional too. The sensibility enjoyed them, but its enjoyment was part of "the organic business." The final cause of poetry—as yet unknown to us—would be the long-range needs of man as a biological and psychological organism which caused him to form sentimental attachments with objects, attachments which brought pleasure to the sensibility, or, as Ransom was now inclined to call it, the id, and moved him to celebrate the attachment in verse.[44]

He continued to flirt with the notion that the organic structure of a poem closely resembled the structure of the world. Arguing that it was the associations in the structure of the world rather than in the poet's mind which caused obscurity in poetry, he asserted that the rapid movement of the poet's mind across these external associations had "the consequence of a tempo in discourse which carries the impression of a density in the content of the natural world. . . . Obscurity is a poetic and ontological device. . . ." And later, discussing the abstract ideas which appeal to us because of their usefulness and the concrete objects which contain them and are, therefore, both useful and capable of commanding our affection by the additional qualities which are not just of practical concern, he wrote, "The relation of the precious object [the concrete] to the specific object [the abstract and useful] within it is thus precisely the same as the relation of the art-work to its own thought-work, the poem to its paraphrase."[45] He was prepared to go even further in 1952, when he reconsidered Aristotle's theory of imitation, which he had described in *The World's Body*: "If 'imitation' is the method of getting the materials for the poetic construction, the imitation which finds such objects as these is freer than Aristotle was prepared for, and the little world it sets up is a small version of our natural world in its original dignity, not the laborious world of affairs. Indeed, the little world is the imitation of our ancient Paradise, when we inhabited it in innocence."[46] It is important to observe that the imitation seems to be of the order

[44] "Poetry: II. The Final Cause," pp. 653-654.
[45] "The Irish, the Gaelic, the Byzantine," *The Southern Review*, VII (Winter, 1942), 534; "Poetry: II. The Final Cause," p. 645.
[46] "Humanism at Chicago," in *Poems and Essays*, p. 100.

of an ontological similarity and not of a one-to-one correspondence between the natural object and the poetic representation he implied in the discussion of a painting in *The World's Body*.

To explain how the precious object contained the specific object, Ransom went back in 1955 to Hegel, from whom he took the term *Concrete Universal*. He distinguished two varieties of universals, the practical and the moral. The first was thoroughgoing: no contingent particulars clung to it. But moral universals appeared in nature and poetry, where they were entangled in all manner of extraneous substance. This, Ransom said, Hegel deplored: he wanted to have his moral universals as tidy and spare as the practical ones. But Kant maintained that beauty was the embodiment of a moral universal in natural details and that poetry represented such beauty by including all the natural surplus. To explain the relation of the moral universal to the details, Ransom resorted, as he had so often in the past, to personification:

"The moral Universal of the poem does not use nature as a means but as an end; it goes out into nature not as a predatory conqueror and despoiler but as an inquirer, to look at nature as nature naturally is, and see what its own reception there may be. The moral Universal takes a journey into nature, so to speak, and the Concrete element is an area of nature existing in its natural conformations as these are given, and discovered, not a Concrete element which it means to ransack for materials which have already been prescribed."[47]

Poets feel a piety toward nature for being so hospitable to the moral Universals. They celebrate nature and represent the Universal in the midst of the Concrete by means of metaphor, which Ransom conceded is not a term used by Kant, though "it would seem a decisive word for his understanding of poetry; it gives us the sense of nature accepting the Universal readily into its infinite system, and lending to it what metaphysical sanction is possible."[48] Perhaps. But one thing Ransom's little fable does not do is make clear just what it is that clings to the Universal in a natural way and yet is irrelevant to it. Indeed, all that we

[47] "The Concrete Universal: Observations on the Understanding of Poetry," in *Poems and Essays*, p. 166.
[48] *Op.cit.*, p. 181.

have in this explanation of poetry is the substitution of *metaphor* for *poetry*, so that the explanation is essentially tautological. It is difficult to discern just where Ransom has gotten much closer to the central problem than he was when he first confronted it back in the Twenties.

VI

Looking back upon Ransom's prose, one sees a remarkable consistency in the assumptions, attitudes, foci of interest, and topics. In the opening section of this chapter it was suggested that the consistency was a consequence of the predilections of his imagination, the informing principle of contrast, the emphasis upon duality and the disparity between the ideal and the actual, the abiding concern with the right relation between man and nature, and the special sympathy with small, independent things that seemed threatened by rationalistic systems and organized authority. All of these, with the possible exception of the predilections of the imagination, were profoundly influenced by Ransom's conception of the mind and especially by his conviction that the patterns of our culture deny the sensibility its innocent satisfactions. Even though Ransom eventually believed that the sensibility did not pursue its needs or achieve its satisfactions apart from the general life of man as a biological and psychological organism, his contexts persistently implied and sometimes directly stated that the reason and sensibility could and usually did work independently of one another if not independently of the total organism. Again and again he suggested that the scientist could suspend the action of his sensibility while his reason formulated general laws, and the artist or the reader of poetry could suspend the action of his reason while his sensibility played upon the qualities of some particular object or event. But the mind is not so compartmentalized; its actions are not so one or the other. Commenting upon Tate's similar conception of the mind, Axton Clark said:

"There is no faculty of will or faculty of imagination existing in haughty isolation and used as we use a hand or a monkey wrench. . . . The sound, carefully grounded view of the human mind that survives vitally in this day is that of a variegated but organic neuro-psychic entity functioning, integrating in different ways and in different directions, but not in compartmental disjunction. . . . Even the most mathematical thought is in fact infused with an emotional obligato."[49]

From Ransom's image of the divided mind, which accorded so well with his dualism and his mode of thinking in systems of correlative, apparently come certain misconceptions which limit the validity and usefulness of his theories of art, poetry, and criticism.

Among the most important are the misconceptions about science and scientists, so often contrasted with art and artists. "Science," he wrote in 1929, "is pragmatic, and bent only on using nature. Scientific knowledge is no more than the knowledge of the uses of nature; it does not credit nature with having any life of its own, and it cannot afford to see in nature any content further than what the scientific terms permit. As a way of knowledge it is possible to us only on condition that we anaesthetize ourselves and become comparatively insensible."[50] Perhaps an engineering student struggling just before an examination to master the formulae for the strength of steel beams might be described as thinking only of uses and as being, for the moment, virtually anaesthetized, but as a generalization this statement displays an unsullied innocence of the history of science and of the way the scientists who make discoveries, who create the scientific images which Ransom compares with poetry, work and feel about their materials. Clark was right in referring to the emotional obligato that accompanies mathematical thought, as any mathematician can testify. Modern scientists try to keep out of their discourse the lyricism, value judgments, and animism which suffuse the writings of Copernicus and Kepler, but they cannot wholly exclude them from their thinking. Actually, they do not constantly attempt to do so, and often these have a significant share in the imaginative processes which precede new advances. The romantic love that leads to knowledge without desire which Ransom attributed to the artist frequently appears in scientific investigation. Despite all the supporting testimony many non-scientists seem unable to believe that scientists pursue and take pleasure in knowledge for its own sake. Moreover, scientists often have strong affections for the instruments and materials

[49] "Poetry Without Purpose," *The New Republic*, LXXIX (June 20, 1934), 149.
[50] "Classical and Romantic," p. 127.

that help them to it and rage against those which seem to bar the way. To realize this one need only hear a physicist or chemist talking about some complicated piece of equipment which he designed and built: he will call it "she" and refer to her temperament, her misdemeanors, her docility when she is in a good mood, using tones that suggest the much-put-upon lover of some high-spirited beauty. The pages of *The Scientific American* or *Nature* show how much life of its own the scientist attributes to a substance and how much animism slips in by way of the metaphors he uses to describe the motions of particles and the behavior of protein molecules. Time and again the most original conceptions have come from a free contemplation of materials which are enjoyed for themselves, from improvisation of forms, and from abrupt, inexplicable insights or massive feelings about the rightness of some pattern—in short, from imaginative processes that much resemble those of the artist. The intuitive leaps of Newton and Poincaré have been duplicated many times in the experience of lesser men—not only in the pure sciences but in technology as well. Buckminster Fuller has said that many of the greatest innovations in engineering came about through the spirit of play.

Unfortunately, scientists have sometimes been obliged to defend their work against inquisitors or to seek the patronage of the powerful by citing the utility of findings made without thought of practical advantage. And in its early years the Royal Society did indeed stress the solution of mechanical problems, while today the public relations expert raises money for research by appealing to our desires and anxieties. But the record generally bears out the words of William S. Beck, a scientist of wide learning in history and the humanities:

"It is not historically true that the major developments of science have been due to a specially strong determination to increase man's command over nature. The Greeks were not pre-eminent in technology but in 'useless' abstract thinking such as geometry. Modern science has been more interested in experimental verification, but it has tried to carry on the tradition that valued exploration and understanding above mere usefulness. . . . Genuine scientific progress in the nature of things cannot take place when science is a wagon hitched to a practical star. And it is time that this realization became part of our culture."[51]

Many scientists understand the limitations of their cognitive modes. They are obliged to be practicing epistemologists, aware that the seemingly best-established laws and catagories are only hypotheses and inadequate figures of speech which will be modified as perception is modified. When writing *God Without Thunder* Ransom caught some distinguished figures of contemporary science saying patently unscientific and silly things. (However, he was a bit unfair when he cited H. L. Mencken as an authority on anthropology.) Yet even as he was making good fun of them, scientists at Göttingen, Cambridge, Copenhagen, and elsewhere were insisting that, as Werner Heisenberg put it later, "In science *the object of research is no longer nature itself, but man's investigation of nature. . . .* The new mathematical formulae no longer describe nature itself but *our knowledge* of nature."[52] The physicists, at least, were not so naive as some of their detractors and admirers made them seem.

Following Hume and Bergson, Ransom rightly insisted on the abstractness of scientific laws and categories; but in his desire to gain approbation for poetry he overstated his case. The scientist can tell us much more and the poet usually tells us much less than Ransom makes out. The scientist cannot give us the unique configuration of qualities and relations within an object or event; on the other hand, the poet can at least point to the object or event and evoke the configuration, which is the truly definitive quality of qualities, relation of relations, and thereby give us a *sense* of the thing-in-itself as a whole and a self. Even so, without departing from his characteristic mode of discourse the scientist can designate an extraordinary number of qualities and relations which are characteristic of an object or event. Taken altogether they do not add up to a complete description of any thing-in-itself, but if we already have some awareness of it as a separate entity the scientist's account may add much to our apprehension of its "thing-ness." The poet, as Ransom says, attempts to utter the proper

[51] *Modern Science and the Nature of Life* (New York, 1957), p. 25.
[52] *The Physicist's Conception of Nature*, tr. Arnold J. Pomerans (New York, 1958), pp. 24, 25.

name of a unique object or event. Insofar as he succeeds he designates (not the same thing as describing) the thing-in-itself. The number of qualities and inner relations which we realize from the designation may be very large or it may be quite small— much smaller than the number of those the scientist can supply. There is no predetermining reason why it *should* be more. The number is a matter of what in *that* context is appropriate to the given poem as poem. The important difference between the poetic and scientific accounts is not in the number of qualities but in the kind—and in the power of the poetic kind to give us, insofar as we attend to it, the feeling that the whole unique thing stands behind the qualities of which we are made aware.

In most of his comparisons, Ransom locates the difference in number. Asserting that any unique event or object is an infinitude of qualities and relations, he says that science gives us very few and suggests that poetry gives them all. We are said to pause along the way in a poem to explore the local details and realize their infinite particularity, which results in our bringing into the total meaning which the poem has for us many aspects which are irrelevant to its logical argument. In support of this he attempts, as in the example to follow, to make distinctions which either state directly or derive from his misconceptions of science—and beyond that, his outmoded theory of the mind.

In his "An Address to Kenneth Burke" he writes:

"No harmony exists logico-mathematically or organically among the heterogeneous properties of a natural object. To assemble the original properties is the work of nature, and the assemblage, if we think about it, always strikes us as arbitrary and contingent, a pure gift or datum, which reason cannot understand though sense witness it indubitably. The image is one thing, and the rational structure is another. The difference between the heterogeneous properties is absolute. Absolute also is the difference between the local imagery of the poem and its logical structure. Their being furnished both comfortably in one poem is not a harmony in a very marvelous sense."[53]

The first sentence states somewhat ambiguously the premise of the argument to follow. The meaning of *harmony* is quite in-

[53] *The Kenyon Review*, IV (Spring, 1942), 232.

definite, but it seems to denote congruity, interdependence, and significant proportion. *Logico-mathematically* is compounded of two roots Ransom uses with singular carelessness, as when he refers to the paraphraseable content of a poem as its "logical structure." The term seems in this context to mean "according to a design or system which can be explained under the principles of logic or mathematics." *Organically* apparently means what it usually does when applied to physical bodies. If it does, then the statement is false. Any competent solid-state physicist can demonstrate an organic harmony among such properties of a piece of germanium oxide as its physical, chemical, electrical, crystallographic, optical, mineralogical, and geological characteristics. A molecular biologist having ordinary professional acquaintance with plant physiology could do even more for a leaf or blade of grass. The second statement is as ambiguous. *Assemblage* can mean "an assembly" or "act of assembling." Either would be arbitrary or contingent, since the presence in the act of assembling of the least effect of unknown or indeterminate forces (and there are always some) makes some stages arbitrary and contingent and thus by strict logic both the whole act and the whole assembly as well, *but only if we acknowledge that some harmony exists organically in the act and the assembly*. Without organic relationships there can be no assembling, no assemblage, no datum: both the act and the assemblage would be infinitely divisible into arbitrary and contingent elements; everything would be arbitrary and contingent and thus, given the meaning of the words, nothing would be. Moreover, the assemblage may be a pure datum which the reason cannot understand wholly (and therefore in the strictest sense cannot understand as a pure datum at all, though it might recognize it as such); but it is *not* a pure gift (i.e., the consequence of purely arbitrary and contingent giving or assembling "by nature"), and the reason can indeed understand much of the "impure" giving. Thus the second statement is not wholly true regardless of the meaning we assign to *assemblage*, and insofar as it is true it contradicts the first statement.

The third statement is semantically careless. *Thing*, "the weakest word in the language," is insufficient to make the distinction Ransom wants. In the sense that the image is a thing, the rational structure is an attribute of it. The next statement must be true, but it is a pure tautology. It cannot be applied to the image and the structure of the natural object because the image is not a property. Nor can it be applied to the local imagery and the logical structure of a poem cited in the next sentence. Local imagery is a class name for participating details. Details are not properties. A structure, in the sense that the term is used in the description of a poem (where it is a dead metaphor), is a property, though it is convenient to speak of it as if it were a separable detail. But *logical* structures are rare in poetry. As we have already seen, Ransom likes to use the term to designate the paraphraseable content, or, to be more exact, the paraphraseable aspect of the total content of the poem. Now theoretically this paraphraseable aspect has a structure, but actually we cannot distinguish this structure, which is a property of an aspect of another aspect (the content) of the whole form-content, which is the poem, a thing-in-itself. What we do distinguish is the structure of the paraphrase, a different thing-in-itself. We hope that by tracing the structure of the paraphrase we may better be able to intuit the structure of the poem. We ignore—we are unaware of—the structure of the paraphraseable content, which is only mentioned here to show how inexact is Ransom's language. Rarely is any instance of these three kinds of structure (structure of the poem, structure of the paraphraseable content, and structure of the paraphrase) logical. Ransom employs the term in order to draw analogies with the rational structure which is an imputed property of a natural object. But the analogies are misleading. A poem is a product of the intelligence: it is a statement, and it can have a logical verbal organization which we may call its logical structure in a metaphoric sense, even though, as we have seen, habit has made *structure* thus used a dead metaphor. A natural object has true structural relations which the intelligence recognizes and reports in rational statements. Hence it is convenient to designate these relations as Ransom does in the third sentence, by the telescoped term *rational structure*. But this term is still another figure of speech. Moreover, in making the structural relations analogous to the structure of a verbal statement, Ransom implies that the natural object does indeed exhibit a logico-mathematical or organic harmony such as he denied it in the opening sentence of the quotation.

By the time we reach the last sentence, which contains the point that Ransom wanted to make in order to support his general argument for the presence in a poem of contingent details which help in the representation of the density and contingency of the natural world—by the time we reach this sentence we are likely to have lost our grip on the words. If we have not, we can see that by overleaping radical differences in kind, Ransom has tried to make some statements about the nature of poetry going back ultimately to misconceptions of what and how much scientists trace in natural objects and events. The combination of the misconception with loose reasoning and, may we say, somewhat arbitrary and contingent wording, results in a view of poetry which permits him to dichotomize the form-content and neglect the aesthetic effect of such harmonious unity as the poets achieve. "Art gratifies a perceptual impulse and exhibits a minimum of reason," he tells us in *The World's Body*. Later, as we know, he backed away from such an extreme position. And he modified his view of scientists and their conduct. But by this time an abiding harm had been done to his theories of poetry and criticism.

Before considering these theories, we should glance at the theory of myth and the good Fundamentalist. It was remarked earlier in this chapter that Ransom's description of myth makes it so similar to poetry—as he defines poetry—that most of what can be said about his views on poetry applies with little modification to the account of myth. One important difference lies in the literalness of belief attributed to the Fundamentalist. One cannot believe in that belief. If he were so critical a naturalist as to have begun by acknowledging a myth to be a man-made fiction and by looking it over carefully to make sure that it was "realistic" before electing to believe in it, the good Fundamentalist could scarcely abandon his critical habits and behave toward his supernaturals as if they were concrete, existent entities—all the while remembering to avoid practicing "magic" and refusing to ask them to intervene on his behalf. In a remark that anticipated his observation in "Poetry: II. The Final Cause" that poetry served the needs of man as organism, Ransom said, "A religion has to justify itself as an economy that makes for human happiness." And "The religion which the Fundamentalist has adopted contains the decision he has taken with respect to his career. He elected it because it seemed to offer him the best definition of his humanity, the best recipe for his happiness."[54] Now, Ransom said that his account was a "logic" rather than a history of how one came to belief in myths; even so, one's position at the end is presumably the same. However one reached it, we have difficulty accepting the premise that one will be able to "elect" the myth on these terms and believe in God. One may well believe that the myth has a cognitive function and can serve as a guide to conduct—as would any significant literary work. But that seems likely to be as far as one can go.

Thereafter Ransom had little to say about religion, choosing instead to argue for the realism of poetry and its efficacy as an "economy" that makes for human happiness. In the process he became the virtual Dean of American Criticism. With the friends against whom he debated and the young men whom he taught and published, he radically changed our approach to poetry, having convinced us that it is a unique and indispensable means of representing human experience, that the value of a poem does not reside in whatever general concepts we can infer from it, and that its elements must be studied with patient and imaginative attention to their qualities and to the poem as a whole. In all this Ransom's example as a reader has been quite as important as his theorizing, though there is far less of it. No one exceeds him in sensitivity guided and restrained by common sense and a feeling for the poem as poem. He tended to neglect it in his theorizing, but he is particularly perceptive in recognizing the general design of a poem, and as a reader he goes straight at it. Then he asks of each detail down to the most delicate discriminations in the weights of accents and variations on the metrical pattern how they affect that design, how they contribute to the poem as a whole. Here his practice quite exceeds his theory of criticism.

In "An Address to Kenneth Burke" he insisted that the "referents" of a poem must not fail to have their functional meanings and later, as we have seen, he objected to the tendency of the new critics to foster disorder in the reading of a poem. Nevertheless, his own writings encourage the reader to neglect the "prose" of a poem (in his contexts almost always a drab statement of the obvious) in favor of the "glittering contingency." Again and again

[54] *God Without Thunder*, pp. 167, 99.

his definition of a poem makes it a metered analogue of a *trompe l'oeil* painting, a verse description invoking in the mind's eye as fully as possible the surface appearance of familiar domestic objects—including people who are reduced to things scrutinized from the outside. Late in his writing he remarked that a poetic imitation was freer than Aristotle would have thought and implied that the important part of the imitation was in the organic parallelism of the poetic construction and the natural world.[55] What he did not acknowledge was that in even the most naturalistic descriptive poem there will inevitably be, by virtue of the selection and arrangement of materials required by the artistic frame of reference, a warping away from the subject and that, regardless of the poet's intentions, this warping will serve an interpretive and evaluative function. He recognized that the need to fulfill a phonetic design would introduce unforeseen material, but he thought this brought the poem nearer to the original. And, as he celebrates the poem as a means through which, freed from appetite and restrained by the form, we may know an object in its fullness, he puts so much emphasis upon the "free" details that they appear to be unencumbered with even a natural order. Nature is said to be chaotic and the poem seems to be invited to be as chaotic as it can so that it will faithfully represent and enable us to know the world's body.

A serious fault in Ransom's theorizing, and in that of many of the currently influential teachers and theorists who stress attention to connotations, is the assumption that the mental image of a natural object or event evoked by verbal reference is qualitatively rich, clear in outline, and nearly exact in verisimilitude. It is on this assumption that Ransom, Tate, Brooks, and others have based their claim that the poet reports for us many more qualities than the scientist can hope to. (Tate, as we shall see, has even said that the poem furnishes us with "complete" knowledge.) According to Ransom, when we have been slowed down and brought to a contemplation of the representation of the subject, we have before us an aggregate of infinite particularity to be studied as we might study some exceptionally thoroughgoing and realistic picture, after which we will be aware of many aspects and qualities we ordinarily overlook. Now, there is abundant evidence—and we

[55] See above, p. 286.

can get as much more as we desire—that *some* properties of the mental image may be strongly realized and felt and that consequently the mental image may have affective force exceeding that of its real-life equivalent, a force that makes the mental image seem more immediate and vivid. And these may well be properties overlooked in the equivalent. The force is a consequence of many things: our being in a receptive mood, our freedom from distractions, and—something that Ransom neglects in his theories—the reenforcement which the details of a well-integrated poem can give to one another. Even so, the mental image of either a detail or of the whole is cloudy, constantly shifting, and surprisingly limited in the number of qualities actually realized. What is important, as we said in our analysis of Ransom's remarks about the absence of harmony among heterogeneous properties, is that the poet, by the particular qualities which he does evoke, gives us the sense of the whole. But a sense that the whole is present is *not* the same as a realization of an infinite number of qualities or even of a very large number.

This writer remembers without effort three particularly vivid scenes from his reading: Lambert Strether having luncheon by the Seine with Mme. de Vionnet in James's *The Ambassadors*, Paul Morel high in a cherry tree watching the sunset in Lawrence's *Sons and Lovers*, and the setting and objects of Frost's poem, "The Silken Tent." In each instance the description is so evocative that he seems to be right on the spot. Yet when he considers the qualities of which he is aware without deliberately stopping, breaking off from his imaginative reconstruction, and by a conscious effort quite foreign to his response to literature forcing himself to list qualities which must by their nature be present in these scenes, the number actually realized is small. The point is that *in their contexts* the qualities realized and felt are enough to make the scenes seem as substantial and palpable as any actual ones, and their emotive effects are stronger than those of most. And if we turn to the splendid image in the first stanza of Ransom's "Blue Girls" we find that it certainly creates an impression of wholeness but that the realized qualities of color, configuration, movement, and personality are much fewer than Ransom's theories suggest. One reason is that the theories emphasize inclusiveness and take no account of how the artistic frame of reference acts to exclude the irrelevant, to focus attention. Moreover, they treat all literature as if it were in the naturalistic mode and say nothing about how symbolism and fantasy affect our realization of the *thingness* of the subject.

Ransom's preoccupation with this assumption and the too narrow conception of poetry which the assumption implies are partly the consequences of his curious ideas about the motivation of artistic creation and of the ways in which a poem comes into being, which in turn derive from his wish to make art and poetry as unlike science as possible. When he says that we make works of art because of our love of natural objects and our guilty nostalgia for the innocent relations we had with them before we applied science and greedily abused them, he overlooks a host of motives—some of them often far more important than any feeling toward the subject matter—to which any artist can testify. Two of the simplest are delight in the qualities of the medium as such and pleasure in handling it. Poets love words and rhythms; a painter can be enchanted with the hues and textures that turn up as he scrapes his palette clean after a day's work; musicians break into smiles over a single note played on a fine instrument. Then there is the satisfaction of arranging details of the medium in a formal order having harmony with enough assimilated diversity to prevent monotony—a satisfaction enjoyed by the creator who works in a non-representational art such as pure music and abstract painting, but one also had by the artist who accomplishes representation of a natural order within an aesthetic order. (It is worth remembering that since Van Gogh and Cézanne most representational painters have been quite willing to do considerable violence to the natural order for the sake of the aesthetic order, particularly in the matter of color.) Then there is the not at all trivial desire for prestige, authority, and plain cash. We need to be reminded today that until the Romantic Period most artists worked on commissions or aimed at specific markets: they had commodities to sell and intended to do just that. Often some of the greatest works of art— Jan Van Eyck's *The Betrothal of the Arnolfini* or Holbein's *The Virgin with the Family of Burgomaster Meyer*, for example—dealt with subjects chosen by the purchaser. Finally, love of the natural object does not account for works whose subjects are hateful or hideous. Ransom once said of Greek tragedy that the plots move with "a great train of free and energetic imagery, and to the handsomest phonetic or musical accompaniment. . . . The focus of dramatic interest is turned altogether upon sensibility; the issue is known, and the plot is not the thing now, the heroic style is the thing."[56] But surely this is only partially true. The style helps to particularize and intensify our realization of the agony of Oedipus, which we cannot love, any more than we can love Oedipus, though we may feel the most profound sympathy and respect for him. If we take other works of art with content which is indubitably hateful—O'Neill's *A Long Day's Journey Into Night*, George Grosz's drawings, Alban Berg's *Lulu*—the "plot" is very much a thing and no splendor of style can distract us from it, especially when it is meant to focus our attention on the plot. Ransom is making a separation, allied to the separation of "structure" and "texture," which, as we shall see, is one of the weaknesses of his position.

Ransom's account of the composition of a poem in *The New Criticism* rightly insists upon the improvisation and compromise present, but, as Murray Krieger has pointed out, describes only one idiosyncratic method of composition and takes no account of the way a poet may discover his "argument" as he shuffles his materials with only a loose general notion of his theme and no strong commitment to it.[57] (Later, as we know, Ransom told Brooks and Warren that as a rule poets went ahead on their own intuition and then looked to see what they had done.) Moreover, *The New Criticism* fails to consider choices made for the sake of consistency and appropriateness in aspects other than the "logic" and the phonetic patterns. And here we are brought back once more to Ransom's contrasting of scientific discourse and poetry. There is a difference *in kind* between them, but the one he describes is misleading in a number of ways. In the first place, it does not arise from the intentions, which are so often cited in his effort to define the kinds. We never know—not even the creator himself knows—exactly what those intentions are; but we know enough to know that Ransom's explanation of the motives of the scientist and artist does not apply in many instances. Nor is the difference in the abstract-concrete or universal-particular polarities, as Ransom so often says. That is a difference in degree because all scientific discourse does not stand

[56] "The Literary Criticism of Aristotle," *The Kenyon Review*, x (Summer, 1948), 399-400.
[57] *The New Apologists of Poetry* (Minneapolis, 1956), pp. 82-84.

at one pole and all poetry at the other, as would be necessary if this were to be a difference in kind. No, the difference in kind results from the presence in a poem of an artistic frame of reference and the fact that the validity of poetic statements is not subject to verification under laboratory conditions. Ransom almost makes this distinction in his discussion of the need for a poem to make sense and satisfy a metrical design, but he does not go far enough in his conception of the frame of reference, which involves much more than the phonetic patterns.

One reason seems to be that he does not consider the phonetic patterns to have an expressive function. When he began writing about the "coexistence" of sound and sense he spoke of art as being, like nature, a mixture. Later, disliking the view of poetry as a moral with decoration, he said that a poem should be a compound, *not* a mixture. But his insistence that poetry consists of universal conceptions of a "scientific" sort, loosened up by free, contingent, and irrelevant local details, together with his idea (at least in *The New Criticism*, and his later emphasis on the argument does not deny it) that the structure is present to support the enjoyable texture, brings him close to the moral-plus-decoration view and certainly implies that poetry is a mixture.

But ideally (that is, according to the ideals that distinguish poetry as a kind of discourse) poetry *is* a compound, and what is not compounded is truly irrelevant and unpoetic. To explain just how it is we need to apply an artistic equivalent of Bohr's concept of complementarity. By this Bohr means that the different pictures which we make in describing the behavior of atoms, though fully adequate to their occasions, are mutually exclusive: according to one the atom is a small-scale planetary system; according to the other it consists of a nucleus surrounded by standing waves. In describing a poem we may consider it as an aesthetic object (using *aesthetic* in its traditional sense rather than in Ransom's) and as a statement about human experience. As an aesthetic object it is seen as an autonomous whole in which the parts work together in harmonious unity. Their interaction makes prominent those aspects of themselves which contribute to the whole and exclude (actually, try to exclude, and their success is considerable) those aspects which do not. Because of their interaction within this artistic frame of reference, whereby the whole exhibits beauty and the parts are arranged so that they work to that end, all the details from the pervasive general ideas to the least of local terms undergo a radical transformation. Ransom is right to speak of the effect of the images, for example, on the argument. But the poem consists of words which do not surrender their referential function, though the character of that function is modified by their interrelations in the poem. As a statement the poem is whole, unique, but not autonomous. Ransom has insisted all along on the uniqueness, the lack of autonomy, and the referential function. But he has not sufficiently related the uniqueness to the artistic frame of reference, since he considers only the phonetic aspect of it, and he has insisted, in all his talk about coexistence and irrelevance, upon the lack of wholeness.

Whatever elements or aspects of elements cannot be assimilated into the unique, whole form-content taken as both an aesthetic object and a statement, or cannot be nullified by the focusing of attention, are blemishes. Ransom, however, thought that too many critics concentrated on the functional relations, which he lumped under "structure" (thereby helping make this key term still more ambiguous). "They like to suppose that in poetry . . . everything that figures in the discourse means to be functional, and that the poem is imperfect in the degree that it contains items . . . which manifest a private independence."[58] We can go further. The blemishes may give a separate pleasure of their own; they may add some naturalistic realism; but these are not a pleasure or a realism which the artist *qua* artist desires. They threaten the *artistic* truth of the work, which is not simple verisimilitude of appearances because the work stands in a symbolic relation to its subject and these blemishes bring disorder into the symbol and the relation. They threaten, too, the beauty of the work, which is not measured in the number of sensations furnished to the sensibility by free and irrelevant details.

But as a theorist, Ransom, who wrote poetry of rare splendor and has always been unusually perceptive of artistic excellence and of the organizational relationships from which it arises, is little interested in beauty. For in his effort to assert the importance of poetry by comparing it with science, he chose to concentrate on

[58] "Criticism as Pure Speculation," *The Intent of the Critic,* ed. Donald A. Stauffer (Princeton, 1941), p. 112.

science's reputed ability to give us knowledge and in the comparison to emphasize the cognitive role of poetry. In our age this is a necessary and courageous choice, and to it we owe much of our renewed respect for and attention to poetry as poetry. But the emphasis does not require him to neglect the ways in which beauty is achieved, especially as these ways affect the cognitive function. And even if he does neglect them, which he has a perfect right to do, though it reduces the scope and value of his theorizing, he cannot in support of the cognitive importance of poetry make assertions which are invalid. One that is often implied and sometimes rather ambiguously stated concerns the resemblance of the organization of a poem to the natural order of the world's body. We are supposed to learn from poetry things we cannot learn from science not because its statements are *about* the world but because they are *like* the world. But, as F. X. Roellinger said, "It seems extraordinary that the way in which the poet happens to solve his structure-texture problems should happen to correspond to the constitution of the world."[59]

Related to this is the idea that the interest of a poem comes almost entirely from its subject and that the value of a poem depends upon its verisimilitude and from the number and vividness of the details it offers for the pleasure of the sensibility. Indeed, Ransom once told this writer that the aesthetic goodness of a work of art was determined by the number of qualities it can tease us into recognizing and enjoying and by the affection for the natural objects which its representation of them can arouse.[60] For a long time he referred to the "biotic" interest of the prose core, and, as we have seen, in "Poetry: II. The Final Cause" he came rather close to the position of I. A. Richards to which he once so vigorously objected, when he said that the local details had a biotic interest too because of the satisfaction they gave to the sensibility, which did not carry on its activities apart from the rest of the human organism. But none of this provides us with a clear measure of the value of the argument or the details (in *The New Criticism* "good" or "positive" details are simply those that add to our awareness of the world's body), or of the objects and events which make up

---

[59] "Two Theories of Poetry as Knowledge," *The Southern Review*, VII (Spring, 1942), 700.
[60] In a conversation on August 26, 1946.

the subject. Ransom never returned to the absurd notion that the value for the observer comes from the marks upon a work of the artist's efforts and pains. (Some of the worst art carries the scars of incredible labor, while some of the best seems almost offensively easy.) He was right to insist on the transfer of value from the real-life equivalents to their representations in the poem, but he was wrong in thinking that all value—all "passion," as he once termed it—comes from the subject. Here, as a consequence of his neglecting the artistic frame of reference, he overlooked its transmutation of the material. In addition to the aesthetic value of the transmuted material there are values imposed on the representation by style, convention, and the formal organization. Moreover, the transmuted material, like the original subject (but not in quite the same way), has values measured by theology, ethics, the historical sense of cultures, and our images of ourselves and our aspirations for self-fulfillment. Ransom recognized this in his later essays when he said that he found the criticism of Blackmur "insufficient" because it lacked ideological emphasis and that poetry represents social behavior and exerts a powerful moral influence.[61] But Ransom does not suggest how the critic shall determine these values. Years before he had written at length to Tate about poetry's testing human values and, ultimately, testifying to their failure, but he did not develop these ideas into a theory of the human significance of poetry as an interpretation and judgment upon human experience. This, plus his neglect of the need to judge the artistic value, may be due, as Krieger says, to the fact that in the end his concern is with the poem-reality relation rather than the poem-reader relation. It is not until he becomes reader himself that attention to these matters appears in his writing and contradicts that astonishing remark in *The New Criticism* to the effect that distinguishing the determinate and indeterminate meanings of poems was the "vocation *par excellence* of criticism."

VII

As one looks back over Ransom's writings on art, poetry, and criticism, the qualities which appear are not always favorable to his standing as a theorist. Though he published nearly thirty essays on

---

[61] "More Than Gesture," *Poems and Essays*, p. 104; "The Community of Letters," *op.cit.*, pp. 112, 114.

these subjects (the exact number would depend on how sharply one defined the subjects) over a span of nearly forty years, he repeated himself again and again and he kept his speculations within a rather remarkably narrow range. Yet though he went over the same ground many times, he retained in his treatment a quality of amateurishness. This is partially an effect of tone, and the informality, modesty, and whimsy which suggest it are refreshing indeed. Often, though, it almost seems that he used key terms in a deliberately loose way in order to preserve the air of lightness and diffidence: as if to say to the reader, "Now don't take this too seriously. Look at the way I use *science*, *logic*, and *prose*—I don't take it very seriously myself." This may be unfair to Ransom, but it is not unfair to say that he uses such terms carelessly and inconsistently. Sometimes he apparently wants them to have their exact sense; sometimes he is manifestly using them figuratively; and sometimes, within the same argument, he wants to have them both ways. Even more amateurish is his treatment of the sciences. When it suits his purpose he lumps them altogether and throws in a few technologies such as engineering and agronomy besides; yet there are differences between, for example, mathematics and theoretical physics, which is reputed to be close to it, so great that some mathematicians claim that their own study is not a science at all. As for the differences between mathematics and the life sciences, even when the latter make use of statistical analysis, these are greater than the differences between mathematics and music. Ransom treats the arts with just about as much cheerful disregard for their significant differences. In 1927 he told Tate, "I think the way of treating poetry separately from the other arts exposes us to almost any sort of error; hardly any error is too extravagant to look likely under this method. But isn't that a poor view of an art which cannot be applied, *mutatis mutandis*, to the other arts?"[62] Yet he often ignored this sensible warning and generalized freely about all poetry—and all literature—in terms of the characteristics of descriptive verse, and about all the arts in terms of this verse and figurative or landscape painting. If he had given more attention to meditative and Symbolist poetry (which he dismissed all too quickly in "Poets Without Laurels" and "Poetry: A Note on Ontology" as "Platonic" and "Pure" poetry) he

---

[62] From a letter written late in the spring of 1927. For a discussion of its date, see note 9.

might have avoided some of his oversimplifications about the concreteness of poetry or about its relation to its real-life equivalents. If he had checked some of his ideas about the arts and the motivation behind them against music, the ballet, architecture, and nonrepresentational painting, he might have said more about the artistic frame of reference, which, even if it were not a central concern, manifestly had much bearing upon the problems in epistemology and the nature of cognition that he was trying to solve.

These are hard words, but they must be used just because we owe so much to Ransom. His style is so ingratiating, his accomplishments as poet, teacher, and editor are so impressive, and the topics to which he addressed himself had so long been neglected by most literary scholars, that his influence has been immense. We must, therefore, be careful to recognize the theorizing for what it is: original, stimulating, limited, wonderfully perceptive, and nearly as often wrongheaded. It is easy to overlook some of its faults because just where it is most confused or ambiguous it appears easy and lucid and because it often reflects the special prejudices of its special audience—such as the prejudice against scientists or that against historical scholars. (We must remember that Ransom has made handsome apologies to both parties.) One of the best ways to see the virtues and faults of Ransom's theories is to read some of his own criticism, which is a model of sensitivity, sympathy, breadth of interest, and resourceful imaginativeness tempered with good sense and honest reporting on the true experience of reading. Another excellent way is to test the theories against his own poetry, which has so many manifest virtues that we soon see what needs to be added to Ransom's theories to cover them all.

Yet we would not read that poetry so well and thus see the limitations of the theories were it not for what the theories have done to bring about the revolution which Ransom wanted to start with Tate. Our appreciation of his poetry—and all good poetry—is a measure of how well the revolution succeeded. In an age of sciences, including a quasi-science of literary studies, he has insisted that we read poetry as poetry. And so we go back to "Necrological," "Janet Waking," "Judith of Bethulia," "Painted Head," and all the others to learn with pleasure what only poems can teach us about the burden and glory of our mixed and disparate destiny.

CHAPTER SEVEN

ALLEN TATE'S PROSE

....

"Man is a creature that in the long run
has got to believe in order to know, and
to know in order to do."

—Allen Tate, "The Man of Letters in the Modern World"

....

I

$\mathcal{R}$ANSOM AND TATE. Think of one and the other comes promptly to mind. The conjunction has become almost habitual, like those of Beaumont and Fletcher, Addison and Steele, Wordsworth and Coleridge—or Brooks and Warren. We can join the friends not because of their poetries, which have always been dissimilar, but because of their prose in which at times the resemblances have been so numerous as to warrant Ransom's friendly allusion to "communal authorship." And the resemblances are significant. So it is convenient to defer consideration of Tate's poetry and move directly to his essays and fiction. There is another reason for thus proceeding. In its texts, if not in its conceptions (which are often surprisingly simple), Tate's is as difficult as any modern American poetry that deserves attentive study, and some acquaintance with his ideas and their evolution, more easily discerned in his prose works, helps one read it. When one knows well both the poetry and the prose, one discovers that the poetry elucidates the prose more than the prose elucidates the poetry. But not at first.

Ransom has always had a genius for working with gifted young men. Yet in the days of *The Fugitive* he was not particularly close to Tate. This may have been due in part to their standings. Ransom was a professor but Tate was more than a bright undergraduate and could not easily assume a deferential role. No obstacles arose between Tate and Davidson, who was on the faculty but who treated Tate as an equal and even looked to him for instruction.

Ransom, however, was less impressed by Tate's show of familiarity with all that was new and daring and, though mild in manner, much more authoritative. Hirsch presided in the loose confederation of the Fugitives, but Ransom was the preeminent member and consequently the one whom Tate would be virtually compelled by his temperament to resist. Ransom defended Tate's right to experiment and admired the thoroughness with which he criticized poetry, including Ransom's own, but he did not think much of Tate's arguments against the restrictions of conventional forms. About all they really agreed on was that the formulas of the sciences were too thin to represent man and his universe, and it was H. C. Sanborn of the philosophy department rather than Ransom who had convinced Tate of this.

Their intellectual association had a tentative beginning in their disputes over contemporary versification in the pages of *The Fugitive* (see Chapter Six), lapsed for a time, and then swiftly became close and deep after Tate settled in New York City in the autumn of 1924 and began sending Ransom copies of his essays and reviews, which led them into discussions of literature and society. In this interval, which lasted until Tate returned to the South early in 1930, Ransom worked out the ideas of "The Third Moment" and *God Without Thunder* and had his strongest influence upon Tate's thinking.[1] Even so this was not the time of their closest communion. Rather, it began with the publication of *I'll Take My Stand* and lasted for ten years. There was much affinity. In his undergraduate days and for a short time thereafter Tate had cultivated a rather self-conscious lawlessness of manner and delivery, but both men were conservatives by disposition. Both formed their philosophies on the assumption that the mind is compartmentalized and requires a careful balancing of the forces of the separate faculties. They believed that in our time the balance was upset, and man, divided against himself, blundered into needless confusion, consequences of which were the disorder and misery of urban industrial society. Both men looked back with nostalgia to a vision, if not the actuality, of the life of the small farmer; yet they preferred, without any sense of self-contradiction, aristocratic, ceremonious societies in which ritual restrained the reason, slowed the tempo of life, and

---

[1] So, at least, Tate himself believes. (From a letter to this writer, September 10, 1953.)

protected the balance of the mind. They mistrusted all ideologies and looked with disfavor upon science and those analytical methodologies which emulated it. Ransom meliorated his suspicions with his wit and general good humor, but Tate rarely let pass an opportunity to show his contempt, particularly for the social sciences. He boasted of his ignorance of them, as if they were so barbarous that no civilized man could be expected to know anything about them except that they had done harm to society and education. (If he had been less truculent he might have been spared some of the humiliations he suffered at the hands of sociologists when he represented the Agrarians before the Southern Policy Association.) Ransom and Tate helped to bring about a revolution in American letters, but it was conservatism, not radicalism, which motivated their opposition to socio-political criticism and the quasi-scientific study of literature.

Yet when *The New Criticism* was published in the spring of 1941, the period of their closest communion was coming to an end. As Agrarianism faded away and the Second World War drew nearer, Tate became more discouraged over the condition of man and more furious with the "scientism" which he blamed for it, while Ransom, who did not look aside from the appalling state of the world, was somewhat more hopeful—or at least less inclined to blame man's difficulties on science and technology. In *The New Criticism* he made a mild but quite definite demurrer against the stand which Tate had taken on the "positivist attitude" in "The Present Function of Criticism" (1940). He had always been a naturalist with strong pragmatic tendencies and once jokingly referred to himself as a "positivist" in a letter to Tate written in 1927. Reflecting on *The New Criticism*, he observed to Tate: "I don't think the positivists [by which he meant the followers of Carnap] will regard me as a convert. . . . I am forced to regard poetic theory as science, though a new science, because about a new or 'different' kind of discourse. That's why I don't want any taboos, restrictions, philosophical censorship, against the analytic work. If that is positivism, I guess I'm a member of the tribe. But so far as the absurd emphasis on scientific discourse as the only discourse goes, I'm far from being one. And I hope I didn't give them much comfort; I didn't mean to."[2] Just the same, there is about this a

[2] The letter is dated "May 23." The discussion of *The New Criticism* fixes the

hint of apology, as if Ransom feared that his friend would feel that he had gone pretty far toward the positivists' position. In the next decade he went much further as he developed a pragmatic theory of poetry resembling the doctrines of relevance which Tate abhorred, while Tate moved on to a belief that the greatest poetry was a proximate incarnation of the Word. In 1952 a review by Ransom of Eliot's collected poems made unmistakably clear how far apart the friends now stood. But their affection for one another remained unimpaired.[3]

It was said in the last chapter that Ransom's principal concern has been with the pluralism of the universe and man's acceptance of both the modest happiness which may be his lot and the destruction of his "dearest values." In his prose Ransom has concentrated on how man shall know Nature and shape his conduct accordingly. Much of his conservatism comes from his agreement with Tate that the universe contains an irreducible measure of evil which optimistic liberals foolishly deny. Usually Ransom has been more interested in problems of knowledge than in problems of conduct, and when, as in his Agrarian essays, he has made conduct his theme, it has often turned out to be conduct for the sake of knowledge. That explains his somewhat curious observation that "the object of a proper society is to instruct its members how to transform instinctive experience into aesthetic experience." Out of context the words seem frivolous. But when we recall what Ransom meant by *aesthetic* we understand that a proper society fosters the contemplation, enjoyment, and knowledge of the world's body.

Ransom frequently alludes to society in his prose, but he has not really written much about man's relation to man. As he defines it, aesthetic experience, in which man's deepest values are realized, is actually something one engages in alone. One is not deliberately withdrawn from men; one is simply not participating with them in any common enterprise. The ideal world of Ransom's poetry and the farm life described in his Agrarian writings are valued in proportion to the freedom and opportunities they give the individual

---

year as 1941. This and all other letters to Tate referred to in this chapter are in the Princeton University Library.

[3] See "Poems of T. S. Eliot: A Perspective," *The New Republic*, cxxvii (December 8, 1952), 16-17.

for enjoying Nature's contingent and infinite particularity. Ransom, a self-designated conservative, is, therefore, actually inclined toward anarchism. He agrees with Tate on the need for restraints between man and nature, but he wants them held to a minimum. He is "conservative" because he thinks liberals attach too much value to regulatory systems. But there is nothing anti-social about his individualism. In his Agrarian essays he put the highest value on easy social intercourse and worked to preserve a society in which it was an ordinary part of life among a people joined by shared experiences and attitudes rather than by economic necessity and law.

For years Tate, too, has had as a principal concern the character of the universe—of Nature—and man's relation to it. Like Ransom he has been particularly interested in how man shall know that character and use his knowledge to direct his conduct. But as Tate sees it, the relationship with Nature should be established from within a community of men rather than in the direct, personal way that Ransom implies. Knowledge is made possible by beliefs transmitted by the community and conduct based on it is sanctioned by the community. Tate is far more concerned than Ransom with the roles men perform in the community, and he tends to reverse the priority of interests found in Ransom and put conduct ahead of knowledge. When knowledge has been his central theme, it has often turned out to be knowledge for the sake of conduct. Richard Foster rightly observes, "Tate has always been less a technical critic [and, we might add, literary theorist] than an essayist using literature as the frame of reference within which he criticizes the mind and life of his time in the light of his convictions about the proper ends of man."[4] One might emend this to read "proper ends of *a* man" or even "proper ends of *a man of letters*," for Tate tends to emphasize the individual, particularly the poet, and to wonder what he needs society for, what he takes from society. As we shall see in a moment, this makes his conservatism quite unlike Ransom's.

The difference in their views is nowhere more significant than in their images of Nature. Ransom's poetry broods upon mortality and the destruction of values and his prose reiterates Nature's in-

[4] *The New Romantics, a Reappraisal of the New Criticism* (Bloomington, 1962), p. 108.

difference to man, its incomprehensibility, and the unforeseeable disasters it visits upon him. Nevertheless, what lingers in the mind is a vision of the garden, the meadow, the airy landscape by Inness. This is not to suggest that Ransom does not mean what he says when he speaks of the suffering that Nature inflicts; rather it shows how much stress he puts upon the natural pleasures and the life-forms that make them possible. Tate exhibits a sensitive awareness of the physical environment even in some of his most overwrought poems, and the descriptions in his *Stonewall Jackson* of the seasons in the Shenandoah Valley suggest how much he himself enjoys natural beauty. Yet the Nature of his speculative prose is curiously hazy and indistinct. (That of his poetry is more vivid and specific.) But not insubstantial. The term seems at times almost as abstract as the physicist's *mass*, and it signifies fewer sensible details and qualities than are found in the Nature of Ransom's *God Without Thunder* or even *The New Criticism*. Nevertheless, though indefinite, it is neither remote nor imperceptible. Its archetypal symbols are not the nebulae but the night, the flood, and the abyss—all as dark, vast, and featureless as Ransom's symbols are small, bright, and vivid. Tate's symbols are immense, but one can be in them—lost in them. Indeed, we may say that Tate's Nature, for all its size, is nearer than that: one is not in the night, the flood, and the abyss, for they are within oneself. To be lost in them is to be lost in oneself. Nature, then, is ultimately human nature; more particularly, one's own nature.

When he writes that Nature is pure, inchoate Quality that threatens to overwhelm man and obliterate his identity and humanity, he is speaking obliquely of the inner disorder of sensations, impulses, tensions, random images, and abrupt and dismaying associations. (It is, as we shall see, highly significant that so many of his poems are set in the confused hours of twilight and deal with the reveries of a dazed and ill-controlled mind.) Nature, he tells us, is evil, by which he partly means that evil is centered in man, in the flux and flow of instinctual and sensual energies. Good, therefore, is far from being Ransom's enjoyment of the infinite particularity of Nature, which in Tate's work is not topographical and Agrarian, is not the Shenandoah Valley nor the Tennessee landscape that charmed Ransom, but a conglomerate of violence and decay that stands for the psychic life of modern man. Good, for Tate, is the security and serenity that comes of escape from the self—the vortex of Quality—through community with others, a community so desperately needed that it cannot be taken for granted as it is in Ransom's prose. Knowledge of the universe is self-knowledge and right conduct is self-control made possible by that knowledge and by a nearly total commitment of the individual to the group which furnishes him with sustaining beliefs and guides to behavior. The danger in a society as disorderly and unstructured as that of modern America, Tate believes, is that the social forms may be insufficient; the individual cannot escape from himself and community—society—does not really exist.

The final function of society is to enable the individual to cope with himself. Tate's emphasis, then, is on what society does for man rather than the other way around, and most of his writing on society charges it with failing the gifted individual, especially the man of letters. His conservatism tends toward the authoritarian and reflects his dismay at the erosion of beliefs and institutions which in his view protect men from the tides of Quality. He is for order, law, and as much regulation as is needed to enforce and preserve them. He argues that under them man is "free"—by which he means that man is at liberty to make up his own set of values in choosing among small matters but in larger ones, though he still must decide for himself, he has the established values and customs of society to direct him and is relieved of the painful and impossible responsibility of trying to control his impulses and feelings with only the impulses and feelings for guidance. Yet where Ransom sympathizes with rebels, Tate equivocates. He approves of hierarchical societies wherein men know their places and keep them. At the same time, his true sympathy is with the exceptionally bold or talented individual who refuses to submit to the restrictions of ordinary men. The seeming conflict is easily resolved, however. The hierarchical society to be approved is one which gives freedom and scope to and reflects the interests and serves the needs of a natural aristocracy of poets, theologians, and quasi-military heroes and statesmen. Any other society—our own, for example—compels the gifted man to oppose it. And that is exactly what Tate has done.

II

Before Tate joined the Fugitives a variety of forces in his life had tended to separate him from his fellows and shut him within himself. His family had moved several times, and his education before Vanderbilt had come from an irregular combination of instruction at home and attendance at various public and private schools. His two brothers were much older than he and could offer him little companionship. If we may judge from the poem "A Pauper" (originally called "Poem for my Father") and the symbolic behavior of the father figure in "Seasons of the Soul," Tate and his father had little in common. (In "The Eye" the speaker compares happy children who grew up to be "fathered gentlemen" with himself, "the mineral man/ Who takes the fatherless dark to bed." "Mineral man" means that he is simply the scientist's mixture of chemicals; he cannot believe he is more.) "Sonnets of the Blood," written after the death of his mother, are addressed to his brothers and are beyond the comprehension of those who do not know the history of his family. But they suggest that Tate's mother was a woman of dominating character, obsessed with religious enthusiasm, unusually high strung, and the source of painful nervous anxiety in her children. Possibly she furnished some of the lineaments of the fanatical woman described in "Mother and Son," which Tate twice placed among "family" poems in his books. Certainly it seems permissible to assume that she would have had great influence upon a sensitive, bookish boy who spent so much time at home and that life in the household was sometimes strained. In the summers, Louise Cowan tells us, Mrs. Tate used to take young Allen back to Fairfax County in Virginia, which she regarded as their true home, though the father's family had lived for several generations in Kentucky and Tennessee. In Virginia Tate saw the ruins of "Pleasant Hill," the family place that had been burned by Union troops, and from the poems "Emblems" and the use of the place's name in *The Fathers* we can surmise that they made a profound impression on him.[5] In Virginia, too, he probably heard family tales of lost greatness—his great-grandfather's acquaintance with Poe seems to have been a point of special pride. Whatever the reason, Tate's roots went back through his mother's family to the Tidewater. He probably felt himself to be something of an alien in the trans-Appalachian communities in which he spent his boyhood.

From Mrs. Cowan's account, from Tate's own description of his behavior in the Fugitive days, and from the letters to and from

[5] *The Fugitive Group: A Literary History* (Baton Rouge, 1959), pp. 36-37.

his friends that have survived it is clear that when he joined the Fugitives he was rebellious, confused about his future, tense, eager to make an impression, revelling in his freedom, and inclined to be contemptuous of his surroundings. Like many a bright undergraduate before him he found the role of the artist a comfort and protection to his vulnerable ego. One result of the great revolutions of the eighteenth and nineteenth centuries was freeing the ordinary man to choose from a variety of social roles, though liberty tended to blur distinctions and make the roles somewhat uncertain. That of the artist offered an ambitious young man the hope of rising swiftly to an eminence from which he might look down upon his fellows who, in the rub of events, seemed to be more favored. Once he had declared his independence of the common life of the times he was free to fancy himself a member of a community bound not by rules but by the fraternity of superior talent and dedication to values beyond the ken of ordinary mortals. At the same time, the revolutions had taken from the artists most of their functions in such once dominant social institutions as the court and the church, and the new society which enabled more men to set up as artists had less use for their work. (American society, as Roy Harvey Pearce has recently pointed out, never granted the artist any real recognition and sanction. Our literature has always tended to be more private than social.[6]) Thus there developed the image of the artist as the bearer of strange, even fearful, knowledge for which he must endure martyrdom. The image offered some wonderful compensations, for, as Geraldine Pelles has said, "In a society where more persons were concerned with material success than ever before, the sentiment of martyrdom often served as a rationalization and exoneration of failure to achieve recognition among those bohemian artists who lived in poverty. They could yet hope to achieve respect among intellectuals for leading a life which, though it might lead to material hardship, seemed faithful to nobler ideals than those that animated the lives of ordinary men."[7] In our own century it has provided the uprooted or discontented with a prototype of the "good Deviant," as Professor Pelles calls him, but there is no assurance that his goodness—his talent and hard labor—will

[6] "Literature, History, and Humanism, An American Dilemma," *College English* (February, 1963), pp. 364-372.

[7] "The Image of the Artist," *The Journal of Aesthetics and Art Criticism*, XXI (Winter, 1962), 132.

earn him the slightest rewards. Enjoying exceptional power over the materials he works with, tempted to suppose himself superior to others but lacking solid proof that he is, the would-be artist may engage in aggressive behavior to punish society for neglecting him and invite retaliation which acknowledges his identity and permits him to play the martyr.

When he joined the Fugitives Tate already knew well this role. As a boy, he tells us in his essay "Our Cousin, Mr. Poe," he spent many moments studying a photograph of Poe and hoping that he would come to resemble him. Later on he had steeped himself in Swinburne's poetry, and he knew Baudelaire by way of Arthur Symons. Most of the Fugitives were stable and rather conventional men, assured of their place in the community. Ridley Wills enjoyed pretending to be the mad young man, but this was part of his general high spirits. Hirsch was a genuine eccentric with serious problems of adjustment to his self-imposed role of withdrawn mystic. He needed to believe in the mantic powers of the poet to justify his curious life. Davidson, too, found comfort in the outland piper, which assuaged his troubled and melancholy spirit. Nevertheless, as we have seen in our examination of the Fugitive group, these men were not really at war with their surroundings and they could count on the support of those nearest them. Their poems on the outcast are at most mildly boastful or sorrowful, not intense and raging. Yet their interest and Wills's encouragement may have had a considerable effect on Tate. Tate rejected much that Hirsch said at the Fugitive meetings; like the other younger members he was annoyed by Hirsch's insistence that great poems had to have conventionally great subjects. Nevertheless, he may well have been impressed—as Davidson had been earlier—by Hirsch's insistence that the poet was a seer and sufferer whose arcane knowledge could be communicated only to the privileged few who deserved it. Certainly it must have been flattering to have Hirsch single out, as he often did, some of Tate's most unusual lines as evidence of profound insight, especially as only Davidson really approved of Tate's poetry, and he sometimes wavered before some of the more experimental. And even those who disliked Tate's poems and thought he went much too far were themselves attracted by *outré* language. What it comes to, then, is this: in a number of ways the Fugitives encouraged rather than inhibited Tate's interest in the role of the artist though none of them except Hirsch were prepared to take it with anything like his seriousness.

A critical moment in Tate's development came with the intervention of Hart Crane in the spring of 1922. It would be difficult to exaggerate the importance of Crane's influence which, among other things, led to the debate with Ransom, described in Chapter Two, over the looseness of Eliot's versification, and to the formulation of a theory of poetry so permissive as to open the way to any kind of self-indulgence—a theory ideally suited to Tate's own need to play the artist and rebel. When in *The Fugitive* for February, 1924, Ransom described the poet as forced to choose between verse that is almost as precise as prose but is free and verse that achieves beautiful technical effects within a stricter form but is an inferior transcript of the "inner thought," Tate replied in the next issue with a proposal that the poet escape this dilemma by way of Baudelaire's theory of correspondences. According to this, impressions on the various senses "correspond." Sounds have some of the qualities of odors, tactile impressions resemble visual images. Man's inner thought, Tate argued, could be represented accurately in metaphors based upon such correspondences, and he praised the modern poet for having "grown so astute that he will be happy only in the obscure by-ways of his own perceptive processes. . . . [He] might tell you that his only possible themes are the manifold projections and tangents of his own perceptions. . . . The external world is a permanent possibility of sign-posts upon which the poet may hang his attitudes, his sensibility. Not the world, but consciousness; hence his difficult abstractness."[8] In his innocence Tate was assuming that there would always be a few people interested in the poet's attitudes and sensibility. The Fugitives may have disliked his poetry, but they were not indifferent to it, and their opposition flattered Tate and permitted him to act the part of literary wildman with the comfortable assurance that the performance would be well attended. He was soon to discover that it was very different in the New York City he so longed for. After reading the essay, Ransom retorted with a friendly letter in which he pointed out that Shakespeare's work is full of such correspondences while many modern poems have none of them. Their presence was no distinction of modern poetry. "This is really a most nonsensical differentia, my

[8] "One Escape from the Dilemma," *The Fugitive*, iii (April, 1924), 35.

fine Allen!!" he wrote. "A good poem is homogenous. I would imagine this is the truer (if tamer) psychology: The poet hates his bondage—the patterns; but he knows it is the condition of his art; and so he takes just as much liberty as he can; if experimentally minded, he goes pretty far, testing (1) whether he will conform sufficiently to remain in his art, or failing that, (2) whether he may not be a Sandburg, and have stuff good enough to stand in any shape, art or no-art."[9] Certainly Tate was going pretty far into the "obscure by-ways of his own perceptive processes," and the poems were anything but homogenous, as may be seen in the mixture of styles in his "Sonnet/ *To a Portrait of Hart Crane*" (*The Double Dealer*, March-April, 1923), which suggests Baudelaire, Swinburne, Davidson, and, of course, Crane himself:

> Unweathered stone beneath a rigid mane
> Flashes insurgent dusk to ancient eyes
> Dreaming above a lonely mouth, that lies
> Unbeaten into laughter out of pain:
> What is the margin of the lovely stain
> Where joy shrinks into stillèd miseries?
> From what remembrance of satyrs' tippled cries
> Have you informed that dark ecstatic brain?
>
> I have not grasped the living hand of you,
> Nor waited for a music of your speech:
> From a dead time I wander—and pursue
> The quickened year when you will come to teach
> My eyes to hold the blinding vision where
> A bitter rose falls on a marble stair.

In this and other poems Tate shows how entirely he had undertaken to be the alienated martyr-seer. He had committed himself far beyond Davidson or even Hirsch. But he had still before him the actual experience of living by it. This was to make a drastic change in many of his attitudes.

As soon as he was able, he fled the "dead time" of the South for New York City, where he entered the foolish, glorious carnival of ephemeral magazines, heroic arguments, and battles with *The*

---

[9] From a letter dated "April 15." The discussion of Tate's essay fixes the year as 1924.

American Mercury so well described by Malcolm Cowley. Before long he had performed the ritual act of repudiating his region and its heritage in his essay "Last Days of the Charming Lady," which was described in Chapter Three. Yet at the very moment of its publication he was discovering how indispensable they were to him. In *The Fugitive* he had proclaimed the absolute freedom of the modern poet and in his own verses had veered in jagged, broken lines after now this impulse and that, this Symbolist and that Decadent, but he was finding in the midst of all the dirt and confusion of the metropolis such freedom and exposure to every whim and sensation unendurable. Raised in a restricting environment among much talk of past and vanished glories he craved liberty and modernity, but once he had them, they ravaged his sensibility. Moreover, he was finding out that New York had even less use for an advanced young poet than Nashville. Characteristically Tate reacted against his surroundings, directing at them the accumulated hostilities resulting from the tensions and frustrations which the role of the poet, so insecure and—particularly with Tate's poetics—so indefinite, could not relieve. He had reached a crisis in his life. Like so many before him (especially among the Southerners) who have felt themselves superior to their environment and their opportunities and have thought that in some vague way they were allied with the elite of earlier times, he attacked the present by comparing its shabbiness and pursuit of inferior values with the heroic life of the past. The first indication of this supremely important change in Tate's attitudes was the awkward, sometimes opaque, but often powerful poem "Retroduction to American History." He agreed with Crane that man needed myths, but thought contemporary naturalism had reduced them to meaningless words and decorations:

> Narcissus is vocabulary. Hermes decorates
> A cornice on the Third National Bank. Vocabulary
> Becomes confusion, decoration a blight. . . .

Man is no longer threatened by monsters; everything has been explained away; there is nothing to distract him from nonentity, to give his behavior dramatic interest or importance:

> . . . scholarship pares
> The nails of Catullus, sniffs his sheets, restores

His "passionate underwear"; morality disciplines the other
Person; every son-of-a-bitch is Christ, at least Rousseau.

The poem ends

Heredity

Proposes love, love exacts language, and we lack
Language. When shall we speak again? When shall
The sparrow dusting the gutter sing? When shall
This drift with silence meet the sun? When shall I wake?

Where should he himself find language? There were many
things, now that he had fled the South and demonstrated his freedom, to turn him back toward his region and its legends: the tales
of his family and his mother's pride in being a Virginian, the Southerner's sense of the past, loneliness for his old friends in Nashville
and the standing he had enjoyed among them, outrage at the treatment of the Scopes trial in the Northern press, those moments in
boyhood when he had hoped to be like Poe, and that compelling
need to be different which, when he was among the conservative
citizens of Nashville, had made him look away to the *avant-gardists*
in the North and now made him exactly reverse his vision. As his
pride and wish to assert himself had encouraged him to assume the
role of rebel and artist, now they inclined him toward an identity
of interests and attitudes with the aristocratic men of action in the
Old South. Moreover, in keeping with that pattern of contradictions so often encountered in talented and rebellious young people,
he who did so many things to dissociate himself from those about
him—by his aggressive behavior, his theory of poetry, his arcane
language and unintelligible lines, and the contentious tone of his
prose—profoundly desired to belong to a group. It may be that one
of the characteristics of his native region most attractive to him was
the close community of loyalties, beliefs, and attitudes. The legend
of the Old South would seem made to his order, but he knew too
much history to accept it and it nurtured on a literature that made
him queasy. Even so, his biography of Jefferson Davis and such
poems as "The Oath" and "To the Lacedemonians" show that the
legend had a considerable effect upon his image of the heroic life
and values.

Where to turn? The actual Old South was gone and its traditions
seemed to have vanished. Anyway, as the "Ode to the Confederate

Dead" suggests, they were no longer available to the modern skeptic. Where might he, imaginatively at least, locate his blood, as he put it in "The Mediterranean"? He hankered for something remote, brilliant, and patrician to which he could give his loyalties and from which he could take standards to guide his writing and give him the measure of his age. Something sufficiently dramatic to permit identification with it—damned by its daring and violence yet saved by a simple faith which lay beyond the reach of skeptical naturalism and resolved all conflicts, brought all the flare and tumult to order. Like other outsiders who believed themselves to be forced into exile by their talents and their loyalty to values too exquisite or grand for the comprehension of their contemporaries he was looking for a group, or society, call it what one will, that was really a fantasy extended from his secret portrait of himself. After reading Eliot, Dante, Spengler, and the French royalist writers Charles Maurras and Henri Massis, he found what he sought in an essentially literary image of the late medieval period and particularly the thirteenth century. Like Ransom's ideal world of gardens and villagers, this image provided a vantage from which to survey the arts, learning, manners, morality, and faith of the present. The terms Tate used to describe it showed unmistakably that he felt about it as many Southerners felt about the legendary Old South in which their forebears were true members of "the Chivalry"; for Tate quite obviously enjoyed a temperamental kinship with the haughty lords, the princes of the church, the dogmatic theologians, and, most of all, that magnificently endowed and prideful genius, Dante. Comparing the present with his lustrous vision, he could be insufferably condescending.

Yet when one gets past the *hauteur* and animus of much of the prose, one has some idea of how dismaying and debilitating the insecurity of the role of artist in America must have been once the old assurances of the easygoing and friendly Southern community had been left behind. Amidst the disorder and anonymity of the vast, noisy, dirty city, medieval life seemed a veritable Golden Age. Men knew who they were and what was expected of them. Definitions were precise. However high one's rank, one was part of the community. People worshipped together and the Church gave all men a collective dignity that sustained each in his role, be he knight or artist. Within a society of fixed classes men were free from the pressure and affliction of confusion. As he developed his image of the medieval world Tate was corresponding with Ransom and Davidson, reading Calhoun, and thinking about making answer to the Northern attacks on the South. Gradually he came around to believing that the men of the Old South had known some of the same certainty about their lives and themselves. The planter, the subsistence farmer, even the slave, had lived by unambiguous customs. By degrees he was brought to the argument that the old orders, elsewhere destroyed by the restless progressivism of western man, had found a last home in the antebellum South.

Simplicity, faith, and stability—these rather than aristocratic splendor were the qualities of life in the Old South emphasized in Tate's first book, *Stonewall Jackson*, published early in 1928. Jackson had small interest in the politics of his time, and since Tate wisely chose to give most of his attention to Jackson's military career after the outbreak of the Civil War, there were few occasions for testy comparisons of the gallant semi-feudal South and the shoddy egalitarian North. But Jackson was a more apt subject than might at first appear. Fatherless, secretive, compulsive, harassed by small guilts, finding in outbursts of destruction a release for his inward strains, he more than a little resembled some of the rootless artists Tate had come to know. Jackson was supported in crises of confusion or self-doubt by his piety and the code of a Southern professional soldier which sanctioned his furious and appalling action. His obsession with honor, concern for salvation, and genius for destroying his fellow men would have made a rich combination for speculative psychoanalysis, as Tate at one point acknowledged, but Tate chose to remain for the most part outside his man and let the actions and events speak for themselves. Leaving aside all but a minimum of political history, Tate presented Jackson through a vivid narrative of his military actions and showed remarkable powers of analyzing the complex campaigns and choosing those natural details best able to evoke the feeling or signify the meaning of a moment. It seems almost incredible that the man who wrote Tate's turgid and clumsily organized poems of this period could also have written such prose, which had all the merits that the poems lacked. It was plain and terse. Details were skillfully arranged to build to cumulative effects of impressive power. Indeed, it is not easy to illustrate the excellence of the writing, for taken by itself

322

a single passage seems a little flat—rather like the lines in a verse-narrative by Frost. But some of the artistry behind the simplicity may perhaps be glimped in the opening of the account of Jackson's last battle:

> "At five-thirty the men of General Howard's corps were still lolling in the open fields of Talley's farm. Suddenly a deer ran from the woods towards the breastworks; then a rabbit; in a few seconds, rabbits, deer, foxes scampered through the meadow.
>
> "In the quiet a brassy screech came out of the woods, lengthening into the cadences of a bugle call. Other bugles took up the noise. Before the men of the Eleventh Corps could get to their feet, a horde of yelling demons, rising out of the earth, were upon them. Far to the north and south the long ragged lines moved forward like a machine. The forest rang with the wild Confederate yell. The lazy pickets of the Federals fired a few scattered shots, and fled."

There is little that is relevant to say about the two armies that is not suggested by this picture of the terrified animals running from the shelter of the woods. Some years later Tate, using a term already tried out by R. P. Blackmur, gave it a name: symbolic naturalism.

The book's few blemishes occur at those points where Tate departs from his narrative to lecture the reader on the blessings of life in a society of fixed classes. His argument, adopted from Calhoun and the royalists, has been dealt with in Chapter Three. It is not an important part of the biography, but it signifies how deeply Tate, who had once demanded an absolute freedom for the poet, was now concerned for order which directed without frustrating the energies of exceptional men. Friendship with Hart Crane and living among writers in New York had taught him, as he said in his novel, *The Fathers*, that "All violent people secretly desire to be curbed by something that they respect, so that they may become known to themselves."

Such faults are more numerous in Tate's biography of Jefferson Davis, which was published a year and a half later. In the interval his loathing of mass society and industrial culture had deepened and, as we have already seen, he had become convinced that the issue of the Civil War was "the Western spirit against the European," "class rule and religion *versus* democracy and science." Since Davis was at the center of the politics of his age while Jackson was out skirmishing in the valleys of western Virginia, Tate had a better opportunity for introducing his proto-Agrarian views. The reader may be irked or amused by the hectoring tone of these passages or such puerilities as the statement "The Southerner, bred to horse-back riding and the use of firearms, was the finest military material in the world, incomparably better than the town-reared clerks and mechanics of the North."[10] (It is no reflection on the skill or valor of the Southern soldier to paraphrase Tate on another occasion and say that if this kind of history is possible, anything is possible.) But whatever the reaction, it may cause the reader to overlook the considerable merits of this uneven work. Davis was a thoughtful man and a master of debate, the South's ablest spokesman after the death of Calhoun. Even so, Tate moved quickly over his career before his election as president of the Confederacy, for he believed that "The vast drama of the war was in a sense the externalization of the interior drama of Davis's soul. Every event was swiftly and subtly, sometimes torturously, recorded upon his sensibility, and the marches of armies and the tactics of battles were the reflections of his own powerful will."[11] In support of this Tate brought to bear his flair for narrative and analysis of complex military operations. In the great theatre of the war he saw Davis as an Oedipus who did not know he was blind. (In his poem "Elegy" he called him Orestes.) To prove his contention Tate did a quite remarkable job of organizing into a coherent and meaningful pattern diverse and widely separated details. At its best, and there is much of that best, the book calls to mind the handling of the materials in Garrett Mattingly's superlative history, *The Armada.*

III

Tate had earned the right to call himself an historian, but it was not a title he particularly desired. For historians, he thought, had helped to discredit the values and the vision of the past which man needed in order to know himself and to act in the present.

[10] *Jefferson Davis, His Rise and Fall* (New York, 1929), p. 102.
[11] P. 251.

In a review of Crane's *The Bridge* he described his friend's efforts to find mythic material in the story of America and added,

"The soundness of his impulse is witnessed . . . by the kind of history in his poem: it is inaccurate, and it will not at all satisfy the sticklers for historical fact: it is the history of the motion picture, of the most naive patriotism. This is sound; for it ignores the scientific ideal of truth-in-itself, and looks to a cultural truth which might win the spontaneous allegiance of the mass. It is on such simple integers of truth, not truth of fact but of religious necessity, that men unite. The American mind was formed on the eighteenth-century Enlightenment, which broke down the European truths and gave us a temper deeply hostile to the making of new religious truths of our own. . . . The age is scientific and pseudo-scientific, and our philosophy is corrupt."[12]

"History . . . of the most naive patriotism" might describe some portions of *Jefferson Davis* or these glib allusions to "religious necessity" and "European truths." But it was not the influence of Hollis's silly little book alone that had caused Tate to introduce such history into a study that had so many excellences. Tate had described Davis as "Morbidly sensitive and emotionally undisciplined; his emotional instability bulwarked behind a boundless intellectual pride." Davis was even something of a man of letters himself and, though its spokesman and elected leader, an alien from his society suffering from some of the loneliness, tumult of feelings, and acquaintance with the abyss known to the poet of our own times. John Peale Bishop saw this at once and wrote that he found the biography more interesting than the biography of Stonewall Jackson, for as a divided, inwardly tormented man Davis was more available to the modern reader.[13] He suffered for want of just those things Crane sought to restore by his mythmaking and Tate professed to see in the Old South and the Europe which he and Ransom described in their Agrarian essays. Much of Tate's "naive patriotism" got into the book by way of his attempts to define the reciprocal roles of the man of letters and his environment and to

[12] "A Distinguished Poet," *Hound and Horn*, III (Summer, 1930), 582-583.
[13] From a letter to Tate, May 26, 1931.

discover what the gifted, lonely man should do among those whose philosophy is corrupt.

Tate had been quickly disenchanted by his venture into the bohemian world. He rejected the aesthetic doctrine of his Fugitive days; yet he still believed the poet capable of transcendent knowledge and thought him about the nearest thing to a tragic hero that the age provided. By virtue of his gifts the poet had some of the hero's tragic awareness, but he no longer had a moral order, sanctioned by superhuman authority, to give a tragic dimension to his experience or that of the protagonists depicted in his work. It was not even possible for him to write great poetry which, Tate claimed, "cannot be written without the background of a perfectly ordered world which men have assimilated to their attitudes and convictions." All he had to go on was "personal forms of some egoistic thrust of will."[14] The New England writers had once had a powerful tradition that "gave an heroic proportion and tragic mode to the experience of the individual," but it was destroyed by individualism, progressivism, and rationalism—the "Western Spirit" backed by the mill industries. Hawthorne inherited a whole world-scheme from the theocratic system, but by the time Henry James began writing it had lost all meaning and his characters were compelled to rely on honor, which "alone is a poor weapon against nature, being too personal, finical, and proud. . . ."[15] For some Southerners such as Katherine Anne Porter the traditions of the Old South still had enough vitality to serve as a frame of reference and release the imagination. Miss Porter's materials, Tate argued, were already defined for her and she could devote her attention to style in the assurance of an ordered experience adequate to it.[16] But most modern American writers resembled Hart Crane, who had no philosophy of history and had to rely on his "locked-in sensibility." The essay on his friend which Tate put together for *Reactionary Essays* out of three earlier pieces is one of the best things he ever wrote and a clear statement of the dilemma of the writer in a mass society as Tate saw it. Crane is, Tate wrote, "the blameless victim of a world whose impurity violated the moment of intensity, which

[14] "The Revolt Against Literature," *The New Republic*, XLIX (February 9, 1927), 329-330; "Edwin Arlington Robinson," *Reactionary Essays on Poetry and Ideas* (New York, 1936), p. 194.
[15] "Emily Dickinson," *Reactionary Essays*, pp. 6, 11.
[16] "A New Star," *The Nation*, CXXXI (October 1, 1930), 352-353.

would otherwise be enduring and perfect. He is betrayed not by a defect of his own nature, but by the external world; he asks of nature, perfection—requiring only of himself, intensity. The persistent, and persistently defeated, pursuit of a *natural* absolute places Crane at the center of his age." [Italics added.] "Every poem is a thrust of that [locked-in] sensibility into the world: his defect lay in his inability to face out the moral criticism implied in the failure to impose his will upon experience."[17] Tate's early poems, written before he had begun to formulate his "philosophy" of history, are thrusts of a somewhat similar sensibility. But since he left off undergraduate playacting and settled down to trying to make his way as a man of letters, he has faced out the moral criticism implied. The mark of his early self-indulgent aesthetic lay long and heavily upon his poetry, but in the end the "philosophy" worked. Tate emerged from what he had once called "the obscure by-ways of his own perceptive processes" and found more to write about than "the manifold projections and tangents" of his sensibility.

Two essays, written and published within a little over a year of one another, mark the beginning of Tate's mature prose writing and are of the first importance to an understanding of that philosophy and the works founded upon it, for in them Tate sets forth his conception of Nature, the mind, and the function of inherited beliefs in mediating between them. The first, "Remarks on the Southern Religion," was published in *I'll Take My Stand* and has been discussed in Chapter Three. The other is "The Fallacy of Humanism," which Tate revised slightly and reprinted as "Humanism and Naturalism" in *Reactionary Essays*. He no longer includes it in collections of his essays, but its final section is even more important in his development than the now well-known "Remarks."

The New Humanism which reappeared after several years of neglect and raised a small commotion in the literary and academic worlds during the late 1920's and early 1930's got most of its renewed energy from the influence of Professor Irving Babbitt,

[17] "Hart Crane," *Reactionary Essays*, pp. 37-38, 30. The earlier pieces are: "A Distinguished Poet," *Hound and Horn*, III (Summer, 1930), 580-585; "Hart Crane and the American Mind," *Poetry*, XL (July, 1932), 210-216; and "In Memoriam: Hart Crane," *Hound and Horn*, VI (Summer, 1932), 612-619.

and when he died in 1933 it withered from sheer inanition. Like the Agrarians, the New Humanists looked to the past for values to set against the disorder and vulgarity of the Machine Age, but they did not have the luck to have a single important writer among them, and their movement, which at the time was far better known than Agrarianism, has been nearly forgotten. In its day it appealed to professors of literature who disliked contemporary writing (the New Humanists said it lacked nobility) and believed that one could study philosophy by reading Homer. It was all very solemn, very genteel, and, despite the Great Names that dropped like rain, very soft on learning. In the spring of 1926 T. S. Eliot suggested to Tate that he write an essay on the attitudes toward the past of Babbitt and Paul Elmer More, Babbitt's chief associate. Nothing came of this at first, but when Tate began to read the New Humanists, and particularly the pronouncements on contemporary literature of Professor Norman Foerster he was outraged. Knowing Tate's own attitude toward the present and past, one might suppose that he would have had some sympathy with the New Humanists, who were aristocratic in preference and detested modern liberal humanitarianism. Yet at this time, when he himself was writing poems on the amorality of the age, Tate was also developing a curious and contradictory doctrine of the irrelevance of poetry and its complete autonomy as art. In a review which approved of Lascelles Abercrombie's thesis that the meaning of a poem cannot be paraphrased, Tate proclaimed, "Its direct corollary is the unavailability of the poetic experience for issuance in action, the *moral futility* of ideas derived from poetry and applied to the improvement or, for that matter, the corruption of man."[18] [Italics added.] It was years before Tate worked out a compromise between this view of poetry and the theory of literature implicit in his remarks on Hawthorne, James, Emily Dickinson, and Hart Crane, where he obviously attached a great deal of value to the morality of the literary idea. For the moment, however, this Doctrine of Inutility put him in exact disagreement with the New Humanists. By early 1929 he was ready with a criticism of their views. Eliot heard of his essay and wanted it for his *Criterion*, where after some polishing it appeared in July, 1929. Soon after it was reprinted in *Hound and Horn* and stirred up a good deal of unpleasantness, as well it might,

[18] "A Philosophical Critic," *The New Republic*, XLVI (April 21, 1926), 281.

for its tone was dogmatic, patronizing, and thoroughly offensive.[19]

The effect of the communion with Ransom between 1925 and 1930 is most apparent in this essay, which Ransom much admired. Though Tate develops in it his idea that Nature is pure Quality and thus Evil, which, as we have seen, reflects an attitude wholly different from Ransom's while agreeing with his emphasis upon particularity, Tate goes right down the line with Ransom on the inadequacies of science and Platonic philosophies in representing Nature. The Humanists, Tate said, were not really so different from the naturalists they wanted to oppose. They were trying to formulate abstract systems to do for man what only religious myths could. Humanists and naturalists tried to substitute Quantity (the abstract, logical series) for Quality (the concrete experience) and misrepresented the world to man, leaving him without adequate means for coping with the onrushing of pure Quality which threatened to overwhelm him. Religion, on the other hand, made just enough of an abstraction to permit man to represent his experience to himself without losing touch with reality.

Tate's argument is so important to the understanding of his later attacks on positivism, his novel, *The Fathers*, and many of his poems such as "Last Days of Alice," "Shadow and Shade," "The Meaning of Life," and "The Meaning of Death" that it is necessary to quote from it at length:

> "The source of Quality is nature itself because it is the source of experience. . . . Pure Quality would be pure evil, and it is only through the means of our recovery from a lasting immersion in it, it is only by maintaining the precarious balance upon the point of collapse into Quality, that any man survives his present hour: pure quality is pure disintegration. The scientist [encountering a Philippine cobra] says, '*Naja samaransis*'; Mr. [Paul Elmer] More, a cadence of the same theme—'Immoral'; Quality is quantified before we ever see it as Quality; and nature becomes a closed system of abstraction in which man is deprived of all experience whatever and, by being so deprived, reduced to an abstraction himself."

It is worth pausing here to note how Tate is drawn by logomachy

[19] For a good brief discussion of the New Humanism, see Frederick J. Hoffman, *The Twenties* (New York, 1955), pp. 139-145.

into statements about science and other supposedly abstract modes more extreme than anything Ransom had said. The argument that the scientist or the Humanist could deprive man of all experience whatever and reduce him to an abstraction is a play on words and pure rubbish. So is all the sententiousness about the precarious balance and surviving the present hour. But to continue:

> "The religious attitude is the very sense (as the religious dogma is the definition) of the precarious balance of man upon the brink of pure Quality. But if you never have Quality, never have the challenge of evil, you have no religion—which is to say, you have no experience either. It is experience, immediate and traditional, fused—Quality and Quantity—which is the means of validating values. . . .
>
> "Religion's respect for the power of nature lies in her contempt for knowledge of it; to quantify nature is ultimately to quantify ourselves. Religion is satisfied with the dogma that nature is evil, and our recovery from it is mysterious ('grace'). . . . It is the indispensable office of the religious imagination that it checks the abstracting tendency of the intellect in the presence of nature. Nature abstract becomes man abstract, and he is at last condemned to permanent immersion in pure and evil Quality; he is forever condemned to it because he can no longer see it for what it is. He has no technique for dealing with evil. . . ."[20]

The tone could only be Tate's, but the premises on science and religion might have come straight off the pages of *God Without Thunder.*

In the essays that followed Tate usually spoke of *positivism* rather than *science* or *naturalism* and under that rubric gathered all tendencies in contemporary culture which seemed to him to "quantify" nature, reduce man to an abstraction, and locate values in instrumental efficiency. In "Three Types of Poetry" (1934) Tate described the mind as made up of the imagination, which is capable of grasping (the metaphor hides a multitude of epistemological problems) the whole quality of an entity or experience, and the practical will, which formulates abstractions for the control of the environment. The latter is the equivalent of Ransom's reason,

[20] *Reactionary Essays*, pp. 140-142.

but the imagination is not his sensibility, nor is poetry said to be produced by the cooperation of the two parts of the mind as Ransom had argued. Rather, a "creative spirit," using the imaginative grasp of the whole, yields poetry in which we can observe "the power of seizing the inward meaning of life." And "The imaginative whole of life is the wholeness of vision at a particular moment of experience; it yields us the quality of experience."[21] (The essay is considered more closely later in this chapter.) There is much circularity here, but the main line is clear. Tate never went as far as Ransom in attempting to account for the operation and motivation of the parts of the mind, for he was more interested in the ethical implications of the results. And being more of a polemicist, he was even less particular in using *positivism* than Ransom had been in using *science*. For Tate positivism was any procedure or moral attitude, emanating from the will, which exhibited "a cheerful confidence in the limitless powers of man to impose practical abstractions on his experience" in the hope of more prompt and fulsome satisfaction of his physical needs. Tate put the matter quite directly in a very bad poem called "Ivory Tower," which he published in his collection *The Mediterranean and Other Poems* (1936) but never reprinted:

> There is a solution to everything: Science.
> Separate those evils strictly social
> From other evils that are eventually social.
> It ends in all evils being social: Deduction.
> Is not marriage a social institution,
> (*Un contrat social*) Is not prostitution
> An institution? Abolish (1) marriage, (2) poverty. . . .
> We are understanding the argument
> That we have got to make men slaves
> Of their bellies in order to get them fed.
> The sole problem is the problem of hunger
> (Or the distribution of commodities). . . .

Social scientists were supposed to be positivists because they tried to discover patterns in the development and behavior of societies which they could manipulate for material ends. Historians were

---

[21] *Reactionary Essays*, pp. 83, 84.

supposed to be positivists because they interpreted the record of human experience as a causal series and thought their interpretations might be used to advantage in public affairs. Literary scholars were positivists because they emulated the scientists. Literary critics were positivists when they argued that the true meaning of a poem could be reduced to a prose statement which could be tested by the empirical methods of the laboratory or applied to social action. Just as the scientist saw a cobra "merely as an instance of the quantification of nature," so positivistic historians and sociologists are presumed to see only what their methodologies allow. Now this generalization is open to all the objections raised in the last chapter against Ransom's description of the scientist. Nevertheless, though Tate pushes it too far, there is a lot of solid truth in his view, as the present efforts to base psychology and sociology on the mathematics of probability make clear. And as we read Tate's fulminations on "Quantification" we should remember that they were written during what Thurber called the Marathon Phase of American life, when "Everywhere, men and women were striving to outfly, outswim, outdance, outwalk, outsit, outtalk, outchew, and outrock one another. . . . If you stared too long at a man who had been sitting on a flagpole for two months, or gaped incautiously at an airplane that had been circling around and around for ten weeks, you were liable to be knocked down by a gentleman walking backward across the country, or mangled by a car in which a sleepless youth was handcuffed to the steering wheel."[22]

Against the moral disarray and exposure to Quality of the positivistic society Tate offered the vision of the moral unity of the traditional society. When Dudley Wynn challenged his account of the traditional society of the agrarian Old South, Tate quickly backed away to the argument Ransom used in defense of myth and he himself had borrowed in "A Note on Milton" (1931): a myth was not something to be believed or disbelieved; it was a framework for comprehensive insights allowing for the largest amount of experience to be given meaningful order.[23] So too the traditional society, which "has never existed, can never exist, and is a delusion. But the perfect traditional society as an imperative of reference

[22] *Credos and Curios* (New York, 1962), pp. 26-27.
[23] *The New Republic*, LXVIII (October 21, 1931), 266-268. For more about Wynn's argument see Chapter Three, p. 148.

—not as an absolute lump to be measured and weighed—has always existed and will continue to haunt the moral imagination of men." Even the medieval era, he conceded, had not known such a society. "We are wasting our time if we suppose that St. Thomas, religious authority, the Catholic church, were more than approximations of a moral ideal by certain men under certain conditions." A great civilized tradition consists of absolutes, points of moral and intellectual reference, which are not imperatives of belief but imperatives of reference. Even the absolutes of religion were imperatives of reference by which men lived until in the slow crawl of history new absolutes took their place. To be viable they must on the whole be unconsciously operative, for

> "We cannot be constantly judging the moral value of human actions and emotions and at the same time see them purely and objectively; we must take some kinds of conduct as inevitable, for our framework of action and feeling, if we are to escape the punishment of having to invent our conduct, a barbaric thing indeed, as we go along. This must all be taken for granted and we must barely be aware that we take it so. That is tradition."[24]

Even such approximations of the traditional society as man is capable of realizing are possible only where there are forms for transmitting them from one generation to another. Such means, Tate said in his essay for *Who Owns America?* can obtain only in a society that gives men direct ownership of property for which they are responsible and does not allow them to separate their moral natures from their livelihood. Returning to this theme in an address to the Phi Beta Kappa Society of the University of Virginia in June, 1936, he asserted that the man of the Old South was a traditional man. By working directly with the land he dominated the means of life and was not dominated by it. Man had never achieved a perfect unity of his moral nature and his economics, but he had not until now failed so dismally. What should be done? "Traditional property in land was the primary medium through which man expressed his moral nature; and our task is to restore it or get its equivalent today."[25] As things turned out, this call to action

[24] "Liberalism and Tradition," *Reason in Madness*, pp. 203, 207, 211, 214-215; "Regionalism and Sectionalism," *The New Republic*, LXIX (December 23, 1931), 159.
[25] "What is a Traditional Society?" *Reason in Madness*, p. 229. For a more

was Tate's last essay on behalf of Agrarianism and it came just one month after Ransom had published his own last effort. It was not, however, Tate's final word. There was still *The Fathers*. In it Tate summed up all he had to say to date on Nature, Quality, Quantification, tradition, property, responsibility, and the Old South.

In the fall of 1933 Minton, Balch, and Company announced that they would soon publish *Ancestors of Exile*, a study by Tate of the disruptive forces in American life. He had worked for a time on a biography of Robert E. Lee but had given it up after deciding that he could not compete with William Douglas Freeman's great work. Now he thought of using the materials he had collected as the bases of a book which would undertake to answer a question which had long bothered him: If the South had possessed a good approximation of a traditional society—and he believed it had in Lee's Virginia—why had it so failed to pass on its "imperatives of reference"? Other cultures had survived defeats as great as the South had sustained. Why, then, were the antebellum Southerners ancestors of the exile which he himself felt so acutely, as his poems of this period plainly show?

In the summer of 1933, while he was still engaged on that study, Tate published his first fiction, the short story "The Immortal Woman," which came out in *Hound and Horn*. A revery hovering between fantasy and reality such as Tate had used in several long poems contrasting the dingy present with the heroic past, it was related by a paralyzed and slightly demented veteran of the First World War who never left his room. He had no life apart from watching the play of light and shadow that marked the seasons and listening to the gossip of the ladies who came to visit his aunt. The past meant nothing to him; neither did the present nor the future. Each fall an elderly woman appeared and sat staring at an empty house across the street from his window. As he was watching her one day he overheard a friend of his aunt describing the Gibson family, which had drifted into misfortune after the father broke up the family estate. One of them had married a Posey and lived in the old house with her crazy sister-in-law, Jane, who never came

extensive discussion of Tate's views on property and their relation to his Agrarianism, see Chapter Four, pp. 182-183.

out of her room, and Little Jane, who inherited violence and madness from both parents. As he listened the veteran watched the woman winding up a ball of twine and realized that she was Little Jane, whose aunt used to make balls of twine and each day give the child a present of scraps. Little Jane was immortal. Like her aunt she had never been in life, in time. "She could neither die nor live." Even as he understood this, the veteran saw a young man fastidiously dressed and walking so lightly that he scarcely touched the ground come up to Little Jane, kiss her, and lead her away. The veteran never saw her again.

Once before the veteran had seen an old doctor named Lacy Beckett pick Little Jane up in his chariot. It might have been his grave, the veteran had thought. Perhaps the veteran had wanted Little Jane to die, but not in the old house. At the story's end one thinks of Emily Dickinson's poem "The Chariot," which begins,

> Because I could not stop for Death,
> He kindly stopped for me;
> The carriage held but just ourselves
> And Immortality.

Did the veteran of a war which Tate believed America had gone into for the sake of its industrial economy—did the veteran realize that he, the crippled modern man, was not really different from Little Jane? That his wheelchair was his chariot? That he was "immortal" because he, too, was outside time—an exile from life who apparently could neither live nor die?

Meanwhile, the study of the American past, which Tate had retitled *The Fathers*, was giving him trouble and though it had been announced for publication he decided to rework it as a novel, perhaps using this story as its conclusion. In the fictional version, which was published in 1938, an elderly Doctor Lacy Buchan (the Lacy Beckett of the story) describes how the Poseys, who had left the land, corrupted and destroyed his own family by taking over its property and responsibility over the means of its livelihood. But by the time Tate had finished telling how George Posey, Little Jane's older brother, had deprived the Buchans of the means of passing on their way of life, there was no need to append the short story and bring the narrative down to the present. George Posey was obviously the man of the future, the modern American. Buchan's father and the men of his generation were the ancestors of exile.

Posey, a sensitive man endowed with energy and imagination, had sought out the Buchans because he had needed "An idea, a cause, an action in which his personality could be extinguished." To cut a fine figure before them he required a horse; so he sold his slave and own half-brother, Yellow Jim. To him another man, a member of his own household, was "liquid capital." But he made his impression and married Lacy's older sister, Susan. Skillful in money affairs, he gradually took over the management of Pleasant Hill, the Buchan farm, without the knowledge of his father-in-law, Major Lewis Buchan, an old-fashioned squire who lived by a rigid code that placed each person, from field hand to patriarch, in an integrated and harmonious pattern wherein each knew his part and did not, like Posey, have to make up his conduct as he went along. (Major Buchan may have been partly modeled on Tate's great-grandfather, Major Lewis Bogan, of Fairfax County, Virginia, whose portrait is referred to in Tate's poem, "The Oath.") Posey put the farm on a paying basis and supplanted the major as the head of the family. Against their father's command, the Buchan sons followed Posey and joined the Confederate forces. But Posey was denied command of the company he had equipped and became a gunrunner, a shadowy figure of ambiguous loyalty moving in darkness outside the community to which he wanted to belong.

Lacy's brother Semmes fell in love with Little Jane, but Susan, who knew the violence and disorder of the Poseys, was determined to prevent the marriage. Yellow Jim had fled from his new owner and returned to the Poseys, and Jane, who was frightened by his efforts to ingratiate himself, so offended his dignity as a human being that he gave way to the Posey violence in him and raped her. In the confusion that followed Jane's mother died of fright, Jane was placed in a convent, Semmes shot Yellow Jim, and George Posey, on an impulse, shot Semmes. Susan went mad. It was suggested that in some way she had used Jim against Jane and initiated the action that destroyed them all.

Lacy had been staying with the Poseys and after the catastrophe he tried to make his way back to his father's farm. But on the way he fell ill with brain fever. In his delirium he imagined that his own grandfather was walking beside him, explaining Posey's failure in humanity by comparing him with Jason. "It is never, my son, his intention to do any evil," the old man said, "but he does evil because he has not the will to do good. The only expectancy that he shares with humanity is the pursuing grave, and the thought of extinction overwhelms him because he is entirely alone." Where Jason sought the Golden Fleece, Posey sought money, and the description of Jason was clearly intended to apply to Posey: "He was a noble fellow in whom the patriarchal and familial loyalties had become meaningless but his human nature necessarily limited him, and he made an heroic effort to combine his love of the extraordinary and inhuman with the ancient domestic virtues. If the Fleece had been all-sufficing would he have taken Medea with him back to Greece?" Posey had tried to practice the domestic virtues, too, and his wife, like Medea, lost her mind and did evil.

At the end Major Buchan, ordered by invading Yankees to leave Pleasant Hill, which he no longer really owned, committed suicide. The house was burned to the ground. Posey made a final effort to join the Confederate Army but was goaded into shooting an old enemy and for the last time fled into the darkness. We know from a remark of the narrator's that he survived the war. Lacy, who lived in the worlds of the Old South and the New, could never bring himself to hate the man who had so mutilated his family, for he saw in him so much of himself.

The novel is a superb example of what Tate himself later called symbolic naturalism, and what it symbolizes are the Agrarian ideas about cash-crop farming as a corollary of industrialism, the humanizing and restraining effects of a ceremonious society made up of families living in the country on their own land, the irresponsibility of capitalism, and Tate's own ideas about the trapped ego and the violence it does when not released by traditions and protected against the surging energies of sensation and impulse. These conceptions are easily identified when one stands away from the novel, but because it is in the mode of symbolic *naturalism* most of them are represented dramatically in the substance of the lives before one's eyes. When it is necessary to add some explanation, Tate has in his narrator a convenient device for shifting from narrative to rumination which keeps its dynamic force because it is part of the experience of a fully realized and vital personality. It is, in short, a part of the action rather than a comment by the author. Like the detail of the animals breaking from cover in *Stonewall Jackson* or the veteran's wheelchair in "The Immortal Woman" the symbols are commonplace but so appropriate and so carefully placed and integrated with one another that they do their work unobtrusively but effectively. Pleasant Hill, the Buchan home, is open to the sunlight and air because it stands on a slight rise in the bland Virginia countryside. The Posey house is shadowy, damp, and shut in by a crowded neighborhood set on low, mist-hung land near the Potomac. Little by little as light and darkness gather about these two polarities we come to understand how they and the complex of details that cluster about them represent two kinds of personality, two ways of life, two relations with Nature, the community, and oneself.

(Perhaps Yellow Jim combines the light of the Buchans and the dark of the Poseys. After Major Buchan he is the most punctilious of them all, the most concerned with family loyalties and the dignity of the individual. Not until his loyalties and dignity have been intolerably affronted does he yield to impulse, and then it is to assert his individuality against the system that had betrayed rather than sustained him. Significantly, it is a Buchan, not a Posey, that follows the code and kills him.)

It is a mark of Tate's skill that he was able to present so clearly within the narrative frame of reference and the limits of the mode he had chosen so many ideas about which he felt strongly and had at times written somewhat intemperately. The restraint served him well, for certain of his ideas, which in his essays arouse a disputatious impulse in the reader, are here tested and proved in a believable image of life. Nothing he has written elsewhere so convinces one of the sustaining powers of custom in times of emotional crisis as the beautifully controlled account of the funeral of Lacy's mother. The only faults occur at those points where for the sake of the "argument" Tate maintains a symbolic consistency which is not underwritten by a naturalistic consistency; where, to paraphrase his own objection to the critics demanding relevance of poetry, he has made politics out of literature. Of course the naturalism of any novel in this mode is an illusion. Selection and arrangement are imposed on the potential materials for the sake of the formal appeal and a unity, coherence, and clarity of meaning which the random and contingent events of ordinary experience do not have. But the organization must be accomplished without interruption of the suggestion of the wholeness and verisimilitude of the representation. At a few points Tate makes just such interruptions.

It is appropriate to the dominant theme and the controlling ideas that Susan be so corrupted by immersion in the inadequately restrained emotional life of her husband's family that she, too, would use a fellow human being for her own ends without regard to its effect on him. It is appropriate, too, that the violence that precipitates the catastrophe be the result of impulse breaking through restraints already weakened by self-centered people who put their own feelings ahead of all custom and consideration of others, as Jane does when she humiliates Jim. We may find it hard to accept as adequate Jim's motivation for the rape of Jane, though Tate succeeds in making the Posey home such a madhouse that we do not boggle much at this. Not, at least, until we come to the explanation that Susan had "used" Jim in the rape. It is not possible to see how she had anything to do with bringing it about or could have foreseen it in time to prevent it. Yet we are supposed to believe that on going to investigate Jane's screams she was not surprised to find Jim in the middle of the night on the upper floor where the women's bedrooms were—that she almost expected to see him there in fulfillment of her purpose.

The grandfather appearing in the feverish dream of a sixteen-year-old boy and discoursing on Jason is a clumsy *deus ex machina*. Dickens would have admired the six-weeks coma which struck Lacy down, but Flaubert would have been appalled at such a handling of the symbolic necessities. It is quite beside the point that the dream seems to have been based on one that actually occurred, to judge from hints in the poems "A Dream" and "A Vision." (The poems are discussed in the next chapter.)

The most difficult character in the book is Major Buchan in whom, even more than in George Posey, we are supposed to find the answer to Tate's question: why did the Old South so utterly fail its descendants? In order to persuade us of the virtues of the traditional society, Tate must show the Major as a vigorous, humane man capable of facing great ordeals without flinching. Then, to account for the collapse of the traditional society, Tate must show him as utterly bewildered by Posey and unable to prevent Posey's intervening between himself and his sons and between the family and its means of livelihood. Lacy tries to explain his father's failure thus:

> "Our lives were eternally balanced upon a pedestal below which lay an abyss that I could not name. Within that invisible tension my father knew the moves of an intricate game that he expected everybody else to play. That, I think, was because everything he was and felt was in the game itself; he had no life apart from it and he was baffled, as he had been baffled by George Posey, by the threat of some untamed force that did not recognize the rules of his game."[26]

"Everything he was and felt was in the game." The traditions, instead of freeing the imagination, inhibited it. They had passed into manners and lost much of their human content. Semmes, the heir of the traditions, is trapped within them and compelled to kill Yellow Jim. They were, in Tate's terms, imperatives of belief when they should have been imperatives of reference which could be modified or replaced in the slow crawl of history. This does well enough as a thesis, but Major Buchan does not illustrate it on the naturalistic level. He is stiff and not very imaginative, but he is not stupid nor lacking in will. We can believe that he would not understand Posey but not that Posey could take his farm away from him and by separating the Buchans from responsible management of their property confuse their moral intelligence or even their plain common sense. This is a splendid novel. Though it is not as widely read as it should be, it is well and properly esteemed among those who know it. If Tate had managed a little more skillfully the fusion to the narrative of the critically important explanations of the Major's bafflement, of Susan's disintegration, and of Posey's lack of the will to do good—if, in short, he had brought a little nearer to perfection the unity of symbolism and naturalism, *The Fathers* would belong among the very best American novels. As it is, there are not many one would want to put ahead of it.

IV

When he was still an undergraduate, Tate was a discerning critic. Though many of his poems have been shapeless or clogged by

[26] *The Fathers* (New York, 1938), pp. 43-44.

detail, his special gift for criticism has always been a sense of the relation of the part to the whole and an acute judgment in matters affecting the harmony of the elements. In an early essay on the nature of poetry he argued that the unity of a poem made it an absolute and gave it autonomy. Unlike the portion of the world for which it stands it is complete and finite. Ideally, the poem would provide the same experience for all readers, but Tate conceded that the variables of the responding intelligence would make it different with each reading, even by the same person. Nevertheless, in each realization their would be "no overflow of unrealized action," and for this reason a poem could not be paraphrased.[27] The problem of how a poem was a self-sufficient thing-in-itself yet stood for a portion of the world was to give Tate difficulties for a long time to come, but from the beginning he held to the view that a poem should be regarded as one whole thing. As a reader he was quick to see the less apparent relations among images and rhythmic variations and to note any superfluous, inadequate, or disproportionate materials. Davidson particularly valued his close reading of his friends' work and with an appealing modesty that shines in his letters sought Tate's advice, saying: "You have given me keener and more helpful criticism than anybody that ever read my poems."[28] In his reviews Tate had little space for matters of style and organization, but when he did his observations were specific, concise, and convincing.

In discussing the nature of poetry he tended to take for granted matters of form and artistic merit and concentrated on justifying poetry as a medium of cognition. In this he resembled Ransom, with whom he discussed the subject many times over the years, but he had much less to say about *how* poetry functions and he never wrote anything that might compare with Ransom's "Wanted: An Ontological Critic." This is regrettable, for the few analyses of poems which he has written show that he was unusually responsive to the effects and interrelations of all aspects of poetry. Early in his speculations he got involved in the problem of the relation of poetry and conduct, and this (even when he denied that there

[27] "Poetry and the Absolute," *Sewanee Review*, xxxv (January, 1927), 41-52. T. S. Eliot saw the essay in the spring of 1926 and wanted to publish it but the arrangements fell through. (From a letter to Tate dated June 22, 1926.)

[28] From letters to Tate dated August 13 and August 23, 1922.

was any relation) has been a main concern ever since—not surprisingly in view of his interest in the condition of society and the role of the man of letters.

At the beginning he was so insistent upon the wholeness of a poem and so determined to protect it from reduction to a "moral" that he argued, as we have seen, the moral futility of its ideas. "The completed poem," he wrote in 1926, "is neither exact nor inexact, but what it is, and does not refer to any other order than its own." A year later he remarked that critics should attend exclusively to the properties of poetry as a fine art—something which he himself, for all his sensitivity to these properties, was certainly not doing.[29] Ransom disagreed. A poem, he said, has many relations with the world and Tate's insistence that it be treated as ultimate, finished, absolute was "a species of idolatry."[30] Though he missed some of Tate's argument, he went straight to a radical confusion. To understand it and its effect on Tate's speculations we must take a moment to consider three aspects of the meaning of a poem:

1. *Representation.* Is a poem (as realized in the reader's imagination) an aesthetically satisfying entity perceived (or, to use Tate's term, "experienced") simply as a thing-in-itself, or does it in some manner represent objects and events outside itself? If it does, we are up against a series of fine problems: the referential functions of language; the differences among pointing to, imitating, and symbolizing; the roles of the medium, the conventions, the poet's style, and the artistic frame of reference; and the distortions introduced by the formal organization.

2. *Knowledge.* What is known? First, the poem as experienced thing-in-itself. Then, if we believe in representation, knowledge by revelation of the subject represented. And there may be knowledge by interpretation: knowledge of universal forms imminent in the particular subject and knowledge of the human values of the representation and the interpretation. But if the distinction of knowledge is validation by evidence, where does one get it and how does one use it?

3. *Relevance.* How much and in what ways does the meaning

[29] "A Philosophical Critic," p. 281; "Poetry and the Absolute," p. 46.
[30] From a letter to Tate, April 3 and 13, 1927. For a discussion of the dating of this letter see Chapter Six, note 9.

of the poem matter to the reader as total human being? Does it matter only because it gives us aesthetic pleasure? Does it matter because it offers in an attractive manner conceptions and information on which we may act? Does it matter because it provides knowledge of our experience which, though not organized for use in practical affairs, helps us to understand ourselves and ultimately to act more wisely and responsibly in fulfilling our humanity? And if we believe that its meaning may help us to understand our experience, is not that meaning subject to judgment according to our conceptions of man and human values?

No one has answered all these questions to the satisfaction of any considerable number of other men. No one ever will. But men vary in the skill with which they seek their own answers, argue from evidence, and avoid illogic and incoherence. Thus they vary in the degree to which they persuade us to accept part of their answers and help us to find answers of our own. To take one ready example, many who do not accept all of Ransom's theory of structure and texture have learned invaluable lessons from his tireless insistence on the richness of poetic details and their abundance of meanings beyond those which can be fitted exactly into the statement of some dominant theme or controlling idea. Anticipating that we will not agree wholly with any man's conclusions, we wish to know how well he has handled his speculations and what he can teach us or drive us to discover for ourselves.

In his argument with the New Humanists and other earlier essays, Tate had acted on certain assumptions about representation, knowledge, and relevance, but his first really thorough consideration of the problems they raised was the essay "Three Types of Poetry," first published in *The New Republic* on three successive fortnights in the spring of 1934. He does not address himself directly to the three aspects of meaning but chooses instead to designate three kinds of poetry which signify three contemporary attitudes and three conditions of the modern mind. The first, "genuine" poetry—for example, the poetry of Shakespeare—comes from "the power of seizing the inward meaning of experience, the power of sheer creation . . . the vision of the whole of life," to which we have already referred in our discussion of Tate's theory of the mind and the character of positivism. The vision of the whole of life can be conveyed in a very few lines.

The eight lines of Blake's "To the Accusers" suffice. Allegorical poetry, the second type, is the product of the practical will. Before the rise of modern science it gave us poems like *The Faerie Queene*, in which the narrative had no inward necessity of its own. (Without committing ourselves to Tate's conception of the practical will we can observe that this is the fault to be found with the unsatisfactory passages in his novel.) Today, Tate says, our culture is dominated by the practical will and obsessed with allegorical literature which competes with science. As an example of what he meant, Tate might have cited, though he did not do so, the kind of poetry called for by Archibald MacLeish in his "Invocation to the Social Muse." When this poem appeared in *The New Republic* in the fall of 1932, Tate answered with a poem of his own, "Aeneas in New York" (*The New Republic*, December 14, 1932), which he has not reprinted. Rejecting the idea that the poet should "bear arms" on behalf of causes, Tate said,

> First we are priests second we are not whores. . . .
> The poet is he who fights on the passionate
> Side and whoever loses he wins; when he
> Is defeated it is hard to say who wins. . . .

The third type is the poetry of Romantic irony, which Tate also attributes to practical will as Ransom attributed much Romantic poetry to the reason. In an argument closely resembling Ransom's, Tate says that when the will cannot make poetry out of science, it rebels against *all* order as "scientific." "The romantic tries to build up a set of fictitious 'explanations' by means of rhetoric, more congenial to his unscientific temper."[31] As an example Tate cites Shelley's lines "Life like a dome of many-colored glass/ Stains the white radiance of eternity," which he says are not poetry. "The will asserts a rhetorical proposition about the whole of life, but the imagination has not seized upon the materials of the poem and made them into a whole. Shelley's simile is imposed upon the material from above; it does not grow out of the material." As an explanation of life it *necessarily* looks toward possible action, but it is meaningless because it is not a practical statement which can be tested. In short, such poetry competes with science and fails.[32] By way of comparison Tate offers "Ripeness is all" and says this

[31] "Three Types of Poetry," *Reactionary Essays*, p. 88.
[32] Pp. 84-85.

figure does indeed grow out of the material. "It is a summation not only of Gloucester's tragedy but of the complex tensions of the plot before the catastrophe in the last scene. . . . [It is] implicit in the total structure, the concrete quality, of the whole experience that we have when we read King Lear."[33]

At this point Tate gets himself thoroughly tangled in problems of representation, knowledge, and relevance: "The specific merit of Edgar's statement as general truth or falsehood is irrelevant because it is an *experienced statement* . . . and the statement remains experienced, and thus significant and comprehensible, whether it be true or false."[34] But a little earlier we were told that good poetry resulted when the imagination seized the inward meaning and provided a vision of the whole of life. Shortly thereafter it is said that such poetry "yields us the quality of experience." Manifestly the test of truth is being applied. Moreover, if the imagination seizes an inward meaning, it is discriminating among several meanings, and we can only suppose that it is engaged upon interpretation.

It is fairly easy to explain what has happened here. Tate is determined to protect the whole poem from reductive readings. (He would have termed them positivistic.) He wants to proclaim the value of poetry and yet insist that it cannot be put to practical uses. In the process of pursuing these aims, which need not conflict, he fails to distinguish four processes: (a) actual, lived-through human experience, (b) the representation of the qualities of that experience in a poem, (c) the experience of reading the poem (itself a part of the first-named process), and (d) the imaginative grasping of the whole of life, which he posits as a consequence of reading the poem. When he says of *Macbeth* that it "is neither true nor false but *exists as a created object*," he has retreated to his position of 1926-1927. Moreover, he has partially accepted the positivists' definition of truth, as may be seen in his remark that Shelley's lines are meaningless because "Practical knowledge can alone fit means to ends."[35] The ending of the essay, however, blandly contradicts the earlier remarks on truth and relevance:

> "When the will and its formulas are put back into an implicit relation with the whole of our experience, we get the true knowledge which is poetry. It is the 'kind of knowledge which

[33] P. 85.   [34] Pp. 85-86.   [35] Pp. 107, 85.

is really essential to the world, the true content of its phenomena, that which is subject to no change, and therefore is known with equal truth for all time.' Let us not argue about it. It is here for those who have eyes to see."[36]

Very well, then. Let's not.

Over the next seven years Tate published a number of statements on poetry and knowledge which did nothing to clarify matters. In "Narcissus as Narcissus" he said, "If the poem is a real creation, it is a kind of knowledge that we did not possess before. It is not knowledge 'about' something else; the poem is the fullness of that knowledge. We know the particular poem, not what it says that we can restate."[37] The honorific phrase "real creation" means nothing. By this argument any gibberish we may improvise is as much a real creation as Tate's "Ode to the Confederate Dead," and we know that gibberish in the way Tate says we know the poem. But of course, as the entire essay makes clear, the "Ode" does indeed offer knowledge about something else: "the cut-off-ness of the modern 'intellectual,'" to use Tate's own words for its theme. For bravado and obscurantism nothing matches his statement in "The Present Function of Criticism" that "The function of criticism should have been, in our time, as in all times, to maintain and to demonstrate the special, unique, and complete knowledge which the great forms of literature afford us. And I mean quite simply, *knowledge*, not historical documentation and information."[38] The argument by italics and the condescending manner toward professional scholars moved Sidney Hook to write the letter, quoted in Chapter Four (page 193), calling into question Tate's competence to discuss philosophical issues. But the same issue of *The Southern Review* that carried Hook's letter offered Tate's "Literature as Knowledge," portions of which showed that Tate was indeed competent when his emotions did not get the upper hand.

In it he brought to bear on a number of theories of poetry the powers of analysis and synthesis he had exhibited in his handling of the Civil War campaigns in his biographies. Starting from the easy example of Arnold, he discussed the ideas of critics who

[36] P. 112.
[37] *Reason and Madness*, p. 135.
[38] P. 9.

believed that the real meaning of poetry, the only part that added anything to human knowledge, was separable from the poem as a whole and could be restated more clearly and accurately, if less persuasively, in expository prose. He demonstrated that though Coleridge recognized the artistic autonomy of a successful poem and the total integration of all its elements into a harmonious unity, he too believed that the meaning was separable. Then Tate considered the theories of Charles W. Morris and showed that his theory of signs in art agreed in all its essentials with I. A. Richards' theories of *tenor, vehicle,* and *pseudo-statement.* The essay ended with praise for Richards' repudiation of his earlier positivistic views in favor of a new theory of the unique cognitive function of poetry. At that point Tate's logic began to disintegrate. What followed tended to bear out Hook.

First Tate quoted Richards' ungrammatical statement (in *Coleridge on the Imagination*) that "Poetry is the completest mode of utterance." Immediately shifting the terms, Tate continued: "It is neither the world of verifiable science nor a projection of ourselves; yet it is *complete.* And because it is complete knowledge we may, I think, claim for it a unique kind of responsibility, and see in it at times an irresponsibility equally distinct." The responsibility is to the "experienced order" (so some kind of truth is involved); the irresponsibility is to the "experimental order" of science. Richards did *not* say that poetry was complete knowledge; he said something else, the meaning of which is obscured by the bad grammar. Apparently by *completest* he meant *richest* or *most comprehensive.* For strictly speaking any utterance is complete as an utterance, though utterances vary in the amount of material they can include. Thus they vary in how nearly they approach saying everything that can be said about a topic. If *complete* be taken to mean saying everything, not one utterance can be complete, let alone "completer" or "completest."

But enough of that. Whatever Richards meant, Tate himself meant that a poem by symbolism of the "mythical order" offered a complete representation of an experience. Then he made another shift and said that a poem's " 'interest' value is a cognitive one; it is sufficient that here, in the poem, we get knowledge of a whole object." There is an important difference between complete knowledge and knowledge of a complete (whole) object, but Tate does

347

not see it. We are back with his old confusion of processes. The essay ends by telescoping representation and cognition, or the completeness of knowledge with the completeness of the subject: "I have been concerned in this commentary with the compulsive, almost obsessed, application of an all-engrossing principle of pragmatic reduction to a formed realm of our experience, the distinction of which is its complete knowledge, the full body of the experience that it offers us."[39] It is all very well to insist on this, but in the end we cannot understand *how* the knowledge to be had from poetry differs from that of common sense or philosophy or even a scientific proposition. We understand only that Tate thinks it differs. The whole matter of the referential function of poetry is so bungled that we are bewildered and finally bored by the incantatory phrases, *vision of the whole of life, wholeness of vision, inward meaning, experienced statement, true knowledge, true content, complete knowledge,* and *experienced order.* Herbert Muller summed things up in a review of *Reason and Madness*:

> "Tate has got himself into an impossible position. He asserts as a fundamental principle that 'literature is the complete knowledge of man's experience,' and that the function of criticism is to maintain and demonstrate this knowledge. This exalted claim is designed to positivists in their place; but unfortunately he does not even begin to demonstrate it in his own criticism. Although he obviously believes that a great deal of literature, especially romantic poetry, does not embody complete knowledge, he gives us no clear criterion for making the all-important distinction. Logically, in fact, he cannot demonstrate it because of another fundamental principle—his objection to the 'Doctrine of Relevance.' "[40]

V

Meanwhile, Tate had been doing some hard thinking about the nature of fiction which was, in the end, to get him out of his difficulties with poetry and meaning. In converting the materials of an historical and sociological study into a novel, he had almost brought off the feat of representing a crisis in history within a narrative

---

[39] Pp. 59-60, 61.
[40] "Three Critics," *The Yale Review*, XXXI (March, 1942), 611.

design that needed no intrusion by its author to make clear the meanings once intended for discursive essays. Soon after completing *The Fathers* he undertook another unusually difficult technical exercise by making a play of James's *The Turn of the Screw*. Eliot read it in the spring of 1938 and liked it. But he had a question which went straight to the heart of those practical problems in literature and knowledge that Tate had been attempting to solve: would those who had not read the story be able to understand the play?[41] Then Tate was appointed resident fellow in writing at Princeton and began work on another novel. Nothing came of this, but Ransom, knowing of his growing interest in the techniques of communicating meaning by showing rather than telling, suggested several times in 1940 and 1941 that he write a "poetics" of fiction for the *Kenyon Review*. Though the poetics was never written, some notion of what it would have been like can be gained from the essays Tate published between 1942 and 1945.

"The Hovering Fly" (1943), though a fully realized and brilliant essay, is clearly a transitional work in the canon of Tate's speculative prose. In it Tate summed up a decade of thinking about literature and knowledge and introduced the concept of symbolic action which he had put into practice ten years earlier in "The Immortal Woman." He described Dostoevsky's use of a fly at the end of *The Idiot* to suggest the human significance of the events that led to the moment and showed how the careful selection and placing of the materials made it possible for such a tiny element to convey so much meaning. "We may *look* at the hovering fly; we can to a degree *know* the actual world," he wrote. "But we shall not know the actual world by looking at it; we know it by looking at the hovering fly."[42] So much is compressed in this apothegm that it is easy to overlook what changes in Tate's thinking (or, if not changes, then clarifications) are there. To begin with, Tate seems to have given up his claims for complete knowledge. (We can *in a degree* know.) Also, it is not simply the experience that is known but its human significance as well. By itself the fly is nothing, but in the tectonic of the novel it represents all that is meant by the abandonment of Nastasya's body by the two men who loved her. Finally, since what we learn about

---

[41] From a letter to Tate, April 12, 1938.
[42] *Collected Essays* (Denver, 1959), p. 156.

the actual world we obtain by looking at the fly rather than the world, the design—the novel as a work of art—is interpretive as well as representational. Interpretive of human values, which means, of course, that it is *relevant*, though Tate does not use that term.

Tate praised the dynamic unity of Dostoevsky's work, by which he meant unity achieved by the organization of experience rather than by the imposition of explanations. In "Techniques of Fiction" (1944) he considered some of the ways whereby naturalistic details interacted to give the reader both an impression of reality and a symbol. Fiction, he argued, is not a literary art if the fictionist fails to abide by the character of his medium and leaves anything to be imagined by the reader. Scenes must seem actual because for the reader they have the effect of containing all that is necessary for actuality.[43] This is exactly how the best scenes of *The Fathers* seem to us. The effect of containing all that is necessary is a long way from the fullness or wholeness of life that Tate once claimed for literature. Yet Tate seems to be saying what he intended all along: literature suggests the wholeness of experience and thereby is able to communicate insights of qualities and relations which cannot be communicated in forms of discourse that are committed at the outset to a partial report. He is on dangerous ground (where he would find plenty of company) in making such an arbitrary statement about fiction as art, but as a requisite for symbolic naturalism his prescription is eminently sensible.

He had always preferred representation in poetry to reflection, which seemed to encourage the moralistic criticism of the Humanists or raise the issue of truth with the positivist. Now he applied his standard for fiction to poetry in three brilliant essays, "A Reading of Keats" (1945), "Johnson on the Metaphysicals" (1949), and "The Point of Dying: Donne's 'Virtuous Men'" (1953). One may think his preference confining. (Is it necessarily less *poetic* to tell rather than to show? What shall one do about the consummate artistry of Pope?) But applied to poems intended to dramatize rather than to expound, such as Keats's odes or Donne's "A Valediction: Forbidding Mourning," it helps to explain the excellence in the organization and the appropriateness and cumulative effects

43 *Collected Essays*, p. 144.

of the details. The first essay is a masterpiece of its kind, gracefully combining scholarship with knowledge of the technical resources and limitations of the medium. The acuteness of the last shows why Ransom long ago went out of his way to praise Tate as a critic. And among them the essays dispose of the old dichotomy which had so long divided Tate's speculations on the nature of poetry. They make it clear that a poem is at least semi-autonomous as a work of art and in that sense is unique and absolute; but at the same time it is about something else that may matter a great deal to us as human beings.

The crowning effort of what Tate once called his self-education in public is the pair of essays entitled "The Symbolic Imagination: The Mirrors of Dante" and "The Angelic Imagination: Poe as God" delivered (in shorter versions) on February 10 and 11, 1951, as lectures at Boston College. Into them he put all that he had concluded about literature as knowledge, the function of tradition and dogma, the moral unity of medieval Europe, the disunity of the present, the dissociation of the modern personality, and the history of the man of letters as a representation of the state of his culture.

In 1950 Tate said that he was not a Catholic. But he had long been studying the Catholic theologians and soon afterward he joined the Church. He had come at last to an all-encompassing Absolute which enabled him to organize into a consistent monistic system the epistemological, ontological, and cosmological assumptions he had so long attempted to unite. A theological naturalist, he rejected revelation in favor of intuitions achieved by modes that were rough corollaries of symbolic naturalism in literature. Under the acknowledged influence of Jacques Maritain he asserted that "The human intellect cannot reach God as essence; only God as analogy. Analogy to what? Plainly analogy to the natural world; for there is nothing in the intellect that has not previously reached it through the senses."[44] In this, of course, Tate abides by the argument of Aquinas that all knowledge, even of things beyond sense, comes to us by way of the senses. Where society enjoys moral unity within traditions backed by the dogmas and authority

---

[44] "Is Literary Criticism Possible?" *Collected Essays*, p. 482; "The Angelic Imagination," *op.cit.*, p. 453.

of an objective religion, the personality is integrated and the imagination is free to explore the natural world and achieve its intuitions of God. But when unrestrained, men strive to know noumenal essences. The practical will outleaps the scale of human action and the intellect moves "in isolation from both love and the moral will, whereby it declares itself independent of the human situation in the quest of essential knowledge," which only angels can know. In the end man destroys himself because he has lost contact with nature and men, and other than himself there is no object for his energies since action directed outside himself has lost all meaning for him. Such has been the fate of man since the rise of science, which is man's attempt to emulate the angelic imagination, and positivism, which seeks to manipulate essences and play at being God. Like the veteran of "The Immortal Woman," like George Posey, like Edgar Allan Poe (as Tate reads the meaning of his work) man is outside the community, outside life—immolated in the Dark Night of the Sense.

At the beginning of this chapter it was noted that Tate eventually changed his conception of Nature, but the change is not as great as it may appear to be. He still argues that raw, inchoate sensations from the natural world destroy man. The important difference is that now he assumes a natural order from which man can by analogy derive those dogmas and traditions needed to guard him from the evil of pure quality. Looking back to "Remarks on the Southern Religion," "Humanism and Naturalism," "Liberalism and Tradition," and *The Fathers* we can trace the direct line of development to the position Tate reaches in these essays. We may even see on it the influence of Ransom's epistemology, though of course the position is far from Ransom's. It is time, therefore, to examine certain premises that have been present in Tate's thinking ever since his disenchantment with experimentalism and his search in the Southern and European pasts for guides to conduct and writing.

For many years he has assumed that psychological need makes tradition and dogma the necessary sources of "imperatives of reference," and he cites the experience of writers (Dante, Donne, Hawthorne, Dickinson, and Yeats) as proof. It will be remembered that in praise of Crane's effort to find in history a cultural truth that would win the allegiance of masses of men Tate wrote, "It is on such simple integers of Truth, not truth of fact but of religious necessity, that men unite."[45] Elsewhere he used "religious necessity" to explain the failure of the Old South and the ineffectiveness of the moral system the Humanists hoped to extrapolate from the literature and cultures of the past. Acting on the assumption set forth in the aphorism used as an epigraph for this chapter ("Man . . . has got to believe in order to know, and to know in order to do"), Tate asked the rhetorical question which signified his inductive leap to God: "Can we believe in the language of humane truth without believing in the possibility of a higher unity of truth, which we must posit as *there*, even if it must remain beyond our powers of understanding?"[46] The answer, of course, depends on how one defines "humane truth." In Tate's argument the implicit definition is circular: humane truth is that which necessitates the positing of a higher truth—an imperative of belief (for an imperative of reference is no longer enough).

Psychological need is no argument for belief in transexperiential entities or even for the necessity of traditions as the source of imperatives of reference. Certainly the mind is likely to be more stable and the emotions more manageable when mental activity is directed at a few relatively simple and uncontradictory goals which permit the *sense* of achievements having value. These goals may or may not be sanctioned by social custom or religious dogmas; such sanction is not a prerequisite of their efficacy. Men have been able to endure incredible suffering or go to their deaths for the sake of unsanctioned goals and beliefs that exclude all possibility of noumena, divine and otherwise.

Even if we grant psychological need as an argument, the fact that a great many people believe in something is not proof of the necessity of belief in *that particular object* for the gratification of the need. They may know of no contrary evidence. They may believe in that object because of the rewards for so doing and the punishment for refusal. If they are happy, effective human beings they might be so *in spite of* rather than because of their belief. The well-established happiness and effectiveness of many Russians cannot be accepted as evidence that the dogmas of Marxist-

---

[45] See above, p. 325.
[46] "Is Literary Criticism Possible?" *Collected Essays*, p. 482.

Leninism are the specific objects of belief necessary for the gratification of their psychological needs.

Finally, even if we allow such proof of numbers as is implicit in Tate's references to medieval Europe, Puritan New England, and the antebellum South, the societies to which he alludes are ill suited to supporting his argument. In each instance the dogmas and traditions on which men were united were supported by coercion and the suppression of opposing views. The unity of the thirteenth and fourteenth centuries to which Tate so many times appealed was real. The cathedrals, the *Summa Theologica*, the feudal orders, the art forms, the great universities, the currency of Latin among the learned—there is no scarcity of evidence. The framework of belief may have been partially established upon postulates that did service for the truth, for even the naturalistic Aquinas, when forced to choose between authority and experimental evidence, chose the former; nevertheless, the unity made possible by that framework entered all aspects of the life of the times. It was backed by dogmas full of superstitions, ignorance, and insoluble contradictions—and by the police surveillance of the priests. Even so, there was more contention than admirers of the times acknowledge, which is one reason for Aquinas's approval of the ferocious punishments inflicted by the Holy Office, a point which Tate's mentors, Etienne Gilson and Jacques Maritain, omit from their commentaries on Thomism. Moreover, the dogmas inflicted on men a heavy sense of guilt, held before them the prospect of an eternity of torture, and then offered them at the price of absolute submission, release from an almost unbearable burden of anxiety. Yet men felt free to despise the bishops who absolved them, and the clergy was an object of hatred and contempt among many. Against the image of the lord and the villein kneeling beneath the same soaring Gothic arches one must place the record of the brutality and license of times, nowhere more conspicuous than among the scholars and clerics. Tate's picture of the European community that supported the symbolic imagination of Dante and inhibited the angelic imagination is partial indeed. The structure of a hierarchical society appeals to those dismayed by the disorder of our own day. But inequality inevitably invites abuses. Perhaps the misery of the serfs has been exaggerated, but their labor made possible the privileges of the clergy and nobility and no

354

organized effort to improve their lot seemed possible. Tate leaves out of his account of the "freedom" of traditional society the tyranny that led to the Peasant's Revolt. In sum, to attribute the breakdown of a system of thought that patched over manifest contradictions and needed the rack and the stake to back up its insistence that no new knowledge was possible, to attribute the collapse of a society in which many lived in the utmost deprivation while a few moved at ease in silks and jewels earned by unceasing labor of the many—to attribute these as Tate has done to the unnatural thrust of the practical will is to posit a determinism as reductive as any positivistic abstractions to which Tate took exception. It is on a par with blaming the disappearance of the bounteous Southern subsistence farm on the malicious contrivance and spiritual corruption of Northern industrialism. Ransom took care of that kind of argument when he said quite simply that the Agrarians never found an answer for the farmer's wife. Tate's appeal to history in support of his conceptions of tradition, the religious community, the role of the man of letters, and his standards for his valuations of our society, has always been one of his least effective maneuvers. He chose the kind of history he had applauded in "The Bridge," but he was not writing poetry.

But to return to the essays: a critical weakness is the indefiniteness of the term *natural order* to designate that which is supposed to mark the limit of the operation of the ordered and balanced mind and to provide the analogues for God. Tate does not make clear how it differs from the orders of science or astrology and what kinds of relations within it, other than love, symbolize God. We are told of Poe that in his work we find "the incapacity to represent the human condition in the central tradition of natural feeling. . . . This primary failure in human feeling results in the loss of the entire natural order of experience."[47] (The *entire* natural order?) But what is *the* central tradition of natural feeling? Central to what? Natural to what? Feeling for what? These questions can be answered only by inference from the whole text of the two essays, and the answers chase one another in a ring. Natural feeling is what you lack when you suffer from the thrust of the will. The thrust of the will is the consequence of a

[47] *Collected Essays*, p. 434.

lack of natural feelings. Natural order is that which is used for analogies by the symbolic imagination. The symbolic imagination functions in an integrated personality. An integrated personality is one in which the symbolic imagination is able to function. The symbolic imagination is that which uses the natural order for analogies.

This is a more sophisticated version in hierological terms of Tate's assertion in "Three Types of Poetry" than the imagination has "the power of seizing the inward meaning of experience, the power of poetic creation . . . the vision of the whole of life." But Tate no longer speaks of a vision of the whole of life. For "every gain [of the symbolic imagination] beyond the simple realism of experience imposes so great a strain upon any actuality of form as to set the ultimate limit of the gain as a defeat." It can formulate only a limited human paradigm of the Word, but through that paradigm we may see what lies beyond the natural world.[48] Whatever the meaning of "natural order," a term taken, apparently, from St. Thomas or his commentators, it refers to some relationship or design obtaining in the natural world, and its presence warrants drawing analogies between God and that world. This is another proposition open to objection. The possibility of analogy depends on how closely one expects the elements to resemble one another and how unambiguous are the terms for their qualities. There are good reasons for believing that human love and divine love (in the Thomist sense) are too far apart for the analogy to have any meaning. The definition of love remains all on one side: the human side in the case of Dante as Tate reads him. Asserting that "the traditional Christian conception of divine love is the love of a God so jealous that he condemns to eternal torment all who have failed to love him as he wants to be loved," Walter Kaufmann argues,

> "As long as we cling to the conception of hell, God is not love in any human sense—and least of all, love in the human sense raised to the highest potency of perfection. . . . When it is asked whether goodness, love, and justice are ascribed to God analogously or symbolically, it should not be forgotten altogether that these terms in anything at all resembling their usual

[48] *Op.cit.*, p. 431.

356

sense, which they have when applied to human beings, simply cannot be applied at all to the God of traditional Christianity."[49]

One may reject Kaufmann's argument out of hand but still find a weakness in Tate's reliance on analogy. Let us return once more to the epigraph which sums up so much of Tate's thinking on all these epistemological problems: "Man . . . has got to believe in order to know. . . ." (It seems to be based upon St. Anselm's words: "I believe in order to understand.") Psychologists and art historians have shown that perception is conditioned by culture.[50] Dante did not see the natural world. He saw the world of thirteenth-century dogma plus whatever personal vision his genius enabled him to have. Now if man must believe in order to know, if knowledge, as Tate suggests, is based on perception of the natural world, and if perception is shaped by what a man believes, then Dante was not proceeding by analogy. Like a medieval schoolman, he looked for evidence for a belief which itself supplied at least some of the evidence. We cannot say how much. But we can say that this is odd analogy. It permits one to suggest that the mantic powers which Tate attributes to the poetic, or symbolic, imagination are extremely vague. Certainly much more evidence for their existence and nature is needed than Tate supplies in these essays or in the brief allusions to Shakespeare, Blake, Wyatt, and Dante in "Three Types of Poetry."

Nevertheless, though one may object to some of the premises and maintain that certain of the key terms are ambiguous, Tate's argument on behalf of poetry as knowledge no longer exhibits the contradictions cited by Muller. Poetry is representational, interpretive, and relevant. How does the new conception of meaning affect the role of the man of letters?

In "To Whom is the Poet Responsible?" (1950-1951) Tate went back to an old irritation: the demands of politically oriented critics that literature serve the commonweal. There are signs of a new certainty about the role of the man of letters in the concession Tate made when he wrote, "There is no doubt that

[49] *Critique of Philosophy and Religion* (New York, 1961), pp. 205, 201, 204.
[50] The best general discussion, which includes a brief historical survey of earlier theories, is to be found in E. H. Gombrich's *Art and Illusion* (2nd ed., New York, 1961).

poetry, even that of Mallarmé, has some effect upon conduct, in so far as it affects our emotions." A few years earlier he probably would not have gone that far. Nevertheless, his opposition to the demands had not diminished a jot. "Because poetry may influence politics, we conclude that poetry is merely politics . . . and thus not good for anything." Or we hold the poet responsible for the morale of the people, as Archibald MacLeish and Van Wyck Brooks had done. But "the poet has a great responsibility of his own: it is the responsibility to be a poet . . . and not to gad about using the rumor of his verse." He is responsible to his own conscience "for the mastery of a disciplined language which will not shun the full report of the reality conveyed to him by his awareness. . . ."[51] Without knowledge of reality men cannot act, but it is not up to the poet to tell them what to do with the knowledge he provides.

In "The Man of Letters in the Modern World" (1951-1952) Tate discussed the role and responsibility in greater detail. It is his most important essay: all of the others, from the earliest pieces in *The Fugitive* through the Agrarian writing to the essays on the symbolic and angelic imaginations, can be said to lead to it (with the obvious qualification that they do many other things besides). The long consideration of the nature of poetry, society, and the relations between the individual and the group or the individual and the natural world and the self, comes to a focus here; all the lines draw inward. The man of letters "must do first what he has always done: he must recreate for his age the image of man, and he must propagate standards by which other men may test that image, and distinguish the false from the true." Therefore his first responsibility is for the vitality of language. With the image of man, with language in which discriminations can be made, we can rediscover in the arts knowledge which is not for control but for understanding of the self. Such understanding enables us to achieve community. At present our secularized society has all but destroyed community, and we dwell in Baudelaire's *fourmillante Cité*, knowing only sensation, and turned destructively against ourselves—incapable of the end of social man, which is communion through love:

[51] *Collected Essays*, pp. 396, 401-405.

"Is the man of letters alone doomed to inhabit that city? No, we are all in it. . . . The special awareness of the man of letters, the source at once of his Gnostic arrogance and of his Augustinian humility, he brings to bear upon all men alike: his hell has not been 'for those other people': he has reported his own. His report upon his own spiritual condition, in the last hundred years, has misled the banker and the statesman into the illusion that they have no hell because, as secularists, they have lacked the language to report it. What you are not able to name therefore does not exist—a barbarous disability, to which I have already alluded. There would be no hell for modern man if our men of letters were not calling attention to it.

"But it is the business of the man of letters to call attention to whatever he is able to see: it is his function to create what has not been hitherto known and, as critic, to discern its modes. I repeat that it is his duty to render the image of man as he is in his time, which, without the man of letters, would not otherwise be known. What modern literature has taught us is not merely that the man of letters has not participated fully in the action of society; it has taught us that nobody else has either. It is a fearful lesson. The rollcall of the noble and sinister characters, our ancestors and our brothers, who exemplify the lesson, must end in a shudder. . . . Have men of letters perversely invented these horrors? They are rather the inevitable creations of a secularized society, the society of means without ends, in which nobody participates with the full substance of his humanity. It is the society in which everybody acts his part (even when he is most active) in the plotless drama of withdrawal."[52]

That is where the prose comes out. And so, as we shall see, does the poetry. Elsewhere in the essay he says ingenuously, "I hope it is understood that I am not imputing to the man of letters a personal superiority; if he is luckier [!] than his neighbors, his responsibility, and his capacity for the shattering peripteries of experience, are greater: he is placed at the precarious center of a certain liberal tradition, from which he is as strongly tempted as the next man, to escape."[53] But despite this demurrer the claims Tate makes are perhaps the most extravagant seen in print since the days of Shel-

[52] *Op.cit.*, pp. 384-385.   [53] P. 390.

ley. They are themselves examples of Gnostic arrogance with but little of the Augustinian humility. So, indeed, is the demurrer. Cannot priests, theologians, and philosophers envision a hell? Do not the analyst and the psychiatrist know the torments of the locked-in sensibility and the need for love and for goals outside the self? Have not Francis Bacon, Max Beckmann, Leonard Baskin, Käthe Kollwitz, and a host of others shown us the loneliness and torment of the age? And who are this banker and this statesman who do not know they are living in the *cité* because they have not read the poets? Perhaps they have seen in battle or in detention camps horrors that most of us know only by report. Perhaps they carry everywhere the shattering sense of their participation in the horrors. It would seem that only one far withdrawn from our society could make such claims. Sidney Hirsch on his couch scarcely surpassed this epitomizing of the poet as crippled divinator.

It would be easy to be misled by the tone of this essay into seeing only complacency and vanity poorly camouflaged. That would be to overlook the candor, the moral responsibility, and the courage with which Tate has faced out the problem which overwhelmed Crane: the failure of the man of great gifts to impose his will upon experience. Since 1925 Tate has thought as deeply on it as any man. Moreover, he has dared to live out the role of the artist which he inherited from Baudelaire, Symons, Davidson, Hirsch, Pound, Eliot, and Crane. Not only has he not surrendered to absolute Quality or absolute Quantity, he has tried through Agrarianism and his essays to take action against the dissociation of the contemporary mind and the alienation of the man of letters. If we protest that his image of our world shows how far he is from it, then our protest proves him very much in the right about part of the image. We have no choice but to argue the matter out with him, which is exactly what many of the essays are intended to make us do. But before one takes the podium, one should be well prepared. The place to begin one's preparation, of course, is with Tate's own work—irritating, honest, indispensable.

....

CHAPTER EIGHT

High in what hills, by what illuminations
Are you intelligible?

—Allen Tate, "Ignis Fatuus"

....

I

A PAINTER once described for this writer the difficulties of two well-regarded colleagues who had come to an impasse. They had studied at a woman's college that encouraged its undergraduates to attempt creative work in the fine arts. The youthful and spirited faculty kept up with the newest experiments in music, drama, the dance, and the visual arts, and students interested in painting were shown how to mix debris with their pigments and urged to splatter them on mildewed sacks and warped boards. A movement had its dedicated followers on the campus within days after it first appeared in New York or Paris. Things were certainly lively and gay; everyone had a fine time splashing about.

Surrounded by so much ebullience and anxious lest they fall behind, the students were disinclined to spend time on the techniques and conventions of the past, which might be just last year. And instead of insisting that they acquire a thorough preparation in the fundamentals of the medium, the teachers, acting on the premise that for the time being it was better to nurture talent than to enforce training, allowed them to go directly into non-representational painting in which any whim or eccentricity was permitted. Naturally, the students wished to prove that they *had* talent, and the measure of their endowment had come to be the shock and intensity of their work. Many of them found themselves entangled in an ascending spiral of violence as they strove to exceed one another in the startling disparities and collisions in their paintings. When they succeeded in compelling attention, it tended to shift from the creation to the creator, who became, whatever the ostensible subject, the ultimate subject in the minds of both the painter

361

and the audience. While judging one anothers' work the students spoke with much confidence and sophistication which almost hid their lack of any firm standards. Confronted with the strident and deliberately disjointed, they could distinguish the newer from the merely new; they could, perhaps, make a rough measure of the force; but they could not tell the good from the bad.

Now, several years out of college and admired among gallery-goers for their resourcefulness and wit, these two artists were tired of the decathlon of novelty. They had just about run through their store of personality and they wanted to pause and look about the world that lay beyond the palette and the shop-talk that always seemed to start with "Have you heard what Y. has been trying? Well, just the other day, more or less by accident, you know, he. . . ." But successful as they had been, neither knew how to paint. They were going to have to go back to school, master the craft, and learn how to see. There was a good chance that, once they had, their admirers would lose interest in them.

It should be understood at once that this report of their difficulties is not given to denigrate experiment in the arts but only to suggest what can happen when really talented beginners are not made to undergo the training which Hans Hofmann, for example, imposes on those who work with him but instead are allowed to proceed at once to imitating the seemingly whimsical surfaces of the great innovators. Having little of the trained taste or the experience with and understanding of the medium which guides the selective judgment of men extending the conventions of the past, beginners often believe quite honestly that they can emulate with fair success or even, such is the boldness of youth, surpass the men whose works they imitate. The social revolutions which allow men to think they may become artists but have made the role of the artist indefinite have been followed by correlative aesthetic revolutions which have obscured the principles of formal order and permitted the ignorant to suppose that they can create by inspiration alone. Where these principles have been neglected or set aside, the tendency has usually been to esteem the intrinsic brilliance or the unexpectedness of the details above their relation to the work as a whole, to put contrast above coherence, and to make the temperament of the creator the actual point of interest.

Allen Tate's Poetry

When Allen Tate joined the Fugitives it was possible for many young men to dabble in poetry under conditions rather like those under which the two painters had prepared. If anything, they were even freer. There were no schools of poetry comparable to the academies of painting and no simple mechanical procedures such as stretching and priming canvas that had to be learned from someone with experience. Free verse, the experiments of the Symbolists, the spirit of iconoclasm following the war, the new developments in music, painting, and the drama reported by the popular press on the lookout for good copy, the aggravating indifference of the public—these encouraged many bright young men of Tate's generation to set up as poets and then do as they damned well pleased. Some wrote odd versicles tricked out in pseudo-classicism, half Dowson and half Pound, scattered the words about the page, collected a small bundle of rejection slips, and found another hobby. But some who were more persistent, ingenious, or plain lucky managed to get their poems into one of the advanced little magazines. This was not as easy as one might think from the number of magazines that flourished and the dismal quality of much that they printed. As the Fugitives found to their cost, the editors of any magazine that lasted more than a few months were soon overwhelmed with unsolicited manuscripts, and often the only way to get into print was to have a friend on the staff or start a magazine of one's own, which could be done for a few dollars. But once the young radical had made it, he could fancy himself the spiritual kin of Pound, Eliot, Cummings, and Williams, even though he might never have written an orderly and intelligent sonnet.

Looking back at *The Fugitive* and other little magazines of its time, Tate once remarked:

"As a rule they give the illusion of authorship to persons of little talent, who would otherwise not get their work printed. But there are always persons of real talent, doing something new and distinguished, who can't get a hearing in the established magazines; for these the little magazine, like the *Fugitive*, is probably better than immediate publication in the big metropolitan journals. In this way the *Fugitive* group developed several distinctive kinds of poetry that we might not have today if the poets had sent their first work to the large journals and had it rejected."[1]

This is right as far as it goes but it overlooks the effect of giving the illusion of authorship to persons of real talent who are doing something "new" and *un*distinguished. Who are, in fact, in the position of the students who suffer from the illusion that they are painters because neither they nor their contemporaries have any way of knowing that they are not, even though they have not crossed the *pons asinorum* of their medium: the still life showing the play of light on glass and rumpled cloth. The encouragement is valuable, but the price in lost time can come high.

In those days Tate was eager for attention, impatient with rules, and already alert to the possibilities for aggrandizement and aggression in the role of the artist as the far-darting visionary. But if the Fugitives chose their best work for publication in the first issue, it would seem from his two contributions that he did not know much about writing poetry or, if he did, could not put his knowledge to work in his own verse. One, a sixteen-line fragment entitled "Sinbad," was a token of many things to come. As in poems to come, Tate used the revery on half-forgotten glories by a dazed mind stumbling through time and space. There are hints of unsanctioned passions, madness, and exhaustion; indefinite allusions to unfamiliar texts; garbled metaphors ("red preserves of love") which suggest a singular obtuseness where connotations are concerned; and a radical structural disorder for which the speaker apologizes: "I beg/ Pardon—I'll go on—unity I don't pretend." One and a half lines later the fragment breaks off. It was not altogether good for young Tate to allow this to be printed.[2]

---

[1] From a letter to Florence B. Pockwinse, quoted in her master's thesis, "A History of the Fugitives and *The Fugitive*" (Boston University, 1938), p. 61.

[2] Permission to quote the poem was denied. The other poem, "To Intellectual Detachment," was somewhat better, but not much. It consisted of three quatrains. The first:

> This is the man who classified the bits
> Of his friends' hells into a pigeonhole—
> He hung each disparate anguish on the spits
> Parboiled and roasted in his own withering soul.

The syntax should have made the teacher in Ransom shiver with dismay.

Two years earlier Tate had published a sonnet in *The American Poetry Magazine* for March, 1920. Entitled "Impossible," it began:

> Do you remember how last year we walked
> Against the purple sun through pearly shade,

From the start he tried to surpass all others in the oddity of his images, the tantalizing elusiveness of his references, and the vehemence of his manner. His effrontery impressed the editors of several other little magazines. In the spring of 1922 *The Double Dealer* printed "Euthanasia," which caught the eye of Hart Crane, and in the next issue, "William Blake":

> Now William pulled the lever down,
> And click-clack went the printing press.
> William was the only printer in town
> Who had peeped while the angels undress.
>
> . . .
>
> And William had high dudgeon for the sightless beadle
> Who worshipped a God like a grandmother on ice-skates,
> For William saw two angels on the point of a needle
> As nobody since except W. B. Yeats.
>
> He browsed in bathetic books—Jacob Boehme
> And Paracelsus—which never mattered;
> But he mentions the Ohio River in a poem,
> So Americans ought to feel flattered. . . .

But enough. For such lines the editors put his name on a list of writers who, they said, gave proof that "The North, the Middle West or the Far West cannot offer a more imposing a more varied or a more capable group of writers than these." Among the Southerners mentioned were James Branch Cabell, H. L. Mencken, Conrad Aiken, and John Gould Gletcher, but no other Fugitive. This was heady stuff.

In many ways the Fugitives seem an odd group for Tate to have joined. They had, certainly, much of the Southerner's taste for unusual language, and Davidson and Hirsch felt the appeal of the mystique of the artist; but in general the group was conservative in its attitudes toward poetry, and one would suppose that Tate might have thought it too stuffy. Ransom, Davidson, Stevenson, and Jesse Wills, who were the most original and accomplished among them, submitted their work to the discipline and limitations of forms and conventions which Tate needed to mould the out-

---

And stopped all breathless—lingered there and talked,
And heard swift pyrotechnics nature played?

pourings of his seething imagination. But arguing the necessity of being truthful to the confusions of the age, Tate chose to defy the forms and conventions before he had mastered them and explored their expressive potentialities. He has said that in those days he was impressed by the precision of Ransom's mind and that in trying to win his approval he developed a habit of precision in writing which constitutes his chief debt to Ransom at that time.[3] But the precision cannot be observed in any of the writing he published then. Perhaps he took pains to find exactly the word he wanted, but he did not pay enough attention to its relation with its context. One cannot make out what he meant with his simile "like a grandmother on ice-skates" or his designation of the works of Boehme and Paracelsus as "bathetic." Such arbitrary and obscure phrasing invited parody, and Stanley Johnson provided it with "Ebullient Bean," which began:

> A. Rauwolf, the cautery viands thought, no doubt,—
> Recalling dusky sisters' calorification in mere sunlight
> And browned men in uniform needing a stomach clout—
> Were vain, O Maracaibo, for his giant Cenobite.

Johnson read the parody at a meeting of the Fugitives during the summer of 1922 and later included it in his novel, *Professor*. There he provided an explanation by the young poet who was supposed to have written it. The portion covering the lines here quoted went thus:

> " 'A. Rauwolf, you will remember, was the man who introduced coffee into Europe' (Davis had discovered A. Rauwolf under "coffee" in Webster's Unabridged). . . .
> " 'Well, A. Rauwolf in eating his breakfast, or meat (the "cautery viands" of the poem), no doubt recalled the coffee beans he had seen in the hot tropical countries where he had travelled; the "dusky sisters" are, of course, the beans heated ("calorification") in the sun. At the same time he would naturally think of the great need of coffee in Europe, as for example among the soldiers ("browned men in uniform needing a stomach clout"). Now, let's go back. A. Rauwolf, then, thought breakfast were vain without coffee (the "O Maracaibo" is a little conceit, I

---

[3] From a letter to the writer, September 10, 1953.

admit)—were vain for his own giant organism, or body—or, in a sense, Cenobite.' "

Johnson's satire is leaden-footed, and one of the cruelest things that can be said of Tate's early poems is that they so much resemble the parody. "Idiot," first published in 1927 and so well regarded by Tate that he reprints it in collections of his verse, has lines that are every bit as opaque:

> . . . Motion, which is not time, erects snowdrifts
> While sister's hand sieves waterfalls of lace.
> With a palm fan closer than death, he lifts
> The Ozarks and tilted seas across his face.
>
> In the long sunset where impatient sound
> Strips niggers to a multiple of backs,
> Flies yield their heat, magnolias drench the ground
> With Appomattox! The shadows lie in stacks.

But though they resisted his campaign on behalf of modernism and sometimes laughed at his excesses, the Fugitives were kindly men who appreciated Tate's unmistakable brilliance, and their recognition meant a great deal to Tate. They liked a good argument, which he could always provide. Their opposition was just enough to goad him toward yet more startling metaphors, for which they gave him space in the magazine. If anything, they were too easygoing, and Hart Crane, who was all for daring, was moved to write, "Don't let your interest in *The Fugitive* woo too many things into too sudden print. Forgive my pedantic bass and lifted finger, but I think you are inclined to too hasty mss. dispatches sometimes."[4] But it would have been hard for Tate to heed the warning had he been so inclined. Davidson, the only Fugitive who really liked Tate's poems (though he did not like "William Blake"), had told him that he was the equal of T. S. Eliot and that when he got more pity and warmth into his poems he would "infinitely surpass him."[5] And not long after Crane had raised his finger Tate learned that Eliot had seen some of his poems in *The*

[4] From a letter dated February 12, 1923. *The Letters of Hart Crane, 1916-1932*, ed. Brom Weber (New York, 1952), p. 123.
[5] From a letter to Tate dated June 25, 1922. Unless otherwise noted, all letters addressed to Tate referred to in this chapter are in the Princeton University Library.

Fugitive and had admired them. The news somewhat assuaged his disappointment when Leiber and Lewis, a New York firm that had agreed in the spring of 1923 to publish a collection of his poems, went into bankruptcy. Other magazines such as *The Wave* and *Folio* were taking his pieces. So let Johnson make fun of him. He had good reason to think that his bold journeys into what, in "One Escape from the Dilemma," he called "the obscure by-ways of his own perceptive process" were taking him toward the bright brave world of the young *avant-garde*. It was not unpleasing to be opposed and misunderstood, for by the Wonderland logic that went with the tradition of the artist as rebel this just showed how superior he was to his circumstances. More's the pity, though, for he was greatly gifted, and his permissive poetics, his playing the outcast, and the too-easy publication were letting him slip around the stern work of learning to think in his medium and were delaying his maturing as a writer. Yet perhaps with his temperament there was no other way. One gets the feeling that no matter which of the arts he had chosen he would have tried to shock and dazzle the beholder before he knew much about it. The recognition of the Fugitives and the generous enthusiasm of Crane may actually have speeded up his passage through an inevitable interval of posturing and bluffing and helped him to get the silly business over a little sooner.

When one takes up the poems published between the founding of *The Fugitive* and the publication, during the autumn of 1928, of *Mr. Pope and Other Poems*, Tate's first volume of verse, what first strikes one is the exceptional violence of the diction and imagery. Even the moist hand of Swinburne, which rests on some of the earliest pieces, cannot much diminish their jagged intensity. This is how Tate described dusk on a rainy autumn evening in "Touselled" (*The Fugitive*, February, 1924. The text is from *Mr. Pope*):

> Unhappily fractured music in the scene
> Spills a hollow bird, perched
> On the bony fall. Drip drip
> Sharply, vertically sharp the drops
> Plunge from the eaves. No wonder an interval

Stalked by twin demons, Day and Night,
Is defeated; it is a bastard hour. . . .

A list of his favorite words evokes the panorama of a holocaust: *curse, broken, pain, steel, blind,* and *burst;* these are followed by *bitter, shatter, storm, mad, anguish, wither, stench, scorched, sick, fear, cut, twisted, crushed, shrieked, spattered, tangled, rage, hurled, bruised, tear, stab, parched, charred, blasted,* and many more. Scattered among these are some of the exotic words such as *arcana, prytaneum, cordax,* and *asyndeton,* affected by Hirsch. In the later pieces these give way to latinate scholarly terms of the kind that Ransom used for humorous irony: *apogees, abnegation, disarticulation, immutable dissimulation* (one phrase) and *restitutions.* But Tate rarely used them with any suggestion of humor, the "Horation Epode to the Duchess of Malfi" being one of the few instances.

It would be difficult to bring together in a single short poem more than a few such terms and the objects or actions to which they allude. Their energies are so great that the strongest formal bonds among the elements would be needed to hold the poem together, and it was just these bonds that Tate neglected. He was a sensitive critic of others' poetry, especially attentive to the relations of the elements to one another and to the design of the whole. Yet when he worked at his own verses he seems to have been so fascinated with singular details in which the primary quality was raw power that he gave most of his attention to them and neglected problems of their appropriateness, the nice distribution of proportions, and the achievement of an overall harmony of parts. Consequently his poems tended to be aggregates of colliding atoms. Sometimes he brought enough of them under control to make a genuine poem. Though it is a slight thing, "Homily" deserves to be quoted in its entirety:

If thine eye offend thee, pluck it out.

If your weary unutterable head
Rivet the dark with linear sight,
Crazed by the warlock of a curse
Dreamed up in some loquacious bed,
And if this head of yours rehearse
The energies spilled into the night

When you fell down and bruised the stars
With the glitter of superior light—

Why, cut it off, piece after piece,
And throw the proud cortex away,
And when you've marveled on the wars
That wove their interior smoke its way,
Tear out the tight vermiculate crease
Where death crawled angrily at bay!

The wry play upon the familiar homily lowers the pitch of the language by making it seem a deliberate and ironic exaggeration. But a few phrases thrust up like spurs of flint and evoke the harassment of the tired head tossing on a "loquacious bed." The fine lines at the end offset the redundancy of *linear* and the floundering syntax and impossible metaphor of "Crazed by the warlock of a curse dreamed up. . . ." The cumulative impact of the details is greater than the separate blows of even the most forceful details of less successful poems. Tate understood this well enough when he read the work of other men, but in his own he apparently tried to make each detail a little landmine, and most of the pieces are overwritten and incoherent. Some are impenetrably private. Many wander about from idiom to idiom. "Lycambes Talks With John (in Hell)," for example, proceeds from the chatty society manner of

Yes, you see,
My dear John Keats, I'm psychoanalyzed!

to the Swinburnian soppiness of

Her eyes like poppies and her silken flanks
Like trembling leaflets kissed by wanton rain;
Her hair a twilight

then on to the terse and colloquial

Him have her? No thanks!

and the pretentious

Archilochus should ne'er that thorax stain.

Even Crane felt he was overdoing it and wrote, "I think you need to cultivate greater simplicity of statement in your emotional things,—however well your present facility suits the more ornamented and artificial congruities of satire or brilliant impressionism."[6] But the most exact criticism came a few years later from Eliot. Returning some of Tate's poems, he said that he liked them, but found in them a tendency toward stridency and overemphasis which he attributed to Tate's attempt to use the strongest possible word at every point. He thought the effort to be exact a good thing but felt that Tate overreached himself.[7]

Yet though the poems are ragged, when read together they have a fairly uniform effect and it is not difficult to make out certain dominant themes, controlling ideas and attitudes, and prevailing interests. Despite the fierce intensity of the elements, the scope of the poems is narrow and shallow and focused on a portrait of the artist as a young man even where the artist is not the designated subject. This is not surprising when one recalls Tate's belief that the proper subject of much modern poetry should be the writer's sensibility and the tendency, described at the beginning of this chapter, of experimental works based on the whims of the creator to direct the attention of the audience to the personality of the artist. A few of the poems are apparently autobiographical and confessional, but their frenetic manner suggests that they are based upon imaginative rather than actual history. Others, usually in the first person, describe such things as the onset of evening or the city at night in terms of their impact on a hypersensitive and tormented mind. Other people appear but distantly. Even the women in the poems about love are vague and faceless, and the emphasis is not upon them but upon the effect which the relation with them has had upon the speaker. Where no mention is made of the poet himself or his *persona*, the verbal surface is so queer that it gets detached from its proper references and directs the reader to the imagination that put it together. Among the abiding impressions one takes from the poems is that of a breathless and hot-eyed young man insisting, "Look at me! Look at me!"

When we do, we see not Tate but the conventional hero of a hundred *künstlerromanen*: Manfred, misunderstood and scorned, plunging through darkness toward madness and exhaustion. Superior to and oppressed by his environment, he is, however, not

---

[6] *Letters*, p. 123.
[7] From a letter of June 22, 1926.

at all the tremulous child invoked by Hirsch and Davidson. As described in the first of two poems entitled "Art," which appeared in *The Fugitive* for December, 1924, he is an aristocrat who shall love to the last day those things for which no others care—"dark precious stones" formed in fires "whereof the reeking fuels/ Were curses and Christ's madness." The ignorance and insensibility of the masses move him to laughter and "a cold satire." Like the protagonist of "Sinbad" he has worn himself out with unholy passions. In "Prothesis for Marriage" the bride-to-be is warned:

> I bring to you my certainty of dust
> Palled in the polite eyes of my serious head;
> The unutterable mask of me, who am dead,
> Bears much of living as lingers in rust—
> A singing verdigris of the tight crust
> Of me. It is a weariness you wed. . . .

He longs for death to release him and thinks with satisfaction of the time when others will come to the places haunted by his memory and recall with awe how he had loved a forsaken beauty. None of them will really understand, however, for

> None will recall, not knowing, the twisted roads
> Where the mind wanders till the heart corrodes.

The best of the poems on the lonely, stricken poet is "Mr. Pope," which was first published in *The Nation* on September 5, 1925. Read by itself, it is an impersonal poem that does not shift attention to the author until the very end, when some readers may find themselves thinking about Tate and wondering why he chose to keep so much of his meaning to himself. But when it is read with the other poems, it can be seen as summing up the constellation of attitudes toward the man of letters and his relations with the world.

> When Alexander Pope strolled in the city
> Strict was the glint of pearl and gold sedans.
> Ladies leaned out, more out of fear than pity;
> For Pope's tight back was rather a goat's than man's.

Crippled and set apart, Pope nevertheless is wholly at ease. By force of character and talent he dominates his surroundings.

Wealthy gentlewomen are intimidated by his abnormal power and the allusion to the goat's back hints that it is malevolent and vaguely sexual.

Then he vanishes. And since he was so assured, he probably went for his own good reasons, which are not told. Others come seeking him, their curiosity a testimony to his continuing fascination:

> . . . he who dribbled couplets like a snake
> Coiled to a lithe precision in the sun,
> Is missing. The jar is empty; you may break
> It only to find that Mr. Pope is gone.

The simile of the snake is vivid though clumsily pieced together. If the couplets are separated enough to be dribbled, they would lack the contiguity of a snake's body. Nevertheless, *dribbled* suggests a fluidity appropriate to both the movement of a snake and the unfaltering production of the master poet. And if the couplets fall one by one like drops, perhaps they coalesce into a pattern resembling in its intricate harmony the marking on a venomous snake's skin. *Coiled* calls to mind both a neatness in the pattern of the couplets and a snake's preparation for striking. The couplets, one infers, are exact and deadly. *Precision* takes away some of the visual clarity, for it is an abstract quality, but it links the couplets with the strict glint and the tight back, and together the images indirectly suggest the tenseness that surrounded Pope. Then, in a last imposition of his will, Pope continues to puzzle and command the respect of those who come after him:

> What requisitions of a verity
> Prompted the wit and rage between his teeth
> One cannot say: around a crooked tree
> A moral climbs whose name should be a wreathe.

Cryptic, self-sufficient, masterful to the end. But this is scarcely the Pope known to history, for he took pains to say exactly what prompted the wit and rage between his teeth. It is, rather, the mysterious artist, maimed, feared, enjoying his last triumph over the ordinary citizen by withdrawing and refusing to let others into his secret meaning.

Earl Daniels argues that the crooked tree may be a symbol of life and that the moral wound upon it signifies the permanence of

Pope's influence.[8] Others see the tree as Pope himself, living on to enjoy the honors that are his right. But Professor Daniels points out that the name *should be* instead of *is* a wreathe; this, he thinks, may mean that Pope has not received the credit due him. "Taken with the first half of the stanza, these lines may be an indictment of the modern failure to value Pope at his true worth; the poet may be hinting that we need to pay more attention to Pope and to the criticisms of the satirists if society is to be what it ought to be, if it is not to deteriorate, so that the urn becomes a definite symbol of the end of everything."[9] This reading has much to commend it, but it seems to require importing more specific meaning than the terms of the poem can sustain. At this time Tate himself was turning to criticism of the social deterioration of the age, and this might be adduced as evidence from outside the poem in support of the reading, but taking the poem by itself the reading is just a good guess and the ending remains uncertain.

During the winter following the first appearance of "Mr. Pope" Tate sent to Warren, who was studying in California, a curious poem entitled "Ignis Fatuus." Apparently it had much personal significance because Tate used it as the epilogue to *Mr. Pope and Other Poems* and then, as he took care to point out in his introductory note, as the prologue to his next collection, *Poems: 1928-1931*.[10] The poem slightly revised now read:

> In the twilight of my audacity
> I saw you flee the world. . . .
>
> Towards the dark that harries the tracks
> Of dawn I pursued you only. I fell
> Companionless. The seething stacks
> Of corn-stalks, the rat-pillaged meadow
> Censured the lunar interior of the night.

If the poem had some special importance for Tate, is he the "I" of the poem? Then who is the will-o'-the-wisp? The Tates were

[8] *The Art of Reading Poetry* (New York, 1941), p. 313.
[9] *Op.cit.*, pp. 313-314.
[10] Between *Mr. Pope* and *Poems: 1928-1931* came *Three Poems: Ode to the Confederate Dead, Message from Abroad, and The Cross* (New York, 1930), privately published in an edition of 125 copies.

living in the country with Crane at about the time that this poem was written. Perhaps Tate saw him as one who was fleeing the world for darkness and misleading others with his false light. Or it may have been someone else, or no one in particular. But when the speaker is unable to keep up and falls back into the ordinary, though terrible, world, that world censures the "lunar interior," which seems to stand for some sort of unnatural madness. The will-o'-the-wisp has passed on into unintelligibility, though its brilliance still compels attention:

> High in what hills, by what illuminations
> Are you intelligible? Your fierce latinity,
> Beyond the nubian bulwark of the sea,
> Sustains the immaculate sight.

The "nubian bulwark of the sea" cannot be explained internally, but if we go outside the poem and suppose that Crane is meant, then the phrase may refer in some way to his poems "Voyages," to his reading about the sea in preparation for writing *The Bridge,* or to the "Atlantis" section of that poem, on which he was working at the time. Whatever is meant, the other man's raging language, which the speaker cannot understand, blazes in the distance and distracts the speaker from all else. (Or such, anyway, seems to be part of the intended sense of *immaculate*.) But at last, unable to do otherwise, the speaker returns to "the green tissue of the subterranean / Worm." He comes back to the natural condition of man and to mortality, for the worm seems to be an allusion to the serpent as symbol of time and to the worms that feed upon bodies. He is "two-handed from / The chase and empty." He wonders what all the disorder means:

> What is the riot
> When the pigeon moults his ease
> Or exile utters the creed of memory?

How shall he interpret his friend's flight from the world in terms of the ancient beliefs from which he has been exiled? The title suggests the answer.

It is tempting to see in this poem a reference to the turning point in Tate's development which occurred in this period. The collection of poems for which it served as an epilogue was written

375

largely under the influence of Crane and his fierce latinity. The collection for which it served as prologue consists of poems in which as an exile Tate looked back to his memory of the creeds and legends of his family and the Old South. Perhaps the poem signifies Tate's intention of giving up exploring the lunar interior and obscure by-ways for a more public poetry. If so, then Daniels's reading of "Mr. Pope" may be right and that poem may be a consequence of Tate's changing his model of the artist from incandescent outlaw to stern critic of the age.

II

Of course, such may not be anything like the intended meaning of "Ignis Fatuus." Nevertheless, from his essays and book reviews and the poems which he now began to write, it is apparent that after a year with Crane and his circle Tate had come to something amounting almost to a crisis of identity. "Most men," Norman Mailer has said, "find their profoundest passion in looking for a way to escape from their private and secret torture." Is such the passion that informs Tate's writing beginning with "Retroduction to American History," which was discussed in the last chapter? It is a truism that the passions of a poem are not those of the poet, even when he intends them to be. The poetic frame of reference interferes with the direct and exact statement of his feelings, though the poem may come close to them. And when the poet is so much given to exaggeration as Tate was at this time, the reader must be especially on guard against false assumptions. Yet taking all the writing together and remembering the discussions of the American scene and the rediscovery of the South which Tate shared with Ransom and Davidson, we may discern behind "Retroduction" and the other poems that followed a real, though at first somewhat superficial, dismay at the disorder and vacuity of contemporary urban life and the seemingly total indifference of the majority of Americans to the art and the values on which Tate had staked his self-respect and his future. Playing at being an artist had assuaged his vanity and compensated for his uncertainties while he was in Nashville among the Fugitives. He could count on some support and attention from the society he attacked and there were some definite and well-understood conventions, social and literary, to be resisted. Rebellion had some meaning when the opposition was so

376

clear, and a rebel was a rebel. But in New York City, anything went—and in such freedom, nothing was. The poetic license to explore the farthest reaches of his inward experience which he had demanded among the Fugitives was taken for granted as part of a bewildering total freedom that threatened to undermine all values and identity. Life was tumult that seemed to get nowhere. There were no restraints upon personality, which ran out into nervous fatigue. Alienation and despair, once just part of the role he had assumed, now, as anxiety chased anxiety through his sleepless head, seemed uncomfortably real. It may be that real secret torture was the possibility that nothing to which he had committed himself mattered or could be made to matter; that only mortality, which he liked to write about darkly, was certain. Anyway, it seems likely that the true measure of Tate's feelings at this time is not the clamorous rage of his early poems on the nullity of American life so much as the longing with which he turned to the remote hierarchical orders of the past in search of guarantors against the chaos that oppressed him.

"Causerie," first published in the British magazine *Calendar* in October, 1926, was the next after "Retroduction" in this series of critiques. At its head Tate placed a fragment from a story in the *New York Times* about a party which the producer Earl Carroll had given at his theatre in honor of Vera, Countess of Cathcart, an admitted adultress in trouble with the immigration authorities. Like "Retroduction" it was a revery by one who could not sleep. At first the *reveur* looks with some amusement on the lack of old-fashioned heroes in our time. Where are the men, he wonders, "with sloops and telescopes, / Who got out of bed at four to vex the dawn?" Then he thinks that they may have sinned, but because what they did had some sort of meaning, they could sleep well, for they were not harried with uncertainty. But modern man, though he has not sinned, cannot sleep. He has lost touch with the past and has no standards of conduct to help him understand and allay his restless anxieties. In what may be a reference to Pleasant Hill, the place in Virginia his own family had lost, Tate has the *reveur* ask:

> Where is your house, in which room stands your bed?
> What window discovers your insupportable dreams?
> In a lean house spawned on baked limestone

> Blood history is the murmur of grasshoppers
> Eastward of the dawn.

One's past counts for no more than the stridulations of insects. Nor does religion help:

> In Christ we have lived, on the flood of Christ borne up,
> Who now is a precipitate flood of silence,
> We a drenched wreck off an imponderable shore;
> A jagged cloud is our memory of shore. . . .

A few years later Tate wrote in one of the key passages of his essay "The Fallacy of Humanism," "If you . . . never have the challenge of evil, you have no religion—which is to say, you have no experience either." Thus when a chorus girl sits nude in a bathtub full of wine and serves drinks, there is scandal but no challenge of evil. "Vittoria [the wicked leading character in Webster's play *The White Devil*] was herself, the contemporary strumpet / A plain bitch," for

> In an age of abstract experience fornication
> Is self-expression, adjunct to Christian euphoria,
> And whores become delinquents; delinquents, patients;
> Patients, wards of society. Whores, by that rule,
> Are precious.

But the rage between Tate's teeth suddenly collapses into peevishness. The heroic past that is the measure of our degradation seems bookish and trivial when the poem ends:

> Was it for this that Lucius
> Became the ass of Thessaly? For this did Kyd
> Unlock the lion of passion on the stage?
> To litter a race of politic pimps? To glut
> The Capitol with the progeny of thieves—
> Where now the antique courtesy of your myths
> Goes in to sleep under a still shadow?

After noting the resemblance of the reference to Kyd to the reference to his play *The Spanish Tragedy* at the end of Eliot's *Waste Land*, the disappointed reader wonders what all the fuss has been about. Surely there ought to be more to the difference than can be found in the implied comparison of Carroll's *Vanities* with pre-Shakespearian bombast.

"Ode to the Confederate Dead," begun late in 1926, first published in 1927, and several times revised during the next decade, is another revery on the difference between the past and the present in which Tate passed beyond the bluster and confusion of the earlier poems to ruminate upon the causes of impotence in contemporary man. Though it is an introspective poem which uses much free association and though in many places it seems painfully contrived, there is in its tone of weary melancholy something which invites the reader's trust that nothing was included to startle, annoy, or simply mystify him.

Latent in the poem, and in all of Tate's writing from this time forward, is the assumption which he put into words in his essay "The Man of Letters in the Modern World": "Man is a creature that in the long run has got to believe in order to know, and to know in order to do." Believe, that is, in certain absolutes by which he can know the meaning of his own conduct. And that, the poem tells us, is exactly what modern man cannot know because his rationalism has made belief impossible by teaching him that his absolutes are illusory. Instead,

> You know, who have waited by the wall,
> The twilit certainty of an animal,
> Those midnight restitutions of the blood
> You know, the immitigable pines, the smoky frieze
> Of the sky, the sudden call; you know the rage
> Of Heraclitus and Parmenides.

Heraclitus taught that knowledge is based upon perception and all unity disintegrates into flux that pours downward into ultimate destruction. (After the destruction comes renewal of unity, but in the poem Tate was concerned only with disintegration and offered no hope of the renewal.) The mind, perceiving the flux, is confused by the disorder; only the gods know order. Parmenides taught that what truly is cannot change or be divided; therefore the phenomenal world in which change appears is a delusion. Their systems do not agree, but in the poem the philosophers symbolize aspects of scientific naturalism. Heraclitus stands for the physicist's argument that the known world consists of the random movement of particles; Parmenides represents the scientific view that the true reality is shaped by impalpable universals and has a structure utterly different from what we think we see. When he revised the poem for publication in *Poems 1928-1931*, Tate replaced Heraclitus with Zeno—not the Stoic but the Eleactic who was a student and disciple of Parmenides known for his metaphysical idealism. The point, however, remained the same: skepticism and the habit of abstraction have brought modern man to the place that he knows only what animals know and in the animal way. He is terrified by the darkening forms in the twilight and by the sudden call. But he can do nothing against them. Between the moments of fear and distraction brought on by darkness and silence

> Lurks mute speculation, the patient curse
> That stones the eyes, or like the jaguar leaps
> For the jaguar's image in a jungle pool, his victim.

Rationalism blinds man or it leaps to destroy that image of himself by which he tries to define and understand his own humanity. When knowledge that the objects of belief which give meaning and value to his behavior are only narcissistic solipsisms is "carried to the heart," man can only wait for death.

Though the revery appears to wander freely, the poem is carefully composed. Like the central figures in "Sinbad," "Retroduction," and "Causerie," the *reveur* is tired and dazed. Fatigue and the uncertain light of an autumn dusk cause him to entangle hallucination and reality, past and present, life and death. He is confused, but the poem is not. Confusion is its subject and not a quality of its organization, which follows a simple pattern: the *reveur* comes to the cemetery, stands thinking as the light fails and sounds die away, and leaves in darkness and silence that signify not only the loneliness and oppression of his environment but the spiritual vacancy within. When he first arrives he is hypnotized by the stare of an angel carved upon a tombstone. He begins to brood idly on the true condition of the bodies of the Confederate heroes, which, according to Heraclitus and modern naturalism, are being reduced to their constituent chemicals and borne away to the sea. For a moment he is able to turn his thoughts to their "immoderate past" and to see them rising from the earth and charging across the ancient battlefields. He even imagines that he hears their shouts, but that inward sound reminds him of the outward silence which engulfs him and reduces him to the condition of a mummy. After considering that the modern skeptic has nothing to say to the heroic believers, he turns away. The cry of the screech-owl recalls for the last time "the furious murmur of their chivalry," and he knows that whereas they once called to one another under the light of a rising sun,

> We have not sung, we shall not ever sing
> In the improbable mist of nightfall
> Which flies on multiple wing. . . .

We cannot even sing an ode to honor the fallen heroes. This one is left unspoken by the solitary man who paused not for some ceremonious occasion but only because his attention happened to be caught by a fragment of crumbling sculpture.

Even after undergoing revisions, which will be considered in a moment, the poem is more difficult than these remarks suggest, but not because Tate was following the principles of composition set forth in his essays in *The Fugitive*. Indeed, this poem is, among other things, an argument against those principles and the preoccupation with the self on which they were established. Nevertheless, the effect of those principles on his style and imagination can be seen in the poem and accounts for some of its difficulty. It turns up in the first lines:

> Row after row with strict impunity
> The headstones barter their names to the element,
> The wind whirrs without recollection. . . .

Strict was one of Tate's favorite words when he composed the ode. All terms and images associated with hard edges, obtruding angles, and sharp, piercing lines appealed to his imagination, which was drawn to their suggestion of pain, pressure, tension, and constraint. Here the word seems intended to evoke a sense of the geometric regularity and vague oppressiveness of the pattern formed by the graves and their markers. But if *impunity* means irresponsibility (a meaning which fits the indifference with which the headstones let the names be effaced by the weathers) then *strict* does not make any sense and seems to be no more than indulgence of a private whim. And why are the headstones said to *barter*? Bartering is usually a slow business, and it may be that the word was chosen to suggest how gradually the names are worn away. Still, in bartering something is given in exchange. What do the headstones take in return for the names? However, the third line is terse, emphatic, and clear; a good line. Then comes

> In the riven troughs broken leaves
> Pile up, of nature the casual sacrament
> Against the sinkage of death.

Riven and *broken* are instances of gratuitous verbal violence and excess. The depressions in cemeteries are not split. The leaves that accumulate in them are damp and mouldy; though they may have been torn from the trees, they cannot properly be called broken. This is too bad, for it takes away some of the power and meaning of the rich and impressive *sacrament*, which should have been approached more unobtrusively so that it could have exerted its full force. It has a fine, but impaired irony, in its suggestion that the casual piling up of the leaves is the only ceremony performed in remembrance of the Confederate dead. Its force is further diminished by the inappropriate jauntiness of the triplet rhythms. Of the next three lines, the first two are just padding:

> Then, in uncertainty of their election,
> Of their business in the vast breath,
> They sough the rumor of mortality.

What a deal of words to say that the leaves were blown about helter-skelter! But the third line is the richest and strongest so far.

And so it goes throughout the poem. There are fine, vivid images such as occur in the description of the Novembers

> Staining the uncomfortable angels that rot
> On the slabs, a wing chipped here, an arm there. . . .

(*Uncomfortable* and *rot* are two of the most exact and suggestive words in the entire poem. It would be difficult to overpraise their visual clarity and emotive aptness.) And there are passages containing foolish exaggeration and ingenuity:

> you know the *rage*
> Of Heraclitus and Parmenides.

. . .

382

> In the *orient of that economy*
> You have cursed the setting sun.

Or wildly mixed metaphors:

> The singular screech-owl's tight
> Invisible lyric seeds the mind
> With the furious murmur of their chivalry.

There is even a lunatic splendor to the confusion of the passage on the curse that stones the eyes or leaps for the jaguar's image. Yvor Winters called the lines "hopelessly bad" when he reviewed *Poems: 1928-1931*. Tate asked him to help with their revision, but he refused. Some years later he came back to them and observed: "The necessity of speculation or a curse *stoning* anything is not clear; and violent action on the part of that which is *patient* is still more perplexing. Nor does one see why a stoner of eyes should leap, like a jaguar, into a pool, nor why the owner of the eyes should not thereby be benefited."[11] Exactly so, though perhaps it was a little ungracious of Winters to publish his observation after having turned down the invitation to improve the lines.

Given a few clues from the essays and reviews Tate wrote in this period, one can see that this difficult poem consists of a few simple conceptions which are not explored by the poetry so much as overlaid with exaggeration, unwarranted epithets, cranky word choices, awkward or downright faulty sentences, and tangled metaphors. One has only to compare it with one of the late, great poems such as "Ode to our Young Pro-Consuls of the Air" or "A Winter Mask" to recognize it for what it is—a piece of rather facile pessimism. (To call it this is not to assert that Tate's own feelings about the present condition of man were only that or without sufficient motivation.) In support of this judgment one can offer, for example, this:

> You hear the shout; the crazy hemlocks point
> With troubled fingers to the silence which
> Engulfs you like a mummy in time, whose niche
> Lacks aperture.

[11] "Poets and Others. I," *Hound and Horn*, VI (Summer, 1932), 676; *The Defense of Reason* (New York, 1947), pp. 530-531.

The prose core—to use Ransom's phrase—amounts to something like the following. The imagined shout of the charging Confederates startles the *reveur* into awareness of his actual surroundings. He sees the hemlocks, which remind him of the silence, a symbol of the emptiness of modern life which compels him to remain in his own time and separates him from the past and the living dead. Thus isolated in the flux and flood of naturalistic process (the Heraclitean downward disintegration), he is as a mummy—as bound and motionless in his death as the soldiers are free and active in theirs. If we ask how the poetry differs from this prose reduction, we ask, among other things (and there are many such other things which we cannot look into now), what additional meanings, given force by the meter and rhythm, the individual details bring to the statement, how well they integrate with one another, what ends, if any, the disparities among them serve, what cumulative contextual effects are achieved, and so forth. We are asking if this is verse or appliqué work.

The hemlocks are called *crazy*. The word seems apt. Seen against the fading sky, their outline would be ragged, crazed. Tossed by the wind that whirs the leaves, they might well suggest an assembly of maniacs. *Troubled* seems a bit too weak for the fingers of the demented, but let that pass. What is more important is that *crazy* in this context achieves an effect that is mainly visual. The overtones of mental derangement suggest that the world itself is mad, an appropriate hint if not followed too far. But *troubled* is too weak to sustain the visual effect and shifts attention from the physical appearance to the putative psychic condition of the trees. That immediately puts us to wondering, "What is troubling them? How do they feel troubled?" Are they upset because the *reveur* forgot about the silence? Or does the silence bother them, too? As we try to answer these questions we see that we are being led off on an excursion that goes nowhere. *Troubled* is redundant if meant only to reenforce the impression of the appearance of the trees and confusing if meant for more.

Then consider the silence. Massive and profound, it pours slowly and heavily upon the *reveur*, engulfing him. For such silence there must be utter stillness with no motion other than its own figurative flood. This would serve well as a contrast to the shouting and running of the soldiers in the vision. Then how can the hemlocks be tossed by the wind, which, if it be strong enough to make them appear to be crazy and troubled, must be noisy? Either the passage contradicts itself or the terms for the hemlocks are unwarranted. The mummy image is good except that mummies are unusually dessicated and the *reveur* is *engulfed*—overwhelmed by the liquid silence. *In time* is too loosely attached to the sentence. It seems to modify *engulfs*, but if it does, then time is the liquid flood. This is an acceptable, if conventional, figure; yet if we read the sentence thus then *silence* cannot properly be the subject of *engulfs*. Since it is, and thus enjoys an advantage over *time*, the latter seems an arbitrary "ideological" appendage. But that is not the end of the difficulties. *Whose niche lacks aperture* could apply to *time*; a niche in time is a familiar metaphor, almost a dead one. But if time is a flood, its fluid substance could not have a niche. Nor could the flooding silence. *Niche* suggests that Tate's imagination moved abruptly from the mummy to a little picture of a bit of sculpture, perhaps the enrobed figure of a saint or knight, standing in a recess in the wall of a medieval church. Then, with that picture still before him, he emphasized how sealed off is the *reveur* by making the niche lack *aperture*, a term appropriate to the setting of a medieval church, but connotatively at odds with the image of a mummy. *Aperture*, by its oddity, raises a final question: what, if it were there, would it open upon? We cannot say.

It may seem that this is a lot of bother to be making over four clumsily written lines, and it would be did they not so well illustrate faults which may be found in all but a half dozen or so of Tate's poems. When these faults come so close together, the details of a poem cannot unite to make poetry or even sense. To understand their main intention, the reader must reduce the passages in which they occur to prose paraphrases and throw away the contradictory and incoherent rest. Commenting on our present insistence that the old distinction between form and content is invalid and that the two are indivisible, George Steiner has said, "They are indivisible only where we are dealing with literature in the most serious, fully realized sense; only where the writer's medium strikes us as inevitable because it is controlled, from within, by pressure of adequate vision. Where such a vision is in default, form and content can and will drift apart. Style, the manipulation of image or verbal sound, will make its independent claims.

Instead of necessary, governed form, we get preciousness and fire-work performance."[12] When he wrote the ode Tate had not learned to think in his medium. He had for too long neglected the organization of the whole for the brilliance or intensity of the part. In "Retroduction" and "Causerie" he had seemed to get away with it, but into the ode he had built enough order to make the failures of concatenation stand out. Like the young artists described at the outset of this chapter he lacked training in his craft, and though he was soon to show more technical mastery and write much better poems, he continued to make blunders which would shame far less gifted, experienced, and serious poets. He knew this poem was too much for him, and, as has been said, he asked Winters to help him with the passage on the jaguar. Robert Penn Warren contributed one line which Tate called the best in the poem but, with his characteristic love of mystifying the reader, did not identify. (It was "Their verdurous anonymity will grow," later changed to "Whose verdurous anonymity will grow."[13]) Then, with the stiff self-consciousness that characterizes his comments on his poetry, he announced in the preface of his *Selected Poems*, "I shall never touch the poem again."

Apart from Warren's contribution, which is surely one of the worst lines in the poem, the changes made in later versions are nearly all beneficial. (In this discussion we shall be considering the final version.) The most obvious is the addition, made in 1930, of what Tate calls "the wind-leaves refrain." As he himself observed, it "makes the commentary more explicit, more visibly dramatic," and " 'times' the poem better, offers the reader frequent pauses in the development of the two themes [the decay of belief and heroic conduct based on it and the disorder of the universe], allows him occasions of assimilation; and on the whole . . . makes the poem seem longer than it is and thus eases the concentration of imagery. . . ."[14] Other changes cannot here be considered in detail, but some examination of those made in lines which have been discussed will suggest their character.

The first line of the poem has not been altered; it retains the defective *impunity*. In the second, *barter* has been replaced by the

---

[12] "Half Man, Half Beast," *The Reporter*, XXVIII (March 14, 1963), 52.
[13] Warren identified the line for this writer.
[14] "Narcissus as Narcissus," *Reason in Madness* (New York, 1941), p. 143.

more accurate and rhythmically suitable *yield*. The troughs are still riven, but the leaves are now *splayed*, which is more vivid and precise. The ambiguous and walloping lines

> of nature the casual sacrament
> Against the sinkage of death

have given way to

> of nature the casual sacrament
> To the seasonal eternity of death

which are manifestly better even though *seasonal eternity* is a pretentious conceit. The last three lines of the opening section now read:

> Then driven by the fierce scrutiny
> Of heaven to their election in the vast breath,
> They sough the rumor of mortality.

The last line, unchanged, is still the only good one. The others are fustian.

The rage of the philosophers remains. Tate probably realized that the term scarcely applied to the thinking of the philosophers he had chosen, for he inserted as an appositive for *rage* the line "The cold pool left by the mounting flood." This seems to be a fancy variant that combines two clichés, cold rage and cold logic, in an effort to suggest that the reasoning of the philosophers and scientists is the product of an obsessive anger against nature and ordinary thought. Just what is meant by the mounting flood is obscure—the more so as pools are left by receding, not mounting, floods. The overwritten lines referring to the Confederates' faith in their cause as "the orient of that economy" have been slightly improved to read

> Lost in that orient of the thick-and-fast
> You will curse the setting sun.

The passage on the hemlocks and the mummy has been emended to get rid of the confusion of metaphors. Tate added a wholly new image:

> You hear the shout, the crazy hemlocks point
> With troubled fingers to the silence which
> Smothers you, a mummy, in time.

The hound bitch
Toothless and dying, in a musty cellar
Hears the wind only.

Tate's reasons for inserting this new image tell us much about his imagination. This, he has explained, is the moment of complete breakdown of the vision of the heroic age, and he chose a *hound* bitch "because the hound is a hunter, participant of a formal ritual."[15] Recalling what Tate had come to believe about the purpose of ritual, we can see why he would wish to relate the disappearance of the vision of heroic conduct to the enfeeblement of a participant in the pageantry of a chivalric society. Had he succeeded, he would have added a small but significant dimension to the poem; but it is asking too much of the image to expect a dying hound to bring to mind the ceremonial conduct of the Old South and the values it dramatized. Even when he has been instructed by Tate, the reader must compel himself to make the association. It is difficult not to think that Tate knew this but took a small, private pleasure from offering a tiny affront to the reader's expectations.

Be that as it may, most of the changes tighten the structure and clarify the meaning. In the decade following the first writing of the ode Tate learned much about the art of poetry and was more concerned with the relation of part to part and of part to the whole. Yet it remains a congested poem more important for its place in the development of Tate's ideas and technique and in the history of Agrarianism than for its poetic merit.

"Ode to the Confederate Dead" was the first writing to show that Tate's interests had gone beyond comparing the past and present to focus on the history of his own region and the problem of coming to terms with it. In the next years he wrote his biographies, worked with Ransom, Davidson, Lytle, and the rest to preserve the remnants of the agrarian Old South, and located in medieval Europe and Old Virginia his image of the authoritarian, traditionalist society directed by responsible aristocrats. Several of the poems written at this time described the disparity between the vigorous, confident ante-bellum South and the trivial, dispirited

[15] *Reason in Madness*, p. 147.

South of the present, and often Tate used the accoutrements of hunting and warfare to represent qualities he admired in the culture of the past. In "The Oath," for example, he told how at the day's end he sat by the fire with Lytle:

> Uncle Ben's brass bullet-mould
> And powder-horn and Major Bogan's face
> Above the fire in the half-light plainly said:
> There's naught to kill but the animated dead.
> Horn nor mould nor major follows the chase.

Idly Lytle asks, "Who are the dead?" and after a moment of meditation answers himself with "By God it's true!" True that the two of them—and all modern men—are the dead, not Tate's ancestors. The fading light, the chill in the air, the sound of the wind, the weariness and silence of the friends—all these are enough to suggest the enervation of the present. But two pieces of hunting equipment and the portrait of a man who had done military service are not enough to persuade us that the past was so different in its vitality unless we happen to belong to the hunting cult. In many ways this is a fine poem, but it comes perilously near to sentimentality. More substance for the condemnation of the present is given in "To the Lacedemonians," another revery in the manner of "Retroduction," "Causerie," and the ode. The speaker is a Confederate veteran who is waiting to take part in a reunion the next day. He describes the modern Southerners as

> people of my own kind, my own
> People but strange with a white light
> In the face: the streets hard with motion
> And the hard eyes that look one way.

Robots blinded by the glare of technology and scientific naturalism, they are damned, but they do not know it for, unlike the veteran, they have no beliefs by which damnation may be defined and made known to them. They have lost touch with the past which he had fought to save. He wonders,

> where have they, the citizens, all
> Come from? They were not born in my father's
> House nor in their fathers': on a street corner
> By motion sired, not born; by rest dismayed.

It had been a matter of special concern to Ransom that the tempo of industrialism had been communicated to all aspects of life and in the introduction to *I'll Take My Stand* and his own essay he had protested that men could no longer pause to savor their surroundings, that they had to keep moving to hide from themselves that they had nothing to make life worth living. For, as Tate puts it here, they

> Lack skill of the interior mind
> To fashion dignity with shapes of air.
> Luxury, yes—but not elegance!
> Where have they come from?

The veteran had

> fought
> But did not care; a leg shot off at Bethel,
> Given up for dead; but knew neither shell-shock
> Nor any self-indulgence. Well may war be
> Terrible to those who have nothing to gain
> For the illumination of the sense:
> When the peace is a trade route, figures
> For the budget, reduction of population,
> Life grown sullen and immense
> Lusts after immunity to pain.

He and his companions will not fight again. All men have become Yankees, "Eyeless with eyesight only, the modern power." The "long cold wrath" of Yankee rationalism has destroyed all that men might live for, leaving the Southerners

> Damned souls, running the way of sand
> Into the destination of the wind!

When this poem was published, Tate had been working with Herbert Agar and developing his views on the irresponsibility of finance capitalism. The passage on war is in effect a little essay in verse reflecting those views. It is the economist rather than the poet who speaks through the callous allusion to self-indulgence; the poet well knew from his study of Jackson's battles that war is terrible even for those fortunate enough to salvage something "for the illumination of the sense." When reviewing Tate's *The*

Mediterranean and Other Poems, published late in the summer of
1936 by the Alcestis Press in an edition of 165 copies, Ransom
remarked that "patriotism," by which he meant Tate's Agrarian
passions and convictions, was eating at his lyricism. (One remembers Tate's remarks about Crane's "naive patriotism.") Though
he did not cite this poem, he returned to the point soon afterward
in a letter to Tate, adding, "What is true in part for you (though a
part that is ominously increasing) is true nearly in full for me:
patriotism has nearly eaten me up, and I've got to get out of it."[16]
As we know, he did. His criticism is amply justified by portions
of this poem in which the veteran talks like a contributor to *Who
Owns America?* This is exactly the kind of poetry that Tate had
deplored as "allegory" in his essay "Three Types of Poetry," published two years earlier, and perhaps some of the vehemence of
his condemnation came from a partial recognition of his own propensity for it.

The best of the poems on the heroic past is "The Mediterranean."
Originally entitled "Picnic at Cassis," it was written, according
to Ford Madox Ford, after he and the Tates had gone late in the
summer of 1932 for a picnic by the sea.[17] Tate was reminded of
the time when Aeneas and his followers had come at last to the
place where they would make their home and found the Roman
Empire. The Trojans, too, had feasted by the Mediterranean, and
the similarity immediately suggested to Tate the differences between the wanderers of the past and those of the present. The poem
begins well.

> Where we went in the boat was a long bay
> A slingshot wide, walled in by towering stone—
> Peaked margin of antiquity's delay,
> And we went there out of time's monotone.

The vivid scene is immediately put before us, and the associations
recalled by *slingshot* and the suggestion of a fortress are exactly
suited to the theme. But at the third line we are stopped by one
of those grating instances of overdoing things which spoil so many
of Tate's best effects. Ben Belitt has cited the line as an example
of Tate's "sterile periphrases" that result from his effort "to

---

[16] The letter is dated "Sept. 17." Someone has added in pencil "1936." There
are many allusions in the letter which show that 1936 was indeed the year.

[17] Ford Madox Ford, *Provence* (New York, 1935), p. 287.

contrive a *furor poeticus* out of rhetoric and cold sweat."[18] The judgment is harsh but just. The fourth line is diffuse and theoretical. But Tate quickly recovers with one of the best images in all of his work:

> Where we went in the black hull no light moved
> But a gull white-winged along the feckless wave

Even the inaptitude of *feckless* cannot mar this. But then the poem slumps into another dreadful periphrasis:

> The breeze, unseen but fierce as a body loved,
> That boat drove onward like a willing slave.

The picnickers make their landfall and have their meal at the water's edge. In their "secret need" for some direction in their own lives they recall how Aeneas and his men, in fulfillment of a prophecy made by the Harpies, had eaten their trenchers (thought by some scholars to be hard bread shaped and used as platters) when at last they came to the end of their search for a homeland. But though the picnickers played at being adventurers,

> What prophecy of eaten plates could landless
> Wanderers fulfill by the ancient sea?
>
> . . .
>
> What country shall we conquer, what fair land
> Unman our conquest and locate our blood?

The manner of these lines is orotund, as befits the reference to the establishment of Rome. But the answer came swiftly in a colloquial idiom, and the shift in the manner helps to signify the indignity of modern man:

> We've cracked the hemispheres with careless hand!

They have nothing to guide them, no mythic prophecy to sustain them. Without will they drift

> Westward, westward till the barbarous brine
> Whelms us to the tired land where tasseling corn,
> Fat beans, grapes sweeter than muscadine
> Rot on the vine: in that land were we born.

[18] Ben Belitt, " 'The Crabbed Line,' " *The Nation*, CXLVI (January 29, 1938), 133-134.

It is not the soil that is tired, for it is bounteous to excess. Rather, it is the people and the culture, too slack now for a Roman destiny. Commenting on the poem to John Peale Bishop, Tate likened it to the last two stanzas of Matthew Arnold's "The Scholar Gypsy," though he thought his poem more realistic because it was less committed to the illusion of a paradise in the past.[19] If the world of Aeneas was no paradise, at least the Rome he founded stood for law, order, and a society whose least citizen, however far he might journey from the capital city, was sure of his status and his duties. And Rome had a special meaning for Southerners because the gentlemen of the Old South had likened themselves to Romans. To be cut off from the experience of Aeneas was, in a sense, to be cut off from that of Jefferson, Calhoun, and Lee as well. However sanguine was the tone of his Agrarian essays, to judge from his poems that is just what Tate felt himself and his generation to be.

III

When he put himself into "The Oath" Tate indicated to the attentive reader that the estrangement from the past described in "The Mediterranean" was for him more than a matter of the social history of his region. In 1928 he had gone to France as a Guggenheim fellow and had stayed until the end of 1929, when he returned to settle in Clarksville, Tennessee. A little more than five years had passed since he had moved to New York City. Now he was back in the South, living among his own kind far from the centers of modernism but near to Nashville, working on his biography of Lee, and participating in all the glorious uproar over Agrarianism. Then Caroline Gordon was given a Guggenheim fellowship and in the summer of 1932 they went once more to France, where they remained until the spring of 1933, when they returned to Tennessee. On this second sojourn abroad Tate worked on his unpublished book of essays on history and morality and talked with John Peale Bishop about the meaning of their Southernism and their family roots in the past. All these experiences, coming after the nightmare of New York and the new desire for stability and community with other men, had made Tate particularly aware of his feeling for the South and

---

[19] From a letter to Bishop written in Toulon on November 7, 1932.

of the failure of his own family to transmit through the generations the means by which he might "locate his blood." *Ancestors of Exile*, the title which he had chosen for his book of essays and later considered as a title for his novel, *The Fathers*, well sums up the ideas and attitudes of a group of poems about his family and its past which he wrote between 1929 and 1933.

The allusions to the family history in the "Sonnets of the Blood" are so difficult for an outsider to understand that we must proceed with care. Even so, we may assume that the death of Tate's mother in the summer of 1929 helped to turn his attention from the general condition of the Southerners described in his Agrarian essays to his personal relationship with the regional past, for it seems that she had made him especially conscious of his Southern ancestry. At the same time, the sonnets hint, there had come down through her side of the family nearly two centuries of trouble which had helped to alienate Tate and his brothers from their native ground. It had been enough to suggest to Tate a similarity to the house of Atreus, though the reader was not told the grounds for the comparison and F. Cudworth Flint was moved to protest that "Mr. Tate at times seemed an Orestes seeking not only an expiation but also a crime."[20]

"Message from Abroad," written in Paris during Tate's first visit to France, describes an ancestor who may have been known to Lytle, to whom the poem is addressed, but is not identified for the ordinary reader. Nevertheless, the intention of the poem is not in doubt. Tate describes how easily one can recover Provence, the Renascence, the age of Pericles, while one's own past is lost, having no monuments or poetry but only the ruins of a house and the memory of a red-faced man who never came to Paris, where the wind blows at the street-corner but does not point the way. The expatriate can learn nothing from his forbears. "Yours," he says to them, "was a secret fate."

> What did you say mornings?
> Evenings, what?
> The bent eaves
> On the cracked house
> That ghost of a hound. . . .
> The man red-faced and tall

[20] "Five Poets," *The Southern Review*, I (Winter, 1936), 666.

Will cast no shadow
From the province of the drowned.

Baffling and ineffably tantalizing are the two poems, "A Dream"
and "A Vision," which were first published separately but were
placed together under the heading "Records" in *Poems: 1928-1931*
and have so appeared in all subsequent collections of Tate's verse.
In the first, a nine-year-old boy, ill with fever, dreams that he is
walking and conversing with his mother's grandfather. (If, as
seems likely, the poem has an autobiographical basis, then this
figure may have been suggested by Major Lewis Bogan, Tate's
great-grandfather, whose portrait was mentioned in "The Oath.")
The two of them come to a country store, which appears to be
empty. Then "a tall fat man with stringy hair" and "eyes coldly
gray" comes out and speaks to them "with a gravely learned air
. . . from the deep coherence of hell." The sky goes black and the
great-grandfather, "all knowledge in his stare," shudders as the
world falls. From the description of the great-grandfather ("In
knee-breeches silver-buckled like a song / His hair long and a
cocked hat on his head / A straight back and slow dignity for
stride") we may take him as a representative gentleman of the
Old South. Tate's mother was proud of her ties with this group.
The tall fat man standing in his greasy galluses before the dog-run
store suggests that class of Southerners which many readers now
associate with the Snopes family. If this be so, then the confrontation of the two figures may have some symbolic significance in
Tate's attempt to explain the failure of the Old South and his own
forefathers to hand on a way of life. But what passed between
them? Above all, what did the great-grandfather learn from the
words of the other man? We are not told. And our curiosity is
piqued all the more when we recall that exactly this incident occurs
in *The Fathers* at the point where the meaning of George Posey's
character and ordeal is being explained to Lacy Buchan. As Lacy
wanders in a delirium, his grandfather Buchan, whose portrait
had hung in the parlor at Pleasant Hill, appears and seems to
walk beside him down the road. (Pleasant Hill, it will be remembered, was the name of the place in Virginia belonging to
Tate's mother's family. Like the house in the novel it was burned
by Yankees.) Lacy's grandfather's hair was long, his hat was

cocked, and his silver buckles, too, were like a song. He and Lacy stop at a dog-run and speak to a fat man with stringy hair and cold gray eyes who tells them that Virginia has seceded and the Yankees are coming. Then he addresses the grandfather in a language that Lacy does not understand. It is after this that the grandfather tells Lacy why Posey is driven down his path of self-destruction. But what did the man say? Is it what the figure in the poem said? What connection, if any, does the encounter have with the history of Tate's family and his sense of disaster transmitted through the blood? Do the forces embodied in George Posey have something to do with it? Is there some significance in the fact, which we learn from the "Sonnets of the Blood," that a member of the family became a captain of industry and thus, as it were, a spiritual heir of Posey? We are not told. Instead, we are tantalized by the reappearance in "A Vision" of what seems to be the same tall man now grown old and near death. A young man, light of heart, is walking home from a visit with his sweetheart.

> A stern command froze him to the spot
> And then a tall thin man with stringy hair
> Fear in his eyes his breath quick and hot
> His arms lank and his neck a little twisted
> Spoke, and the trees sifted the air:
> "I'm growing old," he said, "you have no choice,"
> And said no more, but his bright eyes insisted
> Incalculably with his relentless voice.

That is all. What is his hold upon the boy? What is their relationship? Is he indeed the man who stood before the dog-run in "A Dream"? Is he perhaps some descendant of that man? Is he even the boy's own father? Could he be a poetic image of Tate's father? There is some resemblance between him and the father figures in Tate's earlier "Poem for My Father" (later retitled "A Pauper"—the pauper being not the father but the son) and his later "Seasons of the Soul." Flint, who came right out with what others have felt about the "Sonnets of the Blood," in another review cited these two poems when mildly rebuking Tate for using the traditions of his own family in ways that require rather than bestow illumination.[21] As poems they do little more than excite curiosity, but the student of Tate's work can surmise that there were forces in Tate's past that deeply oppressed him.

Though he has not chosen to say what they were, their effect on the spirit and on the general tenor of the poems about his family is best conveyed by "The Ancestors," which, when it was first published in *The New Republic* in November, 1933, bore the motto "(After J. P. B.)"—a reference to Bishop, with whom Tate had discussed the heritage of the modern man of letters. Looking to that time of day which of all was for him most fascinating and dreaded, the moment of "The flickered pause between the day and night" when ancient failure begs for a new start, Tate described the response of the intuition to something which the reason will not admit:

> The bones hear but the eyes will never see—
> Punctilious abyss, the yawn of space
> Come once a day to suffocate the sight.
> There is no man on earth who can be free
> Of this, the eldest in the latest crime.

It is the abyss described in *The Fathers* as opening beneath all men—the dark depth of pure quality, the original sin or evil Nature that is in all men, however they would deny it with their bright faith in reason and its enterprises. This is the "eldest crime" which the ancestors, unmentioned in the poem itself, pass down to their heirs.

This fine poem links those on the corrupt heritage with another group written in the same period on the nature of evil and the loss of inherited religious beliefs which gave man his only means of coping with it. In "The Fallacy of Humanism" and "Remarks on the Southern Religion" Tate had described nature as a maelstrom of particularity in which all the forms and values by which man knows and governs himself are dissolved. The great virtue of religion, he maintained with Ransom, was its successful representation of evil in its myths and dogmas and its placing of protective barriers between nature and man. In "The Cross" these ideas are

[21] From an untitled review of *Poems: 1928-1931* in *Symposium*, III (July, 1932), 410-411.

made explicit, but the poem must have bewildered the readers of *The Saturday Review of Literature*, where it first appeared on January 18, 1930, who had not been studying his essays attentively, for it is a most difficult work. It tells how

> Long ago
> Flame burst out of a secret pit
> Crushing the world with such a light
> The day-sky fell to moonless black,
> The kingly sun to hateful night
> For those once seeing, turning back.

In the pit stands a "blinding rood." Those who see it lose all desire for the things of the natural world; or if they still long for them they become monsters "instructed by the fiery dead." One thinks of the hellish knowledge which caused the great-grandfather of "A Dream" to shudder as the world fell.

The poem telescopes many symbols and muted allusions which cannot be rearranged for contemplation in any precise order. Roughly speaking, however, it suggests that the true site of the Cross is Hell because Christian doctrine, which instructs man in the meaning of good, also teaches him the meaning of evil. It is, in fact, the source of evil, for without the doctrine there would be none. Here Tate agrees with Ransom, who in *God Without Thunder* praised the myths of the Old Testament for their realism in making God the author of both good and evil. The knowledge symbolized by the Cross destroys natural innocence, and the men who possess it must hate nature or be perverted by their hellish wisdom. The strange conceits, involute reasoning, and diction suggest the influence of John Donne at his most finical, but the terms of the argument do not have the exactness one expects of Donne, and the lack makes the syntax and dialectic exceedingly hard to follow. Even with the hint provided by the title, it is difficult to make out the meaning of the lines

> For love so hates mortality
> Which is the providence of life
> She will not let it blessed be. . . .

Yet on these depends the whole sense of the poem. "Love" is Christianity, the love of God, the love of good, and "mortality" is nature or the natural condition. Moreover, understanding is further impeded by the ambiguity of pronominal references, and by choosing the wrong antecedents one can make the poem yield meanings wholly at odds with Tate's thought. It is only by virtue of the explanation of the poem which Tate set down in a letter to Miss Ursula Eder that the reading given here is presented with any confidence.[22]

Though some of its lines bristle with difficulties, the meaning of "The Twelve," one of Tate's best poems, is somewhat easier to reach. The disciples, now just "twelve ragged men . . . twelve living dead," kneel in prayer to Christ, whose words once

> seared the western heart
> With the fire of the wind, the thick and the fast
> Whirl of the damned in the heavenly storm. . . .

But the wind is empty. Christ does not appear, charity is become a fatherless child, His words no longer matter. So

> the twelve lie in the sand by the dry rock
> Seeing nothing—the sand, the tree, rocks
> Without number—and turn away the face
> To the mind's briefer and more desert place.

It is not hard to make out the failure of belief and the desolation of the modern spirit as the primary themes of the poem, but the conceptions of Christ and Christianity are uncertain. He is called "the victor of Rome," and the poem says that at the Crucifixion, "His eyes cold with that inhuman ecstasy," He "Cried the last word, the accursed last / Of the forsaken. . . ." Two possible interpretations present themselves. Christ's words seared the western heart with knowledge of good and evil and the possibility of damnation. Such knowledge put an end to the old easy relationship with nature and turned it into a stony desert. Or: Christ triumphed over Rome and undermined the rule of human law and order and then took away support for divine law and order when, anticipating the unanswered prayers of His disciples, He cried "Why hast Thou forsaken me?" He denied the sanction behind

---

[22] The letter is dated April 4, 1957. Miss Eder, a close reader of Tate's verse, gave a different interpretation in her doctoral dissertation, *The Poetry of Allen Tate* (University of Wisconsin, 1955).

His own teachings. These readings are not contradictory and both may have been intended. But whether we chose one, both, or neither, it is apparent that Christ's inhuman words were a curse upon life and now His followers have not even the comfort of belief in the curse but are turned back upon the vacuity of their own thoughts.

Such, for different reasons, is the fate of Lewis Carroll's little girl in "Last Days of Alice." Now grown lazy, mammoth but not fat, she has become the symbol of modern man—indeed, of the whole of western civilization. She has passed from the natural world through the narcissistic machinery of science and technology, into the world of abstractions. These are but reflections of her own desires, of her appetitive self, for Tate agreed with Ransom that science is the formulation of man's appetites and the means for satisfying them. When she embraced the image of herself seen in her science, she lost contact with everything outside her that was needed to fulfill her humanity. As Tate put it in "The Fallacy of Humanism," under science "nature becomes a closed system of abstractions in which man is deprived of all experience whatever and, by being so deprived, reduced to an abstraction himself." She is locked within this reduced self, trapped like the solipsistic naturalist of "Ode to the Confederate Dead." The poem ends with a prayer made without hope:

> —We too back to the world shall never pass
> Through the shattered door, a dumb shade-harried crowd
> Being all infinite, function, depth and mass
> Without figure, a mathematical shroud
>
> Hurled at the air—blessed without sin!
> O God of our flesh, return us to Your wrath,
> Let us be evil could we enter in
> Your grace, and falter on the stony path!

"Let us be evil. . . !" Better the hazard of evil and the painful stumbling on the path to grace than the meaningless state and inability to act of Alice.

Such is also the theme of "The Meaning of Life," a wholly successful poem that belongs among the half-dozen or so of Tate's finest works. Unlike "The Oath" and "Last Days of Alice," it

400

holds that some action is still possible and can keep the abstract idea from smothering reality in which man must live if he is to remain a man. Recalling that he had once resolved on abstract principles to refrain from violent action, Tate says,

> I know at thirty-three that one must shoot
> As often as one gets the rare chance—
> In killing there is more than commentary.

The poem concludes with a magnificent image of the force in man that charges him with a passion for concrete experience stronger than any ideas:

> One's sense of the proper decoration alters
> But there's a kind of lust feeds on itself
> Unspoken to, unspeaking; subterranean
> As a black river full of eyeless fish
> Heavy with spawn: with a passion for time
> Longer than the arteries of a cave.

"Time" is history, action, and the cave is Plato's: the abstract, idealistic intellect. But the black river is no simple good thing, for Tate is no nature enthusiast, no primitivist of the instincts. It is the dark flood at the bottom of the abyss; it flows through the lives of the Buchans and the Poseys past the place where Yellow Jim is shot and Brother Semmes dies.

But it is better than nothing. Such, too, is the thesis of "Shadow and Shade," Tate's best and most nearly perfect poem. Two lovers watch the movement of light and darkness on a wall:

> The shadow streamed into the wall—
> The wall, break-shadow in the blast;
> We lingered wordless while a tall
> Shade enclouded the shadow's cast.

Streamed into and the oblique reference to a breakwater give the shadow the palpable substance of dark water, a familiar sexual symbol, resisted by the wall, which may signify such abstract inhibitions as kept Ransom's equilibrists apart. But when all but the air about them has vanished in the concentration of their passion, the lover cleaves his beloved's shadow with his shade even as the shadow streamed into the wall. Then, their love consummated,

I asked fair shadow at my side:
What more shall fiery shade require?
We lay long in the immense tide
Of shade and shadowy desire

And saw the dusk assail the wall,
The black surge, mounting, crash the stone!
Companion of this lust, we fall,
I said, lest we should die alone.

After their lovemaking comes that most ambiguous moment, the hour of dusk, when, it was said in "The Ancestors," "the bones hear but the eyes will never see," and the ancient failure, the eldest crime, begs for a new start. The bright, geometric, empty world of daylight, walls, and reason has been overwhelmed by darkness and instinct. The lovers have fallen—into an imperfect but genuine community. What they have done *matters*. In love, as in killing, there is more than commentary. If, as seems likely, Donne was an influence, then the influence has been wholly assimilated. Tate has made with masterly ease and restraint the point which he failed to get across with all his excited talk about the great and sinful lovers of the past in "Retroduction" and "Causerie." The poem is beautifully articulated and moves with perfect pacing toward the final word which caps the whole. The separate details do not spend themselves in random thrusts away from the poem but gather force as they move toward a total poetic energy far greater than the sum of all the single energies. By the time the last lines are reached, that energy is so immense that we half expect it to burst from the formal order; it does not seem likely that Tate can hold everything in balance until the final tremendous syllable is sounded. But he does, and the effect is stunning. If only, one thinks, he had chosen to obtain the power he so admires by such organization rather than by piling up violent but discrete details. Of the poems published before this one appeared in *The New Republic* on August 9, 1933, only "The Cross" and "The Twelve" approach it in power and beauty and only "The Wolves," though a less tightly constructed poem, may be its equal. "The Paradigm," which also suggests Donne's influence, has one or two superb images, but the figures become raveled and the poem crumples under the strain of its excessive ingenuity.

During the next three years Tate worked on *The Fathers* and collaborated with Herbert Agar in editing *Who Owns America?* To make ends meet he taught English at Southwestern College in Memphis. There was time for only a few new poems, among them "To the Lacedemonians," and of these only "The Robber Bridegroom," the only published poem bearing any resemblance to Ransom's verse, had an artistic merit comparable to that of "Shadow and Shade." Late in 1936 Tate prepared for the press his *Selected Poems*, which was published early in the next year. For it he took thirteen poems from *Mr. Pope and Other Poems*, all of the poems except for one of the "Sonnets of the Blood" from *Poems: 1928-1931*, and all but "Ivory Tower" from *The Mediterranean and Other Poems*. ("Aeneas in New York," the satirical retort to Archibald MacLeish mentioned in the last chapter, has never been reprinted in a book.) The fifty-six poems chosen from fourteen years of writing beginning with the first number of *The Fugitive* represented his best work. It is a small garner that should have been smaller by several poems such as "The Idiot" and some of the "Sonnets of the Blood," which were revised but little improved. Ten, at most a dozen, are distinguished poems. All of these were first published between 1930 and 1936 and most between 1931 and 1933. The rest ranged downward from some good but flawed pieces like "Mr. Pope" through clumsy ones like "Ode to the Confederate Dead" to the calamitous second "Sonnet at Christmas." To be blunt, it does not seem much to show for so many years of work by the one Fugitive who set out to become a professional poet.

Tate's achievement will be considered closely later in this chapter, but we may pause for a moment to note some of the changes that had taken place since *Mr. Pope and Other Poems*. The most striking is the closer integration among details which are scarcely less intrinsically energetic and difficult to control than those in the earlier poems. Tate still lost his grip from time to time and was capable of abominable lapses of taste. In "The Anabasis," written in memory of Lytle's mother, he described her standing on the stairs as "Meridional and true" and cried "Re-corporated be!" But he had gotten far enough away from his absorption in the separate element to be more attentive to the requirements of the whole. His diction and imagery both supported and received more support from his subject so that form and content did not tend to become separated in the reader's mind. And as the elements worked more and more together, they directed attention away from the poet and toward the poem, which was not so insistently personal even when it was based upon Tate's experience or the history of his family. Even so, one cannot wholly put aside the impression that some of the cryptic passages were withheld from the reader in a deliberate attempt, which may have been almost unconscious, to awe him into submission to the poet's will. Yet most instances of obscurity seem to be the consequence of trying to do more things than the space and the nature of the medium permitted. Some of the poems such as "The Eagle" resemble in their organization the compositions of Karlheinz Stockhausen and other followers of Anton von Webern, whose staggering complexities are visible to the eye but cannot be heard by the ear; that is, Tate's passages may yield their secrets to the laboring analytic faculty but they do not evoke any response from the sensibility. Even so, he had come a long, long way toward mastering his art, for he cared more about what he was saying than about impressing the reader with how he said it and with himself as a devilishly clever young man.

IV

If Tate had to stand on his *Selected Poems* he would be remembered as a poet of a few excellent pieces and many others that aimed high, made quite a stir about themselves and their splendid intentions, and fell short of the mark. But though he published little poetry in the six years that followed the appearance of that volume, some of it, taken with the best of his earlier work, entitled him to a place among the important American poets of the first half of this century. These were years of protracted crisis, and the poems are testaments of a withering despair. It is a wonder that they were even written. Many things worked to defeat the spirit. There was the disappointment over Agrarianism, in which Tate had made a profound emotional investment. Because he so needed the assurance of an external order, ties with the past and participation in a stable, conservative culture meant more to him than to Ransom. The Agrarians' failure to win any support from the

Southern community seemed to signify rejection by the society to which, after an interval of withdrawal, he had pledged his loyalties with the fervor of the convert. And the rejection was all the more corrosive because he had been singled out for ridicule by other Southerners. Then came the collapse of *Free America*, the forced abandonment of plans to work with Ransom, Ransom's friendly but firm demurrer from his views on positivism, and the outbreak of the war. The fall of France was for him a personal horror and fearful omen of the triumph of the dehumanized mass mind and its mechanisms over the last remnants of the splendor and spirit of Old Europe. He had loved that land, which seemed akin to the Old South, and now it, too, was gone. Things looked better in America but, as he wrote in the frenzied prose of "The Present Function of Criticism," which is a terrible index of his despair, beneath the bland surface they were the same. In the statements of our war aims and our descriptions of the good world to come he saw the ultimate victory of instrumentalism. Already compelled by his interests and his profession to live on the edge and often against the society of his times, he now found himself thrust further from the center of feeling as men united around slogans and aspirations with which he had little or no sympathy. He was like his own George Posey, shut out after he had made a great effort to escape the confinement of his ego and achieve fellowship based upon attitudes and affections come down from a common past. In his isolation he sometimes wondered if there were anything for which a poet should live.

For three years after preparing *Selected Poems* for the press Tate published no new verse but worked on his dramatization of "The Turn of the Screw," his second (unpublished) novel, and his essays on poetry and criticism. When he reappeared as poet in the autumn of 1939 it was with an appalling exercise in metaphysical conceits called "The Trout Map," which had the unhappy distinction of containing the worst line in all of his work: "The ego'd belly's dry cartograph." It is scarcely credible that one who had written "Shadow and Shade" could allow such a poem to leave his desk; yet with all his achievement he was still capable of the widest variance in taste where his own work was concerned. In the next four years he published ten poems, among them both his masterpiece, "Seasons of the Soul," and a sonnet, the fourth in a sequence entitled "More Sonnets at Christmas," nearly as inept as the "Sonnets of the Blood." But good or bad, the poems had one theme, the unmitigated and hopeless defeat of the spirit.

Four of them described a cretinous, amoral culture in which there was no place for the man of letters. The American Dream had become a false nightmare: it was "false" because it was no hallucination but reality. The land for which the exiles of "Emblems" and "The Mediterranean" had longed and for which the Agrarians had striven had been raped. Yet the nation which had violated it was impotent and onanistic; Walt Whitman, its spiritual father, had left no sons. From such velleity a New Kingdom was supposed to be coming and in "Jubilo" Tate wondered what would become of the poet who had taken no part in the war effort that was to bring it to pass:

> After the dry and sticking tongue
> After our incivility
> Who will inflate the poet's lung
> Gone flat of this indignity
>   Till the Day of Jubilo?

The poet and the scholar, men with a sense of the past such as that which had directed his own meditations and loyalties, were utterly empty and debilitated. Perhaps they could be revived with a transfusion, and if the blood were used up for the Day of Jubilo, science would find surrogates to maintain a semblance of life:

> Salt serum stays his arteries
> Sly tide threading the ribs of sand,
> Till his lost being dries, and cries
> For that unspeakable salt land
>   Beyond the Day of Jubilo.

The whole poem takes its meaning from the phrase "unspeakable salt land," which suggests Palestine, Christ, and the "rocky way" of "Last Days of Alice." It is a *salt* land because it is harsh, lonely, and far from the abundance and ebullience of the New Kingdom. It is *unspeakable* because the poet can no longer tell others about it: he is speechless and his language cannot be understood. But there is another side to this icon. The salt land is a desert where the disciples described in "The Twelve" wander in unbelief, and it is unspeakable because the words which once could be spoken now have no meaning. The poet desires the lost Old Kingdom of God, but does not believe in it.

The best of these poems is the superb "Ode to Our Young Pro-Consuls of the Air," which like the satires of Dryden, Pope, and Swift surpasses its moment to become a great indictment of human folly. Here the occasion was the publication of Archibald Mac-Leish's pamphlet *The Irresponsibles* (1940), a preposterous indictment of contemporary writers for having weakened the moral fiber of western civilization and prepared the way for Hitler. The poem begins with the present scene:

> Once more the country calls
> From sleep, as from his doom,
>> Each citizen to take
>> His modest stake
> Where the sky falls
> With a Pacific boom.

The speaker wonders, "What might I have done / (A poet alone)?" and for answer looks to the childish version of history in which the heroes of the past are reduced to the stature of toy soldiers. He sees that while the bad guys, the decadent writers, were corrupting the simple, nursery-tale world of the good guys, he himself had stood aside. Then came Pearl Harbor.

> It was defeat, or near it!
> Yet all that feeble time
>> Brave Brooks and lithe MacLeish
>> Had sworn to thresh
> Our flagging spirit
> With literature made Prime!

The good citizens of Cow Creek and Bear Wallow, enervated by T. S. Eliot, were revived by reading *The Irresponsibles*. The nation was saved.

Thus far the poem was witty but superficial, resembling in its ingenious rhymes (*Eliotic-patriotic*) the topical verses of Marya Mannes. Then in the last five stanzas Tate, without giving way to any of the undisciplined rage of "Retroduction" or his prose attacks on socio-political critics, turned the poem into a terrible indictment of the new imperialism which destroyed old cultures in the name of the commonweal. Young aviators are pro-consuls of a technology so subhuman that it recalls the Jurassic Period. They range the planet, seeking those civilizations whose values are religious rather than mechanico-reptilian:

> O animal excellence,
> Take pterodactyl flight
> > Fire-winged into the air. . . .

> Take off, O gentle youth,
> And coasting India
> > Scale crusty Everest
> > Whose mythic crest
> Resists your truth:
> And spying far away

> Upon the Tibetan plain
> A limping caravan,
> > Dive, and exterminate
> > The Lama, late
> Survival of old pain.
> Go kill the dying swan.

The pterodactyl and the swan—in their confrontation Tate summed up more than he had said in all his fulminations against positivism. Not only because they are so apt but because they culminate a poem which for controlled order and concentration belongs with "Shadow and Shade" and "The Meaning of Life" at the height of Tate's achievement in formal beauty and artistic merit.

In "The Winter Mask" Tate turned to the private scene and found the nadir of despair. The poem puts the question implicit in the others: in time of war, that winter of the soul, what is there worth living for? The speaker discovers in himself a perverse determination to separate action from belief and live by sense alone. Not even one as wise as Yeats can explain

> Why it is man hates
> His own salvation,
> And finds his last safety
> In the self-made curse that bore
> Him towards damnation:
> The drowned undrowned by the sea,
> The sea worth living for.

This poem denies the qualified affirmations of "The Meaning of Life" and "Shadow and Shade," for the sea worth living for is *not* the dark flood of those poems but rather the "water of life," the holy water of religious belief. When he chooses instead the "last safety" of immersion in the dark flood, which is here called a "self-made curse," man tries to put himself beyond all responsibility for his acts. But this is the same as putting himself beyond all possibility of remaining human and being saved. Man, the poem imports, is mysteriously and compulsively self-destructive.

Tate told John Peale Bishop that he regarded this poem as "a mere warming up" for "Seasons of the Soul," which is written in the same difficult stanza.[23] It could have served as the third or "winter" section of the longer poem, for man's self-destructiveness is a primary theme of "Seasons," as is made plain by the epigraph taken from Dante's *Inferno*, XIII, 31-33: "Then I put forth my hand slightly and tore a small branch from a great thorn tree; its trunk cried, 'Why do you rend me?'" The rending occurred when Dante and Vergil had reached the second ring of the seventh circle of Hell, where dwelt the souls of those who had done themselves injury, and the speaker, now blind and imprisoned in a tree, is one who had slain himself. Though there is no allusion to Hart Crane in the poem, the condition of the speaker calls to mind Tate's description of the locked-in sensibility of his friend, who killed himself; it also reminds one of the solipsism and self-destructive skepticism of the *reveur* in "Ode to the Confederate Dead." By the epigraph Tate signified the importance of the *Divina Commedia* for the poem. There are numerous allusions to the *Inferno*, and the ending takes much of its meaning from the implied comparison between the condition of Dante, who was brought by Beatrice to salvation, and that of the speaker in the poem, who is suing Santa Monica, the Mother of Silences, to tell him if he is dying into an absolute nothingness or will be reborn in grace. The issue is left in doubt, for she does not reply.

When the poem was first published in *The Kenyon Review* in the winter of 1944, the sections bore as titles not the names of the seasons but the names of the elements, fire, air, water, and earth, arranged in the cyclic pattern of Heraclitus, who taught that in times of war and violence all things move downward to the earth

[23] From a letter to Bishop dated February 13, 1943.

whence there leaps anew the flame of life. The poem follows the disintegration of the soul as it progresses toward the grave. At the outset it is poised upon the moment when the dissociations of knowledge and belief, intellect and feeling, mind and body, and meaning and action will begin:

> Summer, this is our flesh,
> The body you let mature;
> If now while the body is fresh
> You take it, shall we give
> The heart, lest heart endure
> The mind's tattering
> Blow of greedy claws?
> Shall mind itself still live
> If like a hunting king
> It falls to the lion's jaws?

The lion may be intended to remind the reader of the one which terrified Dante before Vergil came to his aid (*Inferno*, 1, 43-48). Alone, the soul cannot withstand the summer's whirl of fire, which is natural energy,

> Unless by sleight or fast
> It seize or deny its day
> To make the eye secure.

By some religious dogma, or trick as it would seem to the positivists, or by ascetic denial, the soul must protect itself against the summer. For the child it had been a period of innocence like that interval, referred to in "The Cross," before the knowledge of good and evil was brought to man. But now France has been overrun, war is loose, and the soul of the adult is set upon the downward cycle. Abruptly the scene shifts to Hell:

> Two men of our summer world
> Descended the winding hell
> And when their shadows curled
> They fearfully confounded
> The vast concluding shell:
> Stopping, they saw in the narrow
> Light a centaur pause
> And gaze, then his astounded

Beard, with a notched arrow
Part back upon his jaws.

In Canto Twelve of the *Inferno* Dante and Vergil encounter Chiron, the wise centaur, who parts his beard with an arrow so that he can speak to his fellows and tell them that Dante is alive. When Vergil has explained Dante's mission, Chiron asks the centaur Nessus to carry them over the river of blood. Eventually they come to the forest of the suicides, where Dante plucks the twig mentioned in the epigraph. But in Tate's poem the significance of the encounter with the Chiron is obscure. Perhaps the other man is Bishop, to whose memory the poem was dedicated. He may have served as Tate's Vergil in discussions which took them into an imagined hell. Perhaps, too, the allusion to the meeting is an oblique way of suggesting the temptation to escape the enveloping flames of summer by self-immolation.

In the next section, "Autumn," fire gives way to the air of loneliness. The speaker finds himself in a well that is transformed into a cold and empty hall. In Canto Thirty-three of the *Inferno* Friar Alberigo explains to Dante that the soul may descend into a cistern, the ninth circle of ice, where dwell those who betrayed their own kind, while on earth its body is inhabited by a demon and continues to move about. The speaker remembers his own family and how he tried to escape from it. He sees his father, who resembles the strange figure in "A Vision," and his mother, who will neither look at nor speak to him. Have they betrayed him? Have their bodies been used by demons? Is there, perhaps, some intended analogue with Tate's experience when, after the tumult of his years in New York, he tried to overcome his loneliness by reestablishing ties with the "ancestors of exile"?

In the soul's winter of despair, the reader turns to Venus, all other gods having perished, and like the lover of "Shadow and Shade" tries to find some companionship and awareness of being through lust and immersion in the dark flood. He plumbs the subconscious, the instinctual life, where

> In the centre of his cage
> The pacing animal
> Surveys the jungle cove
> And slicks his slithering wiles

> To turn the venereal awl
> In the livid wound of love.

But this attempt to drown in sensuality is really a form of immolation. Beneath the waters of the winter sea he breaks a branch from a tree of coral. Blood runs and speaks, as once it spoke to Dante.

> "We are the men who died
> Of self-inflicted woe,
> Lovers whose stratagem
> Led to their suicide."
> I touched my sanguine hair
> And felt it drip above
> Their brother who, like them,
> Was maimed and did not bear
> The living wound of love.

Then it is spring, the season of the earth. The speaker remembers the pleasant land of his childhood, and feels the faint stir of life and hope, which he mistrusts:

> In time of bloody war
> Who will know the time?
> Is it a new spring star
> Within the timing chill,
> Talking, or just a mime,
> That rises in the blood . . . ?

At first he thinks it a false star. Why, then, should he like Sisyphus begin his labors all over again? In anger at the uncertainty of his fate he speaks roughly to Santa Monica, the mother of Saint Augustine, who had waited patiently while her son in his unbelief had run through the seasons of his soul and who, when he had come at last to belief, held quiet conversation with him at her window in a garden overlooking Ostia:

> Come, old woman, save
> Your sons who have gone down
> Into the burning cave:
> Come, mother, and lean
> At the window with your son

And gaze through its light frame
These fifteen centuries
Upon the shirking scene
Where men, blind, go lame:
Then, mother of silences,

Speak, that we may hear. . . .

But she has nothing to say to those who have descended to the hellish cave, which may be a symbol of scientific naturalism, since the image suggests Plato's cave, and both Ransom and Tate were inclined to see science and Plato's idealism as forms of abstract thought to which they gave the generic name of "Platonism." The poem ends with the speaker wondering

Whether your kindness, mother,
Is mother of silences.

Perhaps she refrains from speaking because it would be cruel to foretell the fate that is coming with a new cycle of seasons. Even so, the speaker would be glad to have his doubts laid, if only by the knowledge that death is simply death and the naturalistic conception of the universe is the true one. But he is left in uncertainty. The question of "A Winter Mask," "What is worth living for?" has not been answered.

While he was working on this poem Tate read his essay, "The Hovering Fly," as a Mesures Lecture at Princeton, and the poem illustrates well the principle for fiction set forth in that work and later, as we know, informally incorporated into his theory of poetry. It renders its ideas in rich and immediate images that have the power of a symbolic naturalism like that which he later praised in the poetry of Dante. Many of these images—"the gray light like shale / Thin, crumbling, and dry" of the "Autumn" section and the sexual metaphors of the "Winter" section, for example—are especially evocative and linger in the mind when the poem has been put aside. The short lines and the complex and difficult rhyme pattern (ABACBDECDE) give them an extra force and carry the reader across the few awkward and bombastic phrases, such as "sea-conceited scop," which means simply poet confused by desire. Occasionally Tate grew careless with his stanzas, setting the shape of his ideas against them for no apparent reason, or in the passage

413

on the encounter with Chiron quoted above, using the runover line
so loosely that his meter was displaced. And here and there are
patches of the old overwriting:

> Back in my native prime
> I saw the orient corn
> All space but no time
> Reaching for the sun
> Of the land where I was born. . . .

But most of the poem shows the restraint and careful articulation
which gave so much strength to "Ode to Our Young Pro-Consuls
of the Air."

After the structural metaphor of the cycle of seasons and elements, the most important major technical device used is the sequence of references to the *Inferno*. It is only partially successful
because the references are intermittent and erratic. The Chiron
episode is so abruptly introduced and dropped that one cannot understand its purpose, though it helps prepare for the allusion to
the episode in the wood of the suicides. The parallel between Dante
among the thorn trees and the poet in the phosphorescent depths
among the madrepore corals is too contrived, and the symbols of
blood and water get mixed up. The best use of Dante is made in
the implied comparison at the end, which helps to extend the scope
of the poem from the private ordeal of the speaker to the spiritual
disintegration of western civilization. This is excellent, but it might
have been even better if the parallels with Dante's poem had been
more consistently maintained and had been made a more integral
part of the total organization.

Yet when one stands away from the poem, these faults recede
from the memory, and what remains is an impression of great intensity and grandeur of scope and significance. "Seasons of the
Soul" has its blemishes, but all in all it is without question Tate's
greatest achievement in poetry thus far. In the two decades since
it appeared he has published "The Eye," another poem on the failure of the father, portions of which are twisted beyond comprehension, two ephemeral "conceits for the eye," and three sections
of a long autobiographical poem in *terza rima* which is still in
progress. It is not profitable to comment on a work so ambitious
and often cryptic with only discrete portions before us. One waits

with great interest for the finished work. Perhaps it will remove some of the ambiguities of the earlier poems occasioned by allusions to personal experiences.

V

When one looks back across the reach from "Seasons of the Soul" to "Sinbad" and "Impossible," one sees an unbroken line of development in Tate's poetry. Here and there the direction changes by a few degrees as new influences and themes possess his imagination, but there are no sudden breaks or extreme swerves such as occurred in Ransom's work between *Poems About God* and "Necrological." We have referred to the experiments of Tate's earliest poetry; that may be a term too dignified to describe what was often more than not just playing with words. Nevertheless, among the seemingly chancy collocations of eccentric phrases and twitching rhythms one senses a definite imagination at work. Even in the obscurities there is a powerful personal style, which maintains its larger coherence and unity beneath the incoherent lines and gives continuity to the evolution of Tate's verse from the trifling and posing at the outset to the agony and beauty that flash in the latest work. Like Ransom's, this style creates a universe and discovers and judges for us qualities in our own.

What impresses one about that style in the recent poems is just what impressed one on reading the earliest, the predilection for diction and imagery representing a destructive violence before which man is a passive and helpless victim. (When he does act, it is, ultimately, against himself.) As the years pass, there is some diminution in the violence of the manner of the poems, but none in the universe which they make visible nor any in the fear and despair which it inspires. If anything, the violence of the universe is more ferocious and the feelings are more trenchant as the energies of the separate elements of the poems are concentrated by Tate's improving craftsmanship. There is, too, another reason for the intensification related to and perhaps a cause of the superior technique: the presence in the poems of certain archetypal images which polarize the imagination. The violence accumulates and swirls about them; upon them the vision of the universe is formed. They are: action that rips and splinters, fire that blinds and sears, blood

415

that throbs with evil passions and instincts, and darkness that over-whelms the will. Together they form a landscape of horror and terror across which obscure and massive forces push man to the edge of hysteria.

Despite the improved technique and the unifying effect of the polarization, the predilection for violence affects deleteriously the organization of the poems, not so much in the prosody, which tends, after the early fooling around, toward the conventional, as in the ragged syntax, the tangled metaphors, and the grating frictions among the elements and their effects. For the attitude of the poetic imagination toward violence is ambivalent: violence is frightening and fascinating, hated and loved. So fascinating and so much loved, indeed, that, as has been many times observed in this study, exploiting the separate forces of violent words and images, even increasing the frictions among them, often appear to matter much more than integrating the poem, though as a critic Tate was unusually sensitive to and appreciative of integration. The ad-mirer of stability and order wrote poetry that tends constantly toward instability and disorder; the traditionalist and authoritarian was an artist with a penchant for anarchy.

The ambivalence toward violence and the division of sympathies help to account for two curious and related contradictions in Tate's poetry and poetics. The first is that though his poetic imagination is so drawn to the powerful detail that it neglects or violates the poem as a whole thing-in-itself, Tate attaches far more importance to the ideas that appear in his poems than do many poets. Paul Weiss has been quoted for observing that ideas are for most artists simply guide-lines which can be abandoned in the fury of com-position; the creation of a work of art counts for more than ex-position of a particular argument. Judging from the ways in which he interrupted or disfigured the arguments of his poems, one might suppose that Weiss's observation certainly applied to Tate. Not so, however. The ideas mattered immensely to him. Much of the con-fusion in his poetry comes from his inability to effect a harmonious compromise between his interest in detail and his interest in the idea, though often the interest in detail seems to get the best of it. The second contradiction was discussed at some length in the chap-ter on Tate's prose. He to whom ideas in poetry mattered so much attacked what he called the Doctrine of Relevance and insisted vehemently upon their inutility. Even though his ideas were concerned with values and right conduct, it was the application to human affairs of precisely such ideas, taken out of poetry, that he opposed. We have seen how he worked his way out of this contradiction and we will not review his progress here. It is enough to observe that it is related to his interest in the brilliant detail. He was determined that none of the detail's fullness of being should be sacrificed to the Big Idea by either the poet or the reader.

Summing up these general observations we may say—a little too broadly—that the forces of the imagination at work in the poetry were divisive, yet the very division itself is, paradoxically, a feature of a consistent style which presents us with a unique vision of the universe. To understand how consistency obtains among divisive forces, to understand the vision, we must consider that imagination.

In the discussion of Tate's prose it was asserted that the central concern of all of his mature work was the same as the central concern of Ransom's: man's relation to the cosmos and the acquisition and right use of the knowledge needed to guide him in that relation. The cosmos—Nature—was envisioned as a great welter of Pure Quality in which, if he lacked knowledge and did not control his conduct, man would dissolve. It was pointed out that there abided in the prose works three archetypal symbols encompassing Nature: darkness, the flood, and the abyss. The environment they represented tended to be more interior than exterior, not so much the universe impinging on man's senses as one consisting of his responses to the impingement and his passions and instinctual impulses. The poetry, on the other hand, takes its metaphors from man's physical and social milieux, but its universe is wholly interior. Its archetypal symbols are not quite the same as those of the prose though they belong to the same genus and the symbols of the prose often appear among the images of the poetry. But no exact distinction is needed, for the difference is one of degrees of interiorness, concreteness, and particularity. The universe of the poetry which man tries to understand and against which he strives to preserve his being is, like the universe of the prose, a welter of Quality. Recreated in the mind's eye of the reader it is more brilliant, palpable, and substantial; yet it is the subjective world of one poetic imagination. It is many times smaller than the universe of the prose, but

417

we are able to know much more about it. The poetry looks into its deepest recesses.

Such is the character of the poetry that the imagination which created and dwells within this universe becomes for the reader a distinct *persona* of which he is constantly aware. Many things make it so: Tate's role-playing in the early verse, the tendency of the violence and eccentricity of the surface of the poems to deflect attention to the presumptive "personality" of the poet, the themes, the introspective treatment of them, the use of a first-person speaker, and the reference to the speaker's traits. The *persona* is a man of letters whose struggles to know and defend himself against the universe are presented in terms of his relations with the society of the times and, most of all, with himself. His inward experiences test and qualify the ideas set forth in Tate's prose. Thus, for example, the argument for the necessity of myth proposed in the essays on Emily Dickinson and Edwin Arlington Robinson is put to the test of "Causerie," "Last Days of Alice," and "Seasons of the Soul." Obviously, therefore, much of the value of Tate's poetry depends upon the character of the *persona* and its imagined life. How much is it one of us, its interior world our world—or at least our interior worlds, and its imagined life our life?

Though he used autobiographical materials in his poetry, that *persona* is not Tate and never has been, even when he tried to persuade the reader that it was. It is—and the point must be insisted upon—only the poetic imagination manifest in the poems. To carry exactness to the farthest extreme, the *persona* is not even the speaker in the poems written in the first person: it is the imagination addressing us through the mask of the speaker. (The speaker, then, is the *persona* of the *persona!*) No doubt there are moments when Tate much resembles the *persona*. It could not be otherwise, since his actual imagination is responsible for the creation of the works in which the *persona* is displayed. But for that matter there are moments when almost any of us might resemble it. Yet even then there would necessarily be radical differences between it and Tate, for though the poetry is often distraught, the conditions imposed by the poetic medium still suffice to frustrate any direct transcription of the man. Therefore, in attempting to describe the *persona* one is only trying to lay hold upon an important part of the implicit content of the poetry, no more.

418

Two essential forces in the *persona* are a sense of inadequacy and the expectation of betrayal by those things to which it is most deeply committed—especially the doctrines, institutions, groups, and individuals in which it hopes to discover a reason for being and some promise of security. These forces cause an anxiety beside which the concern over mortality in Ransom's poetry seems but a mild uneasiness. Harried by them, the imagination can never be free of perturbation long enough to forget itself. It is tormented and accused by a self-consciousness so unrelenting that all experience becomes oppressive and a cause for fear and guilt. That is why man, as represented by the *persona*, is always the victim. Worse, by his insufficiency he deserves to be. He deserves suffering and betrayal.

Were these the only forces in the imagination there could be no poetry. But other forces resist their paralyzing effect, and in the resistance is the final cause of much of the ambivalence, conflict, and incoherence of the poetry. The sense of inadequacy and the expectation of betrayal threaten the imagination; yet they are loved. With the fear and guilt goes a curious pride in having so much to fear and such cause to feel guilty. The imagination enjoys secondary gains from its feeling of inferiority, which is a refuge and an emblem of a superior sensitivity and talent. Failure is a kind of success known only to the most worthy. It should be obvious how attractive to the imagination is the whole mystique of the artist as the rebellious outsider too fine for this world.

Yet the prose argues the necessity of escaping from the self through community with others made possible by shared traditions which protect one from the whims and impulses which are the modes of Pure Quality in the interior world. The discussion of Crane's tragedy and such poems as "Ode to the Confederate Dead," "The Twelve," "The Wolves," "The Meaning of Death," and the second and third sections of "Seasons of the Soul" show how ravaging are the loneliness and dejection of what Tate called the "locked-in sensibility." Even so, there are signs that the imagination has sought some of its isolation. In these very poems, and more so in less successful ones, it exhibits an unwillingness to go forth toward community. Tormented by insecurity, it wants the assurance of approval and admiration from the readers; but at the same time it rejects the readers and courts their rejection. It dreads betrayal and almost hopes to be betrayed. It seems deliberately to undertake too much, striving to awe the beholder and yet failing in the end so that it may retire within the delicious shelter of inadequacy. It appeals to the interest of just those persons with whom community would seem to be most likely and rewarding, and then by the aggressively antagonistic manner so apparent in the essay "The Present Function of Criticism," by the privacy of many passages in the poetry, by the needless difficulties placed in the way of the reader, and by that arrogance-in-humility which Roy Harvey Pearce has wittily called "speaking down from the Cross" it tries to drive them away. The behavior is punitive, but the real object of the punishment is the self: the poems punish the *persona* by aggravating the reader. There is self-love in the withdrawal into the isolation. But there is also self-hatred as strong—or stronger, and it builds up, for there is no adequate means of releasing it. It abrades the imagination, creating a nervous tension which causes reactions that seem quite out of proportion to the events depicted in the poetry. This, and not alone the fascination with violence, helps to explain the exaggerated intensity of many of the poems.

One may see a rough parallel in the behavior of children. This is not to say that either the poetry or the *persona* is childish, for both are indubitably adult. Rather, the equivocations are simpler and more overt among children. Often a child, doubting that it is worthy of love and anxious lest its trust be betrayed will try to command attention and test the devotion of its parents by withdrawal. If the parents are sufficiently annoyed to ignore it and withhold their love, it becomes frightened and enraged. Its anger will seem to be directed at the parents, whom it tries to punish for their neglect; but it is really more angry with itself for its unworthiness, and it tries to punish itself by hurting the parents whom it loves and by making the return to its former intimacy with them more difficult. The ideal and most dreadful way of realizing all of its contradictory purposes is, of course, self-destruction, which the child may threaten. The child half understands that it has chosen a course leading it into greater anxiety, guilt, withdrawal, loneliness, and misery, but the power of its feelings shreds what is left of its self-control and it has no pattern of conduct to follow in extricating itself. What it wants most of all is to submit to the absolute authority of the parents and to be made to take its place in the hierarchical structure of the family where its role is clearly defined for it. Then it no longer has to control its feelings with only the feelings themselves to serve as guides. It knows what to do: obey. Responsibility is assumed by the overlords, leaving the child free to exercise its preferences and powers of choosing in small matters that do not threaten the orderly structure of its little world. If for a moment one thinks that only children find themselves in such jeopardy, one need only remember the brilliant portrait and analysis of George Posey in *The Fathers*. The whole discussion of tradition in Tate's prose shows how exactly he understood the torture of being absolutely free and exposed to unchecked feeling. He pushed Calhoun's arguments too far in *Jefferson Davis*, but its premises were founded upon sound insights into the tensions of the contemporary spirit.

If the parents are patient and sympathetic, the child's needs can be met. For one thing, the parents are there: they are real and visible. Their gestures of love and authority can be seen. The child can take them as absolutes. Later on it can treat them as "imperatives of reference," to use Tate's excellent terms. But the *persona* revealed in "Ode to the Confederate Dead," "Last Days of Alice," "The Twelve," "Sonnets at Christmas," "A Winter Mask," and "More Sonnets at Christmas," cannot believe in any absolute which might validate the dogmas and traditions which would slow it on the path that seems to lead toward self-destruction by immersion in Pure Quality. Again and again Tate argued in his prose the necessity of belief and then asserted in his poems that belief was not possible. In 1950, shortly before he joined the Roman Catholic Church and affirmed at last his belief in an absolute, he wrote: "As I look back upon my verse, written over more than twenty-five years, I see plainly that its main theme is man suffering from unbelief; I cannot for a moment suppose that this man is some other than myself. . . . [Man's] disasters are probably the result of his failure to possess and be possessed by a controlling sense of the presence of redemptive powers in his experience."[24]

There is, of course, one certainty remaining to the unbelieving imagination: death, the supreme withdrawal for the superior spirit and the supreme punishment for the guilty and inadequate one. In it the conflict of self-love and self-hate, the ambivalence toward

[24] "Religion and the Intellectuals," *The Partisan Review*, XVII (March, 1950), 250-251.

violence, and all the many opposing forces of the imagination and the poetry are laid to rest. Readers as attentive as Samuel French Morse and Howard Nemerov have separately observed that mortality is Tate's main theme.[25] The writer prefers Tate's judgment that the main theme is unbelief, but death is everywhere in the poetry. It is the noumenon within the archetypal symbols of both the prose and poetry; it is the essence of the Nature which seems so charged with energy. The *persona* as man of letters inhabits the kingdom of death; he dwells where Tate in his essays assigned the modern poet—in hell. His name, if he had one, would be entered after those of Julien Sorel, Captain Ahab, Roderick Usher, Stephen Dedalus, and Joe Christmas on the list of "noble and sinister characters, our ancestors and our brothers," who exemplify, Tate has said, the lesson that in our society nobody participates with the full substance of his humanity and all act a part in "the plotless drama of withdrawal."

Repeatedly in this discussion the point has been made that the outer world is a symbol of the *persona's* inner world. But now the direction of reference must be reversed as we ask to what extent that inner world is a symbol of the spiritual condition of the outer world. Or, to be more accurate, we should ask how much the inner world of the contemporary man of letters depicted here resembles the interior worlds of most men of our time. Do all men live in a *fourmillante Cité*, as Tate maintained in "The Man of Letters in the Modern World"?

The canon of the work in which the answers must be sought is small. If the squibs of *The Golden Mean* are not counted, the total number of Tate's published poems comes to slightly less than one hundred and fifty. About fifty of these appeared in *The Fugitive* and other little magazines but were never reprinted in a book. From the remainder he chose only seventy for *Poems 1922-1947,* published in 1948—seventy poems to represent a quarter of a century's work since the founding of *The Fugitive*. Not many of these, perhaps a dozen at the most, are satisfying works of art having enough inner harmony and coming near enough to perfect

---

[25] Samuel French Morse, "Second Reading," *Poetry*, LI (February, 1938), 262-266; Howard Nemerov, "The Current of the Frozen Stream," *Furioso*, III (Fall, 1948), 55-56.

wholeness of being to give pleasure *as poems* and not as miscellanea. The others have fine things in them; none lacks interest and all but a few impress by the intensity of the feeling and the originality and penetration of many—sometimes even a majority —of their lines. Even so, the faulty elements usually have as much effect, and often more, upon the reader as the good ones. Thus when defects appear, the interaction of the parts of a poem is not simply suspended but broken. There are places in each of Tate's volumes (pages 73 through 90 in *Poems 1922-1947*, for example) to which one can turn and read for some minutes and wonder, in spite of the excellence of many lines and the unforgettable impression made by some details, whether Tate really had much feeling for the poem as a poem—which is to say for the art of poetry. Then one comes to such a perfectly realized work as "Shadow and Shade" or to a poem like "The Mediterranean" in which the harmony among the splendors quite overbalances the scattered faults, and one thinks, "If this be not a poet, who is?"

Yet when the measure of Tate's achievement is taken, the value of the poetry comes more from the knowledge of the human condition which it provides than from its artistic excellence. This probably does not much trouble Tate, for he said in "The Man of Letters in the Modern World" that the final purpose and extrinsic end of the literary arts is self-knowledge. Outside of poetry there can be knowledge without artistic excellence. Within poetry there can be, too; but by as much as the poems providing such knowledge lack artistic excellence they are not poems and it is not of that unique order which Ransom and Tate have taught us to desire. This is not to say that such knowledge is wholly unpoetic or that it cannot be immense. Rather, it is to say that the most illuminating representation, the deepest penetration of the substance, and the subtlest and most original interpretation result from just that interaction among the elements which is the source of artistic excellence and our sense of the poem as poetry. Tate's work offers the reader a great deal of knowledge, enough to warrant the closest attention in spite of its defects. Nevertheless, those defects do not just mar the formal beauty and limit our aesthetic pleasure; they diminish the richness of the content and the value of the knowledge. Describing the breeze propelling a sailboat as being "fierce as a body loved" does more than disrupt the tone of "The Mediterranean" and turn the mind to an image that has no relevance whatever; it blurs the clarity and lessens the authority of the other images and subtracts appreciably from the power and scope of their accumulating contextual meanings and the unique knowledge which they bear. Fortunately, though the rarest and finest knowledge is missed in all but a few poems, there are many passages and many more single phrases and images that reach far into the interior darkness which is the special province of this poetry. Tate's absorption with the striking individual detail may have spoiled much of his work, but undeniably some of the details have great intrinsic value. There is, for example, the superb beginning of "The Paradigm." The poem quickly got out of control and crumbled into a confusion of separate images, but the simile of the first quatrain reveals more than many whole poems:

> For when they meet, the tensile air
> Like fine steel strains under the weight
> Of messages that both hearts bear—
> Pure passion once, now purest hate. . . .

There are many things as good as this. Moreover, they are representative of a powerful and consistent style which, when we read enough of the poems, has its own cumulative effect, even though so many of the individual pieces are fragmented; it posits its own vision. It is as if this effect were some great, shadowy poem in itself. Taking this "poem" and the more successful actual poems we may ask how well the poet has performed the duty which Tate assigned him, rendering the image of man as he is in his time, an image which would not otherwise be known. How inclusive is it and how true?

The image is very exclusive. There are great ranges of human experience which the *persona* never goes near. One of these is love. A few poems touch on sexual desire, but in them the emphasis is upon the psychic disturbance or the problems of alienation and incapacity for meaningful action. For the poems abstract from those areas of experience which the *persona* enters just those aspects immediately significant to the themes of belief, self-discipline, moral confusion, and the ends of man as they figure in the philosophy or the anxieties of a man of letters of a particular sensibility. The image of man is made so exclusive not so much by the predominance of an individual in special circumstance as by the limitations placed upon that individual's participation in the common life of men. The *persona* much resembles Hamlet before his return from England. Hamlet, too, is an individual in special circumstance, a prince with a particular sensibility. Yet all of us see some of our life in his and catch a glimpse of ourselves in the mirror of his soul. Imagine the play transformed into a series of reveries upon loneliness, belief, knowledge, the disorder of life, the grossness of society, and the greatness of the past from which Hamlet has been cut off by the intervention of a pragmatic man of affairs. Many things revealed in the exchanges between Hamlet and other characters would be lost, but many things might be gained from the concentration. Then imagine that in the reveries there was no reference to Horatio, Polonius, and Laertes; that Ophelia was reduced to the faceless anonymity of the girl in Tate's youthful Oenia poems or the beloved of "Shadow and Shade"; that Gertrude had no more substance than the woman in "Mother and Son" or "Sonnets of the Blood" and Claudius was just one of the multitude in "Retroduction to American Society," "Causerie," and "To the Lacedemonians." Hamlet would approach the condition of the *reveur* of the "Ode to the Confederate Dead," who is a representative embodiment of the *persona.* Confined by the *reveur's* narcissism, to use Tate's own term, Hamlet would scarcely be the comprehensive image that he manages to be while still being utterly the Prince of ancient Denmark. His great question, immanent throughout Tate's poetry, would remain, but the scope of the inquiry into it would be drastically reduced.

To be or not to be. Is there anything worth living for? In either form it is an ultimate question. Tate's prose attempts some answers, if only by implication, but the poetry just puts the question and describes some of the conditions which the answers, if any there be, must take into account. Even to ask the question is to engage in what Fichte called the vocation of man: the preservation of his identity and his ability and desire to be held accountable for his choices and actions. Pursuing that vocation has brought Tate up against some of the most difficult problems of our time: the nature of reality now that the old cosmologies have been discredited; how that nature is known; what man can believe in when his knowledge is uncertain and subject to sudden change; what gives his conduct meaning; the relation of the individual to the group; the appalling effects of the modern environment upon the spirit. His image of man confronting these problems and asking the question is the poet in hell. The conditions are almost all infernal.

They are real enough. Few have escaped the seasons of the soul. There is no experience depicted in the poem we have not lived, no passion described or evoked we have not known. We have been shaken by the sense of inadequacy, the expectation of betrayal, the anxiety, the guilt, the self-love and self-hatred, and in his prose, particularly in his novel, Tate has explained why we are so vulnerable to them in our time. But there is more, and it is not in this poetry. There are other conditions by which the answer to Tate's question must abide.

It was said that the ideal world implicit in Ransom's poetry is insufficient as an image of our deepest human values. The ideal hell implicit (and often nakedly explicit) in Tate's poetry is too. This is not an ingenious quip. For that ideal hell defines some of those deepest values by showing how they are denied, corrupted, or destroyed. (To show that hell is lonely is to define the value of communion.) But there are other values beyond the scope of this poetry. They, too, might perhaps be defined only by showing their denial, corruption, or destruction. The contemporary world may be a hell more vast than that symbolized by the interior hell of a modern man of letters. Or it may be less hellish. The measure cannot be had from this poetry. Its archetypal symbols are not enough. The *persona* is not enough. But they are true, and ignore them we dare not. Tate has not flinched from the duty of the man of letters as he himself defined it. If there is more to be shown, what he shows at least validates his claims for the literary arts, "without which men can live, but without which they cannot live well, or live as men."

We shall never answer Hamlet's question, the question of these poems, if we deny what they can teach us.

CHAPTER NINE

ROBERT PENN WARREN: THE LONG APPRENTICESHIP

....

"That landscape lost in the heart's homely deep."
—*Robert Penn Warren, "Lullaby: Moonlight Lingers"*

....

I

*T*HERE is a landscape full of boyhood's grief and glory known to those who grew up before the war—the last one, or the one before—on farms or in small towns of the Mississippi Valley. Though lost in the heart's homely deep, it may be found in the works of Robert Penn Warren.

Now that only ten percent of the people work at farming and the towns are dormitories, now that fields are braided with electric fences and the woodlots are posted, there are not many places where a boy between eight and fourteen can wander alone out of the sight and sound of the interstate highways. Once he could roam all day until it was time for his paper route or the chores and no one cared. Nothing could happen to him, anyway, as he soaked up impressions of the motionless clarity of a summer morning, of the flash of riffles where the creek ran thin over gravel, of the hawk resting on the shelf of afternoon light above the layered shadows. There were places he pretended were secret and called his, such as the opening in the woods where the grass was lush and untrampled, and sometimes he thought of hiding in one of them until long after sundown. Then let them call and call. Yet he could not have said why he wanted that.

Then there was the marsh with the grey stumps and the wild lilies. When he tried to pick a lily, gas bubbled up fatly and the stem was slimed and slick. Someone said there was a catfish four feet long on the bottom and once when the sun was high he thought he saw it, but it was only a log. At night he sometimes heard things being killed out under the trees, heard a rabbit scream and the awful thumping of the earth. Next morning he found tufts of fur and nearly vomited. He then felt as if eyes were watching him and as if, somehow, his fear and nausea made him to blame. Other nights he would hear a far-off train whistle or a dog's bark and later, when all other sounds were still, the creak of a shed door in the night breeze, and he would feel lonely and deprived.

As a boy grew older these things in some strange way seemed connected with his own body, though he tried not to think about it. Perhaps he found the grass of his secret place flattened and nearby an empty pint bottle and wondered about strange pleasures from which he was excluded. Then he would shiver with fright for in the darkness the catfish waited for him and the eyes saw, even though he did not believe in the catfish and the eyes could not belong to anything bigger than a coon. The morning smiled blandly and pollen sifted in the sunlight, but he knew the terror of the commonplace. And the disgust: aware of his body he began to notice the bodies of adults and those of old people filled him with revulsion. He noticed especially the mouths: the sagging lips pink and wet as a baby's, the decayed teeth, the liver spots on the fumbling hands, the swollen goiter. He could scarcely abide the touch of his grandparents, and he felt ashamed but could not help it.

Then abruptly his childhood came to an end and though he might wander the fields again it was never the same. Perhaps a great windstorm tore down the barn where he had played in the haymow and kept his treasures. Perhaps the creek flooded and left filth on the trees that stank for days. Perhaps he shot a bird that would not die but flopped horribly in the grass as he ran away— and for long afterward he would wake in the morning and there would be only a few minutes before he would remember the bird. Perhaps his parents had found him in one of his secret places helping his cousin unbutton her dress. Perhaps he quarreled with his mother and suddenly began to shout all the filthy things that came in his dreams, and for days he went about as if stunned. With a passion of misery he would not have believed possible he longed for his innocence and the old, careless, unthinking relation with the world and his family. It was like the longing for a lost toy, only many times worse. Then, queerly, it was as if he might set things right if only he could find the toy buried somewhere under sodden, decaying leaves. If only he had not left it out in the rain. But no,

428

there wasn't a chance, and everything reminded him of the old happiness or the new guilt. The whiteness of a flower could shake his heart. A great, hairy mole on his grandmother's cheek reminded him of his own monstrously growing and evil body. At night one light on a hillside made him desolate: he could imagine the kerosene lamp on the checkered oil-cloth and he almost burst into tears.

And now, a man, he sometimes thinks of a meadow at morning as he stands on a street corner waiting for the light to change. Then he thinks of the lost toy and the end of childhood and he groans and strikes his palm with his fist. He remembers the secret places and the dead thing and the swamp and thinks, "If only. . . ." Then the light changes and he smiles at his childishness. But his deepest need is to come to terms with these memories. To accept the fact that the toy is gone, the grass is trampled, the barn is down, the old people he loathed when he should have loved them have died, and he is what he is and there is no going back. Nor any reshaping of this world to look like the lost landscape. He is banished from Eden into manhood and must earn his own redemption.

Robert Penn Warren knew some version of that boyhood, knew the longings, knew the terms by which one must discover and redeem the self. All of his mature writing is established upon that knowledge.

His father's house stood on the edge of the village of Guthrie in southwestern Kentucky. Open country was just a few minutes away down the road. During the summers he roamed the wilderness around his grandfather's farm, which had changed little since the Civil War. It was rough land with caves, gorges, limestone shelves, and many a hiding place. There was a spring from which Warren drank on hot days. Its waters flowed away to a pool full of quicksand in which it was said a man and his team of oxen had disappeared. At night Warren lay on a scratchy mattress filled with new straw and listened to the sound of his grandfather's breathing or an owl's hoot. It seemed as if in that land all nature was a little more vivid and intense than elsewhere in the Mississippi Valley. Perhaps the wind blew harder in Oklahoma and the summer dust was deeper in northern Mississippi, but taking everything —the hail storms, the grass made rich by lime, the bright swiftness of the streams and the torpor of the rivers, the great age of the

trees, the sweetness of the morning air, the variety of the horizon
—take all these, and Warren's Kentucky had about it a beauty and
violence and sadness remarkable even for the South and it forever
shaped his imagination, his style, his vision of man. He has lived
many places, but when he seeks for radical symbols of the human
condition, his mind reaches back to the land he knew as a boy, for
such is his vision that many of the moments in man's search for
himself and the meaning of his fate are rooted in childhood experiences and can be represented by his sense of and reaction to the
country. In his own way Warren is concerned, like Ransom and
Tate, with man's relation with Nature and the knowledge he needs
for right conduct within that relation. But in his writing, that Nature is unusually concrete and specific. One can almost point to its
place on a map. No other modern American—not even Faulkner
or Frost—has given us a more present and palpable world.

II

There was none of it in the poems that have survived from
Warren's undergraduate days. The two that depict nature take their
images not from the country over which Warren had wandered
but from the library shelf.

He was sixteen when he took Davidson's course in the survey
of English literature. Though it covered the usual span from Beowulf to Hardy, it was not the usual course, for Davidson encouraged his students to write imitations of the authors studied instead
of the usual themes. To receive credit the imitations had to be
exact, and Davidson corrected them with meticulous attention.
Those who wrote them learned much about style. It was for this
course that Warren wrote his first poetry in college, though he
had already taken English 9 under Ransom, which was the only
course in writing he ever had. It was Ransom's whim to teach the
principles of composition by analyzing Shakespeare's sonnets, and
Warren heard a great deal about structure and the relation of the
part to the whole.

It was about then that he read *Poems About God*. "I was then in
the full tide of the boyish discovery of poetry," he recalls,

"and my taste ran to the grand and romantic, to resounding lines
and sweeping gestures. What was peculiar about this little book

was that, without resounding lines and sweeping gestures, it gave me the same mystical shiver I got from Keats and Blake or the sonnets of Shakespeare. It dealt with none of the materials I found so exciting in those other poets. It dealt, simply, with the world of rural Tennessee. It put that mystical shiver, as it were, into the back pasture. In other words, it opened my eyes to the fact of poetry in, even, the literal world."[1]

Yet in spite of his feeling for the mystical shiver in the back pasture (which is a good way to describe the effect of such a poem as his own "Boy's Will, Joyful Labor Without Pay, and Harvest Home [1918]") Warren went on trying to write about the grand and romantic.

Being practicing poets gave Ransom and Davidson prestige among the students interested in writing, who took their courses and thus became acquainted with one another. Some of them formed the Poetry Guild and in the spring of 1923 published a booklet called *Driftwood Flames*, which they dedicated to Ransom, though he had no connection with the enterprise. Andrew Nelson Lytle contributed two poems (one in French), and Warren five, in which he echoed Swinburne and the English Decadents. "I am sowing wild oats / On rocky hills and steep," one boasted, "And when my harvest whitens / I shall not be here to reap." Another, Heaven knows why, was reprinted entire in *The Bookman* during the summer. Years afterward Tate could still remember its opening quatrain. Warren had shown him the poem when they met for the first time in Curry's office soon after Tate's return to Vanderbilt. Perhaps the meeting made the impression, for "The Golden Hills of Hell" is not a memorable poem:

> O, fair the Golden Hills of Hell,
> > Where lightly rest the purple lilies;
> There, as all the saints tell
> > Lightly nod the lilies.

> Dim beyond the scarlet river,
> > Slenderly and slow they nod,
> Glimpsed from where the splendors quiver
> > On the minarets of God.

[1] "John Crowe Ransom: Some Random Remarks," *Shenandoah*, XIV (Spring, 1963), 19.

> False tales the saints tell
> Of the slender lilies;
> For I have knelt on the Hills of Hell
> Among the withered lilies.

Warren was younger than his classmates, shy, and inclined to withdraw into solitude. Occasionally other students would set upon him and tease him to the point of tears. These qualities and the vague, languid masochism of this poem might lead one to suppose that Warren would be attracted by Davidson's mystique of the outland piper. But though "Iron Beach," another poem he contributed to the pamphlet, describes some sort of outcast shouting defiance from the world's edge, the forlorn singer does not appear in Warren's early work, and he soon turned to sterner stuff.

"Crusade," which earned Warren a place in the competition for the Nashville Prize offered by the Fugitives in 1923, consists of the recollections of a soldier in the service of Count Raymond of Provence on the night following the capture of Jerusalem:[2]

> We have not forgot the clanking of grey armors
> Along the frosty ridges against the moon,
> The agony of gasping endless columns,
> Skulls glaring white on red deserts at noon;
> Nor death in dank marshes by fever. . . .

The soldier remembers how the crusaders took their vows in a thronged cathedral, the sunlight on the long green wash of breakers, the "Tattered mail rusting on hot hard sands," the long struggle for the tomb of Christ, and thinks,

> This low malignant moon gives no surcease
> Nor any opiate of forgetfulness
> For the sob and choke of remembered sorrow . . .
> We have no solace in this bitter stillness.
> We shall be still enough tomorrow.

Warren may have had Browning somewhere in the back of his mind as he wrote this, but the substance comes straight from innumerable boys' books. Yet, puerile as it is, it exhibits some modest virtues. In marked contrast to the disorder of Tate's "Sinbad," the

---

[2] See Chapter Two, pp. 77-81.

quasi-narrative is brisk and orderly. With the perspicacity of hind-sight one can see here some of Warren's characteristic interest in history and flair for anecdote. The poem piles up too many details of the same kind and the colors are so intense and contrasted that the effect in the mind's eye is garish and vulgar, but it is undeniably vivid as "The Golden Hills of Hell" was not. Henceforth, indeed, Warren's poems might have many defects, but they were always firmly concrete and *there*.

When he entered the contest Warren was rooming with Ridley Wills, Tate, and William Cobb, a graduate student. It would be pleasant to report that the young writers spent their time com-muning about the art of poetry, but such was not the case. Like all college boys they talked a lot about sex, liquor, assignments, and campus politics. Only once in a while did they talk about writing. Warren looked up to Tate and Wills because they were Fugitives and were constantly referring to books he had never heard of. He read the queer magazines Tate brought in and was impressed when Tate's poems appeared in *The Double Dealer* and *The Modern Review*. He had a sensitive ear for idioms which would serve him magnificently in his fiction and some practice at imitating poets under Davidson's tutelage; so it was easy for him to assemble a pastiche of Pound and Eliot entitled "After Teacups," which the Fugitives accepted for publication in the issue for August, 1923. Its opening reads like some cancelled lines from the *Cantos*:

> I was not on the parapets at Cretae
> Dreading sails black against the red low moon,
> When my ruin overthrew me.
> Nor did it claim me with the plunge of Grecian spears. . . .

After a time the poem shifted to the manner of "Prufrock":

> But dissolution clutched me
> Descanting at Mme. Atelie's salon
> Of balls at Nice and coursing at L'Enprix.
> I sipped my tea with marked exactitude,
> Refusing claret. . . .
> Outside a spring swarmed up the avenues,
> Spattering hydrangeas with a gust of bloom.

The notion of an eighteen-year-old boy from a Kentucky village writing this is so delightfully ridiculous that one is inclined to think that Warren was making fun of the masters. But perhaps not, for he wrote other poems at this time no less pretentious and manifestly intended to be taken seriously. And seriously is just how the Fugitives took them all.

It would have been easy to imitate Tate, and Warren did once:

> Now has brittle incandescent day
> Been shattered, spilling from its fractured bowl
> The so trite dusk upon a street and soul
> That wait their own and evening's decay.
> Will not a midnight grant deliverance
> Of dusk and all its bitter casuistries. . . ?

The language is Tate's own, and the touches of assumed ennui, the self-pity, and the longing for dissolution are right in character. But "Autumn Twilight Piece" has beneath its canopy of metaphors an orderliness of syntax and structure not often found in Tate's verse and never in the poems he was writing at this time. Perhaps Warren managed his material better because he was not trying to stagger the reader with every syllable. He had little interest in the artist as rebel. He listened to Tate discourse on Eliot, Crane, Baudelaire, and the Symbolists, and when he joined the Fugitives he sided with the modernists, but he did not go in for Tate's aggressive and self-conscious experimentalism. He had beneath his timidity his own penchant for violence, and, as the fabulous talkers in his novels show, he exulted in the swing and swirl of gorgeous rhetoric; yet even when most ostentatious, he eschewed the arcane. The grandiloquence he put into the mouths of his characters consisted of fragments and rhythms from the tall story, the Bible and pulpit oratory, political addresses, and those passages from Shakespeare and the poets that schoolboys memorize—that is, it came from the rich verbal resources of the Southern imagination and not from specialized vocabularies such as Ransom, Tate, and Hirsch drew upon. Moreover, Tate, for all his own obsessive *avant-gardism*, did not urge his friends to write as he did. As a critic of their work he was, as we know, attentive to contextual meanings, structural coherence, and the harmony of tonalities, and, like Ransom, he tried to help others do what they wanted and not what he himself would have done. Warren appreciated Tate's perceptiveness and patient attention and sought his advice. He thought, as had Davidson, that Tate's criticism was far more helpful than any he got at the Fugitive meetings. Tate's instructive care for Warren's writing, not only when they roomed together but for the decade thereafter, is one of the best things in the record of the Fugitives.

The weeks after his admission to the group early in 1924 were hard for Warren. His spirits were low and by the end of the term his health was so poor that he left without finishing all his course work. His depression is reflected in a group of four dispirited poems written in this period called "Death Mask of a Young Man." Over the next months he wrote so many poems on the mortality of the flesh—nearly half of those he published in *The Fugitive* were on that theme—that Tate warned him against obsession. Yet this was his first original and personal poetry, and in "The Wrestling Match" one sees unmistakable traces of the imagination from which would come "The Return: An Elegy" and even *Brother to Dragons*:

> "Here in this corner, ladies and gentlemen,
> I now present 'Mug' Hill, weight two-hundred-ten,
> Who will wrestle here tonight the 'Battling Pole,'
> Boruff—" who, as insistently the stale
>
> Loud voice behind asserts, is good as hell.
> "Is good as hell, I says," and then the bell
> Stabs up to life two engines of flesh and bone,
> Each like a great bronze automaton
>
> That by black magic moves stupendously,
> Moving with a machine's intensity,
> To some obscure and terrible conclusion
> Involving us as in an absurd vision.
>
> The truculent dull spirit is involved
> There to contend above, while is dissolved
> In sleep the twisted body on the bed.
> The barker said—or was it this he said:
>
> "Ladies and gentlemen, I now present—"
> The voice here sank in some obscene intent—

435

"That which is body so you all may see
The bone and blood and sweat and agony

And thews that through the tortured years have striven
To breach the flesh so sure to spill when broken
The only breath, a cry, and the dark blood
That forever we would keep if but we could."

Warren was preoccupied with the body's organs and processes. Subsequently in his fiction he would describe with the most minute care textures of skin or the articulation of the bones of his people, and over and again he went for symbols to the moist, bulging, convolute inwardness of the body. Innumerable writers have described the horrors of bodies shattered in war or crushed beneath the wheels of technology, but only Aldous Huxley matches Warren in evoking nightmares of revulsion and fear by means of details of quite whole and healthy bodies or disgust by dwelling upon abnormalities and signs of decay. In each writer the loathesomeness is actually a twisted sentimentality, for the feelings roused so often far exceed their occasion.

In that melancholy spring Warren wrote three sonnets which were published during the following August in *The Double Dealer* as "Portraits of Three Ladies." Two were trifles of no interest, but the third was something else altogether:

Strangely her heart yet clutched a strange twilight,
One that had lured with dreams down a cypressed way
To glens where hairy-haunched and savage lay
The night. Could ever she forget that night
And one black pool, her image in the water,
Or how fat lily stalks were stirred and shifted
By terrible things beneath, and how there drifted
Through slimy trunks and fern a goatish laughter?

Sometimes at dusk before her looking glass
She thought how in that pool her limbs gleamed whitely:
She heard her husband watering the grass
Or his neat voice inquiring, "Supper dear?"
Across the table then she faced him nightly
With harried eyes in which he read no fear.

Warren had written better poems already and would write more before the year was over. The first two lines are below the level of his pieces in *Driftwood Flames,* and the poem as a whole quite fails to unite two sets of conventions then much esteemed by undergraduates: the eroticism of Cabell (satyrs, midnight pools, and gleaming limbs) and the boob-baiting of Lewis and Mencken, which had for a favorite butt the oaf who is complacently unaware of his wife's sexual hungers. Up to a point this is the sort of poem college boys everywhere were writing. The difference (and the interest) is in the *hairy-haunched* night and the fat lily stalks moved by some vague horror beneath the waters of the black pool. For the first time—in print, anyway—Warren uses the obscure but powerful associations evoked by pubic hair and the wet surfaces and dark coil of entrails and genitalia to suggest mystery and terror latent in the ordinary. He reaches past clichés to touch for a moment the fantasies and fears rooted in the anxieties and sexual dreams of late childhood and early adolescence. He laid hand on the deep and awful tensions represented by the images of the hairy and fat-petalled flowers that lean and confer in "Revelation" and the "ovoid horror / Which is furred like a peach" in "Original Sin" or the swamp of bestiality into which Jerry Beaumont sinks in *World Enough and Time.*

Actually, however, there were few indications of the measure of his talent in the poems Warren wrote as an undergraduate. There is little to suggest that he had been a Fugitive, but he believes that being taken into the group was one of the most fortunate things that ever happened to him. For from it and the signal honor of being asked to join he got invaluable encouragement to write and to measure his work against far higher standards than he otherwise would have thought to apply. If his were only learner's poems, he was learning well and the poems, though indistinguished, exhibit real technical competence. About half were sonnets. (He did not publish any more until "Sirocco" in 1955, which might be called a sonnet of sorts.) Within that form and the various stanzas—usually quatrains—he used, he tried many variations, particularly with the rhythms, for though circumspect in grammar and syntax he liked irregularity of movement and shaped his lines to resemble spoken discourse made up of long sentences broken into short staccato phrases. To counteract any looseness he laced his lines tightly with alliterations, consonance, and internal rhymes and skillfully matched the progress of the discourse to the stanzaic divisions, though, as may be seen in "The Wrestling Match," he was already sophisticated enough to run over from one stanza to another in order to emphasize an element, such as the word *stale* at the end of the first stanza, which had primary importance for the tonality of the poem but only secondary importance for the structure of the sentence of which it is a part. Among the Fugitives only Ransom had gone further than this beginner in developing *functional* variations on conventional patterns; yet because he did not go in for Tate's Baudelarian correspondences, neologisms, and ellipses his poems appear to be less daring than one would expect those of a young man in his position to be. Their modes are dramatic or anecdotal rather than lyric, and only in the poems on the illnesses and death of young men does Warren begin to approach the directly observed and experienced. He had not yet begun to use the riches he had so long been assimilating. He seems to have written poems mainly for the sake of writing poems. About the landscape and life he knew so well he had as yet nothing in particular to say.

III

In the fall of 1925 Warren went west to do graduate work in English at the University of California. It was the first time he had lived away from his region and his own kind of people, and for a while his life was charged with excitement. He liked the brilliance and variety of Berkeley and especially of San Francisco, but he found the discussions of literature less interesting and informed than those he had grown used to at Vanderbilt and he decided he would be better off at Yale. He arranged to transfer to that university at mid-year, but when his mother heard of this she intervened with the authorities of both universities. Warren was furious but he stayed at the University of California for two full years, during which he became engaged to Miss Emma Brescia of San Francisco. He had little time for writing poetry, but when he did, he did not describe his travels, his love affair, or his night wanderings in the city. (In a letter he refers to a poem, "San Francisco Night Window," which was never published.) Instead, his thoughts went back to his family, Kentucky, the history of his region and the yarns he had heard from his mother's father, who had been a cavalry officer under Forrest. Like Jerry Calhoun, Willie Stark, and Amantha Starr, Warren was discovering his place and its past by leaving them. He had always read history, but now he became especially interested in the Civil War, and as he did his attention focused on crazy John Brown.

Feeling more independent than he ever had at Vanderbilt he could acknowledge the strength of his ties to his home and people by writing poems about the country around his grandfather's farm and about a son's mixed feelings toward his parents. He could also acknowledge the force of Ransom's poetry by imitating it in "The Last Metaphor," which he wrote during his first year at Berkeley, though it was not published until five years later. It was not a good poem, but in some lines Warren caught Ransom's idiom exactly:

> So he took counsel of the heart alone
> To be instructed of this desolation,
> And when the tongue of the wind had found cessation
> After such fashion he lifted up his own. . . .

Ransom's idiom would have ill served his awakening consciousness, as one may see from "Garden Waters," which was written in 1926. The second stanza reads like something Ransom might have written before he got around to tightening up the lines:

> In this man's garden as in any other
> Where decent waters through the night have flowed
> Is converse of a musical small clamor. . . .

But where Ransom might have been reminded of how the brook looked by day and gone on to say something about its waiting impatiently to be at its proper business of sparkling in the sun, Warren was reminded of "the voiceless waters of dream / Monstrously tumbled . . ." and of the fact that even a brook may hide some decaying and abandoned thing:

> The obscure image of the season's wreck,
> The dead leaf and the summer's chrysalid.

It might seem that Tate's jagged cacophony would be nearer Warren's purpose. Among the poems Warren submitted for the Fugitive anthology was "Letter of a Mother," written during his

439

first year in California. It described conflicting feelings which went deep with Warren and he thought it his best poem. But it was a clumsy copy of Tate's at his most pretentious (with one utterly inapt line of purest Ransom: "Whose sweet process may bloom in gratitude"). A son "defined upon the superscription, / Inherits now his cubicled domain / And reads" a letter from his mother which overwhelms with longing his mind, described as

> a subtile engine, propped
> In the sutured head beneath the coronal seam,
> Whose illegal prodigality of dream
> In shaking the escheat heart is quick estopped.

(At the Fugitives' reunion Tate claimed to be the only one who had used *escheat*. Ransom had used it in *Poems About God*.) Even though his flesh cries out across the plains,

> The mother flesh that cannot summon back
>
> The tired child it would again possess
> As shall a womb more tender than her own
> That builds not tissue or the little bone,
> But dissolves them to itself in weariness.

His loneliness was making Warren aware of the comfort of the very dependency he had struggled against, and he put into his poems the fears and guilts engendered by his both loving and rejecting his parents. "Pro Vita Sua" was another poem on the same material written at this time in a confusion of wrong voices, but when in 1929 Warren returned to the theme in "The Return," he spoke for himself. (This poem, which he eventually placed at the end of the Kentucky Mountain Farm sequence, must not be confused with "The Return: An Elegy," written in 1931.) After describing how a leaf falling on the smooth surface of a stream meets its image moving toward it from the depths, he wrote:

> So, backward heart, you have no voice to call
> Your image back. . . .
>   And he, who had loved as well as most,
> Might have foretold it thus, for long he knew
> How glimmering a buried world is lost

The Long Apprenticeship

In the water's riffle, the wind's flaw;
How his own image, perfect and deep
And small within loved eyes, had been forgot,
Her face being turned, or when those eyes were shut
Past light in that fond accident of sleep.

These lines, the best and most personal he had yet written, contain the germs of many works to come: the trauma of separation, the longing for the lost past and its security, the feeling of betrayal, the recognition of the human fallibility of the parent, the sad acceptance of change, and the search for the self. Warren also used here two of the symbols that recur in his later treatments of these themes, the pool as analogue of the womb state and the eyes in which one fears and hopes to live until one has been forced to concede that one's identity and being come from within.

While remembering his region and brooding on its history, Warren was studying fiction under Chauncey Wells, whose analyses of stories so interested him that he tried writing some of his own. Though he told Davidson they were terrible, they quickened the narrative impulse in his poetry. One result of the many forces playing upon his imagination is "Pondy Woods," a patched-up jumble of genres and styles that includes elements of the folk ballad, the erudite fable such as Ransom wrote (though none of this poem was in his idiom), the verse narrative of Masters and Frost, with, here and there, suggestions of Eliot's satiric sketches. It veers erratically between realism and fantasy, frontier humor and urbane irony, as it describes Big Jim Todd's flight from a sheriff's posse. Though it was published in the *Second American Caravan*, when Warren was twenty-three, it is at best an interesting failure. Warren let himself go with an exuberant recklessness that in years to come sometimes served his purpose well but often marred and vulgarized his work. Though it gets out of control, violent and irreverent juxtaposing of incompatible conventions and traditions is clearly intended to shock the reader into attention but it tends instead to call to mind the cynical roughhousing with words in the columns of sentimentally tough sports writers.

"Nigger, you went this afternoon
For your Saturday spree at the Blue Goose saloon,
So you've got on your Sunday clothes,

441

On your big splay feet got patent-leather shoes.
But a buzzard can smell the thing you've done;
The posse will get you—run, nigger, run—
   . . . your breed ain't metaphysical."
The buzzard coughed. His words fell
In the darkness, mystic and ambrosial.

        . . .

"The Jew-boy died. The Syrian vulture swung
Remotely above the cross whereon he hung
From dinner-time to supper-time. . . .
Nigger, regard the circumstance of breath:
Non omnis moriar, the poet saith."

Pedantic, the bird clacked its grey beak,
With a Tennessee accent to the classic phrase. . . .

Earlier there had been hints of the tough-guy manner in "The Wrestling Match" and "Easter Morning: Crosby Junction" (*The Fugitive*, June, 1925), but not until this poem did Warren so indulge himself without regard for his material. (The measure of his indulgence can be had only from the entire poem, which is too long for quotation here.) In his novels he created some wildly wonderful talkers such as Bill Christians of *Night Rider*, Duckfoot Blake and Jason Sweetwater of *At Heaven's Gate*, and Willie Stark and Jack Burden of *All the King's Men*, who gave scope for hilariously inappropriate allusions, grotesque metaphors, abrupt zigzagging from one usage level to another, and quotations from the Bible, Shakespeare, and sampler maxims. Their lines are legitimate means of characterization, though Warren overdid his effects with Blake, who becomes a fantastic clown in a grimly naturalistic novel, and with Burden, the narrator of *All the King's Men*, whose compulsive scoffing makes him at times a poor medium through which to project, even obliquely, the personalities of other characters, in particular Anne and Adam Stanton. All of these great talkers except Christians use the tough-guy manner as an armor against feeling. They belittle others so that they need not take seriously their emotional or other obligations toward them. Warren's weakness for the manner betrayed him into the crudity of such stories as "The Patented Gate and the Mean Hamburger" and "The Confession of Brother Grimes." There is reason to think

442

he liked it so much because it sometimes served him as a cover for his own susceptibility. When he put himself into *Brother to Dragons* he had "R. P. W." speak so incessantly in this manner that he appears, especially by his obtuse disregard for the feelings of the other speakers, downright stupid. It is, therefore, difficult to accept his shift of sensibility, signified in the poem by a shift to an oracular tone, just as it is difficult to accept a similar shift in Burden's delivery which is supposed to go with a new sense of responsibility toward others. Nevertheless, though the manner often grinds on the reader, it shows in the later works that Warren has powers of verbal invention and improvisation such as few writers of our time can claim.

There are touches of the manner in "The Return: An Elegy," but in that superb poem they are wholly successful. Written when Warren was twenty-six, it is the first poem that justifies taking him seriously as a poet. Its subject is a son's inability to acknowledge and cope with his feelings at the death of his mother. Around it Warren developed the theme adumbrated in "Letter of a Mother" and "The Return": the conflict between the wish to deny reality and return to the protected state of childhood and the drive toward maturity and accommodation with reality. Associated with this are such secondary themes as the necessity of facing the guilts that have come with the destruction of childhood innocence and the dependence of love and sorrow on accepting the humanness of others and their inevitable entanglement in the physical processes of the world. Warren has worked with these themes throughout his career; yet in this first really thorough treatment of them he did almost as well as he ever would.

Warren chose to represent the son's struggle in its true inward locus, and for this he took the mode of the revery. He was obliged to penetrate to the level of the preconscious, and he demonstrated what had been faintly hinted in the third of the "Portraits of Three Ladies" and the passage in "History Among the Rocks" about the disquieting effect of an apple falling in the night, his understanding of and courage in examining feelings, especially of fear and revulsion, which most of us but dimly comprehend because we are ashamed to acknowledge them. At the outset the *reveur* cannot acknowledge them, either.

The east wind finds the gap bringing rain:
Rain in the pine wind shaking the stiff pine.
Beneath the wind the hollow gorges whine
The pines decline
Slow film of rain creeps down the loam again
Where the blind and nameless bones recline.

> they are conceded to the earth's absolute chemistry
> they burn like faggots in—of damp and dark—the
>   monstrous bulging flame.
> calcium phosphate lust speculation faith treachery
> it walked upright with a habitation and a name
> *tell me its name*

> The pines, black, like combers plunge with spray
> Lick the wind's unceasing keel
> *It is not long till day*
> The boughs like hairy swine in slaughter squeal
> And lurch beneath the thunder's livid heel.
> The pines, black, snore *what does the wind say?*

> *tell me its name*

The format is part of the representation. It helps to signify the movement among the three levels of consciousness on which the *reveur* wavers between recognition and denial, or at least transformation, of reality. On the highest level the mind would exorcise the dead thing by pretending that it is nameless and going off into apostrophes to the pines. The order of consciousness on the second level (indicated by indentation and the dropping of most of the punctuation and the capital letters at the beginning of the line) can admit that as time passes bones are modified in the process of nature and that they once belonged to something having a name and place, but that is as far as it can go. It is on the lowest level where primal forces of love, fear, and guilt move with the least check that the issue in which they are involved can be raised by the imperative *tell me its name.* The italics suggest the power of the forces. Presumably when the italics are used on higher levels they indicate that the primal forces are thrusting upward to those levels and violating the higher modes of perception and cognition. Not until they are allowed to emerge upon the highest level can the *reveur*

444

finally accept his mother's and his own true nature and physicality, gain control of his feelings, and direct them toward realizing himself as a man participating in an adult relationship.

When on the highest level the mind tries to deny or transform reality by rhetoric, the primal forces, if at first not strong enough to prevent the attempt, can at least so bend it that the rhetorical figures on which the mind seizes turn out to be linked to what the mind fears and is trying to evade. The results are like those slips of the tongue that give away one's true thoughts. Thus, for example, the pine boughs suggest hairy animals being slaughtered. The rhetorical question *"What does the wind say?"* instead of leading away from the issue, weakens the mind's resolve so that the forces on the lowest level can erupt with the demand that the dead thing be named.

But the mind dodges by assuring itself, "I have a name: I am not blind," revealing that one reason for its inability to face the death of the mother is its fear of the death of the self. Then it tries to belittle the issue by reverting to the less civilized second level and behaving so outrageously that the problem will, as it were, be driven off:

> give me the nickels off your eyes
> from your hands the violets
> let me bless your obsequies
> if you possessed conveniently enough three eyes
> then I could buy a pack of cigarettes

The tough-guy manner suggests how overwhelming are the real feelings. But the sneer does not work, for to make it the *reveur* has been forced to come nearer to admitting the true identity of the dead person.

Returning to the highest level he thinks of death and decay in terms of a fox for whom nature spreads a catafalque. The ritualistic associations of the image cannot help him, however, and he slips downward to "the old bitch is dead" and at once recoils: "What have I said!" He tries to pretend that the words have no meaning and he, no responsibility: "I have only said what the wind said." For a moment he regains his poise and by rhetoric is able to keep reality at bay:

> By dawn, the wind, the blown rain
> Will cease their antique concitation.

It is the hour when old ladies cough and wake,
The chair, the table, take their form again
Earth begins the matinal exhalation

Reality has slipped around the guard of language, for in casting about for material to use in the peroration the mind compulsively chooses the old ladies. At once the forces on the third level demand, *"does my mother wake"* and the dead person has at last been identified. But the mind refuses the question and turns to the scenery. Yet the forces can no longer be denied and their power is shown by the suddenness with which the mind reverses itself and answers the question. So doing, it faces the ultimate threat: *"the old fox is dead."* The mother is an animal; she is part of the natural world as the old fox is and thus has qualities which inspire fear and revulsion as well as love. By admitting her animality, the mind recognizes her as a real person. The rest of the poem shows how the *reveur*, once this crisis is past, can release his true feelings toward her. In a flickering moment he tries to escape once more, this time into an idealized childhood, but fact intervenes:

turn backward turn backward in your flight
and make me a child again just for tonight
good lord he's wet the bed come bring a light

At the last having run the risk of dishonoring his mother by admitting his real feelings, he can honor her with the true measure of real love and sorrow. The return is not just to the home and sonship but from illusion to reality and the human condition. To himself.

The revery may have been suggested by the example of Tate, who at this time was revising his "Ode to the Confederate Dead" and consulting Warren about his difficulties with it. The shifts in the levels of consciousness remind one of the ode and of Eliot's *Waste Land*, which probably influenced both poets powerfully but indirectly. Warren may also have had in the back of his mind Stephen's ruminations about his mother in Joyce's *Ulysses*. Even if he did not, a comparison is instructive, for it shows how much less the poet needed to do to suggest the inward leaps of the mind and still get his meaning across. The typography and changes in rhythm and pace indicate movements that Joyce could suggest only by much reiteration. Moreover, where Joyce achieves a massive effect of great power, Warren has a greater intensity made possible by closer and more complex interaction among the tightly organized elements. The formal effect of the organization enables the reader to examine without shying away the brutal aspects of the whole experience, which are just those he would suppress in such an ordeal, and see the pathos in the crudity. The poem does what few elegies can do without violating their intention: it shows us what grief is really like but does not surrender to it. Warren took great risks and won. Here, manifestly, was a major talent.

In the fall of 1927 Warren finally made it to Yale, and not long afterward Tate helped him obtain a contract for a biography of John Brown, which was published in the fall of 1929.[3] It is a good book for a young man, for it has vividness, dramatic presence, and a strong feeling for country life and the grain of the land, but it is not really a good study of Brown. Its proportions are wrongly conceived. Unfortunately, since Warren had a gift for such things, there is little effort to understand the self-righteous young man who flogged his brothers, memorized his Bible, thought himself superior to his circumstances, and because he could not attain the ideal world of his desire, yearned for death. One needs to know the young Pharisee before one can approach the old fanatic, but Warren, who was carrying a full program of graduate work and had to get his facts almost entirely from earlier biographies, did not sufficiently elucidate the patterns of Brown's early development or relate it to factors other than the struggle over slavery. Though he did not rely on any models, he may have been influenced without knowing it by the spate of biographies in the manner of Lytton Strachey. Warren was intrigued by the disparities in his man, especially between his noble sentiments and his ferocious violence, but when pointing these out he often lapsed into a Stracheyan flippancy akin to the tough-guy style. His ironies could show the confusion of Brown's behavior but not the deep disorder beneath it. Thus he did not explain how the man who wielded the Sword of the Spirit had embezzled, stolen, and murdered. Later he would have done better, for in Brown he encountered the proto-

[3] For an account of the writing and publication of this book see Chapter Three, pp. 141-142.

447

type of many figures in his fiction: the lonely egotist trapped in himself and prevented by his monomaniacal self-absorption from taking men and the world for what they are and getting along with a provisional version of life. Sometimes, as in the cases of Jerry Beaumont of *World Enough and Time* and Lilburne Lewis of *Brother to Dragons* the egotist is an idealist who, like Brown, would go outside the law for the sake of his Good and do a deed of darkness in the glare of his incandescent idea. Sometimes he prefers withdrawal into inaction. But either way he refuses to accede to the human condition and struggles to escape from life because it does not conform to his dream or destroys himself in his determination to force it to conform.

At about this time Warren wrote "Athenian Death," a poem on Alcibiades later published in *The Nation* (October 31, 1936), but never reprinted in collections of his verse. Proud, violent, and with no direction but that of his whims, Alcibiades is another of Warren's egotists, whom he sees as our brother, the representative modern man,

> So packed of truth and perfidy,
> Of rage and charm, that we may get
> Thus magnified and perfectly
> Our image glassed in grander grace. . . .

Obviously such figures resemble the abstractionist as Ransom described him in *God Without Thunder*. Warren had read part of the book in manuscript during the fall that his biography appeared, but by then it could not affect his study. He had been out of touch with Ransom since he left Vanderbilt, and whatever influence Ransom's ideas had on him would have come by way of Tate or from the warnings against excessive Platonism that Ransom threw out to his students when Warren was an undergraduate. At best they were at this time known to Warren only in a general way. They doubtless encouraged him to follow the bent of his own thinking but they did not furnish him with any specific conceptions which he was conscious of using. Later he was much stimulated in his criticism of abstract idealism by reading and talking with Ransom and Tate, but while he gladly acknowledges the power of their thought in helping him to refine his ideas Warren believes that initially his convictions, like Ransom's fury against abstraction, came from his experience and observation rather than the work of any particular thinker.

Writing the story of John Brown helped to renew Warren's interest in fiction. Through Tate he met Katherine Anne Porter, whose stories he read carefully for he began to see in them some of the functions of technique such as he had long known in poetry. Then he met Ford Madox Ford, and from him, Miss Porter, and Caroline Gordon he heard his first really close talk about the craft of fiction. Not long afterward Paul Rosenfeld, who had accepted his poems "Pondy Woods" and "Genealogy" for the *Second American Caravan,* suggested that he write a story for a subsequent edition of the anthology. With the biography out of the way, Warren began work in the winter of 1929-1930, while he was in his second year as a Rhodes Scholar at Oxford. For his material he went back beyond the academic worlds in which he had spent nearly a decade to the place of his boyhood about which he had heard so much local history.

Laid in Kentucky in 1907, the time of the Black Patch Tobacco War, "Prime Leaf" tells how an elderly tobacco farmer involves his family in disaster by joining an association formed to raise the price of tobacco by keeping it off the market until the buyers meet the farmers' terms. When the association resorts to night-time violence, the old man resigns. His barn is burned and his son shoots a neighbor who led the arsonists. The father makes arrangements for the son to turn himself in, but as the son rides to town, he is shot from ambush and killed.

The story moves slowly at first. Warren, who had talked with Lytle during the previous summer while home on vacation, had become interested in the Agrarian explanation of the troubles of the cash-crop farmers and he put too much of this into the opening. The real interest of the story is not in local history but in the conflict between the father and son. The older man is domineering, proud of his masculinity, and inclined, without knowing it, to undermine his son. The son does the heavy work, but the father insists on making the decisions about the farm, and he does much, symbolized by his shooting a hawk, to deflect to himself the loyalty and admiration of his grandson. His daughter-in-law tends to side with him when the two men are opposed. The son is jealous, sullen, and dissatisfied. To make things more difficult, life has become too complex for the simple code of the older man, which is based on self-sufficiency. In the end he sacrifices first his crop then his son to the code. Morally he was right, but Warren suggests that his tyrannical pride was compelling him on a course that would in one way or another eventually destroy his son.

There are many touches that show how much Warren had learned about fiction. The organization of the material is more sophisticated than the writing, which is amateurish and inferior to that of *John Brown*. As an example of his skill there is the old man's boast as he prepares to shoot the hawk, "I still do most of the shooting around the house." He does, but it is the son who, taking the initiative, shoots the night rider and, having acted for himself, brings about his own death. Still, it was the father who arranged the dangerous journey for the son—almost as if he were unwittingly shooting the son for having asserted his will. One remembers his boast. Then there is the delicate and really professional refinement of having the daughter-in-law tell the old man that his son has capitulated and will go along with the decision to join the association. A simple thing, but it reveals more than many explanations about the emotional forces beneath the surface of the family relations. It was the kind of symbolic action that Ford savored. It was some time before Warren wrote another story as good as this one, but doing it—and seeing it in print, for Rosenfeld accepted it for the *Fourth American Caravan*—helped to get him started. Within a year after finishing it he had begun his first novel. Henceforth he was committed to both poetry and fiction.

IV

In September, 1930, Warren married Miss Brescia and settled in Memphis, where he had a position in the English Department of Southwestern University. He saw his Agrarian friends occasionally, but he was not one of the inner group. In the next year he went to Vanderbilt to replace Ransom, who was absent on leave. Davidson was there and Tate was living in Clarksville and came to Nashville often. When Ransom returned Warren was kept on and they became fast friends, though seventeen years and differences in rank separated them. Two years later Warren moved to Louisiana State University. His stay among the Agrarians and the interval of close companionship with Ransom were surprisingly brief. This needs to be remembered when one thinks of the intellectual communion among the three principal Fugitive-Agrarian writers. Much that Ransom and Tate had come to agree on through their correspondence was fully exposed to Warren while he was at Yale and visiting the Tates on weekends. At that time Warren was much impressed by their argument that a man needed myths or traditions and that scientific rationalism had destroyed the bases of responsible judgment and action, leaving man unable to cope with the contingent universe. At Nashville these ideas were much in the air and Warren responded to them. Yet he was not sympathetic with Tate's views on the hierarchical societies of the past, partly because he had never taken any interest in a lost Golden Age. Agrarianism encouraged further his interest in Southern history and Lyle Lanier convinced him that progress was an illusion in whose name men burdened themselves with needless confusion and suffering. But much as he loved his region and the rich substance of its past, he did not share the passion of Tate and Davidson for the vanished grandeur of the Old South. Nor did he much respond to that image of the satisfying life which Ransom and Tate signified in their Agrarian essays with the term "European." Though he was to put more of the philosophy of Agrarianism into his imaginative writing than any other member of the group, he used only a little of its social and still less of its cultural theory. One can understand him better for knowing something about Agrarianism, but only if one observes how independent he was.

This was for him a time of great personal difficulty. The Depression was approaching its nadir, and the state of young college teachers was perilous. Warren's annual appointments at Vanderbilt were made with the expectation that they would not be renewed. During the summer before the school year of 1933-1934 he was without a job and all but penniless. His wife was dangerously ill and he himself was tormented by a series of small sicknesses. Throughout it all he worked away at fiction hoping to make a little money. In the spring of 1931 a publisher had suggested that he write a novel and by the following August he reported that it was one fourth done.[4] He finished it during the summer of 1933, when he was nearly exhausted by worry and ear and throat infections. Set in Kentucky during the period 1910-1914, the novel, to which he gave the title *God's Own Time*, described a family much like his own. For it he sought a model in the works of Hardy, with the result that it was too like a play: there were too many scenes, gestures, and speeches and too few opportunities for commenting on the meaning of the action within the framework of the narrative. But he learned many things about what a novelist working with the conventions of the symbolic naturalism of Flaubert, Conrad, Ford, Porter, and Gordon could *not* do and remain faithful to his medium. The novel was rejected. So were the stories, among them "When the Light Gets Green" and "The Unvexed Isles," which he wrote in this bad season. Even so, he began at once on his second novel, which he finished in 1935 but left untitled. This, too, was set in central Kentucky, and described the conflicts of a school and family during the Twenties. Warren submitted the novels to nearly every publisher in New York without success. In 1936 he told a story that he later used in *At Heaven's Gate* to a publisher who agreed to bring out the novels after Warren had written the story. But Warren disliked the arrangement and withdrew from it. Neither of these early novels has yet appeared.[5]

Less than a year after the desperate summer of 1933, Warren was offered a post at Louisiana State University, where he would be working with his old friend and fellow Rhodes Scholar, Cleanth Brooks. It was a good appointment without the uncertainties he had known at Vanderbilt, and better things were to come, for during the following March the president of the university proposed that he and Brooks serve as managing editors of a new review for which Charles W. Pipkin would act as editor-in-chief. They were guaranteed $10,000 for a start and told to ask for more if it was needed. By the following summer the first number of *The Southern Review* came off the press. In it was "Letter from a Coward to a Hero," Warren's best poem to date. Before the war brought it to an end early in 1942 their magazine was the most distinguished

---

[4] From letters to Tate dated April 24, 1931, and August 10, 1931. All of the letters from Warren to Tate referred to in this chapter are now in the Princeton University Library.

[5] From a conversation with Warren, January 6, 1954.

quarterly in the country, comparable in its style and excellence to Eliot's *Criterion*. Ransom's *Kenyon Review* had a narrower scope and greater significance in the history of our literature, but it was not so fine nor interesting a magazine. *The Southern Review* offered poetry and fiction by Stevens, Auden, Katherine Anne Porter, Eudora Welty, and Warren, but its great distinction was in its criticism and essays on Southern culture. Ransom, Tate, Brooks, Yvor Winters, Blackmur, and F. O. Matthiessen argued over the nature of poetry while others wrote explications of particular works which were remarkable in those days for their thoroughness and depth. John Peale Bishop's essay on *Finnegans Wake*, for example, was for long the best piece on that book. Tate, Davidson, Owsley, and George Marion O'Donnell defended the South with vigor and often with outrageous condescension. The magazine was not intended to reflect the view of any group, but the Agrarians and their friends and students appeared in it frequently and gave it much of its tone and merit. The editors were liberal and welcomed dissenting opinions, though in general the magazine spoke for a conservative position.

Fine as it was, other collaborations of Brooks and Warren were to have much more lasting importance. With Jack Purser they published *An Approach to Literature* in 1936. This anthology for use in the last years of high school and first years of college provided examples of close reading and attention to function that characterized the criticism in *The Southern Review*. Teachers and students alike found it so rewarding that Brooks and Warren prepared a more sophisticated book, *Understanding Poetry*, which first appeared in 1938 and, in a third edition, was still selling well twenty-five years later. This has been unquestionably the most influential guide to the study of literature of our time, and more than anything else it brought about the revolution that Ransom and Tate wanted by establishing as dogma for a generation of students and teachers that the significant meaning of a poem came from the total interaction of its elements arranged in their own unique and inviolable order and exceeded any paraphrase. The two young editors got the discussion of the poem as poem out of the quarterlies and into the classroom.

When the book appeared it was thought that it owed much to the example of Empson's *Seven Types of Ambiguity*. In his *Mod-*

ern Poetry and the Tradition (1939) Brooks acknowledges his indebtedness to Empson—and to Tate, Yeats, Ransom, Blackmur, Richards, and other critics. But none of those cited had published a critical system. Rather, they showed what poems could yield under close scrutiny, so that Brooks's references to synthesizing their ideas is a bit misleading. He and Warren knew the work of Empson and Richards, his teacher, when they prepared their anthology, but though they admired them as readers, there was nothing in the espousal of ambiguity which the editors had not heard already in discussion with Ransom and Tate, and Warren doubts that Empson had any influence whatever on their approach. Actually, they were reaping the harvest of their experience as poets and of all the talk about poetic technique in which they had participated since they were undergraduates at Vanderbilt. It was the environment in which they had matured more than the work of any theorist or critic that shaped their method, though if one man were to be cited as a force acting upon that environment it would have to be Ransom, not because of any single writing but because, as so often with aspects of Warren's thought, Ransom's ideas were in the air.

When the list of influential modern critics is recited, Warren's name is often included, but this is mainly a testimony to the extraordinary effect of *Understanding Poetry* and *Understanding Fiction* (1943), on which he also collaborated with Brooks, for though he has written a few superb essays on the dominant themes in the works of other poets and fictionists such as Coleridge, Ransom, Conrad, Hemingway, and Welty, he has not substantially affected our critical vision of any writer nor, except through the textbooks, modified our perspective in the ways that Ransom, Tate, and Brooks have done. His one essay in poetics to date, "Pure and Impure Poetry," first presented as a Mesures Lecture at Princeton in 1942, summarizes their ideas on the differences between concrete pluralistic poetry and abstract monistic scientific discourse. His ontology of a poem resembles Ransom's, but he avoids the problem of imitation and representative form. He assumes that poetry makes statements about (not resembling) experience and he wants them to be faithful to the full substance, to the "impurity" as well as to the pure idea imbedded in it. He makes a fine case for the validity and value of poetic knowledge and shows himself to be an alert and sensitive reader, but it cannot be said that he adds anything to our theories of literature and criticism.

Warren was so busy with fiction and preparing for his classes when he first came back to Tennessee that it is not surprising that he neglected poetry. In 1930 he wrote only one poem that was published; in 1931-1932, only two. (One of them was "The Return: An Elegy.") In 1933-1934 he did better in spite of the troubles that beset him, for he finished his first novel and before he was deeply into his second he wrote ten or eleven. By the end of 1935 the count 'of those that actually reached print stood at seventeen, a small total for five years.[6] Though he used regional materials in his fiction, Warren did not follow the direction in which he had been moving since he went to California but turned aside after "The Return: An Elegy" to write poems having small resemblance to anything he had done before. He was teaching Elizabethan and seventeenth-century drama and poetry. Following his predilections and the examples of Ransom and Davidson he emphasized the diction, imagery, and organization of the works considered and the relation of a writer's style to his vision. He himself read Shakespeare with a new attention and passion. The dramatist appealed to his taste for imposing language and his deepening sense of the irony and bafflement of man's fate. His father and grandfather had enjoyed quoting scraps of poetry distinguished by the music and splendor of the diction, but whatever affinities Warren inherited had until now been pretty well kept under except for his imitations of Tate and his brief indulgence of what has here been termed the tough-guy manner. Perhaps Ransom's opposition at the Fugitive meetings to the Southern propensity for florid language had something to do with it. Now he let himself go more and more. The study of Shakespeare increasingly affected his writing, not only in its rhetoric but in the organization of scenes in his fiction, the depiction of character by means of action, the symbols, and the concentration upon the theme of self-discovery. When, years afterward, Warren looked back upon the long preparation, it seemed to him that Shakespeare and Dante were the most important influences upon both his poetry and his fiction.[7]

For the present, however, John Donne and the metaphysical school had a more obvious effect on his work than Shakespeare.

[6] Information about the dates of the writing of the poems discussed in this chapter was furnished by Warren during the autumn of 1953.

[7] He was quite emphatic in making this point in a conversation on January 6, 1954. Dante's influence, which came after the time now under discussion, is taken up in the next chapter.

Tate, too, was studying Donne (his essay, "A Note on Donne," was published in the spring of 1932), and his influence could be seen in "The Cross" and "Shadow and Shade," while Ransom wrote the most metaphysical of his poems, "Painted Head," the only one on which Donne may have had some influence. Both men liked to cite Donne's verse for having the tension and texture needed to complicate the abstract argument, and their opinions carried weight with Warren. From Donne and the metaphysicals he learned about compression and weaving together intricate metaphoric variations, but the poems he wrote at this time were not very good—not for the man who had written "The Return: An Elegy," anyway.

They are ingenious enough, "yoking by violence together" the apparently contradictory or inapt and compelling the reader to agree that, yes, a connection of sorts can be discerned after all. But the yoking does not lead beyond itself as it does with Donne's conceits or Ransom's oddly assorted phrases, to the discovery of qualities which familiarity and inertia have made us overlook. For example, there is "Problem of Knowledge":

> What years, what hours, has spider contemplation spun
> Her film to snare the muscled fact?
> What hours unbuild the done undone,
> Or apprehend the actor in the act?

A lot of bother to say a simple thing the hard way! Now Warren had, as it turned out, a remarkable gift for putting before the reader little nuances of desire and anxiety on the very fringe of awareness. Usually he did this by choosing some exactly right and, though commonplace, singularly evocative detail, such as the allusion to the waiting mail in "End of Season." Often these details were related to the observations of childhood described at the beginning of this discussion and their force came from their association with deep, and sometimes long-suppressed, feelings going back to one's early years. But at other times he might try to get at the nuances by piling up qualifications, exceptions, contradictions, and paradoxes, and often these would overbalance and topple his argument. The line "What hours unbuild the done undone" represents this kind of self-defeating fussiness, which, on a much larger scale, mars a number of the ruminative passages of *Brother to Dragons* when the language strains toward some ultimate mystery. Similarly in

World Enough and Time the narrative keeps turning back upon itself in order to nag questions whose complexity the reader fully appreciates. In "Calendar" the speaker wonders if the dead remember "an age that knew no hap / Of coil, nor jar," or whether it is their wrong that makes the wrong of our time. And what of the ages to come?

> In midnight's poise
> Long past our hence-going
> Will our hurt in the wind's voice
> Speak so to men unknowing
> Of our hugged joys
>
> Then overpassed
> And frailer than summer's heart
> That locked in the burr from frost
> With the wanton year may start
> And glad time's waste?

The dutiful reader can start at either end of that question but his attempt to make sense of it will come to little. Does *glad* function as a verb (gladden)? What is the antecedent of *that* in the third line from the end? Is *locked in the burr from frost* a non-restrictive participial phrase, or is it part of a fragmentary relative clause, *That* [*is*] *locked in the burr from* [*the*] *frost*? Questions such as these seem picayune, but because they cannot be answered, the poem cannot be understood. It overreaches itself.

In some of the poems the cleverness collapses into phrase-mongering. "Toward Rationality," for example, begins:

> Brothers, stones on this moraine of time,
> And I, a stone: for you were Xerxes' guests
> In littoral picnic by the unfettered brine.
> This commentary, perhaps, will discommode.

It does indeed. For the poem continues:

> The cortex-knotty apple draws by blue
> Occasion from the lambent air, what?

The baffled reader may well reply, "Don't ask me." Here is something rare in Warren's work, an obscure poem. It was one of four poems published in *The American Review* in May, 1934. Two of

457

the others were as labored and almost as opaque, but not "Eidolon," which is by turns pretentious in an academic way and sensitive in its invocation of the mystery and sad loneliness of night in the country.

> All night, in May, dogs barked in the hollow woods;
> Hoarse, from secret huddles of no light,
> By moonlit bole, hoarse, the dogs gave tongue.
> In May, by moon, no moon, thus: I remember
> Of their far clamor the throaty, infatuate timbre.
>
> The boy, all night, lay in the black room,
> Tick-straw, all night, harsh to the bare side. . . .

He could hear "Far off . . . unappeasable riot." In nearby rooms lay "the man, clod-heavy, hard hand uncurled; / The old man, eyes wide, spittle on his beard." Beyond,

> In dark was crushed the may-apple: plunging, the rangers
> Of dark remotelier belled their unhouselled angers.

In the morning the boy found

> blood black on
> May-apple at dawn, old beech-husk. And trails are lost
> By rock, in ferns lost, by pools unlit.
> I heard the hunt. Who saw, in darkness, how fled
> The white eidolon from fanged commotion rude?

It is a strange poem, mixing melodrama, the specious smartness of the ellipses, and the fustian of "belled their unhouselled angers" with a real feeling for the boy's sense of exclusion from some frightful yet longed-for rite. What validates the feeling and offsets the silliness of the unhouselled angers and the "fanged commotion rude" is that tick-straw in the side.

It is helped by the rhythmical force. For some time Warren had varied his line by adding unaccented syllables and crowding the accented ones together. Often, as in "Pondy Woods" and "The Return: An Elegy," he used long phrases cast in the syntax of ordinary speech, and his rhythms tended to be rapid and slurred while the accents pattered lightly within the lines, which frequently ran over. When he wrote his metaphysical poems, he put strong syllables side by side so that they formed nervously hovering accents, spondees, or simply two feet with no unaccented syllable or pause between them. To add emphasis, he broke his lines into short, staccato phrases. It was partly for this that he developed the elliptical mannerism of "In May, by moon, no moon, thus: I remember" and "Tick-straw, all night, harsh to the bare side." Finally, he packed his verse with alliteration, consonance, and assonance, which added weight and helped locate the accents of some of the most irregular lines. He was learning to manage the pacing well. By thinning out the differences among the strong accents, he made some of his lines carry the reader along so swiftly that he could not decide where to put pressure or come to rest. Then, having rushed the reader along, Warren would bring him to a full stop or a long pause before detonating in his ear a cluster of syllables weighted by alliteration and consonance. For those who take pleasure in rhythmical energy and variety, there are a multitude of delights in such lines as

> Dogs quartered the black woods: blood black on
> May-apple at dawn, old beech-husk. And trails are lost
> By rock, in ferns lost, by pools unlit.

Bad as some of the poems of this interval may be (and "Pacific Gazer" is probably his worst), Warren was learning much from writing them.

One poem used the seventeenth-century modes with stunning success: "The Garden," awarded the H. H. Levinson Prize given by *Poetry* in 1936, three years after it was written.

> How kind, how secret, now the sun
> Will bless this garden frost has won,
> And touch once more, as once it used,
> The furled boughs by cold bemused.
> Though summered brilliance had but room
> In blossom, now the leaves will bloom
> Their time, and take from milder sun
> An unreviving benison.

After a description of the summer garden that exquisitely balances vivid naturalism with ceremonious formality, the poem ends,

> But he who sought, not love, but peace
> In such rank plot could take no ease:

459

Now poised between the two alarms
Of summer's lusts and winter's harms,
Only for him these precincts wait
In sacrament that can translate
All things that feed luxurious sense
From appetite to innocence.

Marvell's "Thoughts in a Garden" comes at once to mind, and one's first reaction is a mixture of awe and pleasure at Warren's mastery of Marvell's kind of poetry. Simply as mimicry, the poem is remarkable, but it is no pastiche as were the earlier imitations of Tate and Ransom. The elements are perfectly right with respect to the seventeenth-century idiom and tone, and they are also perfectly right for one another in the constellation of this poem. Style and substance are wholly merged.

To appreciate them one needs to remember how Marvell delighted in the abundance of *his* garden:

What wond'rous life is this I lead!
Ripe apples drop about my head;
The luscious clusters of the vine
Upon my mouth do crush their wine;
The nectarine and curious peach
Into my hands themselves do reach;
Stumbling on melons, as I pass,
Ensnared with flowers, I fall on grass.

Aware of the season's brevity, he wants to keep the summer and its riot. But Warren speaks of a briefer and more precious moment —a single autumn day "poised between the two alarms." Marvell's poem tries to banish thoughts of time and decay with the present abundance, but Warren's faces them. Warren takes the way Ransom would have chosen—to measure the garden's value by acknowledging its mortality. His poem is the more adult (being like Donne's poetry without the sardonic harshness); yet its meaning depends much upon our memory of the youthful lightheartedness of Marvell's poem. Warren took a chance in reminding us of such a master, but he was equal to the occasion.

He admired gamblers who, as he said in "Resolution," knew "Time's secret pulse" and made their dares against time and decay, aware that in the end they would lose. He could admire, but not so much, the hero with no fear whom he described in "Letter from a Coward to a Hero," published soon after he turned thirty.

> What did the day bring?
> The sharp fragment,
> The shard,
> The promise half-meant,
> The impaired thing,
> At dusk the hard word,
> Good action by good will marred . . .
> All
> In the trampled stall:
> > *I think you deserved better;*
> > *Therefore I am writing you this letter.*

The speaker recalls the scenes of childhood, with their innocence and assuring light, and wonders how the hero's courage was made strong enough to outlast the changes that came with growing up. For himself,

> Though young, I do not like loud noise:
> The sudden backfire,
> The catcall of boys,
> Drums beating for
> The big war,
> Or clocks that tick all night and will not stop.

Out of his familiarity with the little terror—it may, after all, be only a mouse in the wall—he warns the hero:

> You have been strong in love and hate.
> Disaster owns less speed than you have got,
> But he will cut across the back lot
> To lurk and lie in wait.
> Admired of children, gathered for their games,
> Disaster, like the dandelion, blooms,
> And the delicate film is fanned
> To seed the shaven lawn.
> Rarely, you've been unmanned;
> I have not seen your courage put to pawn.

461

"At the hour when lights go out in the houses" and the mind is troubled by the cry of killdeer and the sound that may be surf or a distant cannonade, the coward writes, "You are what you are without our aid." He seems to be one of the Captain MacWhirrs, too boyish and unimaginative to be troubled. But in the last line—in fact, in the last word—Warren adds his subtlest touch to the portrait:

> No doubt, when corridors are dumb
> And the bed is made,
> It is your custom to recline,
> Clutching between the forefinger and thumb
> Honor, for death shy valentine.

Why *valentine*? Commenting on the poem Cleanth Brooks says that the comparison earlier in the poem of the hero with a pointer that is not gun-shy is used "to qualify and define the coward's attitude toward the hero. The virtues of the pointer are solid virtues—but they are hardly the virtues of imagination." Yet, "the poem does not veer off into mockery of the hero." To resolve the conflict between his admiration and a certain impatience with the hero's immaturity, the speaker ends with a bit of humor. "The whimsical compliment, *though* compliment, at the same time reduces the hero to a small boy, and, ironically, a shy young boy."[8] Yet is it that simple? Is there not a delicate hint of perversity in the childlike behavior of the hero? Not only does he not fear death, he likes it. He sends it shy tokens of his affection. Perhaps he plays games with it. He resembles the figures in the later poem "Terror" who are compelled to seek danger in order to get enough sensation from outside themselves to know that they are alive. They are without "an adequate definition of terror," which means that they are also without an adequate definition of love, guilt, regret, time, death. They have never grown up. Here the last word cuts deeply into the mystery of human nature and lays bare some of the psychic roots of fear and evil. The imagery of Tate's "The Wolves" is powerful and his poem is more sustained and effective than this one. (Warren almost throws the poem away with the cheap sarcasm of "For sleep try love or veronal, / Though some prefer, I know, philology.") Still, there is nothing in "The Wolves" that gets

[8] *Modern Poetry and the Tradition* (Chapel Hill, 1939), pp. 83, 85.

quite so far under the surface as the allusion to the valentine. It was Warren's special gift that he could understand the worries, usually released only in nightmare, that would lead from dandelions on the well-kept lawn right back to death itself.

For those who are not heroes, *what will avail?* he asks in "Question and Answer," and in "History" suggests an answer: Nothing, for "Only the act is pure," and the meaning of the act is corrupted and lost in time. So it is with the act of love and love itself. Lovers, he had written in "Resolution," know even better than the gamblers—the huddled jockey, the matador between the bull's horns, the pitcher when the score is tied and the sun low—how time mars all things. The girl in that poem, like the girl in Ransom's "Vaunting Oak," thinks she can defy time with her love and cries *"There is no Time."* But her lover knows better. In 1935-1936, as he was completing his second novel and before he had begun working on *Night Rider*, Warren wrote four great poems on the mortality of love: "Picnic Remembered," "Monologue at Midnight," "Bearded Oaks," and "Love's Parable." In style they stand somewhere between the metaphysical poems of 1933-1934 and the Marvellian "The Garden." They explore and develop metaphysical conceits, but they are not so dense and tangled as the earlier poems, though their tone and idiom is unmistakably influenced by seventeenth-century verse. Thus "Picnic Remembered":

> We stood among the painted trees:
> The amber light laved them, and us;
> Or light then so untremulous,
> So steady, that our substances,
> Twin flies, were as in amber tamed
> With our perfections stilled and framed
> To mock Time's marvelling after-spies.

The variations on the master metaphor are imaginative and the account of the decay of love attains profound sadness restrained by great formal dignity. But the tension of form and feeling is not maintained. At the end Warren shifts from narrative to comment and stumbles into banality:

> . . . is the soul a hawk that, fled
> On glimmering wings past vision's path,

Reflects the last gleam to us here
Though sun is sunk and darkness near
—Uncharted Truth's high heliograph?

The same thing had happened earlier with "Question and Answer," which ended by answering its question *what will avail?* with the suggestion that man be as a stone or hurl defiance at God. Though he asserted that meaning is lost in time, Warren felt compelled to sum up his poems with generalizations appealing to big, vacant, capitalized terms such as "Truth." Later on in his fiction a similar need to explain his narratives gave him unceasing difficulties. To involve his explanations in the dynamic of the story he resorted to interpolated tales, journals, and comments by observers. His success was various. Willie Proudfit's story is forced upon the structure of *Night Rider*; Jack Burden's reflections fit easily into *All the King's Men*, for he is the narrator, but often they are limited by his sensibility; Jerry Beaumont in *World Enough and Time* and Amantha Starr in *Band of Angels* weary the reader by returning again and again to the same propositions. Warren sometimes could not leave well enough alone, not trusting his material to project its own meaning. In "Bearded Oaks," however, he struck off a perfect ending. After describing, a little too lengthily, how two lovers have escaped for a moment into serenity in which "history is thus undone," the speaker concludes:

> We live in time so little time
> And we learn all so painfully,
> That we may spare this hour's term
> To practice for eternity.

Such simplicity did not come easily in the tumult of Warren's prodigious talent. More to his liking was the accumulation of similes in "Love's Parable," which does not have the precision of feeling of "Picnic Remembered" nor the virtuosity of "The Garden" and is perhaps too abundant but is nonetheless a magnificent poem. It carries its burden of riches with scarcely a falter right down to the final syllable.

> As kingdoms after civil broil,
> Long faction-bit and sore unmanned,

Unlaced, unthewed by lawless toil,
Will welcome to the cheering strand
A prince whose tongue, not understood,
Yet frames a new felicity,
And alien, seals domestic good:
Once, each to each, such aliens, we.

That time, each was the other's sun,
Ecliptic's charter, system's core;
Locked in its span, the wandering one,
Though colder grown, might yet endure
Ages unnumbered, for it fed
On light and heat flung from the source
Of light that lit dark as it fled:
Wonder of dull astronomers.

"All on easy axle roved." Now the lovers "have seen the fungus eyes / Of misery spore in the night" and "How proud flesh on the sounder grows / Till rot engross the state of men."

And marked, within, the inward sore
Of self that cankers at the bone,
Contempt of very love we bore
And hatred of the good once known. . . .

The lover wonders, "Are we but mirror to the world? / Or does the world our ruin reflect. . . ?" and concludes:

O falling-off! O peace composed
Within my kingdom when your reign
Was fulgent-full! and nought opposed
Your power, that slack is, but again
May sway my sullen elements,
And bend ambition to his place.
That hope: for there are testaments
That men, by prayer, have mastered grace.

The astronomical tropes and the image of the lover revolving around the beloved that appear in the poem suggest Donne, but the diction and the other images show that Shakespeare, particularly through his sonnets, was a more important agent in Warren's

465

imagination. The poem could have been written only by one who had steeped himself in Shakespeare's works. The strength of Warren's affinity for that work is suggested by the images of morbid conditions of the flesh such as ulcers and suppurative infections. Like Shakespeare, Warren was obsessed with the canker rotting the substance beneath the winsome surface, and henceforth he used some form of the metaphor many times in his works to suggest a secret evil within the most innocent-seeming occasion. Only the symbol of the dark pool appears as often in his writings.

In the fall of 1935, the Alcestis Press published in an edition of 165 copies a collection of Warren's verse entitled *Thirty-Six Poems*. All of them but "Genealogy" were subsequently included in Warren's *Selected Poems*. Only one, "To a Face in the Crowd," had been written before Warren went to Berkeley. The four poems on the decay of love were finished too late to be included. Then in 1936 Warren was granted a Houghton Mifflin fellowship and settled down to work on *Night Rider*. He was thirty-one. He had been writing poetry seriously for fourteen years. He was not to return to it for another four. An interval in his development was over.

They were student poems. Such an observation seems absurd in the face of his achievement in the best of them. Nevertheless, he was still learning, experimenting, feeling his way among a variety of style and modes, doing, in fact, what he had done for Davidson as an undergraduate. He had not followed most of the poets of his generation and gone to school to Baudelaire, the Symbolists, the Imagists, Pound, Eliot, and Cummings, though, as we know, he had once imitated Pound and Eliot in the same poem. He knew all about the little magazines; he had been down to the Village and over to Paris. Even so, he learned his lessons in the library and the graduate seminar and not on the Left Bank. He had not yet declared his independence. Sometimes he spoke in his own voice, as in the Kentucky Mountain Farm series, "The Return: An Elegy," "Resolution," "Letter from a Coward to a Hero," parts of "Eidolon," and a few other pieces, but then he would turn aside to try out the tones of another man. It was not simply imitation, though it is hard to say just what it was. Later, when he had found his style, it was to be full of echoes of Shakespeare, the

King James Bible, Milton, western Kentucky dialects, the Methodist hymnal, folksongs, and, for good measure, bits of Wordsworth, Coleridge, and Tennyson. But these were as fully assimilated into an idiom all his own as were the elements of fairy tales and the essays of seventeenth-century churchmen into Ransom's. What he did was not imitation because he learned to think in the styles that he tried. In "Love's Parable," for instance, he examines his material through Shakespeare's style (or one of them, anyway) and sees it with something akin to Shakespeare's sensibility. Though he was slow in coming into his own, that was a good deal to have done even at thirty-one.

Curiously, just when Agrarianism was deepening his interest in his region and its past he ceased to make much use of regional material in his poetry, though he used much of it in his fiction. And though he had been brought to Agrarianism by his dislike of many aspects of industrial civilization, he wrote no poems on the evils of urban life or the defacement of the country. Concerned over the loss of individual freedom and identity, he wrote no poems on the oppression of the individual. Nor any on the decline from past greatness, for when he spoke of the effects of time he focused upon the changes taking place in the span of one's life. He was inclined with Ransom to think that all ages were much alike. (That was one good reason for reading history—not to escape the drabness of the present but to understand it.) He was still assimilating ideas as he was assimilating styles. By the time that conceptions which might definitely be termed Agrarian began to appear in his writing the Agrarian interlude was over, and when his thinking came most to resemble that of Ransom and Tate—or at least the portion that furnished the philosophical bases of Agrarianism—he had, by his own testimony, put Agrarianism aside and largely forgotten it under the pressures of wartime.

Perhaps he wrote so little about his region because he was on guard against local colorism. The Fugitives had promptly rejected any proposal from outside the group that they write on Southern themes, and they were harsh in their criticism of anything redolent of sentimental sectionalism. Warren, as we know, was persuaded by Tate of the writer's need for tradition—a right relation with a place and its past. This being so, as he wrote in "Not Local Color" (1932), "the merely quaint, that pitfall of the so-called local color school, arouses . . . a peculiar and violent distaste. The idea of local color is incomplete and unphilosophical; it does not provide a framework in which human action has more than immediate and adventitious significance."

A few years afterwards, soon after he had started on *Night Rider*, he observed in "Some Don'ts For Literary Regionalists":

"Regionalism is not quaintness and local color and folklore, for those things when separated from a functional idea are merely a titillation of the reader's sentimentality or snobbishness. . . . Regionalism does not mean that a writer should relinquish any resource of speculation or expression that he has managed to achieve. . . . A writer's worst dishonesty would be to deny, on the ground of theory, part of his own temper and own resource; to limit, arbitrarily, the sensibility he would bring to his material."[9]

Perhaps he was so diffident because he had not yet found his own right relation to the past, which, it was said earlier in this study, is the great problem of Southern writers of his generation and the one immediately before it. In nothing was he more Southern than in his sense of man's desire to give his conduct a meaning lasting beyond the need of the moment. He knew Southern history and he had a rare sense of the land—probably only Owsley equalled him in this. But despite his acceptance of Tate's beliefs about the need for tradition, he did not have his friends' aggressive concern for Southern tradition as such. To put the matter a little too simply, he himself was concerned with certain inward aspects of man's universal search for his true identity. When he took for his poetry images from his region it was because he understood them well enough to know they would evoke the interior event. And so it was even with so regional a novel as *Night Rider*. By the time he had finished it, he had found his relation to history. It was not the legend of a lost superior civilization but a parable of men in all times to be understood for all times. Look at it long enough and there was no need to worry about mere local color.

[9] "Not Local Color," *VQR*, VIII (January, 1932), 154; "Some Don'ts For Literary Regionalists," *The American Review*, VIII (December, 1936), 148, 149.

V

In September of 1904, less than a year before Warren was born, a group of tobacco growers met in Guthrie and formed the Planters' Protective Association. The American Tobacco Company had a monopoly in that area and had driven prices so low that farmers could not even make expenses. It was the intention of the Association to force prices up by keeping crops out of the market.

Southern farmers had united before. On the frontier in 1875 some had formed the Southern Farmers' Alliance against the land syndicates. It evolved into a secret society with rituals that gave its oppressed members a feeling of importance. When Dr. C. W. Macune was its head, he dreamed of turning it into a national organization, and at one time there were 35,000 official lecturers out spreading the word. When goaded far enough the farmers were ready for violent action. The South had not forgotten the first Klan. In 1889 a mob rode into Delhi, Louisiana, and wrecked several stores in a childish attempt to cancel indebtedness. Thus when the Planters' Protective Association failed to raise prices despite the fact that it had 30,000 members in western Kentucky and Tennessee and 8,000 in Virginia, there were precedents for direct action, and between 1906 and 1908 bands of night riders scraped plant beds, destroyed crops and barns, whipped and sometimes murdered men, and dynamited warehouses. The violence was finally brought under control by the state militia after threatening the breakdown of all law and order in some sections. One of Warren's earliest recollections was of the National Guardsmen stationed in Guthrie to keep the peace, and throughout his boyhood he heard tales of the Black Patch Tobacco Wars. From these he had taken the material for "Prime Leaf," his first published story. Now he went back to them for *Night Rider*.

Percy Munn, the protagonist, is a lawyer who lives on a tobacco farm outside Bardsville, Kentucky. Urged by friends to whom he cannot say "no," he joins an association of tobacco farmers and in time becomes a leader of the night riders who use force to keep crops off the market. His days and nights are separate. By day he defends a client against a charge of murder, though he has to resort to an illegal night search to get evidence leading to acquittal. He is gradually drawn more deeply into the lawlessness of the darkness, which spills over into his orderly daytime life. He loses his wife and his home, kills his client, who had betrayed the night riders, has an affair with the daughter of his best friend which causes the friend to have a stroke and eventually die, is accused of a murder he did not commit, goes into hiding, and at the end is shot by soldiers while fleeing. Yet throughout this violent career he is a strangely passive man. Others make most of the decisions that affect his life. He is talked into joining the association and then the night riders; he is asked to speak at a rally and does, but cannot remember what he said; his mistress takes the initiative in beginning and ending their affair; others decide where he shall hide out; and he is killed at last when the nephew of the man with whom he had been staying reveals where he is. The nephew had been outraged when his former mistress, whom he had not asked to do so, visits him at his hidingplace and comes in the night to his bedroom to talk to him. About the only important thing he does of his own accord is to draw the fire of the soldiers by shooting at them first, though he does not know why. He has no loyalties, not even to himself. As long as things go along in familiar ruts he is supported by the routine of the community, but once a crisis breaks out, his utter separateness is revealed. He half-heartedly tries to find some sort of identity and attachment in violence, but he fails. The climax of the story's meaning comes in the final interview with Lucille Christians. She tells him that she had been trying to warm herself at his vitality but now knows he is as cold as she. In truth he has long been dead before the soldiers' bullets find him. He can scarcely be said ever to have been alive.

The social history in the novel exactly illustrates the Agrarian explanation of the evils of cash-crop farming. The farmers are at the mercy of the market, which is controlled by large, impersonal corporations feeling no responsibility for their welfare. They are, as Ransom had argued in his essay "Land," over-capitalized; they produce so much that the buyer can set the price. If they raised only what they needed, they could defy outsiders, and those like Bill Christians who come nearest to being subsistence farmers are the ones best able to keep decisions in their own hands. But finance-capitalism corrupts the community, takes responsibility for the affairs away from the citizens, undermines the law, and destroys the trust that enabled men to live together. The novel also gives support to Ransom's ideas about the effect of farm life on character. Munn and the other hollow man of the novel, Senator Tolliver, have left the land to pursue such abstractions as law and political power and have cut themselves off from the past, their families, and despite the appearance of camaraderie, the community. By comparison Bill Christians, Captain Todd, and Willie Proudfit love and serve the land, though they have been trapped into a false economy. Willie, who had been a buffalo hunter in the West, returned to the hard drudgery of farming to save his soul. He had come to understand that in hunting for pay he had become no more than a part of a killing machine.

Herbert Agar, to whom Warren told the story before he started writing it, recognized its cogency at once and talked about it to the Houghton Mifflin Company. Though the firm had turned down both of Warren's earlier novels, it acted on Agar's urging and sent Warren forms to apply for the fellowship which he eventually won. Agar's interest and the aptness of the novel as an illustration of Agrarian economics make it easy to exaggerate the importance of Agrarianism for it. No doubt it helped Warren to understand the history of his region, though there is nothing so sophisticated about the explanation that understanding could not have come by way of the tales about the tobacco wars. To read it as an Agrarian novel is to miss the point that the real story, like the real one of "Prime Leaf," lies elsewhere. Here social history is used as the occasion for acting out a psychic history. In an essay on Eudora Welty, Warren commented on her use of allegory and made an observation that applies quite as well to his own more naturalistic fiction: "It is a method by which the items of fiction (scene, action, character, etc.) are presented not as document but as comment, not as a report but as a thing made, not as history but as idea. Even in the most realistic and reportorial fiction, the social picture, the psychological analysis, and the pattern of action do not rest at the level of mere report; they finally operate as expressive symbols as well."[10] Thus it is with the Agrarianism of *Night Rider*.

Expressive of what?

[10] "Love and Separateness in Eudora Welty," *Selected Essays* (New York, 1958), pp. 167-168.

The novel is Warren's first extended fictional portrait of the lonely egotist cut off from others by inadequacies that keep him from establishing his separate identity and fulfilling himself as a man. If he were self-sufficient he would be sufficient for others as well. But like others who do not know who or what they are and for that reason must depend on those around them even when they deny them, he is forced back upon himself. Since there is no true self there, he ends in nothing. The inadequacies are not closely studied in the portrait of Munn. The accumulating violence about him drastically changes Munn's life, but not his character, for there is little to change. He lacks awareness of much except raw force and he has next to no moral imagination. Compared with such later characters who are afflicted with similar inadequacies as Sue Murdock, Jerry Beaumont, or even the cloddish Jerry Calhoun and careening Willie Stark, he has little curiosity about his own nature. He is dull and usually apathetic. That the novel is so absorbing is a tribute to the excitement and historical significance of the events and the skill with which Warren reveals his character in behavior.

He had married a pretty, childish woman. Both of them were so incapable of love, both were so empty, that even in their most tender moments he had to hurt her in order to make an impression. Lucille Christians was a more energetic woman, but, as she tells him, " 'We never talked any . . . not like other people. What we were to each other, it was all closed up, shut in. It was cut off from everything else, everything we had been. From part of what we were, even then.' " And so it is with all things. Even when he is most involved with the organization and shares in its most desperate undertakings, he feels apart from the other men. At times his loneliness oppresses him. Standing at night by a hotel window, he sees some unknown man walking down the street and has an impulse to dress and hurry after him because then he would have a destination. It seems to him that others have some secret that sustains them, and he peers furtively into their faces to startle the secret and know it. He feels dimly the lack of meaning in his behavior: "What was the center of his life, he demanded of himself. He could not say." " 'People have to have something to look forward to,' " he says to Lucille, " 'something to move toward, to hope for. Some direction.' " But when they try to make love after her father has learned of their affair and lies paralyzed, the act fails them. "He knew a loathing, suddenly, of himself for the emptiness of the act he had performed: a vicious and shameful pantomime, isolated from all his life before it and from any other life, cut off in time, drained of all meaning, even the blind, fitful meaning of pleasure. He was infected by her emptiness. Or her emptiness had discovered to him his own."

Yet for all that, he seeks isolation from the disturbing contact with others because he fears committing himself and exposing himself to their demands upon him. He "fears to take the full risk of humanity." He shuts out all memories lest they threaten the serenity of his withdrawal. At the outset we see him in a jostling crowd of men, fastidiously separating himself from the press of their bodies. Yet soon afterward he speaks to them and moves them, though he does not know what he said. Later, recalling the moment of fusion and fulfillment, he has the habit of raising his hand as if to utter some great truth, but no words come. He has no truth in him. At the end, as he runs toward darkness, he feels a great delight.

> "He fell again, and, rising, saw to one side and above him on the slope, vaguely against the field and paler sky, the standing form of a man. But there—there, beyond that form—would be the woods, the absorbing darkness, the safety, the swift and secret foot. As he lifted the revolver, he was certain. He was certain. But without thought—he did not know why—at the long instant before his finger drew the trigger to the guard and the blunt, frayed flame leaped from the muzzle, he had lifted his arm a little toward the paleness of the sky."

It is the old gesture of the raised hand, made for the last time, *he did not know why*. Then he fires, "without concern for direction" and as he dies "he drowsily heard the voices down the slope calling emptily, like the voices of boys at a game in the dark." The voices had no meaning for him: men could not reach him. In his delight he has moved back toward childhood, games, dependency, and beyond to the safety of darkness and the primal and ultimate unconsciousness.

He had never grown up. In this novel we are not told why, though Warren suggests that his trouble goes back to his relations

473

with his mother, a widow who was cold and remote but sometimes tried to love him in frightening bursts of violence rather like Munn's own behavior toward his childish wife. Tolliver, who is both a kind of father-surrogate and *alter-ego* to Munn, had also grown up without a father under the care of a twisted and neurotic woman. Even so, Captain Todd, the most stable, self-sufficient, and humane man in the story, cannot pass on enough understanding to save his son from darkness. Ironically, the son, like Lucille Christians, whose father was also a strong, self-sufficient man, looks for direction to Munn. But each man must earn the meaning for his life by his own efforts. Otherwise the night takes him. Standing in an unlighted room Munn has an intimation of this:

> "It came to him that all he knew was the blackness into which he stared and the swinging motion and the beat of the blood. But was he staring into blackness, a blackness external to him and circumambient, or was he the blackness, his own head of terrific circumference embracing, enclosing, defining the blackness, and the effort of staring into the blackness a staring inward into himself, into his own head which enclosed the blackness and everything?"

Munn never finds out, for the blackness obliterates all.

The passage recalls Tate on the abyss, and Munn and George Posey much resemble each other. Each grew up without a father in an unnatural relation with an emotionally unstable and demanding mother. Each left working directly with the land to pursue abstract social power: money, in the case of Posey, and law in the case of Munn, though Posey has a passion for the power of money and an indifference to its specific uses quite different from Munn's attitude toward the law. Each seems to be at the center of the community; yet in the event each proves to be outside it and cut off from others by his incompleteness as a man. Each engages in extra-legal conduct under cover of night and is drawn into destructive violence that affects his relation with his wife. Each turns to a closely-knit and affectionate family in hope of discovering a purpose, though the family of Professor Ball, which Munn enviously observes, does not much resemble the Buchans of *The Fathers*. But the similarities point up differences. Posey is more like Willie Stark or even John Brown, for he is energetic, independent, and decisive, and seeks to impose his will upon others, whereas Munn is passive and acts, however violently, only in fits and starts; others impose their wills on him, which makes him mutinous, for he wants most of all to be left alone. Posey is a warmhearted, vital man with a great capacity for love. In fact, we are told that he loves his wife too much. But Munn is cold and loveless. Where Posey is destructive from excess of passion, Munn is destructive in grasping spasmodically for it. Ultimately, the differences come to this: Posey relishes life and fears death because he cannot accept it as an inevitable part of the process he enjoys too freely; but Munn fears life and wants to escape into death. Because Posey is so charged with energy, he was already creating tumult around him before the Civil War came and weakened the restraints imposed upon him by the community. But Munn could have drifted along indefinitely if tumult had not entered his life from the outside. Nevertheless, both men illustrate in their behavior an observation by Eric Hoffer, which goes to the heart of Tate and Warren's concern with identity and guides to conduct:

"The crumbling of a corporate body, with the abandonment of the individual to his own desires, is always a critical phase in social development. The newly emerging individual can attain some degree of stability and eventually become inured to the burdens and strains of an autonomous existence only when he is offered abundant opportunities for self-assertion and self-realization. He needs an environment in which achievement, acquisition, sheer action, or the development of his capacities and talents seems within easy reach. It is only thus that he can acquire the self-confidence and self-esteem that make an individual existence exhilarating or even bearable.

"Where self-confidence and self-esteem seem unattainable, the emerging individual becomes a highly explosive entity. He tries to derive a sense of confidence and of worth by embracing some absolute truth and by identifying himself with the spectacular doings of a leader or some collective body—be it a nation, a congregation, a party, or a mass movement."[11]

Not only does this account for some of the behavior of Posey and

[11] Eric Hoffer, "The Awakening of Asia," *The Reporter*, x (June 22, 1954), 16-17.

Munn, it partially explains why the Buchans were drawn to Posey and why Lucille Christians and young Todd were drawn to Munn. In the novels to come Warren demonstrated the validity of this observation many times. Each has the "crumbling of a corporate body" as background for the individual's search for self-confidence and self-esteem, which are really steps in his search for himself. *At Heaven's Gate* describes the labor troubles and financial panic attending the downfall of a financier whose career somewhat resembled that of Colonel Luke Lea of Tennessee. *All the King's Men* describes how the impoverished masses identified themselves with and kept in power a leader resembling Huey Long, whose spectacular doings brightened their drab lives. The protagonist of *World Enough and Time* uses for his private drama the confusion of a crisis in Kentucky during the 1820's over the power of the courts. The flames of the Civil War and Reconstruction form the backdrop of *Band of Angels*. In *The Cave* a village is invaded by the agents of the mass media, who convert reality into nightmare and men into beasts that prowl labyrinthine fantasies. In each work the crisis weakens or destroys the customs and authority of the community and compels men to rely on their own resources and consciences. When the crisis ebbs, the self-sufficient survivors have earned the knowledge they need to push on, and they may have formed an alliance with another survivor as Jack Burden does with Ann Stanton, but significantly, nothing is said about the rehabilitation of the community. Presumably they may have enough fellow-feeling to form some loose confederation until time blurs their hard-won self-knowledge and a new crisis breaks out. Tate had argued that the individual is saved by society, but *Night Rider* seems to infer that society, such as it is, is saved, if at all, by those who first can save themselves. Part of the salvation, we learn from later books, comes from being able to accept the humanness of others and form a loving relationship. Where Tate emphasizes restraint Warren emphasizes release. Though the lust of the inadequate man is onanistic and destructive, the love of the mature and self-sufficient man is creative and sustaining. Established upon respect for the self and the beloved it provides its own restraints. Warren goes further than Tate in showing the horror in man, that "brother to dragons," yet in the end his works show far more expectation and hope of him.

Warren asks of poetry a sense of contact with reality,[12] and that is just what *Night Rider* gives from the opening paragraph on. Over and over again one is impressed at the way some minute but meticulously chosen detail charges a scene with life and immediacy. Grown men meet at a schoolhouse, and Warren tells us they were embarrassed at sitting in the cramped seats of childhood. That puts us there. Bill Christians in his nightshirt listens to Munn's report on a raid and tugs at the hairs on his chest and rolls them between thumb and forefinger. It is as if we were standing beside him listening too. Writing in praise of Katherine Anne Porter's style in *Noon Wine*, Warren said,

> "Here the style is of the utmost transparency, and our eye and ear are captivated by the very ordinariness of the ordinary items presented to us. . . . Miss Porter has the power of isolating common things, the power that Chekhov or Frost or Ibsen or, sometimes, Pound has, the power to make the common thing glow with an Eden-like innocence by the mere fact of the isolation. It is a kind of indicative poetry."[13]

Exactly that may be said of the writing in *Night Rider*.

It makes the characters live. One seems to know them unusually well, and yet when one stops to list exactly what one had been told about them, it is not much. Most of them are lightly sketched, but everything counts. What we know of them places them so near us that we take their wholeness on faith and feel that if pressed we could supply an accurate account of those aspects which have not been shown us. Munn, the only character presented in something approaching the round, must have presented difficulties. He is so lacking in vitality that much "indicative poetry" is required to plant him firmly in a believable world. To make matters harder, he serves as the central intelligence. It is not what happens but how he feels about it that makes the story and he is not capable of feeling much. Others must force the action past its turning points, and while this keeps the story going it imperils the proportions and propriety. Thus, for example, it is quite in character that Willie Proudfit's prudish nephew should be offended when Lucille Christians goes at night to Munn's bedroom, but

---

[12] *Fugitives' Reunion*, ed. Rob Roy Purdy (Nashville, 1959), p. 142.
[13] "Irony with a Center: Katherine Anne Porter," *Selected Essays*, p. 144.

this seems too slight an incident and he too slight a character to precipitate the catastrophe. Moreover, since Munn is too passive to make a good register of events, Warren has to include the overly long story of Proudfit to buttress his meaning.

Proudfit had gone west, worked as a hunter, lived among the Indians and witnessed the ritual "ghost dance" to bring the buffalo back, and had come back to his native region to raise tobacco. He had seen a communal society destroyed by technology (rapid firing guns) and a lust for profit that took no account of the lives of others—that is, he had seen among the Indians an equivalent of what the corporations were doing to the agrarian society of the South. Tate objected to the story and late in 1938 Warren sent him an explanation of its purpose:

"First . . . the exhausting, on psychological grounds, of the possibility of going West, etc. Second, the reference, almost as in terms of oblique fable, of the 'ghost dance' to the night-riding, a kind of dancing of the buffalo back by ritual—outmoded, too— of personal violence. Third, the reference to Munn's private situation in general. This may be stated along these lines: Proudfit is a man who has been able to pass beyond his period of 'slaughter' into a state of self-knowledge. If he is not at home in the world, practically (losing his place, etc.) [for the decline of tobacco prices threatens Proudfit with ruin], he is at least at home with himself, has had his vision. It is an incommunicable vision, and is no solution for anyone but himself. He is, in a way, a foil for Munn, who has tried to embrace his vision by violence (discovery of humanity leading him into the act, murder, which is the cancellation of humanity, the act which defines isolation). But more specifically, as the tale relates to Munn's decision: Munn feels, as it were, that though he cannot achieve the vision, he can, perhaps, by a last act of violence, inject some rationality into his experience, he can round it out in terms that on mechanical grounds at least would be comprehensible—that is, by committing his murder [of Senator Tolliver, who sold out to the tobacco companies], he can in a way justify his present situation, for he is on the run for a murder he did not commit; and the murder of the Senator would be the first completely personal and private murder for him. [But Munn did not go through with it, and immediately afterward he is shot.] Fourth, the Indian business, obliquely again, implies the tribal loyalties, the conflict within the tribe. . .; all this has some extensions into the situation among the people involved in the tobacco troubles."[14]

The imbedded short story used as oblique commentary was to be a favorite device with Warren. In *At Heaven's Gate* he interspersed among the chapters sections of a "statement" by Ashby Wyndham. Its style wonderfully suggests the speech of the hill people of eastern Kentucky and Tennessee, but to this end Warren used spelling and phrasing that would not appear in a written account and the disparity, trivial as it is, makes one uneasy. Wyndham's confession turns out to be the little stone that sets off the avalanche in Bogan Murdock's rickety financial empire, and is thus fortuitously connected to the main body of the work. The statement is as important for the meaning as Proudfit's tale was for *Night Rider*, but it is almost as separate. The fourth chapter of *All the King's Men* contains a superb novelette written mostly in the grave epistolary style of the antebellum South. Nowhere does Warren mimic a style more effectively. Its very tone, by contrast with the breezy vulgarity and callousness of Burden's delivery, is a profound comment on Burden's disability as a human being. Cass Mastern's story of how he betrayed his best friend and came at last to accept responsibility for his evil carries the knowledge Burden needs to achieve full humanity, and the crisis of the novel occurs when Burden understands the relevance of the story for himself. It has, then, a more significant place in the *action* than the stories in the two earlier novels. Yet it makes a long interruption and, much as one appreciates its intrinsic merit, one wonders if a novelist of Warren's resourcefulness could not find some way to make his point without wrenching apart the fabric of his narrative.[15] *World Enough and Time* contains a brief story by Munn Short, who describes how he came to recognize his responsibility toward other men; it is appropriate, but unneces-

---

[14] From an undated letter. At its close Warren sent Tate good wishes for 1939.

[15] In the autumn of 1959 word went out that Warren was reworking the Cass Mastern story as a play entitled "Listen to the Mockingbird." On April 25, 1960, the *New York Times* carried a story saying that the play had been acquired by the Theater Guild and that Vincent J. Donahue was interested in staging it. At this writing it has not been produced.

sary. In *Band of Angels* Hamish Bond tells Amantha Starr of his earlier wanderings. Of all the imbedded narratives this is the one most nearly integrated with the central narrative, for Bond is a principal figure and his story provides information about another such figure, Rau-Ru, as well. Even so, its length and complexity further imbalance an already clumsily proportioned work. *The Cave*, however, has no such story.

Each story serves in its way a purpose equivalent to the third Warren listed for the Proudfit tale. That is, in each the narrator describes how he passed through an interval of confusion and violence into a state of self-knowledge, how he had his vision and is at home with himself. This has made him self-sufficient in the turmoil that has disrupted the "tribal loyalties" of his society. And that, spelled out often in terms of images from the landscape lost in the heart's homely deep and the conflicts that have their origins, ultimately, in childhood and the relation with parents, was, as we shall see, to be Warren's great theme. What saved men was not the community and its traditions but the courage and capacity to grow into adulthood—to confront and master the terror of the ordinary and accept the responsibility that is part of self-fulfillment. The words Warren set down in explanation of Conrad's *Nostromo* apply exactly to *Night Rider* and the great works ahead, and it will be remembered that Warren consulted Conrad's novel for guidance: "The victory is never won, the redemption must be continually re-earned. And as for history, there is no Fiddler's Green, at least not near and soon. History is a process fraught with risks, and the moral regeneration of society depends not upon shifts in mechanism but upon the moral regeneration of men."

CHAPTER TEN

ROBERT PENN WARREN:

THE ACHIEVEMENT

....

"History is blind, but man is not."

—*Robert Penn Warren,* ALL THE KING'S MEN

....

I

*I*N the spring of 1940, Robert Penn Warren published two poems which may have puzzled an attentive reader. "Love's Parable" was formal, literary, grave. "Crime" was ragged and melodramatic to a degree that none of his verse had been since his Fugitive days. The reader would not have known it, but four years stood between them. The first was written in 1935-1936, the second not long before it appeared. In the interval the burden of time and things had pressed heavily on Warren, and a profound shift had taken place in his imagination. His hold on his medium had loosened.

The darkness on the horizon of his earlier poems had moved over the envisioned land. History and hallucination were so entangled that they could scarcely be distinguished let alone separated. Simply to be a man with a man's ordinary past now seemed such an affliction that we should, in the words of "Crime,"

> Envy the mad killer who lies in the ditch and grieves,
> Hearing the horns on the highway, and the tires scream:
> He tries to remember, and tries, but he cannot seem
> To remember what it was he buried under the leaves.

For us "memory drips, a pipe in the cellar-dark" and in the attic the letter names our name and mourns. "Nothing is lost, ever lost." There seemed to be, as Warren said years afterward, no forgiveness for being human.

The months passed and more poems appeared: "Terror," "Pursuit," "Original Sin: A Short Story." In their nightmare vision, trivial things suddenly became the contorted and abhorrent images

481

of accusation and apprehension, and the most ordinary objects were streaked with terror. The coldness of a puppy's nose, thought of the germs nestling in a kitten's fur, notice that one's bank account was overdrawn, or a glimpse of an arthritic hand could pinch the heart. In these poems Warren was groping, at times with an almost lubberly uncouthness, beyond the familiar forms of action and explanation to those depths of the spirit where fantasies of fear and self-disgust coiled and drifted. All that he brought to light—an abandoned doll, "the old hound that used to shuffle your door and moan"—testified against man. He was cowardly, faithless, guilty. Well might he envy the mad killer and dread "the cricket's corrosive wisdom under the trees."

Night Rider had been well received, and Warren was granted a Guggenheim fellowship which enabled him to spend the academic year of 1939-1940 in Italy. There he saw for himself the storm troopers and "the criminal king, who paints the air/ With discoursed madness and protruding eye" described in his poem "Terror." As he said later, all about was the "unmasking of blank power. . . . You felt that all your work was irrelevant to this unmasking of this brute force in the world—that the dehumanizing forces had won." He had become an Agrarian in protest "against a kind of dehumanizing and disintegrative effect on your notion of what an individual person could be," but now Agrarianism seemed naive and futile, and he ceased to think about it.[1] But its effects were not easily put aside. The play "Proud Flesh" and the novel *At Heaven's Gate* on which he was working were, philosophically at least, more Agrarian than *Night Rider*. In them he was trying to show how the dehumanizing forces had won by applying to recent social history Agrarian-Distributist conceptions of technology, finance capitalism, and the power state. Dante and Machiavelli, whom he was reading at the time, furnished him with a gloss.

He had begun to learn Italian at Louisiana State University and during the summer of 1938 he had enrolled in a course of intensive study of the language at the University for Foreigners at Perugia. Now, after working on Petrarch, he read Dante for

[1] *Fugitives' Reunion*, ed. Rob Roy Purdy (Nashville, 1959), pp. 208, 210.

as long as five hours a day.[2] He felt toward Dante an affinity as strong as that which he had felt for Shakespeare. He was particularly impressed by the shock techniques of Dante's metrics and by his way of mixing elevated modes with the harshly colloquial. He himself had for some time experimented with metrical irregularities and abrupt shifts in style. "Crime" has several startling twists which probably show some of the effect of studying the Italian master. One such is

> But what was it? . . .
> He [the mad killer] cannot say, nor formulate the delicious
> And smooth convolution of terror, like whipped cream. . . .

In Italy, in Chapala, Mexico, where he spent the summer of 1941, and in Baton Rouge, to which he returned before moving to the University of Minnesota, he wrote a dozen poems which he judged good enough to keep. Seven of them ("Crime," "Original Sin," "End of Season," "Revelation," "Pursuit," "Question and Answer," and "Terror") he published with the four poems on the decay of love in a little pamphlet called *Eleven Poems on the Same Theme* in 1942. Despite the great shift of sensibility that occurred between 1936 and 1940, the title was not misleading, for all the poems dealt with some aspect of the guilts and anxieties resulting from the corruption of human values under Time.[3] "Revelation" looks back to a crisis, adumbrated in "Letter of a Mother," "The Return," and "The Return: An Elegy," which, more and more, Warren was coming to regard as one of the great dividing moments of life: the recognition of separateness from one's parents forced upon one by misconduct toward them. In short, the moment of the ending of childhood's innocence and security. Describing such a moment, Warren skillfully evoked the hypersensitivity of the senses when the mind is stunned and disordered by the violent disruption of a fundamental emotional relation:

> Because he had spoken harshly to his mother,
> The day became astonishingly bright,

[2] From a letter to Tate, written in Rome and dated December 14, 1939. The letter and all others to Tate referred to in this chapter are now in the Princeton University Library.

[3] All twelve poems written in 1940-1942 were included in Warren's *Selected Poems* (New York, 1944). The five not in the pamphlet *Eleven Poems on the Same Theme* bore the heading "Mexico is a Foreign Country: Five Studies in Naturalism."

The enormity of distance crept to him like a dog now,
And earth's own luminescence seemed to repel the night.

With a superb thrust of insight Warren recovered the child's fright and shame and, most remarkable, his way of seeing his environment:

By walls, by walks, chrysanthemum and aster,
All hairy, fat-petalled species, lean, confer,
And his ears, and heart, should burn at that insidious
                            whisper
Which concerns him so, he knows; but he cannot make out
                            the words.

Then the poet's grip relaxed and the poem fell off into ostentatious allusions to civil war in Rome, *Macbeth*, and Brahma, among which the fine line that carried the point of the poem ("In separateness only does love learn definition") was all but hidden. In "Original Sin" similarly acute perceptiveness was marred by even sillier overwriting. The two opening lines are on the level of horror comics. But in the second stanza Warren suddenly touched on the real horrors that beset children and haunt the adult mind. Of the attempts to flee one's pervasive sense of guilt he wrote,

You thought you had lost it when you left Omaha,
For it seemed connected then with your grandpa, who
Had a wen on his forehead and sat on the veranda
To finger the precious protuberance, as was his habit to do,
Which glinted in sun like rough garnet or the rich old
                          brain bulging through.

Helpless before his revulsion and conscience-stricken at his failure to love a relative whose appearance frightens him, the child falls into the sin of rejecting others. Later, hoping in manhood to make a fresh start, he compounds it:

You have moved often and rarely left an address
And hear of the deaths of friends with a sly pleasure,
A sense of cleansing and hope. . . .

He suffers from the inability to face himself as did the protagonist of "The Return: An Elegy." It is startling that a poem so honest and revealing could fumble into such bombast as:

The Achievement

Never met you in the lyric arsenical meadows
When children call and your heart goes stone in the bosom;
At the orchard anguish never, nor ovoid horror,
Which is furred like a peach or avid like the delicious
                                    plum.
It takes not part in your classic prudence or fondled axiom.

Yet even in the midst of such rubbish there is a flash of light into
the darkness of irrational fears when Warren links the benign, but
furry, peach with uterine monstrosities. Such truthfulness prevails
and has made this one of Warren's best known and most admired
poems.

But Warren protests too much, and there comes a point when
the reader begins to suspect a morbid relish in the accumulating
references to tumors and malformations. Linking the growth on
the grandfather's head to the child's sense of its unworthiness
showed brilliantly how the roots of anxiety and guilt may go
back to trivial things observed in childhood. So was the insight
into the healthy man's feeling abashed by a hunchback and appealing for his sympathy in "Pursuit." But scattered among such
passages are obsessive and gratuitous ones like those in "Terror"
that allude to "lunar wolf-waste" and "the arboreal / Malignancy,
with the privy breath, which watches / And humps in the dark."
These are no better than the terrible green moons, bats, and bowls
of blood that Warren put into "Midnight" nearly twenty years
earlier.

Despite the raffishness of many of their lines, the poems bring
into meaningful order glimpses of an inner landscape where the
spirit and the moral sense stumble along the edge of hysteria.
It is an ultimate of the human condition where all sounds tighten
to a scream, light stabs like a blade, and things grind painfully
or bloat like viscera. The figures that pace that night are grotesques,
maimed, and perversely fond of what has stunted or crippled them.
Or they are shape-shifters who in an instant can turn themselves
inside out and become the very opposite of what they seem. The
weak are the oppressors, the lovers are the betrayers, the betrayers
are the betrayed. Decay is in everything. Facing so bleak a world—
the inner analogue of the one in which Warren had dwelt and
watched love yield to Time and the blank power prepare for war—

485

one could withdraw from the human communion, numb himself, or try to make his way through understanding back to some kind of emotional and moral stability. Warren's account in the long works to which he was turning of how men coped with the nightmare constituted his vision of our age. He could still believe that if history was blind man was not. Not always, anyway.

II

As he broods on the disasters that brought down his friend Willie Stark, Jack Burden, the real protagonist of *All the King's Men*, Warren's third published novel, comes to understand something that Tate had been insisting since 1926: "Reality is not a function of the event as event, but of the relationship of that event to past, and future, events. . . . Direction is all. And only as we realize this do we live, for our identity is dependent upon this principle."[4] But what determines the direction? Does man live in an agony of will or is he jerked and prodded by the spasms of some necessity which Burden at one point calls the Great Twitch? How shall he know the direction and answer the question that confronts Warren's protagonists: "Who am I?"

Running through the stories of their attempts to evade or answer that question is a single great Ur-narrative or fable. No one work contains the whole of it, but *World Enough and Time*, Warren's fourth novel, and *Brother to Dragons*, the "tale in verse and voices," come nearest.[5] Nor does any work present its version in quite the form given here, for as he developed the fable Warren was making his way more deeply into its substance. Yet wide apart as the variants are—ranging in locus from the towns of Kentucky in the 1820's (*World Enough and Time*) to the business world of the 1920's (*At Heaven's Gate*)—there is in them what Warren has called, speaking of the theme of *Brother to*

[4] *All the King's Men* (New York, 1946), p. 407. In this section aspects of Warren's novels and his two long narrative poems are discussed without consideration of the order and circumstance of their writing. In the next section his works are discussed separately in chronological order.

[5] The discussion of Warren's writings in this chapter does not include the novelette *Wilderness* (New York, 1961), the children's books *Remember the Alamo* (New York, 1958) and *The Gods of Olympus* (New York, 1960), and the collection of poems, *You, Emperors, and Others* (New York, 1960). His novels *The Cave* (New York, 1959) and *Flood* (New York, 1964) are considered only incidentally.

Dragons, "a human constant," and one good way to understanding and appreciating them is to begin with it. The fable has a place in Warren's writing comparable to the parable of the innocent abroad in Henry James's or the tale of the lonely egotist learning to survive in the destructive element in Conrad's. Like these two novelists, Warren returns again and again to certain types: whining older women who think they deserved better of the world, indulged and selfish girls, fathers whose awkward devotion annoys the beloved child, exuberant shouters and doers, monomaniacal idealists, sentimental cynics, and older men saddened by the weight of their wisdom. Virtually all of his characters down to the least ones have presence. But they are not so individual as Conrad and James managed to make their own typical figures. Still, among them they encompass a greater range of eras, settings, classes, occupations and skills, speech levels and idioms, and plain day-to-day experience. To tell their story Warren brings before the reader an exceptional quantity and variety of sheer physical detail. Yet there are curious omissions and limitations of perspective. Warren sees much and tends to see it in the same way.

It would be proper to describe his fable as resembling a myth, had not that term been so abused in recent discussion of fiction. Many things give it a mythic quality and scope. One is the number of allusions to myths and legends and the literatures that have nurtured on them such as the Bible, sixteenth- and seventeenth-century English poetry and drama, Renaissance Italian verse, and the evangelical works of the Old South. Another is the constant suggestions by means of similes, personifications, and "pathetic fallacies" that the physical world is some somnolent, sphinx-like monster and man himself a fabulous beast—a "brother to dragons and companion to owls," as Job named him. The imagery evokes the pulse and flow of vast currents in the cosmos that move men in their "thrust toward timelessness, in Time." In "The Ballad of Billie Potts" man is said to feel the same compulsion to return to the place of his origin that moves the bee, the eel, and the goose that flies to the northern marshes. "The salmon heaves at the fall, and, wanderer, you / Heave at the great fall of Time," for you are "Brother to pinion and the pious fin. . . ." Amantha Starr tries to explain her sense of being compelled by forces beyond the understanding of man when she says, "It was as though your life had a shape, already totally designed, standing not in Time but in Space, already fulfilled, and you were waiting for it, in all its necessity, to be revealed to you, and all your living was merely the process whereby this already existing, fulfilled shape to Space would become an event in Time."[6] How the archetypal shapes become events in Time is the substance of Warren's fable.

Though only the stories of Amantha Starr and of Sue Murdock in *At Heaven's Gate* go back that far, the fable begins with early childhood. A young child scarcely differentiates between the external world and itself. Protected and irresponsible, it is little aware of change, hardly at all of time, and it tries to suppress knowledge of anything that perturbs it. If it does not recognize it, perhaps the perturbation will vanish. The parents' permissive behavior and the fantasies of children's stories help the child to deny any unpleasantness that intrudes. For a long time it is able to claim "King's X." Later on the older child and the adult, no matter how realistic and mature, look back to that time of ease and security with longing. Some try to behave as if it still prevailed. Thus Laetitia Lewis of *Brother to Dragons* thinks when trouble comes,

> "Oh, no—this isn't me, not me,
> Not bad like this to me—for I'm Laetitia,
> I'm little Tishy—" and I played beside the river
> And sang a song to make the river run,
> And the river ran and sparkled, it was summer,
> And birds sang, too, and I was nice and good,
> And minded Mama. . . .

At last the child, who may by now have reached adolescence, is forced to recognize that reality cannot be manipulated to conform to his whim. Part of that reality is himself: he sees that he falls far short of the idealized image in which his ignorance, security, and inexperience had enabled him to believe. The crisis may come suddenly, as it does to the boy who had spoken harshly to his mother, or the boy in "Blackberry Winter," when, on the day after a storm that has upset his environment, an inexplicably

---

[6] *Band of Angels* (New York, 1955), p. 265.

sullen stranger appears at his home, and as it does to Amantha Starr, when she is seized as a Negro slave at the funeral of her father, whom she has just discovered to be a bankrupt adulterer. Or it may come slowly, as it does to Jack Burden in the succession of his mother's marriages and to Jerry Beaumont in the series of shocks that culminate in his first sexual intercourse. "Court-martial," a poem first published in *The Yale Review* in the spring of 1957, describes a boy playing in the shade during a summer's day on a remote and tranquil farm. With the self-confidence of childhood he thinks he knows more about the Civil War than his grandfather, who had been a cavalry officer, and he sets out with his toy soldiers to "untie the knot of History." By chance he asks his grandfather what the word *guerrilla* means and learns that during the war the old man had caught and hung bushwhackers. Suddenly he sees his grandfather as a young man involved in violence. The bright air grows dark as he realizes "The world is real. It is there." His childhood is over.

This is the moment when for the first time one perceives directed toward oneself the force of time, change, and evil. As Warren describes it, the crisis often reveals the human fallibility of the parents whom the child had taken for granted as the compliant agents of its desires and guardians of its comfort. Suddenly they have become part of the world that is *against* the child, who feels abandoned and unloved just when he most needs support. ("In separateness only does love learn definition.") Significantly, many of the characters in Warren's fictions have only one parent on whom all the anger and sense of betrayal are focused. So it was for Percy Munn, Lucille Christians, and Senator Tolliver in *Night Rider*. So it is for Jerry Calhoun, Ashby Wyndham, and Jason Sweetwater in *At Heaven's Gate*; for Jack Burden, Anne and Adam Stanton, Willie Stark, and Sadie Burke of *All the King's Men*; for Jerry Beaumont of *World Enough and Time* (and Rachel Jordan's father was hardly in her life and died while she was young); for Amantha Starr of *Band of Angels*; for Ikey Sumpter and Rachael Goldstein in *The Cave*; and for Brad and Maggie Tolliver, Yasha Jones, Lettice Poindexter, and a number of minor characters in *Flood*. When both parents are living, one may so dominate the household that the situation is much the same, as it is in the families of Sue Murdock of *At Heaven's Gate*,

Percival Skrogg of *World Enough and Time,* and Hamish Bond
and Tobias Sears of *Band of Angels.* Sometimes the single or
dominant parent is cold and remote; sometimes the parent loves
but cannot communicate with the child; sometimes a warmly sympathetic parent is rejected by the child. For, whatever the relation,
the child has difficulty accepting the humanness of the parent,
because that would require admission of the child's humanness,
too. The *reveur* in "The Return: An Elegy" could not at first
reconcile himself to the physicality of his mother. "R.P.W." points
out in *Brother to Dragons* that the "most happy and difficult conclusion" is to accept the father's own acceptance of his humanness
and limitations—his "failure."

> It is most difficult because that reconciliation
> Costs the acceptance of failure. And can we,
> Sunk in our saeculum of desire,
> Pay that cost?
> Most difficult because that reconciliation
> Signifies the purification of vanity.

Often the relation with the parent is complicated by powerful
sexual feelings. Sue Murdock thinks she hates her father but her
deepest desire is to replace her weak, alcoholic mother, and her
love affairs are doomed by her tendency to cast her lovers in the
roles of agents for or against her father. She cannot accept them
as themselves. Anne Stanton long remains unmarried partly because she serves her father and her father's memory. When his
image is destroyed, she turns to Willie Stark, symbol of the
devious political power that overcame her father, and clings to
him in the same dependent, daughterly way. In *Band of Angels*
Warren takes pains to point out the similarity between Amantha
Starr's relation with her father and her relation with her first
lover, middle-aged Hamish Bond, who pets and pampers her and
serves as her target for angers and shield against reality. Many
of the male characters are sexually confused or retarded. Slim
Sarrett, a homosexual, makes up fantasies about his mother's supposed prostitution. Jack Burden thinks that his father was a failure
who could not keep the love of his beautiful young wife, and his
difficulties of adjustment are compounded by the way his mother,
who has kept her charm, practices on him the tricks she uses

to control other men. Jerry Beaumont takes for his wife the woman seduced by the man whom he had come to regard as a father, and his love-making is haunted by images of Rachel in the arms of Colonel Fort. And though Hamish Bond loathes his mother, he is for years driven by his need to make her regard him as the man his father failed (in her eyes) to be.

Thus the people of Warren's fable reach adulthood ill prepared for its risks and responsibilities for they have not yet outgrown the dependencies and self-centered daydreams of childhood and ado-lescence. Wavering between thinking themselves too good for the world and too weak and unworthy to cope with it, they want to return to the pre-experiential innocence. Jack Burden describes their feelings well in a key passage early in *All the King's Men*. Of the instant before some threatening knowledge is forced upon one, he says it is

> "like the second when you come home late at night and see the yellow envelope of the telegram sticking out from under your door. . . . While you stand there in the hall, with the envelope in your hand, you feel there's an eye on you. . . . The eye knows what's in the envelope, and it is watching you to see you when you open it and know, too. But the clammy, sad little foetus which is you way down in the dark which is you too lifts up its sad little face and its eyes are blind, and it shivers cold inside you for it doesn't want to know what is in that envelope. It wants to lie in the dark and not know, and be warm in its not-knowing."[7]

Many of them carry in their heads an image from the time when to all effects they still lived in the foetal state. For Jack Burden it is a summer of carefree swimming when he would dive to depths beyond the sights and sounds of the world. His memories focus on the picture of Anne Stanton as a little girl floating whitely in dark water under a gathering storm. Amantha Starr recalls "a grassy place, a place with sun, maybe water running and sparkling, or just still and bright, and myself sitting there." The characters dream of finding a new place where they can reorder things to conform to the image of the lost world. Jerry Beaumont wants "Some place in the West, a silent, wooded valley where the great

[7] Pp. 11-12.

trees let only a green light down like the light under water when you dive deep and where everything is still." By thus in effect recovering the lost world, they would recover the lost childish identity. The chorus in "The Ballad of Billie Potts" explains how the journey West is really a search for the self:

> There is always another country and always another place.
> There is always another name and another face.
> And the name and the face are you, and you
> The name and the face, and the stream you gaze into
> Will show the adoring face, show the lips that lift to you
> As you lean with the implacable thirst of self,
> As you lean to the image which is yourself.
> To set the lip to lip, fix eye on bulging eye,
> To drink not of the stream but of your deep identity. . . .

Narcissistic as it is, the image gives some meaningful direction to their conduct, and Jerry Beaumont boasts to Rachel, " 'We will make the world what we will.' " Others prefer to find some strong person to act as a buffer between themselves and the rub and grind of circumstance, leaving to him the burden of decision. Al Suggs, the policeman of "Proud Flesh" who is the prototype of Sugarboy in *All the King's Men*, says of Willie Talos, who became Willie Stark:

> I was nameless, but he has now named me.
> And aimless, but he has now aimed me,
> And flung me, and flings me—Oh, errand
> Blind with the glittering blindness of light.

"When our individual interests and prospects do not seem worth living for," writes Eric Hoffer, "we are in desperate need of something apart from us to live for. All forms of dedication, devotion, loyalty and self-surrender are in essence a desperate clinging to something which might give worth and meaning to our futile, spoiled lives. Hence the embracing of a substitute will necessarily be passionate and extreme."[8] So it is for Al Suggs-Sugarboy, and for Anne Amos-Anne Stanton in her affair with Talos-Stark and for the mobs that put him in office. But he needs the mob as it needs him. Talos tells the people, "Your will is my law. . . . Your

---

[8] *The True Believer* (Mentor edition: New York, 1958), p. 24.

good is my good. . . . Your hope is my hope." Stark says much the same thing: "Your will is my strength. . . . Your need is my justice." When others cannot stand between them and reality, the characters may numb themselves with alcohol (Dorothy Murdock), overwork (Keith Amos-Adam Stanton), sensuality (Jerry Beaumont), or a narcotic idea such as Jack Burden's belief that life is a series of unrelated events in which one's actions are so determined that one is not to blame for anything. Poor mad Lilburne Lewis of *Brother to Dragons* carries the logic of numbing the self all the way and brings about his own death.

Jerry Beaumont, the most thoughtful and self-conscious of Warren's protagonists and in some ways the one most desperate in his struggle with reality, tried all the modes of evasion and of imposing the vain, impossible self-image upon the world. Looking back upon his career he sees that he began with an effort to "justify" himself,

> "not by the world, which he would deny, but by the idea. *The idea is all,* he had thought.
>
> " 'For . . . it is the first and last temptation, to name the idea as all, which I did, and in that error was my arrogance, and the beginning of my undoing and cold exile from mankind. . . . What becomes of the idea, if we place it apart from our warm world and its invisible fluids by which we live?'
>
> " 'He had thought that the idea in and of itself might redeem the world, and in that thought had scorned the world. But that thought . . . had led to a second error, which must always follow from the first when we find that the idea has not redeemed the world: the world must redeem the idea. 'Then in this thought . . . man will use the means of the natural world, and its dark ways, to gain that end he names holy by the idea. . . .'
>
> "But there is a third error, he says, that follows from the second: to deny the idea and its loneliness and embrace the world as all, or, as he puts it, 'to see communion only in the blank cup of nature, and innocence there. . . . But that innocence is what man cannot endure and be man. . . .' "[9]

Those who can, learn at last that evasions, whether by dominance

[9] *World Enough and Time* (New York, 1950), p. 459.

or by withdrawal, will not suffice. Lucy Lewis, mother of Lilburne, tells her brother, Thomas Jefferson:

> . . . whatever hope we have is not by repudiation,
> And whatever health we have is not by denial,
> But in confronting the terror of our condition.
> All else is a lie.

And Jack Burden thinks, "If you cannot accept the past and its burden there was no future, for without one there cannot be the other, and . . . if you accept the past you might hope for the future, for only out of the past can you make the future." But past and future have meaning only when one accepts one's kinship with other men. "You are not you except in terms of relation to other people. If there weren't any other people there wouldn't be any you because what you do, which is what you are, only has meaning in relation to other people."[10]

The climax of the fable comes when the protagonist prepares to act upon this knowledge and achieve his identity within the human communion. He may not make it, but, as Warren says in *Brother to Dragons*, there is a glory and meaning in the effort. Writing of the contrasts and tensions between the dream and the act in Eudora Welty's stories, he made an observation that applies exactly to the several versions of his fable:

> "The dream must be carried to, submitted to, the world, inno-cence to experience, love to knowledge, knowledge to fact, individuality to communion. What resolution is possible is, if I read the stories with understanding, in terms of the vital effort. The effort is a 'mystery,' because it is in terms of the effort, doomed to failure but essential, that the human manifests itself as human."[11]

Certain key terms and symbols turn up many times in the narratives. The most important terms are Time and History, which are virtually synonymous. The most important symbols are light and darkness, water, cancers, and watching eyes.

Time signifies the whole of reality as man apprehends it, which is as a series of events. Even "things" and ideas or values are

---

[10] *All the King's Men*, pp. 461, 136.

[11] "Love and Separateness in Eudora Welty," *Selected Essays* (New York, 1958), p. 167.

really processes that change; that is, history. The egotist tries to establish his dream against or outside Time, and one reason for his rejecting the father is that the father embodies the past and illustrates the inevitable mutability of human affairs. On occasion Warren uses Time in an altogether different sense. Those who do not understand what Jack Burden painfully learns—that the past and the future form a continuum and one cannot have one without the other—think of Time as morally neutral, discrete happenings. This being so, they can always go West and make a fresh start with a new name and face. For, as the chorus puts it in "The Ballad of Billie Potts":

> they have been dipped in the healing flood.
> For they have been dipped in the redeeming blood,
> For they have been dipped in Time
> And Time is only beginnings. . . .
> For Time is motion
> For Time is innocence
> For Time is West.

In the end Billie Potts comes back to the homestead, obeying the compulsion of all things to fulfill themselves by going against Time. Now it would seem that this is inconsistent with Warren's argument for the necessity of submitting to Time, but it is not. What they go against is Time as a flood of inchoate particulars. They obey the force of some absolute which is itself beyond Time but works on them through Time. Thus the apparently morally neutral event is imbued with human significance and History as fact is transmuted into History as myth. Put in Jack Burden's terms this means that they are enabled by something (here a vague cosmic force, elsewhere an Idea) outside Time to accept the past, have hope for the future, and live *in* Time, which they no longer see as "motion . . . innocence . . . West." The irony is that they may be slain on the homeward journey from the West to the community of men. Billie and Jerry Beaumont are.

The world in which man struggles is steeped in the blackness that once overwhelmed Percy Munn. Darkness is a quality of Time as process. Often it signifies the concrete, sensual, sub-human—the "black inwardness and womb of the quagmire" in which Jerry Beaumont, as his third error, seeks to drown himself.

From another perspective it may be the darkness of the cellar and the cave where, in the cold dampness and decay, memory drips and evil broods,

> hulked
> In the blind dark, hock-deep in ordure, its beard
> And shag foul-scabbed, and when the hoof heaves—
> Listen!—the foulness sucks like mire.

"The beast waits." But now and then light strikes through: light, remembered from childhood, and signifying variously the idea, the pure, the innocent, the hope aspired to. Warren seems particularly moved by light gleaming upon water, sifting softly through pollen in the spring air, or thrusting through a cover of leaves to illuminate some quiet glade or splendid tree. Over and over his characters think of happiness and serenity in terms of such a spot. In "Gold Glade," first published in *Encounter* in the spring of 1957, the speaker tells how as a boy he came upon an affirmative vision which has stayed by him throughout his life. After he had wandered through the gathering shadows and declivities of an autumn woods,

> There, in gold light, where the glade gave, it stood.
>
> The glade was geometric, circular, gold,
> No brush or weed breaking that bright gold of leaf-fall.
> In the center it stood, absolute, and bold
> Beyond any heart-hurt, or eye's grief-fall.
> Gold-massy in air, it stood in gold light-fall.

It seemed at that instant that "There could be no dark." Yet of course dark came. Years afterward he could not remember where the great golden shagbark had stood but he was sure that

> solid in soil that gave it its birth
> It stands, wherever it is, but somewhere.
> I shall set my foot, and go there.

In a sense that light, that hope, is earned. The boy had overcome his fearfulness and made his way to it. And it was surrounded by the shadow of time and the world. But there is another kind of light—too intense, too white, beyond the shadow of reality. It is the blank incandescence of the abstract and pure idea such as blinded Jefferson in *Brother to Dragons,* so that he stumbled into the labyrinth where the beast waited.

Water, the most important of Warren's symbols, is virtually the physical universe itself, or the changing processes, the fluid continuum of birth, growth, decay, and death that we know as nature. Like nature it is by turns luminous and dark. As the clear bright stream or the sun-dazzled sea it represents the joyous and innocent and seems to promise healing and redemption, as it does to the self-thirsty wanderers in "The Ballad of Billie Potts." But far more often it is seen as the dark pool, which first appeared in "Portraits of Three Ladies," and which, of all his symbolic images, seems most to engage Warren's imagination. A firmly specific yet extraordinarily complex symbol it hides in its depths all the primal mystery, horror, and fat putridity of death-and-birth, all the pervasive sexuality and bestial energy that make up the processes of matter and man's own body and arouse in Warren a fascination and loathing. One example out of the hundred or more scattered through his works may suffice more than any attempt at analysis to convey those qualities which Warren associates with the image. In a description of an aged, deformed river pirate it is said that he

> "had been spewed up out of the swamps and jungles of Louisiana, or out of some fetid alley of New Orleans—out of that dark and savage swill of bloods—a sort of monstrous bubble that rose to the surface of the pot, or a sort of great brute of the depth that swagged up from the blind, primal mud to reach the light and wallow in the stagnant flood, festooned with algae and the bright slime, with his scaled, armored, horny back just awash, like a log."[12]

Analogous to the great brute or the rotten log that lies in the depths of the dark pool are the cancers and tumors that fatten in the moist darkness of the body, favorite symbols of swift-growing corruption in the moral will. Warren consciously thought of Talos as a malignancy in the body politic and with this and Talos's arrogant lecherousness in mind chose the *double entendre* "Proud Flesh" for the title of the play that became *All the King's Men.* Allusions to carcinomata are most numerous in these works but

---

[12] *World Enough and Time,* pp. 428-429.

are scattered throughout Warren's later works. Widespread, too, are the watching eyes that represent the condemnation and hostility which figures in the fable at times feel everywhere about them. Even in their most private moments they have the sense that they are observed, their defenses penetrated and their inadequacies and guilts noted with sly relish. No explanation, no show of boldness or gesture of hearty good-fellowship avails: the eyes watch and accuse, and in their gaze all joy and self-esteem wither.

For all the naturalism of the settings in which these symbols appear, their ultimate configuration is surreal—a Mercator's projection of an inward terrain where man gropes between attenuated moments of happiness among images of fear, disgust, and self-condemnation (for the eyes that watch are really his own). And since the theme of the fable is man's search for himself beyond the overextended boundaries of childhood and adolescence it is fitting that the dominant symbols go back to the observations of early years and evoke childish longings and anxieties.

III

In his introduction to the Modern Library edition of *All the King's Men* Warren says that the idea of writing a verse play on a Southern dictator came to him one afternoon during the winter of 1937-1938, when he was writing *Night Rider*. To achieve greater dramatic force he based the dictator's power on his ability to fill the secret needs of others and made him an idealist whose power tainted his ends. Warren planned to use a chorus to point out the psychological and ethical meaning of the action. Years afterward Frank Owsley recalled that in the earliest stages the chorus was made up of motorcycle policemen, exemplars of tyrannical force. But in the end it consisted of surgeons who rigidly insisted upon naturalistic determinism and saw men as simple mechanisms. The change shows how the scope of Warren's conception grew.

Though he wrote a few speeches, Warren did not really get down to work on the play until his year in Italy. As he finished sections he mailed them to Ransom and Tate for criticism, and a few days before Christmas of 1939, he sent them the final scene. Then he turned aside to poetry and *At Heaven's Gate* until the following summer, when he went to North Bennington, Vermont, to consult with Francis Fergusson, under whose eye he rewrote much of it. They hoped to produce it at Bennington College, but nothing came of this and it was not staged until 1947. It has not been published.

"Proud Flesh" might be roughly described as *All the King's Men* without Jack Burden. It begins where Governor Willie Talos, prototype of Willie Stark, is arranging to have a public hospital built by Gummy Larson, who will give Talos his political support in return for the contract and some "sweetening." Then Talos's son is fatally injured in a football game. Transformed by his suffering, Talos, who has been having an affair with Anne Amos (Anne Stanton), decides to return to his wife and have the hospital built without graft. Outraged, Tiny Harper, the State Highway Commissioner who had set up the deal, tells Anne's brother, Keith, about the liaison, and Keith, a surgeon who was to have been head of the new hospital, shoots Talos and is killed by Talos's bodyguard. Just before the shooting, Talos makes a speech admitting having used corruption to achieve his ends and asks, "From the bottom of my heart, and from the secrecy of my soul, I ask it. Is it my only way?" He admits that he has loved power and says that now he will use it to destroy anyone who stands in the way of the will of the people. Amos, too, has his moment of self-justification immediately before the end. Remembering all the "uninvolved delight" of boyhood, he says that he has sought only innocence. It is clear that Warren was thinking of the dehumanization by power to which he referred at the Fugitives' reunion.

The play dramatizes what Tate had so long insisted and the great Southern writers have understood so well: a man must have something to live for. Others look to Talos to provide the something ("I was nameless, but he has now named me. / And aimless, but he has now aimed me."), but he has discovered that he has nothing for himself. Man is not a machine as the surgeons had claimed and operational efficiency does not justify all. His crisis of self-knowledge comes when he hears a radio commentator ask where his lust for power will lead him. He flings the radio to the floor, but it goes on speaking, for it has become the voice of his deepest need:

> He fears nothing not himself, but fears that emptiness
>   of self the cricket names and calls to.
> He fears nothing but self, but since he knows the horrible
>   nothingness of self, he fears only nothing, therefore.
> But yet fears the more.

When Anne Amos learns of his incertitude, she asks,

> If you are fragmentary, what of us others?
> What of me, for my need by your needlessness only
> Is answered?

But it is too late for them, for Amos has resolved to destroy "the essential deformity / Wherein all rectitude of nature is reviled," to cut the malignancy out of man and society and restore the lost innocence.

Gun, motorcycle, scalpel, hospital, political machine, phallus, even human beings—all are instruments which men have made into ends. The play presents in terms similar to those of Ransom's *God Without Thunder* and the introduction to *I'll Take My Stand* modern man's enslavement to technology and his failure in love and respect for the humanity of his fellows. It reads well, but it is too declamatory and too crowded with overlapping characters (twenty-two plus surgeons, reporters, and patrolmen) for the stage. Warren needed more room than the medium provided.

He had it in *At Heaven's Gate*, finished in the summer of 1942, which explores the same theme with more thoroughness and depth.

The action moves between two poles embodied in Bogan Murdock, a financier, and Mr. Calhoun, a simple dirt farmer. The reader is conscious of the polarity, but the characters are not. Only a few of them even know who Mr. Calhoun is. His son Jerry finally works his way through to a rough comprehension of what the two men represent. In taking Jerry as a lover, Murdock's daughter Sue is deliberately choosing between the two worlds of the fathers, but not until afterward does she meet Mr. Calhoun. She senses the polarity, but does not really understand it. The men are different in every way—so much so that if Calhoun is wholly a man, and he is, Murdock must be wholly inhuman. That is just what Duckfoot Blake tries to tell Jerry. " 'Bogan Murdock ain't real. Bogan is a solar myth, he is a pixy, he is a poltergeist. . . ,

just a wonderful idea Bogan Murdock had. And that is why Bogan
Murdock is a great man. . . .' "[13] Indeed, he is great in power:
wealthy, cultured, physically graceful, absolutely at home in the
New South of finance-capitalism, he gets what he wants. If, for
example, he and his friends wish to start a fox-hunting club, he
simply has his agents call in the mortgages on enough farms. He
has no idea of whose farms they are. But Mr. Calhoun is poor,
ignorant, agonizingly clumsy, and ill at ease among city people. His
farm is one of those taken for the club. Murdock is unloving, self-
centered, and served by others on whose humanity he feeds to
fill his emptiness. He is a parasite who lays waste the land with
his mines, quarries, lumber companies. Mr. Calhoun is affectionate,
selfless, and full of humanity which he puts without stint to the
service of others. He loves the land and works with his own hands
to take from it without greed what he needs. Murdock is a leader
of the industrial and mercantile New South, while Mr. Calhoun
(it is a mark of respect for his innate dignity that one always thinks
of him as *Mr.* Calhoun) is a yeoman from the agrarian past now,
by the economics of cash-crop farming, placed like Bill Christians
at the mercy of the financiers.

Even more than *Night Rider* this novel is an Agrarian critique.
It was first conceived when the Agrarians were preparing *Who
Owns America?* and its representation of the irresponsibility and
abstractness of the world of the great corporations might have come
straight from the essays of David Cushman Coyle, Lyle Lanier,
Richard B. Ransom, and Tate, or from the arguments of Agar
and Owsley, which Warren knew well. Jerry is the All-American
hero of the Success Story: from farmboy to financier by the stick-
to-it-iveness learned on the football field. He believes in Progress,
and he progresses, shedding the past and his father for the future
and Murdock. But he is desperately unsure of himself and he
feels that everyone from a bellboy to a governor is watching him
and judging him by a secret knowledge of how the world turns
and that he will fail in their eyes for want of it. Sue Murdock is
the All-American girl-friend: glamorous, popular, a dabbler in
the arts and a sportswoman. She is as willful and almost as selfish

---

[13] *At Heaven's Gate* (New York, 1943), p. 373. Strangely enough, Yasha
Jones, the quasi-saint of *Flood*, bears a close resemblance to Bogan Murdock,
though it is asserted that he is capable of deep love. The assertion does not make
him either real or human.

as her father, and like him she lives off the labor and vitality of others. Yet she senses how empty is his world and responds to the humanity of Mr. Calhoun. Confused and wavering, she nevertheless knows that " 'It's not a question of what you want to be. . . . It's a question of what you are.' " She is trying to find out what she is. Jerry is trying to deny what he thinks he is.

She is the means of bringing into the novel Jason ("Sweetie") Sweetwater, a labor organizer, and Slim Sarrett, a poet, who furnish additional points of view through which to look at Murdock. Both men understand the emptiness behind his power (and Sarrett has the satisfaction of pointing it out to Murdock himself). Both know that a man must have something outside himself to live for and that his guide must be established upon a realistic knowledge of the world and the self. Yet both of them live by dreams of themselves that are—morally, anyway—as narrow and selfish as Murdock's. Neither one, by following his dream, can discharge the responsibilities entailed by his relation with Sue or satisfy her need for love. Like Murdock, they are divorced from the natural order, for they use Sue without respect for her integrity as a person. In the end Sarrett protects his fantasy life by killing her.

The novel is Warren's most searching study of the parent-child relationship, and it is there, even more than in the Agrarian social criticism, that we find the explanation for the sterility of contemporary life. The abstractness and emptiness of technology are the correlatives and perhaps even the consequences of the failure in personal relations that begins in childhood. All of the central figures except Mr. Calhoun and Duckfoot Blake have rejected their families and the fathers who embody the past they want to abolish. Murdock, with his sound instinct for using others, keeps up an appearance of loyalty to his aged father, who is a tool for shaping public opinion by appealing to its nostalgia for the aristocratic Old South. Sue had to leave home to survive, but she had small chance of achieving an independent identity and maturity because her inability to forgive her father tied her to him and compelled her to attach herself to men who, different as they might seem, were like him underneath. Sweetwater's father lived in the legend of the Old South, and his fatuity drove his son frantic. Part of the son's brutality comes from his determination to be as unlike his father as he can. Sarrett's rejection is the most unnatural. His simple, middle-class Georgian parents have no part in his romance of himself, and he invents a preposterous story in which his mother is supposed to be a whore and himself the spiritual son of all her lovers, a Son of Man. Warren's portrait of Sarrett is a sardonic judgment on the myth of the artist as martyr and shows how an adroit manipulator can use the myth as an instrument of power. Jerry Calhoun's rejection of his kind and faithful father is most cruel, but it is not unnatural. For in some of the most perceptive writing of all his fiction Warren shows how impoverished was Jerry's boyhood and how excruciating his father's patient clumsiness. Kind as he was Mr. Calhoun could not avoid outraging his son. The honesty and authority of Warren's account gives pathos to Jerry's career and enables us to think that under the layers of his smugness and selfishness there is still enough sensitivity to enable him to realize that he had desired his father's death. In that recognition there is hope of reconciliation and of escape from vanity. He isn't much, but Jerry is the best man of his group.

At Heaven's Gate has a range and richness beyond the power of this summary to suggest. Still unduly neglected, it is in many ways a splendid work, and one critic has said flatly that after *All the King's Men* it is Warren's most important work of fiction.[14] For measure one might compare it with the better known *The Cave*, which it somewhat resembles. (Slim Sarrett and Ikey Sumpter are blood brothers; Rachel Goldstein is a lot like Sue Murdock; Monty Herrick suffers the same obscure shames and longings that afflict Jerry Calhoun.) *The Cave* exhibits great technical sophistication. The writing is everywhere sinewy and assured. *At Heaven's Gate* is rickety and often painfully inept, as in a montage describing Jerry at a country club dance. Its crisis is brought about by a nearly total outsider, who, except for the accident of being related to one of Murdock's partners, has no place in the narrative, though the interpolated story of his journey in search of salvation is important to the theme. (He does not find it, for he carries Christian humility and unworldliness to the point of dehumanization and fails in his responsibility to others.[15]) The point of the

[14] John Lewis Longley, Jr. "'At Heaven's Gate': the Major Themes," *Modern Fiction Studies*, VI (Spring, 1960), 13.

[15] I am indebted to Professor Longley's excellent essay for this interpretation of Wyndham's pilgrimage.

novel comes too late and too abruptly when Duckfoot Blake, who all his life has carefully protected himself from involvement with others suddenly has a change of heart and shouts at Jerry, " 'Everything matters.' " The way this is presented suggests, almost, that Warren himself had stumbled on the point at the last minute. Anyway, beside *The Cave* this is a gawky novel, but it has an honesty and understanding (not shrewdness, understanding; there is plenty of shrewdness in *The Cave*) which the later novel does not show. There is not one character in *The Cave* so immediately present as Jerry Calhoun, shallow though he be, nor anything so penetrating as the account of Jerry's suffering as he watches his father fumbling with some tool. Beside the characters of this novel, those of *The Cave* seem like paper figures cut from the pages of Warren's earlier works. For *At Heaven's Gate* is like the poems of the period of its writing: it impresses by the rightness of some of its details rather than by the mastery over the whole. Yet with all its imperfections it is the best novel about business and businessmen since Dreiser.

In the spring of 1943 Warren returned to "Proud Flesh." His understanding of the effect of power on the spirit had grown with his thinking about Murdock. So had his understanding of responsibility and self-knowledge. He needed the scope of the novel and someone more self-conscious than Talos-Stark and more contemplative than Keith-Stanton; so he added Jack Burden as narrator. But if Burden was to understand how man struggles against responsibility and self-knowledge, he himself would have to be responsible for something he would like to repudiate. Therefore it was given to him to turn up the evidence that led to Anne's affair and the deaths of his two friends and Judge Irwin, his own true father. As Warren described Burden's twistings to avoid commitment to life and acknowledgment of his share in events, he exposed the moral nihilism of the determinism and pragmatism behind which Burden tried to hide. But, as in *At Heaven's Gate*, Warren went beyond this to the psychological bases of Burden's evasions. The dominant theme was no longer corruption by power but the achievement of adult identity through accepting the *burden* of guilt and the accidents of time and change. Burden, who was not even in the play, became the protagonist of the novel, but because throughout most of it he was passive and withdrawn, Stark was needed to charge the scene with action and the history of his corruption kept its central place in the narrative structure.[16]

The novel gave Warren the space he needed to show Stark's early idealism and how it enabled him to act when others were bewildered by lack of purpose. But his idealism suffers the same impediment that marred Talos's: it defined good in instrumental terms and man as a thing among things. Though he never becomes the monster that Murdock was, Stark at times can reaffirm himself only by bullying others. But he cannot bully Jack Burden, who is too clever to allow anyone but Anne Stanton to have any hold upon him. Separated from both his real father and the man whose name he bears and whom he supposes to be his father, and believing that his mother does not love him, he is too unsure of his own worth to risk getting involved in life. Anne senses this and will not marry him. So he drifts, putting his cleverness at the service of others who decide how it shall be used. He and Stark well serve each other's needs.

While working on the novel Warren paused to write "The Ballad of Billie Potts." To escape punishment for an unsuccessful attempt at murder Billie goes West and takes a new name. But it means nothing. There is no past in it. It is just "the agitation of the air." So Billie goes home and is killed by his parents, who do not recognize him. Told that the bearded stranger they have robbed and buried is their son, they uncover his body, confirm his identity, and speak his true name, which now has a past, a history, a content. He had fulfilled his destiny. Jack Burden, when he learns of the affair between Anne and Stark, goes West. He is able to come back at once for he succeeds in persuading himself that everything is pre-determined. Actually, he is still fleeing. But like Billie he has in him "the long compulsion and the circuit hope" that in the end proves stronger than his longing to preserve the irresponsibility and dependency of childhood. He acknowledges that he is the brother in guilt of Tiny Duffy (once Tiny Harper), who told Adam about his sister and brought about the assassination. He is reconciled to his mother and, a man at last, he marries Anne. They take into their home Ellis Burden,

---

[16] In "Proud Flesh" there was a reporter named simply Jack, who had been the boyhood friend of Keith Amos. He had only a few words to speak.

symbol of the past and the "father" Jack had so long denied with contempt.

Adam Stanton is in his way as much of an instrumentalist as Stark, but he is less of a man and realist. He wants people to behave like chemical elements. In the operating theater he can treat them almost as if they were, and he solves their emotional problems by prefrontal lobectomies. When they misbehave like human beings, he unforgivingly rejects them. The hospital, supreme symbol of their limited ideas of good, brings him to Stark— and to their mutual destruction rather than their redemption. Both men desire the well-being of others, but—man of action and man of abstract ideas—they need the man of moral imagination that Burden succeeds in becoming or they can only destroy one another. Burden is a writer: politics and science need poetry.

Jerry Beaumont, protagonist of *World Enough and Time*, Warren's next long work, written in 1947-1950, is both a man of action and a man of ideas who in time becomes a man of moral imagination. But until then he suffers from what Burden, speaking of Stanton and Stark, calls the "terrible division of the age," which for him is a division of the self. Each side of him tries to redeem the other and cannot. When he accedes to moral understanding, it is only to know that man cannot live by either word or deed alone and to wonder if there is a way whereby they can be reconciled. The novel is Warren's longest, most complex, and darkest work, and at its end Beaumont can only wonder, "Oh, was I worth nothing, and my agony? Was all for naught?" The last words of the novel repeat the question as if to challenge the reader to provide his own answer.

It was enough for Jack Burden to accept responsibility to fulfill himself. His responsibility seemed simple and clear enough. But Beaumont in effect asks, "Responsibility to what? What are the forms of responsibility? What is justice? How is it related to truth? Where does a man find the truth, in his heart or in the world's eye? Or in his belly, perhaps, which knows the truth of necessity?" The novel of his quest is based on accounts of a celebrated murder in early Kentucky. One Jereboam Beauchamp killed a Colonel Sharpe. While awaiting execution he wrote a confession published in 1826. Katherine Anne Porter came on a copy of it at the Library of Congress in 1944 and showed it to Warren, who had been appointed Consultant in Poetry and had the study next to hers. After reading it he looked up the record of the trial, the letters of Beauchamp's wife, and a pamphlet written by Leonidas Sharpe, the Colonel's brother. Beauchamp's confession simply stated the facts, but his wife exulted in their fidelity to their private ideal of justice. That was Warren's real *donnee*.

Of all Warren's protagonists, Beaumont most resembles John Brown. He yearns for something to give his life importance, and unlike Jack Burden is eager for great responsibilities—but to what? Self-conscious, brooding, inclined like Jerry Calhoun to melancholy and the feeling of being left out, he can understand nothing except in terms of himself. His concern for the meaning of his acts is greater than that of the characters in Warren's other works, and his self-absorption is so complete that responsibility can only be to his private vision. Yet the vision must be acknowledged by others, and for that he must compel them to assent to his values. So he is driven to act in the world and is caught between conflicting ideas of truth and justice. He had already shown signs of the extremes he would go to. As a boy he liked to study a picture of a young woman being burned at the stake. It aroused his sexual desire. Sometimes he thought of how he would rescue her, sometimes of how he would die with her, and sometimes of how he himself would put the flame to the faggots. He would become so excited that he would have to leave the house. Later he goes to a revival meeting and, exalted with the Spirit, couples with a loathsome creature in a thicket. Then in a frenzy of revulsion he strikes her down and flees to a nearby river, where he lies in the water in a state of near unconsciousness. He discovers in himself a terrible separation of mind and body, idea and action. Henceforth he is never to be free of a sense of unworthiness that mars all experience, and he becomes unspeakably cruel to others because first he is so cruel to himself.

For a time he reads law with Colonel Fort, who takes the place of his father, who died when Beaumont was young. Informed that Fort had seduced Rachel Jordan, he sees at last his chance for a grand gesture. He nags her into saying she will marry him if he kills Fort. Like himself, she is inclined to melancholy and romantic visions. When they meet she is reading the *Symposium* to forget the world. Beaumont takes the book from her and reads aloud the passage describing how through love men may come to contemplate the Idea of Absolute Beauty. In her relation with Fort she had shown herself capable of earthly human love and forgiveness, but Beaumont seduces not her body but her soul by persuading her to sacrifice a fellow man to their dream of the Absolute.

Fort is involved in the conflict between the Old Court and the New. In the 1820's extreme poverty was widespread in Kentucky, and it was proposed to relieve the poor by extending the time limit on debts. This conflicted with the federal and state constitutions, but the Relief party argued that the will of the majority was superior to the law. When the state supreme court (the Old Court) found against the Reliefers, they planned to get enough members into the legislature to enlarge the court (New Court) and get another ruling. Fort had been for Relief but had come to believe that chaos would result if men could change the law to suit their convenience. Beaumont had put aside his resolve to kill Fort, but two members of the Relief party trick him into doing it on the night before Fort was planning to offer a compromise between the law and the needs of men. Fort had served in the world and knew that all man lives by may be a delusion but he has nothing else. He knew that the word is tainted by the deed. Yet undaunted he had sought and apparently had found some reconciliation. In killing him Jerry slew a wise, good man.

Jerry is accused, arrested, and tried. He lies when he pleads not guilty, but otherwise sticks to the truth. Yet the lies of others convict him and he is sentenced to hang. What then is truth, what justice? He escapes with his wife and goes to a swamp in the West where nobody cares who he is or what he has done. He ceases to care himself, and sinks into bestiality: he who had aspired to be more than human becomes less. Then he learns that he had been tricked and cries that everyone has used him, even Rachel. But she, at this last betrayal, tells him the truth about himself: he has used them all. Then she kills herself. Understanding himself at last, he starts back to give himself up, but he is killed before he is able to rejoin the human community.

Plainly a novel of ideas, *World Enough and Time* carries more rumination and interpretive comment than may be found in any other of Warren's fictions. In the confession that is "quoted" to give his view of events, Beaumont broods endlessly on his motives. (In the real confession Beauchamp did not.) Then the anonymous narrator broods upon Beaumont's brooding, pointing out the delusions and the ironic difference between what he professes and what he does. Warren himself sometimes addresses the reader directly, arguing that truth changes under time and that the narrator may have his own delusions. Some of the passages are virtually essays. There is, for instance, a section of some sixty lines comparing the old-fashioned duel with modern warfare which is neatly organized into example, analysis, comparison, and conclusion.[17] Most of the commentary is given over to insistence upon the ambiguity of all things. Thus, "You never knew when the doubleness you embraced might become simplicity, or when the single to which you looked or on which you laid your hand might divide like smoke, or to what strange corner the familiar street down which you walked might lead. The common word in your mind or mouth betrayed you. What did the word mean, after all?"[18] Warren lets pass no chance to debate that question, and at last one tires of the interpolated questions, the examples, the long—too long—stories about minor characters such as Sugg Lancaster, which clog the narrative. Yet the pattern of the central narrative is simple and straightforward, with fewer major incidents than are found in either *At Heaven's Gate* or *All the King's Men.* Warren moves easily among his several points of view and the focus is kept steadily upon the meaning of events, even when they are most vivid and violent. *World Enough and Time* is much too large, but it is by far the most skillfully constructed of Warren's novels until one reaches the codetta on the last three pages, which is an artistic disaster. Printed in italics, it describes modern Kentucky to make the point that men are not much nearer to justice and the reconciliation of the world and the idea. Parts of it are in the worst tough-guy manner, but no felicity of style could make it anything but supererogatory. It is a particularly obvious example of Warren's own failure to reconcile the world of fiction with the idea he intends it to illustrate. Here as in a number of other

[17] *World Enough and Time*, pp. 117-118.
[18] P. 303.

places he has dulled the image of events with more discussion than it needs or can sustain.

But "There must be a way . . ." and in *Brother to Dragons* Warren triumphantly found it.

On the night of December 15, 1811, Lilburne and Isham Lewis, sons of Thomas Jefferson's sister Lucy, butchered a young Negro slave at their home near Smithland, Kentucky. They were arrested and released on bail, but before they could be brought to trial, Isham shot Lilburne, who was supposed to shoot him, too, but didn't. Isham escaped and later died in the battle of New Orleans. Jefferson never made any recorded reference to the crime.

Warren heard a distorted account of it when a child, but did not read about it until 1943. Next year, while at the Library of Congress, he ran across allusions to it in abolition literature and a book on slavery in Kentucky. Intrigued, he looked up accounts of the crime in old newspapers and journals. It seemed just another gruesome story, but it stuck in his head because it happened in Jefferson's family. He went to Smithland in the summer of 1946 to climb the hill whereon the Lewis home had stood and to have a look at the court records. They went back to 1775. It took some digging, but he found the papers on the case. Rheumy old men and little boys hung around as he read through them, peering over his shoulder and asking, "D'ya think he done it?" In view of the conception of man set forth in the *Declaration of Independence*, Warren wondered what Jefferson made of it. Perhaps if he had been able to find out, the story would have been laid to rest. As it was, he was driven to pondering how the energy from the night side of life, how all the darkness and sadism, might be used for something constructive.

He considered writing a novel about the crime. (In 1880 a citizen of Smithland used it as an incident in a novel.) But he saw that would not do. The day-to-day circumstances were not a point of interest, which focused naturally upon the philosophical significance. To bring that out would require a disproportionate amount of comment. A friend from the theater suggested that he make a play of it. A chorus would be needed to point out the meaning, and Jefferson was the logical choice; but since his reaction rather than the action would be the center of attention, the chorus would overwhelm the play. While on a visit to Ransom after his investigation at Smithland, Warren wrote some lines of a poem in ballad form. When he came back to it during the next summer he found himself up against the old problem: the events simply would not sustain the form. So he put everything aside and went to work on *World Enough and Time*.

When the novel was done he went back to his material and this time he had the right shape for it: the tale would be told in rhymed and unrhymed verse by a colloquium of speakers meeting in "no time and no place" and speaking when moved to by inner necessity. By this means Warren could give his interpretive comment a human dynamic and a broad range of feelings and points of view while achieving dramatic presence and vivid characterizations. Lilburne had found an insanely simple way to cut through the ambiguity of things and affirm his loyalties and identity. After the event he would have little need to speak of it; so he was given only one speech, and his words on other occasions were reported by his wife and brother. George, the murdered slave, had only three lines. But the others spoke at length and told as much about their own struggle for fulfillment as they did about Lilburne's. Among them was "R.P.W.," a mask of Warren himself, put in to link 1811 to the present and show that the "no time" of the poem was all time and the issues debated made up a human constant. He had gone back to the Lewis place in the winter of 1951. That trip had a special importance for him, for he felt that he had been able to accept all the accident and evil in human experience which the place had symbolized during his first visit. It was in a special way the kind of return to the landscape lost in the heart's homely deep he had described in "The Return: An Elegy," "The Ballad of Billie Potts," *All the King's Men* (Jack Burden's return to Burden's Landing at the novel's end), and *World Enough and Time* (though Jerry Beaumont never got there), and was to write about in "Gold Glade" and other later poems. In token of his acceptance he had picked up some acorns before going down to join his father, who had waited in the car. He ended the poem with the words, "Let's go home."

Jefferson was the protagonist, but since he was not an actor in the original event, something had to happen to him to make the story move. Warren chose to have him look back on the crime as a representation of all that was dark in American history and had shadowed and befouled his dream. What happened to him was that he changed his mind about man—twice. The second time his sister Lucy persuaded him that he had been wrong in coming to think that man is entirely evil. She had had her own frightful problem, for she had fathered the monster who committed the murder in her name. To furnish her with grounds for arguing with her brother and him with a reason for listening to her, Warren brought in Meriwether Lewis, Jefferson's distant cousin whom he had treated as a son, to accuse Jefferson of betrayal by failing to prepare him for the evil and irrational that drove him to suicide. Meriwether's accusation, for Warren, was the turning point of the poem. He had the shape of his meaning.[19]

As Warren presents him, Jefferson is another man of ideas. He knew the evil in nature and man, knew "that all night long / History drips in the dark. . . ." Nevertheless, he believed that man is capable of innocence and to make it prevail must "redeem Nature." Thus he fell into his first great error. He defined good by means of an inadequate image of man and the world. Confronted by Lilburne's act he swung to a second error. Still oversimplifying, he now asserted that man and Nature were only evil.

> Lilburne is an absolute of our essential
> Condition, and as such, would ingurgitate
> All, and all you'd give, all hope, all heart,
> Would only be disbursed down that rat hole of the ultimate
> > horror.

One came at last, he said, to the center "Where Nothing screams nothing." So he decided to locate all meaning in pain, "the only real thing." From this it seemed to him to follow that "There's no forgiveness for our being human," for there is nothing from which forgiveness might take its meaning.

But though he had decided that only pain is real, he still repudiated Lilburne on moral grounds. His sister, who admitted that in some way she failed to love her son enough and must therefore share responsibility for his act, maintained that love, not

---

[19] This account of the search for the right form is based on Warren's remarks in the foreword to the poem, a conversation on January 6, 1954, and a talk entitled "The Natural History of a Poem," which Warren gave before the English Institute on September 11, 1953.

pain, provides an absolute by which all can be most nearly comprehended and men behave humanly. She pleaded with Jefferson not to forswear his love for Lilburne. It was here that Meriwether entered and accused his uncle of teaching him the great lie "that men are capable of the brotherhood of justice." As Lucy was to Lilburne, so Jefferson was to Meriwether, and when Jefferson conceded this, his sister told him that his repudiation of Lilburne was rooted in his fear of himself as "capable of all." To deny the mixture of good and evil that is in all men, even himself, he had stricken Lilburne as Lilburne had stricken George. She urged him to confront "the terror of our condition." When he did, he realized that

> Nothing we had,
> Nothing we were,
> Is lost.
> All is redeemed
> In knowledge.

Looking back to what the crime has meant to the speakers, "R.P.W." thinks,

> We have yearned in the heart for some identification
> With the glory of human effort, and have yearned
> For an adequate definition of that glory. . . .

That yearning argues for him the necessity of believing in virtue.

> In so far as man has the simplest vanity of self,
> There is no escape from the movement toward fulfillment.
> And since all kind but fulfills its own kind,
> Fulfillment is only in the degree of recognition
> Of the common lot of our kind. And that is the death of vanity.
> And that is the beginning of virtue.

So instructed, he sees that to yearn for glory is itself a kind of glory. Jerry Beaumont's question is answered. All is not for naught.

Though shorter than the novels, *Brother to Dragons* surpasses all of them in the measure of experience and thought brought into meaningful order. It has the richness and clarity of the best interpretive passages in *World Enough and Time* with the passion and intensity of the best narrative passages in *At Heaven's Gate*

and *All the King's Men.* The variety and range of tonalities in
the voices is remarkable, extending from the grave but impassioned
idealism and even more impassioned horror of Jefferson, through
the simpering and whining of Laetitia Lewis, Lilburne's wife, to
the "show me" cynicism of some of "R.P.W.'s" speeches and the
sad gentleness of Lucy Lewis's. Nowhere has Warren put on such
a virtuoso display of his ear for idioms or put his gift to better
use. Moreover, he managed to fit the natural rhythms of the
idioms to the exigences of verse drama, and he used every phonetic
means to give force to the colloquial discourse. One may take for
example these lines from the climactic exchange between Lucy and
Jefferson:

> JEFFERSON: . . . whatever my failings, I feared no man.
> LUCY: Yes, one.
> JEFFERSON: Who?
> LUCY: His name is Jefferson.
> I mean yourself. I mean the deepest fear.
> Yes, when you had learned in that report from Kentucky
> What evil was possible even in the familial blood,
> Your fear began, the fear you had always denied, the fear
> That you—even you—were capable of all. . . .
>
> In vanity and virtue and your fear,
> You struck. You struck Lilburne down—and yet strike
> Poor Lilburne down, and over and over again, the axe
> Falls. The axe falls, and you cast him forth in the fire. . . .

How *fear, struck,* and *falls* toll in the ear! How skillfully the
words and pauses are set in the lines! Where a phrase is repeated,
a different relation to the meter gives its elements fresh interest
and slightly different values. On the first appearance of the combination *you struck,* the words are so placed that the emphasis is
on the action. This is appropriate to the suggestion that Jefferson's
fear and vanity had brought him to such a pitch that he sought
relief in violence. The object mattered, for the instant, less than
the striking. But then attention shifts to what—or whom—he
struck. The position of the second appearance of *you struck* is such
that there is less emphasis on it this time, and much emphasis
on *Lilburne.* Then, since Jefferson's continuing to strike is a

shocking thing, *yet strike* is given the force that comes from being put at the end of the line and the extra force of running over into the next line, where *Poor Lilburne*, the object of the verb, gets a little more weight from the runover and its place at the beginning. This may seem like a small point, but it takes a great craftsman to give the same verb three different weights in the same line and have them agree so well with his meaning.

There are times, however, when Warren's pleasure in the clangor of sounds overcame his judgment and resulted in redundancy and empty ostentatious rhetoric. Instances abound: "Could nestle, nuzzle, smug and snug," "That frets and freaks with joy," "The fat sump and cess of common consciousness," "Agony of will / And anguish of option," "Muck, murk, and humus, and the human anguish." Slick. Very slick, indeed.

But compared with a far deeper flaw these are only blemishes of the surface. Jefferson and R.P.W., the speakers who make most of the interpretive comments and are supposed to validate the ideas by the changes in their beliefs and attitudes, are not quite believable even under the special terms of the poem. The difficulty in accepting them does not come from our knowledge of the real Jefferson and the real Warren outside the poem, but it is certainly increased by that knowledge. It is convenient for Warren's reading of American history to have Jefferson bear his own name in the poem, but even if he had changed the name, as he changed the names for *World Enough and Time*, we would still have trouble accepting the characters. Briefly, Warren overdoes things. He makes both men so simpleminded, violent, and coarse in places that we cannot believe it when they shift to grave regard for others and delicate discriminations of thought and feeling. Indeed, when Meriwether enters with his bullet-torn head and Jefferson greets him with "Well, Crack-head, who are you?" one is tempted to lay the poem aside in disgust. *This* is the author of the *Declaration?* True, Jefferson is an agony of revulsion, but one cannot imagine his giving way to such grossness. What has happened here is what we have seen before: Warren is trying too hard to make a point about an idea. In this great poem he managed better than ever before to give flesh to the word, but there are places—many of them—where the argument took precedent over the art.

Warren had labored for three decades toward the achievement

of *Brother to Dragons*. One might say that he began with the third of the "Portraits of Three Ladies" with its glimpse of the dark pool and the hairy horror and had striven through the earlier poems and the successive versions of his fable to the moment of acceptance, understanding, and reconciliation with nature and natural man signified by the ending of the poem. Now the danger would be that having delineated his vision in its most appropriate form he might begin to parody himself.

When the reader takes up *Band of Angels*, his heart may sink at the first words, "Oh, who am I?" Surely, he may think, Warren's characters have asked that question often enough. Amantha Starr, who asks it this time, is another egotist trying to escape from things as they are. The pampered only child of a Kentucky planter, she learns at his death that she has colored blood and she is sold into slavery. The man who buys her puts himself, as her father had, between her and reality. She thinks she wants freedom, but what she really desires is to do as she pleases and let someone else take all the responsibility. She wants to remain a privileged child forever. From imposing on her father, who felt guilty because she was illegitimate and her mother had died in childbirth, she has become adroit at dominating men by making them feel that they have abused her fragile innocence. She takes what she can but will not forgive her father or her lovers for being what they are. Only after much wandering and suffering does she win freedom by accepting them and their claims upon her. At last she has something outside her own willfulness to tell her who and what she is.

Part of her story is based on the actual experience of two supposedly white girls who were seized at their father's grave and sold into slavery. Around this macabre bit of Americana Warren has arranged a great many facts, gathered by patient research, about the slave trade, the capture and occupation of New Orleans during the Civil War, and the political tumult of the early Reconstruction. There is more history in this novel than in even *World Enough and Time*, and a lot of it is superb. Warren's theme had lost none of its intrinsic importance, but the characters without exception are trivial, regardless of how solemnly they comport themselves and speak. Moreover, Warren's insistence upon the ambiguity of the world had become a habit and the reader soon gets accustomed to seeing everything turn into its opposite. Love is immediately succeeded by hatred, joy by disaster, comfort and safety by peril and confusion. The dear friend is the dark betrayer; the selfless ascetic, the rapacious voluptuary; the magnanimous officer, the timid boy at heart. What in the earlier books is anguish is here self-pity and petulance; what was depravity is just vulgarity. There are many marks of Warren's imagination on the work, but it is a failure. The writing looks tired. Happily, there were better things soon to come.

Seen in retrospect, nearly all of Warren's principal characters are emotionally stunted. They have never really grown up, however boldly they confront the world, however sophisticated their knowledge of its ways. For to be truly adult is to be prepared to cope with life without the protection and security extended to children, and this, in the last analysis, they cannot do, despite the force and confidence that some of them may show. They demand adult freedoms and privileges, but they evade adult commitments and responsibilities, even when they have given themselves utterly to some abstract ideal that seems intended to serve the common weal and for that ideal endure hardships which would daunt all but the most courageous and self-disciplined. For that ideal is a barrier behind which they can withdraw from the just rights and demands of others, especially those others from whom they themselves ask the most.

Their deepest need is for the love of other adults, but they cannot inspire it because they cannot face the responsibilities it entails: they cannot give adult love in return. In *Flood* Brad Tolliver compulsively destroys his marriage to Lettice Poindexter because he cannot respond to her need for love that transcends sexuality. Thus Jack Burden loses Anne Stanton's love because he will not enter man's estate. Like so many others, he wants the unearned love given to children and all safety and irresponsibility that goes with it. Cut off by their inadequacy from the human communion, the characters lack identity, which, as Jack Burden comes to understand, is defined in terms of one's actions toward others. But they cannot even begin to seek it in any meaningful way until they are ready to accept the risks and burdens of adult behavior. They must give up infantile self-images and role-playing and accept themselves as mixtures of good and evil, nobility and baseness, dignity and absurdity, strength and weakness, wisdom and ignorance. For some it is not possible even to try. Percy Munn is too passive. Lilburne Lewis is mad. Laetitia Lewis is too stupid. Bogan Murdock and Slim Sarrett are perverted beyond any hope of redemption. But others have a will to maturity, a drive to fulfill themselves in human terms (rather than the superhuman terms of the Pure Idea or the subhuman terms of pure sensuality), that compels them to seek the communion and the discovery of the self. For, as Warren said in his address, "Knowledge and the Image of Man," "Each of us longs for full balance and responsibility in self-knowledge, in a recognition and harmonious acceptance of our destiny."[20]

However protected and comfortable, most of them had difficult childhoods because, in the language of the literature, their dependency needs and longing for love were unfulfilled. Sue Murdock, for example, grew up amidst wealth, but in the passage of *At Heaven's Gate* that tells us most about her, she deliriously identifies the doctor who has just performed an abortion on her with her father. Her lover has left her, their child has been taken from her and destroyed, and in her feverish nightmares she remembers her childhood loneliness and how it was in some inexplicable way related to losing something such as a locket or a ring or a silver spoon. Father, lover, doctor—all took away love that she has needed since she was a little girl. As John Lewis Longley, Jr., has pointed out, it is at this moment when she has been used and abandoned by all that she receives her last letter from her father urging her to go away.

Because their needs are unfulfilled, the characters believe at their most secret core that they are unworthy of love, and they turn inward, even though, paradoxically, some of them reach out to cling to a stronger person, a surrogate of the parent who, like Sue's father, has failed them. Their narcissism may make them vain, selfish, and self-righteous. Nevertheless, for all their pridefulness, they cannot accept themselves, cannot admit that they are just flawed human beings like their parents. With the arrogance of the radically fearful they may set up impossibly high standards for themselves to show that they are different from

[20] "Knowledge and the Image of Man," *Sewanee Review*, LXIII (Spring, 1955), 189.

others and then cruelly punish themselves, as do Jerry Beaumont and his wife, for failing to measure up. But whether they attack the world or withdraw from it, beneath the seemingly overweening self-love that characterizes their behavior is actually an ultimate inability to love themselves in a healthy way (they think they do not deserve to) which keeps them from giving and taking adult love. That is the substance of Lucy Lewis's great insight. She explains to her brother, Jefferson, that he must accept the Lilburne in himself; he must confess himself only a man and a brother to dragons. With the humble and contrite acceptance of the self come the possibility of loving others and beyond it the possibility of communion and identity. In the end self-acceptance, the capacity to love, communion, and identity all are one. They are, in a word, maturity. Toward this all life lifts and yearns.

IV

In April of 1957, readers of the *Yale Review* were confronted by:

> The sun is red, and the sky does not scream.
> The sun is red, and the sky does not scream.
> There is much that is scarcely to be believed.
> The moon is in the sky, and there is no weeping.
> The moon is in the sky, and there is no weeping.
> Much is told that is scarcely to be believed.

Much indeed. For "The Necessity for Belief" was the last of ten new poems by Warren which showed that another great shift had occurred in his imagination. No longer need the sun signify the grinding, bloody agony of the spheres, nor the moon the ineffable sadness of the deprived heart. It was as if the poet could scarcely believe what his poems told him: hope and joy were possible.

The knowledge was earned. In "Court-martial," as we have already said, Warren described once more the child's first encounter with the violence and ambiguity of the world that exceeded his little notions of History. "School Lesson Based on Word of Tragic Death of Entire Gillum Family" was an even finer description of the encounter, for reality bursts not only upon some school children but upon the reader as well, and with something like its original shock. As Ransom took the reader off guard in "Janet Waking,"

so Warren tricks him into a stock response; the impact of reality
is greater and the complacency of the reader's response is exposed
in the contrast between what actually happened and how the reader
feels about it. At the outset the verse is jaunty and patronizing:

> They weren't so bright, or clean, or clever,
>> And their noses were sometimes imperfectly blown. . . .

These are the Gillums, who came six miles to school from out
back where "the whang-doodle whooped and the dang-whoodle
snorted." Old Slat Gillum loved them and wanted them to have
their chance, but one day they don't show up and word comes
that the father has slain the entire family with an ice-pick. And
"When the sheriff got there the school bread was long burned to
a crisp." That is the "indicative poetry" that helps to change all.
Abruptly the other scholars and the reader are compelled to go
behind the attitudes suggested by the jeering tone of the poem
and see the Gillums there—and dead. Their schoolmates are left
with two lessons to ponder: the qualities of the event (they
struggle to take in the fact that, yes, it really did happen) and
"another lesson, but we were too young to take up that one"—
the lesson of the sudden madness that is in things. And still man
endures and there is hope. "Foreign Shore, Old Woman, Slaughter
of Octopus" describes how, after a day of "picnic and laughter"
and the pointless killing of an octopus, an old woman walks on
the beach as the darkness gathers. She knows "that what came
will recur" and is undismayed. And the poet thinks,

> This is not my country, or tongue,
>> And my age not the old woman's age, or sea-age.
> I shall go on my errand, and that before long,
>> And leave much but not, sea-darkling, her image.
> Which in the day traffic, or as I stand in night dark,
>> may assuage
> The mind's pain of logic somewhat, or the heart's rage.

One remembers "Pursuit" and another who went with troubled
heart to the shore and how, at the hotel, he spoke to an old lady
in black, who croaked like a toad or Norn.

Warren called the sequence "Promises." One month later the
English magazine *Encounter* published nine more poems bearing

the same title and dedicated to Warren's son, Gabriel, born in the summer of 1955. The promises are wrested from the circumstance of violence and despair. "Dark Woods," a long poem having three nearly independent sections describes the heart turning inward to its own blackness. The speaker acts out the inner event by walking more and more deeply into the dark woods until, among reminders of death, he comes to a blossoming dogwood. After a surge of joy he wishes to destroy its bland beauty, and he wonders, "Could the poor heart's absurd / Cry for wisdom, for wisdom, ever be answered?" Later on, returning to the darkening woods, he is able to accept change, death, and his own queer reaction to the tree's shimmering perfection and tells himself to remember how, like other men, he had gone into the darkness and known anger and despair. "Summer Storm (circa 1916), and God's Grace" describes an instance of the outer irrational trouble that afflicts man as "Dark Woods," an instance of the inner. It is superbly clear and vivid, bringing at once to mind the eerie stillness and hypersensitivity just before a storm bursts:

> In that strange light all distance died.
>   You know the world's intensity.
>   Field-far, you can read the aphid's eye.
>
>   . . .
>
>   A half a county off, now spy
>   The crow that, laboring zenith-high,
> Is suddenly, with wings askew,
>   Snatched, and tumbled down the sky.

Warren was so sure of the force of his material that he could risk treating it with some of the giddy humor that may overtake one in the midst of overwhelming violence. He tells how "with a squawk, / The henhouse heaved, and flew away." The gamble, like the gamble with making fun of yokels in "School Lesson . . . ," pays off with heightened reality. But then, having brought off this feat, Warren nearly destroys his poem with a puerility that recalls the crudities of Ransom's early poem "Noonday Grace":

> And God got down on hands and knees
> To peer and cackle and commend
>   His own sadistic idiocies.

By itself this is bad enough. To make things worse it mars the somber dignity of the plea at the end of the poem that the men who do not whine when hit by such a catastrophe be given "one summer just right,"

> And if a man wake at roof-roar at night,
> Let that roar be the roar of God's awful grace,
> and not of His flail.

The remote and fearful majesty imputed to God by these lines is denied by the image of a sadistic idiot on hands and knees.

Having in these and other poems set forth man's afflictions, Warren finds among them some things such as the great shagbark hickory of "Gold Glade" that endure "absolute and bold" and are a promise and not a trick to disarm man before the blow falls. And speaking directly to his son in "When the Century Dragged," which is the first section of "Infant Boy at Mid-Century," he foresees a time when the son will spurn his parents and pass on

> To pause, in high pride of undisillusioned manhood,
> At the gap that gives on the new century, and land,
> And with calm heart and level eye command
> That dawning perspective and possibility of human good.[21]

This is embarrassing. It is hard to believe that one long schooled in the hard ironies of life would thus betray his deepest feelings with a tableau straight from a W.P.A. post-office mural. Such a lapse of judgment and taste suggests that Warren had suddenly chosen to deny all that he suffered and labored to learn about man. But in the next section, "Modification of Landscape," he grants that in his son's time there may be "expansion, we hope, of the human heart-hope, and hand-scope," but warns that "flesh will yet grieve on the bone, / And the heart need compensation for its failure to study delight." "The new age will need the old lies" because "there's natural distress / In learning to face Truth's glare-glory, from which our eyes are long hid." In the last section

---

[21] This is the text of *Promises, Poems 1954-1956* (New York, 1957). In *Encounter* the lines read:
> To print, in the high pride of undisillusioned manhood,
> Sand of new century, where you in your fullness, will stand,
> And with calm eye and uncurled lip, command
> That dawning perspective and possibility of human good.

he asks his son to remember that the father's age was not the worst of times and had persons of private virtue who can watch his achievement without envy.

These poems show that Warren was somewhat unskilled in the poetry of happiness, most difficult to write. He had, as he suggested in *Brother to Dragons,* lived out some personal version of his great fable and had come to terms with himself. He was late a father, being forty-eight when Rosanna, the first of his two children, was born. Now he was seeing the substance of his fable not as the guiltily rebellious son but as the father tormented by the prospect of the inevitable fate that would overtake his children and knowing that he, in his turn, would be rejected for the sake of some ideal vision to which he could not measure up. In 1954, when his daughter was one year old, he wrote five poems, published in the *Partisan Review* in the spring of 1955, in which he sought to bring into order the mixture of delight in her beauty and apprehension induced by all the death and misery about her. The Warrens had spent the summer in a partially restored fortress at Porto Ercole by the sea just north of Rome. There, as he tells in "Sirocco," a dry wind, blowing through dust and the blaze of sun on water, threatened the flowers which his daughter so resembled. To this unease was added fear of the "filth of fate" embodied in the defective child next door. The creature had a beautiful older sister who had taught it to greet passers-by with a gesture of benediction. Her untroubled beauty and faith enraged the poet. "Fool," he thought in "The Child Next Door," "doesn't she know that the process / Is not that joyous or simple, to bless, or unbless. . . ?" Then, to his daughter,

> I think of your goldness, of joy, how empires grind,
> stars are hurled.
> I smile stiff, saying *ciao,* saying *ciao,* and think:
> this is the world.

His love has made him vulnerable to the meaningless cruelty of the world and his blessing is desperate, for he knows that the process is not that joyous or simple. The most he can hope for is that man may be wise enough to take joy from beauty.

Yet the poems show his own hopefulness growing with his

happiness. The children throve at Porto Ercole. Watching them, he thought of his parents, his boyhood, and the Kentucky countryside. Out of his memories came the shambling but infinitely touching poem, "What was the Promise that Smiled from the Maples at Evening," in which he described the kind of enigmatic loneliness that so troubled Sue Murdock. To a little boy, excited by watching older boys shooting nighthawks, darkness is suddenly inviting and sad, and on an impulse he hides in it and will not come when his parents call. It is his first experience with the obscure mixture of melancholy, obstinancy, and guilt which drew him into the darkness and loneliness out of the security and affection in which he was lapped. Years afterward, he gropes for an explanation, as Sue Murdock had done, and thinks that something was lost—something somehow connected with a door that creaks where it hangs. He asks his own son to understand that his parents wish him well, and remembering his own parents, decides that if something was lost and the promises they died to fulfill were not realized, they at least achieved a serenity and glory in reaching toward them. In "Founding Fathers . . ." he had written that one generation could not speak to another, but his own fatherhood enabled him, after all the years when something was lost, to hear what his parents had to tell him and answer their call through the darkness.

One has the sense that it is such an emotional reunion with the past that made it possible for Warren to write of hope and to describe one wonderful day of boyhood in "Boy's Will, Joyful Labor without Pay, and Harvest Home (1918)," published in *Botteghe Oscure* during that same bountiful spring of 1957. Years later, with a "heart stab blessed past joy or despair," he can see in his mind's eye the day's end and "That field, pale, under starlit air." It is an image suffused with what Lucy Lewis called "the blessedness of the human condition." And it stands against Time, which is no longer the wholly destructive force that it was in the *Eleven Poems on the Same Theme*. Life sinks down, light and warmth fail, flowers wither in the wind, parents die, yet goodness and joy recur. Warren could even assert in "Lullaby: A Motion Like Sleep" that all things move toward a fulfillment in "Time's irremediable joy." It is inconceivable that he could have written that phrase as recently as the period when he was working on

Brother to Dragons. In "Lullaby: Smile in Sleep," the most remarkable poem of that remarkable spring, he went still further
and, in effect, opposed the whole tenor of his fable to tell his son:

> What if angry vectors veer
> Around your sleeping head, and form?
> There's never need to fear
> Violence of the poor world's abstract storm.
> For you now dream Reality.
> Matter groans to touch your hand.
> Matter now lifts like the sea
> Toward that cold moon that is your dream's command.
> Dream the power coming on.
> Dream, strong son.
> Sleep on.

It would be difficult to exaggerate the depth and massiveness of
the change these lines signify. Warren had always insisted that the
Flesh required the Word, that the Action demanded the Idea.
But he had insisted much more on the dangers of the dream of
the Word and Idea and on the disasters that overtook those who
proposed to redeem nature. And now, after that extraordinary
epitome "you now dream Reality," he qualifies his claims, remembering that his son "will, of course, see all / The world's brute
ox-heel wrong, and shrewd hand-harm." All the infidelity and
betrayal. He even warns indirectly that in time the son, too,
will fail, for he likens the son's dream of reality to the image
toward which the diver moves in the instant before he starts his
downward plunge. Still, the dream will serve his son as

> now, dreaming, you serve me,
> And give our hope new patent to
> Enfranchise the human possibility.
> Grace undreamed is grace forgone. . . .

In 1958 Warren published these poems and a queer sequence
of nightmares of sexual fear and guilt called "Ballad of a Sweet
Dream of Peace" in a collection entitled, appropriately, *Promises.*
His using this title for a third time suggests how significant it was
for him. Though the poems vary widely in merit, the best—
"Sirocco," "The Child Next Door," "School Lesson. . . ," "Dragon

Country," "Founding Fathers," "Foreign Shore. . .," and "Boy's
Will . . ."—are with "The Return: An Elegy," "The Garden,"
and "Picnic Remembered" the finest verse Warren has yet given
us.[22] Most of the poems are intricately formal and have nearly as
much hard, ceramic surface as Ransom's: yet at first one has an
impression of great slovenliness and incompleteness. The impression comes from the unusually rough lines and distorted snytax of
the poems one first encounters in the volume and from the
rambling, inconclusive organization and thinking of "The Flower"
and "Colder Fire," the fourth and fifth. Bewildered by the long
lines and the nervous flutter of hovering accents, one may fail
to see that the first two poems, "Sirocco" and "Gull's Cry," are
Shakespearean sonnets, and that in "Gull's Cry," the development
of the dominant idea is carefully matched to the sonnet form.
Indeed, one must go back to 1933-1934 to find poems as carefully
wrought as these. The formal order and formidable surface permit
Warren to speak of personal feelings with an intensity which
would disturb if they were not so manifestly under control. One
feels uneasy when Warren lets his grip go slack in "The Flower"
and "Colder Fire," in which he fumbles around like a raconteur
who has forgotten the point of a story and hopes to recall it by
circling the area where he thinks it is. These poems have some
lovely and moving passages, but "Moonlight Observed" is as
trashily sentimental as the lyrics of popular songs from which its
images derive.

In some poems Warren invents stanzas so elaborate that if he
did not call attention to the form by repeating key lines the reader
might not notice that the stanzas are not irregular verse paragraphs. "Lullaby: Moonlight Lingers" uses a stanza of 16 lines
rhyming *aababbcccddefeff*. The numbers of feet are: 4, 4, 4, 3,
5, 2, 4, 7, 3, 4, 4, 4, 4, 3, 6, 3. The phrasing of the stanzas ap-
proximates a uniform pattern: the five, six, and seven foot lines
end in full stops, and the distribution of the sentences is about
the same in each. "Lullaby: A Motion Like Sleep" uses a stanza
of 11 lines rhyming *ababcdcdeee*, in which the numbers of feet
to the line are: 4, 4, 3, 5, 4, 4, 4, 5, 4, 2, 2. Each stanza ends with
some variant of "Sleep, my son. / Sleep son." The poem is

---

[22] This is said with the poems of *You, Emperors, and Others* in mind. The
scope of this study does not permit examination of that volume.

beautifully made and its demeanor, if one may call it that, dignifies the remarkable abjuration to "dream Reality." In the slow-paced gravity of the poem the abjuration seems a great dare against Time and the terror of the human condition and not just an uprush of fatherly fatuity.

Such tightly coherent forms are needed to help bind Warren's crazed and twisted syntax. He transposes major elements of his sentences, as in "Far to that blueness the heart aches." Often he widely separates coordinate elements. Thus, instead of writing, "We brought you to a place of ruined stone and sea-reaches," he offers the jagged, "To a place of ruined stone we brought you, and sea-reaches." Back in 1940-1942 he sometimes dropped articles out of his sentences, as when in "Original Sin: A Short Story" he wrote, "Which glinted in sun like rough garnet." By *Brother to Dragons* the omission of articles had become a characteristic of his style. In *Promises* it seems almost obsessive: "Rosemary, thistle, cluth stone." Resembling it is the piling up of fragmentary clauses consisting of predicates without subjects, or of subjects and adverbs or subjects and predicate adjectives without verbs:

> White goose by palm tree, palm ragged, among stones
>   the white oleander,
> And the she-goat, brown, under pink oleander, waits.

And:

> Said, "Mister," in bed, the child-bride; hadn't known
>   what to find there;
> Wept all the next morning for shame; took pleasure
>   in silk; wore the keys to the pantry.

Scattered among these are many homemade compounds, more often than not combining two alliterative, monosyllabic words such as *hawk-heel*, *blaze-blue*, and *gleam-glory*.

With these eccentricities Warren achieves a rich consort of rhythmical and metrical variations. He inverts feet, adds and drops syllables, and divides accents so often that in some poems it is impossible to decide whether the movement is predominantly iambic or trochaic, let alone identifying the meter. He is especially fond of putting accented syllables side by side, as in "range easy" and "the heart aches." Sometimes the accented syllables are separated by punctuation which creates a pause between them and gives additional force, as in "Sleep, my son. / Sleep, son." Mingled with such spondaic effects are many hovering accents, and one is compelled to go over some of the lines many times before determining what pairings are spondaic and what hovering. It requires some thoughtful meditation on the meaning, not just of the lines, but of the whole poem, to determine the rhythmical pattern of

> A hill, no. Sea cliff, and crag-cocked, the embrasures
> commanding the beaches. . . .

Or,

> Head back, gray eyes narrow, thumb flat along knife-blade,
> blade low.

There are so many secondary pauses that the accents tend to bunch together and many lines read like series of irregular explosions.

Years earlier Ransom suggested in "A Poem Nearly Anonymous," that Milton may have gone back over his smooth lines and deliberately roughened them to make his own voice heard through the anonymity of the pastoral elegy. Whether he did or didn't we cannot know. But Warren roughened his. When he reprinted "Founding Fathers . . ." he added to these lines words, here placed in italics, which were not in the version published in *Encounter*:

> There was always a grandpa, or cousin *at least,* who
> had been, of course, a real Signer.
>   · · ·
> Or the mold-yellow Bible, God's Word, in which,
>   *in their strength,* they had also trusted.

In "Lullaby: Smile in Sleep" the line

> As though season woke in the winter underwood

was changed to

> As though season woke in the heart's cold underwood.

The distribution of accents is not changed, but in the second version there is a tension between the meaning and the meter by virtue of the force which *cold* has which the second syllable of *winter* did not. Many other instances could be adduced, but these are enough to bear out the observation by James Wright that the distortions are part of "an extreme exaggeration of a very formal style." Wright believes that Warren is a master of prosody who chose "to fight through and beyond his own craftsmanship in order to revitalize his language at the sources of tenderness and horror."[23] From this one might suppose that the distortions come from a refusal to impose form upon feeling, but close study of the lines and comparison of early and late versions show, rather, that the distortions are, as Wright sees, not a denial but an extension of craftsmanship. Writing of Edgar Varèse's *Ionization* (a composition for thirty-seven percussion instruments), Paul Rosenfeld referred to the "pulsatile and frictive choir . . . functioning as a sonorous unit." The same might be said of Warren's verse, in which the distortions are not adjunctive but integral. The feeling does not discover them; they discover the feeling. The poems that seem at first to be careless and unfinished actually have the elegance of a painting by Tapies or sculpture by Richier.

In keeping with the formal control is the curiously restrained and simple diction and imagery. The syntax may be wrenched but the language and idioms are colloquial. "Gull's Cry" has some of the cant that disfigures *Brother to Dragons*, as in "the astonishing statement of sun," which means only "bright sunlight," and "the irrelevant anguish of air," which apparently refers to small gusts; but as a whole the collection is notably free of this. And free, too, of the abstract commentary toward which, as Frederick P. W. McDowell observed, all of Warren's later work has tended. Perhaps the short forms and complex structures made him work on his material so hard that he got it just right and could trust it to make its way without ancillary explanation. Only in the loose mode he used for "The Flower" does he indulge in it, apparently because he realized that his poem was getting out of hand and chose to bring it back into focus by explaining rather than beginning again.

Visibility has always been a quality of Warren's work, but never before have its scenes and events been rendered with so much precision and palpability. Particularly lovely are the Mediterranean vistas, drenched in sunlight and suffused with gold, pale blue, and

[23] "The Stiff Smile of Mr. Warren," *Kenyon Review*, XX (Autumn, 1958), 647, 646.

white, and set off in their transparent lightness against the masses of dark boulders and the coastal range. The poems describing the Kentucky of Warren's boyhood are just as "painterly." "Summer Storm," for example, has some of the qualities of the work of Thomas Hart Benton and a similar gusto, flamboyant humor, and affection for the rural life of the Mississippi Valley. It would be easy to put that poem on canvas. Then, as one grows used to the way that, in these poems, "The world is real. It is there," one becomes aware of the measure of lived-through experience in that so solid realm that Warren has put before the reader. Proportionately, there is more of it rendered in "Founding Fathers. . .," "Country Burying. . .," and "Boy's Will . . ." than in much of the fiction, for all the fiction's turbulent action and profusion of details. "Christmas Gift" and "Blackberry Winter," Warren's two best stories, can match these poems. So can some of the best scenes in *Night Rider,* such as the description of Percy Munn on the train at the beginning or the account of his initiation into the night riders. But there are no scenes in *All the King's Men, World Enough and Time,* or *Brother to Dragons* comparable to the description of summer night in the country at the end of "Boy's Will . . ." or of the old woman on the sands at evening in "Foreign Shore. . . ." It was just in the period that he was writing these poems that Warren told the reunited Fugitives that for him the test of poetry was the sense of contact with reality. One may disagree and think that more is demanded. But just because these poems so admirably meet Warren's own test they give the more one might ask for.

The finest of them are incomparably better than most of the American poetry of their time. In scope, tragic sense, mastered substance, inventiveness, and plain power *Promises* surpasses all other volumes of verse published in this country since the Second World War. Significantly, the best poems are set in that "landscape lost in the heart's homely deep" to which his most promising early poems looked back and to which, after a long pilgrimage of the imagination, he could at last return to confront what we have elsewhere called its grief and glory. He, too, fulfilled his promises.

V

Man, Warren everywhere insists, is both in and out of Nature. That is the definitive fact of his history, the cause of all the grief and glory. And it demands of him not only the emotional maturity described earlier in these pages, but philosophical maturity as well. "As men," he has said, "we have in common certain capacities that make us men, the capacity to envisage ourselves in relation to nature and other men, the capacity for self-criticism, the capacity for a disinterested love of excellence." Each must "accept his responsibility for trying to realize his common humanity at its highest" and work for a society in which others can realize theirs.[24] *Common humanity, highest, in relation to nature, self-criticism, love of excellence.* Such terms indicate that his great fable and the epilogue that is *Promises* must be understood in ontological and ethical as well as psychological terms. By his own definition in the essay on *Nostromo* Warren is a philosophical poet and novelist "for whom the urgency of experience . . . is the urgency to know the meaning of experience." And the urgency has grown with the years. McDowell is right when he says that despite Warren's mistrust of abstract thinking, philosophical and ethical speculation has come to absorb him.[25] Or had down to *Promises.* In each successive version of the fable the "documentation of the world," as Warren called it, strives ever more "to rise to the level of generalization about values" as it did in Conrad. As a consequence, Warren, who wrote no essays on the philosophy of Agrarianism, began in his poetry and fiction with some of the premises of that philosophy expounded by Ransom and Tate and explored them far more deeply than ever his friends had done even in their overtly philosophical writings. Thus, though little involved in the activist side of Agrarianism, Warren, as we have said elsewhere, was in this way, at least, the most Agrarian of writers. One need only put *World Enough and Time* beside *The Fathers* to see this. In its endless brooding upon the problems of man's duality, his relations with nature, and the dangers of abstraction Warren's novel is as philosophical as *God Without Thunder* and far more deeply penetrating. One can go further and maintain that Warren not only surpasses the other Agrarians in incorporating philosophy into imaginative writing but is the most profoundly and comprehensively philosophical of the major American writers of our time.

[24] "Knowledge and the Image of Man," pp. 183, 184.
[25] Frederick P. W. McDowell, "Psychology and Theme in *Brother to Dragons*," *PMLA*, LXX (September, 1955), 565. McDowell's essay is the best short study of Warren's work yet to appear. My indebtedness to it is obvious.

Yet he is not schematic and deductive in his mode but artistic. Only in his weaker passages is the philosophy not assimilated by the narrative and the poetic or fictive frame of reference. He does not lapse into allegory, but he sometimes lapses into melodrama. That is, he may represent a characteristic act with violence and emotional intensity quite exceeding the occasion, motive, and personalities of the actors in order to supply a philosophical point with emphasis which his story by its necessities cannot provide. Such excess all but destroys the recent novel *Flood*.

Diction, imagery, character, and symbolic actions and settings all direct our attention to the psychological level of meaning in his versions of his fable. But he believes that "the story of every soul is the story of its self-definition for good or evil, salvation or damnation,"[26] and the elements of the fable are so ordered as to bring about a symbolic extension from this primary level to an ontological level and thence, through and beyond it, to an ethical level. Of course, recognition of the three levels comes, if at all, only when we stand off and ruminate upon the meaning. In the narrative itself they are all one and the key terms of the meaning— *nature, man, human, love, virtue, glory, responsibility*, and *redemption*—apply to all of them at once. Thus, for instance, we understand that reconciliation with the self and the father on the psychological level leads to, requires, and even participates in reconciliation with the tension between fact and idea and with the ambiguity of nature on the ontological level, and these lead to, require, and participate in humility, loving forgiveness, and acceptance of the brotherhood of men on the ethical level.

In 1954 Warren took part in a conference on the Unity of Knowledge at Columbia University, and in his speech, which has been cited several times in this chapter, summed up the philosophy of his own work. "Only by knowledge," he said, "does man achieve his identity . . . because it gives him the image of himself." And

"the image of himself necessarily has a foreground and a background, for man is in the world . . . with continual and intimate interpenetration . . . which in the end does not deny, but affirms his identity. . . .

"Despite this . . . man's process of self-definition means that

[26] "Knowledge and the Image of Man," p. 182.

he distinguishes himself from the world and from other men. He disintegrates his primal instinctive sense of unity, he discovers separateness. In this process he discovers the pain of self-criticism and the pain of isolation. But the pain may, if he is fortunate, develop its own worth, work its own homeopathic cure. In the pain of self-criticism he may develop an ideal of excellence, and an ideal of excellence, once established, implies a de-personalized communion in that ideal. In the pain of isolation he may achieve the courage and clarity of mind to envisage the tragic pathos of life, and once he realizes that the tragic experience is universal and a corollary of man's place in nature, he may return to a communion with man and nature.

"Man can return to his lost unity, and if that return is fitful and precarious. . ., all is the more precious for the fact, for what is now achieved has been achieved by a growth of moral awareness. The return to nature and man is the discovery of love, and law."[27]

Once he is able to love, he can leave the West and come back to the homestead. He can live with both the dark pool and the golden shagbark and all that they stand for in himself and others.

As an ontologist Warren, like Ransom, is a persistent dualist, as these two symbols suggest. Nature is both evil and good, destructive and creative, beautiful and revolting, comforting and terrifying. If man cuts himself off from it entirely, he becomes a monster such as Percival Skrogg; but if he immerses himself wholly within it, he becomes a no less horrible monster such as La Grand' Bosse or the catfish under the winter's ice which

> sleeps with eye lidless, and the brute face
> Is the face of the last torturer, and the white belly
> Brushes the delicious and icy blackness of mud.
> But there is no sensation. How can there be
> Sensation when there is perfect adjustment?

That is why, as "R.P.W." says in *Brother to Dragons,*

> despite all naturalistic considerations . . .
> We must believe in virtue. There is no
> Escape.

[27] "Knowledge and the Image of Man," pp. 186-187.

Yet we must not for the sake of that virtue

deny Nature
And leap beyond man's natural bourne and constriction
To find some justification for the natural.

If it be not the perfect adjustment of the catfish, neither is virtue any transcendent absolute sanctioned by a divine authority. For Warren, as for Ransom, God is a metaphor used to represent the fullness of the natural. What, then, does he mean by saying that we must believe in virtue *despite* all naturalistic considerations?

Man makes his own definitions of glory and virtue. Nature may provide the appropriate imagery but

whatever the gleam of massive magnificence or
glimmer of shy joy
May be, it can only resemble the moon
And is but mirror to the human heart's steadfast and
central illumination.
If there is glory, the burden, then, is ours.
If there is virtue, the burden, then, is ours.

Yet this still does not tell us how man can be enough above nature to struggle toward a definition of glory (the struggle itself being, as he says, a kind of glory) when the natural is all there is. One may say, however, that it is proper to Warren's belief in the limitations of knowledge for man to see himself both in and out of nature and not be able to explain how this is so. And that is where the matter rests.

The resemblance at many points between his thinking and Ransom's is very great. As we know, he did not form his ideas by studying Ransom's works or sitting at his feet. But on the evidence of his essay "John Crowe Ransom: A Study in Irony," published in 1935, we can be sure that before he began his major work he thoroughly understood his friend. The resemblance is most fundamental and significant in their insistence upon the radical pluralism of all things as man knows them. Like Ransom, Warren is wary of systems and rejects Hegelian third terms that resolve the fundamental dichotomies of human experience. His grimly absolutist and self-righteous idealists such as Jefferson and Jerry Beaumont resemble the ruthless, warlike Christ of Ransom's

"Armageddon." His kindlier idealists such as Tobias Sears remind one of Ransom's Captain Carpenter. His men of abstract intelligence and will such as Bogan Murdock, Adam Stanton, and Percival Skrogg are similar to the "scientist" of Ransom's *God Without Thunder* and *The World's Body,* and are the least believable of his characters, for they suffer from the same limitations and distortions that were pointed out in the discussion of Ransom's conceptions of science and scientists. But the figure in Ransom's work who perhaps best fits into Warren's story of the man caught between idea and action is the friar of "Necrological."

Like Ransom, Warren is quick to see polarities such as illusion and reality, timelessness and Time, order and violence, light and dark, history and poetry, and to find in their permutations the ineluctable ironies and mysteries of human experience. "Man," he wrote in his essay on *Nostromo,* "must make his life somehow in the dialectical process of these terms. . . ." But he does not tend to think in systems of correlatives, probably because, though he sees man as dual and divided, he does not see the mind as compartmentalized. Indeed, he often goes Ransom one better and argues that opposite poles actually may contain one another. As McDowell says, for Warren "every act and emotion carries within it not only its own impulsion but its contrary possibility. A fervently accepted good, therefore, has more possible evil in it than a lukewarm virtue, while an unabashed evil carries with it latent violences that augur the possibility of heartfelt conversion."[28] Warren's psychology is more up to date than Ransom's.

Though they agree on the plurality of Nature, their visions of it are radically different and have been since the earliest days, as was pointed out in the comment on Warren's poem "Garden Waters." Both warn man against letting abstractions blind him to its complexity, Ransom because then man gives up the innocent pleasures in particularity, Warren because then man forgets that he is a brother to dragons and that to spurn Nature for the idea is to spurn himself. In the end the right attitude toward Nature, Ransom argues, brings man temperateness and serenity with which to endure natural catastrophes and to enjoy natural beauty. But for Warren the right attitude makes possible bearing the burden of responsibility for the natural evil in oneself and facing up to

[28] "Psychology and Theme in *Brother to Dragons,*" p. 578.

the terror of the human condition which is part of the greater terror of Nature. In *Promises,* however, he asserts, without a supporting ontological argument, that there is a good "Beyond any heart-hurt, or eye's grief-fall." Wisely, he lets his images authorize themselves for those who wish to believe.

In his insistence on the darkness and terror, Warren comes close to Tate's ontology. Both warned that man loses his identity by immersion in the dark natural chaos. And for both that chaos is but the outward sign of inner disorder. Yet there is a significant difference. Tate sees it as a tumult of sensations and discrete impressions over which there plays a lightning of nervous tension. Though he has written of the Dark Night of the Senses, his chaos is singularly free of sensuality. But Warren's is a swamp of sensuality in which man sprawls in delicious torpor. There his nerves are not stretched and torn as they are in Tate's but numbed. For Tate, then, Nature as chaos is made up of jagged fragments; for Warren it is made up of some amorphous slime. Warren's nature is pervasively genital; Tate's is not. For each ontology is, as it were, a poetry of ethics. Both men argued the necessity of what Tate called "imperatives of reference" to guide man in the black confusion of the world and his own mind; but there again is a significant difference. Warren's referents are tentative, provisional, and tainted with man's ignorance. At best they are but Conradian illusions that sustain man though they bear the blemish of his vanity and selfishness along with whatever glory and virtue he can dimly surmise. Tate, on the other hand, takes them as given by the community and tested in the long history of its common experience. In his early works he conceded that they might be altered over the generations, but later he came to think of them as imperfect counterparts of transexistential absolutes fixed beyond time or change. He argued that they relieved man of some of the burden of responsibility and enabled the locked-in egotist to escape himself. Warren's referents put the burden squarely upon man and enabled the egotist to accept himself—though in so doing he could and must accept other men. The tendency of Warren's thought is individualistic; the tendency of Tate's is authoritarian.

But the most curious difference of all is that Warren's ethics are Christian and Tate's are not. (Of course they are not anti-Christian.) Tate's derive from the code of the gentleman and go back through the image of the Virginia aristocrat to the ideals of ceremonious conduct of the British upper classes. The ultimate source is the pagan humanism of Greek philosophy and the writings of Cicero. The virtues of his system are those of the feudal lord: courage, dignity, restraint, courtesy, humility, and respect for the worth of others based upon a sense of one's own worth. Warren, we may be sure, would assent to the value of all of these virtues, but the ones which he emphasizes are contrition, humility, forgiveness, charity, and love. Now both men give place to humility, but they are not thinking of the same thing. Tate's is that of the knight or the Confederate captain who is too strong, too controlled, too unselfconsciously confident to make any claims. Warren's is that of the sinner who hopes he may be saved—the humility of Jack Burden when he admits that he is no better than Tiny Duffy or of Jerry Beaumont when he prepares to shake the hangman's hand. In his poems, essays, and novel Tate condemns our age for its materialism and triviality which rob conduct of meaning. In the end one comes to feel that much of his moral indignation comes from plain dislike of the milieu and the things in which many men find fulfillment and happiness. There is in his condemnation a suggestion of simple exasperation with the contentment of others. Granted that complacency in a time of gas ovens and labor camps can and should sometimes infuriate us all, Tate often seems less concerned with that than with the fact that others do not suffer the particular kinds of loneliness and disappointment that beset the man of letters. It is hard to think that there is not a good deal of such resentment in "Retroduction to American History," "Causerie," "To the Lacedemonians," and "Jubilo." Warren, however, condemns the age for lack of love and charity and for using men and nature as if they were mere things. Here once more his thought veers toward Ransom's, for in *God Without Thunder* Ransom indicted modern man for ravaging the world's body and the body of his beloved to satisfy his appetites. Yet, as we have seen, Ransom's values are aesthetic. Warren's are more nearly in the Christian tradition of the worth of the individual soul. In fact, without professing literal belief in Christian theology, Warren is something of a Protestant in his emphasis upon the individual's responsibility for his conduct and the necessity of *earning* redemption by good works and in his acceptance of Original Sin as part

537

of the human condition. But he interprets the Sin according to his ontological premises. As McDowell points out, in Warren's work man does evil because he does not have enough self-knowledge to avoid it, and he always will since complete self-knowledge is impossible to obtain.[29] And he is naturally wicked in wishing to abandon the struggle to know and surrender himself to irresponsibility. It is here that the psychological and ethical levels of meaning in Warren's fable come together. By an exquisite irony of man's fate, the longing to return to the lost innocence of childhood is sinful because it encourages one to use others to that end and because it impedes one's progress toward mature, if limited, wisdom which may partially redeem. "In so far as he is to achieve redemption [man] must do so through an awareness of his condition that identifies him with the general human communion, not in abstraction, but immediately. The victory is never won, the redemption must be continually re-earned."[30]

As he said a good philosophical novelist should, Warren has tested his beliefs in the arena of reality. No living writer using English—certainly none with his philosophical predilections—has brought into his imaginative works such an abundance and variety of the things man has lived among in past and present, in country and city, in high station and low, at his labor and his leisure. And the things are not just named. They are, as has been so often said in these pages, almost protrusively there. And the characters! From children to the most aged; from squalid creatures of the backwash of the advancing frontier to the urbane masters of corporations; farmers, laborers, public relations men, riverboat bullies, financiers, students, lawyers, ministers, politicians, debutantes, soldiers, and surgeons, all rendered against settings appropriate to them. Warren's scope is enormous. But there is a thinness to the people and thence to the meaning which he seeks in their lives.

Warren has depicted, sometimes with a marvelous delicacy and accuracy, portions of our psychic life which we do not understand because we shy away from them or because, since they extend far back into childhood, we have succeeded in suppressing them. Those portions and the images and actions through which they

[29] "Psychology and Theme in *Brother to Dragons*," p. 575.
[30] *Selected Essays*, p. 54.

come to light are presented over and over again while other portions are neglected or not given the importance they have in the real histories of men. Of course, all literary characters are reductions. As E. M. Forster says, Homo Fictus is more elusive than his cousin Homo Sapiens and lives a queer half life in which proportions and relations are very different from those we ourselves encounter. But as we read we forget the difference. We pretend that Homo Fictus is Homo Sapiens and that he does all the boring, routine things which we do, though we are glad that the writer has not bothered to mention them. We take it on faith that behind the parts of his world and his experience that we are shown is a whole world and a whole experience and that they are just about the same as ours. We can do this even with fantasy provided that in the end Homo Fictus, being some sort of man, does not escape man's fate. Or rather, we can do this unless something keeps reminding us of the difference. In Warren's work something does. It is the obsession with mortality.

The shadow of death lies, now faintly, now darkly, across almost all of the work from the poems in *Driftwood Flames* onward. It even drifts in the bright sunlight of the Mediterranean poems. It is everywhere in that landscape of childhood to which, it has been argued here, so much of the work looks back. Perhaps it helps to explain the insatiable craving for love to put between the self and reality that, unsatisfied, leads to the unfulfilled needs and belief in their unworthiness of the principal figures in Warren's fable, though one cannot assert this with any surety. It does, though, account for the great importance of Time in the fable. In 1924 Tate cautioned Warren against the obsession, but to no good, and one has only to recall the remarkable number of images associated with bodily decay in *All the King's Men* to get some notion of how the obsession charged the imagination behind that novel. Nowhere is fear of death given as a motive for the instrumentalism of Willie Stark and Adam Stanton. Yet that may be the ultimate and best explanation of their absorption with biotic efficiency and well-being symbolized by the hospital which is their common concern. Fear of death and of guilt which warrants punishment—often self-inflicted—that takes away a little, or even all, of one's life—this fear accounts for some of the emotional force and contextual associations of the metaphors Warren uses

so well in "End of Season," "Pursuit," "Original Sin," and some
of the poems in *Promises* to penetrate to far reaches of the mind.
Indeed, in his representation of man's history all experience after
the moment of first selfconsciousness and separateness from nature
is a form of dying.

Often it seems that the great obsession of Warren's work is not
mortality but sexuality. Mention has been made of the genital
character of his image of Nature beginning with the reference to
the dark pool and hairy haunches in the third of the "Portraits
of Three Ladies." And in the fiction sexuality is frequently predominant in the descriptions of characters, their relations, and
their attitudes toward one another. Men measure themselves and
other men in terms of their sexual energy. Women are described
in terms of their "juiciness" and suppleness in bed. When other
appetites are mentioned they are often made to seem correlatives
or sublimations of erotic desire, as when Jack Burden, after describing their sexual life, imagines his first wife, Lois, eating chocolates
in a particularly lubricious manner. But there is nothing remotely
salacious in the references to the sexual act, which is a "shameful
wrench and contortion of the flesh," a mere twitch or spasm. It
is not joyous and invigorating. It is, rather, an autoerotic assault
which uses up part of one's vitality and wears and taints one's
victim. Though some of the characters have children, the sexual
relationships that form part of the narratives neither create life
nor deepen love and understanding of the beloved and the self.
In sum, sex is a paramount part of experience and hence of dying.

There is no need to insist on the importance of the instinctual
drives to self-preservation and sexual satisfaction nor on their
relation to suppressed feelings that go back to childhood, and Warren is right to emphasize their place in the long struggle toward
maturity and knowledge and acceptance of the self. The fault is
in oversimplification. Warren has brought together a vast gallery
of people, but from a little distance they all begin to look too
much alike. There is too much terror, too much decay, too much
sexuality, too much narcissism, too much disgust. Or, rather, there
is not too much if these be seen amidst other qualities of character
and behavior. Self-knowledge is more than recognition of one's
capacity for wrongdoing. Glory is more than bearing up under a
nearly overwhelming load of self-loathing and fear of the grave.

The Achievement

There are kinds of undemanding affection, rightful self-esteem, unaggressive humor, loyalty, aesthetic delight, and good strong confidence that need to be taken into account when Warren's ideas are tested. The hopeful poems of *Promises* reach out toward them and in time they may force a new total vision of man and his world that is as broad as Warren's present one but of greater depth and subsurface variety. If it be argued that no writer can present the whole of life, one can answer that at least a writer can present a more representative portion to back up his claims about the whole. By the very urgency of his generalizations and the portentousness of his delivery Warren invites us to inspect the evidence; it turns out to be very sound evidence indeed, but, for all its great quantity, not wholly adequate.

There is a principle of art that Mies van der Rohe put into three words: "Less is more." By the logic of reversible equations, we may say that "More is less," and so it is with Warren's work. The oversimplification of human experience we here complain of is an effect of an abiding fault of his writing, excess. Only a few short pieces are free of it—"The Return: An Elegy," "The Garden," "Sirocco," "The Child Next Door," "School Lesson . . ." and "Dragon Country" (surprisingly, for they are seemingly reckless), "Boy's Will. . . ," and the marvelously restrained story "Christmas Gift." Perhaps there are others. But elsewhere the work lacks discrimination and control. Warren has stupendous powers of improvisation but often wants powers of invention, which are not the same, for invention is both richer and more disciplined. He can fabricate scenes; he can release a torrent of language of unmatched energy and create an effect of intensity; he can think of innumerable questions to turn the meaning back upon itself and reiterate the ambiguity of all things; he can think of yet one more way to say essentially what he has said before. Often his gift for improvisation enables him to make a great display and hurry past some point where he ought to linger and explore. Explore not the language *about* the situation but the situation itself. Because he does not pause, the obsessions can predominate. Driven by them the words and images surge along until they pile up on some pluralist paradox like wreckage on a bridge abutment, marring the work with disproportions, inappropriatenesses, repetitions, inner contradictions and fragmentations and limiting the meanings expressed. More *is* less.

To put the matter in the harshest terms, all but a few works show a streak of vulgarity. Warren cares too much about the raw material of his art and not enough for the formal order and for the elements after they have been assimilated and transmuted by it. For all his gifts and energy (and no living American writer except perhaps Norman Mailer has nearly so much), for all his dedication and earnestness, he lacks some *literary* understanding and thus some final understanding—and truth.

Such words come hard to one who admires Warren's work and believes, as does this writer, that he is our foremost living novelist, at times one of our best poets, and among the half-dozen or so great literary figures of twentieth-century America. His work is deeply flawed. But it is never mean, and it has a greatness that survives all. The greatness comes from three things. First is his vision of evil. Forster said, "As a rule, evil has been feebly envisaged in fiction, which seldom soars above misconduct or avoids the clouds of mysteriousness." But Warren gets beyond these because he sees it as violation of the integrity and dignity of the individual. To represent evil you must believe in and be able to represent the integrity and dignity too. Few can, and today most of them are Southerners. Second is his understanding of how the impulse to violate comes from deprivation that goes far, far back and for which others are much to blame. Men do evil to others because somewhere, sometime, at a critical juncture, others failed them. Last is his magnanimity. He can reconcile himself to failure, knowing men cannot help it, being only men. Through the medium of his incomparable "indicative poetry" he lends us charity so that we, too, may be reconciled. Reconciled to our own failure as well as the failure in the lives that touch ours. And reconciled to the glory that costs so much.

That is the proof of his greatness. We read him and become aware of the conditions that identify us with the human communion, not in abstraction, but immediately. He said, "The victory is never won, the redemption must be continually re-earned." For us, with his help, some of it is.

INDEX

Index

Graves, Robert, *On English Poetry*, 262
Grosz, George, 300

Hardy, Thomas, 211, 283, 452
Harris, Joel Chandler, 13
Hawthorne, Nathaniel, 326, 328
Hegel, G. W. H., 261, 287
Heisenberg, Werner, 291
Hemingway, Ernest, 3, 46, 454
Heraclitus, 379-380, 409-410
Hirsch, Goldie, 15-16
Hirsch, Nathaniel, 16
Hirsch, Sidney Mttron, vii, 79, 84, 86, 89-90; and American letters, 3-4, 90; as Fugitive, 3-5, 16-17, 31, 32-35; diction, 8, 51; esoteric learning, 5-6; *The Fire Regained*, 3, 7-10, 16; "The Little Boy Pilgrim," 51; "The Mysteries of Thanatos," 10; mysticism, 5-6, 19-20, 35; "The Passion Play of Washington Square," 10; qualities of his poetry, 51; travels, 5-6
Hobson, J. A., *Rationalism and Unemployment*, 175
Hoffer, Eric, 475, 492
Hofmann, Hans, 362
Holbein, the Younger, Hans, *The Virgin with the Family of Burgomeister Meyer*, 299
Hollis, Christopher, 163, 167; *The American Heresy*, 133-135
Hook, Sidney, on Tate's theory of literature, 193, 346
Hoss, Bishop E. E., 12
Hume, David, 291
Huxley, Aldous, 436

I'll Take My Stand, 89, 140-141, 144-145, 147-171, 173, 175, 182, 186, 189, 199, 262, 390, 500
Imagists, The, 466
Indiana School of Letters, 195n, 283
Ives, Charles, 44n

James, Henry, 326, 328, 487; *The Ambassadors*, 298; *The Turn of the Screw*, 349
Jarrell, Randall, 8on, 208n
Jefferson, Thomas, 133-134, 163, 175, 510-515 *passim*
Johnson, Gerald, 140-141
Johnson, Stanley, 16, 21, 84, 85, 87; "Imprisonment," 62-63; "Pier," 61-

62; *Professor*, 85-86; qualities of his poetry, 61-63; "Sermons," 57
Joint University Library, as repository of Fugitive-Agrarian materials, vii, viii, 35n
Joyce, James, 24, 180, 446-447
Jung, Carl Gustave, 270

Kabbala, The, 3n, 90
Kant, Emanuel, 261, 277, 287
Kaufmann, Walter, 356-357
Keats, John, 44, 431
Kenyon School of English, 195, 283
The Kenyon Review, 195, 196, 283, 349
King Lear, 344-345
Kirkland, James M., 12, 110, 141, 172
Kline, Henry Blue, 144, 170, 171
Knickerbocker, W. S. 177, 200
Kollwitz, Käthe, 360
Krieger, Murray, 300, 304
Ku Klux Klan, 108
Kyd, Thomas, "The Spanish Tragedy," 378

Laforgue, Jules, 44
Lanier, Lyle, 132-133, 173, 174, 182, 186, 451, 501; "A Critique of the Philosophy of Progress," 169-170
Lawrence, D. H., *Sons and Lovers*, 298
Lea, Colonel Luke, 476
Lewis, Sinclair, 133, 437
Lincoln, Abraham, 134, 180
Long, Huey, 476
Longstreet, Augustus Baldwin, 158
Lovengood, Sut, 158
Lowell, Amy, 22
Lowell, Robert, 8on, 222
Lytle, Andrew Nelson, vii, 8on, 143, 149, 172, 185, 186, 195, 196-197, 214, 388-389, 394, 403, 431, 449; feeling for farm life, 168; "The Hind Tit," 166, 167-169; "The Lincoln Myth," 167

Macauley, Robie, 8on
Macbeth, 345
MacLeish, Archibald, 358; "Invocation to the Social Muse," 344; *The Irresponsibles*, 407
Macune, Dr. C. W., 469
Mailer, Norman, 376, 542
Mallarmé, Stéphane, 358
Mannes, Marya, 407
Maritain, Jacques, 351, 354

545

Index

Index